FAMILIES

A Sociological Perspective

FAMILIES

A Sociological Perspective

David M. Newman

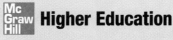

Boston   Burr Ridge, IL   Dubuque, IA   New York   San Francisco   St. Louis
Bangkok   Bogotá   Caracas   Kuala Lumpur   Lisbon   London   Madrid   Mexico City
Milan   Montreal   New Delhi   Santiago   Seoul   Singapore   Sydney   Taipei   Toronto

 **Higher Education**

A Division of the McGraw-Hill Companies

This book is printed on acid-free paper.

1 2 3 4 5 6 7 8 9 0 WCK/WCK 0 9 8

ISBN: 978-0-07-340416-5
MHID: 0-07-340416-0

Editor in Chief: *Michael Ryan*
Publisher: *Frank Mortimer*
Sponsoring Editor: *Gina Boedeker*
Marketing Manager: *Leslie Oberhuber*
Director of Development: *Rhona Robbin*
Developmental Editor: *Jennie Katsaros*
Production Editor: *Catherine Morris*
Manuscript Editor: *Kay Mikel*
Design Manager: *Andrei Pasternak*

Text Designer: *Anne Flanagan*
Cover Designer: *Ashley Bedell*
Illustrator: *Dartmouth Publishing*
Photo Research Coordinator: *Natalia Peschiera*
Photo Researcher: *PhotoFind, LLC, Toni Michaels*
Production Supervisor: *Tandra Jorgensen*
Composition: *9.5/12 ITC Garamond*
   by Thompson Type
Printing: *45# New Era Matte, Quebecor World, Inc.*

Cover: Simple Stock Shots/Images.com

Credits: The credits section for this book begins on page C-1 and is considered an extension of the copyright page.

Library of Congress Cataloging-in-Publication Data

Newman, David M., 1958–
   Sociology of families / David Newman. — 1st ed.
      p. cm.
   Includes bibliographical references and index.
   ISBN-13: 978-0-07-340416-5 (alk. paper)
   ISBN-10: 0-07-340416-0 (alk. paper)
   1. Family—United States. 2. United States—Social conditions. I. Title.
   HQ536.N5235 2008
   306.850973—dc22

                                                   2008033020

The Internet addresses listed in the text were accurate at the time of publication. The inclusion of a Web site does not indicate an endorsement by the authors or McGraw-Hill, and McGraw-Hill does not guarantee the accuracy of the information presented at these sites.

www.mhhe.com

About the Author

David M. Newman is currently Professor of Sociology at DePauw University in Green-castle, Indiana. He received his PhD in Sociology from the University of Washington in 1988. He teaches courses in Deviance, Mental Illness, Family, Social Psychology, and Research Methods and has won teaching awards at both the University of Washington and DePauw University. He has published numerous articles on teaching and has presented several research papers on the intersection of gender and power in intimate relationships. He has authored three books, *Sociology: Exploring the Architecture of Everyday Life* (and co-edited an accompanying anthology), *Sociology of Families, and Identities and Inequalities*. When not hunkered down in his third floor office or complaining about lower back pain, he enjoys running, swimming, crossword puzzles, and arguing with his sons.

Brief Contents

Contents

PART II

Families and Social Inequalities   80

PART IV

Families Over the Life Course   266

PART V

Families and Challenges   348

13 Intimate Violence   348

Preface

You'd have a hard time finding a topic as emotionally compelling and as personally interesting to people as family. Tell folks you're writing a book about families and you're bound to hear some anecdote ("My family's nuts! You should write about them."), an opinion about a family-related social problem ("See how out-of-control kids are today? It's because parents aren't disciplining them enough. You should write about something useful like *that*!"), or a request for advice ("I hope this book of yours will tell me how I can get my son to help with the dishes without me having to ask all the time.").

Everybody, it seems, has something to say or some strong feeling about families. Whether spoken of reverently as the moral foundation of society or referred to disparagingly as the greatest obstacle to happiness and freedom by some rebellious teenager, "family" permeates our lives and defines who we are as a culture like no other institution.

Type the word "families" into an Internet search engine and you'll discover hundreds of categories and thousands of sites devoted to some component of families, whether it's academic research on some feature of family life (marriage, divorce, children, and so on), the positions of political interest groups devoted to some family issue, or services provided by nonprofit family organizations. Move beyond these organizational sites and you'll find something even more interesting: thousands of *personal* family Web sites—individual families simply presenting information about . . . well . . . themselves.

Many of these sites present the sort of personal information you typically see in those letters some people stuff in their Christmas cards each year. You know, "Fred finally got his real estate license and we couldn't be prouder"; "Suzie loves her new position as goalkeeper on the travel soccer team"; "Our trip to Disneyworld was a dream come true." Some contain elaborate digital family photo albums with pictures of weddings, christenings, bar mitzvahs, children's softball games, prom night, beloved pets, summer vacations, and so on. Others offer even deeper peeks into people's private lives by providing detailed family trees, religious testimonials, political opinions, downloadable copies of wedding vows, or favorite cookie recipes.

What do you suppose would motivate people to open up the intimate details of their families to the vast, anonymous world of the Internet? It's not as if there are all these people out there dying to know about Joe and Martha Klotzman's fondness for Tupperware parties. Instead, the Klotzmans and others are taking this technological opportunity to make a public statement about their commitment to and pride in their families.

Highlighting the importance of family in people's lives is nothing new. For as long as there have been people pondering the human condition, there have been scholars, poets, novelists, musicians, and clergy examining, studying, celebrating, bemoaning, and making predictions and writing about every conceivable aspect of family life. Open a newspaper or turn on a television and you'll find no shortage of contemporary "experts"—from Dear Abby to Dr. Phil—who are more than willing to offer their two cents about the joys and sorrows of families. So how does one write about something so eternally important without treading over well-worn ground?

THE STORY

I knew from the start that I didn't want this book simply to be an encyclopedia of information that would be useful only in the context of a college course and thus easily discarded at the end of the semester. I wanted it to be a sort of intellectual guidebook—not only *informative* in terms of current sociological knowledge of families, but *meaningful* in terms of contemporary family debates and *applicable* to students' own family experiences. In other words, I wanted to write a book that would connect to people's personal lives while, at the same time, showing how sociologists understand and explain families.

That may sound simple, but it turned out to be a formidable task. One of the challenges I faced is that a student's first college textbook on family—or first course on family, for that matter—is never his or her introduction to the topic of family. Everybody has grown up in one type of family or another. Consequently, all students bring with them a lifetime's worth of personal information, data, values, expectations, and assumptions. Most have some experience with siblings or grandparents or cousins. Many have seen their parents divorce and remarry. Some have even formed their own families. Indeed, when it comes to a topic like family, everyone is a potential expert.

With such direct knowledge come some deeply held beliefs about what a family is and how it should work. These preconceived notions pose an interesting dilemma to instructors—and, by extension, to textbook authors. Certainly we want our students to see their own experiences in the material we present. I've found in my own classes that students are more engaged and learn more when they find the subject matter immediately relevant to their lives.

But at the same time we all want our classes and our textbooks to be more than just an album of personally familiar snippets of family life. That "it-happens-to-me-therefore-it-must-be-true-for-everyone" approach to family-related topics can be a serious obstacle to learning. Classroom discussions that stay at this level become merely exchanges of personal yarns, and little is learned about understanding the subject sociologically.

A textbook on family must go beyond simply telling stories that students can relate to. It must show how professional scholars go about understanding the social patterns that underlie those family matters that everyone seems to have some experience with or some opinion about. A textbook should provide the intellectual tools needed to *understand* the broader social implications of family experiences, *appreciate* the applicability of the sociological perspective to people's everyday lives, and critically *evaluate* the social information about families that bombards us every day. In short, it must strike a balance between the personal and emotional relevance of the material on one hand and scholarly analysis of it on the other.

THE PHILOSOPHY

Sociologists may have many things in common, but our assumptions, perspectives, and attitudes can be quite different. Some sociologists focus on broad demographic information about large groups of people; others concentrate on the everyday interpersonal experiences of individuals. Some write from a specific political position or theoretical perspective; others are more pluralistic in the ideologies and theories they use.

This book reflects my sociological perspective—one that draws heavily on the interrelationship between the everyday experiences of individuals and the society in which they live. I believe family is both an individually lived experience and a systematic social institution. Our private lives are always a combination of the idiosyncrasies of the family to which we belong and the broader social rules and expectations associated with families in general. In that sense, our families are strongly influenced by large-scale social forces like culture, history, economics, politics, religion, the media, and so on.

However, we, as individuals, are also vital contributors to structural forces that influence our lives. I will argue that much of what we experience in our families is a product of negotiation, whether at the cultural/political level or the level of individuals. Sociologists refer to this approach as a *constructionist* perspective. Whether we're talking about whom we consider our relatives, how to start (or end) an intimate relationship, how to give birth, what it means to be a child or an adolescent, how to balance the demands of work and family, or what we take for granted as "appropriate" family behavior, we actively give meaning to "family" in our everyday experiences. Moreover, as individuals, couples, or groups, we can, through our actions, change, modify, or reinforce existing elements of family.

THE DESIGN

I have organized this book into five parts, each with a unique theme and purpose. Part I, *Families and Society,* contains three chapters that provide a broad foundation for examining the specific aspects of family life that will come later in the book. In these chapters, I explore important questions such as "What is a family?" "What is the current health of families?" and "How do sociologists study families?" Part II, *Families and Social Inequalities,* looks at the impact that race, gender, and social class have on family life, both as sources of personal and group identity and as sources of inequality. Part III, *Families and Relationships,* focuses on how people establish intimate relationships, how they live within them, and how they balance their demands with the demands of work. Part IV, *Families Over the Life Course,* examines some of the important developmental stages that people face: the entry into parenthood, the experiences of childhood and adolescence, and the strains of adulthood and later life. Finally, Part V, *Families and Challenges,* looks at the problems and difficulties many families face (violence and divorce). The closing chapter peers ahead and examines the challenges families will likely face in the future.

Despite the five-part organization of this book, you will quickly notice that all the parts are interrelated. One of the difficulties in writing a book on family is that family matters don't align neatly in distinct and conceptually independent chapters. For instance, you can't talk about relationship formation, the dynamics of marriage, the balance of work and family, children and child rearing, and so on without taking gender, race, and social class into consideration. A topic like divorce is closely related to economics, child rearing, work, social policy, perhaps even intimate violence. Hence you'll notice that within a particular chapter I often reference similar material found in other chapters. Rather than calling attention to my redundancy, these references reinforce the interconnectedness of family experiences.

A few common stylistic elements can be found in all of the chapters. For instance, each begins with an anecdote—sometimes from current events and sometimes from my own life—that illustrates the key theme of that chapter. Throughout the book, key terms are highlighted in the margin. In addition, all of the chapters include a summary of key points at the end, to clarify important concepts, ideas, or theories. Finally, each concludes with a section, called *What Does It All Mean?* This section is designed not just to summarize what students read in the chapter but to get them to think critically about the material. I envision these sections as sources of classroom conversations and discussions.

The Special Features

The trend in textbooks these days is to stuff them with as many special features as is possible. Often these components are visually distinct from the main text. But with so many of them, it can be difficult to determine where the main text ends the special section begins. I've designed the special features in this book to be less conspicuous and intrusive while at the same time providing additional useful information or opportunities for active learning:

- *Taking a Closer Look* features provide an in-depth look at a specific example of information presented in the chapter or a discussion of an important piece of research.

- *Going Global* features explore family-related phenomena as experienced in other cultures.

- Most of the carefully selected photographs in the book convey important information by painting provocative sociological portraits of family life. In some chapters, I have included multipage photographic essays—extended treatments of an issue raised in the chapter. Other photographs briefly illustrate the connections between family life and legal or policy issues. As students study these visual features, they will be practicing the skills of observation that can make them more astute participants in their own families and in the social world at large.

- Each chapter ends with an exercise called *See for Yourself* that encourages students to study the "real world," much as professional sociologists do, to get a better understanding of the similarities and differences among families. These exercises—akin to mini-data-gathering ventures—give students an opportunity to actively engage information from the chapter. They range from systematic observational exercises to content analyses to brief interviews. Some of these exercises require more of a time investment than others, and instructors can condense, modify, or otherwise tailor the exercises to suit their interests, needs, and goals.

Words

As sociologists, we know the power of language in shaping ideas, values, and attitudes. I have tried to be very careful in my choice of terminology. Consider, for instance, the title of this book: *Families: A Sociological Perspective*. You will notice that I use the word *Families* and not *The Family.* One of the key themes of this book is that families are extremely diverse in form and function. No single family structure can serve as a prototype for everyone. Hence in the title and throughout the book I have opted for the more inclusive (and I think more accurate) term "families." Only when referring to the *institution* of family or referring to a specific family (for example, "When she became the head of the family . . .") do I use "the family."

RESOURCES FOR INSTRUCTORS AND STUDENTS

An array of electronic resources is available for extending the concepts and pedagogical methods of the book. The Web site for this book (www.mhhe.com/newman1) contains a variety of resources for instructors and students, including chapter quizzes with feedback, key terms, Powerpoint slides, and the instructor's manual and test bank.

Acknowledgments

Writing a book like this one is an enormously time-consuming endeavor that simultaneously requires total seclusion and utter dependence on other people's expertise, guidance, goodwill, and patience. Although it's my name that appears on the cover, many people contributed their time, suggestions, opinions, and sometimes simply emotional support to bring this project to completion.

First, I'd like to express my heartfelt appreciation to Gina Boedeker, Jennie Katsaros, Rhona Robbin, and Elisa Adams for their support, optimism, and impeccable editorial and substantive suggestions throughout the entire grueling process of putting this book together. Even though McGraw-Hill is a huge company, every one of them took the time to read multiple versions of this book, not something that many publishing teams would be willing to do. And for that, I am eternally grateful. In addition, I appreciate the numerous helpful comments offered by our many reviewers:

Richard Ball, Ferris State University
Sampson Lee Blair, The State University of New York at Buffalo
Jennifer Meehan Brennom, Kirkwood Community College
Susan Cody-Rydzewski, LaGrange College
Philip Cohen, University of North Carolina at Chapel Hill
Janet Cosbey, Eastern Illinois University
Lillian Dees, Texas State University—San Marcos
Lance Erickson, Brigham Young University—Provo
Christine Fruhauf, Colorado State University
James Gadberry, Athens State University
Bethany Gizzi, Monroe Community College
Carol Hodgson, Rowan-Cabarrus Community College
Susan Holbrook, Southwestern Illinois College
Donna Holland, Indiana University/Purdue University—Ft. Wayne
Erma Lawson, University of North Texas
Tina Martinez, Blue Mountain Community College
Michallene McDaniel, Gainesville State College
Carol Mosher, Jefferson Community College
Tina Norris, Kent State University
Catherine Robertson, Grossmont Community College
Ovetta D. Robinson-Heyward, Midlands Technical College
Marie Saracino, Stephen F. Austin State University

Beth Anne Shelton, University of Texas at Arlington
Jerry Shepperd, Austin Community College
Sudha Shreeniwas, University of North Carolina at Greensboro
Paula Snyder, Chaffey College
Michelle Tordsen, Minnesota State University-Mankato
Elizabeth Tracy, Rhodes State College
Nicole Warehime, University of Oklahoma
Debra Williamson, Lansing Community College

I'd also like to thank Catherine Morris for guiding the book through the production process and Kay Mikel, who did a wonderful job copyediting the final version of the manuscript.

I especially want to express my sincere gratitude to the many colleagues and friends who offered assistance along the way. In particular, Jodi O'Brien, Christopher Bondy, Rebecca Upton, and "Sister" Mary Susan provided valuable illustrative examples and cross-cultural information. Finally, I'd like to thank my students and my own family who, whether they realize it or not, inspire me to continue learning.

Good luck.

David M. Newman
Department of Sociology and Anthropology
DePauw University
Greencastle, IN 46135
E-mail: dnewman@depauw.edu

FAMILIES
A Sociological Perspective

1

Defining Families

In 2005 a Louisiana couple whose home was destroyed by Hurricane Katrina was forced to relocate in Chicago. They said of the people there, "They took us in with open arms. . . . It's like we're all *family* here. That's what it feels like." A year later the political group MoveOn.org published a book on the tragedy titled, *It Takes a Nation: How Strangers Became Family.*

A proverb among the Mende of Sierra Leone says: "The stranger who tells our stories when we cannot speak not only awakens our spirits and hearts but also shows our humanity—which others want to forget—and in doing so, becomes *family*" (Beah, 2007, p. 81).

The Olive Garden Italian restaurant chain has a marketing campaign that features the tag line, "When you're here, you're *family*." The idea of family pervades the company's Web site: "Olive Garden is a *family* of local restaurants focused on delighting every guest with a genuine Italian dining experience. . . . We offer a comfortable, home-like setting where guests are welcomed like *family*."

In each of these examples we see the varied, fluid, and sometimes unexpected ways people use the term *family,* and the powerful connotations that term has. Could the displaced Louisiana couple have expressed their gratitude by saying, "It's like we're all *neighbors* here"? Could the suffering Mende thank people who have informed the world of their plight by referring to them as *supportive allies*? Could Olive Garden inspire feelings of comfort in potential customers if its advertisements read, "When you're here, you're *an important customer*"? Certainly not.

The really curious thing, though, is that none of these examples used the word *family* to describe the relationships most of us usually think of as family—husbands and wives, parents and children, brothers and sisters, grandparents, aunts, uncles, cousins, and so on. Instead, people use *family* to induce images of love, commitment, generosity, protection, and warmth.

In this chapter, we'll examine the vital issue of how family is defined. Who gets to be called a family and who is excluded from this definition are not simply differences in labels. The categories of "family" and "nonfamily" have different values and privileges in the culture.

IDENTIFYING FAMILIES

Perhaps no word evokes as much emotion or carries as much political weight as *family*. It permeates our lives and defines who we are as a culture. We're all born into a family of one sort or another and will spend at least part of our lives inside some type of family.

Ironically, as recognizable as it is, family is also a remarkably elusive term. Ask 10 people to define it and you're likely to get 10 different responses. We may want to think that family is a natural feature of human life, but in fact its meaning—not to mention how people feel about it and what they expect from one another within it—is **socially constructed.** This means that what we believe to be "real" is always a matter of what we collectively define and agree upon as real (Newman, 2007). Your relationships to others *become* family relationships when you refer to yourselves and treat each other as a family (Berger & Kellner, 1964).

For instance, when I talk about the "Newman family" I am describing something that is organized in a particular way; something that has identifiable boundaries that determine who's in it and who's not. But this thing called the Newman family does not have an objective reality separate from people's definitions of it. In fact, although we may refer to it—thereby giving it meaning—no two members experience or define it in exactly the same way. Newman family means something entirely different to my younger son than to my older son or, for that matter, to me. And it certainly means something even more different to those outside it.

One of the most fundamental and deceptively simple questions facing people who study family is this: Just what exactly *is* a family? The answer has very real and critical consequences for all of us. People defined as family may be in line to receive a whole host of tangible benefits, such as eligibility for certain types of housing, tax breaks, inheritances, health care coverage, and travel insurance, not to mention legitimate recognition within their community. Even our right to spend time with certain people sometimes depends on whether or not we're considered that person's family. For instance, all 50 states have some type of law that grants grandparents and sometimes other relatives the right to visit children over the objections of parents. The state of Washington goes even further, giving anyone, even those without any defined relationship to the child, the right to petition for visitation rights. Petitions are successful if the court concludes the individuals play such an important family-like role in the child's life that regular contact would be in the child's best interest (L. Greenhouse, 2000a).

Not only are those who fall outside the definition of family ineligible for certain benefits, but their relationships may be considered illegitimate, inappropriate, or immoral as well (Hartman, 1994). One of the key ideas to keep in mind as you read this book is that our views about which family forms are acceptable, normal, desirable, and praiseworthy also determine our views about which forms are abnormal, problematic, and in need of repair or condemnation.

The "Official" U.S. Definition of Family

Taken to its logical extreme, the idea of family as a social construction would mean that a family can be whatever an individual says it is. If I choose to consider my mother's best friend, my mail carrier, or even my dog as members of my family, I can. But we don't live our lives completely by ourselves, so we don't have complete freedom to define our own families. At some point we need others to ratify or recognize our own personal sense of family. Not only do we come into fairly regular contact with people who want to know what our family looks like, we also must navigate a vast array of organizations and agencies that have their own definitions of family and that may, at times, impose them on us. For instance, local, state, and federal governments manage many programs that provide certain benefits only to families. The federal government regularly compiles up-to-date statistics on the number of individuals, married couples, and families that live in this country. Obviously it must have some idea of what a family (or what a marriage) is before it can start counting.

This information is often used by legislators and researchers to support their arguments about the state of U.S. families and their need for legal protection. For instance, shortly before I first wrote this chapter, the U.S. Census Bureau released figures showing that only about half of the nation's households contained married couples (cited in Roberts, 2006). Such information will no doubt be useful to groups wanting to bolster programs designed to strengthen marriage.

The Census Bureau's official definition distinguishes between *households* and *families*. **Households** are all persons or groups of persons who occupy a dwelling such as a house, apartment, single room, or other space intended to be living quarters.

■ **social construction of family**
The meaning we attach to family is a matter of collective definition and human agreement.

■ **household**
All persons or groups of persons who occupy a dwelling intended to be living quarters.

■ **family**
A group of two or more people related by blood, marriage, or adoption and residing together.

■ **nuclear family**
Small family unit consisting of a married couple with or without children, or at least one parent and his or her children.

■ **extended family**
Relatives outside the nuclear family, such as grandparents, aunts, uncles, and cousins.

Households can consist of one person who lives alone or several people living together. A **family,** on the other hand, is a group of two or more people (one of whom is the householder—the person in whose name the unit is owned or rented) related by birth, marriage, or adoption and residing together (U.S. Bureau of the Census, 2006b). This official definition also defines what social scientists call the **nuclear family**—the small unit consisting of a married couple with or without children or at least one parent and his or her children.

According to the official definition, a family is always a household, but a household is not always a family. Over the past several decades, the growth of "nonfamily households" (people living with friends, roommates sharing an apartment, cohabiting couples, young single people, and so on) has been dramatic. In 1960, 15% of all households were nonfamily; today the figure is over 30% (Figure 1.1).

Right away you can see that the official definition limits who does and doesn't count as family. Grown children who maintain their own households and no longer live with their parents are not counted as part of their parents' families (though the parents would no doubt think otherwise). And what about **extended families**—grandparents, aunts, uncles, and cousins who extend beyond nuclear families? Most of us would consider them to be part of our family too, even though they don't live with us. And the official definition excludes close friends and other nonrelated folk whom we may *treat* as members of our family.

How useful is this conventional definition of family in everyday life? What does it imply about the nature of people's relationships and their responsibilities to others within and outside their families? To address these questions, let's take the official definition of family as a starting point and break it down into its component parts.

Two or More People: Family *as a Social Group*

A popular nationwide Italian restaurant chain, *Buca Di Beppo,* serves all its meals "family style," meaning that the portions are purposely large so two or more people can share them. One person would have a difficult time eating there alone. Likewise, according

FIGURE 1.1
The Diversity of U.S. Households
Source: U.S. Bureau of the Census, 2006a, table H1.

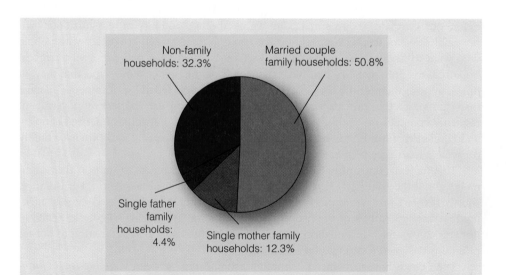

to the Census Bureau definition, one person cannot be a family. Why not? In sociological terms, families contain not only individual people but also named relationships: husband-wife, parent-child, sister-brother, and so on. These relationships imply connections, bonds, attachments, privileges, and obligations *between* people.

Of course, any type of close social group contains connections between people. Teachers form bonds with students, bosses with employees, coaches with players. But the intensity of involvement between family members is usually stronger than it is in these other groups. And the range of activities we share with family members tends to be much broader than contacts with friends, coworkers, or other people in groups to which we belong. We do pretty much everything with certain family members across a range of situations: eating, sleeping, playing, punishing, fighting, convalescing from illness, having sex, and so on. Such close involvement adds a unique emotional element to family relationships.

Another big difference between families and other close groups is that families tend to last for a considerably longer period of time (Klein & White, 1996). We're born into a family that already exists, and it endures for our lifetime. Even after we become adults and start our own families, our parents are still our parents and our siblings are still our siblings no matter what we think of them. Some people may choose to informally "disown" some of their family members by deciding never to have contact with them, but they don't cease to be their family. We can certainly have lifelong relationships with close friends, but families are the only groups that virtually require lifetime membership.

The strong prospect for continuing interaction gives families a history and tradition we rarely find in other social groups. Given how common divorce has become (see Chapter 14), this idea of permanence applied to families may seem hopelessly outdated. However, we still assume that people don't get married with the intent of getting divorced.

Living Together: Family *as Common Residence*

Another implication of the official definition of family is that the family group shares a common residence. In most people's minds, family is closely associated with a sense of place. Think of how often you equate *family* with *home*. Indeed, for many social scientists, common residence is *the* defining characteristic of family (e.g., Murdock, 1949). The individuals who make up a family constitute a single identifiable entity that can be located in the same space.

That view is common, but it's not universal. Among the Kipsigis of Kenya, for instance, the mother and children live in one house and the father lives in another (Stephens, 1963). The dominant household forms among the Ashanti of Ghana are frérèches or dwellings that consist only of siblings (Bender, 1979). Traditionally, wealthy European families sent their children away to boarding schools, where they spent the majority of their childhood.

Consider the "commuter marriage." In U.S. society, a **commuter marriage** is one in which spouses spend at least several nights a week in separate residences, yet they are still married and intend to remain that way. Marriages in which spouses live apart much of the time have always existed. Careers such as the military, the merchant marines, professional sports, and entertainment often require one spouse to travel for long periods. Today, however, commuter marriages are likely to occur because the husband and wife both have careers that require commitments to different locations. Although the

■ **commuter marriage**
Marriage in which spouses spend at least several nights a week in separate residences.

difficulties of such arrangements are substantial, no one would deny that the people in them are families.

Remember also that having a common household residence does not, in and of itself, determine whether a unit is a family. Perhaps you live with a roommate. Not only do you share an address but you are likely to share domestic chores and household expenses too. You may even feel very close to each other, sharing personal experiences, helping out in times of need, and so on. Yet most people wouldn't consider roommates family. Your common residence is likely to be the result of economic convenience rather than long-term emotional commitment.

Some cities have tried to restrict definitions of family to limit the kinds of people who are allowed to live together in the same household. Black Jack, Missouri, for instance, does not allow two unmarried adults who have a child together—either by blood, adoption, or foster care—to live in dwellings zoned for single families (Currier, 2006). In an effort to reduce overcrowding inside homes, the city of Elgin, Illinois, is considering a measure that would limit residence in dwelling units to single nuclear families. Four or more people who are *not* related by blood, marriage, or adoption would be presumed not to be a family. However, they would be allowed to continue living together if they could prove they were the "functional equivalent" of a family by, for example, living and cooking together and by sharing expenses (Zimmer, 2006). Similarly, in 2006 concerns with suburban overcrowding led the city of Manassas, Virginia, to try to redefine "family" in its zoning code so that large extended immigrant families could not live in "single-family" dwellings (Caldwell, 2006).

Related by Birth: Family *as Kin*

■ **kinship**
Who is related to whom across generations.

The official definition suggests that families consist of people who are related to one another across generations, what social scientists call **kinship.** Kinship is a way of recognizing some people as special and distinct from others (Gittens, 2001). But how do we determine such relationships? Most people would argue that two individuals are kin if they have a blood—that is, a biological—connection. Since reproduction occurs in all human societies, it's easy to assume that kinship is determined in a similar fashion everywhere. However, sociologists and anthropologists are quick to point out that kinship is as much a human creation dependent on social rules and cultural traditions as it is an automatic biological fact. Kinship, in other words, is not a synonym for blood/ biological ties (Gittens, 2001).

At birth everyone inherits two separate bloodlines, raising the question of which bloodline—the mother's or the father's—is to be more important for determining an individual's kin. These designations are vital because they determine not only names but authority, ownership of property, and inheritance.

■ **patrilineal descent**
Kinship system in which family connections are traced through the father's line.

In some societies, kinship is established only through the father's line, a system called **patrilineal descent.** A woman typically takes her husband's name and children downplay or ignore their connections with members of their mother's family, showing allegiance and loyalty to kin on the father's side. So, for instance, a mother's sister—whom we'd call an "aunt" in the United States—has no culturally recognized role in a patrilineal family.

■ **matrilineal descent**
Kinship system in which family connections are traced through the mother's line.

In other societies, the kin group is made up of people connected by mother-child links, or **matrilineal descent.** Here a child's status and heritage are traced only through the mother's blood relations, and the father's kin are not considered part of the family. The Hopi, a Pueblo group in the American Southwest, are a matrilineal society. The relationship a Hopi child maintains with his or her father's relatives may be affectionate, but it includes little direct cooperation or culturally recognized authority.

Finally, in some societies, such as the United States, children trace their descent and define their kin through both parents' bloodlines, a system known as **bilateral descent.** Although U.S. women typically take their husband's name when they marry and children take their father's name, descent and inheritance are usually linked equally to both parents. We may distinguish between our *paternal* and *maternal* grandparents and even like one set better than the other, but we recognize both equally as kin. Neither side of the family is expected to exert special influence and power over the children.

In bilateral descent societies, the potential for kin relationships can be quite extensive. If you were to map out a family chart of kin on both sides of your family, its size and complexity could be immense. But at some point we all stop counting distant kin as family. Barack Obama and Dick Cheney are *eighth* cousins, but neither man considers the other family.

■ **bilateral descent**
Kinship system in which family connections are traced through both the mother's and the father's line.

Related by Marriage or Adoption: Family *as a Legal Unit*

Family isn't simply a group made up of biologically connected kin. The law also determines which people can be members of our family. For instance, adopted children have the same legal and family status as biological children.

Moreover, in many societies marriage is the legal cornerstone of an official definition of family. Most of us take for granted that **monogamy**—the marriage of one man and one woman—is the fundamental building block of family. Some people may have several spouses over their lifetimes, but in the United States they are allowed only one at a time (what sociologists call serial monogamy). And families can exist without a married couple, such as a single parent and his or her children. But monogamous marriage continues to be the only adult intimate relationship that is legally recognized, culturally approved, and endorsed by the Internal Revenue Service. It is still the one relationship in which sexual activity is not only acceptable but expected.

■ **monogamy**
The marriage of one man to one woman.

Monogamous marriage, like family in general, is a patterned way of life that includes a set of commonly known roles, statuses, and expectations. Although the expectations of husbands and wives are always changing, and will differ from one couple to the next, they are far better understood than expectations for any other type of relationship, such as a "significant other," "life partner," or "boyfriend, girlfriend." Furthermore, no other intimate relationship has achieved such status or is privileged as highly as marriage. Despite public concern about its disintegration, legal monogamous marriage remains the cultural standard against which we judge all other types of intimate relationships.

Traditional heterosexual marriages have long benefited from legal and social recognition. According to the Government Accounting Office, marriage partners in the United States today enjoy more than a thousand legal rights and benefits not available to other adult relationships (cited in Conley, 2007). They can, for example, take part in a spouse's health insurance plan and pension program, share the rights of inheritance and community property, make a claim on a spouse's rent-controlled apartment, receive Social Security and veterans' benefits including medical and educational services, file joint tax returns, determine the spouse's medical and burial arrangements, and receive crime victims' recovery benefits (Hunter, 1991; Sherman, 1992). In addition, spouses are granted visitation rights when the partner or his or her children are in a hospital or prison (reported in Ingraham, 1999).

common-law marriage
Agreements by which couples who have not had their relationships validated religiously or civilly are considered legally married if they've lived together long enough.

Even though legal marriage is undeniably important, not all states agree about who can and can't marry. Today some states, such as Pennsylvania, still recognize **common-law marriage.** These marriages are agreements by which couples who have not had their relationships validated religiously or civilly are considered legally married if they've lived together long enough. Some states allow first cousins to marry, others don't; and the minimum legal age for marriage varies from state to state, as does the recognition of marriage contracts across state lines (Johnson, 1996). Despite these variations, it's hard to imagine a society that is not structured around the assumption that the vast majority of adults will live in monogamous marriages.

■ GOING GLOBAL

Plural Marriage

polygamy
A marriage in which an individual has more than one spouse at the same time.

polyandry
A marriage consisting of one wife and multiple husbands.

polygyny
A marriage consisting of one husband and multiple wives.

Many cultures around the world do not limit marriage to two people of the opposite sex, or even to two people. Some societies allow an individual to have several spouses at the same time in an arrangement known as **polygamy.** Anthropologists have estimated that about 75% of the world's societies accept some type of polygamy, although few members within those societies actually have the resources to afford more than one spouse (Murdock, 1957; Nanda, 1994).

In some parts of the world, **polyandry** permits one woman to have more than one husband. In certain areas of northern India, for instance, women can marry a set of brothers. The practice stems from economic pressures. This area's terrain is rugged— steep forests and mountains leave only about a quarter of the land suitable for farming. With so little land to support a larger population, having all sons in one family marry the same woman ensures the control of childbirth and keeps the family wealth under one roof (Fan, 1996). It's estimated that roughly 10 out of 100 families in this region practice this form of polyandry.

Even in the United States, certain groups practice **polygyny,** or the marriage of one man to several wives. Somewhere between 20,000 and 60,000 members of a dissident Mormon sect in Utah live in polygynous households (cited in McCarthy, 2001). Although their marriages are technically illegal—Utah outlawed polygamy as a condition of statehood in 1896—few polygynists are prosecuted. In fact, 2001 marked the first time in 50 years that a person was convicted on polygamy charges. However this case doesn't mean that Utah is cracking down on polygamy. In this case a man with five wives and 25 children had decided to discuss his polygynous marriage openly on national talk shows, violating an unspoken rule that such arrangements would be quietly tolerated if the participants didn't speak publicly about them.

Family as a Social Institution

social institutions
Patterned ways of solving problems and meeting the needs of a particular society.

The official definition of family considers whom we live with and whom we consider our kin. But sociologists also talk about family as a **social institution.** Institutions are the building blocks that organize society. They are the patterned ways of solving the problems and meeting the requirements of a particular society. Although people may differ over what a society "needs" and how best to fulfill those needs, all societies must have some systematic way of organizing the various aspects of everyday life. Key social institutions in modern society include the family, education, economics, politics and law, and religion. Some sociologists add health care, the military, and the mass media to the list.

Reproduction is essential to the survival of humans as a whole, and all societies must have a way of replacing their members. Within families, sexual relationships among adults are regulated; people are cared for; children are born, protected, and socialized; and newcomers are provided a family identity that gives them a sense of belonging. Just how these activities are carried out varies from society to society. Indeed, we've already seen that different societies have different ideas about which relationships qualify for designation as a family. But the institution of family, whatever its form, remains the center of social life in virtually all societies.

To be a member of a family group means more than simply being connected to other individuals in named relationships. It also means having certain legal and culturally recognizable rights and responsibilities, which are spelled out in the formal laws of the state and the informal norms of custom and tradition. Parents, for instance, have legal obligations to provide basic necessities—food, shelter, clothing, nurturance—for their children. If they fail to meet these obligations, they may face legal charges of negligence or abuse.

Along with spelling out obligations, the institution of family includes some assumptions about authority—about who has the legitimate right to control or influence the lives of others (Hunter, 1991). In other societies, someone outside the nuclear family may hold this authority, such as the father's brother or the community at large. In U.S. society, parents have the legal right to control their children. However, in cases of multiple parents (birth parents, adoptive parents, stepparents, foster parents, and so on) the lines of authority may be murky. Courts must sometimes determine who has legitimate authority over children, as in custody cases in which biological parents have attempted to regain custody of children put up for adoption.

Conflict over family authority can sometimes have grave consequences. In 2003 a bitter dispute became the lightening rod for a national debate about the legal parameters of family. Terri Schiavo, a severely brain-damaged Florida woman, had lived on life support for 13 years. State law allowed her husband to make life-or-death decisions. He wanted to remove her from life support. Two years later, over aggressive opposition by her parents, religious interest groups, and even some federal legislators, he was granted his wish.

Terri Schiavo in 1990 before collapsing into a "persistent vegetative state" . . .

. . . and 13 years later before she was taken off life-support equipment; she died in 2005.

Family as a Cultural Symbol

Judging from the strong emotions evoked by debates over the definition of family, it's clear that family is important not just for whom it includes or for how it meets society's needs, but for what it stands for. Many people fervently believe that as the family goes, so goes the country. Hence,

> the task of defining what the American family *is* [is] integral to the very task of defining America itself. . . . Obviously more is at stake than a dictionary definition of "the family." The debate actually takes form as a political judgment about the fate of *one particular conception of the family and family life* [emphases in original]. (Hunter, 1991, pp. 177, 180)

In U.S. society family has become a powerful symbol of decency. You can be assured that if you go out to eat at a family restaurant, you'll probably not see a fully stocked bar or scantily clad servers. Disneyland and Disneyworld are considered family theme parks because they emphasize the wholesomeness of the activities they provide. You'll find no pubs, strip clubs, or gambling halls there. Likewise, every video rental store has a "family movie" section. But the films you'll find here aren't necessarily about families. Instead the label *family* identifies films devoid of graphic sex and violence, with themes children and adults can enjoy together.

Some people believe that a definition of family that goes beyond the official definition demeans family's symbolic importance. From their perspective, family means only the most traditional type: married parents and their children. If people have the right to define a family however they see fit, they would empty family of its symbolic meaning and power. The significance of marriage, in particular, rests on its uniqueness—the belief that it is not one lifestyle among many but the fundamental intimate arrangement in society. Some fear that when relationships that aren't marriages start being treated as if they are, marriage loses its cultural value and relevance.

But to many others, the popular rhetoric of "family values" is little more than a thin cover for a particular political agenda. In their view, those who deplore cohabiting heterosexual and homosexual couples, the increasing numbers of single and working mothers, the growth of nonfamily households, and the high rates of divorce are making an explicit judgment about the sorts of human relationships we ought to define as "appropriate."

STRUCTURAL FAMILIES OR EMOTIONAL FAMILIES?

To those who argue for a more inclusive definition, the shape and configuration of a family are less important than the emotional bonds that can exist between people. Should, or can, our official definition of family go beyond people who are structurally tied to one another by law or by blood to include people tied to one another by their commitments, love, and interdependence?

Families We Choose

Despite the official definition and political attempts to limit family definitions, in everyday usage we are likely to use the word *family* to describe a group of individuals who have achieved a significant degree of emotional closeness and sharing, even if they're not related. Indeed, an approach to defining family that relies more on feelings and less on formal structure is appealing to many family scholars. Compare the following definition once proposed by the American Home Economics Association (now called the American Association of Family and Consumer Science) to the Census Bureau definition we examined earlier:

> two or more persons who share resources, share responsibility for decisions, share values and goals, and have commitment to one another over time. The family is that climate that one "comes home to" and it is this network of sharing and commitments that most accurately describes the family unit, regardless of blood, legal ties, adoption or marriage. (quoted in Christensen, 1990, p. 36)

Notice how this definition highlights emotional ties, obligation, and cooperation, not formally recognized relationships and living arrangements.

A prominent sociologist once argued that we ought to define family as "a unit comprising two or more persons who live together for an extended period of time, and who share in one or more of the following: work (for wages and house), sex, care and feeding of children, and intellectual, spiritual, and recreational activities" (D'Antonio, 1983, p. 92). Another suggests that any definition of family should emphasize commitment and have, at its core, the expectation that adults care for and protect children, "no matter what living arrangements they enter into" (Giddens, 2007, p. 31).

Changes in society and in contemporary lifestyles have led many people to construct nonfamily care networks to supply them with the kinds of emotional satisfaction and assistance that most people typically seek from officially recognized kin (Hansen, 2005). You may know of situations in which **fictive kin**—people other than legal or biological relatives—play a family-like role in providing for the emotional and other needs of others. For instance, instead of marrying or relying on children or siblings, as they approach retirement age, many single older women these days are forming lasting bonds with longtime friends that include, among other things, dividing chores, pooling financial resources, and purchasing insurance policies or homes together (Gross, 2004). Or perhaps you have a close family friend whom you've referred to for years as "Uncle So-and-So" or "Aunt So-and-So," even though he or she isn't a sibling of either parent. In some situations, choosing whom you identify as family is left to your discretion. The family status of in-laws and step-relatives, for instance, is often left to the judgment of individual families. The powerful emotional connections we can form with these "chosen relatives" shows that, in practice, family is rarely limited to formally recognized kin relations.

■ **fictive kin**
People other than legal or blood relatives who play family roles by providing for the emotional and other needs of others.

■ TAKING A CLOSER LOOK

Fictive Kin in Ethnic Communities

Fictive kin have historically played an important role in certain ethnic communities. For instance, in some Latin American communities, *compadrazgo* is a form of fictive kinship in which adults outside the blood family are named as protectors of newborn children. Unlike contemporary forms of godparenting, which are often merely symbolic, *comadres* and *compadres* form close, lasting bonds with family members, ensuring their involvement throughout the child's life. In times of economic hardship they are expected to provide security to the family (Kana'iaupuni, Donato, Thompson-Colón, & Stainback, 2005).

In her book *All Our Kin,* anthropologist Carol Stack (1974) describes fictive kin relationships in a Midwestern black neighborhood called "the Flats." The people in this community used many kinship terms to refer to relationships based on caring, loving, and close friendship. These "kin" felt the sort of obligations, responsibilities, and loyalties we typically associated with blood relations. Stack found that the community's informal system of parental rights and duties determines who is eligible to be a member of a child's "family."

This system often conflicts with the official law of the state concerning parenthood. For instance, a girl who gives birth as a teenager might not raise and nurture the child. Although she may live in the same house as the baby, an **othermother**—her mother, grandmother, aunt, older sister, cousin, or an adult female friend—may do the actual child rearing (Collins, 2002). Young mothers and their firstborn daughters or sons are often raised as sisters or brothers. The child learns to distinguish his or her "mother" and "father" (the biological parents) from his or her "mama" and "daddy" (the people who raised him or her). Usually—Stack estimates about 80% of the time—the mother and the "mama" are the same person. But in those other cases, the "mama" can be someone else, when relatives conclude that the mother is not emotionally ready to nurture the child and fulfill her parental duties. The "mama's" relatives and their husbands and wives also become a part of the child's extended family.

In sum, social circumstances can sometimes alter traditional ideas about kinship. People can be recognized as family not because they have biological ties but because they assume the recognized responsibilities of kin—they "help each other out" in times of need.

■ **othermother**
An adult woman who raises a child when relatives conclude that the child's biological mother is not old enough or emotionally ready to fulfill her parental duties.

The Controversy Over Same-Sex Marriage

For some people, family is less a matter of whom they choose to include than whom they are legally *prevented* from including in their family. One of the most contentious debates about the definition of family today is whether same-sex couples should be granted the right to marry and thereby create culturally and legally legitimate families.

Current Legal Status

In some countries, gays and lesbians can have their relationships legally ratified. Belgium, Spain, and the Netherlands allow gay couples to legally marry, as do several provinces in Canada. France, Denmark, Portugal, and Germany allow same-sex couples to enter "civil unions" or "registered partnerships," which grant them many of the legal and economic benefits and responsibilities of heterosexual marriage (Lyall, 2004).

The matter is far from resolved in the United States, however. Vermont legalized civil unions (but not marriage) for same-sex couples in 2000, extending benefits like inheritance rights and full medical, dental, and life insurance to "domestic partners." Since then, similar laws have been approved in Connecticut, California, Oregon, New Hampshire, and New Jersey. In 2007 California became the first state to allow overnight "conjugal" visits for gay and lesbian prison inmates and their partners (McKinley, 2007).

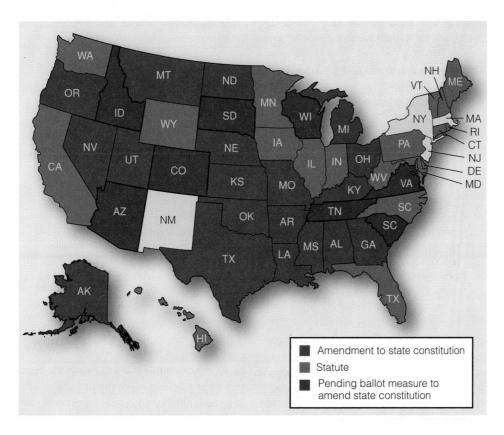

FIGURE 1.2
State Laws Banning
Same-Sex Marriage
Source: New York Times,
2006.

In addition, according to the Human Rights Campaign, a national advocacy group, more than 8,000 employers—and 215 Fortune 500 companies—provide domestic partner benefits for their gay and lesbian workers (cited in Joyce, 2005). In 2004 Massachusetts became the first state to grant same-sex couples the right to legally marry, provided they are state residents. California followed suit in 2008.

But most states, 44 at last count (Figure 1.2), have moved in the opposite direction, either enacting statutes that define marriage as a union of a man and a woman or including bans against same-sex marriage in their state constitutions (National Conference of State Legislatures, 2005). Courts in New Mexico and Oregon have nullified same-sex marriages that had been permitted by some cities (Mehren, 2005). In 2006 the New York State Supreme Court ruled that denying same-sex couples the right to marry does not violate the state constitution. In 2005 the Michigan state legislature ruled that its law defining marriage as a relationship between one man and one woman meant that gay and lesbian state workers are not entitled to health benefits for their partners (Lyman, 2005).

At the federal level, the 1996 Defense of Marriage Act formally reaffirmed the definition of marriage as the union of one man and one woman; authorized all states to refuse to accept same-sex marriages from other states if they ever become legal; and denied federal pension, health, and other benefits to same-sex couples. However, because the Constitution's "Full Faith and Credit Clause" requires each state to recognize the lawful actions of others states, some opponents of legal same-sex marriage worry that federal courts could overrule the Defense of Marriage Act and force states to recognize gay marriages performed elsewhere (Masci, 2004). In 2006 the U.S. Senate began debate on a constitutional amendment that would strictly limit marriage to heterosexual couples.

The Argument to Legalize Same-Sex Marriage

Although domestic partnership or civil union laws and policies go a long way toward legally recognizing long-term gay and lesbian relationships, many people feel such changes are inadequate. Advocates of same-sex marriage argue that allowing gay and lesbian individuals to legally marry would result in a more secure, stable, and protective relationship. After the Court of Appeals in New York ruled that the state could bar same-sex couples from legally marrying, the chief judge who opposed the ruling stated:

> The true nature and extent of the discrimination suffered by gays and lesbians is perhaps best illustrated by the simple truth that each one of the plaintiffs could lawfully enter into a marriage of convenience with a complete stranger of the opposite sex tomorrow, and thereby immediately obtain all of the myriad benefits and protections [of] marriage. Plaintiffs are, however, denied these rights because they each desire instead to marry the person they love and with whom they have created their family. (quoted in Wolfson, 2006, p. 3)

Without legal status, such family relationships can sometimes be difficult to preserve. For instance, homosexual partners of victims of the September 11, 2001, attack on the Pentagon were not eligible for the same survivor benefits offered to heterosexual spouses in the state of Virginia (Farmer, 2002). In contrast, the governor of New York issued an executive order making same-sex surviving partners of victims of the attack on the World Trade Center eligible for aid of up to $30,000 from the state's Crime Victim Board (Dahir, 2002).

In addition to citing these sorts of practical problems, some advocates of gay marriage argue that legalizing it would lead to greater public acceptance of homosexual people in general. Having the right to legally marry and start families would combat the all-too-common belief that gay relationships are solely about sexual activity and would force heterosexuals to acknowledge that gay couples can be seriously committed to each other and take on traditional family responsibilities. Far from being a repudiation of family, then, the desire to legally marry acknowledges the ideal of family.

The Argument Against Legalizing Same-Sex Marriage

Public opinion on legalizing same-sex marriage is, at best, mixed. Although acceptance of gays and lesbians in the military, in the workplace, as elementary school teachers, and as politicians has grown over the past several decades, support of laws allowing gay couples to marry is tepid. A recent study found that only 32% of U.S. adults favor a law that would allow homosexuals to marry, and only 45% favored allowing same-sex couples the right to enter civil unions (Pew Research Center, 2007). Even people who consider themselves supportive of gay rights in general are ambivalent about legalizing gay marriage (Seelye & Elder, 2003).

Most opposition to legalizing same-sex marriage comes from conservative religious groups that feel such legal recognition would destroy U.S. families and society. In 2004 a prominent evangelical minister proclaimed in apocalyptic terms that if same-sex marriage were legalized, "the family as it has been known for five millennia will crumble, presaging the fall of Western civilization itself" (quoted in Coontz, 2005, p. 273).

Ironically, some opposition to legalizing same-sex marriage comes from a small number of gays and lesbians. They argue that legalizing same-sex marriage would be a civil rights victory but would render gays and lesbians even more invisible to the larger society and undermine the movement to establish a separate and unique gay culture and identity (Ettelbrick, 1992; Johnson, 1996; Stacey, 2001). Some fear that homosexual married couples would be expected to behave just like heterosexual married couples, amounting to acceptance of a heterosexual standard for what a successful intimate relationship ought to look like (Lewin, 1996). In fact, some gay opponents of homosexual marriage argue that the absence of marriage as a regulating institution in their intimate lives actually gives them the space to define their families in richer ways, to include friends, neighbors, and community (Johnson, 1996).

In the end, the debate over legalizing same-sex marriage may be more symbolic than practical. Canadian same-sex couples did not run in droves to courthouses to marry when such an option became legal in certain provinces there. Although there are no official statistics, gay rights organizations put the number at only about 3,000 marriages nationally in the first year. Of those, about 1,000 were U.S. couples who returned to the United States after getting married (Mulkern, 2004). In Massachusetts, the number of same-sex marriages has dropped steadily since 2004 (Belluck, 2008).

Moreover, long-term gay and lesbian households have existed for decades—operating much like heterosexual marriages—without legal marital status. Over one third of lesbian households and one fifth of gay male households include biological children under the age of 18. Eight states and the District of Columbia now allow unmarried same-sex couples to adopt, and 40% of private adoption agencies report placing children with same-sex couples (Coontz, 2005). Indeed, even without legal recognition, the family structure for most gay parents tends to be based on a conventional heterosexual model: two parents living in one household (Bowe, 2006).

In sum, more is at stake in this debate than the emotional rewards of formalizing shared commitment in a loving relationship and the practical rewards of legal recognition of gay and lesbian marriage. This issue is fundamentally about what arrangements we as a culture believe deserve the label "family." These beliefs can ultimately shape the law, public policy, and the contours of our everyday lives.

FAMILY PRIVACY AND AUTONOMY

One of the most powerful values associated with definitions of family in U.S. society today is that family is, or should be, private. **Family privacy** means that a family can exercise discretion and be protected from unwanted outside interference, whether it be from nosy neighbors or governmental agencies. Families are assumed to be the best judges and guardians of their own interests and needs. Privacy is usually linked to **autonomy**—the ability of families to make their own decisions about their futures or about the treatment of their members.

■ **family privacy**
The ability of families to keep their everyday activities confidential and to be protected from outside interference.

■ **family autonomy**
The ability of families to make their own decisions about their future or about the treatment of their members.

The Cultural Ideal of Family Privacy

Although family privacy is something most people in the United States take for granted, there is nothing "natural" about it. Societies create privacy when members agree that certain aspects of family life are legitimately off limits to others (Nock, 1998b). In general, in the United States we include in this category such matters as sexuality and other displays of affection, grieving, and family conflict (Fox, 1999).

Family privacy is maintained by powerful social norms and everyday expectations. For instance, we are advised to "keep our noses out" of other people's family affairs.

The violation of this norm—when we feel the urge to scold somebody else's child, for example—can create profound discomfort in us and extreme anger in others. Such norms, of course, vary from society to society. In many cultures, community members are expected to discipline any children who are misbehaving.

At first glance, the question of whether or not family life is—or should be—private and autonomous appears obvious and simple. After all, we decide with whom we will form relationships, what those relationships will look like, if and when to have children, and how we will treat other members of our family. Indeed, few of us would question the appropriateness of these decisions being solely our own. Moreover, we shudder at the idea of outsiders having access to the most intimate moments of family life. Witness the emotional debate over whether the media should cover families grieving the loss of loved ones killed during the war in Iraq.

Many people in our society today feel that what goes on in a family should always be protected from community interference, public scrutiny, and state regulation. Family life, they believe, is best left to families—not the government, courts, or other public agencies (Gubrium & Holstein, 1990). Such privacy is a cornerstone of family law (Sprague, 2002) and is essential to the development of liberty and freedom (Feshbach & Feshbach, 1978; Fraser, 1987).

Some sociologists argue that privacy helps contribute to family stability. Once marital problems are made public, the marriage may start falling apart at an accelerated rate. Conversely, the couple may have a better chance of working out their problems if outsiders mind their own business. In addition, family privacy can help its members develop a feeling of being a unified, cohesive group, which is healthy for that family as well as for the larger society (Berardo, 1998).

Unfortunately, the high value that our society places on family privacy has made it difficult for us to recognize the problems that privacy can cause. For more than 4 years, a Missouri man lived in an apartment complex with a boy he had kidnapped. None of the neighbors noticed anything strange, even when another boy, also kidnapped, began living there. They simply assumed they were a family. To many, this story was a cautionary tale about the price of minding one's own business. Said one sociologist, "In public life nowadays, we have a norm of noninvolvement. It's almost considered a faux pas to get into someone's face and say, 'How's your family life?'" (quoted in Saulny & Sander, 2007, p. 25). As we'll see in more detail in Chapter 13, when abuse remains concealed, abusive family members feel less pressure to stop, and their victims have a harder time seeking outside help.

The Location of Privacy

The home provides the symbolic as well as the physical boundaries between private and public, between family and nonfamily. Our homes are the places where we most expect to be left alone or to deal with others if and as we choose. Home denotes a physical location where we can relax, express ourselves candidly, show affection, enjoy sexuality, and reinforce family ties (Allen, 1988).

Home Sweet Home

A number of legal provisions protect the privacy of the home. The Third Amendment to the U.S. Constitution prohibits the quartering of soldiers in private homes during peacetime, reflecting the notion of home as a place where people are entitled to undisturbed seclusion. The Fourth Amendment guarantees individuals the right to be secure in their houses against unreasonable searches and seizures.

To be sure, friends, neighbors, distant relatives, strangers, people selling things or soliciting donations, and various others breach the privacy of our homes from time to time. But allowing their presence is clearly a courtesy we extend. They are visitors, and we expect them to behave that way. Unlike household members, who can use the phone or bathroom at will, check what's in the refrigerator, or turn on the TV whenever they want, visitors must seek and receive permission to do these things. Even people who have known a family for years and have slept or eaten in their home many times may be somewhat reluctant to shed the visitor role and really make themselves "at home" by entering without knocking or taking food without asking. Much of the humor of a character like Kramer on the popular 1990s television show *Seinfeld* derived from wanton disregard for this norm as he continually barged into his neighbor's apartment.

In everyday life the private home gives people a place where they can behave in ways that outsiders might discourage if they constantly watched and evaluated us. As you're well aware, we all do and say things in the privacy of our own homes and in the company of family members that we wouldn't dream of doing or saying in front of strangers or even close friends.

Over the years, innovations in household amenities have contributed to increasing family privacy by moving family activities from visible, public locations into the home. Telephones, for instance, allow people to communicate with one another without being in their immediate presence. Refrigerators make it unnecessary to visit the market every day to buy perishable food. Air conditioning allows us to spend hot, stuffy summer evenings inside instead of on the front porch or at the local ice cream parlor. With the Internet, fax machines, text messaging, and home shopping cable networks, a family can practically survive without *ever* leaving the privacy of its home.

Ironically, however, technology also poses one of the greatest challenges to family privacy in contemporary society. When we surf the Internet, for instance, we leave a record of the Web sites we've visited and purchases we've made that is accessible to businesses and marketers. Recently, data mining has become a common practice that searches large amounts of data for revealing patterns, raising additional privacy concerns.

Front Stage and Back Stage

To some sociologists—most notably, Erving Goffman (1959)—the distinction between private and public behavior is crucial to understanding family life. Goffman argued that social life often requires us to be like actors on a theatrical stage, performing so that others will see us in a particular way. Think of these people who observe our behavior as the "audience." The "roles" we play are the images of ourselves we are trying to project. And the "dialogue" consists of our communications with others. The overarching goal is to enact a performance that is believable to a particular audience, and that allows us to achieve the goals we desire.

Different locations require different sorts of performances, so sociologists distinguish between public, **front stage** interaction and private, **back stage** interaction. In the theater, front stage is where performances take place. These performances are presented for the eyes and ears of the audience and are meant to convey a believable image. When applied to everyday social interaction, front stage is where people carry out interaction performances and maintain appropriate public appearances in front of

■ **front stage**
Region of social life where people carry out interaction performances and maintain appropriate public appearances in front of others.

■ **back stage**
Private region of social life where people can be authentic and can knowingly and sometimes cynically violate their front stage performances.

others. For restaurant workers, for instance, front stage is the dining room where the customers (the audience) are present. Here the servers (the actors) are expected to present themselves as upbeat, happy, competent, and courteous.

In contrast, theatrical back stage refers to the wings and dressing rooms where people remove makeup, rehearse lines, rehash performances, and slip "out of character." In social life, back stage is synonymous with privacy. It's where people can prepare for upcoming front stage encounters or comment on those just completed. It's also where people can knowingly and sometimes cynically violate their front stage performances. Going back to the restaurant example, back stage is the kitchen area where the once-friendly, courteous servers now shout, shove dishes, and even complain about or make fun of the customers.

The distinction between front stage and back stage is crucial to family life. Much of the time we spend with our family members is spent in public—at restaurants, grocery stores, Little League games, school plays, neighborhood parties—where audiences expect families to present a cohesive and consistent image of themselves. Have you ever witnessed a married couple fighting in a shopping mall or a parent screaming at a child in a supermarket? These scenarios violate the unspoken expectation that families not "air their dirty laundry" in public. Hence, family members—especially spouses—often feel compelled to hide conflict and criticism of each other when they are on front stage.

Fortunately for society, however, most families do have access to a back stage area in their private households where they need not be concerned with how others judge their looks, actions, or statements. Karen Fowler, one of the individuals who spent nearly six weeks living under constant camera surveillance for the television show *Big Brother,* claimed that the stress of having no privacy and constantly being watched nearly caused her to have a nervous breakdown ("Indiana Woman Says," 2000). It doesn't require cameras to disrupt our privacy, however. If you've ever had guests in your house for a long time, you know how disruptive they can be to family life. It's not just that they represent an extra mouth to feed or complicate social plans. Their presence robs the family of the ability to "go back stage" in its own home.

Family privacy means more than an escape from worrying about our public image, however. Underlying the distinction between front and back stage behavior is the belief that the most authentic family experiences occur in the privacy of the home (Gubrium & Holstein, 1987). This is where a family's *true* feelings and characteristics emerge. Most of us believe we can see the *real* family only in its private moments, "behind closed doors."

For example, parents who are harsh and abusive to their children in private may work hard to appear loving and gentle in public so outsiders won't judge them negatively. Likewise, the incompatible married couple may maintain a façade of cordiality when with friends. Thus the back stage aspect of the household is not only intrinsic to family life but is also, at times, camouflaged, hidden, or protected (Gubrium & Holstein, 1990).

This notion has implications for real, accurate knowledge of families. We know what our own families are really like because we've seen them back stage. However, despite our curiosity about other people's family relationships, we usually don't have access to their back stage, so we can only know them in terms of their public presentations and discourse. The gap between public images and private realities may be quite wide. If, in fact, the "true" nature of family interaction remains hidden from public view, our understandings of families may be inaccurate or incomplete. It's ironic that privacy, so essential to family life, is also a cultural value that can obscure our understanding of it.

PERSONAL DESIRES AND FAMILY OBLIGATIONS

Within families, people face the dilemma of how to balance the pursuit of their private, personal desires with their feelings of obligation to loved ones. Consider the 20-year-old college student who wants desperately to be an actress but whose parents are counting on her to take over the family dry-cleaning business after graduation. Or what about the 50-year-old son who must turn down a promotion in a different state because he needs to live close to his elderly, ailing parents.

The way people juggle family obligations and personal interests varies from society to society. Scholars often distinguish between collectivist and individualist cultures. **Collectivist cultures** are those in which members tend to subordinate their individual goals to the goals of the larger group, and to value obligation to others over personal freedom. In contrast, **individualist cultures** are those in which individual rights, self-realization, personal autonomy, and personal identity are likely to take precedence (Dion & Dion, 1996; Triandis, 1995). Keep in mind that in no society does every citizen live his or her entire life according to collectivist or individualist principles. These terms describe the values and ideals that tend to be emphasized in a given society.

Collectivist Cultures

In collectivist cultures, such as those found in most Asian societies, people view the family unit as members who are interdependent and highly involved in one another's lives. Duty, sacrifice, and compromise are considered desirable traits. Collectivism doesn't mean a complete negation of the individual's well-being or interest, however. Instead, people assume that maintaining the group's well-being is ultimately the best guarantee of the individual's well-being (Hofstede, 1984; Sinha, Sinha, Verma, & Sinha, 2001).

In collectivist cultures, family obligations can last forever. In rural parts of China, for example, people believe that individuals continue to exist after death, and surviving family members are obligated to tend to all their wants or needs. Because an unmarried life is considered to be incomplete, parents of dead bachelor sons will go to great lengths to ensure their dead child's contentment. One way to do that is through a folk custom called *minghun,* or "afterlife marriage." Parents will search for a dead woman to be their dead son's bride. Once they have found—and paid for—a corpse, the pair are buried together as a married couple. The price can be steep, sometimes amounting to several years' worth of income, but people describe this custom as their parental duty and an expression of family loyalty (Yardley, 2006).

Shame is a powerful means of social control in collectivist cultures. Because each person is a reflection of the entire group, his or her singular actions can disgrace everyone in that group. This belief gives family members a great stake in the behavior of other family members. And shame is not limited to living relatives. In China, for instance, an individual's present misbehaviors can dishonor all ancestors as well as all future generations.

In collectivist cultures, personal identity is often subsumed within the family's identity. In traditional India, for instance, feelings of status and prestige derived more

■ **collectivist cultures**
Cultures in which members tend to subordinate their individual goals to the goals of the larger group, and to value obligation to others over personal freedom.

■ **individualist cultures**
Cultures in which individual rights, self-realization, personal autonomy, and personal identity are likely to take precedence over family obligations.

In China's rapidly aging society, couples like this one from the village of Baodeng have no grown children to care for them in their old age.

from strong identification with the reputation and honor of the family than from individual achievements (Roland, 1988). The tradition of arranged marriages—employed in as many as 80% of cultures outside the United States (though they are rarely the only means of marriage)—fits with this orientation toward family status (Pasupathi, 2002). Personal well-being in marriage is not so much a matter of emotional intimacy as it is in individualistic societies, whose members assume marriages are based on individual feelings of romantic love (Dion & Dion, 1996).

■ GOING GLOBAL

Family Obligation in Japan

Traditional Japan offers a good example of collectivist family ideology. Until the last decade or so, the sense of familial responsibility was quite strong in Japan. When Japanese men and women reached their mid-20s, pressure to marry—to please parents and peers and to fulfill social obligations—tended to mount rapidly. As recently as two decades ago, between 25 and 30% of Japanese marriages were arranged (Applbaum, 1995). In addition, most people had a strong, lifelong commitment to their relatives. Most Japanese elderly lived with one of their children.

But things in Japan are changing. Arranged marriage is becoming less and less popular. Prior to World War II, well over half of Japanese marriages were arranged. By the late 1990s that figure had dropped below 10% (Figure 1.3).

The Japanese emphasis on family responsibility now plays against a societal backdrop of an intense desire for individual social mobility. Workplace pressures are strong, and long hours away from family are the norm—especially for men. On average, Japanese workers put in about four more hours a week on the job than their U.S. counterparts, amounting to about 200 more work hours per year ("Length of Workweek," 2001).

Perhaps we shouldn't be surprised, then, that collectivism appears to be losing some of its influence among younger Japanese. In one study of Japanese attitudes, older people were more likely to hold traditional collectivist attitudes toward their families and their place in society than younger people, who were found to be more dedicated to improving their own lives and to valuing their own achievements rather than collec-

FIGURE 1.3
Arranged and Love Marriages in Japan, 1930–1995
Source: "Tying the Knot," July 28, 1998. http://web-japan.org/trends98/honbun/ntj980729.html.

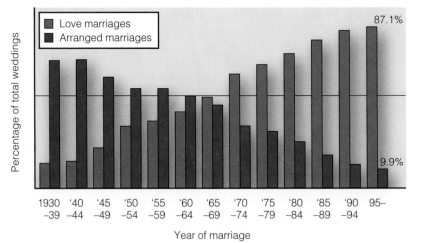

tive achievements (Ishii-Kuntz, 1989). Even though their primary loyalty is still to their families, many young Japanese report resentment at being forced to subordinate their personal interests to a tightly organized educational and employment system. Not coincidentally, the number of three-generation Japanese families living in the same household has steadily declined over the past several decades (cited in Strom, 2001).

Individualist Cultures

In sharp contrast, cultures like those of western Europe, the United States, Canada, and Australia tend to value individual freedom, autonomy, personal development, and self-gratification over group obligation and duty. Interestingly, in some individualist societies family obligation is written into the law, perhaps to ensure that individuals who otherwise may feel little moral obligation to assist family members in need will do so. In France, for instance, a law known as *obligation alimentaire* spells out which family members are required to give support to others and under what circumstances. The first priority is to spouses. The second is to ascendants and descendants (parents, grandparents, children, grandchildren, and beyond—without limit). The third priority is to in-laws, unless a divorce occurs. Even if an individual's spouse dies, a person's obligation to in-laws persists as long as there are surviving children (Twigg & Grand, 1998).

U.S. culture has always celebrated independent people whose success—usually measured in financial terms—is based on their individual achievement and self-reliance (Bellah, Madsen, Sullivan, Swidler, & Tipton, 1985). A key task in "normal" self-development in such an environment is the eventual separation from one's family. Most of us take for granted that someday we'll leave the home of our parents and start our own families, where we'll be expected to devote most of our emotional and economic attention. In fact, we sometimes see childhood chiefly as preparation for the crucial event of leaving home. I seriously doubt that when typical U.S. teenagers imagine their future, it includes still living with their parents when they're 40 or 50 years old.

But not every segment of U.S. society downplays their family obligations. A survey of 2,352 U.S. adults between the ages of 45 and 55 found that fewer than 20% of whites care for their elderly parents or in-laws, compared to 28% of African Americans, 34% of Latinos, and 42% of Asian Americans (American Association of Retired Persons, 2001). People born outside the United States are much more likely to provide such care (43%) than those born here (20%). Ironically, this study also found that while Asian American adults provide the most care to their elderly parents of any ethnoracial group, they are also the most likely to feel guilt over not doing enough, reflecting a powerful sense of collectivist obligation.

Critics of U.S. individualism note that it creates an economic, cost-versus-benefit, "What's in it for me?" approach to intimacy and family. As in an economic transaction, we're initially attracted to and more likely to stay with those we think can provide us with the highest "payoff" at the lowest cost (see Chapter 7 for more on the process of relationship formation). Feelings of obligation and responsibility are rarely part of the equation. When people ask themselves questions like "Am I getting what I want from this relationship?" "Am I getting as much as my partner is getting?" "Would I be more satisfied with someone else?" they are implicitly applying highly individualistic calculations to their intimate lives (Bellah, 1995). These questions, critics argue, replace other questions like "Didn't my marriage vows commit me to try to make this relationship work?" and "What can I do to make my partner feel happy and fulfilled?"

Although some degree of cost-benefit thinking in intimacy is inevitable—after all, we're not likely to form a relationship with someone who provides us with no desirable or satisfying outcomes—relationships formed only in terms of personal gratification may fail to fulfill their traditional function of providing people with stable relationships that tie them to the larger community (Bellah et al., 1985). Take, for instance, the phenomenon of interracial or interfaith marriage. In a culture that prides itself on the ideal of individual rights and freedom, marriages between people of different racial, ethnic, or religious backgrounds ought to be perceived as little more than individual people acting on their right to fall in love with whomever they want. However, for groups whose numbers are declining or are already small, such marriages can be perceived as threats to an entire culture and heritage.

Family Obligation and Social Policy

Some scholars fear that the more individualistic a society is, the more difficult it becomes for people to experience the things we typically associate with family relationships: strong emotional interdependence, mutual caring, and a high degree of sensitivity to others' needs and desires. From this perspective, society will suffer unless family obligation—especially, parents' obligation to their children—becomes the guiding force in public policy (Bellah et al., 1985; Etzioni, 1993). In families without children, an emphasis on the individual rights of the adults may be appropriate. But families with children are engaged in activities with vital social consequences. When parents have children, they enter into an unspoken social contract with the larger society. Hence, many people feel that individual freedoms may need to be restrained in the interests of family obligation (Galston, 1995a).

For instance, some states have imposed mandatory waiting periods for couples contemplating divorce, and others are debating whether to restore the old requirement of proving fault in cases where only one spouse is seeking divorce. These measures are designed to make it especially difficult for couples with children to divorce.

Such policies reflect a preference for intact, two-parent families. People who support these policies don't necessarily believe that all single-parent families are somehow "dysfunctional" or that all parents seeking divorce are selfish. After all, millions of single parents successfully provide good homes for their children. Nor does the endorsement of two-parent families necessarily imply nostalgia for the traditional male-breadwinner families of the 1950s. Many supporters of divorce law reform simply want to point out that, on balance and all else being equal, two-parent families are best suited to the task of raising children and that family policy ought, therefore, to focus on strengthening two-parent families (Galston, 1995a).

The crusade to heighten the value of marriage in U.S. society by suggesting policies designed to make individuals think more about their family obligations is an idea few would argue with. But whether we realize it or not, the pursuit of individual interests has become an acceptable part of family life. As one author put it, "we marry to make ourselves happy" (Smiley, 2000, p. 62). Even the staunchest critic of individualism would have trouble congratulating a woman who stays with a man who beats her because she vowed to stay married "for better or worse." Few people want to return to an age when it was nearly impossible for women to divorce their husbands or earn enough money to support themselves. And few of us feel that parents should sacrifice all their worldly pleasures and personal happiness so that their children or their elderly parents can live a little better (Schwartz, 1987).

Perhaps individual self-fulfillment isn't necessarily incompatible with family. If you think about it, family obligations are difficult to satisfy unless a person is first personally fulfilled. Can an unhappy person ever be a good, thoughtful spouse? Can a person in a miserable marriage ever be a complete and effective parent to his or her children? Research continually shows that people who are personally satisfied with and gratified by their relationships are more committed to seeing them work. In other words, it's easier to remain in a relationship when you're happy than when you're unhappy (Cox, Wexler, Rusbult, & Gaines, 1997). Remaining in loveless or conflict-ridden marriages often costs both the spouses and their children dearly (Riley, 1991).

And what about the argument we hear that parents who devote significant time and energy to their careers are selfishly neglecting their familial obligations? Ironically, such an argument rests on the assumption that parents alone raise their children. But we all have a stake in the successful development of children, and we all ought to be committed to ensuring their well-being. Other societies protect children not by punishing working parents but by changing the social structure to provide adequate institutional support for children. Sweden, for instance, shows a societal commitment to children through prenatal and postnatal medical care and liberal parental leave policies, childhood immunization, adequate nutrition, access to preschool programs and well-funded schools, elimination of child poverty, safe neighborhoods, and the prevention of unwanted pregnancies through sex education and the availability of contraceptives.

Finally, the contention that U.S. adults have completely abandoned all their social, familial obligations and commitments in the pursuit of self-fulfillment is most certainly an overstatement. After all, family—with its enduring emphasis on interdependence and attachment—has survived despite our enormous cultural emphasis on individualism and self-reliance. Couples still marry, the desire to have and raise children remains high, and the vast majority of older adults who need care receive it from their families.

Indeed, research suggests that we haven't become a society of individuals totally isolated from our families. For instance, more U.S. adults than ever have grandparents who are alive, and the ties between grandparents and grandchildren may actually be stronger than ever (Bengtson, 2001). Most U.S. adults stay in contact with family and provide advice, emotional support, and financial help when needed. Close ties between siblings and with an extended network of aunts and uncles, cousins, and other kin often persist over the life course, providing a critical source of support (Horwitz, 1994). So even against a cultural backdrop of extreme individualism, collective interests and ties remain strong in U.S. families.

WHAT DOES IT ALL MEAN?

Family is a vital component of our everyday lives, but it is not something we can easily define or into which we can easily place people. The debate over what a family is, how private it should be, and how people should balance their personal needs with their family responsibilities reflects profound questions about what we, as a society, choose to value and embrace.

It's not all that surprising that the issue of defining families reflects deep emotional divisions. You've seen in this chapter that there's more to family than meets the eye. Some cultures have ideas very different from ours about what sorts of family arrangements are normal and natural. And in this society, most people's lives depart in some way from the traditional nuclear family depicted in the official definition and in popular images of family. For that reason, throughout this book I will avoid talking about *the* family, as if there were some single entity that all agree constitutes family. Whenever possible, I'll use the plural form, *families,* to reflect a more inclusive concept.

As you think about all these issues, consider the following questions:

1. Should society's recognition of family be limited to blood and legal relations, or should we be able to choose whomever we want to be our family? What is society's interest in controlling which arrangements we call family?

2. In the near future, do you think the concept of family will expand to acknowledge the validity of many diverse relationships and living arrangements, or will it contract, reinforcing the legitimacy and desirability of the "traditional" family?

3. When and under what conditions should society protect and tolerate a family's privacy and autonomy? When should it breach them?

4. Do you think that individual self-fulfillment is incompatible with family responsibility? Would it be possible or desirable to abandon our cultural emphasis on individual achievement in favor of a more collectivist approach to everyday life?

5. How far should family obligation extend? Most people agree that we have some obligation to help our parents, but what sort of help should we feel obligated to offer siblings? And at what point should maturing children be forced to fend for themselves instead of relying on their parents?

SUMMARY

■ Even though *family* is one of the most important components of everyday life and serves as the foundation of society, it is a deceptively difficult term to define.

■ The official government definition of family determines eligibility for a variety of social programs and economic benefits, but it often comes up short in reflecting people's actual experiences.

■ Sociologists recognize that family is not only a lived experience but a social institution that provides patterned ways of solving problems and meeting the needs of society.

■ One of the key debates is whether our definition of family ought to be based on formally recognized blood or legal relationships or reflect people's emotional connections to one another.

■ One of the most controversial illustrations of the family definition debate concerns the movement to legalize (or legally prohibit) same-sex marriage.

■ Privacy and autonomy are not universal features of family life. They are maintained by powerful social norms and everyday expectations.

■ The high value we place on family privacy in this society can make it difficult to recognize the problems it can cause.

■ We often associate family privacy with a physical location—the home—and we make distinctions between interactions that occur in private spaces (back stage) and those that take place in public spaces (front stage).

■ Individuals often struggle to balance their personal desires with their feelings of obligation to their families. The outcome of this struggle is influenced by whether people live in a collectivist or an individualist culture.

■ Some social critics argue that U.S. society has become too individualistic and that people too easily downplay or disregard their family obligations.

Go to the Online Learning Center at **www.mhhe.com/newman1** to test your knowledge of the chapter concepts and key terms.

KEY TERMS

back stage   19

bilateral descent   9

collectivist cultures   21

common-law marriage   10

commuter marriage   7

extended family   6

family   6

family autonomy   17

family privacy   17

fictive kin   13

front stage   19

household   5

individualist cultures   21

kinship   8

matrilineal descent   8

monogamy   9

nuclear family   6

othermother   14

patrilineal descent   8

polyandry   10

polygamy   10

polygyny   10

social construction of family   5

social institutions   10

SEE FOR YOURSELF

In the past, photo albums and home movies provided friends and relatives with a visual glimpse into the private lives of families. Today, the Internet serves a similar purpose. Thousands of families maintain personal Web sites devoted to presenting the intimate details of their lives to anyone with a computer. What people choose to include on family Web sites can tell us a great deal about how they define family and what they see as the proudest features of their family experiences.

For this exercise, examine and analyze the contents of these Web sites. The easiest way to gain access to a list of family Web sites is to go to http://dir.yahoo.com/Society_and_Culture. Click on "Families." Then click on "Family Home Pages." Randomly select 50 or so (more if you have time) and try to document the different categories of information families include about themselves: factual information (e.g., size and location of family), specific celebrations, likes and dislikes, opinions on political or social issues, links to other Web sites, and so on. Do these pages tend to focus on nuclear families, or do they include information about extended family members? Do they tend to be "traditional" (that is, mother, father, and children) or are less traditional family arrangements represented (such as same-sex couples or single-parent families)? Are certain racial, ethnic, or religious groups over- or underrepresented? Did you notice any differences in the home pages of U.S. families versus families from other societies? What do the content and design of these home pages tell us about the nature and importance of family in people's lives? How can you explain the willingness of these families to expose such private aspects of their lives to the vast public domain of cyberspace?

2

Declining Families/ Enduring Families

On April 20, 1999, two students at Columbine High School in Littleton, Colorado, went on a shooting rampage, killing 13 people and wounding 24 others before committing suicide. It was one of the deadliest high school shootings in U.S. history. In the aftermath, people around the country searched for quick explanations. Some blamed the proliferation of violence on television, movies, and video games and the easy access to weapons in a gun-ridden society. Others talked about how the killers were bullied and intimidated by so-called jocks on campus, leading to festering feelings of resentment. Still others bemoaned the culture's alleged de-emphasis on religion and subsequent "moral breakdown."

But much of the anger that spilled out in the weeks, months, and years after the massacre eventually found a more tangible target—the gunmen's families. A national poll found that 83% of U.S. adults believed the parents were at least partly to blame (cited in Brooks, 2004). Social commentators began using terms like "parental irresponsibility" to try to make sense out of the tragedy. The killers' parents, they claimed, were insufficiently involved in their kids' lives. Eight months after the shootings, the police released a videotape the boys made prior to the shootings in which they talked about staging dress rehearsals, gathering shotguns and pipe bombs, and hiding ammunition in their houses. One recounted the time his parents walked in on him when he was trying on his black leather trench coat, with his sawed-off shotgun hidden underneath. The other boy recalled the time his mother saw him carrying a gym bag with a gun handle sticking out of the zipper. She assumed it was his BB gun (Gibbs & Roche, 1999). The father of one of the boys worked out of his home and saw his son every day but noticed nothing out of the ordinary.

The local community was quick to blame the boys' parents too. Victims' families filed wrongful death lawsuits against them. One of the lawsuits accused the parents of being "negligent in the duties and responsibilities of parental supervision," contending that "by omission and inaction" the parents "facilitated the actions" of their sons (Sink, 1999). Fearful of further legal action, the parents have never really spoken publicly about the incident. Indeed, in 2007 a judge ruled that depositions by the parents of the gunmen would remain sealed until 2027 (Cullen, 2007).

But it didn't take long for the accusations to move beyond the boys' parents to families in general. Some attributed the massacre—as well as other incidents of youth violence—to the growing numbers of children growing up with two working parents or in single-parent households:

> The breakdown of two-parent families is more than obvious. Just 40 years ago . . . fathers were responsible for the welfare of the family. Moms generally stayed home. It was safe to walk to school or go to the movies unattended. . . . It is now so common for young people to grow up in divorced households that the term "broken family" is . . . a forgotten expression in the popular culture. Fathers are living apart from their natural children. Mothers no longer stay at home, but work as a head of the household. As a result, women in our society have lost their feminine identity and the moral authority of fathers is undermined by a society that no longer embraces the structure of the family. (Jeremiah Project, 2007, p. 1)

In the end, there was no definitive single explanation for this tragedy. Nevertheless, sentiments like these reflect a broader sense of dread that the institution of family is crumbling, and taking the entire society with it. Disturbing media stories about apathetic kids, illegal drugs, poverty, domestic abuse—not to mention school shootings—symbolize the fraying of the country's social fabric. Journalists, politicians, and social commentators often use words like endangered, vulnerable, decaying, disappearing, collapsing, declining, and doomed to assess the current health and future prospects of U.S. families.

Not everyone agrees that families are in such dire straits, however. Some scholars argue that as an institution, family is as strong as ever. Although many of today's families may bear little resemblance to the traditional families of our nostalgic past, these scholars believe they still work for the most part and hence are here to stay. Indeed, it's their ability to change in response to shifting economic, political, and cultural forces that makes families strong.

In Chapter 1 we examined some of the controversies that arise in trying to define family. In this chapter we'll look at how definitions of family determine people's feelings about the state of family. How we define family is closely linked to whether we see it as an institution that is weak and in danger of disappearing, or as one that maintains its strength even as it changes its form. Let's see whether we can get past the rhetoric to examine a variety of facts about the current state of U.S. families and then try to assess just how much trouble they really are in.

THE FAMILY DECLINE PERSPECTIVE

Many people today believe that "alarming" changes in the institution of family have robbed it of its traditional influence over people's everyday lives, and of its importance in society. This view reflects what we can call the **family decline perspective.** Supporters of this perspective point to the strong movement in recent years, in the United States and other Western societies, away from traditional nuclear families and toward an assortment of households claiming to be families. They argue that the institution of family has lost many, if not all, of its traditional functions. Let's take a closer look at this perspective.

■ **family decline perspective**
An approach to understanding families that regards recent changes in family life as a sign that the overall importance of family as a social institution is eroding.

The Waning Institutional Influence of Family

We saw in Chapter 1 that family operates simultaneously at two levels—as a lived personal experience and as a social institution. Throughout our history, the institution of family has been the center of many important activities. In families, children have received educational and religious training, both children and adults could expect emotional nurturing and support, and sexual activity and reproduction have been regulated. The family was also the economic center of society, and family members worked together to earn a living and support one another financially.

But as the economy shifted from a family-based system in which families produced all they needed to survive to a wage-based system in which family members sold their labor outside the home in exchange for money, so too did the role that families played in people's lives (this economic transformation is discussed in more detail in Chapter 9). In the 19th century, the teaching of skills and values that was once a part of everyday home life began to take place elsewhere, principally in schools. A large part of the history of childhood and adolescence in the 20th century was a steady decline of parental authority and influence, and an accompanying increase in the influence of educators, peer groups, and the mass media.

To those who subscribe to the family decline perspective, the family's role as a source of emotional security and nurturing has disappeared as it has become less able to shield its members from the harsh realities of modern life (Lasch, 1977). The absenteeism rate of fathers, the apparent decline in the amount of time parents spend with their children, and the increasing proportion of a child's life spent alone, with peers, or in day care all attest, they claim, to the loss of this function (Popenoe, 1993).

We can measure the strength (or weakness) of family as an institution not just in terms of how well (or how poorly) it performs important social functions, but by the strength of the hold it has over its individual members. Strong families maintain close ties among members and direct their activities toward collective goals. But today, according to the family decline perspective, individuals have become increasingly more autonomous, less bound by their sense of obligation to family, and less committed to its norms and values (Popenoe, 1993). According to this perspective, further signs that the family may be in decline include the steady erosion of the belief in mutual assistance among family members, of family loyalty, of concern for the perpetuation of the family as a unit, and of the subordination of individual interests to the interests and welfare of the family as a group (Popenoe, 1993).

Social Change and Family Structure

Those who believe the family is in a state of decline express alarm that the traditional nuclear family is becoming less common. Family structure in modern industrialized societies has indeed undergone greater and faster change in the past several decades than in any previous period of human history (Skolnick & Skolnick, 2007). We've seen a dramatic and pervasive weakening of the expectation that people will marry, remain married, have children, and maintain separate roles within families for men and women. The transition from singlehood to marriage no longer carries the strong sense of obligation and commitment it once did.

Family has been changing since the beginning of recorded history. But, according to family decline theorists, recent changes—beginning in the 1960s—have been unique and much more serious. They believe that something can and should be done to restore family to its natural state and its rightful place in social life (Glenn, 2000).

The "Fall" of Marriage

The centerpiece of the family decline argument is concern over the state of traditional marriage. Many social scientists have argued that marriage not only is the most culturally approved intimate relationship, it also provides important benefits to spouses. For instance, some evidence suggests that married people are better off economically than people who cohabit. Married men make between 10 and 40% more than single men with similar educational attainment and employment history (Popenoe & Whitehead, 2004). People who are married may also have more emotionally and sexually satisfying lives than either single people or people who cohabit. One study even found that married men and women face lower risks of dying at any point than those who had never married or who had experienced divorce (Waite, 2000b). (See Chapter 8 for more detail.) What's not altogether clear, however, is whether marriage *causes* these benefits, or whether people who are poor, uneducated, and unwell are less likely to marry in the first place (Lerner, 2004).

Despite these apparent advantages, family decline supporters point to statistics that seem to indicate more U.S. adults are rejecting or at least postponing marriage. Over the last three decades or so, the marriage rate among those aged 15 and older has dropped from 16 per thousand people to 11.7 per thousand (U.S. Bureau of the Census, 2006b). In 1970, 67% of people in this age group were married; today that figure is 53% (U.S. Bureau of the Census, 2006a). And U.S. residents now spend more of their adult lives single than married (DePaulo, 2006). A number of factors may affect the drop in marriages, including the delaying of first marriage until older ages, the reduced tendency of divorced persons to remarry, and the increase in the number of people who simply choose to remain single.

One factor that can't be ignored is the increase in unmarried cohabitation. Between 1970 and 2005 the number of cohabiting couples increased by more than 1,000%, growing from 523,000 to about 6 million (U.S. Bureau of the Census, 2008). They now make up more than 5% of all U.S. households, up from 3% in 1990. In the past, cohabiting couples were likely to be poor people who couldn't afford to get married. Today, they come from all classes and all age, ethnic, and racial groups. Cohabitation is also common among divorced individuals, many of whom have children. It is estimated that at some point during their childhood, 1 in 4 people is likely to live in a family headed by a cohabiting couple (Graefe & Lichter, 1999).

Social policies may motivate many people's decision to live together rather than marry (Waite & Gallagher, 2000). For instance, marriage reduces welfare eligibility for individuals, and the standard income tax deduction is often lower for working married couples than for two singles. Domestic partnership policies of private companies, cities, or even states—designed to grant cohabiting couples many of the same benefits that married couples receive—may deter marriage if couples believe they can gain the same benefits whether they're married or not.

Another oft-cited sign of the reduced importance of marriage in people's lives is the increasing number of women who are bearing children while unmarried (Cherlin, 1992). According to an organization of well-known sociologists and other family experts, marriage is declining as the principal location for childbearing and child rearing, with devastating consequences for millions of children (National Marriage Project, 2001). Nowadays, many young people see sex as independent of marriage. About two thirds of teens in one study indicated that they felt it was all right for unmarried 18-year-olds to have sex if they have a strong affection for one another (Whitehead & Pearson, 2006), and the percentage of high school seniors who think having a child outside marriage is acceptable has grown over the past 20 years (Masci, 2004).

In 1980, 18% of all births in the United States were to single women; by 2005 the proportion had increased to 37% (Hamilton, Martin, & Ventura, 2006). In fact, in 1998, for the first time on record, the majority of first children (53%) were born to or conceived by an unmarried woman. Similar increases have occurred in most industrialized societies (Figure 2.1). Contrary to popular belief, these single mothers aren't just teenagers. Less than a quarter of out-of-wedlock births occur to women under the age of 20 (U.S. Bureau of

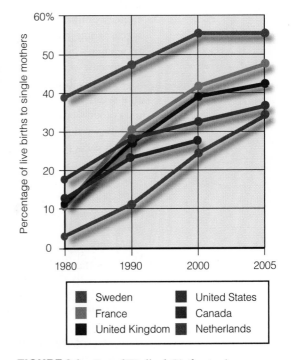

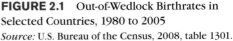

FIGURE 2.1 Out-of-Wedlock Birthrates in Selected Countries, 1980 to 2005
Source: U.S. Bureau of the Census, 2008, table 1301.

the Census, 2008). In fact, between 1991 and 2005, births to teenage mothers declined by 35% (Hamilton, Martin, & Ventura, 2006).

Changing Family Roles

Other changes that have had a powerful impact on families—even among married people—are those that break down the traditional separation between male and female family roles (Goldscheider & Waite, 1991). In the past several decades, the women's movement has encouraged large numbers of women to reject the idea that motherhood and family are their primary destiny and to strive for success and independence through career achievement. Today the rate of labor force participation is higher among mothers than it is for women in general (U.S. Bureau of the Census, 2008). In fact, the fastest increase in female labor force participation has been among mothers of children under the age of 2 (Bianchi & Casper, 2000).

Similar changes in the gender-based division of labor are occurring worldwide, even in countries that have historically had fairly traditional gender expectations. In Greece, for example, rates of female labor force participation increased from 33% in 1980 to 53.4% in 2005. During that same time span, Ireland saw its rate increase from 36% to 60.9% (U.S. Bureau of the Census, 2008). Women worldwide are finding that they must earn more money to provide their children with an adequate life (Lewin, 1995).

With more women entering the paid labor force, wives are becoming less dependent on their husbands for economic support than they were in the past. Indeed, the higher a wife's income relative to her husband's, the greater the likelihood of separation or divorce (Cherlin, 1992). Furthermore, families in which both parents work can experience conflict over the balance between work and family responsibilities. Given these forces, some fear that husbands and children will cease being the most important part of women's lives, and that the family will relinquish even more of its nurturing functions to day care centers and others outside the family.

Equally disturbing to proponents of the family decline perspective is the effect that women's labor force participation has on society at large. There is evidence that as women's labor force participation increases, so does the demand for public funding and public delivery of social support like better health, education, and welfare services (Huber & Stephens, 2000). As their numbers grow, working women become more successful at pressuring the government to spend more on such services.

Some observers also see a link between a lack of parental presence at home—especially mothers'—and rising rates of teenage suicide, growing juvenile arrest rates, more and earlier drug use and sexual activity, and falling SAT scores. A 2001 study of more than 1,100 children in 10 U.S. cities found that those who spend a lot of time in child care were more likely than children cared for primarily at home to be aggressive, defiant, and disobedient (cited in Stolberg, 2001). Another researcher has found that so-called latchkey children—those unsupervised by adults after school is out for the day—suffer from heightened rates of psychological disturbance, delinquency, and drug use (Galambos & Maggs, 1991).

The Declining Importance of Children

Family decline proponents also argue that as a culture we've become less child-centered. For instance, since 1960 there has been a steady decrease in fertility rates as well as in the number of households with children. This trend may be linked to falling rates of marriage. In a 1980 national survey, 64% of men between 18 and 34 agreed that people who want children should get married. But in 2002, only 51% felt this way. For women, the figure dropped from 56% to 42% (National Marriage Project, 2005).

People are having fewer children than they did a half century ago. In the early 1960s, the average U.S. woman had 3.5 children over the span of her life. Today, it's closer to 2.0 (Population Reference Bureau, 2007). Why are people having fewer children? Some parents choose to have fewer children so they can devote more time and resources to raising them. Certainly economic pressures have convinced many couples to limit the number of children they produce. But equally important, increasing numbers of women are getting married later and delaying childbearing until after they've graduated from college and established careers. For example, in 2000 Massachusetts became the first state in which more babies were born to women over age 30 than under 30 (Goldberg, 2000). When couples wait to marry and begin childbearing, the number of children they eventually have is bound to be reduced. In addition to having fewer children, more couples than ever are choosing not to have children at all. Between 1976 and 1998, the percentage of women between 40 and 44 who were childless almost doubled—from 10% to about 19% (Bachu & O'Connell, 2000).

■ TAKING A CLOSER LOOK
The Social Costs of Small Families

A reduction in the size of families is not proof, in and of itself, of family decline. Strength is not always in numbers. But according to the family decline perspective, having fewer children suggests that people are less committed to traditional family ideals. Small families can cause long-term problems. The U.S. birthrate is currently at about the level necessary to replace the current population in the next generation. In parts of western Europe and Scandinavia the birthrate is actually below this level (Population Reference Bureau, 2007). Many people fear that the economy will decline if society fails to produce ever-increasing numbers of consumers. Some fear that other cultures with larger populations will render their own culture obsolete. And there's also concern that declining numbers of entry-level workers will not be able to make up for the larger number of retiring workers.

Low birthrates have become such a concern in some parts of the world that countries have taken an active role in trying to get their citizens to have more children. In low-fertility countries such as Italy, Sweden, and Scotland, government officials are debating whether to offer would-be parents large tax breaks or even outright bonuses for having children. One town in Quebec pays couples $75 for their first child, $150 for their second child, and $750 for each child after that. In addition, it reimburses families with three or more children 50% of the costs for their children's music lessons and other cultural activities (Krauss, 2004). And in Japan, some companies will pay their employees bonuses—as much as $10,000—for each child they have (Sims, 2000).

A decrease in the number of children being born can have consequences for individual families too, especially in their ability to care for needy members. The past several decades have witnessed a dramatic shift in the age structure of U.S. society. More people are living into their 80s and 90s than ever before. Hence, families are expanding *vertically* (more generations living per family) at the same time they're shrinking *horizontally* (fewer individuals per generation). The consequence may be a shortage of family members to share in caring for elderly parents in the future. With few or no siblings to help them, many people—particularly women—in their 40s, 50s, and 60s will have to cope with the burden of caring for their parents on their own in addition to the usual demands of work and family, adding further strain to family relationships.

Burgeoning Rates of Divorce and Single-Parent Families

For much of the history of human civilization, the death of a parent was the most likely form of family disruption. Separation and divorce were kept rare by social, religious, and legal restrictions. But they are relatively common experiences for contemporary U.S. families (see Chapter 14 for more detail).

The causes of the high divorce rate are many and may include things like higher expectations for marriage, a reduction in the influence of religion, and the stress of changing gender roles. Moreover, the more common divorce is, the more "normal" and less stigmatizing it becomes.

The number of children who live with both of their parents has dropped over the past two decades (Figure 2.2). Some children live in single-parent households because they were born to unwed mothers, but many others are there because of divorce. For children, divorce sets in motion a series of changes, each with the potential to disrupt their lives. Children may have to move to a new home in a new neighborhood, make new friends, and go to a new school. Because the overwhelming majority live with their mothers, their standard of living may decline due to women's generally lower earning capacity and the common failure of fathers to pay child support (U.S. Bureau of the Census, 2008).

In addition, children raised by single parents after a divorce receive less adult supervision, and the relationship they have with their noncustodial parent diminishes over time (Kerr, 2004). To some sociologists, the disappearance of fathers is one of the most serious changes that has taken place in U.S. families. Several sociologists (McLanahan & Booth, 1991; McLanahan & Sandefur, 1994; Popenoe, 1996) have found that children who grow up in divorced, fatherless households are more likely than other children to:

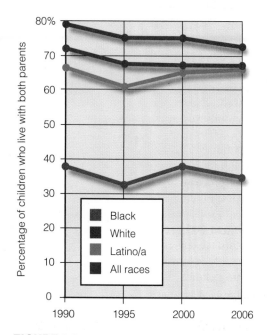

FIGURE 2.2 Proportion of Children Who Live With Both Parents by Race, 1990 to 2006
Source: U.S. Bureau of the Census, 2008, table 65.

■ Earn poorer grades in school and perform worse on standardized tests

■ Be absent from or drop out of school

■ Commit violent crime and engage in drug and alcohol abuse

■ Be victims of child abuse and neglect

■ Suffer from eating disorders and depression

■ Be poor and, when they reach adulthood, have lower earnings

■ Marry early, have children early, and divorce

Once considered an event to be avoided unless absolutely necessary, marital separation has come to be seen as an improvement in some cases. Few people today feel that a couple in a troubled marriage should stay together "for the sake of the children" (Adelson, 1996). Given these attitudes, couples have increasing difficulty committing themselves wholeheartedly to their marriage. As a result, many couples take protective steps, such as prenuptial agreements, that may undermine the quality of the relationship and create the impression that failure is inevitable. Not surprisingly, there has been a steady erosion of the expectation that marriage is permanent. Furthermore, children of divorce may grow up expecting that their own future marriages will not last. A high divorce rate, therefore, can have cumulative and long-lasting effects on cultural perceptions of marriage.

THE FAMILY TRANSFORMATION PERSPECTIVE

These trends are understandably a cause for concern. Most social scientists of all political persuasions, for example, agree that children in single-parent and stepfamilies have a greater risk of suffering from emotional, behavioral, and academic problems than children who grow up in intact, two-parent families (Glenn & Sylvester, 2006). But saying there is an increased risk doesn't mean that these problems are inevitable or even common. Most children, no matter what their family structure, don't have problems.

Indeed, many social scientists oppose the notion that the institution of family is in steep, perhaps irreversible, decline. They disagree that a family's structure is a more important predictor of members' well-being than the relationships and processes that take place within it. For instance, parental supervision, control, involvement, and sensitivity create a favorable environment for children regardless of whether they live with one parent or two, or whether they live with biological or stepparents (Acock & Demo, 1994; Lansford, Ceballo, Abbey, & Stewart, 2001). In addition, these social scientists say that by accepting the notion that the idealized, "traditional" family is something to be preserved, the family decline perspective misses the crucial sociological point that historical and cultural changes influence family structures and encourage new arrangements (Giddens, 2007).

This perspective, which I'll call the **family transformation perspective,** maintains that family—both as a living arrangement and as a social institution—is not disappearing at all but instead is becoming more diverse and complex as it adapts to changing cultural and economic circumstances (Mintz, 2006). Although changes in work, family, and sexual opportunities for men and women can create significant instability and uncertainty in people's lives, they can also introduce greater democracy, equality, and choice into our family relationships (Stacey, 1996). According to this perspective, we cannot measure family strength by how closely a family's structure resembles a traditional ideal, but rather by how well a family functions, no matter what its composition.

■ **family transformation perspective**
An approach to understanding families that maintains that family–both as a living arrangement and as a social institution–is not disappearing but instead is becoming more diverse and complex as it adapts to changing social and economic circumstances.

Rethinking Traditional Ideas of Family

Supporters of the family transformation perspective ask us to rethink our traditional ideas about what family is or should be. They see "nontraditional" family forms like dual-earner families, childless couples, single-parent families, and heterosexual and homosexual cohabiting couples as viable alternatives. The difficulties that all families face today may be as much a matter of rapid demographic, economic, and political change as of family decline; more a failure of social policy than a failure of individual families (Elkind, 1994).

Those who support the notion of family transformation take issue with the argument that the collapse of the traditional family is the prime cause of societal decay. They emphasize that many of today's family problems are consequences rather than causes of social problems. For instance, the key problem facing many families is money. Material deprivation can have a serious impact on adult partners as well as children (Kerr, 2004). Stable employment and sufficient income is necessary for establishing stable, nurturing relationships, whether between two adults or between adults and children.

As we'll see in more detail in Chapter 6, poor people bear the disproportionate burden of economic downturns in a society. They are far less likely to marry and far more likely to divorce than more affluent people (Mintz, 2006). The losses in real earnings and high-paying jobs due to the decline in industrial manufacturing, the ghettoization of women in low-wage work, and global restructuring that exports jobs to other countries may wreak more havoc on families and on society than the effects of feminism, sexual revolution, divorce, cohabitation, and individualism. When significant economic changes take place, it's inevitable that families will feel their effects. For instance, the competitive pressures of the international capitalist marketplace have forced many businesses and industries to make greater use of so-called disposable workers—those who work part time or on temporary contract—in order to maintain profits. These jobs offer no benefits and no security and thus add instability directly into family life.

Taking a Long-Term, Historical View

Supporters of the family transformation perspective argue that many of the claims of institutional decline in family are based on flawed, somewhat nostalgic images of what families used to look like. For instance, one of the principle images people have about families is that they used to be more harmonious and more stable than they are today:

> It is a pretty picture of life down on grandma's farm. There are lots of happy children, and many kinfolk live together in a large rambling house. Everyone works hard. Most of the food to be eaten during the winter is grown, preserved, and stored on the farm. . . . The family has many functions; it is the source of economic stability and religious, educational, and vocational training. Father is stern and reserved and has the final decision in all important matters. . . .
>
> All boys and girls marry, and marry young. . . . After marriage, the couple lives harmoniously, either near the boy's parents or with them. . . . No one divorces. (Goode, 1971, p. 624)

But most family historians argue that this nostalgic image is distorted. The traditional U.S. family of the past never really existed in the form it takes in our collective imagination. In truth, from the time of the Puritans to the early 21st century, each succeeding generation has been concerned about some crisis of the family (Hareven, 1992; Skolnick & Skolnick, 2007). Families have always been diverse in structure and have always had trouble protecting members from economic hardship, internal violence, political upheaval, and social change. By glorifying a mythical past, we foster artificial or limited standards of a "normal" family and, in the process, ignore the potential value of other family forms.

We often look back with warmth and fondness on historical images of family life, like this one from the 1950s, even though these nostalgic images bear little resemblance to what life was like for many families.

Colonial Families

It's common when describing life in colonial America for people to focus exclusively on families of European origin. But we must remember that several different types of families coexisted during this period. The Iroquois in the Northeast, for instance, lived in longhouses that accommodated large, extended families. In some colonies, contact between Europeans and Native Americans was often violent and coercive, but that wasn't the case in other areas. In the Carolinas and Georgia, for instance, there were many mixed marriages as Native American women often voluntarily married Englishmen (Berkin, 1996). African American slaves—whose nuclear families were routinely and purposely torn apart by their owners—secretly built extended family networks through co-parenting arrangements and the adoption of orphans (Coontz, 1996).

For all types of families during this era, death was a common occurrence. Almost half of all children died before reaching adulthood; half of those who survived didn't reach age 50. The average length of an 18th-century marriage was less than 12 years (Skolnick, 1991). Short life expectancies meant that the majority of children spent time in a single-parent family or stepfamily. Even children fortunate enough to come from intact families usually left home well before puberty to work as servants or apprentices in other people's homes. Mothers were much less involved in the care of their children than even the busiest of employed mothers today. And since it was common to send children away from home to work or learn a trade, many children depended more on siblings, neighbors, and masters for their upbringing than on their parents.

Male authority in families was taken for granted, and slight disobediences by women and children were considered punishable offenses. Children were not protected from sexuality, either in action or in discussion. Indeed, many parents at the time believed that children were inherently corrupt beings. So a key task of parents and other caretakers was to "break the will" of children and conquer their naturally evil tendencies (Mintz, 2007). Harsh physical punishment and humiliation were thus considered legitimate forms of parental authority.

Nineteenth-Century Families

At the beginning of the Revolutionary War, small family farms and shops flourished for white residents, and a wife's work was valued as highly as her husband's. But by the middle of the 19th century, industrialization and wage labor had taken men away from small family farms and businesses, leaving wives without their former economic partners. For the first time, men became known as the family breadwinners. By the post–Civil War era, the participation of women in the paid labor force was at an all-time low (Coontz, 1996).

Working-class children entered the workforce by the thousands, however, often toiling in horrible conditions for 10 hours or more a day. It was estimated that in the early part of the 19th century, half the workers in northern factories were children under age 11 (Coontz, 1992). In the South, children worked in the fields. Slave children were not exempt from field labor unless they were infants, and even then their mothers were not allowed time off to nurture them.

Although close to 20% of U.S. children now live in poverty, about the same proportion lived in orphanages in the late 19th century, often because their parents simply couldn't afford or didn't want to raise them. Rates of alcohol abuse, school dropout, and child abuse were all higher during the 19th century than they are today (cited in Coontz, 1992).

One of the most pervasive myths about 19th-century U.S. families is that they were usually large and extended, with a massive and perpetually available support network of grandparents, aunts, uncles, and other relatives living together. Historical research shows, however, that U.S. families have always been fairly small (Goode, 1971; Hareven, 1992). The highest proportion of extended family households ever recorded in this country was only around 20%, and it occurred between 1850 and 1885 (Hareven, 1978). Even then, these families were usually rural and were large for economic not emotional reasons. Farm families needed lots of members to produce enough to survive. Children were valued more for their labor than the opportunities for love they provided (Zelizer, 1985).

Early and Mid-Twentieth-Century Families

Concerned that longer life spans would put a strain on marriages, experts and clergy began advising people to direct all their emotional, nurturing, and sensual energy into their marriages. Although such encouragement introduced new levels of intimacy, it also raised spouses' expectations about what they should get out of their marriages, leading more couples to express dissatisfaction over what they weren't getting (Coontz, 2005). Not surprisingly, in the early 20th century, the United States had the highest divorce rate in the world (although it was quite low by contemporary standards). Social

Before laws were established to protect them, many children worked long hours side-by-side with adults early in the 20th century.

commentators bemoaned the fragility of the nuclear family and pined for the "good old days." Birthrates dropped among the highly educated, prompting some state legislatures to pass laws prohibiting abortion in order to boost the nation's birthrate.

Contrary to nostalgic images, the poverty brought about by the Great Depression of the 1930s didn't bring families closer together. It's true that divorce rates fell during this decade, but with jobs and housing scarce, many couples simply couldn't afford to divorce. Marital unhappiness, domestic violence, and desertion increased dramatically. Economic stress often led to harsh parenting practices, which left many children with emotional as well as physical scars. Marriage rates and birthrates plummeted.

The divorce rate rose sharply again right after World War II. In 1946, 1 in 3 marriages ended in divorce, most likely due to the brief courtships that took place before young men shipped out and the stress of separation when they were overseas. In one study of fathers who returned from the war, 4 times as many men reported unhappy, even traumatic, reunions as remembered happy ones (Tuttle, 1993).

The Baby Boom of the 1950s

For people who could recall their family's struggle to make ends meet during the Depression or who had experienced instability and family separation during World War II, the opportunities to buy a home and have a big family during the 1950s represented

■ **baby boom**
An era roughly from the late
1940s to the early 1960s
marked by high marriage
rates, low divorce rates, and
high birthrates.

an attractive promise of security and fulfillment (Acock & Demo, 1994; Mintz & Kellogg, 1988). The result was the **baby boom:** births rose from 18.4 per 1,000 women during the Depression to 25.3 per 1,000 in 1957 (Mintz & Kellogg, 1988).

For many who fret over the current state of U.S. families, the 1950s stand out as the "glory days," a reference point against which to measure and interpret recent changes in family life. Looking back, it probably was the most family-oriented period in U.S. history, a dramatic reversal of what had occurred during the previous 50 years. Half of all women in the 1950s married while still teenagers. The divorce rate declined sharply, to about half what it is today. Life revolved around marriage:

> [Marriage] was how practically everyone embarked on his or her "real" life. It was the institution that moved you through life's stages. And it was where you expected to be when your life ended. (Coontz, 2005, p. 226)

For the first time in history the vast majority of U.S. children could expect to live with married biological parents throughout their childhood. Although society had serious problems to deal with—poverty, racial discrimination, lack of educational opportunity—the lives of many white middle- and working-class children were now markedly better than they were before the 1950s.

Economic prosperity for some people further bolstered the pro-family features of this era. Per capita income rose by 35% between 1945 and 1960. The increase in ownership of single-family homes between 1946 and 1956 was larger than the increase during the preceding 150 years. Eighty-five percent of new homes were built in the suburbs, away from the turmoil of crowded cities (Coontz, 1992).

New values regarding families also developed in the 1950s. The belief that people could find all the satisfaction and amusement they needed within the nuclear family had no precedent in history. According to one popular magazine of the time, the defining characteristic of the ideal family was "togetherness," a "new and warmer way of life" in which men and women sought fulfillment not alone but as a family sharing a common experience (cited in Mintz & Kellogg, 1988). U.S. adults consistently reported in surveys that home and family were their primary source of happiness and esteem. Fewer than 1 in 10 believed an unmarried person could ever be truly happy. Indeed, people who didn't marry were thought to suffer from "emotional immaturity and infantile fixations," "unwillingness to assume responsibility," the selfish "pursuit of career ambitions," and even "deviant physical characteristics" (Ehrenreich, 1983).

It certainly appears as if families of this era were strong, stable, and culturally valued, an appropriate model against which to compare today's families. Unfortunately, the reality was far more painful and complex than nostalgia would suggest. Twenty-five percent of U.S. citizens were officially poor, and in the absence of food stamps, housing programs, and other forms of government aid, poverty could be deadly. At the end of the 1950s, a third of U.S. children were poor, a figure significantly higher than today's. High school graduation rates were lower than they are now, and while the vast majority of white middle-class mothers were housewives, close to half of all black women with small children had to work outside the home to support their families (Coontz, 1992).

Other popular ideas about the nuclear families of the 1950s also turn out to be myths on closer inspection. By 1960, for instance, fewer than half of U.S. families consisted of traditional single-earner married couples, and nearly one fourth were dual-earner couples (Masnick & Bane, 1980). Unmarried people were hardly sexually abstinent in the 1950s either. Between 1940 and 1958, the nonmarital birthrate tripled (Coontz, 1997).

Even among families that approximated the middle-class ideal, life was not always carefree. Prior to the introduction of the Salk vaccine in 1955, tens of thousands of children were crippled by polio each year. Because of the risk that a minor ailment could grow into a more serious disease, parents were told to be watchful for the tiniest symptoms, such as a sore throat, headache, stomach cramps, fever, neck stiffness, and so on (Mintz & Kellogg, 1988).

People in white, middle-class suburbs could effectively ignore conflict and turmoil, but elsewhere there was tremendous hostility toward people defined as somehow different: Jews, African Americans, Puerto Ricans, the poor, homosexuals, and so on.

Alcoholism, battering, and incest were rampant among all classes during the 1950s but more often than not were swept under the rug. Researchers in Colorado found 302 battered child cases in a single year, although virtually none was publicized (cited in Mintz & Kellogg, 1988).

Less dramatic, but perhaps more widespread, was a high but hidden level of marital unhappiness (Coontz, 2005). One researcher at the time found that fewer than a third of the couples she interviewed were happily married (Komarovsky, 1962). *Esquire* magazine called working wives a "menace"; *Life* magazine called female employment a "disease" (cited in Coontz, 1992). Yet ironically, psychologists and psychiatrists were writing that most psychological problems people had could be traced to domineering mothers who spent too much time doting over them as children. The frustration many women felt from being forced into tightly defined domestic roles led to a soaring increase in the incidence of mental illness and the use of tranquilizers and alcohol (Warren, 1987).

Men were also pressured into accepting family roles. They sometimes lost jobs or promotions because they weren't married. Bachelors were considered "immature," "infantile," or "deviant." Those who were married and had children often resented the long hours they had to spend at work to support their families.

Many had buried themselves in the private concerns of family, home, and career. Now there were signs of restlessness and change (Skolnick, 1991).

The Sixties and Beyond

Many people who came of age in the 1940s and 1950s married, had children, and settled into careers by the time they reached their mid-20s. But by the 1960s it was becoming clear that this life pattern was a poor fit with social reality. The rising educational demands of modern society were keeping young people in school longer and prolonging adolescence (Skolnick, 1991). People were forced to reexamine the foundation of family they had taken for granted: sexual norms, gender roles, and marital patterns.

U.S. families began to undergo changes as dramatic and far-reaching as those at the turn of the 20th century. More people began postponing marriage or choosing not to marry at all. Birthrates plummeted, as they had during the Depression. The number of divorces in 1966 was 3 times higher than in 1950 (Mintz & Kellogg, 1988). This trend created a sharp increase in the number of female-headed households. New sexual norms allowed people to experiment with new forms of family, such as cohabitation.

To observers in the 1960s and 1970s, the institution of family seemed under fierce attack. But, in many ways, the 1960s marked a resumption of cultural trends that had been put aside since the 1920s. Issues like shifting sexual codes, women's rights, household division of labor, child care, and marital satisfaction were merely reemerging.

In part because of women's active protest against their limited roles as housewives and mothers, new family issues began to appear that are still with us: the demand for equal responsibilities for both spouses in work, household, and child care; the

---

liberalization of divorce laws; paternal rights and joint custody arrangements after divorce; premarital contracts spelling out marital and economic rights and obligations; cohabitation and singlehood as viable living arrangements; the right of unmarried women to bear and retain custody of their children and the right of married couples not to have children at all; the legitimacy of homosexual relationships.

Families have experienced some dramatic changes throughout our history. But from the family transformation perspective, when social commentators lament the decline of the traditional family, they are invariably referring to a romanticized and idealized image. Calls for a return to the good old days are, in fact, calls to return to something that has never truly existed, except maybe in nostalgic media images.

Media Images of Family

Many of our ideas about what families are—and whether we believe they're strong or in trouble—come from the media: books, newspapers, magazines, films, and, especially, television. These images affect people's expectations about and interactions within their own families (Douglas, 2003).

For almost 60 years, television has served as a high-powered cultural lens on U.S. families (Stacey, 1996). For most of that time, the families presented in prime-time programs, daytime soap operas and talk shows, reality shows, news stories, and commercials have been conventional and narrow in scope, fostering a largely inaccurate version of reality.

TV Families, 1950–2000

One study of all long-running, prime-time TV families from the 1950s to the 1990s found that two thirds were married couples living together with their children or nuclear families sharing a household with one or more members of their extended families (Moore, 1992). The overwhelming majority (88%) was middle class or higher, and 94% were white. Only 14% of the programs featured childless couples.

In the late 1950s and early 1960s, shows like *Leave It to Beaver, Ozzie and Harriet, Make Room for Daddy, Father Knows Best, The Donna Reed Show,* and *The Dick Van Dyke Show* provided optimistic, homogenous images of American families. With some notable exceptions—the childless, working-class Kramdens in *The Honeymooners* or the urban, interethnic Ricardos in *I Love Lucy*—these early television families were happy, prosperous, suburban, and white. They consisted of husband-father breadwinners and nurturing wife-mothers whose primary task was to look good in an apron and keep peace among the children. You would have been hard-pressed to find on television the sorts of people and families that, in reality, characterized much of American society at the time: the old, the nonwhite, the non–middle class, or people in nontraditional households (Coontz, 1992).

Viewers at the time were presented with nuclear families that had no serious economic problems or embarrassing histories. The most pressing problems could be solved in 30 minutes with a few wise words from Dad or a plate of Mom's chocolate chip cookies. It's no wonder that when people today look back on families of the past, they gravitate toward these blissful "good-old-days" TV images. To this day, syndicated reruns of these old shows remain popular.

But the social upheavals of the late 1960s and early 1970s motivated networks to create shows that were more relevant and realistic. The working-class families on *All in the Family* and *Good Times* demonstrated that family life wasn't always a middle-class haven. Conflict was a part of their day-to-day existence. They addressed issues such as racism, sexism, and economic inequality head on.

TV families were even becoming a little less traditional in their structure. To be sure, *The Brady Bunch* featured a sugar-coated white, middle-class, suburban family, but the Bradys were a blended family that sometimes had to deal—albeit cheerily—with dilemmas posed by the presence of stepsiblings and stepparents. The 1970s show *One Day at a Time* featured a divorced woman raising two children alone. Popular shows like *The Mary Tyler Moore Show* and *Laverne and Shirley* featured single women whose emotional nurturing came primarily from close friends rather than family. These characters enjoyed freedoms that had previously been taboo for women on television.

During the 1980s and 1990s, nuclear television families reasserted their dominance—most notably through shows like *The Cosby Show, Family Ties,* and *Home Improvement*—even though the actual number of people living in intact nuclear families continued to decline. Although many popular shows—*Roseanne, Married With Children,* and *The Simpsons*—portrayed the ugly side of family life, the tone was humorous and the generally positive emotional interactions that we associate with family relationships remained.

TV Families, 2000 to the Present

In the 2000s, the television portrayal of families has become more diverse and sharp-edged. The dysfunctional-but-intact family can still be seen in recent comedies such as *Malcolm in the Middle, Everybody Loves Raymond, Arrested Development,* and *Family Guy* or in shows that document the antics of celebrity families such as *The Osbournes* or *I Want to Be a Hilton.* Elsewhere the problems are more destructive. Dramatic shows such as *The Sopranos, The O.C.,* and *Desperate Housewives* portray family life in stark, unsentimental terms.

Some of the most popular television shows in recent years—most notably *Friends, Sex and the City,* and *Will and Grace*—focus on the lives of young, hip single people. However, these shows are not antifamily by any stretch. In fact, many of the anxieties and travails their characters experience stem from a gap between their singlehood and their desire for a traditional family life of marriage and children.

The recent popularity of so-called reality television has added new twists to the depiction of families. Sometimes—as in *Extreme Makeover: Home Edition* in which families facing enormous tragedy are given new or remodeled homes—the depiction of families is quite sympathetic. Other times, however—as in *Nanny 911* and *Honey, We're Killing the Kids*—families are presented as hotbeds of tension, anger, chaos, and negligence that can only be "saved" through the intervention of "experts." Some shows even go so far as to create family tension for entertainment purposes, as in the various spouse-swapping shows that have appeared on the air recently.

In general, television images of families have changed in some remarkable ways over the years. Women now play a more dominant role than they once did in family shows, gay characters as well as single-parent and minority families are more common, and both mothers and fathers are more frequently seen outside the home (Douglas & Olson, 1996). However, television still tends to portray traditional gender roles within families. In television commercials, for instance, men are shown less often than women doing housework and spending time with children and are rarely shown caring for daughters (Kaufman, 1999).

The formulas of contemporary family programs also remain quite similar to those aired in the 1950s (Cantor, 1991). Television families have rarely tackled big problems

Though prime-time cartoon families like the Simpsons or the Griffins from Family Guy *are often portrayed as dysfunctional and conflict-ridden, they also reflect a traditional family structure.*

like the changing economy or ethnic conflict and political unrest abroad. Rather, fictional families act out morality plays about appropriate beliefs and behaviors. The 1950s arguments over teenagers kissing and wearing too much makeup have evolved, in the 2000s, into arguments over sleeping with a boyfriend or purchasing contraceptives. But the dynamics of the situations remain remarkably similar, and parents and children almost always resolve their differences by the end of the show. No matter how nontraditional the lifestyle, the central virtue of family togetherness is still depicted as the main source of individual happiness and well-being for adults and children alike.

The significance of these trends is that TV shows are far more than entertainment; they shape our ideas about what a family is and is not, how its members should relate to one another, and how a family should relate to the world. But television viewers are hardly passive recipients who absorb every message uncritically. For example, 9- to 13-year-old girls in one study tended to dismiss as unrealistic families that did not look and act like their own. They did, however, accept the family-oriented values they saw on television, probably because they were consistent with those they received at home (Fingerson, 1999). In short, we learn from the people in our lives, as well as from the media, to dismiss and discount alternative forms of families and to laugh at or dislike unconventional characters who challenge our accepted notions about family life (Currie, 1997).

CHALLENGING THE NOTION OF FAMILY DECLINE

The current statistics on marriages, births, and divorces seem to be signs that all may not, in fact, be well (Figure 2.3). But is it possible that a high divorce rate, falling marriage rate, and low birthrates are not as harmful as the family decline perspective leads us to believe? Let's take another look at the evidence—this time from the family transformation perspective.

Marriage and Divorce

Although family expectations have shifted some-what over the past three decades, our feelings about intimacy and family seem to be quite stable. The majority of us still want the love, af-fection, companionship, and emotional security that go with long-term relationships. The num-ber of teenagers who think a good marriage and family life are important has increased since the mid-1970s ("The Institution of Marriage," 1999). And most U.S. adults who marry are still com-mitted to the idea of having healthy and happy children. In 2006 the Centers for Disease Con-trol and Prevention reported that the majority of men and women believed it is better to get married than to go through life single (cited in Jayson, 2006). Such feelings suggest that marital expectations remain embedded in our culture.

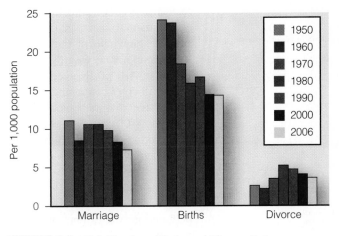

FIGURE 2.3 U.S. Marriage, Birth, and Divorce Rates, 1950 to 2006
Source: U.S. Bureau of the Census, 2008, table 77.

Furthermore, even though cohabitation has become more popular in recent years, it doesn't seem to threaten the existence of marriage, which remains valuable and dis-tinctive in people's minds (Cherlin, 2007). Most cohabiting relationships either end or evolve into legal marriage within a few years (Brien, Lillard, & Waite, 1999). The most notable effect of cohabitation is that it delays marriage for people who live together first. Also, the older people are prior to marriage the less likely they are to divorce, so cohabi-tation, for some, may actually have a stabilizing effect on marriage.

Another aspect of marriage that concerns supporters of the family decline per-spective is the high number of children born to unmarried adults. Most people assume that unwed births occur to couples who have casual sex and are not committed to one another. However, according to one recent nationwide study, 82% of unmarried mothers and fathers are romantically involved, 44% are living together at the time of the child's birth, and more than 70% of mothers say there's a strong possibility of marrying the baby's father. Even among unmarried parents who are not romantically involved, about half of mothers say they are friends with the father. In addition, 81% of fathers pro-vide financial help during the pregnancy, and 75% visited the mother and the baby in the hospital (McLanahan, 2006). These figures indicate that out-of-wedlock births don't always mean that only one parent is involved in the child's life.

What about divorce? Divorce undeniably creates serious problems for families and for society. But some social scientists argue that its negative impact has been exagger-ated. Throughout history, significant numbers of people have endured intact but mis-erable marriages. Just because they weren't divorcing in large numbers—for religious or social or financial reasons—doesn't mean their marriages were solid and satisfying (Coontz, 1992). Moreover, separation and desertion were common alternatives to legal divorce in the past.

Despite the high rate of divorce—and growing rates of cohabitation and voluntary singlehood—marriage remains the living arrangement of choice for the majority of U.S. adults. In 2006, for example, 89.7% of women and 87.6% of men aged 45 to 54 had been married at some point in their lives (U.S. Bureau of the Census, 2008). Over the past several decades a consistent 96% of the U.S. population has expressed a personal desire for marriage. Even individuals whose own parents had divorced show a rather strong commitment to marriage (Landis-Kleine, Foley, Nall, Padgett, & Walters-Palmer, 1995).

The high rate of remarriage indicates that people who are unhappy with their spouses do not necessarily become disillusioned with the institution of marriage. Overall, about 70% of divorced individuals in this country are likely to remarry, and many more will enter cohabiting relationships (Cherlin & Furstenberg, 1994). Many remarried couples feel that their second marriages are happier and more satisfying than their first (Kain, 1990).

Another concern raised by divorce is the effect it has on children. Most social scientists agree that children develop best when they live with two happily married adults. But some researchers have found that children's academic or psychological well-being doesn't suffer that much when they have little contact with their noncustodial fathers. Indeed, many of the factors that create the most serious problems for children can also be found in two-parent, intact families: low income, poor living conditions, and lack of parental supervision (Cowan, 2006).

Furthermore, some research suggests that children's behavioral problems—particularly those of younger children—are caused not by the divorce itself but by exposure to conflict between parents, both before and after the divorce (Ahrons, 1998; Booth & Amato, 2001; Hetherington, 2002; Stewart, Copeland, Chester, Malley, & Barenbaum, 1997). If we look at those kids whose parents are unhappily married or display a great deal of conflict, we find that differences in the frequency of problems between children of divorce and children in intact families virtually disappear (Furstenberg & Cherlin, 1991). In fact, children who grow up in intact families in which there is frequent parental conflict may actually have *more* problems. In short, the simple fact of being exposed to a breakup may not be as important in the development of a child as the way parents relate to each other and to the child. It seems that a stable, conflict-free family with at least one responsible, caring, nurturing adult is a child's best path to becoming a well-rounded adult (Furstenberg & Cherlin, 1991).

In sum, even though single-parent families have been criticized in the media and by politicians, the problems that children experience in them cannot always be attributed to poor childrearing values, lack of rules, or low expectations for children. Instead, the disadvantages of single-parent families tend to stem from sustained economic hardship—a factor that can impede children's development in two-parent households just as easily (Acock & Demo, 1994; Gerson, 2000).

Gender Expectations and Family Roles

To supporters of the family decline perspective, changing gender roles in society have created unclear expectations in marriages, making these relationships less stable and more difficult to maintain. For instance, as more and more women become capable of supporting themselves financially, they no longer require marriage for their economic survival (Coontz, 2005; Kipnis, 2004). But supporters of the family transformation perspective argue that changing expectations needn't lead to negative outcomes in marriage:

> [Marriage] remains the highest expression of commitment in our culture and comes packaged with exacting expectations about responsibility, fidelity, and intimacy. Married couples may no longer have a clear set of rules about which partner should do what in their marriage. But they do have a clear set of rules about what each partner should *not* do. And society has a clear set of rules for how everyone else

should and should not relate to each partner. These commonly held expectations and codes of conduct foster the predictability and security that make daily living easier. (Coontz, 2005, p. 309)

Some feminist sociologists (e.g., Stacey, 1994) have argued for years that the traditional breadwinner-homemaker marriage makes women economically dependent, reduces their influence in the family, and makes their survival in the event of a divorce more difficult. Thus supporters of the family transformation perspective argue that the recent increase in couples whose partners are both employed is an important development in making marriages fairer. Furthermore, they point out, the family decline argument that parents' (particularly mothers') decision to enter the paid labor force is motivated by the selfish pursuit of career ambitions ignores the economic realities facing many families, which require both parents to work to support the household.

Yet an important question remains: Is mothers' employment outside the home in fact hurting children? One study found that 75% of young men and women who grew up with working mothers were happy their mothers worked (Gerson, 2002). Another study found that children whose mothers have high-paying, complex jobs have greater verbal and cognitive abilities than other children (Parcel & Menaghan, 1990).

Some researchers have found that despite women's increasing participation in the paid labor force, their time with their children has not diminished dramatically (Bianchi, 2000; Sandberg & Hofferth, 2001). Only about 12 to 14% of children between the ages of 5 and 12 spend some time home alone after school and on average only about an hour a day (cited in Berger, 2000). In fact, there's some evidence that mothers actually spend more time with their children (and less time in housework, socializing with friends, and other adult activities) than they did four decades ago (Bianchi, Robinson, & Milkie, 2006). They have accomplished this not by cutting back on time at work but by reducing time spent on housework and free time with their husbands, friends, and relatives.

The belief that working mothers create problems for their children is thus not so much a conclusion based on a body of research as it is a function of broader cultural attitudes. Children's well-being doesn't depend solely on whether a mother works, but rather on her satisfaction with work and family, the availability of quality child care, and the active participation of fathers (Gerson, 2000).

▪ GOING GLOBAL

Examining Cross-Cultural Evidence of Family Change

Sociologists Sharon Houseknecht and Jaya Sastry (1996) examined the issue of family decline by comparing family life in different societies. They ranked four countries—Sweden, the United States, Germany, and Italy—on several indicators of possible family decline: rising median age at first marriage, increasing percentage of the population never married, lower marital birthrates and higher nonmarital birthrates, increasing divorce rate, increasing percentage of single-parent households, increasing percentage of working mothers, and declining average household size.

They found that Sweden, by far, ranked highest in overall "family decline" based on these factors, followed, in order, by the United States, Germany, and Italy. They then compared these countries on various measures we typically associate with the well-being of children: average reading and writing proficiency, percentage of children in poverty, rate of child abuse deaths, teen suicide rates, juvenile crime rates, and rates of juvenile drug offenses.

The comparisons across countries did not clearly support either the family decline or the family transformation perspective. On one hand, the data from Italy support the family decline perspective. Italy showed the lowest levels of family decline and the most positive levels of child well-being on four indicators (lowest child abuse death rate, teen suicide rate, juvenile crime rate, and drug offense rate). And children in the United States—second only to Sweden in the severity of family decline—were the least well off of the four countries on four of the six indicators of well-being (highest percentage of children in poverty, and highest rates of child abuse death, teen suicide, and juvenile drug offenses).

However, Sweden represents an interesting exception that lends support to the family transformation perspective. Swedes take pride in the fact that they are a nation of individuals, and their family policies reflect that attitude. Married couples receive no tax benefits and cannot file joint income tax returns. There is no tax deduction for children. Swedes aren't particularly religious, and without financial incentives, it's not surprising that many couples don't bother to marry. About half the babies in Sweden are born to unwed mothers, though very few are born to teenagers. Half of Swedish marriages end in divorce, and unmarried parents separate 3 times as often as married ones. Approximately 1 in 5 Swedish families is a single-parent family ("Home Sweet Home," 1995).

Despite all these "problems," the Swedish birthrate has increased steadily since 1970 ("Home Sweet Home," 1995), and children rarely suffer. Sweden has several generous state-supported policies that assist children—such as parental leave, subsidized day care, and leave for taking care of sick children. Fewer than 7% of Swedish children live in families with less than half the average income. Perhaps as a result, Swedish children showed the highest educational performance of the four groups in the study, the lowest percentage in poverty, and nearly the lowest child-abuse death rate.

These findings may alarm some, but they are also cause for hope. As long as society finds a way to support the types of long-term, committed, interdependent relationships that people actually create, there will always be family. It may not look much like a family looked 30 years ago, and it may have vocal detractors with very real and legitimate concerns, but it will still be a family to those within it.

FAMILY POLICY IMPLICATIONS

The issue of whether the institution of family is in trouble, or is simply adapting in form to shifting social circumstances, is not solely an academic debate. It has definite policy implications that will affect the way we all live.

From the family decline perspective, the so-called marriage movement has tried to influence legislation to strengthen heterosexual marriage. One prominent sociologist minces no words when he describes how families can be improved: "If the nuclear family is to be revived, we *must restore the cultural importance of voluntary, lifelong monogamy*" [italics in original] (Popenoe, 1999, p. 30). He goes on to suggest specific focal points for policy efforts, which include promoting sexual abstinence among teens; reining in the entertainment industry through organized protests and boycotts of objectionable material; spreading the word about the emotional, economic, and health benefits of monogamous marriage; educating people about the demands of modern marriage; disseminating information about the damaging effects of divorce on children; discouraging the formation of "alternative lifestyles"; and renewing the culture's emphasis on children.

These ideas have found a degree of support in local, state, and federal governments:

- "Community marriage policies" have been signed in several hundred cities over the past several years. Clergy in a town or city agree to perform marriage ceremonies only for couples who have been through a process of premarital counseling and preparation. In some cities, successful married couples are recruited to act as mentors. The aim is to reduce the high proportion of marriages that end in divorce.

- A few years ago, Florida instituted a mandatory marriage and relationship class for high school seniors. The state of Oklahoma has used $10 million of welfare money to pay for rallies and a year-long public speaking tour by a husband and wife team of Christian "marriage ambassadors" (Lerner, 2002).

- During the 2004 presidential campaign, George W. Bush publicized a major initiative to provide federal funds to states, local governments, and private charities for a range of marriage-related programs designed to help poor couples sustain "healthy marriages." In 2006 Congress approved a $750 million five-year plan to pay for it. The program, administered by a division of the Department of Health and Human Services, helps engaged couples gain access to marriage education services where they can learn how to sustain a "healthy" marriage through conflict resolution, financial management, and parenting skills (Administration for Children and Families, 2006a). The obvious goal is to strengthen and increase the proportion of traditional nuclear families. Cohabiting same-sex and opposite-sex couples are excluded.

The assumption underlying all these programs is that if we convince enough young people to marry and convince enough married couples to stay married, then society will benefit in the long run. The belief that we just need to return to the good old nuclear family and everything will be fine, however, allows the public and the government to avoid responsibility for undertaking remedies such as intervening in destitute neighborhoods, providing affordable housing and health care, ensuring that all young people have access to quality education, and creating needed jobs. According to the family transformation perspective, we, as a society, have two choices:

> We can come to grips with the [contemporary] family condition by accepting the end of a singular ideal family and begin to promote better living and spiritual conditions for the diverse array of real families we actually inhabit and desire. Or we can continue to engage in denial, resistance, displacement, and bad faith, by cleaving to a moralistic ideology of *the family* at the same time that we fail to provide social and economic conditions that make life for the modern family or any other kind of family viable, let alone dignified and secure. (Stacey, 1996, p. 11)

Lack of stable employment and financial resources limit people's ability to be supportive partners and effective parents (Reich, 2004). Twice as many men who earn over $25,000 a year marry than men who earn below that figure (cited in Lerner, 2004). Like its more conservative counterparts, the Center for Law and Social Policy (2006) endorses federal and state policies that help children grow up with their two biological, married parents whose relationship is healthy. However, it also realizes that such arrangements are not always possible and so it advocates creating policies that help all parents—whether married, unmarried, cohabiting, separated, divorced, or remarried—cooperate better in raising their children.

The larger policy question is whether the government should be involved at all in people's private decisions to get married or stay married.

WHAT DOES IT ALL MEAN?

You can see that there's no clear answer to the question, Is the institution of family falling apart or undergoing a metamorphosis? Nor is it clear whether the structure of a family is a more, or less, important predictor of members' well-being than the processes that go on within it. What some consider a loss of stability in that structure, to others represents an expansion of freedom. People on both sides of the issue have compelling arguments. And scholars on both sides genuinely care about the state of U.S. families. It's probably accurate to say that there is some merit to both the family decline and the family transformation perspectives. It does little good to trivialize the real problems brought about by certain family structures, but it also does little good to couch discussions of the contemporary state of families in the vocabulary of alarmism and panic.

Certainly, we shouldn't ignore the very real problems that unwed parenthood or divorce can create. On the whole, children usually do better with two parents than one. And many people suffer when their families break apart. But at the same time, condemning single mothers, divorced parents, or voluntarily childless couples as the culprits behind the destruction of society seems unfair and simplistic. Surely some unwed parents shirk their parental responsibilities, but others do a splendid job in raising their children. Some divorces do irrevocable harm to children, but others create better situations for everyone involved. Some married couples do decide not to have children for selfish reasons, but others are motivated by a real concern for society and find other ways to contribute to its perpetuation. In short, despite the heated rhetoric we hear on all sides of the debate, there is no formula that can predict which family forms are most likely to keep society functioning smoothly.

As you ponder the issues examined in this chapter, consider the following questions:

1. Do you think U.S. families are in decline, or are they simply adjusting to shifting social circumstances?

2. How useful in the search for an accurate image of contemporary U.S. families is information about families of the past? What is the connection, if any, between families of the past and current family forms?

3. Why do you think there's such a pervasive tendency in the media to focus only on the problems facing U.S. families? How do media images of family affect people's own family experiences? Do the media (television, in particular) *create* images of family that viewers then use to form their own attitudes about family, or do they simply *reflect* the reality of family life as people experience it?

4. Do you believe that high rates of voluntary childlessness, cohabitation, working mothers, divorce, and so on are dangerous trends in U.S. society?

5. Imagine that you've been given the responsibility of designing a set of government policies that will help families in the 21st century. What would be your top two or three priorities? Why?

SUMMARY

■ To some critics, recent changes in the structure and function of family—such as increasing rates of cohabitation, divorce, dual-earner households, out-of-wedlock births, and voluntary childlessness—have diminished its importance in society.

■ To others these changes indicate the strength of family as an institution that can adapt to shifting social circumstances.

■ Despite our nostalgic views, in each succeeding generation, family has faced enormous threats that have led people to express concern over its very existence.

■ Media depictions of family affect people's perceptions of its well-being as well their expectations and interactions in their own families.

■ Research about the state of U.S. families (especially in comparison to families in other societies) serves to influence social policy.

Go to the Online Learning Center at **www.mhhe.com/newman1** to test your knowledge of the chapter concepts and key terms.

KEY TERMS

baby boom   42

family decline perspective   31

family transformation
perspective   37

SEE FOR YOURSELF

You've seen in this chapter why it's important to understand families of the past when assessing the state of contemporary families. One way to find out how families have changed over time is to document and analyze the trajectory of your own family over the years. To complete this activity, you'll need to interview several people in your family who can act as sources of information about previous generations. You may focus on one side of your family or both sides. If you have multiple sets of parents, you can focus on your biological family, your stepfamily, or both. Face-to-face interviews are better, but you may have to conduct your interviews over the phone or on email to save time. In addition, you should make use of existing family records (for example, old letters, diaries, photographs, videos, heirlooms, and so on) that may provide insight into the lives of family members in previous generations. You can go back as far in time as you think is necessary to gather sufficient information.

Your task is not to simply chart the births and deaths of those who came before you in your family, but to sociologically analyze and interpret people's everyday lives in each generation. You will use your relatives' lives as a source of data—"case studies," if you will—of what family life was like in the past. It might be helpful to focus on one or two of these family-related issues:

■ Childhood and education

■ Dating and courtship

■ Marriage and divorce

■ The balance of work and family

■ Male and female roles

■ Sexuality

■ Health and illness

Try to look for patterns in their experiences that could be linked to broader sociological concepts, such as race, ethnicity, gender, social class, or religion. In addition, find out how your family first arrived in the United States. If some of your past relatives lived their whole lives in another country, you can examine how their family experiences differed from those of your relatives who immigrated to the United States or who lived their entire lives here. Pay particular attention to how people's lives were influenced by larger historical or social forces (wars, economic depressions, cultural upheavals, prejudices, epidemics, and so on). How did your relatives' experiences compare to what you've read about past families in this chapter?

Do you think that your family experiences have been typical of other Americans or unusual? To what extent have *your* family experiences been shaped by the experiences of previous generations in your family? What sorts of ideals, values, beliefs, and traditions have you "inherited" from family members in previous generations?

Please note: Whenever you use people to gather information about a particular issue, you must have your plan reviewed and approved by the appropriate committee on your campus (usually called the Human Subjects Review Committee or Institutional Review Board). Make sure you consult with your instructor before you begin interviewing people to see how you acquire this approval.

3

Measuring Families

ensus
2000

This is the official form for
easy, and your answers are
help your community get w

art Here

Please use a
black or blue pen.

4.

many people were living or staying in this
e, apartment, or mobile home on April 1, 2000?

Number of people

DE in this number:
oster children, r
eople st
oth p

5. WH

Wha

On February 13, 1986, a Connecticut newspaper reporter working on a Valentine's Day story phoned sociologist Neil Bennett at his Yale University office (Cherlin, 1990). Bennett and two colleagues were studying the effects of educational attainment on women's probability of getting married (Bennett, Bloom, & Craig, 1986). Bennett told the reporter that some preliminary data showed that college-educated women were less likely to marry than women who had never attended college. Furthermore, their marital chances worsened with age. Those who were still single at age 30 had only a 20% chance of ever getting married; those who were 40 and still unmarried had only a 1% chance of ever marrying.

The reporter incorporated these predictions into the Valentine's Day article. The next day, the Associated Press picked up the story. *Newsweek* magazine ran a cover story declaring that successful single women in their 30s were more likely "to be killed by a terrorist than find a husband." The magazine said the figures "confirmed what everyone expected all along: that many women who seem to have it all . . . will never have mates" (Salholz, 1986, p. 55).

A kind of collective panic was aroused. Those who weren't saddened, depressed, or frightened by the news were angered by the suggestion that marriage was essential for women's happiness, and that women who didn't marry, or didn't want to marry, were somehow defective and doomed to a miserable life.

In the end, the predictions were not very trustworthy. Remember that the statistics being cited were future projections, not hard data. To make such projections, researchers must assume that when current 20-year-olds become 40 social conditions and behavior patterns will still be the same. But unforeseen cultural and historical circumstances can alter marital patterns over time. For instance, women's labor force participation has increased dramatically since the 1980s. Women have more options than ever before, and it might be that waiting to marry is more appealing than it used to be (cited in McGinn, 2006).

Moreover, researchers at the U.S. Census Bureau, using the same data but different projection formulas, reported that college-educated women in their 30s had a 32 to 41% chance of marrying, and a 40-year-old had a 17 to 23% chance (Moorman, 1987)—not high but certainly not as dire as Bennett's predictions. Recent data indicate that the marital chances for a 40-year-old single woman today are over 40% (cited in Yellin, 2006).

In 2006, *Newsweek* issued a retraction of the story it published 20 years earlier. But the damage, to a certain extent, had already been done. For two decades, the desperate "terminally single woman" (Yellin, 2006) has been a popular fixture on television (e.g., *Sex and the City*) and in films (*When Harry Met Sally, Must Love Dogs, While You Were Sleeping,* and *27 Dresses,* to name a few). The cultural message was clear: Being married and having a satisfying family life are still essential for personal fulfillment, even for women with successful careers.

Clearly, of all the topics that scholars research, none are more popular or have more immediate personal relevance than those that deal with intimacy and family. People want to understand how families are formed, why people within them act the way they do, why some relationships succeed and others fail, how best to raise children, and so on. In fact, maybe you are taking this course because you want some answers to questions you can apply to your own life.

This chapter provides a broad overview of theory and research as it applies to family. How do sociologists and other social scientists go about answering questions regarding family experiences? What factors help us evaluate the trustworthiness of social research? These questions are critical because they provide a foundation not only for understanding what research findings mean and how they're generated but for assessing whether they're credible. Because we're exposed to so many statistical claims regarding intimacy and family, we need to be critical, informed consumers of this information.

EVERYDAY VERSUS SOCIAL SCIENCE RESEARCH

Social research is all around us. Throughout our lives we are flooded with a sea of research statistics: which detergents make clothes brighter, which soft drinks are preferred by most people, which chewing gum most dentists recommend. Many of the important decisions we make, from purchasing a car to voting for a political candidate, are supported by some sort of research.

Whether you realize it or not, every time you seek out the opinions of others, try to gauge the attitude of a group of friends, or draw conclusions about some event, you are engaging in a form of research. Say, for example, that you thought your score on the next exam would improve if you studied with others. So you formed a study group. After the exam you compared your grade with the grade you received on the previous exam. If you noticed any significant improvement, you'd likely attribute your better performance to the study group. This is the essence of research: You had an idea about some social process (studying with others improves grades), and you went out and tested it to see whether you were correct.

Although useful and common, this kind of casual, everyday "research" can be fraught with problems. We may make inaccurate or selective observations, overgeneralize on the basis of a limited number of observations, or draw conclusions that protect our own interests (Babbie, 1992). For instance, maybe your exam performance would have improved anyway simply because you were more familiar with what the instructor was looking for.

Characteristics of Social Science Research

In contrast, the way social scientists go about answering questions is a systematic, careful, and controlled process of collecting information, interpreting that information, and drawing conclusions. To that end, researchers usually do the following:

- Design and choose questions in advance, and ask them in a consistent way of a large number of people.
- Use sophisticated techniques to ensure that the characteristics of the people in a study are similar to those of the population at large.
- Methodically record observations across a variety of situations.
- Use computers to generate statistics from which we can draw confident conclusions.

Furthermore, social research is subjected to the scrutiny of colleagues and critics, who will point out any mistakes and shortcomings. In published articles, researchers are obligated to report not only their results but also the methods they used to collect data and the conditions surrounding the research. Such detailed explanation allows **replication** of the study—that is, it allows other researchers to perform a similar study themselves to see whether they obtain the same results. The more a particular research result is replicated, the greater its acceptance in the scholarly community. This process

■ **replication**
The practice of researchers performing similar studies to see whether they obtain the same results as a previous study.

helps to correct flawed research and ultimately replace it with more accurate and better designed studies (Furstenberg, 1999).

Interpreting Social Science Research Results

Social science research, then, is a more sophisticated and structured form of the sort of individual inquiry we use every day. Because published research tends to be couched in scientific and highly sophisticated terms, the general public is likely to assume that the information is accurate and credible. However, when presented in the popular press, social science research is often oversimplified. Small differences between groups—for example, that children from divorced families are 20% more likely to fail first grade than children from "intact" families—take on more weight when published uncritically in the popular press (Furstenberg, 1999). Unfortunately, our tendency to believe research findings just because they appear in print can sometimes get us into trouble.

In April 2001, the U.S. Census Bureau released a report titled "The 'Nuclear Family' Rebounds," which claimed that the number of children living in a traditional nuclear family with their biological mother and father had increased between 1991 and 1996 (U.S. Bureau of the Census, 2001a). Newspapers and magazines proclaimed that traditional U.S. families were making a comeback. Whew! But was such an optimistic conclusion warranted? Probably not. It turned out that a rise in the number of people of marrying age accounted for the rise in the number of marriages. True, more people were getting married and having children, but because the population as a whole was larger in this age group, increases were occurring in other types of households too: childless married couples, unmarried cohabitors, and single-parent families.

Indeed, barely a month later the Census Bureau released a profile of U.S. families based on new data from the 2000 census. These figures showed that the proportion of U.S. households consisting of married-couple families with children had, for the first time, dropped below 25%. And the number of unmarried heterosexual couples living together had risen from 3% of all households in 1990 to 5% of all households in 2000 (U.S. Bureau of the Census, 2001b). These figures are holding steady today (U.S. Bureau of the Census, 2008). Indeed, if we add same-sex couples to the mix, approximately 1 out of 10 couples living together today are unmarried (cited in Roberts, 2006).

To be informed consumers of social research—and to form accurate conclusions about family life—we must always ask ourselves these questions: How accurate is this information? and How well does information about a specific case generalize to the entire society?

THEORETICAL PERSPECTIVES ON FAMILY

■ **theory**
A set of statements or propositions that seek to explain or predict a particular aspect of social life.

Most social research is guided by a particular theory. A **theory** is a set of statements or propositions that seek to explain or predict a particular aspect of social life (Chafetz, 1978). Theory does not mean a conjecture or a speculation, as many people think. Instead, a theory is a kind of model for how we believe the world works. Furthermore, theories deal with phenomena as they exist, not with morality or ideological preference. In other words, they describe the way things are, not the way they ought to be.

Research and theory closely depend on each other. Theory without research is abstract and speculative. We may *believe* that certain factors in an intimate relation-

FIGURE 3.1 How Sociological Theory Views Families

Perspective	Key Assumptions About Families
Structural Functionalism	Families fulfill certain roles to keep society as a whole functioning smoothly.
Conflict Perspective	Inequality is an inherent part of families. Some family members benefit more than others from these arrangements.
Feminist Theory	Inequality within families and society is structured along gender lines. Males benefit more from family practices than do females.
Social Exchange Theory	Enduring family relationships and interactions are those that offer the greatest rewards and have the fewest costs.
Symbolic Interactionism	Families are created through day-to-day interactions. Communication is central to the creation and maintenance of family bonds.
Sociobiology	Individual, couple, and family patterns are determined by biology.

ship lead to conflict, but unless we acquire actual information about conflict from real couples, our ideas will be just that: ideas. At the same time, research findings without any underlying theoretical reasoning are simply a string of meaningless bits of information (Mills, 1959). Contrary to popular belief, numbers never speak for themselves; we must interpret them. Theories help us interpret research "facts" by treating observations as examples of general principles or processes (Klein & White, 1996).

Sociologists use a variety of theories to explain the structure and dynamics of families. Each theory makes different assumptions about human nature and social behavior (Figure 3.1). Yet they are not necessarily mutually exclusive. Some theories are broad frameworks that attempt to explain the origin of families and the existence of family as a social institution. Others focus more narrowly on specific family issues, such as mate selection, interpersonal communication, power relations, or conflict.

We'll look at six theoretical perspectives that social scientists often use to explain certain aspects of family life. Note, however, that although some research is clearly linked to a particular theoretical perspective, researchers typically draw upon multiple theories to better understand a particular behavior or experience.

Structural Functionalism

Some sociologists see families as essential for survival because they serve as an individual's primary source of emotional and practical training in society. This image of family reflects a theoretical perspective in sociology called **structural functionalism.** Structural functionalism emphasizes how a society is structured to maintain its stability. It portrays society as a massive organism with various social institutions working together to keep it alive, maintain order, and allow individuals to live together relatively harmoniously.

■ **structural functionalism**
A theoretical perspective that assumes that society is structured to maintain its stability; families serve as an individual's primary source of emotional and practical training in society, a necessary institution for the survival of the larger society.

When we use this framework, family becomes not simply a place in which people live out their intimate lives but an important—even necessary—institution for the very survival of the larger society (Parsons & Bales, 1955). Structural functionalism forces us to look at the family in terms of its contribution to society. To that end, it identifies several important functions best performed by the family:

- *Control and regulation of reproduction.* All societies need to have a system by which new members are produced. Obviously, children can be, and with increasing frequency are, born outside "conventional" families. But most societies do not encourage—and in many cases strongly discourage—reproduction outside the family setting.

■ **socialization**
The process by which individuals learn the values, attitudes, and behaviors appropriate for them in a given society.

- *Socialization.* **Socialization** is the process by which individuals learn the values, attitudes, and behaviors appropriate for them in a given society. Families provide members with a sense of self and identity, as well as a set of beliefs and attitudes. It's within families that we get our first sense of our own worth in the eyes of others, and our first taste of what's expected of us as males or females. Over the last century or so, families have surrendered much of the responsibility for socialization to educational institutions. Schools transmit the skills and values we believe are necessary to being a good citizen in society. But balancing the relative influence of schools and families can create conflict. Some families are glad to relinquish responsibility for educating their children to schools, but others want to retain control. When parents protest against the teaching of certain subjects in school or the reading of certain books, when they fight for the right to choose the schools their children attend, or when they reject schools altogether and opt to homeschool their children, they are attempting to reclaim the family's right to train their children.

- *Emotional support.* Although the institution of family may play a less prominent role in socializing children than it did in the past, it continues to serve the necessary function of providing affection and emotional security. To some, a family's most useful service to society is to be a "haven in a heartless world" (Lasch, 1977), where one can find safety and protection and escape the stresses and strains of public life. Families are supposed to provide intimacy, warmth, and trust, an antidote to the dehumanizing and alienating forces of modern society.

According to some structural functional theorists, families serve these social functions most efficiently when different members are responsible for carrying out specialized tasks. For example, many theorists have argued that the traditional husband-breadwinner/wife-homemaker household is the superior family arrangement because it allows individuals to focus on what they do best to ensure the health and well-being of all members (Parsons & Bales, 1955). Such arguments support the status quo by reinforcing the idea that a traditional gendered division of labor is in the best interest of families and hence in the best interests of society as a whole.

Structural functionalism was the dominant theoretical tradition in sociology for most of the 20th century (Skolnick, 1996). Within the past 3 or 4 decades, however, it has been criticized for failing to ask *why* people create certain social arrangements, and how they might exploit or otherwise disadvantage certain groups or individuals.

In an attempt to reclaim their institutional role as principal socializers, many parents are opting to teach their children at home. This 6-year-old is one of four siblings who are "unschooled" (the parents are teaching their children without using any textbooks, curriculum, or formal assessment).

Conflict Perspective

In contrast to structural functionalism, the **conflict perspective** examines society in terms of conflict and struggle. Its focus is not on how all the elements of society contribute to its smooth operation and continued existence, but on how social structure promotes divisions and inequalities within and between groups. Social order arises not from the pursuit of harmony but from dominance and coercion. Social institutions—political, religious, educational, economic, or family systems—foster and legitimize the power and privilege of some individuals or groups at the expense of others. The key question that the conflict perspective asks is, Who benefits from and who is disadvantaged by particular social arrangements?

Conflict sociologists see families both as an element of a larger class system and as a microcosm of society. They are particularly likely to focus on the link between families and larger systems of political and economic inequality. For instance, how does racial discrimination in politics, education, and employment affect family life? How does a family's socioeconomic position affect its ability to act on its own behalf? How do economic trends such as corporate downsizing, falling wages, and the globalization of economic marketplaces change the power structure and create conflict in families?

Inequality can exist *within* a particular family too. Because families are organized principally around age and gender, the benefits of family life tend to be distributed unequally between parents and children, men and women, boys and girls (Thorne & Yalom, 1982). Relationships can be characterized as a competitive struggle to control scarce social, emotional, and economic resources within the family. Conflict can arise over a wide range of issues—from how loud the television should be to whether or not the family should relocate to another city. It's the rare parent who is able to avoid battling

■ **conflict perspective**
A theoretical perspective that examines society in terms of conflict and struggle, focusing on how social structure promotes divisions and inequalities between groups.

with his or her children over meals, homework, fashion, hygiene, and sibling quarrels. Likewise, spouses commonly compete with each other over how to spend money, where to go on vacations, and how to raise children. Sometimes the competition occurs through bargaining and negotiation, other times through force and aggression.

The conflict perspective paints a rather pessimistic picture of family life. Its emphasis on conflict and coercion tends to overlook the cooperation, agreement, and stability that exist in many families. Nevertheless, it sensitizes us to the reality that people in families often have incompatible needs, and with limited resources some will get what they want and others won't.

Feminist Theory

■ **feminist theory**
A theoretical perspective that attempts to explain women's subordination in families by arguing that men's power within families is part of a wider system of male domination.

One particularly noteworthy and influential extension of the conflict perspective is **feminist theory.** This approach assumes that men and women experience family differently and may want different things from their family experiences. It attempts to explain women's subordination in families by arguing that men's dominance within them is part of a wider system of male domination. The 19th-century German philosopher Friedrich Engels (1884/1972) argued that in primitive human groups sexuality was casual and unregulated, making it difficult to establish who a child's father was with any certainty. So the first family form was based on the biological link between mother and child, and a person's family identity was likely to be traced through the female line. Women, therefore, wielded significant power.

Gradually, though, a pattern of stable sexual relations between heterosexual pairs arose in the interests of establishing more permanent bonds between people. The result, according to Engels, was the subjugation of women, who came to be regarded by men primarily as their sexual property. Hence, the monogamous, married-couple family form so common today emerged hand-in-hand with the first form of systematic oppression in human society: that of women by men. Engels felt that women in contemporary society could be emancipated only if the monogamous, male-dominated family were abolished.

Similarly, contemporary feminists argue that the way gender is defined and expressed in families is linked to the way it's defined and expressed in the larger society. For instance, women have been encouraged—or in some cases, required—to perform unpaid household labor and child care duties while men have been free to devote their energy and attention to earning money and power in the economic marketplace. Women's lower wages when they do work outside the home are often justified by the assumption that their paid labor is secondary to their husbands'.

But the oppression of women exists not just in specific household arrangements but also in the cultural *ideology* of family. In the distant past women were considered the sexual property of men, and the marriage contract legally obligated women to abide by the wishes and desires of their husbands. Although such formal contractual obligations no longer characterize marriages, overall male dominance in society and general beliefs about women's "proper place" are still closely linked to gender inequality in families.

■ GOING GLOBAL

Child Brides

Female oppression can sometimes be seen in the marital patterns of a particular society. In many developing societies, marriages are not love relationships, they're contracts between families. Families of men (or the men themselves) often pay money or offer property to parents of girls (called a "bride price") in exchange for the right to marry their daughter. Girls are valued for the work they perform and for their ability to reproduce. Because men want to marry virgins who will be able to bear children for a long time, parents feel compelled to marry off their daughters as soon as possible. And the younger the bride, the higher the price she can bring (Bearak, 2006).

The rate of child marriage in some areas of the world is staggering (Figure 3.2). More often than not, these child brides are married to men in their 30s or older. Parents may feel that marrying off a young daughter to an older man can help them economically and keep the girl "safe" from unwanted sexual advances.

But such differences in age can have devastating effects. Married girls usually have few social connections, limited resources, and virtually no power in their new household (Chong & Haberland, 2005). Because they are typically pulled out of school to

This 11-year-old Afghan girl wanted to be a teacher, but her parents forced her to quit school when she became engaged to this 40-year-old man.

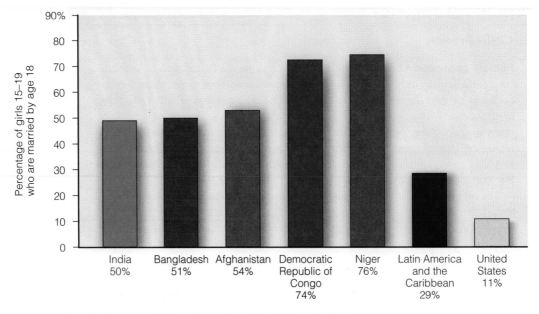

FIGURE 3.2   Rates of Child Marriage Around the World
Source: United Nations Population Fund, 2005.

get married, they have lower educational attainment than girls who marry later. Hence, they have virtually no opportunities for independent employment and self-sufficiency. In addition, they are more likely to be in a polygamous marriage and may be at greater risk of violence. They tend to be virgins and find themselves thrust into unwanted sexual relations with relative strangers. Tens of millions of young girls are having babies before their bodies are mature. Not surprisingly, pregnancy-related medical conditions are the leading cause of death for girls between 15 and 19 worldwide (UNICEF, 2005).

Social Exchange Theory

■ **social exchange theory**
A theoretical perspective that assumes humans' intimate choices are motivated by the same forces that drive economic market-places: a desire to maximize rewards and minimize costs.

Like the conflict perspective, **social exchange theory** uses the principles of economics to explain family experiences. But it pays special attention to the way individuals make decisions and choices. In particular, it focuses on why we are attracted to some people and not others, and why we pursue and remain in some relationships and avoid or leave others.

Social exchange theory assumes that humans are motivated by the same forces that drive economic marketplaces: a desire to maximize rewards. Rewards can assume many forms: money, desired goods and services, attention, status, prestige, privilege, approval by others, and so on. At the same time we are also motivated by a desire to minimize our costs—to avoid unpleasant, undesirable, or painful experiences. Humans will choose a particular line of action over others because it produces the best profit (profit being rewards minus costs).

When applied to intimacy and family, social exchange theory implies that those relationships that are the most "profitable" to both partners will be the most satisfying and the most likely to last. Intimate relationships provide obvious rewards—love, sexual access, warmth, desirable characteristics of the partner, and companionship. But they present certain costs as well—time and effort spent trying to maintain the relationship, undesirable characteristics of one's partner, bickering, and so on. Research has shown that people who indicate high levels of happiness have partners who provide many rewarding experiences and few costly ones (Birchler, Weiss, & Vincent, 1975; Rusbult, 1983; Vincent, Weiss, & Birchler, 1975).

Unlike the rewards and costs of purely economic exchanges, which are objective and defined in terms of money, rewards and costs in an intimate, family context are likely to be matters of subjective definition. What one person defines as rewarding (e.g., sensitivity) another may define as costly (e.g., wimpiness). Even so, such preferences are, in many ways, embedded within the larger society's definitions of desirability. As long as we have generally agreed-upon standards of a person's attractiveness and worth and as long as certain people have a competitive advantage over others in terms of what they can offer to a relationship, our preferences and our relationships will share some features of the economic marketplace (Becker, 1981).

Social exchange theory also directs our attention to people's expectations derived from past experiences. If our present relationship exceeds our expectations—that is, if it's "better" than any relationship in which we've been involved before—our satisfaction is likely to be high. On the other hand, if our present relationship doesn't provide us with what we have come to expect, we probably won't be very happy.

We also compare the attractiveness of a present relationship to the kinds of rewards we think are available in other possible relationships (Thibaut & Kelley, 1959). If an individual perceives that an available alternative would be more rewarding than the present relationship, he or she will be less likely to remain. But when people feel that they have few, no, or only more costly alternatives, they tend to stay in their relationship, even if it is far from satisfying.

The social exchange perspective provides important insight into how and why relationships form and continue. However, it tells us relatively little about how people subjectively define certain traits or behaviors as rewarding or costly in the first place. Furthermore, it assumes that people act rationally when it comes to intimate relationships and family experiences, an assumption that may be dubious at best.

Symbolic Interactionism

Another major sociological perspective on family is **symbolic interactionism.** This perspective attempts to understand society and social structure by looking at personal day-to-day interactions of people as individuals, pairs, or groups. These forms of interaction take place within a world of symbolic communication. The symbols we use—language, gestures, posture, and so on—are influenced by the larger group or society to which we belong. When we interact with others, we constantly attempt to interpret what people mean and what they're up to. Most human behavior, then, is determined not by the objective facts of a given situation but by the subjective meanings people attach to it.

This perspective presents an image of family as a reality that we must negotiate. *Family* is not a "thing" that is self-evident. If you think about it, you can't really "see" a family. You can only see people and infer from the way they live, treat one another, and resemble one another whether they can be considered a family. Furthermore, people's experiences *within* families are always a matter of their own definitions rather than some objective reality. Marital equality, for instance, is not a characteristic waiting to

■ **symbolic interactionism**
A theoretical perspective that attempts to understand society by looking at day-to-day interactions of people as individuals, pairs, or groups; the larger group or society to which we belong influences the symbols we use to communicate—language, gestures, posture, and so on.

be found or achieved; it's an interpretation that partners construct—sometimes alone, sometimes together—and apply to their relationships (Harris, 2006).

In everyday life we use language to refer to many objects that we can't see: feelings, attitudes, nations. We come to know these "things" through our experiences with them. We learn their shape and give them meaning when we speak of them, act toward them, and respond to them (Gubrium & Holstein, 1990). Think about your own family. You can probably describe the characteristics of the people in it and their feelings for and relationships to one another. You can also talk about its structure, its geographical location, its financial wherewithal, and its quirky traditions. In doing so, you give shape and meaning to this "thing" called family.

Simple enough, right? But is the family you describe the same one your parents or siblings would describe? Probably not. Our definitions depend on everyday experiences such as housework, leisure time, financial and physical well-being, and so on. Two individuals in the same family are unlikely to "see" the same thing. For instance, children have very different family experiences than parents and therefore are likely to define family differently. Consider a child's perception of a single-parent family. If a divorced parent remarries, does that automatically turn the single-parent family into a married-couple family? It probably would to the parent, who now has another adult with whom to share parenting responsibilities. But it may not be perceived that way by the child, who may rebel against the idea that his or her parent's new spouse is now a parent. The child may still "see" a single-parent family even though two adults are present (Trost, 1988). And how do those people at the edges of a particular family—grandparents, aunts, uncles, cousins, close friends—see it?

Finally, even if everyone in your family could agree on a definition of what it is, that definition may bear little resemblance to the self-definition of the Nguyen family or the Garcia family or the Davis family or, for that matter, the vast majority of families that exist in the world today.

In sum, although all families consist of identifiable statuses, roles, and norms, each individual family adapts these structural features to its own everyday experiences. The reality of family life is not fixed and inevitable. It is created, sustained, and changed through the day-to-day interactions that take place among members.

Sociobiology

■ **sociobiology**
A theoretical perspective suggesting that all human behaviors are influenced to some degree by strong biological forces and that biology always interacts with culture to create certain family forms; the fundamental assertion of this perspective is that we are endowed by nature with a desire to ensure that our genetic material is passed on to future generations (also known as *evolutionary psychology*).

Some theorists focus not so much on the social patterns that underlie family relationships but on biological imperatives. They assume that some features of family life—why people form relationships, why men and women act differently in them, or why people have children—are the natural end products of a long evolutionary process. This perspective, known as **sociobiology** or *evolutionary psychology,* seeks to understand human behavior by integrating relevant insight from the natural sciences into traditional sociological thinking. It suggests that biology always interacts with culture in creating certain family forms (Walsh & Gordon, 1995).

Several varieties of sociobiology exist: Some argue that cultural influence is minimal, and that underlying physical states determine *all* intimate animal behavior (whether we're talking about humans or mole rats); others acknowledge the strong effect of social experience and the environment. However, the fundamental assertion of the sociobiological perspective, no matter what its emphasis, is that we are endowed by nature with a desire to ensure that our genetic material is passed on to future generations (Lindsey, 1997).

Hence, sociobiologists believe that human families mirror the biological characteristics of our species' mating behavior and reproductive systems (van den Berghe, 1979).

Family patterns in humans, they argue, evolved over millions of years to ensure that mothers and infants remain closely attached, and that adults mate and produce healthy offspring who survive to adulthood, when they too will reproduce. A central tenet of this perspective is that the dominant family forms existing today—most notably the nuclear family—are those that are the most effective in ensuring species survival (Buss, 1994).

THEORY AND RESEARCH

The concepts and propositions that form the bases of family theories are not easy to observe empirically. We can't directly see concepts like "marital satisfaction," "gender expectations," or "attachments to parents." To test their theories, sociologists must translate abstract propositions into predictions (called hypotheses) that specify how certain measurable components (called variables) influence one another. Only then can they conduct actual research about some aspect of family life.

Hypotheses and Variables

A **hypothesis** is a researchable prediction that specifies the relationship between two or more variables. For example, perhaps you suspect—because of the tenets of conflict theory and social exchange theory—that household income is related to marital happiness. You might hypothesize that as income increases, marital happiness would also increase. To test this hypothesis, you would need to figure out a way to measure the variables family income and marital happiness over time and compare them statistically.

A **variable** then is any characteristic, attitude, behavior, or event to which we can assign two or more values or attributes. For example, the variable "sex" usually has two values: male and female. The variable "attitudes toward divorce" has values ranging from very favorable to very unfavorable. The variable "marital status" has several categories: never married, cohabiting, married, separated, divorced, widowed.

Social researchers distinguish between independent and dependent variables. An **independent variable** is the factor that we presume is influencing or creating changes in another variable. The **dependent variable** is the one that depends on, is influenced by, or changes as a result of the independent variable (Newman, 2006). If you believe that different levels of income create different levels of marital happiness, income would be the independent variable and happiness would be the dependent variable.

Modes of Research

Once a sociologist has formulated a hypothesis and identified the key variables, the next step is to decide which mode of research will be best for gathering the data needed to support or refute the hypothesis. Although the answers to important sociological questions are not always simple or clear, the techniques sociologists use to collect and examine data allow them to draw informed and reliable conclusions about human behavior and social life. Let's look at the types of research from which we can choose.

Experiments

An **experiment** is typically a research situation designed to elicit some sort of behavior and is conducted under closely controlled laboratory conditions. In the ideal experiment, the researcher randomly places participants in two groups and then deliberately

■ **hypothesis**
A researchable prediction that specifies the relationship between two or more variables.

■ **variable**
Any characteristic, attitude, behavior, or event to which we can assign two or more values or attributes.

■ **independent variable**
A factor that is presumed to cause changes in or to influence another variable.

■ **dependent variable**
A factor that is assumed to depend on, be caused by, or change as a result of another variable.

■ **experiment**
A research method designed to elicit some sort of behavior; typically under closely controlled laboratory conditions.

introduces changes into or otherwise manipulates the environment of one group of participants, called the "experimental group," and not of the other, called the "control group." The researcher takes care to ensure that the groups are relatively identical except for the changes—the variable that he or she manipulates. Then the researcher can attribute any observed or measured differences between the groups to the effects of the experimental manipulation (Schutt, 2006).

Experiments have a significant advantage over other types of research: The researcher can directly control all the relevant independent variables. Thus, he or she can draw conclusions about one variable causing changes in another more convincingly than in other types of research. The artificial nature of laboratory experiments, however, may make participants behave differently than they would in their natural settings, leading some people to argue that experimentation in sociology—and, in particular, in family research—is practically impossible.

To overcome this difficulty, some social researchers have created experimental situations (sometimes called "quasi-experiments") outside the laboratory setting. In 1974 two social psychologists, Donald Dutton and Arthur Aron, devised an experiment to determine the degree to which physiological arousal influenced men's feelings of sexual attraction. In the experimental condition, the researchers had an attractive female assistant stand in the middle of a fear-inducing suspension bridge—a 450-foot wobbly footbridge that swung in the wind 250 feet above the raging Capilano River in British Columbia. When she saw a lone male hiker walking along the bridge who appeared to be between the ages of 18 and 40, she would approach him and ask whether he would be interested in participating in a study she was doing on "creativity in scenic places." If he agreed, she'd ask him to write some brief stories based on a picture she'd show him. When the man was done writing the stories, she would tell him, "I'm sorry I can't tell you any more about the study until it is over, but it will be over tonight, and if you want you can phone me to learn more about it." She would then give him her name and phone number.

For the control condition, the researchers found another bridge upriver, built of heavy cedar beams and only 10 feet above a shallow stream. There, the female assistant followed exactly the same procedure.

Dutton and Aron hypothesized that men on the rickety footbridge would perceive their state of physiological arousal (which was actually fear) as attraction to the female researcher. Therefore, they would be more likely to call her later that day than those on the safe bridge, who had no physiological basis for feeling sexual attraction.

In the experimental condition on the rickety bridge, 9 of 18 participants (50%) called the interviewer later that day; in the control condition on the more solid bridge, only 2 of 16 (12.5%) called her. In addition, the stories the participants in the experimental condition wrote contained significantly more sexual imagery than those written by participants in the control condition. The researchers concluded that physiological arousal is indeed linked to the level of sexual attraction people feel for others (Aron & Aron, 1986).

Surveys

When sociologists want to draw conclusions about an entire population, experiments are impractical or impossible. So they often employ survey research, the most common sociological method. **Surveys** require that the researcher pose a series of questions either orally, on paper, or electronically.

Survey researchers typically use standardized formats to ask all participants the same questions in roughly the same way, and they use large samples of the target popu-

■ **survey**
A form of social research in which researchers ask respondents a series of questions, either orally or through a questionnaire.

lation. Respondents should be able to understand the questions the way the researcher wants them to be understood, and the questions should measure what the researcher wants them to measure. Of course, for the research to be meaningful, respondents are expected to answer the questions honestly and thoughtfully.

All of us have had experience with surveys of one form or another. Every 10 years we are required to fill out questionnaires for the U.S. Census Bureau, the source of most statistical data on families. At the end of some college courses you have probably filled out a form whereby you can evaluate your instructor and the course.

One survey that has provided the basis for much family research is the *National Survey on Families and Households*. First conducted in the late 1980s, it includes information derived from interviews with more than 13,000 respondents. A second wave of the survey, conducted between 1992 and 1994, and a third wave between 2001 and 2003 include interviews with surviving members of the original sample. The sample covers a diverse array of households, including single-parent families, families with stepchildren, cohabiting couples, and recently married persons. A great deal of family information was collected from each respondent, including family arrangements in childhood, dating experiences, experiences of leaving home, marital and cohabitation experiences, contact with kin, and economic well-being, as well as education, childbearing, and employment histories. Much of the research discussed in this book is based on analyses of data collected from this survey.

The major advantage of surveys is that they are fairly inexpensive. Researchers can collect information from large numbers of people in a relatively short time. But the disadvantages are equally obvious. Can a researcher gain an understanding of the rich nuances of family life through a highly structured questionnaire? Certainly not. At best, surveys provide a quick, somewhat shallow glimpse into family life that may oversimplify complex issues. Furthermore, through surveys researchers learn about what people *say* they do, not about what they may actually do (Gelles, 1995).

Another problem associated with surveys is what sociologists call the **social desirability bias**—the tendency for respondents to report what they believe are the most socially acceptable or appropriate answers (Larzelere & Klein, 1987). Even on anonymous surveys, people want to depict themselves in a favorable light. Hence, they will often accentuate positive attributes and downplay or hide negative ones. In research on marital satisfaction, for example, couples have a tendency to report more satisfaction and happiness than actually exists. Similarly, in research on marital power, some studies have found a "powerlessness bias"—with each partner claiming the other is more powerful—because claiming power is perceived to be socially undesirable (Brehm, 1992).

Nevertheless, surveys remain useful for research on certain areas of family life that, for ethical or practical reasons, are simply not amenable to direct observation (e.g., sexual intercourse, violence).

Field Research

In **field research** sociologists typically seek to obtain in-depth information about some issue or question through direct observation. This means spending a significant amount of time with individuals, examining the context of their lives to gain familiarity with their everyday experiences. Field researchers tend to rely less on quantitative data and typically pair their findings with long quotes from and stories about real people as opposed to sets of statistics, tables, and charts. That research frequently provides rich and detailed information about people's family experiences.

■ **social desirability bias**
The tendency for study participants to report what they believe are the most socially acceptable or appropriate answers.

■ **field research**
A type of research in which the researcher goes out and observes events as they actually occur.

For her book *Families on the Fault Line,* sociologist Lillian Rubin visited the homes of 162 working-class and lower-middle-class families who lived in a variety of cities all across the country. Twenty years earlier she had studied some of these families as part of a previous research project. She had kept in touch with some of them over those 20 years, being their friendly adviser when needed. Whenever possible, she spent time with wives, husbands, and teenage children—eating meals and sitting in living rooms. Because of the nature of the topics Rubin was studying, it wasn't always easy to get people to cooperate. So she devised a strategy:

> Experience long ago taught me that my best chance for getting cooperation is to approach the woman in the family first. If I could convince her, she almost always became my ally in helping to persuade the other family members. So I phoned the woman, introduced myself, and explained what I was doing and why it was important for me to talk with her. . . . Some of the women were able to secure the promise of cooperation from their husbands and, where they had any, their teen-age children, even before I arrived on the scene. In other families, it had to wait until afterward, by which time I had become something of a family event, provoking the curiosity of other family members sufficiently so that they didn't need much convincing to talk to me. (Rubin, 1995, pp. 14–15)

Field research is a useful method of studying families because it allows the researcher to observe the subtle attitudes and behaviors that we can't artificially create in a laboratory setting or find in paper-and-pencil questionnaires or structured interviews. Rubin's vivid accounts of working-class people's frustrations, anger, fears, hopes, and dreams could not have been obtained through any other research method.

As a general rule, it's always better to observe people interacting than to ask questions about their interactions because their answers may be inaccurate or biased to give a good impression of themselves or their families. For instance, observing a parent disciplining a child usually produces more accurate information than asking that parent how she or he has disciplined the child in the past.

But field research does have its drawbacks. For one thing, it usually requires a significant investment of time. Arlie Russell Hochschild's (1997) examination of how people balance their work and family lives required in-depth observations and interviews of employees at a single corporation over 3 years. Furthermore, because fieldwork is so time consuming, researchers can conduct only a limited number of interviews and observe only a limited number of people. Hochschild may have collected rich information about people's work/family trade-offs, but she studied only one corporation. It's risky to generalize from the experiences of a small group of workers in one company to all workers in all sorts of work environments.

The possibility also arises that the researcher will unwittingly change people's behavior simply by being there. As you well know, people act differently when they know they're being watched. However conscientious researchers are in minimizing their influence on participants, the fact remains that their presence changes things.

Unobtrusive Research

All the research methods discussed so far require the researcher to have some contact with the people being studied: giving them tasks, asking them questions, or watching them. The problem with these techniques is that the very act of intruding into people's lives may influence the phenomenon being studied. Sometimes sociologists make use of another research technique that requires no contact with people at all. **Unobtrusive research** is an examination of the evidence of social behavior that people create or leave behind. Several types of unobtrusive research exist, including analysis of archived data, content analysis, and historical analysis.

One type of unobtrusive research is the analysis of data that were produced for purposes other than scholarly research but that scholars can nevertheless use to learn about human behavior (Webb, Campbell, Schwartz, & Sechrest, 1966). I mentioned earlier that one of the most popular and convenient sources of data on families is the U.S. census, which collects demographic information about all U.S. citizens every 10 years to keep an ongoing record of changes in the population. Sociologists can analyze these data to understand family patterns such as changing marriage, divorce, or premarital childbearing rates. Because the census has been conducted since 1790, we can compare current conditions with past conditions to discern trends in family life.

The biggest advantage to using archived data is that there are few costs associated with obtaining large amounts of data that would otherwise be prohibitively expensive for one individual or research group to gather. However, the researcher has no control over the questions people were asked.

Another popular form of unobtrusive research is **content analysis,** the study of recorded communication—books, speeches, poems, songs, television commercials, and the like. Content analysis can tell us about cultural perceptions of family life that would be hard to capture through other means.

Sociologists Sarah Brabant and Linda Mooney (1999) were interested in the messages people received about families based on how families and race were portrayed in Sunday newspaper comics. They studied three cartoon families (*Dennis the Menace, Calvin & Hobbes,* and *Curtis*) by analyzing all the strips from these cartoons appearing in 1994. They found that the comic strip *Curtis,* which depicts an African American family, showed more family unity and social engagement than the ones that depicted white families. White families were portrayed as more isolated from other families and the community at large, and from one another.

A limitation of content analysis is that it may tell you more about how one person or group of individuals—poets, songwriters, cartoonists—feel about an issue than what is really going on. Often, the media present an idealized version of family and social life. At the same time, media can inform us about changing cultural perceptions of the ideal, especially when we examine content over a long period.

Related to content analysis and analysis of archived data is a third type of unobtrusive research: **historical analysis** of existing historical documents. Family is not a static entity. Not only do families change over the lifetime of individual members, but the social definition of family also changes over time within a society. Charting those changes and reconstructing the lives of past families requires a detectivelike examination of what people in the past have left behind.

Historian Lawrence Stone (1979) was interested in how massive shifts in worldviews and value systems between 1500 and 1800 affected British families. Existing statistics from the distant past are often unreliable, and he could not observe or survey people who have been dead for centuries. So Stone examined every possible type of evidence to pick up hints about how these changes were being incorporated into people's everyday lives. He studied personal documents, diaries, autobiographies, memoirs, letters, wills, marriage contracts, and divorce decrees. He sifted through birth, marriage, and death records of towns, villages, and cities. He studied the architectural designs of homes to see how the physical properties of the household affected family interaction.

■ **unobtrusive research**
A form of social research in which the researcher examines the evidence of social behavior that people create or leave behind.

■ **content analysis**
The study of recorded communication–books, speeches, poems, songs, television commercials, and the like–to determine variations in social trends over time.

■ **historical analysis**
A research method that relies on existing historical documents as a source of data.

Realizing that accounts of social phenomena can usually be found in the informational and entertainment media of the time, he also examined novels, plays, poems, and popular art of the day.

The key problem encountered in historical analysis is the interpretation of these records. Historical researchers have no way to check the accuracy of diaries, memoirs, autobiographies, and letters, and therefore must treat these records with a high level of critical scrutiny. Many of these documents are often quirky and idiosyncratic. A letter cannot "tell us more than what the author of the document thought—what he thought happened, what he thought ought to happen or would happen, or perhaps only what he wanted others to think he thought, or even only what he himself thought he thought" (quoted in Stone, 1979, p. 25). The best way to overcome these problems, Stone felt, was to examine as many documents as possible, not to rely on a single person's unique interpretation of events.

Furthermore, reliance on written records necessarily limits any study of the past to a picture presented by those who were literate and articulate and who had sufficient leisure time to write detailed accounts. This requirement, of course, excludes the majority of people, particularly in the distant past, who could not write a word, let alone keep detailed, thoughtful, and frank diaries of their family life. Women, too, tended to be excluded from the world of literacy long ago. Hence, most written records reflected a distinctly male perspective on events.

Nevertheless, despite the built-in limitations of historical information, historical analyses like Stone's are able to provide a compelling account of at least some people's experiences with marriage, birth, death, lineage, sexuality, child rearing, and the role of gender in family life.

THE TRUSTWORTHINESS OF FAMILY RESEARCH

Most family sociologists see research not only as personally valuable but as central to improving human knowledge and understanding. But we, as consumers of this information, must always ask ourselves how accurate it is. I've noted that much of what is reported in the popular media is either inaccurate or misleading. To evaluate the results of family research, we must examine for ourselves some important elements of the research process: units of analysis, samples, indicators, and the researcher's values and interests.

Units of Analysis

Families are made up of individuals, but as we saw in Chapter 1, they're much more than groups of people who happen to live together. Some family researchers focus on individual family members, some on families as a whole, and some on the institution of family as a part of society's structure. With so much possible variation in who or what they study, family researchers must be careful to specify whether the units they wish to study—called **units of analysis**—are individuals, couples, nuclear families, households, extended families, or the institution of family.

Studying individuals in families is not the same as studying families themselves. For instance, if you are interested in whether children from rich families are more likely to attend college than children from poor families, the units of analysis are individual children. But if you are interested in whether families with higher incomes are smaller than families with lower incomes, the units of analysis are individual families.

■ **units of analysis**
Who or what a researcher is studying, such as individuals, couples, nuclear families, households, or extended families.

It's not always easy to identify the appropriate units of analysis. Much research on "families" relies on information acquired from one family member, who reports on the characteristics of the entire family. This strategy is easier and less time consuming than surveying all members of a family, but it assumes that each family member sees the same reality. If you were interested in determining whether rich and poor families differ in the way household tasks are divided, would you be comfortable assuming that the one person from each household you surveyed would have the same perspective as all other members about who does what around the house?

Family members often disagree on even the most fundamental facts. One study of children whose parents had divorced found disagreement about the number of people considered to be in the family. The children listed absent parents as family members, but the custodial parents did not (Furstenberg & Nord, 1985).

Nor can husbands and wives always provide valid data on their partner's attitudes or perceptions (Deal, 1995). Spouses have been known to disagree on the most obvious facts about their relationship: how they met, how long they've been married, how often they see friends, and so on. In fact, according to one prominent sociologist, even happily married husbands and wives disagree on three of every four questions they're asked about their marriage (Bernard, 1982). Data on socially disapproved or sensitive family issues such as marital violence, marital conflict, and sexuality are especially likely to produce disagreement among partners (Szinovacz & Egley, 1995).

How much can we trust our conclusions about the nature of U.S. families if the data fluctuate depending on which family member provides the information? One way around this problem is to acquire information from both members of a couple (Schweingruber, Anahita, & Berns, 2004). Then we can compare partners' answers and look for systematic differences in their perceptions of the relationship. In one study, the estimated marital violence rate when data were gathered from only one partner was 50 to 80% lower than the violence rate indicated by couple data, where violence is taken to exist if either partner reports it (Szinovacz & Egley, 1995). Similarly, estimates of the amount of injury to wives caused by marital violence are substantially higher when wives' reports or couple data are used rather than husbands' reports.

Samples

In determining the accuracy of published research, we must also know something about the people who participated in the study. Sometimes researchers can gain insight into the dynamics of family life by making meticulous, detailed observations of a small number of families. More often than not, however, researchers are interested in drawing broad conclusions about the attitudes, behaviors, or characteristics of large groups of people—college students, women, U.S. adults, and so on. Directly interviewing, surveying, or observing all the people in these categories is impossible, so researchers must select a smaller **sample,** or subgroup, of respondents from the larger population.

Ideally, the characteristics of the sample should approximate the characteristics of the entire population of interest. A sample is said to be **representative** if its relevant characteristics are typical of the population as a whole. For instance, a sample of 100 divorced people should include roughly the same proportion of men and women that characterizes the entire adult population. The likelihood of choosing a representative sample is enhanced if the researcher selects participants randomly. **Random selection** means that each person in a population has an equal chance of being selected. Drawing names out of a hat—provided that the names of everyone in the population are

■ **sample**
A subgroup of individuals selected from the larger population for study.

■ **representative sample**
A small subgroup that is typical of the population as a whole.

■ **random selection**
Sampling procedure in which each person in a population has an equal chance of being selected.

in the hat—would be an example. Random in this sense doesn't mean haphazard or arbitrary, however. In fact, it is usually quite a bit more systematic than pulling names out of a hat. Some researchers will compile a complete alphabetized list of members of a population and select every *nth* person (that is, every fourth or fifth or tenth person) on the list. Others will arrange a list of the population so that members are grouped in terms of some important variable. For instance, a researcher might list all the women and all the men and then randomly select a certain number from each group to ensure that the gender of the participants accurately represents the gender distribution in the population.

Random selection guards against any conscious or unconscious bias a researcher may have (for instance, hand picking only happy spouses if he or she wishes to show that domestic violence is not a serious problem in contemporary marriages). Techniques for randomly selecting representative samples have become highly sophisticated, as you can surmise from the accuracy of polls conducted to predict election results.

A sample that is not selected randomly runs the risk of being biased. Suppose you were interested in studying dating experiences on your campus. You decide to stand in front of the main library between 9:00 p.m. and 10:00 p.m. on a Saturday night and interview each student who shows up at the library at that time. Such a strategy— known as **convenience sampling**—may be handy and take less effort, but it can result in a biased sample because not every student had an equal chance of being selected (Schutt, 2006). Do you think the dating experiences of students who go to the library on a Saturday night are different from those who don't? If so, any results you obtain are likely to lead you to some inaccurate conclusions about your student body.

In some physical sciences, like chemistry, sampling is less of an issue. A chemist needs to study only a small quantity of liquid nitrogen because one vial of that substance is not likely to be all that different from others. Human beings, however, vary widely on every imaginable characteristic. We can't make a general statement about all U.S. families on the basis of interviewing members of one family. For that matter, we can't draw conclusions about all families from observing a sample consisting only of white families, only working-class families, or only families with pre-school-age children. Samples that are not representative can lead us to inaccurate and misleading conclusions about the population.

Sometimes, too, the people who choose to participate in a study are different in important ways from those who choose not to. For instance, those who decline to participate in a voluntary survey of domestic violence could be more likely than volunteers to have something to hide. Hence, the data derived from a sample of volunteer respondents will, in all probability, underestimate the rate of violence.

Indicators

What does powerlessness look like? Can you see "marital dissatisfaction" or "traditional gender expectations"? How would you recognize a family's social class? None of these concepts can be observed directly. So sociologists must measure **indicators** of the variables we cannot measure directly. Researchers evaluate events and behaviors commonly thought to accompany a particular variable, hoping that what they are measuring is a valid indicator of the concept they are interested in.

For instance, suppose you believe that people's attitudes toward divorce are influenced by the strength of their religious beliefs, or "religiosity." You might hypothesize that the more religious someone is, the less accepting he or she will be of divorce. To

■ **convenience sampling**
A nonrandom method of sampling in which participants are selected on the basis of convenience.

■ **indicators**
Measurable events, characteristics, or behaviors commonly thought to reflect a particular variable.

test this hypothesis, you must first figure out exactly what you mean by "religiosity." You could determine whether the participants in your study identify themselves as members of some organized religious group. Would this accurately measure how religious they are? Probably not. Many people identify themselves as Catholic or Jewish or Moslem but are not religious at all. Likewise some people consider themselves to be quite religious but don't identify with any organized religion. So this indicator would highlight group differences but fail to capture the intensity of a person's beliefs or the degree of religious interest.

Perhaps a better indicator would be some measurable behavior, such as the frequency of attendance at formal religious services (Babbie, 2007). Arguably, the more often a person attends a church, synagogue, or mosque, the more religious he or she is. But here, too, we run into problems. Regular church attendance may reflect things other than the depth of religious commitment, such as family pressure, habit, or the desire to socialize with friends in the congregation. Furthermore, many very religious people are unable to attend organized religious services because they are frail or disabled.

Frequency of prayer might be a better indicator. People who pray a lot are presumably more religious than people who don't pray at all. But some nonreligious people pray for things all the time.

The point is, whichever indicator you use, you are going to affect the type of information you get and thus the conclusions you are able to draw. Surveys are particularly susceptible to inaccurate indicators. A loaded phrase or an unfamiliar word on a survey question can dramatically affect people's responses in ways the researcher didn't intend.

If a respondent misinterprets what the researcher intended to ask, then the researcher will inevitably misinterpret the respondent's response. For example, people often comprehend terms referring to sexual behavior differently. To some people, a "virgin" is someone who has never had penile-vaginal intercourse. But to others, a "virgin" is someone who has never experienced an orgasm—manually, orally, or otherwise—in the company of someone else. Using a question like "Are you a virgin?" as an indicator of sexual activity can create an inaccurate estimate if respondents are interpreting the term differently.

You can see that, for most sociological variables of interest, indicators seldom perfectly reflect the concepts they are intended to measure. Hence, as you read published research findings, try to determine whether the questions people are being asked truly reflect what the researchers intend them to reflect, and whether the indicators are likely to elicit socially desirable—and not necessarily truthful—responses.

Values and Interests

In addition to units of analysis, samples, and indicators, the researcher's own values and interests can influence the conclusions drawn from social research and thereby influence sociological information about families. Ideally, research is objective and non-biased and measures what is, not what should be. The study of social events, however, always takes place in a particular cultural, political, and ideological context (Ballard, 1987; Denzin, 1989).

In fact, because family is such a politically charged topic, research in the area is sometimes designed to support narrowly defined political interests. Many people who write about families have strong commitments to certain policy positions, which are revealed in the ways they present empirical evidence (Furstenberg, 1999). You can be reasonably certain that research supported by conservative political organizations, such as the Family Research Council or the Alliance for Marriage, will uncover the harmful effects of mothers working outside the home. But it's equally likely that research supported by more liberal organizations, such as the Institute for Women's Policy Research, will find less damaging, even positive effects of mothers' working. It is always tempting to accept the evidence that supports our position and discount the evidence that refutes it, but we must be more open-minded if we want an accurate understanding of families.

We must remember that sociologists are people too, with their own biases, preconceptions, and expectations. Sociologists' values always determine the vantage point from which they will gather information about a particular social phenomenon. In fact, their values can influence the questions researchers find important enough to address in the first place (Reinharz, 1992). For instance, most research on homosexual parenting asks whether lesbian and gay parents subject their children to greater risks or harm than heterosexual parents. Because antigay researchers are looking for evidence of harm, researchers who are sympathetic to homosexual parents defensively seek evidence that the children of homosexual parents are not unduly harmed (Stacey & Biblarz, 2001).

Similarly, the historical tendency for family researchers to be men has affected the questions they ask in studies of the effects of women's work on their families (Acker, 1978; Thorne & Yalom, 1982). The term *labor force* has traditionally referred to those working for pay and has excluded those doing unpaid work, such as housework and volunteer jobs—forms of employment that are still predominantly female (see Chapter 9). The result of such bias is that findings on labor force participation are more likely to reflect the significant elements of men's lives than women's.

■ TAKING A CLOSER LOOK

Family Privacy and Research Ethics

Research on families often deals with sensitive topics and activities. And, as we saw in Chapter 1, the most compelling and interesting elements of family life occur beyond the watchful eyes of others. Indeed, unless we use a hidden camera, the very act of observing people changes the nature of the phenomenon we're studying. Private family life immediately ceases to be private once people become aware they're being studied.

Even paper-and-pencil surveys sometimes require the disclosure of very personal information—like sexual satisfaction or marital conflict—that can be embarrassing or damaging to participants' self-esteem. To a person who has just lost his or her job, answering a simple question like "What is your annual income?" can be a devastating admission of failure.

Sociologists, therefore, must take special care to balance the risks posed to participants with the benefits to society of studying something we all have an interest in: the intimate aspects of family life (Bussell, 1994). Family researchers must try to protect the rights of individuals and minimize the amount of harm or disruption they may experience as a result of being part of a study. Most researchers agree that no one should be forced to participate in research, that those who do participate ought to be fully informed of the possible risks involved, and that every precaution ought to be taken to protect the confidentiality and anonymity of participants.

Sometimes the desire to secure the most accurate information possible conflicts more directly with ethical considerations. Consider sociologist Laud Humphreys' famous 1970 book, *The Tearoom Trade,* a study many sociologists found ethically indefensible. Humphreys was interested in studying anonymous and casual homosexual encounters among strangers. He decided to study such interactions in "tearooms"—places, like public restrooms, where male homosexuals used to go for anonymous sex before the AIDS epidemic significantly curtailed such activity. Because of the secretive and potentially stigmatizing nature of the phenomenon he was interested in, Humphreys couldn't just come right out and ask people about their actions, nor could he openly observe them. So he decided to pose as a lookout, called a "watchqueen," whose job was to warn of intruders as homosexual men engaged in sexual acts in public restrooms. By misrepresenting his identity, Humphreys was able to conduct very detailed field observations of these encounters.

But he also wanted to know about the regular lives of these men. Whenever possible he wrote down the license numbers of the participants' cars and tracked down their names and addresses with the help of a friend in the local police department. About a year later he arranged for these individuals to be part of a simple medical survey being conducted by some of his colleagues. He then disguised himself and visited their homes, supposedly to conduct interviews for the medical survey. He found that most of the men were heterosexual, had families, and were respected members of their communities. In short, they led altogether conventional lives.

Although this information shed a great deal of light on the nature of anonymous homosexual acts, some critics argued that Humphreys had violated the ethics of research by deceiving these unsuspecting participants and violating their privacy rights. Others, however, supported Humphreys, arguing that he could have studied this topic in no other way. In fact, his book won a prestigious award. But close to 40 years later, the ethical controversy surrounding this study persists (Galliher, Brekhus, & Keys, 2004).

In sum, despite potential problems associated with samples, indicators, and ethics, social research remains an effective and efficient way of providing us with information about families. Our task is to be careful and critical consumers of such information, questioning how and from whom it was collected.

WHAT DOES IT ALL MEAN?

To some degree, everyone is an expert on families. That expertise is based on personal experiences with our own families. However, such information is inevitably biased and idiosyncratic. Systematic social science research provides a more sophisticated understanding of family experiences and patterns.

After reading this chapter, you should have a good sense of what family research is, how it is related to theory, how it is done, and what some of its potential pitfalls are. The development of a body of trustworthy knowledge about families depends on solid research techniques.

Most of us learn about the findings of family research not by studying scholarly journals but by reading or hearing others' interpretations of such research. These presentations typically reduce complex statistical findings to brief, easily digested summaries. In the process, much of the information we need to judge the validity of the conclusions (sample, method, indicators, and so on) is left out. Thus it's important that we maintain a healthy skepticism and critically examine the family claims made by social critics, politicians, pundits, talk-show hosts, and Web sites. But we must also employ our critical faculties when we do study scholarly journals, because even the most objective, ethical scholars are human beings subject to inadvertent blind spots and biases.

As you review what you've learned in this chapter, consider the following questions:

1. Given the "private" nature of family life, can we ever really know what families are like? Are some phenomena that occur in families so personal that we simply should *not* study them?

2. Think of the "facts" you "know" about U.S. families (trends in marriage, cohabitation, divorce, childbearing, and so on). Where did you learn this information? Do you consider some sources more trustworthy than others? Why? What are the possible shortcomings of drawing conclusions about all families from our own family experiences?

3. Suppose you were given the task of finding out why some people are happy and satisfied in their long-term intimate relationships and others aren't. What research technique would be the best way to study this issue? Why? How would you distinguish happy/satisfied from unhappy/unsatisfied people? What would you consider "long-term?"

SUMMARY

- To some degree, everyone is an expert on families. That expertise is based on personal experiences with our own families. However, such information is inevitably biased and idiosyncratic. Systematic social science research provides a more sophisticated understanding of family experiences and patterns.

- Sociological research is grounded in a handful of theoretical perspectives: structural functionalism, the conflict perspective, feminist theory, social exchange theory, symbolic interactionism, and sociobiology. Each perspective has something to offer in the effort to understand families and the institution of family; each has shortcomings.

- Sociologists provide useful information about families through a variety of research techniques: experiments, field research, surveys, and unobtrusive research.

- Although systematic research is more trustworthy than informal observation, we still must be careful consumers of published research information about families. The nature of the people being studied, the way certain phenomena are measured, and the researcher's own values and interests can all skew the results of a study, rendering our beliefs about family life inaccurate.

Go to the Online Learning Center at **www.mhhe.com/newman1** to test your knowledge of the chapter concepts and key terms.

KEY TERMS

conflict perspective 61
content analysis 71
convenience sampling 74
dependent variable 67
experiment 67
feminist theory 62
field research 69
historical analysis 71
hypothesis 67

independent variable 67
indicators 74
random selection 73
replication 57
representative sample 73
sample 73
social desirability bias 69
social exchange theory 64
socialization 60

sociobiology 66
structural functionalism 59
survey 68
symbolic interactionism 65
theory 58
units of analysis 72
unobtrusive research 71
variable 67

SEE FOR YOURSELF

One of the most frequently used sources of data on families is the U.S. Bureau of the Census. As mandated by the U.S. Constitution, the Census Bureau compiles a complete count of the U.S. population every 10 years, called the decennial census. The most recent count took place in 2000. For the decennial census, a survey form is sent to every household, as well as to institutions such as prisons, college dormitories, and nursing homes. The Census Bureau also collects annual data from a sample of the population. From these surveys, you find an astonishing amount of information about how people in the United States live, including information on such family-related topics as cohabitation, marriage, divorce, childbirth and child care, sexual activities, labor force participation, and income.

This activity will require you to answer some simple questions about family life by gathering statistical information from an easy-to-use link on the Census Bureau Web site called *The 2008 Statistical Abstract* (www.census.gov/compendia/statab/). When you click on this link, you will see the table of contents of this document broken down into different sections. Scroll down the table of contents until you see "Index" and click on the highlighted page numbers. This will take you to a detailed index of specific topics that you will need to find to answer the questions. The numbers given after each entry refer to table numbers (not page numbers). When you find what you think might be useful tables, return to the table of contents and find the section that contains the table you're looking for. Click on the blue page numbers of that section and you will be taken to the tables. Find the table you're looking for by scrolling down.

Once you've gotten the hang of navigating this Web site, see if you can find the statistical information that would help you answer some important questions about families such as these:

■ What percentage of U.S. households contain a married couple?

■ What percentage of U.S. households are female-headed, single-parent families?

■ What is the median income for U.S. families? What is the median income for U.S. households? Why are these two figures different?

■ What has been the trend in the poverty rate of U.S. families over the last 5 years? How does this trend differ for different ethnoracial groups?

■ Do black, white, Latino/a, and Asian American families differ in size? If so, how?

4

Gendered Families

A five-year-old boy, left, who ◆
identifies as a girl, plays with
a friend.

Break on Through to the Other Side

Our entire society is organized around the principle that "male" and "female" are stable, universal, and unchanging sex categories into which every person can be unambiguously placed. However, things aren't always so straightforward.

In the early 1950s, George Jorgensen was in the U.S. Army. After his discharge, George traveled to Copenhagen, Denmark, changed his name to Christine, and made modern medical history by undergoing the first sex change operation. Note how Christine's clothing, makeup, hair,

and smile convey traditional femininity. It's these visible changes—perhaps more than the surgical sex change—that turned George into Christine. We have to rely on such cues to determine sex because anatomical indicators are generally hidden or invisible.

Unlike sex, which is harder (but not impossible) to change, individuals can intentionally manipulate gender. The classic example is the cross-dresser. The beauty queen in the photo is actually a man, who was crowned Miss Tiffany 2005 in Thailand's Miss Transvestite Pageant. "Success" in the pageant depends upon looking and acting the part, what sociologists refer to as "doing gender." It's not enough that he dress like a woman, he must also behave in ways that are clearly feminine. The same is true in everyday life, for everyone. Labels—"sissy" (for effeminate males) or "tomboy" (for females with masculine ways)—await those who are viewed as acting inappropriately.

Cross-dressers may look and act like members of a different sex, but they don't *become* a different sex. Transsexuals—who want to be a different sex—often use hormonal and surgical methods to assist in a permanent sexual reassignment. Robert Eads was born "Barbara" and spent the first 40 years of her life as a woman. She was married to a man and gave birth to two sons. She divorced her husband after the birth of his second son, and lived for some time as a lesbian. In the 1980s, Eads began to transform into life as a man through testosterone treatment and a double mastectomy, though he never had genital reconstruction or a hysterectomy. In 1999, Eads died of ovarian cancer.

predisposing them to be more independent and directive later on and predisposing girls to be more warm, nurturant, and interested in relationships with others. They acknowledge that some of these differences may result from factors in the postnatal environment. But because the differences appear so early, they attribute most of the effect to genetic, hormonal, or prenatal influences.

Others, however, have argued that even at so early an age a wide variety of factors other than biology can affect physical developmental, such as how much parents encourage the child and how much opportunity a child has to learn these activities (Carli, 1997). For example, in African cultures where mothers actively teach their babies to crawl, children reach this milestone significantly earlier than children raised in cultures where crawling is not taught (Super, 1976). Likewise, in the United States, giving infants practice in sitting or stepping can accelerate the age at which they learn these abilities.

The Cultural Flexibility of Gender

Using biology to explain gender differences later in life is the subject of much debate. Many anthropologists and sociologists note that because gender expectations are invented and defined by human beings, they can be quite flexible. What it means to be masculine or feminine can vary from place to place. Although certain gender stereotypes and expectations are shared by everyone in a particular culture, such perceptions can and often do differ by subgroup, depending on race, social class, sexual orientation, age, physical appearance, and so on. For instance, sociologist Noel Cazenave (1984) examined the way different groups define the "ideal man." Comparing responses from his survey of middle-class black men to results from another survey of predominantly middle-class white men, he found that black men placed greater emphasis than whites on such things as being self-confident, competitive, successful at work, aggressive, warm and gentle, and protective of their family.

The best-known research illustrating variations in ideas of masculinity and femininity was conducted by the anthropologist Margaret Mead (1963). Mead studied three cultures in New Guinea in the 1930s. Among the mountain-dwelling Arapesh, men and women displayed similar attitudes and actions. They showed traits we would commonly associate with femininity: cooperation, passivity, sensitivity to others. Mead described both men and women as being "maternal." These characteristics were linked to broader cultural beliefs about people's relationship to the environment.

South of the Arapesh were the Mundugumor, a group of cannibals and headhunters. Here, too, males and females were similar. However, both displayed traits that we in the West would associate with masculinity: assertiveness, emotional inexpressiveness, insensitivity to others. Women, according to Mead, were just as violent, just as aggressive, and just as jealous as men. Both were equally virile, without any of the "soft" characteristics we associate with femininity.

Finally, there were the Tchambuli. This group did distinguish between male and female traits. However, their gender expectations were the opposite of ours: Women were dominant, shrewd, assertive, and managerial; men were submissive, emotional, and seen as inherently delicate.

More recently, anthropologists have examined communities in which women have significant power and status. For instance, among the Agta Negritos of northeastern Luzon in the Philippines, women participate in all the subsistence activities men do, including hunting, fishing, and bartering. Consequently they have considerable author-

In many countries, such as Ghana, women hunt, fish, or barter alongside men.

ity over decision making in the family (Estioko-Griffin & Griffin, 1997). In some regions of Ghana, trade of local food crops in central markets is dominated by women, who are expected to financially support their husbands and children (Clark, 1994).

Studies like these are important because they show that definitions of masculinity and femininity are not universal. Women need not be the passive nurturers of children; men need not be the aggressors and breadwinners. Moreover, gender expectations are strongly shaped by the social context. For instance, some studies show that when women are rewarded for behaving aggressively, they can be just as violent as men (Hyde, 1984). Conversely, when men are the primary caretakers of their children, they can be as nurturing, sensitive, and physically affectionate as mothers (Risman, 1989).

We've seen, then, that sex and gender are separate, though related, concepts. Thinking of them as the same thing leads us to overlook extensive similarities between the sexes and wide variations within each sex. For instance, men as a group do tend to be more aggressive than women. Yet some women are much more aggressive than the average man, and some men are much less aggressive than the average woman. Indeed, social circumstances may have a greater impact on aggressive behavior than any innate, biological traits.

Assuming that gender differences are natural also ignores the fact that even within the same culture, gender expectations change. In just the past few decades, for example, it has become more socially acceptable for women to be assertive and ambitious. If such traits were purely biological, they would not have become more prevalent so rapidly.

Human genetics evolve on a millennial scale, not within a generation or two. Finally, if we rely on biology to explain gender differences, we overlook the wide cultural and historical variations in people's conceptions of masculinity and femininity.

In the end, what's important is how we, as a society, perceive and respond to the differences we see between males and females. It would be silly to argue that there's absolutely *no* connection between sex and gender, or that there are no biological or physical differences between males and females that influence their lives. But even biological predispositions aren't completely free of social influence. The members of a society can decide which sex differences to amplify and which they can and should ignore.

LEARNING GENDERS

If we're not born with a gender, how do children come to understand their gender in a way that is consistent with larger cultural dictates? Both boys and girls learn at a very young age to adopt gender as an organizing principle for themselves and the social world in which they live (Howard & Hollander, 1997).

Gender Differentiation in Infancy

Sexual differentiation has clear biological influences. But the gender differentiation process is social and begins the moment a child is born, or earlier if the fetus's sex is known before birth. Usually a physician, nurse, or midwife immediately declares whether the child is a boy or a girl. Indeed, this identification is the first thing most people—parents included—want to know. It's still common in many hospitals for infant boys to be wrapped in blue blankets and infant girls in pink ones. For better or worse, from that point on, the gender developmental paths of males and females diverge. The messages that children will eventually receive from families, books, television, other children, and schools will teach and reinforce culturally defined gender expectations and attitudes.

If you asked parents whether they treated sons any differently from daughters, most would probably say no. Yet considerable evidence shows that what parents do and what they say they do are two different things (Lytton & Romney, 1991; McHale, Crouter, & Whiteman, 2003). In one early study, when 30 first-time parents were asked to describe their newborn infants, they frequently used common gender stereotypes. Those with daughters described them as "tiny," "soft," "fine-featured," and "delicate." Sons were seen as "strong," "alert," "hardy," and "coordinated" (Rubin, Provenzano, & Luria, 1974). A replication of this study 20 years later found that parents continue to perceive their infants in gender-stereotyped ways, although to a lesser degree than in the 1970s (Karraker, Vogel, & Lake, 1995).

Parents begin the gender socialization process even before their children become verbal. Research has found that mothers talk differently with their daughters and sons, even as infants. One study found that mothers of 6-month-olds are more likely to ask their daughters interpretive questions that require some kind of response: "Look at you playing with the beads. Are you going to slide the red bead next?" In contrast, they are more likely to direct their sons' behavior, by providing instructions such as "Come here" or simply getting the child's attention by calling out his name. In addition, mothers comfort and hug their daughters more than their sons (Clearfield & Nelson, 2006).

New parents can be especially sensitive about the correct identification of their child's sex. Even parents who feel there's too much emphasis on sex and gender nevertheless spend a great deal of time ensuring that their child has the culturally appropriate physical appearance of a boy or girl. This sensitivity is not surprising given the centrality of sex and gender in our culture and our desire for clarity. When others misidentify the sex of their baby it can be an embarrassing, even painful experience for some parents, which may explain why parents of a girl baby who has yet to grow hair (a visible sign of gender in this culture) will often tape pink ribbons to the bald baby's head. In many Latin American countries, families have baby girls' ears pierced shortly after birth, providing an obvious visual indicator of the child's sex and gender.

Gender Differentiation in Later Childhood

Early on, children learn to distinguish the female role from the male role, learn to see a broad range of activities as exclusively "appropriate" for only one gender or the other, and come to identify themselves accordingly. Most developmental psychologists believe that by the age of 3 or so most children can accurately answer the question "Are you a boy or a girl?" (Kohlberg, 1966). But to a *very* young child, being a boy or a girl means no more than being named Jason instead of Jennifer. It is simply another characteristic, like having brown hair or 10 fingers. The child at this age has no conception that gender is a category into which every human can be placed.

At around age 5 children tend to see gender as an invariant characteristic of the social world—something that is fixed and permanent. They may say things like "men are doctors" and "women are nurses" as if they are inflexible, objective "truths." Even at this early age, most children have developed a fairly extensive and often incorrect repertoire of gender stereotypes that they then apply to themselves (Martin & Ruble, 2004). They also use these stereotypes to form impressions of others and to guide their own perceptions and activities. A boy, for instance, may avoid approaching a new girl who has just moved into the neighborhood because he assumes she will be interested in "girl" things. Acting on this assumption reinforces the original belief that boys and girls are different. In time, though, children's attitudes toward gender will probably become a bit more flexible, although such flexibility may not be reflected in their actual behaviors (Martin & Ruble, 2004).

Parents, siblings, and other significant people in the child's immediate environment serve as the earliest models with whom the child can identify and whom the child can ultimately imitate. Sometimes the lessons are purposive and direct—as when parents provide their children with explicit instructions on proper gender behavior, such as "Big boys don't cry" or "Act like a young lady."

Decades' worth of research show that parents continue to interact differently with their sons and daughters as the children grow and develop. For instance, when parents were instructed to tell their school-age children stories about their own childhoods, they were more likely to highlight themes of autonomy and independence when they had sons than when they had daughters (Fiese & Skillman, 2000). Fathers spend more time and engage in more physical play with their sons than with their daughters, whereas mothers are more emotionally responsive to girls and encourage more independence with boys (Lanvers, 2004; Raley & Bianchi, 2006).

Parents also influence their children's gender through the things they routinely purchase for them, such as clothing. Not only do clothes inform others about the sex of an individual, they also send messages about how that person ought to be treated.

Clothes direct behavior along traditional gender lines (Martin, 1998) and encourage or discourage certain gender-typed actions. Even very young girls understand that some behavior is not appropriate when in a dress. Consider the following scene at a children's preschool with a group of 5-year-old girls:

> Four girls are sitting at a table—Cathy, Kim, Danielle, and Jesse. They are cutting play money out of paper. Cathy and Danielle have on overalls and Kim and Jesse have on dresses. Cathy puts her feet up on the table and crosses her legs at the ankle; she leans back in her chair and continues cutting her money. Danielle imitates her. They look at each other and laugh. They put their shoulders back, posturing, having fun with this new way of sitting. Kim and Jesse continue to cut and laugh with them, but do not put their feet up. (cited in Martin, 1998, p. 498)

You can see that feminine dress and adornments restrict girls' movements, which leads them to take up less space with their bodies. Dresses don't lend themselves easily to rough and dirty play. Likewise, it is difficult to walk quickly or assertively in high heels and skirts. Everyday clothes for boys and men rarely restrict physical movement in this way.

Toys, too, serve to distinguish between the sexes. Toys have always played a significant role in teaching children about prevailing cultural conceptions of gender. In the 1950s—a time in U.S. history when most adults had endless faith in the goodness of technological progress—erector sets and chemistry sets were supposed to encourage boys to be engineers and scientists. Dollhouses and baby dolls taught girls to be modern homemakers and mothers during a time when girls typically assumed they'd occupy those roles in adulthood.

A quick glance at Saturday morning television commercials or toy store shelves or manufacturers' Web sites reveals that many toys and games remain segregated along gender lines. "Girls' toys" still revolve around themes of domesticity, fashion, and motherhood and "boys' toys" emphasize action and adventure (Renzetti & Curran, 2003). Gender-specific toys foster different traits and skills in children and thereby further segregate boys and girls into different patterns of social development. Typical "boys' toys"—like construction sets, military gear, and sports equipment—encourage invention, exploration, competition, and aggression. Typical "girls' toys"—such as, dolls, plastic jewelry sets, and kitchen appliances—tend to encourage creativity, nurturing, and physical attractiveness.

For the most part, toy manufacturers are still quick to exploit the gender-distinct roles children are encouraged to pursue when they become adults. They know full well that those few adults who do object to gender-specific toys will face disappointed children scowling at the sight of some gender-neutral alternative (Williams, 2006). Fisher-Price offers the "Little Mommy" doll, a soft, cuddly baby that drinks from a bottle and comes with a potty seat for toilet training. Playmates Toys' "Amazing Amanda" laughs, talks, cries, asks for hugs, and changes facial expressions. Mattel makes a pregnant version of Barbie's friend Midge (called "Happy Family Midge"). She comes with a distended tummy that, when removed, reveals a 1 3/4-inch baby nestled in the doll's plastic uterus. The doll comes with everything a girl needs to play out the birth and care of the new baby, including diapers (pink if it's a girl; blue if it's a boy), a birth certificate, bottles, rattles, changing table, tub, and crib. All these dolls clearly teach young girls the cultural value of motherhood, a role most girls are encouraged and expected to enter later in life. You'd be hard-pressed to find a comparable toy popular among boys that prepares them for future roles as nurturing fathers.

It's important to note that the process by which children learn gender is not a passive one in which they simply absorb the information that bombards them. As part of the process of finding meaning in their social worlds, children actively construct gender as a social category. From an early age, they are like "gender detectives," searching for cues about gender, such as who should and shouldn't engage in certain activities, who can play with whom, and why girls and boys differ (Martin & Ruble, 2004, p. 67).

Doing Gender

Gender isn't acquired in the sense that once we learn it, we have it for a lifetime. Many sociologists believe gender entails an active learning component: that is, it is an accomplishment rather than a fixed attribute of each individual (Lorber, 2005; West & Zimmerman, 1987). True, young children acquire knowledge about gender through socialization and, in most cases, learn to display behaviors and attributes appropriate for their gender. But what they learn are the gender rules that allow them to be perceived as masculine or feminine. Simply learning these rules doesn't make a person feminine or masculine.

To become masculine or feminine, we must "do gender" appropriately and continuously through everyday social interactions. Indeed, the sexual dichotomy itself could not be maintained unless people present themselves in ways that allow others to categorize them as male or female (Ridgeway & Smith-Lovin, 1999).

How do we "do gender"? We do it by behaving in ways that are considered appropriate for our gender. For women, that means not acting in masculine ways (for example, sitting "lady-like," paying attention to appearance, wearing makeup and jewelry, not burping in public). For men, it usually means not acting in ways that are typically defined as feminine, such as not overtly displaying certain emotions and not nurturing others, especially other adults.

Is it possible not to do gender? Not really. We might not do gender well or we might do it in culturally inappropriate ways, but if we try not to display or do gender at all, others will do it for us. Sociologist Betsy Lucal (1999) describes what it's like to be a woman, identify as a woman, but be mistaken for a man because she is large, has short-cropped hair, and dresses in masculine clothing:

> Each day, I experience the consequences that our gender system has for my identity and interactions. I am a woman who has been called "Sir" so many times that I no longer even hesitate to assume that it is being directed at me. I am a woman whose use of public rest rooms regularly causes reactions ranging from confused stares to confrontations over what a man is doing in the women's room. (p. 781)

According to Lucal, she can choose not to do femininity (that is, not to act in ways that conform to cultural expectations for women), but she cannot choose not to do gender. People she encounters always attribute one or the other gender; it just so happens they sometimes make a misattribution. But for Lucal, as for most of us, gender is a significant part of her identity, and she is deeply embedded in the "gender system." Her failure to do traditional femininity doesn't means she's not a woman or that she doesn't want to be seen as a woman. According to Lucal:

> I am not to the point of personally abandoning gender. . . . I do not want people to see me as genderless as much as I want them to see me as a woman. . . . I would

like to expand the category of "woman" to include people like me. . . . I do identify myself as a woman, not as a man or as someone outside of the two-and-only-two categories. (pp. 793–794)

The Rewards and Costs of Doing Gender

To understand why we care so much about doing gender appropriately requires thinking about gender on both individual and cultural levels. On an individual level, we may do gender to experience the rewards and privileges that come from acting in ways consistent with people's gender expectations. For instance, by acting incompetent at housework—a characteristic typically associated with masculinity—a man may be able to get a female friend or partner to cook and clean for him. Women who wear makeup at work are more likely to be seen as attractive, healthy, and competent than women who do not (Dellinger & Williams, 1997). Both men and women who do gender "well" may find that they are more successful at attracting mates.

The way we do gender also may help us avoid hostile reactions, whether because of our own characteristics, as in Betsy Lucal's case, or because of the social context. For instance, doing gender can be difficult for men in predominantly female occupations, such as nursing, where their masculinity is likely to be questioned by the people they serve (Williams, 2004). In these cases, men may employ special strategies (such as emphasizing the tough, physical nature of their work) to accentuate their masculinity.

In other cases, an individual may lack the social or personal resources to do gender appropriately. Unemployed men, for example, especially those who perceive breadwinning as integral to their masculinity, face a difficult dilemma—how to seem masculine when circumstances don't allow them to do gender the way they think they should. Many unemployed men may resist doing housework or child care even more vehemently than they would if they were employed to avoid further threats to their masculinity.

In general, the social costs of violating gender norms are not felt evenly by girls and boys, or by women and men. Consider the different connotations and implications of the words *tomboy* and *sissy*. The *tomboy* may fight, curse, play sports, and climb trees, but her entire sexual identity is not called into question by the label. In fact, in some situations she is just as likely to be included by other children as shunned, as when, say, she is asked to play in informal games of football or basketball with neighborhood boys. Girls, in general, are permitted to do "boy things" (Kimmel, 2004). Indeed, being a tomboy, if considered negatively at all, is typically seen as transitory, a stage that a girl will eventually outgrow. How many TV shows or movies have you seen in which a pugnacious tomboy reaches puberty, sprouts breasts, discovers boys, discards her rough-and-tumble ways, puts on makeup and a dress for the first time, and unveils to stunned friends and family her true feminine beauty?

For boys, life on the other side of the gender fence is much more precarious. The chances to play girl games without ridicule are rare, and the risks for doing so are steep. The *sissy* is not simply a boy who enjoys female pursuits. He is suspiciously soft and effeminate (Farr, 2006). His sissy behavior is likely to be seen as reflective of his sexual nature, a sign of impending homosexuality.

Part of the reason for this asymmetrical response to gender-crossing behavior is the structural gender inequalities that exist in society. Simply put, in a society built around and for the interests of men, stereotypically masculine traits (strength, assertiveness, confidence, and so on) are likely to be valued culturally and interpersonally. Hence, many women conclude that their own success requires such traits. Even young children learn that these traits are valued more highly than stereotypically feminine traits:

Boys and girls both understand the inequality between women and men, and understand, too, that their less-than-equal status gives girls a bit more latitude in the types of cross-sex (gender-inappropriate) behavior they may exhibit. Girls think they'd be better off as boys, and many of them declare that they would rather be boys than girls. By contrast, boys tend to see being girls as a fate worse than death. . . . [A little boy comes] to understand that his status in the world depends upon his ability to distance himself from femininity. By exaggerating gender difference, he both assures and reassures himself of his higher status. (Kimmel, 2004, pp. 132–133)

On a broader level, doing gender appropriately sustains and legitimizes the larger institution of gender (Ridgeway & Smith-Lovin, 1999). Because every aspect of our social life is gendered, if we collectively declined to do gender, we would have to dismantle and reorganize the way we work, relate, eat, parent, show emotions—everything. Further, by doing gender in culturally appropriate ways, we submit to the view that gendered social arrangements are natural and normal.

Although women have made significant strides into traditionally male occupations, men have been slower to enter traditionally female occupations; it's still rare to see men who teach kindergarten.

Androgynous Socialization

Nevertheless, some parents today, concerned about the overemphasis on male-female distinctions and gender stereotyping, are pushing for less restrictive ideas about gender (Lips, 1993). To diminish gender distinctions, some parents and child development experts advocate **androgynous socialization**—bringing up children to have both male and female traits and behaviors (Bem, 1974). Advocates for androgynous socialization see no biological reason, except for a few anatomical and reproductive differences, to differentiate between what males and females can do.

Yet parents' ability to carry out androgynous socialization may be limited (Sedney, 1987). Four- and 5-year-old children often engage in strongly gender-stereotypical play, regardless of the attitudes and beliefs expressed by their parents (O'Brien & Huston, 1985). In fact, sociologists have found that even children raised in feminist households—where they are taught that men and women are equal and that no activity needs to be sex-linked—act in ways that are fairly gender stereotypical when with their peers (Risman & Myers, 1997). Findings like these have led some researchers to suggest that the effects of androgynous socialization are more likely to show up in adulthood rather than in childhood, after individuals have developed the cognitive maturity and the confidence to incorporate nontraditional ways of doing gender into their everyday lives (Sedney, 1987).

But some sociologists question whether parents or anyone else has the ability to change deeply ingrained gender lessons (Lorber, 1994). Gender structures every organization and shapes every interaction in society, often in ways we are not consciously aware of. Individual parents may have little hope of seriously altering their children's understanding of gender. Remember the case of Aurora/Zachary, whose parents lost custody of their child because they failed to properly gender socialize him/her? The efforts of some parents to break gender barriers can quickly be undermined by the larger society.

■ **androgynous socialization**
Bringing up children to have both male and female traits and behaviors.

GENDER AND POWER IN FAMILIES

Gender is an important component of family life, not just because it influences people's experiences and behaviors, but also because of the privileges and ultimately the power it provides some people and not others. Feminist theorists have argued that the problem with current gender arrangements is not just that males and females act or feel differently. The problem is that sex differences are perceived as gender differences, which then get translated into power differences:

> Females are born a little smaller than males. This difference is exaggerated by upbringing, so that women grow into adults who are less physically strong and competent than they could be. They are then excluded from a range of manual occupations and, by extension, from the control of technology. The effect spills over into everyday life: ultimately women have become dependent on men to change the wheel of a car, reglaze a broken window or replace a smashed roof slate. (quoted in Lorber, 1994)

This author is talking about how gender differences can lead to female dependency in the workplace and in day-to-day activities. Power differences also exist within marriages and families. We need to understand them not because they shape men's and women's lives so profoundly, but because doing so can help us understand gender inequality within the larger context of a society.

power
The ability to impose one's will on others.

For our purposes, **power** is an individual's ability to impose her or his will on others (Lipman-Blumen, 1984). Those with power can exercise it by punishing (or threatening to punish) others or by rewarding them. Power is most obvious within families when members either enact, over time, some sort of changes they want—because they have the ability to put them into effect—or are thwarted because others are able to use their power to create obstacles (Komter, 1989).

Power is an integral part of family relationships because, as in all relationships, it determines how people relate to one another and how decisions are made. When people perceive that they have power, they are inclined to exert dominance in everyday interactions with their partners (Dunbar & Burgoon, 2005).

orchestration power
The ability to decide what course of action will be taken.

implementation power
The ability to decide how a course of action will be accomplished.

The key to understanding the distribution of power in families is not necessarily knowing who makes the *most* decisions but who gets to decide *which* decisions will be made. Sociologists distinguish between **orchestration power,** making decisions about what will be done, and **implementation power,** making decisions about how it will get done (Safilios-Rothschild, 1976). If a wife decides the family will take a trip and tells her husband to make all the decisions concerning travel arrangements and hotel accommodations, who really has the decision-making power? Although the amount of power people have in their intimate relationships depends on many individual and situational factors, gender has a considerable impact on power differences in contemporary couples (Ridgeway & Smith-Lovin, 1999).

Contemporary Gender/Power Relationships in Families

At first glance, we might assume that women hold tremendous power within their families because the private, family domain is so closely associated with women's traditional roles. But studies of power within marriage reveal a different story (Howard & Hollander, 1997). Sociological research has consistently shown that power imbalances are the rule rather than the exception in intimate and family relationships, and that it is typically men, not women, who possess power.

Half a century ago, researchers noted that husbands tended to have more power over their wives than wives have over husbands, particularly when wives were not employed outside the home (Blood & Wolfe, 1960). Although power in contemporary couples is more equal, or egalitarian, than it was in 1960, subtle (and sometimes overt) power differences are still likely to be at work in contemporary marriages. In one study, researchers interviewed 61 married couples who had faced important work and family choices to determine what factors influenced their decisions (Zvonkovic, Greaves, Schmiege, & Hall, 1996). Most of the decisions revolved around the adjustments the wife should make—namely, whether she should increase or decrease the number of hours she spent at work. The decision factors were those that traditionally affect women: constraints such as having a young child, or opportunities such as having children near an age where they could more easily look after themselves. But when the decisions concerned the husband's job, the couples tended to focus only on whether he ought to switch jobs and not on whether he should increase or decrease the amount of time he spent at work.

When the husband's job was the focus of attention, both partners tended to know what the other wanted, and both spouses tended to want the same thing from the decision. But when the decision revolved around the wife's job, there was significant disagreement about the most favorable outcome and a general lack of understanding of the other spouse's desires. For example, in one couple, the wife enjoyed her part-time job and believed it had beneficial effects on her and on the marriage. Yet her husband viewed her job as just one in a series of rather unimportant temporary positions. The researchers attributed this sort of disagreement and uncertainty to ambivalence about the wife's participation in the labor force in the first place.

Interestingly, most couples maintained that the decisions they made were "joint" or "mutual." In reality, however, most of the time the husband's preferences prevailed. Husbands' unspoken power over work and family decisions was reflected in one wife's description of how she and her husband make important decisions: "We usually talk and come to full agreement, or I give in and do what he wants on . . . [a] majority of things. I love him, and minor disagreements are a part of life" (quoted in Zvonkovic et al., 1996, p. 98).

The intersection of gender and power within intimate relationships can operate in other important ways. For instance, women are more likely to know their husbands' work friends than men are to know their wives' work friends. This tendency could be a function of women being more supportive of their husbands' friendship networks. But it also reflects the differential importance of husbands' versus wives' occupations. Women are more likely to move with their husbands' work opportunities than men are to move with their wives' work changes. Hence, women's work and friendship ties with others outside the relationship may be sacrificed as a result of a move made because of a husband's job (Ridgeway & Smith-Lovin, 1999).

■ GOING GLOBAL

Hidden Power in Japanese Couples

The intersection of gender and power in families can be complex in rapidly changing societies. In Japan, for instance, women have historically occupied a visibly subservient position both in society and in families. At one time women were expected to walk several steps behind their husband so as not to offend his dignity by stepping on his shadow (Kristof, 1996b). Wives were legally prohibited from using different surnames from their husbands. Although more than 65% of Japanese women work outside the home (U.S. Bureau of the Census, 2008), they earn about 65% of what Japanese men earn, one of the largest gender gaps in the industrialized world (French, 2003). Indeed, a cross-national study of seven industrialized countries—the United States, Norway, Sweden, Canada, the United Kingdom, Australia, and Japan—found that women in Japan are significantly less likely than women in the other countries to hold supervisory or managerial positions in the workplace (Wright, Baxter, & Birkelund, 1995).

Within Japanese families, however—even though women are still expected to clean, cook, and tend to the needs of their husbands—women exercise a surprising degree of authority. Many wives control the household finances, giving their husbands monthly allowances as they see fit. Recent surveys have found that about half of Japanese men are dissatisfied with the amount of their allowances. Many wives refuse to give their husbands cash cards for the family bank account. If the husband wants to withdraw money from the account, the bank will usually phone the wife to get her approval. Japanese men are even starting to take on some of the housework responsibilities, a development that would have been unthinkable a decade ago. One man summed up the situation this way: "Things go best when the husband is swimming in the palm of his wife's hand" (quoted in Kristof, 1996b, p. A6).

By now, you can probably tell that the balance of family power isn't always obvious. For instance, when a wife anticipates her husband's angry response to her desire for him to do more around the house, she may decide to stifle her concerns to avoid what she thinks will be certain conflict. Thus he has successfully exerted power over her by preventing her from speaking her mind without any direct confrontation. Such "invisible" power is important because it can maintain inequality even in those marriages that appear harmonious and conflict-free.

If women exercise their power within families only covertly, they may have more power than sociologists have been able to observe. Some researchers suggest that women operate from a position of "negative dominance"—for example, withdrawing love or provoking men's guilt feelings to impose their will. This strategy may be strong enough to balance the overt power of their husbands (Holter, 1970).

Anthropologist Susan Rogers (1975) observed this sort of covert power in her studies of peasant societies over 30 years ago. Although men's public authority made them appear dominant, women actually controlled tremendous informal power in the family. Here's how one couple demonstrated what Rogers called a "myth of male dominance":

> Mme. François wanted a motorbike for fetching the cows from pasture. She argued at length with her husband, who insisted that they could not afford one for at least a year. Two weeks later, she had a motorbike. When I asked her about it, she might very well have said, "I control the budget and I wanted it, so too bad for him, I went out and bought it." But rather, she winked and said simply, "Pierre changed his mind." (p. 741)

Publicly, women in this community insisted that the husbands were in control and showed them deference when in public. But privately, Rogers suggests everyone in the community—men and women alike—seemed to understand that men's power was in fact a myth.

Does the same phenomenon exist in contemporary U.S. society? Without question, many women who are dependent on men for goods and services have probably learned how to influence their partners in such a way that their needs, or their families' needs, are met. But the male dominance we see in contemporary U.S. marriages doesn't appear to be entirely mythical. One important difference between the women in the peasant societies Rogers studied and women in highly industrialized societies like the United States is that in preindustrial, peasant societies, men and women are equally dependent on each other socially and economically. But in industrialized societies, gender relations have evolved in such a way that women typically control fewer resources than men and are therefore less powerful. As this gap diminishes, mostly as a result of women's successes in the labor force, women have regained greater power in their relationships.

Resources and Dependence

A key factor in power differences within families, according to social exchange theorists, is **dependence**—the degree to which one person relies on the other for important resources. If your partner has something you want or need—money, love and affection, understanding and support, companionship, information, sex—you'll be motivated to comply with his or her wishes, obey his or her commands, or put up with other undesirable or costly behaviors in order to get it.

> ■ **dependence**
> The degree to which one person in a relationship relies on the other for important resources.

Each person brings a variety of resources to her or his intimate relationships (e.g., money and other possessions, status, attractiveness, emotional support, sex and affection). We exchange the resources we have for a desired benefit from our partner. The more resources individuals believe they contribute to a relationship, relative to their partners, the more they expect in return and the more power they're likely to believe they're entitled to (Safilios-Rothschild, 1976).

But control over a resource creates power differences only if we highly value the resource and perceived it as essential. Moreover, it must be something that we can't obtain elsewhere. So if you don't care about sex or financial security or if you have other prospects for acquiring them, you won't depend on your partner to provide these things, and he or she will not be able to use them to exercise much power over you.

When we depend on people to provide resources that we desperately want but that are unavailable elsewhere, we find ourselves in a position of powerlessness. Power and dependence are *inversely* related. That is, the more dependent a person is on a partner to meet his or her needs, the less power he or she is likely to have in the relationship. This is as true for emotional resources as it is for financial ones. For instance, a partner who loves more is more dependent and therefore more likely to be submissive. Such submission can be used as a means of keeping the other partner happy, thereby maintaining the stability of the relationship (Winton, 1995).

Because men and women tend to control different types of resources, dependence and power in families are entwined with gender (Howard & Hollander, 1997). Men's higher earnings and greater access to prestigious occupations have historically given them more power and privilege inside their families. Women who don't work outside the home or who are burdened with the care of young children have considerably fewer opportunities to earn money and are particularly likely to be economically dependent on their partners.

But family power is rarely absolute. Traditional male breadwinners, who can use their economic wherewithal to exert power over their wives, may nevertheless depend on their wives to provide the physical, psychological, and emotional support that enables them to work outside the home. In short, they can be as emotionally dependent on their wives as their wives are economically dependent on them (Hertz, 1986). In addition, women are often able to claim significant power in families because of their role as "kinkeeper"—the person who controls those relationships that cross generations or that involve relatives outside the nuclear family (Kranichfeld, 1987). These bonds place women at the very center of family life.

Furthermore, as women have entered the workforce in greater numbers, they have begun to acquire the economic resources that enable them to participate more forcefully in family decision making (Blumstein & Schwartz, 1983; Rubin, 1995). They may still defer to their husbands in many situations, and they still retain primary responsibility for domestic work (see Chapter 9). Even so, employed women in general are more likely than nonemployed women to feel they have the right to have their say at home and contradict their husbands. One wife, who oversees a large laboratory, explains why: "I make decisions at the office from nine to five and I think it would be a little strange if I came home and was treated like a pussycat" (quoted in Blumstein & Schwartz, 1983, p. 141).

Conversely, women who drop out of the paid labor force often experience a noticeable decrease in their ability to make family decisions at home: "We don't get along as well as we used to when I was working because then he used to listen to me more than he does now. He tends to boss me around the way he tends to boss his students" (quoted in Blumstein & Schwartz, 1983, p. 142). Some evidence suggests that more and more college-educated women—even those in professional programs at elite universities—plan to delay entering the labor force, to leave it entirely, or to cut back to part time to raise children (Story, 2005). One recent book argues that the major impediment to women's achieving independence, power, and hence full equality in society is not obstacles to advancement in the workplace but the continuing expectation that they sacrifice their careers to take care of their families (Hirshman, 2006).

That one partner has more financial resources than the other is not the crucial fact here; rather, it's the meaning couples attach to these resources (Pyke, 1994). The effect that a resource like money has on marital power depends on whether couples consider it a gift or a burden. For instance, a woman whose husband sees her employment as a threat to him rather than as a contribution to the household will derive less power from her wage earning. This is particularly true when the husband is chronically unemployed or works in a low-status, menial job that increases his dependence on his wife's wages. A woman's employment in these situations may be such a sore spot for her husband that she is actually expected to compensate for it, perhaps by doing more work around the house or by deferring to his authority. Sensitive to her husband's feelings of failure, a woman may feel the need to soothe his threatened ego by consciously downplaying her own employment status (Hochschild & Machung, 1989).

Conversely, a nonemployed woman married to a man who values her domestic work may actually derive more power from that role. She may be grateful to him for enabling her not to work for pay, and he may value her choice to stay home, especially when children are present. If her nonparticipation is perceived as her choice, staying out of the workforce may actually reflect her power and her ability to make decisions on her own behalf.

The Role of Cultural Ideology

For all its importance, money isn't the only factor influencing power/gender relations in families. It's highly unlikely that, even if they earned more than men, women would be able to claim the lion's share of power and influence in families. Conceptions of power and family are deeply embedded in our society. Indeed, despite some changes, gender inequality has persisted in U.S. society despite women's movement into the labor force in the past few decades and their increasing representation in male-dominated occupations such as law and medicine (Ridgeway, 1997). Thus *cultural ideology* may overshadow the effect even of monetary resources on family power.

In our culture, certain family members gain power from social norms, traditions, or laws. That is, we allow certain people in the family to exert power over others because of the positions they occupy rather than because of any special or noteworthy characteristics they as individuals might have. The authority of a parent over a child, for example, is considered legitimate to the extent that the norms and traditions of the larger society uphold this power relationship, or perhaps even require it.

In some segments of U.S. society, as in other male-dominated cultures, men control most, if not all, of the important social institutions: politics, economics, religion, the media, and education. By virtue of their higher social status, they can also claim they have the legitimate right to exercise power over their wives and children.

Although many in the United States would deny the traditional claim that men have the plain and simple right to enforce their will within their families, we often justify the same power differential in more socially acceptable—but still ideological—terms. For instance, some women now subordinate their careers to their husbands' on the grounds that doing so maximizes family resources and is the most efficient way to serve the interests of all family members (Pyke, 1996). Though wrapped in seemingly rational language, this belief still has the effect of undermining women's long-term economic interests and limiting their claims to family power (Hirshman, 2006).

Women's economic well-being may also be offset by cultural ideologies that value them primarily for the noneconomic resources they provide. In Korea, for example, researchers have found that wives who go to work outside the home actually *lose* power in their marriages (Balswick & Balswick, 1995). Since Korean wives already have the responsibility and authority to spend the family's money, they gain little personal power from earning money themselves. But the nurturing resources—such as showering husbands with care and attention after a day's work—are highly valued in Korean society, more than any extra income wives may provide to their families. By working outside the home, wives lose the emotional power they had.

The diversity of U.S. culture yields vastly different conceptions of women's and men's "places" in families. Among some groups—such as recent immigrants from Latin America, Africa, and Asia—male dominance and authority are the norm. Husbands in these families can wield significant power within the household. Among other groups in the United States, however—such as Unitarians and Reform Jews—families are more likely to approach gender equality. In these more liberal groups, you may find individual women who are more dominant than their husbands. Even so, there is no group within contemporary society where women systematically hold greater power than men.

The Cultural Devaluation of Women

One of the most insidious outcomes of the power differences within society is that power translates not only into prestige, status, and independence but also into social worth. Groups that systematically lack power both within and outside families, such as children, women, and minorities, often are devalued in society.

We can see signs of women's devaluation in everyday social practices. Consider the unwanted attention that many women must endure. Women riding on crowded

New York City subways are routinely touched, groped, or flashed. Such incidents have become so common in Tokyo and Mexico City that rail companies have introduced "women only" cars to protect women from unwanted fondling. As one reporter put it, "Just as some men reflexively check to see if they have their wallets on a crowded train, women check their bodies" (Hartocollis, 2006, p. B11).

Female devaluation isn't just an annoyance; it can sometimes be fatal. In some countries parents place much higher value on sons than on daughters. Typically, sons carry the family name, inherit ancestral property, and care for parents in old age. Researchers estimate that approximately half a million female fetuses—or about 10 million over the past two decades—have been aborted by parents who didn't want a daughter after ultrasound tests revealed the child's sex (Jha et al., 2006). Indian parents are even more likely to abort a female fetus if they already have a daughter.

Even when daughters are born, families in some cultures often invest resources to ensure their son's future at the expense of their daughter's. Families short on food commonly see to it that male children are well fed, even if it means taking food from female children. As a result, girls tend to grow up sicker. Many female babies are so undernourished that they die within the first year (Bryjak & Soroka, 1992).

In some developing countries in Africa and Asia, laws dictate that a daughter's inheritance automatically goes to her husband upon marriage. Furthermore, widows often have no inheritance rights in property owned by their husbands and thus may lose their homes, the land they've worked on, their household possessions, even their children when their husbands die (Owen, 1996). What value daughters do have in such societies lies in their ability to get married. Among the Masai of Kenya, for example, parents of girls as young as 9 give them to adult men to marry in exchange for money, livestock, food, or any other needed commodity. Sexual coercion and violence within marriage has been documented in such diverse settings as South Asia, Latin America, Africa, and the Middle East. Women's powerlessness and cultural norms that stress men's entitlement to sex lie at the heart of the problem (Population Council, 2004).

Worldwide, women lack the legal and familial protections that men enjoy. Consider these examples:

- The Iranian constitution states that the value of a woman's life and her testimony in court is half that of a man's. Iranian women cannot travel anywhere without their husbands' permission (Watson, 2005).

- In Kenya, when a woman's husband dies, she loses her land, her livestock, and all household property. In addition, widows are transferred to a male relative of the deceased husband, who takes control of the property (Lacey, 2003).

- In Kyrgyzstan, it's estimated that more than half of all married women were abducted by their soon-to-be husbands in a centuries-old legal custom known as *ala kachuu* (which literally means "grab and run"). If they are kept in the man's home overnight, their virginity becomes suspect, their names disgraced, and their future marriage chances destroyed. So most women (about 80% according to estimates) eventually relent and marry their abductor, often with the urging of their own families (Smith, 2005).

- In Senegal, single women who are rape victims may be killed by their families because as nonvirgins they can no longer command a high dowry. A married woman who has been raped may be killed by her "dishonored" husband (Morgan, 1996).

■ About 60% of married Pakistani women who file rape charges—which require four male witnesses for a conviction—are later criminally charged themselves for having sex outside marriage (cited in Fisher, 2002).

Destructive practices often are so entrenched in a culture they're accepted as part of everyday life. Take, for instance, the practice of female genital mutilation (FGM), a procedure that entails the removal of a girl's clitoris and/or the destruction of the labia and vulva, often under highly unsanitary conditions and without anesthetics (Amnesty International, 2004). A decades-long worldwide campaign to end FGM has led many countries to ban the practice. However, it persists as a local custom in 26 countries, and over 3 million girls a year are subjected to it (Cohn, 2007).

In the African and Middle Eastern countries where FGM is practiced, women are expected to be virgins when they marry. The ritual, therefore, serves to control young women's sexuality and ensure their "marriageability." Indeed, a girl who has not undergone this procedure may be considered "unclean" or a prostitute by local villagers and therefore unmarriageable. Ironically, it is often women themselves—usually mothers and grandmothers—who enforce the practice of FGM (Crossette, 1995). But such pressure is not motivated by cruelty. In fact, these older women may have the girls' best interests in mind. If a young woman's marriage chances, and therefore her future economic security, require that she be subjected to FGM, her very survival is at stake.

Although these practices may seem extreme to us, many U.S. women also experience abuse, mutilation, and murder rooted in gender inequality. Consider a new trend in cosmetic plastic surgery called "designer laser vaginoplasty"—surgical enhancement of the vulva—for "purely aesthetic" purposes. Plastic surgeons in the United States will also perform "hymen repairs" so that a woman will bleed when she has sexual intercourse, to signify that she's a virgin. Although these surgeries are elective and performed under sterile conditions by trained professionals, we can wonder how different they really are from FGM. Nor is the devaluation of women through murder an unknown practice here: roughly 1 in 3 female murder victims in a given year is killed by a husband or live-in boyfriend (Catalano, 2006; see Chapter 13 for more detail).

In sum, everyday family life for countless numbers of women worldwide is an extremely dangerous enterprise. Gender inequality, both within and outside families, can literally be life threatening.

But the news isn't all bad. Educational gaps between boys and girls are closing in many countries (Figure 4.2). Adult women worldwide have increased their participation in the paid labor force and are making greater financial contributions to their families, thus gaining some power in their intimate relationships. Likewise, in some societies, women are becoming a political and cultural force that can no longer be ignored. Greater awareness of sexual exploitation and violence may eventually reduce—though perhaps not totally eliminate—traditional tolerance for sexual harassment, rape, and spouse abuse.

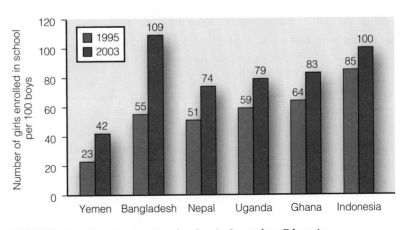

FIGURE 4.2 **The Closing Gender Gap in Secondary Education**
Source: Ashford, 2005, figure 1.

WHAT DOES IT ALL MEAN?

The sociological study of families relies heavily on the analysis of gender. Most contemporary scholars would argue that it is really not possible to study family without understanding gender. Our gendered selves inform all our family experiences.

As we'll see in later chapters, every aspect of family life is shaped by gender. Not only do parents respond to their daughters and sons differently, men and women also parent in different ways. Further, the work men and women do in and outside the home is strongly gendered. Dating behaviors, and experiences with sexuality, aging, divorce, and much more, are also gendered. All these experiences "produce different feelings, consciousness, relationships, skills—ways of being that we call feminine and masculine" (Lorber 1994, p. 14).

By doing gender in this way, we are constantly reinforcing the existing social organization of gender, making it difficult for new gender expectations to emerge. Nevertheless, gender relationships in our society, and by extension in U.S. families, are slowly but noticeably changing.

Yet as long as we continue to subscribe to the concept of two-and-only-two sexes or genders and to see gender differences as inherent and natural, we are likely to accept the differential treatment of men and women as inevitable. As a result, the power differences in families that are based on gender are likely to persist. As you think of the material covered in this chapter, consider the following questions:

- Can you envision a society that is not structured around the sexual dichotomy? How would such a society differ from the one in which you currently live? How would our ideas about intimacy and family change?

- Do you think parents should try to raise their children androgynously? What would be the advantages of such an upbringing? What would be the disadvantages?

- Can you think of specific examples in which gender has affected your own intimate or family experiences? How did your gender interact with other aspects of your identity, such as age, race, ethnicity, or religion?

- Do people in one country have an obligation to try to do something about practices in other countries that devalue or harm women when those practices are considered appropriate within the context of that culture?

SUMMARY

- Whereas "sex" is typically used to refer to a person's biological maleness or femaleness, "gender" designates psychological, social, and cultural aspects of maleness and femaleness.

- Although most people take for granted that there are two, and only two sex categories, cross-cultural and biological evidence suggest that these categories are neither exhaustive nor mutually exclusive.

- Reliance on biology to explain gender differences overlooks the wide cultural and historical variation in conceptions of masculinity and femininity.

- Parents, siblings, and other significant people in a child's immediate environment provide early lessons—both subtle and direct—on how he or she should behave with regard to gender.

- Gender isn't something that is simply acquired through socialization. It is also something we "do"—created and reinforced continuously through everyday social interaction.

- Gender differences are often translated into differences in power and dependence within families.

- Gender inequality takes an enormous economic, psychological, and physical toll on women worldwide.

Go to the Online Learning Center at **www.mhhe.com/newman1** to test your knowledge of the chapter concepts and key terms.

KEY TERMS

androgynous socialization   95

dependence   99

gender   83

implementation power   96

intersexuals   84

orchestration power   96

power   96

sex   83

sexual dichotomy   83

transsexuals   84

SEE FOR YOURSELF

Gender is said to be pervasive—governing every aspect of life and society—yet invisible. Gender signs are so ubiquitous that we usually only notice them when they are missing or ambiguous (Lorber, 1994).

To help you gain an understanding of the power of gender, intentionally violate a gender norm. Consider the many ways gender is done in everyday society. Pick any aspect of "doing gender" and deliberately act in a way inconsistent with how you identify yourself. It can be as simple as not getting up immediately to clear the table after dinner or leaving the dishes unwashed (if this is part of how you do gender). If you are a woman, consider sitting in a very public place, like the mall, in a very "unladylike" posture. If you are a man, consider asking someone for help opening a jar or avoid automatically getting into the driver's seat on a date. Avoid actions that are too obvious (for instance, a man wearing a dress to class).

Be as daring as you feel comfortable being, but make sure the activity is not illegal or likely to be harmful to you or anyone else. Try committing your "violation" on several occasions, with several different audiences (males and females; older people and younger people; people you know and strangers).

Pay careful attention to how you feel when preparing to do this activity and when you're actually doing it. Is it fun? Is it scary? How uncomfortable do you feel? Consider the source of these feelings.

Make note of others' reactions to you. If possible, arrange to have a friend or fellow classmate watch from a distance to see how others react to you. The additional observer may see things you don't and can also help confirm your impressions.

Finally, explore what your experiences with doing gender "inappropriately" indicated about the pervasiveness of gender in all aspects of social life.

5

Diverse Families/Similar Families

Descendants of Thomas ◆
Jefferson gather at Monticello.

I teach at a private liberal arts university in the Midwest. My students are predominantly white, and many come from wealthy families. As a way of introducing the topic of race in a sociology course I teach, I ask the class a series of questions. First, I ask them to list the features they think characterize African American families, Latino/a families, and Asian American families.

They have little trouble identifying long lists of differentiating traits, though they're quick to point out that most are stereotypes they don't believe. Some of the stereotypes are positive, such as "Asian American families are supportive and tight-knit"; others are distinctly negative, such as "African American families are weak and unstable."

I then ask the students to list the traits that typify white families. Here the discussion usually grinds to an awkward halt. The question troubles them. But I don't come to their rescue. I let them struggle. After a while, some variation of the following conversation typically ensues:

> *Student:* What kind of white family are you talking about? . . . There are too many kinds of white families and it'd be impossible to generalize.
> *Me:* OK, what kinds of white families are there?
> *Student:* Some white families are poor and they're different from rich families.
> *Me:* Uh huh. Go on.
> *Student:* Some white families are very religious and others aren't. Also they might be of different nationalities, live in different parts of the country. You know, they're all different. There's no way you can come up with common traits.
> *Me:* You're absolutely right! [The student usually beams with pride at this point for being a good sociologist.] But why didn't you ask me what kind of African American family or Latino/a family or Asian family I had in mind when I asked you to characterize them? Surely there are rich Asian and poor Asian families. There must be religious Latino/a and nonreligious Latino/a families out there. There are African American families that live in big cities and others that live on farms. (Newman, 2007, p. 15)

My point in these conversations is not to humiliate my students or put them on the spot (though they'd probably disagree); it is to illustrate how intertwined race and ethnicity are with our perceptions of family. Being a member of a majority racial group conferred on my students the privilege of thinking about their "whiteness" in terms of individual differences and not in terms of common group traits. Yet when considering other groups, they were more inclined to form broad generalizations, even though there is just as much diversity among African American, Latino/a, and Asian families as there is among white families. The lesson is clear: It's as misleading and erroneous to talk about *the* African American family, *the* Latino/a family, or *the* Asian American family as it is to talk about *the* white family or, for that matter, *the* American family.

My students aren't the only ones who have difficulties describing white families. The U.S. Bureau of the Census publishes a compendium of population statistics each year called the *Statistical Abstract of the United States.* The index contains family-related entries for "black population," "American Indian, Alaska Native population," "Asian and Pacific Islander population," "Native Hawaiian population," and "Hispanic origin population" but not for "white population."

Clearly white families—or more accurately, white, middle-class families—are the standard against which we measure "other" families. We tend to consider as "variations" the family patterns that differ markedly from the idealized image of the white, middle-class family—whether the differences are based on race, ethnicity, religion, or something else. People often view these differences either as curiosities that need to be examined, as "dysfunctional" barriers to a minority group's success that members must overcome, or as "shortcomings" upon which to blame many social ills.

But does that mean we should disregard all ethnoracial (or for that matter, religious) differences and simply view all families as, well, families? No. Although we should be careful not to overgeneralize, race and ethnicity do provide important links to inequality and, ultimately, to family experiences.

This chapter examines the roles of racial, ethnic, and religious identity in family structure, focusing on both the commonalities and the differences across groups. We'll discover that describing the effects of race, ethnicity and religion on family experiences simply as a matter of "differences" is woefully inadequate when we consider some of the historical and societal complexities that both divide and unite families with diverse backgrounds.

THE SOCIAL CONSTRUCTION OF RACE AND ETHNICITY

To most people, **race** is a category of individuals who share common inborn biological traits, such as skin color; color and texture of hair; and shape of eyes, nose, or head. We generally assume that people we place in the same racial category also share behavioral, psychological, and personality traits that are linked to their physical similarities. Sociologists typically use the term **ethnicity** to refer to the non-biological traits—such as shared ancestry, culture, history, language, patterns of behavior, and beliefs—that provide members of a group with a sense of common identity. Whereas we think of ethnicity as something we learn from other people, we commonly think of race as an inherited and permanent biological characteristic that we can easily use to divide people into mutually exclusive groups (Newman, 2007).

But the concept of race is neither as natural nor as straightforward as this definition implies. Some people who consider themselves "white," for example, may have darker skin and kinkier hair than some people who consider themselves "black." And it turns out that there may be as much or more biological variation *within* so-called races as there is *between* them. In addition, since the earliest humans appeared, they have consistently tended to migrate and interbreed. Some surveys estimate that at least 75% of U.S. blacks have some white ancestry (cited in Mathews, 1996). The famous naturalist Charles Darwin (1871/1971) wrote that despite external differences, it is virtually impossible to identify clear, distinctive racial characteristics. Indeed, there is no gene for race. No gene is 100% of one form in one racial group and 100% of a different form in another racial group (Brown, 1998). Certainly there are physical differences between people who identify themselves as members of different races. But it's our collective imagination that organizes, attaches meaning to, and perhaps alters the meanings of those differences.

So what ultimately ties people together in a particular racial group is not a set of shared physical characteristics—because there aren't any shared by all members of a particular racial group—but the shared experience of being identified by others as members of that group (Piper, 1992). During the process of growing up and creating an identity for ourselves, we learn three important things: the boundaries that distinguish group members from nonmembers, the perceived position of our group within society, and whether membership in our group is something to take pride in or be ashamed of (Cornell & Hartmann, 1998). In other words, race is a social construction.

▪ **race**
A category of individuals labeled and treated as similar because of some common inborn biological traits, such as skin color, texture of hair, and shape of eyes, nose, or head.

▪ **ethnicity**
The nonbiological traits—such as shared ancestry, culture, history, language, patterns of behavior, and beliefs—that provide members of a group with a sense of common identity.

We can see the fluid, socially constructed nature of race in historical changes in the categories used by the U.S. government in its decennial population censuses (Lee, 1993). In 1870, there were five races: White, Colored (black), Mulatto (people with some black blood), Chinese, and Indian. White people's concern with race-mixing and racial purity led to changes in the social rules used for determining the status of mixed race people, particularly in the South. The 1890 census thus listed eight races, half applying to black or partly black populations: White, Colored (black), Mulatto (people with three-eighths to five-eighths black blood), Quadroon (people who have one-fourth black blood), Octoroon (people with one-eighth black blood), Chinese, Japanese, and Indian. In 1900, Mulatto, Quadroon, and Octoroon were dropped, so that any amount of "black blood" meant a person had to be classified as "black." Between 1930 and 2000, some racial classifications (such as Hindu, Eskimo, and Mexican) appeared and disappeared. Others (Filipino, Korean, Hawaiian) made an appearance and have stayed ever since. Individuals filling out the 2000 census form had a wide array of racial categories from which to choose: White, Black, American Indian or Alaska Native, Asian Indian, Chinese, Filipino, Japanese, Korean, Vietnamese, Native Hawaiian, Guamanian or Chamorro, or Samoan (Newman, 2007).

Racial/ethnic categories in the U.S. Census are still fairly arbitrary. For instance, there is no "Asian" category; instead Asian Americans must choose a specific nationality. However, "Blacks" and "Whites" are not required to indicate their nation of origin. Latino/a is not included at all in the list of races on the latest census form. With the exception of the category "Mexican" in 1930, Spanish-speaking people have routinely been classified as "white." But because Latino/as can be members of any race, the Census Bureau now allows for "Hispanic origin," although as an ethnicity not a race.

■ TAKING A CLOSER LOOK

✳Multiracial Identities

I n 1992 the U.S. Bureau of the Census reported that for the first time in history the number of biracial babies increased at a faster rate than the number of single-race babies (Marmor, 1996). Between 1970 and 2000, the number of children whose parents are of different races grew from 900,000 to over 3 million (Lee & Edmonston, 2005).

For centuries the United States has adhered to what sociologists call a **hypodescent rule** to determine the racial identity of people with mixed-race backgrounds; that is, an individual is always assigned the status of the subordinate group. Common law in the 19th-century South determined that a "single drop of black blood" made a person black. Today, some ethnic groups informally establish identity in a different way. Among older Japanese Americans, a child who is predominantly Japanese with some white blood is considered white by the rest of the community and is not fully admitted into the ethnic group. Not surprisingly, a study of 1,500 offspring of Asian Anglo couples found that the majority of these children (52%) identified themselves as Anglo. The rest viewed themselves as Asian (38%) or a combination of the two (10%) (Saenz, Hwang, Aguirre, & Anderson, 1995).

In the mid-1990s, biracial individuals began lobbying Congress and the Bureau of the Census to add a multiracial category to the 2000 census form.

■ **hypodescent rule**
A determinant of racial identity of people with mixed-race backgrounds, whereby an individual is always assigned the status of the subordinate group.

They argued that the change would add visibility and legitimacy to a racial identity that has historically been ignored. But many civil rights organizations objected to the inclusion of a multiracial category (Farley, 2002). They worried that it would reduce the number of U.S. citizens claiming to belong to long-recognized minority groups, dilute the culture and political power of those groups, and make it more difficult to enforce civil rights laws (Mathews, 1996).

In the end, the civil rights organizations won. For the 2000 census, the government decided not to add a multiracial category to official forms. Instead it adopted a policy allowing people to identify themselves on the census form as members of more than one race. The new guidelines specify that those who check "white" and another category will be counted as members of the minority group (Holmes, 2000). According to the U.S. Bureau of the Census (2008), 1.6% of the population—or about 4.7 million people—identify themselves as belonging to two or more races. As you might expect, people under the age of 18 were more than twice as likely as people over 50 to thus identify themselves (Jones & Smith, 2001; Lee & Bean, 2004).

Some sociologists caution, however, that the Census Bureau's method of measuring multiracial identity—checking two or more race categories—does not adequately reflect the way multiracial people personally experience race. The National Longitudinal Study of Adolescent Health, which contains information on the racial identity of a nationwide sample of more than 11,000 adolescents, shows that the way people racially classify themselves can be fluid, changing from context to context (Harris & Sim, 2002). For example, almost twice as many adolescents identify themselves as multiracial when they're interviewed at school than when they're interviewed at home. Furthermore, nearly 15% expressed different racial identities across different settings. This research is important because it shows that the census data on multiracial identity don't necessarily account for everyone who self-identifies as multiracial in everyday situations.

RACE, RACISM, AND FAMILY

Ethnoracial identity is not enough to explain people's family experiences. The historical conditions under which any group enters U.S. society are also crucial in determining the degree of economic success and achievement it will experience, which in turn influences family and community life. Not surprisingly, throughout history, those groups whose skin color and traditions are very different from those of the white majority face harsher obstacles upon arrival. Some have been treated with derision and suspicion; others have been forced from their land, persecuted, or even enslaved.

So some ethnoracial minority groups have had to adapt their families to deal with hardships imposed by the larger society. Extended families, single parenthood, "fictive kin," dual-earner couples, and many other deviations from the mainstream culture's family ideal are among adaptations these groups have made to demanding societal circumstances. Even though these patterns are products of historical conditions and don't reflect diminished importance of family (K. Newman, 2005), observers often blame them for a particular group's social and economic difficulties:

> Latinos, among whom extended family networks play a crucial role in integrating family and community, [are] criticized for being too "familistic"—their lack of social progress . . . blamed on family values which [keep] them tied to family rather than economic advancement. African-American families [are] criticized as "matriarchal" because of the strong role grandmothers [play] in extended family networks. (Dill, Baca Zinn, & Patton, 1994, p. 16)

But are family patterns found in ethnoracial minority groups really all that unique? If so, what are the social, historical, and economic conditions that created these differences?

Native American Families

The story of Native Americans includes racially inspired massacres, the takeover of their ancestral lands, their confinement on reservations, and unending government manipulation. Successive waves of white settlers seeking westward expansion in the 18th and 19th centuries pushed Native Americans off any land that the settlers considered desirable. A commonly held European belief that Native Americans were "savages" who should be displaced to make way for civilized whites provided the ideological justification for conquering them.

According to the Fourteenth Amendment to the U.S. Constitution, "All persons born or naturalized in the United States, and subject to the jurisdiction thereof, are citizens of the United States and of the state wherein they reside." But despite the broad wording of this amendment, Native Americans were excluded from citizenship. In 1884 the U.S. Supreme Court ruled that Native Americans owed their allegiance to their tribe and so did not acquire American citizenship upon birth. Not until 1940 were all Native Americans born in the United States considered U.S. citizens (Haney López, 1996).

Most Native Americans have migrated from the reservations over the years, but about 18% remain and life there can be bleak (U.S. Bureau of the Census, 2007). Today, only African Americans have a higher poverty rate and only Latino/as have a higher school dropout rate than Native Americans (U.S. Bureau of the Census, 2008). Deaths from cirrhosis of the liver—a disease associated with severe alcoholism—are twice as high among Native Americans as among the rest of the population (National Center for Health Statistics, 2003). In such an environment, the maintenance of strong family ties, traditionally a key determinant of identity and status in most tribes, is difficult.

African American Families

Of all ethnoracial minorities in the United States today, African American families are the most negatively portrayed. The stereotypical image projects marital violence, broken homes, large numbers of children, and a resulting cycle of poverty, illegitimacy, crime, welfare, and unemployment. Black men, especially poor black men, are typically portrayed as being on the outer fringe, either uninterested in or incapable of participating in the lives of their families (Hamer, 2007). How accurate are these images, and how have they developed throughout history?

Slavery, Racism, and Blocked Opportunities

The experiences of African American families have been unique among ethnoracial groups in this country because of the direct and indirect effects of centuries of forced

Although slaves were forbidden to officially marry, many had secret wedding ceremonies.

servitude. Because slaves were not allowed to enter into binding legal contracts, for instance, there was no legal basis for marriages between them. Slave owners determined which slaves could (or even had to) "marry" and which "marriages" would be dissolved.

From their purely economic perspective, slave owners had an interest in keeping slave families intact. For one thing, it was believed that "married" slaves would want to have children. Children had economic value because they represented future slaves (Burnham, 1993; Staples, 1992). In addition, "married" slaves were thought to be more docile and less inclined to rebel or escape. However, when financial troubles forced the sale of slaves to raise capital, many slave owners had no misgivings about separating the very slave families they had once advocated. The threat of separation "hung like a dark cloud over every slave couple family" (Burnham, 1993, p. 146).

In this environment, African American families became an important means of survival and showed a remarkable capacity to adapt and endure. It was within families that slaves received sustaining affection, companionship, love, and support. It was here that they learned to cooperate with one another to avoid punishment and retained some degree of self-esteem.

Even when individual families were broken apart, the values of marriage and two-parent households persevered. Sociologist Herbert Gutman (1978) examined marriage licenses, birth records, and census data from 1855 to 1880 and found that two-parent, intact black families prevailed both during slavery and after emancipation. In counties and towns in Virginia, Mississippi, South Carolina, and Alabama, between 70 and 85% of black households contained both a mother and a father.

After slavery, blacks had the freedom to legally marry, and they did so in large numbers. Just about every element of black society—churches, newspapers, social organizations—worked hard to convince newly freed blacks of the virtue of formalizing their marriages (Hill, 2005). Children were of special value to emancipated slaves, who could easily remember having their children sold away during slavery. Indeed, by 1917, 90% of all black children were born into existing marriages (Staples, 1992).

During the late 19th century, the strong role of women in black families emerged. Racism and legal, social, and economic exclusion made it extremely difficult for black men to find employment adequate to support their families and to maintain their dominance in them. Survival dictated that black women enter the labor force. In 1900, 41% of black women were in the labor force compared to 16% of white women (cited in Staples, 1992).

Despite the difficulties left over from slavery, African Americans were able to create impressive norms of family life over the years. At the same time, though, their family structures were widely disparaged in the larger society. Negative images received a sort of official legitimacy in 1965 when Daniel Patrick Moynihan, then an assistant U.S. Secretary of Labor, wrote a report titled *The Negro Family: The Case for National Action.* When this book was written, the South was still highly segregated. And in the North as well as the South, blacks were at the bottom of all relevant social and economic categories. It's not surprising, therefore, that politicians at the time would cite deficiencies in black families as the key cause of their social and economic disadvantages.

Moynihan argued that the root of the problems blacks experienced was not economic deprivation but the inherent weakness and deterioration of black families. He described black families as a "tangled pathology," whose key feature was the absence of fathers and the unusually large amount of power held by women. Moynihan felt that this "variant" family structure resulted in, among other things, low self-image, low IQ, high rates of school dropouts, delinquency, unemployment, violent crime, and drug abuse—especially among sons.

This sentiment has not fallen out of favor. In 2005 a columnist (who happens to be black) wrote:

> You don't have to be Sherlock Holmes to know that some of the most serious problems facing Blacks in the United States—from poverty to incarceration rates to death at an early age—are linked in varying degrees to behavioral issues and the corrosion of black family life, especially the absence of fathers. (Herbert, 2005, p. 31)

To add fuel to the fire, the conditions Moynihan described with such alarm 4 decades ago seem to have gotten worse. Black families, it seems, have experienced broad trends and changes more rapidly and with greater intensity than other sectors of society (Tucker & Mitchell-Kernan, 1995). For instance, blacks have consistently had a lower marriage rate than whites and wait longer to marry. Yet blacks begin sexual activity and childbearing earlier. This combination has resulted in a dramatic racial difference in nonmarital births and single-parent households (U.S. Bureau of the Census, 2008).

However, it would be misleading to discuss these features of African American families without examining the broader economic effects of racial inequality, which continue to hamper educational advancement and block access to high-paying jobs. The unemployment rate for African Americans is twice that of whites, and blacks comprise almost 30% of the long-term unemployed in this country (Economic Policy Institute, 2006). For those who are employed, there's a greater chance of underemployment, inconsistent employment, and lower wages. As a result of these trends, 34.2% of African

American children live in poverty, compared to 17.1% in the general population (U.S. Bureau of the Census, 2008).

Long-term exposure to these economic conditions can seriously affect family stability. Sociologists Stewart Tolnay and Kyle Crowder (1999) compared blacks living in northern inner-cities with those who recently migrated from the south. They found greater marital stability among those who had migrated. But they suggest that exposure to "destabilizing conditions" found in the north—such as higher rates of poverty, unemployment, and adults on public assistance—is likely to lead to greater marital instability and a decreased likelihood of children growing up with both parents present.

Unstable economic conditions can have a dramatic effect on marriage chances. When men don't work or don't earn sufficient wages, they may grow less interested in becoming husbands because they are constrained in their ability to perform the provider role in marriage (Hamer, 2007). Black single men who are in stable employment are twice as likely to marry as single men who are sporadically employed or unemployed (Testa & Krogh, 1995). In addition, black men's anxiety about being able to provide for their families also increases the likelihood of marital difficulties and divorce, particularly in early marriage (Hatchett, Veroff, & Douvan, 1995). This argument, of course, assumes that male employment is perceived to be a necessary requirement for marriage.

While black men have historically had limited employment opportunities, black women have seen their opportunities increase. In 2005, about 1.4 million black women were enrolled in American colleges and universities, compared to 774,000 black men (U.S. Bureau of the Census, 2008). Between 1977 and 1997, the number of bachelor's degrees awarded to black men increased by 30%, while the number increased by 77% for black women (cited in "Report on Black America," 2000). Because they are relatively successful compared with black men, black women have less financial incentive to marry than other U.S. women. Consequently, they're much more likely to be single mothers than women in other ethnoracial groups (U.S. Bureau of the Census, 2008).

African American Family Diversity

The stereotype of black family pathology popularized by Moynihan more than 40 years ago persists today. For instance, when asked why African Americans are likely to suffer from low income, poor jobs, and inadequate housing, most non-African Americans reject the idea that blacks are intellectually inferior. But many continue to believe that African Americans lack the motivation or willpower to escape poverty (Figure 5.1).

The pervasive image of black family weakness ignores the diversity of African American family life. The African American population consists of families with widely different histories and experiences. Not all have ancestors who entered the country enslaved, for example. Some

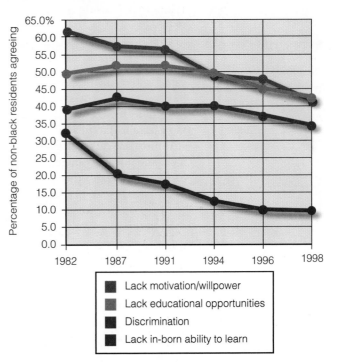

FIGURE 5.1 Changing Explanations for African Americans' Misfortunes

Source: National Opinion Research Center, 1998.

More African American families can be considered middle class than ever before.

came to the Americas free; others came as indentured servants who worked off their indebtedness and went on to lead free lives. Today, African American families come from different classes, different religions, and different geographical areas. Although most have had to deal with some degree of discrimination and oppression, their family structures are quite diverse. The despair of poverty, single parenthood, underemployment and unemployment, and lack of opportunity may be higher among African American families than other groups, but that doesn't mean these problems are uniformly experienced by all blacks.

In short, the image of black families as "pathological" overlooks the families that don't fit this negative stereotype. Consider these facts:

■ One third of African Americans have incomes, educations, and lifestyles that place them in the middle class. Between 1980 and 2004, median household income for blacks increased from $23,372 to $30,134—though, as it has for other ethnoracial groups, income has dropped a bit in the past few years. During those same years, the poverty rate among black families dropped from 29% to 22.1% (U.S. Bureau of the Census, 2008).

■ It's true that fewer than half of all African American adults are married. But contrary to the contention that all black men are averse to marriage, approximately 90% of those who are college-educated with annual incomes over $25,000 are married and live with their spouse (Holmes, 1996).

■ The birthrate for unmarried black women between the ages of 15 and 44 fell from 90.5 per 1,000 women in 1990 to 67.2 per 1,000 in 2004 (U.S. Bureau of the Census, 2008).

In some ways, African American families might actually be stronger than other families. Family relationships remain a crucial form of emotional and economic support. For instance, one survey of African Americans found that over 90% considered themselves close to their families (Hatchett & Jackson, 1993). Another study found that lower-middle-class blacks are more likely than lower-middle-class whites to claim a long-term goal of providing their children with a strong and loving family (Hill & Sprague, 1999). Blacks tend to have large extended families, often including both blood-related kin and people informally adopted into the family system (McAdoo, 1998). Furthermore, loyalty and responsibility to others in the family are often highly valued.

Asian American Families

When researchers examine the difficulties ethnoracial minority families face in the United States, they often consider Asian American families to be the "exception" because of their well-publicized occupational and economic success—especially among highly educated people of Chinese, Indian, and Japanese descent. Japanese Americans, for instance, are sometimes labeled the "model minority" because they tend to show respect for the cherished U.S. values of hard work, achievement, self-control, dependability, good manners, thrift, and diligence (Kitano, 1976). But like all stereotypes, this one doesn't describe all Asian American families and can mask the disadvantages they do experience.

Immigration and Racism

Like many other ethnoracial groups, Asian Americans have endured a history of prejudice and discrimination that has had a long-lasting impact on the structure of their families. For instance, in the second half of the 19th century, industrialists in the western United States recruited Chinese immigrants to work in the mines and build the transcontinental railroad. But from the outset they were treated with hostility. Widespread fears that hordes of Chinese would take scarce jobs and eventually overrun the white race fostered the image of the "yellow peril."

Initially, working in this country was a means of gaining financial support for the immigrants' families back in China. The goal was to earn enough money to return to China and purchase land there, and most workers assumed they were here temporarily. Indeed, U.S. law in the late 19th and early 20th centuries actually prevented Chinese laborers from becoming naturalized citizens.

In addition, Chinese men who arrived before 1882 were not allowed to bring their wives and were prevented by law from marrying whites (Dill, 1995). Thus, for many years, the predominant family form among the Chinese in the United States was a **split household,** in which financial support was provided by one member (the father) who lived far from the rest of the family. Men were sometimes separated from their families for 20 years or more. Many children grew up never knowing who their fathers were. Wives who remained in China had to raise children and care for in-laws on the meager earnings their husbands in the United States sporadically sent them. These families became interdependent economic units that spanned two continents (Glenn & Yap, 1994).

■ **split household**
A family arrangement common among 19th-century Chinese immigrants in which financial support was provided by one member (the father) who lived far from the rest of the family.

Even when Chinese immigrants were able to create and maintain intact families here, prejudice, violence, and discrimination kept them poor and segregated. By necessity, Chinese American communities—which would eventually become the "Chinatowns" we can see in many large cities today—were tightly structured and insulated against the threats from the dominant white society. In these close enclaves people learned to become self-reliant, creating their own businesses and organizing their own social clubs.

The collectivist nature of Chinese culture required the sacrifice of individual needs and desires in favor of the overall welfare of the family unit (Coltrane & Collins, 2001). In traditional Chinese families, children were taught to be loyal and obedient to their parents and to value educational achievement. Although many Chinese wives were more or less equal producers in family businesses, they were expected to assume major responsibility for the household and child care (Wong, 1998). Fathers tended to have final authority and wielded unquestioned power; others—wives and children—were expected to be obedient (Kitano & Daniels, 1988).

Early Japanese immigrants, who arrived around the turn of the century, had similar experiences. In response to prejudice and discrimination, they too created separate, insulated communities where children were taught the Japanese language and culture in schools established by their parents. They learned the importance of hard work, obedience to authority, and self-sacrifice. Tight families and a strong work ethic enabled many Japanese families to pool resources and achieve substantial success. However, this success motivated lawmakers to enact legislation that limited Japanese people's ability to own or lease land. Fearing rapid growth in the Japanese population, Congress enacted the National Origins Act of 1924 barring all further Japanese immigration (Takagi, 1994).

Hostility toward Japanese reached its peak in the early 1940s following Japan's attack on Pearl Harbor. Vocal special-interest groups, influential members of the government, and the military held the Japanese American community responsible for the surprise attack. The military used suspicion, fear, and racial prejudice to successfully pressure the government to suspend Japanese American citizens' constitutional rights. Eventually President Franklin D. Roosevelt signed an executive order authorizing a suspension of Japanese American citizens' constitutional rights and their internment in camps surrounded by barbed wire and watchtowers.

Internment had a devastating impact on Japanese families and the Japanese American community. As part of the registration process, internees were forced to express their loyalty to the United States and renounce their ties to Japan. Many second-generation Japanese (those born here) felt more American than Japanese and thus could express loyalty to the United States more easily than their parents. When they did so, however, Japanese-born parents felt their children were betraying their heritage (Broom & Kitsuse, 1956). In addition, the camps undermined the traditional status and authority of Japanese American parents. Many interred in the camps were farmers. When the war ended, they found that their farms had been taken over during their absence, and they were forced to resettle their families in urban areas. Urban living provided many young Japanese Americans with their first opportunity to work and live independently of their parents, making it especially difficult to retain their traditional way of life (Takagi, 1994).

Both Chinese American and Japanese American family structures have emerged as adaptive strategies for survival in a racially hostile environment. Because people were forced to turn to their relatives for support, families took on an important economic as well as emotional role in their lives. With such a strong familial foundation, it is not sur-

After the attack on Pearl Harbor in 1941, American families of Japanese descent were uprooted and transferred to internment camps, placing overwhelming pressure on family relationships.

prising that many Asian American families have achieved high levels of educational and professional attainment and earnings exceeding those of the rest of the population.

Contemporary Asian American Families

As Asian immigrant families adapt to the dominant culture, they are more likely to adopt behaviors characteristic of other U.S. families. For instance, because Asian Americans tend to come from cultures in which relatively few women work outside the home, the contemporary need for two earners in a household has created conflict between young couples and members of older generations who expect a more traditional family structure.

U.S.-born Asian men and women are significantly more likely than foreign-born Asians to marry outside their ethnic group (Lee & Fernandez, 1998). And fewer than 1 in 5 Asian Americans belong to an all-Asian kin group including aunts, uncles, siblings, spouses, and in-laws (Goldstein, 1999). Such trends make it even more difficult to retain traditional cultural values. Nevertheless, Asian Americans are twice as likely as whites to live in extended families and half as likely to live alone. More workers in a family mean more earnings, which may explain why household income is higher among Asian Americans than any other group (U.S. Bureau of the Census, 2008).

Yet again we must be aware of the variation *within* the Asian American population. Asian Americans come from some 28 Asian countries or ethnic groups. In fact, people of Asian descent rarely think of themselves as a single racial group (Espiritu, 2004). They have different languages and cultures and different reasons for migrating to the United States. For the most part, Chinese, Japanese, Korean, Indian, and Filipino immigrants came to this country seeking a better life. They have been here the longest, have a higher proportion of native-born individuals, and are less culturally distinct than those recently arrived from Vietnam, Cambodia, and Laos, who are typically political immigrants or refugees (Parke & Buriel, 2002).

Chinese, Japanese, and Korean families are significantly smaller than Vietnamese, Cambodian, and Laotian families and less tied to the traditions of their countries of origin. The more recent arrivals often try to re-create the family structure of their homeland. Immigrant Vietnamese families, for instance, may incorporate friends and neighbors into their extended kin networks, enabling them to maintain some semblance of their traditional, complex extended families despite the disruption of migration (Kibria, 1994).

Latino/a Families

One of the fastest-growing segments of the U.S. population is Spanish-speaking people who have migrated from Mexico, the Caribbean, Central America, and South America. According to the U.S. Bureau of the Census (2006b, 2008), close to 15% of the U.S. population is Latino/a, compared to 12.5% in 2000 and about 9% in 1990. Experts project that by 2050, 1 out of 4 Americans will be Latino/a and by 2100, 1 out of 3 will be Latino/a (Saenz, 2004).

But, as is true of other ethnic groups, there is tremendous cultural and familial diversity among those considered Latino/a. Even race is a source of some debate. We've seen that the Census Bureau characterizes "Hispanic origin" as an ethnicity, not a race. Hence, Latino/as can be of any race. This distinction has not been received well by many Latino/as who consider themselves a separate race. There were so many Latino/a respondents to the 2000 census (about 42%) who refused to identify themselves by any of the racial categories available on the census form that "some other race" became the fastest growing category in the United States (Swarns, 2004).

Early Immigrant Families

The diversity of the Latino/a population in the United States stems from distinctly different immigration histories. For instance, because Puerto Ricans were granted U.S. citizenship in 1917, their immigration to the United States has been relatively easy and, at times, actively encouraged by the government (Sanchez-Ayendez, 1998). Most Puerto Ricans live in the large metropolitan areas of the northeast.

When Fidel Castro came to power in Cuba in the late 1950s, Cuban immigrants poured into the United States. Because they were fleeing a Communist political regime that was at odds with U.S. political ideals, their initial entry into this country was met with enthusiasm (Suarez, 1998). Many of the early immigrants were middle-class Cubans who had the means to climb the occupational ladder; a few were wealthy executives and business owners who were able to set up lucrative businesses, particularly in Florida. Today, Cuban American families have the highest median income of any Latino/a group.

The experience of people of Mexican descent in the United States has been quite different. Mexican Americans make up the largest segment of the Latino/a population, and many are not descendants of immigrants at all. In 1848, following war with the United States, Mexico lost more than half its territory, giving up all claims to Texas and ceding much of what is now Arizona, New Mexico, Utah, Nevada, and California (Dill, 1995). Although Mexicans who had been living on the U.S. side of the new border were supposed to be granted all the rights of U.S. citizens, their property was routinely confiscated, and they lost control of mining, ranching, and farming industries. In the early 20th century, life continued to be a daily struggle for survival. Since then, many poor immigrants from the interior of Mexico have crossed the border to seek work, some becoming permanent U.S. residents and some returning seasonally to their home villages.

Roles in traditional Mexican families were strongly defined by gender. Women were valued first and foremost for their household skills. In rural areas they might also be responsible for tending gardens and looking after animals. But high rates of widowhood—due to the hazardous nature of the work available to men—and temporary abandonment by men in search of employment created sharp increases in female-headed households from the mid-19th to the early 20th century (Griswold del Castillo, 1979). Women (and children) began joining the labor force primarily as maids, servants, laundresses, garment workers, cooks, and dishwashers.

Eventually entire families participated in the labor market, particularly in seasonal, itinerant farm labor that helped increase earnings and keep the family together. Mexican Americans in extended families fared better economically and experienced less downward mobility than people in smaller, nuclear families (Dill, 1995). Extended families could assist newly immigrating relatives in finding housing and employment and pool their resources to pay for food, housing, transportation, and schooling (Gelles, 1995).

Contemporary Latino/a Families

Because of the influx of immigrants with large families and Catholic proscriptions against birth control, Latino/a families tend to be relatively large. In 2006, for instance, 17% of Latino/a families had three or more children under 18 in the household, compared to 11% for African Americans and 8% for non-Hispanic white families (U.S. Bureau of the Census, 2008). Not surprisingly, Latino/as are more inclined than either Whites or Blacks to consider having and raising children to be the primary purpose of marriage (Pew Research Center, 2007).

Latino/a families also tend to be more stable than families in other ethnoracial groups. In 2006, for example, 7.9% of the Latino/a population was divorced, compared to 12.1% of Blacks and 10.8% of non-Hispanic Whites (U.S. Bureau of the Census, 2008). And despite a greater percentage of single-parent families among Latino/as than among Whites, fewer cases are due to the breakup of a marriage.

Compared to African American and white households, a smaller percentage of Latino/a households contain *no* employed adult member (U.S. Bureau of Labor Statistics, 2006). Yet Latino/as tend to be more economically disadvantaged than Whites, with some variation by subgroup. For example, 8.1% of white families live below the poverty line, but 22% of Mexican American families and 23.5% of Puerto Rican families live in poverty. By contrast, only 9.1% of Cuban American families live in poverty (U.S. Bureau of the Census, 2008).

A sense of familial responsibility and mutual obligation continue to play a prominent role in Latino/a families (American Association of Retired Persons, 2001; Hines, Garcia-Preto, McGoldrick, Almeida, & Weltman, 1997). Their large kinship networks can best be described as **expanded families** (Horowitz, 1997). Even though they don't live in the same household, relatives often live in the same neighborhood and interact on a regular basis. Within expanded families, members are able to exchange important services such as babysitting, meals, personal advice, and emotional support (cited in Becerra, 1992). Rather than being labeled a freeloader, a person who can survive without money for a long time by going from relative to relative is considered to have a strong, cohesive family (Horowitz, 1997). But in recent years, in light of the rapidly growing elderly Latino/a population, fulfilling familial obligations has become more difficult.

■ **expanded families**
Large kinship networks in Latino/a communities in which even though relatives don't live in the same household, they live in the same neighborhood and interact on a regular basis.

Of all the popular images of Latino/a families, one of the most prevalent is the concept of *machismo*. Machismo is often equated with male dominance, pride in masculinity, honor in being the economic provider, and a sexual double standard. According to this stereotype, the father is considered the head of the household, the major decision maker, and the absolute power holder in the family (Becerra, 1992). Manhood is expressed through independence, strength, control, and domination. By extension, Latina women are considered self-sacrificing and passive caretakers of the entire family.

But the ideals of machismo are frequently contradicted by the economic demands of contemporary life, and most scholars agree that the degree of male dominance associated with machismo has been exaggerated (Taylor & Behnke, 2005). Over time, more and more women have become heads of households and entered the paid labor force. And contemporary Latino men share child care, decision making, and household tasks as much as non-Hispanic white men do (Coltrane, Parke, & Adams, 2004; Hurtado, 1995).

Once again, we see that common stereotypes and generalizations about particular ethnoracial groups fall short in characterizing the family experiences of all or even most members of those groups.

Diversity and Assimilation

melting pot
A metaphor popular in the late 19th and early 20th centuries that depicted U.S. society as a place where different ethnicities and nationalities would blend together to form a new cultural pattern.

In the late 19th and early 20th centuries the **melting pot** was a popular metaphor; it depicted U.S. society as a place where different ethnicities and nationalities would eventually blend together to form a new cultural pattern. Although few people today desire a society where everyone looks or acts the same, the pressure toward **assimilation**—the process by which members of ethnoracial minority groups change their own ways to conform to those of the dominant culture—remains strong. Indeed, many new immigrants believe that if they gradually lose their differences and adopt the lifestyle of the majority, they can get high-paying, stable jobs and become successful members of mainstream society (Waters & Jiménez, 2005).

assimilation
The process by which members of minority groups change their own ways to conform to those of the dominant culture.

But assimilation contains an inherent trap: The only way for a group to conform to the dominant way of life is to abandon many of the traditions, including family traditions, of the culture it left behind. Furthermore, throughout history, assimilation has sometimes been imposed on certain groups. Native Americans were forced to abandon their traditional family lifestyle by Whites; black slaves were forced to take new names and forgo the family and social traditions of their native cultures.

multicultural society
A society in which groups maintain not only their ethnic identities but also their own languages, arts, music, foods, literature, religions, and family forms.

Thus some members of ethnoracial minority groups consider assimilation an undesirable goal. Instead they promote a **multicultural society** in which groups maintain not only their ethnic identities but also their own languages, arts, music, foods, literature, religions, and family forms. They believe that multiculturalism enriches society. With the steady influx of foreign-born, non–English-speaking people into this country, it is difficult if not impossible to think of the United States as one culture and Americans as one people.

religion
A system of beliefs about the purpose of the universe and the intervention of God (or some other divine force) in human lives that serves as a major source of cultural knowledge, plays a key role in the development of people's ideas about right and wrong, and aids in the formation of people's identities.

RELIGION AND SPIRITUALITY IN CONTEMPORARY FAMILY LIFE

In many ways, **religion**—a system of beliefs about the purpose of the universe and the intervention of God (or some other divine force) in human lives—is like race and ethnicity. It is a fundamental component of many people's identities. It is practiced in many forms and adds to the diversity of U.S. society. Throughout our his-

Oct 29
Loma linda

tory, adherents of certain faith traditions have been dominant, and others have been the targets of various forms of prejudice and discrimination.

But religion also is a social institution that spells out a set of family expectations and obligations. Rules against certain intimate and family activities can be particularly strong in some religious traditions. Religious rites of passage that parallel key aspects of family life—baptisms, bar and bat mitzvah ceremonies, confirmations, and weddings—not only reaffirm an individual's religious identity but impress on her or him the rights and obligations attached to a new status within a particular community (Turner, 1972).

So what role does, and should, religion play in contemporary family life? Do families need religion to function successfully?

Signs of U.S. Religiosity

Structural changes in society have made religious affiliation somewhat unstable in recent years. For one thing, as people move from one location to another, many of the ties that bind them to the same religion—most notably networks of family and friends—are broken. Only about 45% of adults attend religious services regularly (The Barna Group, 2005). Over the past couple of decades, many of the most powerful religious groups have experienced a decline in membership. For instance, between 1990 and 2000, the Lutheran Church suffered a 3.2% drop in membership, the Episcopal Church 5.3%, the United Methodist Church 6.7%, the Presbyterian Church 11.6%, and the United Church of Christ 14.8% (American Religion Data Archive, 2002).

To some people, these figures are a sign that U.S. citizens are turning away from religion. For instance, people are now less likely to marry someone of the same religion than they once were ("Breaking the Rules," 2002). Conservative critics believe that growing secularism, or a decline in the importance of religion in people's family lives, is at the root of many contemporary social problems, such as high rates of divorce, cohabitation, premarital sexuality, AIDS, and violence.

But other signs indicate that religion is not losing its influence in U.S. society. Indeed, at the same time that membership in some religions has shrunk, that of so-called conservative churches (Roman Catholic Church, Church of Jesus Christ of Latter-day Saints, Assemblies of God, Christian Churches, and Southern Baptists) has increased (American Religion Data Archive, 2002). And new religions are constantly emerging. Of the 1,600 or so religions and denominations in the United States today, half were - founded after 1965.

Furthermore, immigration has helped fuel an increase in non-Christian religions. More than 4 times as many immigrants as native-born Americans report non-Christian religious affiliations (Cadge & Ecklund, 2007). Between 1990 and 2001, membership in a variety of non-Christian religious groups grew significantly, including Muslim, Buddhist, Hindu, Unitarian/Universalist, Scientologist, Baha'i, Taoist, New Age, Eckankar, Sikh, Wiccan, Druid, and Santerian. During that same period of time, the number of Muslims and Buddhists in the United States more than doubled and the number of Hindus more than tripled (U.S. Bureau of the Census, 2008).

Religion may not look the same as it did 50 years ago, but it still remains a fundamental part of most people's lives. Indeed, compared to most other Western democracies, such as Canada, Australia, Germany, France, and Great Britain, people in the United States stand out for the depth of their religious beliefs (Zoll, 2005). And consider these facts:

- Eighty-four percent of U.S. adults say that religion plays a big role in their lives (Zoll, 2005). In contrast, 52% of Norwegians and 55% of Swedes say that God doesn't matter to them at all (cited in Ferguson, 2004).

- Eighty-three percent of Americans pray in a given week (The Barna Group, 2007), and 31% pray more than once a day (American Religion Data Archive, 2004).

- U.S. adults are 3 times as likely to say they believe in the virgin birth of Jesus (83%) as in evolution (28%; Kristof, 2003).

- Forty-five percent of the population believes "It is necessary to believe in God in order to be moral and have good values" (American Religion Data Archive, 2002).

- Over half of U.S. adults feel the lesson of the September 11, 2001, attacks was that there is too little (not too much) religion in the world. Close to half say they believe that the United States has special protection from God (Pew Forum on Religion and Public Life, 2002).

In short, religion remains a significant part of everyday life. We still consider ourselves "one nation under God," and our money still proclaims our trust in God. Athletes publicly thank God for their victories. Sales of Christian books, computer games, videos, and toys go up each year. Enrollment in evangelical colleges has grown steadily over the past decade, as has the number of families choosing to homeschool their children for religious reasons (Talbot, 2000).

How Religion Strengthens Families

One of the key aspects of religion is that it constrains human behavior, or at the very least it encourages members to act in certain ways. This normative aspect of religion has important consequences for people's family experiences. Religious beliefs can play a role in virtually every stage of family life: dating, marriage, sexuality, childbearing decisions, parenting techniques, responses to illness and death, household division of labor, divorce, and so on. For instance, in recent years, more and more churches have begun requiring engaged couples to participate in premarital counseling and religious education programs before the wedding. In highly religious families, the Bible or the Koran or the Talmud may serve not only as a source of faith and inspiration but as a literal guidebook for every aspect of family life.

One more formal mechanism through which religion can strengthen family bonds is participation in regular religious services. Clergy often preach the importance of positive relationships among family members, thereby validating people's commitments to their spouses and their children (Pearce & Axinn, 1998; Sherkat & Ellison, 1999). Even couples who have not participated much in religious activities before having children decide to start attending services once their children reach a certain age. There is indeed some evidence that the presence of children increases church membership and attendance among young families (Stolzenberg, Blair-Loy, & Waite, 1995).

In most religions, people are reminded regularly of the value of marriage and family (Wilson & Musick, 1996). Some church-based educational programs teach communication skills to engaged or recently married couples so they will be better equipped to handle problems and disagreements when they arise. Others provide specific child-rearing instruction; for instance, conservative Protestant denominations emphasize children's strict obedience to their parents and the use of corporal punishment when they don't obey.

Religious organizations and families are often strongly interdependent (Call & Heaton, 1997) and mutually reinforcing (Roof, 1999). In some cases, they both draw upon the same emotional bonds and symbols. So intertwined are some families with their religious communities that they view their place of worship as a second home and the members of the congregation as a second family (Wuthnow, 1998). For others, church and family are virtually indistinguishable. The common use of terms like "father," "mother," "brother," and "sister" in churches of various sorts reinforces the connection between religious organizations and family.

Religious organizations can create strong social ties by linking friends and family members in the same social group. From time to time they also offer more formal support for families (Pearce & Axinn 1998). For example, many African American churches have long-standing traditions of providing financial assistance to needy families. These churches can draw on their preexisting organizational skills and spiritual traditions to mobilize their better-off members in the service of those in the community who lack the resources to help themselves (Chatters, Taylor, & Jayakody, 1994).

Religion also provides families with a shared system of spiritual beliefs that reinforces bonds and supports members through difficult times. Belief systems are important because they shape our convictions, attitudes, biases, values, and assumptions. They trigger emotional responses, guide our actions, and inform our decisions (Walsh, 1998). For example, virtually every religion—from Christianity to Zoroastrianism, Judaism and Islam to Taoism—promotes some version of "the golden rule" ("to love others as ourselves") and encourages its members to subordinate their selfish, personal desires to the interests of their family (Vela, 1996). Such principles can inspire commitment, tolerance, and unconditional love.

It's not difficult to imagine such rules fostering positive interactions. One study found that parents with conservative religious ideologies are more likely to praise and hug their children and are less likely to yell at them than are parents with less conservative beliefs (Wilcox, 1998, 2000). Consider how this 8-year-old girl, raised in a strict Catholic family, describes what such rules mean to her and her family:

> One way religion is used in our family is that Jesus told us to worship Him and serve Him. We also read our Bible in school, church, and home. Mother reads it to us at night or sometimes in the afternoon. We go to church and communion every Sunday. We also serve Jesus by the way we treat each other at home. We treat each other nicely. If someone falls down, we help them up. When my little baby sister cries, I give her the pacifier." (quoted in Vela, 1996, p. 166)

Active commitment to religious or spiritual belief systems—often through participation in religious rituals—can elicit loyalty and provide family members with a sense of purpose (Durkheim, 1965). In some religions, informal religious rituals also promote family togetherness, as this Seventh Day Adventist explains:

> Ritual gives you a sense that all is well. . . . That is the wholesome service of family ritual. One ritual that I have found to be valuable is the candle light supper on Friday evening to welcome the Sabbath. . . . Hopefully the house is clean and the chaos is over. Many times on Friday evening I will sit on the sofa and read. Often my two oldest daughters will snuggle up beside me and talk. We can talk about anything they want to talk about. . . . Another is I kneel by the children's beds, put my arms around them, and pray with them. I will thank Jesus for the incredible, awesome child. (quoted in Vela, 1996, pp. 154–155)

Specific religious beliefs can also help families weather adversity. In times of stress, which can be disruptive to families, a dominant religious or sacred belief system often provides "answers" to difficult questions and serves as a guide for behavior. Through such beliefs, family members can begin to understand painful, uncertain, and frightening events, making them less vulnerable to hopelessness and despair (Walsh, 1998).

Given the influential role religion can play in everyday life, it's not surprising that higher levels of religiosity and specific religious traditions tend to be associated with aspects of family life that many people would consider "positive" (Wilcox, Chaves, & Franz, 2004). For instance, religiosity has been linked to higher levels of marital commitment and stability (Call & Heaton, 1997; Larson & Goltz, 1989), more positive parent–child relationships (Pearce & Axinn, 1998), lower rates of cohabitation (Thornton, Axinn, & Hill, 1992), lower rates of adolescent antisocial behavior (Simons, Simons, & Conger, 2004), and lower rates of voluntary childlessness (Heaton, Jacobson, & Fu, 1992).

One area of family life that has received quite a bit of scholarly attention is the intersection of religiosity and divorce. Prohibitions against divorce still exist among some U.S. religious groups. Catholics, Jews, and fundamentalist Christians have historically been stricter about marital dissolution than mainstream Protestants. In fact, the divorce rate tends to be highest among couples who are unaffiliated with any religion, perhaps because they are less bound by social conventions and face fewer sanctions than those actively involved with their faith (Call & Heaton, 1997). In addition, interfaith marriages tend to be less stable than marriages between people of the same religion.

Ending a marriage is much more difficult within a religious community, not only because of obvious constraints against divorce but also because such communities offer so much support for staying together (Larson & Goltz, 1989). One study found that among Catholics and Protestants, the likelihood of divorce goes down as church attendance goes up (Figure 5.2). In another study of people in long-term marriages (40 years, on average) most respondents said that religious faith was one of the most important factors enhancing their marriage (Robinson, 1994).

But no religious group, not even one that explicitly forbids divorce, is completely immune to members wanting to end their marriages. Despite the Catholic Church's clear and strong opposition to divorce, 1 in 4 Catholics who have ever been married has divorced (Pew Research Center, 2007).

Furthermore, means other than divorce exist to accommodate people who are unhappy in their marriages but whose religious beliefs are strong enough to prevent them from divorcing. Every year in the United States, more than 50,000 Catholic marriages are annulled (Woodward, Quade, & Kantrowitz, 1995). An annulment is a church declaration that a marriage was invalid from the beginning and therefore never existed in the eyes of God or the church.

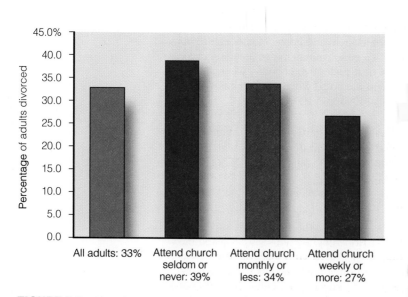

FIGURE 5.2   Church Attendance and Divorce
Source: Pew Research Center, 2007, p. 44.

How Religion Stresses Families

For families with a fairly traditional structure (married, with children, and heterosexual), religion typically has a positive, reinforcing effect. For families that don't fit this mold, however, religion may create considerable stress. Problems can arise when the structure or practices of a family don't coincide with religious doctrines—as is often true of unmarried cohabiting heterosexual couples, homosexual couples, families with homosexual members, single-parent families, divorced couples, childless couples, and any other families that do not fit the traditional model. When religious organizations take unambiguous, categorical stands on issues such as sexual behavior, divorce, and gender roles, families with different values or ways of doing things will receive little comfort. Research indicates that children in religious families whose parents divorce are more likely than children from "intact" families to either renounce religion entirely or switch to a different religion in an effort to seek a more supportive environment (Lawton & Bures, 2001). Among fundamentalist Christians, divorced individuals sometimes feel compelled to change churches to avoid facing old friends (Ammerman, 1987).

The tendency for people to turn away from their houses of worship when they violate religious doctrine shows us that the relationship between religion and family ties is a complicated one. As mentioned earlier, most people assume that low levels of religiosity cause a variety of family-related problems. However, it may be that the relationship works in the opposite direction as well: that people who engage in what their religion defines as problematic or perhaps sinful behavior withdraw from the congregation and become less religious as a result of the way others treat them. In fact, some evidence suggests that divorced or separated individuals stop attending services because they feel rejected, or were rejected, by clergy or fellow members (Glenn & Supancic, 1984).

Similarly, in those religious groups that are most opposed to sex outside marriage, the decision to cohabit or engage in premarital sex leads young people to reduce their religious participation. Such withdrawal is especially likely among those who were originally the most religious (Thornton et al., 1992; Thornton & Camburn, 1989). It is very difficult to commit yourself to a group that believes your actions have reserved you an eternal spot in the fiery pits of hell. Ironically, religion may have little to offer those who are arguably most in need of the social support a religious community can provide—divorcing couples, single-parent families, rebellious teenagers, and conflicted homosexuals.

Interfaith Marriage

It can be very stressful for families to be devoutly religious in a society they perceive to be at odds with a godly lifestyle. In predominantly religious societies, because almost everyone is a devout member of the same religion, parents don't have to worry about their children acquiring "undesirable" beliefs from friends, teachers, colleagues, or spouses. The problem only exists in culturally and religiously diverse societies in which children are likely to be exposed to friends, teachers, and later on coworkers and potential marriage partners who are significantly less religious than they are, or who have very different religious beliefs.

This situation poses a serious problem for highly religious parents and their churches. At young ages, devout parents may control their children's social environment and restrict their friendship choices to those with compatible religious beliefs to ensure that their children acquire and retain orthodox religious beliefs (Kelley & DeGraaf, 1997). When children get older, these parents often worry about their marital choices. In a society such as our own—where individuals have considerable choice over mates, are likely to interact with many persons of different religions, and feel less pressure to switch faiths upon marriage—interfaith marriages have become more common (Roof, 1999). These parents are likely to worry that their grandchildren will be raised in a different religious tradition or without any religion at all.

On a more general level, religious leaders are often concerned that interfaith marriage will result in more secular values throughout society. In 2004, the Vatican issued an official church document discouraging marriage between Catholics and all non-Christians, especially Muslims (Feuer, 2004). The Pope's concern was that such marriages would further weaken people's religious beliefs and values, lead to the raising of children in a different faith, or encourage family members to abandon religion entirely.

Marriage between people of different faiths is especially troublesome in those religions whose numbers are already small. The situation facing U.S. Jews provides a good example. The percentage of Jews in the U.S. adult population has declined from 4% to about 1.4% in the past 50 years (Safire, 1995; U.S. Bureau of the Census, 2008). Although only 1 Jew in 10 married a non-Jew in 1945, close to 1 in 2 does so today. A lower birthrate among Jews compared to other groups, coupled with the likelihood that interfaith couples will not raise children as Jews, explains, in part, why the Jewish population has been dropping steadily (Goodstein, 2003).

Some Jewish leaders fear that the outcome of the trend toward greater interfaith marriage will be not only the shrinking of the Jewish population but also the erosion and perhaps extinction of an entire way of life. They believe that the survival of U.S. Judaism depends on maintaining the integrity of traditional Jewish values and institutions. Young people who decide to marry outside the faith "are threatening to transform Judaism into a religion of half-remembered rituals, forgotten ancestors and buried beliefs" (Rosen, 1997, p. 7).

Promoting "Oppression"

Problems also can arise for individuals when families are too successful in meeting their religion's expectations. In some situations, living up to religious teachings can come at the expense of an individual's own happiness or well-being. For example, according to the Koran,

> Men are the protectors and maintainers of women. . . . Therefore righteous women are devoutly obedient. . . . As to those women on whose part ye fear disloyalty and ill-conduct, admonish them, refuse to share their beds, (and last) beat them (lightly). (translated by Yusufali, 2001, p. 1)

■ GOING GLOBAL ■

The Taliban

When we think of religious ideologies as being "oppressive," we typically think of radical regimes in other countries that use religious texts to reinforce conformity and justify their persecution of dissenters. For example, in 1996 the Taliban, a radical fundamentalist Islamic movement, took control of Afghanistan. Before the takeover, women accounted for 70% of Afghanistan's teachers, 50% of its civil servants, and 40% of its physicians. The Taliban immediately issued religious edicts forbidding women to work outside the home, attend school, or leave their homes unless accompanied by a husband, father, brother, or son. They were not permitted to wear white socks—because white is the color of the Taliban flag—or to wear shoes that make noise as they walk.

These restrictions had a profound effect on women's physical and mental health. About 62% of Afghani women experienced a decline in access to health care shortly after the takeover. Most were so frightened of being flogged or beaten in the streets that they were often reluctant to seek what little help was available to them. One study found that 86% of Afghan women showed signs of anxiety, and 97% demonstrated evidence of major depression (Rasekh, Bauer, Manos, & Iacopino, 1998). It's worth noting that in recent years, since the overthrow of the Taliban, the everyday lives of Afghan women have improved somewhat (U.S. Department of State, 2003). However, the Taliban have not given up. According to the Afghan Minister of Education, there are about 1,350 girls' schools in the country. But over a span of 6 months during 2006, Taliban attacks disrupted or shut down more than 300 of them. Even today, 79% of Afghan women have not learned to read or write (Moreau & Yousafzai, 2006).

The Taliban are an extreme case, but the potentially harmful consequences of families adhering to strict religious belief systems can be found in more democratic societies and within other religions as well. For instance, although there's no evidence that violence against women is more frequent in highly religious Judeo-Christian families, abused women who are religious may be more vulnerable in the aftermath of the abuse. They're unlikely to leave (because of the promise before God to stay until "death do us part") and commonly express feelings of guilt because they feel they've failed God in not being able to make the relationship work. Such feelings are reinforced by a religious ideology that typically depicts women's roles as wife and mother as essential to their self-worth and that condemns divorces (Nason-Clark, 2004).

Some religions hold that children enter the world with a wayward will and that it is up to the parents to break that will so the child can better respond to parental guidance and submit to the will of God (Greven, 1991). But many parents have taken this directive to "break the child's will" as a mandate that allows them to inflict severe physical punishment, pain, and sometimes injury for the child's own good and not out of their own anger or vindictiveness (Capps, 1992). In 1984, 90 state troopers and 50 social workers raided the compound of the Northeast Kingdom Community Church in Island Pond, Vermont. They rounded up 112 children—ranging in age from 9 days to 17 years—and took them to a courthouse in nearby Newport where they could be examined for evidence of mistreatment. The children were eventually released to the custody of their parents. Church members didn't dispute that they used corporal punishment, usually with thin rods, to discipline the children. But they claimed they did so in accordance with their God-given right to discipline and in a spirit of love:

> Discipline comes from love. Without discipline, children will not have any respect for God or for authority. They have no sense that there are consequences for disobedience. Discipline is not a joyful experience, it hurts, but [children never feel] unwanted or unloved. (quoted in "Trip Home to Stand," 2000, p. A16)

In 2000 a conservative religious leader in Eau Claire, Wisconsin, showed a group of parents how to inflict corporal punishment. Demonstrating on a teen-age boy, he stated "You spank them right here on the gluteus maximus, which God made for that purpose" (quoted in "Conservative Leader Urges Parents," 2000). The minister urged parents to start spanking children around age 2, claiming that it builds self-esteem because it lets children know that they are loved. However, research on corporal punishment has found that such disciplinary tactics are likely to result in overly aggressive and easily frustrated children (Crary, 2000).

In other situations, the harm caused by religious beliefs is less direct. Consider, for example, parents who refuse to seek medical treatment for their sick children because of their religious beliefs. Most states allow parents to refuse certain medical procedures for their children on religious grounds, such as immunizations, eye drops for newborns, screenings for lead poisoning, and physical examinations (CHILD, Inc., 2006). But it is unclear what ought to be done when parents' religiously inspired actions result in the injury or death of a child. Thirty-nine states allow religion as a defense in cases of child abuse or neglect. Nineteen states have religious defenses to felony crimes against children. Delaware, West Virginia, and Arkansas allow religious defenses in cases of murder.

WHAT DOES IT ALL MEAN?

As you've seen in this chapter, race, ethnicity, and religion can play powerful roles in people's family experiences. Families from all ethnoracial groups—even those that are the most destitute—demonstrate incredible resilience, surviving difficult and sometimes debilitating social circumstances. These families—particularly African American, Asian American, and Latino/a families—are more often than not a source of strength for their members, providing crucial support and nurturing. Families can play a significant part in helping individual members of racial and ethnic minorities overcome the disadvantages they face in mainstream society.

As U.S. society becomes increasingly multiracial, we will be forced to deal with a number of critical issues. Can a society that has been strongly committed to assimilation truly appreciate racial, ethnic, and religious diversity? What would such appreciation look like? Is it possible to address and reduce large-scale economic and educational inequalities without threatening the cultural uniqueness expressed by different groups?

In the past, religious and family institutions had a mutually supportive relationship. Religion served to legitimate marriage and child rearing and to support and guide family life. In exchange, families were an extension of the religious community, inculcating religious values, beliefs, and practices. Although society has not become completely secular, as some have feared, this close relationship between family and religion has weakened due to a wide variety of challenges facing contemporary families. The benefits to be gained from the close tie between family and religion are therefore not experienced by as many in the United States as in the past.

As you think about the material in this chapter, consider these questions:

1. Popular conceptions of *the* family in U.S. society are typically based on a narrow, white, middle-class image. Consequently, family types that do not conform to this image have often been perceived as deficient, abnormal, or even dangerous. How do the structures of minority families represent historical adaptations to broader social and economic conditions? Is it useful to focus on race and ethnicity as the defining features of minority families?

2. When it comes to understanding families, should we emphasize the similarities that exist across ethnoracial and religious groups, or should we emphasize the differences that give these groups their unique culture and identity? Do you think we as a society should aspire to assimilation or multiculturalism? And do you think we will ever reach a point when racial and ethnic categories are irrelevant in people's lives?

3. Have you or someone you are close to grown up in an interfaith or interracial family? What do you see as the disadvantages? Is children's racial and religious identity necessarily weakened in such families? What are the advantages?

4. Should religious organizations compromise their position on various issues (such as premarital sex, divorce, or homosexuality) if their message makes some groups or individuals feel unwelcome? How could such compromises benefit families, religious organizations, and society in general? At what costs?

5. Should parents have complete freedom to homeschool their children if they believe public (and even parochial) schools cannot instill proper religious values? What role should the government play in ensuring that these children receive adequate educational experiences? Should religious organizations help subsidize these children's education?

SUMMARY

- The characteristics that distinguish one racial group from another have less to do with biological differences than with what a society defines as socially significant.

- The dramatic growth in the number of multiracial children is challenging traditional conceptions of race.

- The family forms that characterize particular racial or ethnic groups reflect the historical and eco-nomic conditions under which that group entered the United States. Minority families must adapt to differing degrees of social exclusion.

- Focusing on the unique family characteristics of certain racial or ethnic groups sometimes obscures the diversity that exists *within* those groups.

- When evaluating the role of religion in family life, it's important to consider how religion can create stress in families along with how it can help them.

Go to the Online Learning Center at **www.mhhe.com/newman1** to test your knowledge of the chapter concepts and key terms.

KEY TERMS

assimilation 122	hypodescent rule 110	race 109
ethnicity 109	melting pot 122	religion 122
expanded families 121	multicultural society 122	split household 117

SEE FOR YOURSELF

U.S. society—especially the economic opportunities it provides and the obstacles it sets in place—can look quite different to people from different racial and ethnic groups. To gain a better understanding of how race and ethnicity influence people's family experiences, interview a few adults from each of the following groups:

- White, European
- Non-white, Latino/a
- Asian American
- African American
- A multiracial couple or family

If possible, interview both husbands and wives, and also try to maximize diversity within each group. For example, for Latino/a adults, try to locate someone of Mexican descent and someone of Cuban descent. For Asian Americans, see if you can interview people of different nationalities.

When you interview your respondents, first ask them to discuss their cultural heritage(s). When did their families come to the United States? What were the circumstances? Do they have any knowledge of relatives living in the countries of origin? Consider how the circumstances and historical context of their arrival here affected contact with and knowledge of distant relatives who live in other parts of the world.

Ask them about family traditions, such as weekly or daily rituals and holiday celebrations. Are some of these traditions linked to their racial or ethnic backgrounds? In what ways? What are the most powerful and important cultural traditions? You might want to ask if it's difficult to maintain these traditions. Do their family traditions include members of their extended families? In general, what role do these other relatives play in their lives?

Finally, ask about experiences with racial or ethnic discrimination. What have these experiences taught them about living and surviving in the United States? About the importance of family?

Use your findings to consider whether, when it comes to family, people should emphasize the similarities that exist across racial and ethnic groups or the differences.

6

Unequal Families

I lived the first 10 years of my life in relative comfort. My parents, my two older siblings, and I lived in a two-story house just outside New York City. We had a big yard and a basketball hoop hanging over the driveway. We had a part-time housekeeper. There was even a small pond behind the house. We were living the prosperous, fairy tale, suburban, middle-class life that characterized the "baby boom" era of the early 1960s.

My father owned a business in Manhattan and wore fancy suits to work. My parents seemed glamorous to me. They had lots of lavish dinner parties, where they laughed with their equally glamorous friends, drank scotch, and listened to Frank Sinatra records. They went out a lot too, often eating at those restaurants where people got up to dance between courses of the meal. Our family flew to Miami Beach every spring and stayed at a hotel for a week.

My father's childhood was rough. He was one of four brothers of poor immigrant parents. He spent World War II fighting in France, Belgium, and Germany. He was fond of saying that he'd seen too much suffering and misery in his life and never wanted his children to experience it. Don't get me wrong. We weren't spoiled or extremely wealthy. But neither were we deprived of anything that we wanted.

Then, just like that, it all changed.

As I was finishing third grade, my father's business went bankrupt. We lost everything, and my parents moved us to southern California. My father ran a shabby dry cleaning store his brother owned. We lived in a small apartment across the street from the eternally busy Ventura Freeway, and the 24-hour sound of traffic formed the soundtrack of my childhood. I was embarrassed to have friends over. I didn't want them to see where or how I lived.

My father didn't wear suits to work anymore. He wore short-sleeved white uniform shirts with a "Wesco Cleaners" patch on one side and his name, "Chuck," sewn on the other. He drove a broken-down van that started up only when it felt like it. My parents didn't go out anymore, and we no longer took vacations. Although we weren't destitute, our life was by no means luxurious.

Life became much more stressful. I heard my parents say "we can't afford it" far too many times to count. They constantly worried about money. My father rubbed his head all the time and snapped at us; my mother cried a lot.

The legendary vaudeville singer Sophie Tucker once said, "I've been rich and I've been poor—and believe me, rich is better." At age 10 I already knew exactly what she meant.

As a society, we don't seem willing to admit to what Ms. Tucker readily acknowledged: that access to economic resources and material comfort can determine the quality of our lives. Instead we often engage in a "conspiracy of silence" about social class and its effects on families (Hansen, 2005). We're fond of saying things like "Money can't buy happiness" and "All you need is love." The truth is, though, that money—or more accurately, social class—frequently can be the thing that separates comfortable families from beleaguered ones; happy families from miserable ones.

Of course, the relationship between wealth—or the lack of it—and family life is not always straightforward. Wealthy families are not immune from misery, disappointment, and pain. New, upscale, high-security subdivisions can leave wealthy residents feeling isolated and unfulfilled (Kilborn, 2005). Rich children are often tightly monitored and controlled by their parents under restrictions that can create enough resentment and rebellion to poison a family.

At the other end of the spectrum, poor families certainly experience a great deal of trouble and heartbreak, but many are also strong, supportive, and emotionally gratifying. Many successful adults who grew up in abject poverty have prospered from the love and guidance of their parents.

As one sociologist recently put it, "understanding contemporary families is possible only by understanding class, and vice versa" (Hansen, 2005, p. xvi). In this chapter, we'll examine the influence of broad economic forces on family dynamics and structure across the economic spectrum.

SOCIAL STRATIFICATION

Inequality is woven into the fabric of all societies through a structured system of **stratification,** the ranking of entire groups of people that perpetuates unequal rewards and life chances in a society. Just as geologists talk about strata of rock, which are layered one on top of another, the "social strata" of people are arranged from low to high. All societies, past and present, have some form of stratification, although the degree of inequality between strata can vary.

Class Inequality

Contemporary industrialized societies are likely to be stratified on the basis of **social classes**—that is, groups of people who share a similar position in society based on their wealth and income. Social class distinguishes one group's pattern of behavior from another's and determines access to important resources and life chances. We live in a society that is solidly structured along the lines of class distinctions.

Theoretically, class systems are different from other systems of stratification—such as *caste systems* found in South Asia and some parts of Africa, which base social position on heredity—because in class systems there are no legal barriers to **social mobility,** the movement of people from one level to another. In practice, however, mobility between classes may be quite difficult. As much as we'd like to believe otherwise, the opportunities to move from one class up to another are not available to all members of society, especially families of color.

To rank families on the basis of class, contemporary sociologists usually compile information on quantifiable factors such as household income, wealth, occupational status, and educational attainment, but the boundaries between classes are not particularly clear. Some have argued that there are no discrete classes with clearly defined boundaries but only a socioeconomic continuum on which individuals are ranked (Blau & Duncan, 1967). Nevertheless, class designations remain a part of both everyday thinking and social research. Here are some common understandings sociologists often use to determine who makes up various classes in U.S. society:

- **Upper class** (which some sociologists define as the highest-earning 5% of the U.S. population): owners of vast amounts of property and other forms of wealth, major shareholders and owners of large corporations, top financiers, rich celebrities and politicians, and members of prestigious families

- **Middle class** (roughly 45% of the population): college-educated managers, supervisors, executives, owners of small businesses, and professionals (for example, lawyers, doctors, teachers, and engineers)

■ stratification
The ranking of entire groups of people that perpetuates unequal rewards and life chances in a society.

■ social class
A group of people who share a similar position in society based on their wealth and income.

■ social mobility
The movement of people from one class level to another.

■ upper-class families
Prestigious families that own vast amounts of property and other forms of wealth, and that consist of major shareholders and owners of large corporations, top financiers, and rich celebrities and politicians.

■ middle-class families
Families that typically consist of college-educated managers, supervisors, executives, owners of small businesses, and professionals (e.g., lawyers, doctors, teachers, and engineers).

Social class often determines the degree to which families can keep their private lives private. Owning a washer and dryer is a luxury beyond the means of many poor and working-class families who must wash their clothes in public.

■ **working-class families**
Families that typically consist of industrial and factory workers, office workers, clerks, and farm and manual laborers; most working-class people don't own their own homes and don't attend college.

■ **poor families**
Families that typically consist of people who either work for minimum wages or who are chronically unemployed. They are sometimes referred to as the *lower class* or *underclass.*

■ **Working class** (about 35% of the population): industrial and factory workers, office workers, clerks, and farm and manual laborers; most don't own their own homes and don't attend college

■ The **poor** (about 15% of the population): people who either work for minimum wages or are chronically unemployed; sometimes referred to as the *lower class* or *underclass* (Walton, 1990; E. O. Wright, Costello, Hachen, & Sprague, 1982).

Those in the higher social classes control nearly all the nation's income. The richest 5% of U.S. families receive 21% of the nation's total income, and the richest 20% control nearly half the income. The average annual income for the richest 5% of families is more than $173,000; for the poorest 20% of families, the average annual income is under $25,000 (U.S. Bureau of the Census, 2007). And the gap grows larger each year (Figure 6.1). Between 2003 and 2004, the income of the richest 1% increased 12.5% while the income of the bottom 99% increased only 1.5% (cited in Krugman, 2006). The gap between rich and poor is larger in the United States than in any other industrialized country in the world.

Inequalities in income lead to even more striking inequalities in wealth. A lifetime of high earnings and inheritance from privileged parents creates a lasting advantage in ownership of property; of durable consumer goods such as cars, houses, and furniture; and of financial assets such as stocks, bonds, savings, and life insurance. The most prosperous 20% of U.S. households hold about 85% of the nation's wealth (up from 81% in 1983). And the wealthiest 1% of U.S. households, who have enjoyed two thirds of all increases in wealth over the past two decades, now own 34% of the wealth. At the same time, the bottom 80% of households control a mere 15% of the nation's wealth (Mishel, Bernstein, & Allegretto, 2007). There are 4 times as many households with a net worth over $10 million today as there were in 1989 (Uchitelle, 2006c).

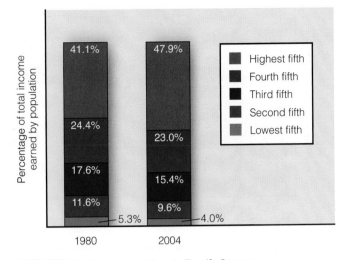

FIGURE 6.1 Increasing Gap in Family Income
Source: U.S. Bureau of the Census, 2007, table 678.

Social Class in Everyday Life

But social class is about more than income, wealth, and occupational prestige; when we talk about social class, we are making broad generalizations about what large groups of people look like and how they live. Class standing can determine a whole host of life chances, including access to higher education, satisfying jobs, and quality health care. Take, for example, college admissions. Most people assume that admissions decisions are based solely on a student's merit. To get into a top college, you generally need to show high academic achievement (reflected in high school grades) and intellectual potential (reflected in scores on standardized aptitude tests like the SAT). What could be fairer than using these sorts of objective measures to determine who gets an elite education that will open doors for a lifetime?

However, SAT scores may depend as much on parents' financial status as on a student's own intellectual aptitude. Obviously, simply coming from a well-to-do family doesn't guarantee a high score on the SAT, but it can help. If you were fortunate enough to attend high school in an affluent, upper-class neighborhood, chances are your school offered SAT preparation courses. In some of these schools, students take practice SAT exams every year until they take the real one in their senior year. Wealthy high schools are also significantly more likely than mid-level or poor high schools to offer advanced placement courses, another important tool that college admissions officers use to measure applicants (Berthelsen, 1999). Even if a school doesn't provide such opportunities, wealthy families often shell out thousands of dollars for private SAT prep courses, college admission summer camps, and "dress for success" counseling to give their children additional advantages (Kirp, 2004). Access to these opportunities pays off (Figure 6.2). Five of every six qualified high school seniors whose families earn more than $75,000—but less than half those whose families earn less than $25,000—enroll in a 4-year college (Kirp, 2004).

Social class influences health too. For an annual fee ranging anywhere from $1,500 to $20,000, wealthy families can buy "boutique," "premium," "deluxe," or "platinum"

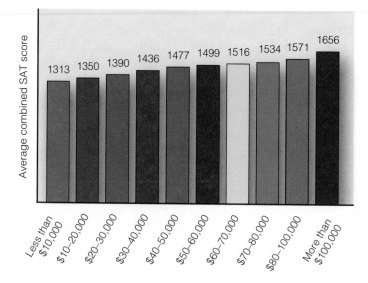

FIGURE 6.2 Average SAT Scores by Family Income Level
Source: National Center for Fair and Open Testing, 2007.

medical services: special access to their doctor via 24/7 cell phone, fax, and e-mail; same-day appointments with a guaranteed waiting time of no more than 15 minutes; nutrition and exercise physiology exams at the patients' homes; doctors or nurses to accompany them when they go to see specialists; and routine physicals that are so thorough they can last up to 3 days (Belluck, 2002; Garfinkel, 2003; Zuger, 2005). The extra fees allow doctors to reduce their patient load so they can provide more personalized attention. One physician provided a common justification for the growing disparity: "Is it health care for the rich? I guess so. But when you come to my clinic, I'm not concerned about the national health care picture. I'm concerned about you" (quoted in Tyre, 2005, p. 53).

Research shows that those at lower levels of the stratification system are more likely to die prematurely from homicide, accidents, or inadequate health care than are people at higher levels. People whose families earn less than $5,000 a year can expect to live about 25% fewer years than people from families that earn more than $50,000 (Deaton & Paxson, 1999). Even after controlling for age, sex, race, family size, and education, the risk of death steadily decreases as income goes up (Marmot, 2004).

Everyday physical comfort is also linked to social class. For instance, Virgin Atlantic Airlines now offers its first-class passengers leather armchairs with matching ottomans that turn into double beds. Emirates Airlines offers first-class passengers their own enclosed suites complete with minibar, 19-inch television, bed, and "dine on demand" room service (Rosato, 2004). Space for such amenities comes at the expense of ordinary passengers in coach sections where legroom and elbow room are typically minimal and food service has all but disappeared. First-class sections usually contain more flight attendants per person than coach sections, and the attendants respond more quickly to call buttons. In addition, first-class passengers have access to shorter check-in lines at airports, and, since September 11, 2001, some of the nation's airlines have set up special express security lines for them so as to avoid unnecessary delays (Squadron, 2005). Such exclusive personal attention creates feelings of power and privilege.

Conversely, people in the lower classes routinely face annoying barriers in their daily lives. In poor households, dwellings are smaller and more crowded than those of more affluent households, making privacy structurally difficult to obtain. Thin walls separating cramped apartments hide few secrets. Family members have little semblance of privacy—whether from one another or from neighbors. In addition, poor families must often make use of public facilities (health clinics, laundromats, public transportation, and so on) to carry out the day-to-day tasks that wealthier families can carry out privately.

Those who seek out government assistance subject themselves to periodic inspections, thereby losing even more of their privacy. In San Diego investigators make unannounced visits to homes of people applying for welfare, looking through garbage cans, medicine chests, and laundry baskets in search of evidence of fraud. Applicants are not required to let them in, but they'll be denied benefits if they refuse (Liptak, 2007).

Social Class and Family

Obviously class exerts enormous influence on what families look like and how people conduct themselves within their families. Of course, families within the same social category—whether we're talking about race, ethnicity, religion, or social class—do not represent a monolithic group. There is often as much diversity within a category as between categories. Nonetheless, class standing affects the kinds of resources families have and the kinds of challenges they face.

Upper-Class Families

This description of the upper class, formulated 50 years ago, still rings true today:

> a group of families whose members are descendants of successful individuals of one, two, three or more generations ago . . . the top of the social class hierarchy. They are brought up together and they are friends. They intermarry and have a distinctive style of life. There is a primary group solidarity that sets them apart from the rest of the population. (Baltzell, 1958, p. 60)

Members of upper-class families tend to be born into formidable wealth (Langman, 1988), which provides political and economic power as well as insulation from the rest of society. A variety of exclusive institutions—including upscale neighborhoods, private schools, social clubs, resorts, cultural organizations, and social activities—protect their position in society and provide members with a particular lifestyle and perspective on the world. In addition, parents often use their money and social power to create a sort of protective bubble around their children in which they learn what it takes to carry on the tradition of family wealth and success (Kendall, 2002). Because inheritance and pedigree are passed down through the children, parents believe it is crucial that they be raised to value their social position and understand the responsibilities that come with it.

Though it's unwise to paint families of any social class with broad, generalized strokes, some features of family life do seem more common in the upper class than in other classes. For instance, an important aspect of upper-class families seems to be the rather traditional role that women play (Ostrander, 1984). Wives often see their role in the family as supportive rather than primary and may consider it their duty to put their husbands' interests ahead of their own:

> He's the brain in the family and it's my role to see that he's at his best. I've subjugated everything to that. When he comes home in the evening, this house must be

(Text continues on page 142.)

Katrina Families

When Hurricane Katrina and the flooding that ensued devastated New Orleans and the Gulf Coast of Mississippi, thousands of families lost everything they had. But the storm and its aftermath didn't affect all residents equally. The neighborhoods with significant flooding had a lower median income, a higher poverty rate, and a higher percentage of households without a vehicle than areas that experienced little or no flooding (Schwartz, Revkin, & Wald, 2005).

Those of us watching the tragedy unfold on television could not help but notice the obvious fact that the vast majority of the evacuees who suffered for days in the sweltering darkness of the Superdome and convention center in New Orleans were poor people of color who came from the most vulnerable parts of the city. These were individuals who either didn't have the necessary transportation to evacuate prior to the hurricane or who stayed behind to tend to sick and elderly relatives who couldn't be moved. This disaster—as well as those that have occurred before and since—reminds us that in times of tragedy, a family's social class standing can literally mean the difference between life and death.

A family uses a boat to evacuate their home in Chalmette, 11 miles east of New Orleans.

More than 340,000 people were eventually evacuated to various locations and shelters throughout the United States. Close to 20,000 people ended up here, in the Houston Astrodome. In this place, people couldn't meet minimal requirements of family life. The activities families normally do alone, or in the company of intimates, the evacuees had to do in the presence of unknown others. They slept next to strangers, showered and used toilets next to strangers, dressed and undressed next to strangers, and ate next to strangers.

Many families that were able to escape overcrowded shelters ended up living temporarily in motels, church basements, or private homes. Although these locations were much more comfortable than the shelters, everyday routines of private family life continued to be disrupted.

Hurricane Katrina killed more than 1,000 people in the Gulf Coast region. Most of these people died not because of the torrential rains and high winds that accompanied the hurricane, but because of the flooding that occurred when the levees that ordinarily protect the low-lying areas of New Orleans (which were in need of repair to begin with) were breached.

perfectly quiet. . . . He wants me to be pleasant, pretty, and relaxed. I never bring a problem to him, except during forty-five minutes set aside on Sunday mornings for that purpose. (quoted in Ostrander, 1984, p. 39)

Such an attitude seems tremendously out of date in the 21st century. However, like women in many 19th- and 20th-century families, these women see such supportive behavior as their essential contribution to their families. They take for granted that their job—their part of the bargain in exchange for a life of luxury—is to "run the house-hold." Even though they rarely do the actual cooking, laundry, and cleaning themselves, they make decisions about how other people—whose labor they have purchased—perform the housework.

Many upper-class women also tend to have a rather traditional perspective on the mother role. Children's preschool years are typically spent at home in the presence of mothers and nannies, nurses, or other private, in-home caretakers. From kindergarten through college, children in the highest social strata are usually enrolled in private schools (Domhoff, 1998). There they are set apart from children of other classes or, as one upper-class mother called them, "ordinary people" (quoted in Ostrander, 1984, p. 85). Mothers play a dominant role in enforcing these high standards of behavior and struc-turing the child's participation in "appropriate" activities and organizations. For instance, they may take an active role in selecting their children's friends, often by setting up play groups with other mothers from their own social network or by providing opportunities to play at country clubs or private clubs in the neighborhood where they will associate with children of other club members (Kendall, 2002).

The popular belief that upper-class women leave the raising of their children to nannies, au pairs, or other hired caretakers may therefore be largely mythical. Many of these women feel it is important to be present in their children's lives, particularly when they are young, even if these other caretakers do take over much of the hands-on, day-to-day care (Kendall, 2002). Upper-class women often arrange their own activities, particularly volunteer work, so they can be home for their children.

What many upper-class parents seem to want most for their children as they get older is a "compatible marriage"—that is, a marriage to someone of equal class stand-ing. Marrying someone below "one's station"—or "marrying down"—means not only accepting that person as an equal partner but also blurring class distinctions in the next generation should the couple have children (Kalmijn, 1991). Parents thus try to ensure that their children engage in class-exclusive recreational activities and join organizations whose membership is by invitation only. Social clubs are places where "acceptable" people of the same kind can meet, ultimately resulting in acceptable marriages (Dom-hoff, 1998; Ostrander, 1984).

Evidence of the tendency for upper-class individuals to marry one another and therefore retain their class standing can be found in the consistency over time of the families listed in *The Social Register*, a directory of names and addresses of powerful and wealthy families that form the social elite in the United States. One study of the list-ings over a span of 55 years found that around 80% of the families listed in 1940 were still there in 1995 (Broad, 1996).

The "New Rich"

Unlike those elite, upper-class families in which vast amounts of wealth are inherited over generations, other affluent families experience a rapid increase of wealth and social mobility through their own personal achievements. These families are usually headed by high-level executives in large corporations, founders of successful new companies, highly compensated lawyers, doctors, scientists, entertainers, and elite professional athletes. They are the **new rich,** people who have made, not inherited, their fortunes. Some executives and professionals were born into poor or working-class families or belong to a disadvantaged racial or ethnic group, but they have been able to climb the social ladder and create a comfortable life for themselves and their families.

Like their upper-class counterparts, newly rich parents can transfer advantage to their children not just through direct financial assistance but also through what sociologists call **cultural capital**—reputations, connections, skills, knowledge, and so on that can be exchanged for economic benefit (Becker, 1981). Even if they don't inherit a cent, children of affluent parents acquire a recognized family name and the respect and privilege that go along with it. Hence, they are likely to have access to opportunities and social advantages that are beyond the grasp of most. Later on, these advantages have a positive effect on children's standard of living by increasing, among other things, the likelihood of attending college, purchasing a luxurious car, and owning a home (Spilerman, 2004).

Sudden wealth can create its own brand of family difficulty. Children of the newly rich often have little appreciation for the lifestyle their parents provide them (Brown, 2000). They live in a world where "middle class" is equated with poverty, where families that go to Hawaii only once a year are considered bottom rung, and where having parents who are "only" doctors is embarrassing. But unlike those upper-class children whose wealth has spanned generations and whose inheritance and pedigree will likely sustain them in adulthood, these children are intensely anxious about their own ability to achieve the vast amounts of wealth to which they've become accustomed. They see their parents working faster and harder to avoid falling back, and they internalize these pressures. Many psychologists and counselors have devoted their practices to treating what has come to be called "sudden wealth syndrome," a cluster of symptoms that includes marked anxiety, persistent and distressing thoughts of money, cycles of depression in response to stock market volatility, insomnia, irritable mood, feelings of guilt, and identity confusion (Money, Meaning, and Choice Institute, 2006).

Middle-Class Families

Neither rich nor poor, middle-class families consist of the millions of people who occupy the vague center of the population. Though this social class is the largest, it is also the hardest to define. The middle-class is simultaneously ubiquitous and invisible:

> The vast majority of Americans think of themselves as "middle class." There is also the folk lexicon of subdivisions of this category—"upper middle," "lower middle," and just plain "middle." . . . The term "lower middle class" is very much disliked by those who might be so categorized, apparently because of the presence of the word "lower." . . . The plain "middle class" is the most slippery category. It is either used as the modest self-label for the upper middle class . . . or it is the covering label for the lower middle class. . . . Either way there is almost no "there" there; to be plain middle class is almost always to be "really" something else, or on the way to somewhere else. At the same time, the "middle class" is the most inclusive social category; indeed almost a national category. . . . It is everybody except the very rich and the very poor. (Ortner, 1998, p. 8)

Middle-class families exist between two important constituencies in modern society, the working class and the upper class, and so they share certain interests and concerns

■ **new rich**
Families that have made, not inherited, their fortunes.

■ **cultural capital**
Reputations, connections, skills, knowledge, and so on that can be exchanged for economic benefit.

of both groups (Zweig, 2000). For instance, as in most working-class families, both husbands and wives in middle-class families are likely to work in the paid labor force to maintain their standard of living. But like members of the upper class, they enjoy relatively secure financial circumstances that allow them to purchase services to help manage the demands of work and home, such as child care or housecleaning—luxuries not available to less economically privileged families (Newman, 1999a).

Of course, significant variations in income, status, and lifestyle exist among so-called middle-class families. Those who are considered "upper-middle-class" (such as physicians, lawyers and other well-paid professionals) may have more in common with upper-class or newly rich families than with lower-middle-class families. For instance, one study of upper-middle-class wives found that their role in the marriage is very much like that of upper-class wives: keeping the household running smoothly, encouraging their husbands emotionally and professionally, moving when their husbands' jobs require it, and so on (Fowlkes, 1987). These women, for the most part, support their husbands by playing an adjunct role in the family. But women in lower-middle-class families are likely to resemble working-class wives, whose own role in the workplace is essential to the family's well-being.

The ambiguous social and economic position of middle-class families shapes family life in significant ways. Wives' employment in middle-class families, especially those of the upper-middle-class, may not be the absolute necessity that it is in families with fewer economic means. When husbands earn relatively high incomes, they may view their wives' earnings as supplemental or even unnecessary (Ferree, 1984). Although a husband may be proud of his wife's accomplishments, he may see himself as the one who has to sacrifice so that his wife is able to work and therefore feels justified in overseeing family spending. Even today, middle-class women may pay for luxury items and designer goods with cash rather than credit cards to avoid their husbands' detection and disapproval (Vora, 2007).

Nonetheless, many middle-class couples do profess to place high value on the ideal of equality in marriage (Cancian & Gordon, 1988; Rubin, 1976). The reality of everyday life for most couples, however, may be very different. For couples in which the spouses work alternating shifts (that is, one works nights, the other works days), household tasks are often divided along traditional gender lines (Deutsch, 1999) (See Chapter 9 for a more detailed discussion of work and family issues.) Yet even though middle-class marriages aren't always more equal than those in other social classes, the *expectation* of equality may be greater. As a result, when middle-class women confront inequality in their marriages, they may be more angry and mystified by it than other women.

The ideology of equality also tends to filter into the parent–child relationship. Shared parenting, or at least greater involvement of men in fathering their children, is a value expressed more among the middle class than other groups (Deutsch, 1999; LaRossa, 1992). But here, too, the reality is often very different from the ideology. For the most part, in middle-class families—like families of other classes—women assume primary responsibility for child care.

The importance of understanding middle-class values and lifestyles is clear when we consider that "middle class" is often equated with what is "mainstream" in U.S. society (Pattillo-McCoy, 1999). Middle-class norms often define for our culture what is desirable and, therefore, what others should strive for (Newman, 1999a). By comparison, families in lower classes are often viewed as deviant or problematic. For example, people in the middle class typically value autonomy, including autonomy among adult siblings and between adult children and their parents (Newman, 1999a), so the U.S. ideal becomes individual independence. Those in lower-class families who find strength in the extended family bonds they rely on for survival may begin to wonder whether they shouldn't be living like the middle-class families they see on TV and in the movies.

But even for families squarely within the middle class, the realities of contemporary life—including divorce, unemployment, lack of quality child care, and so on—can sometimes limit their ability to live up to the values associated with their class standing.

Working-Class Families

Clearly the stresses associated with affluence pale in comparison to the stresses felt by families that constantly struggle to make ends meet. The most important characteristic of working-class families is their dependence on hourly wages, which makes them particularly susceptible to downturns in the economy that can result in layoffs, plant closings, and unemployment (Rapp, 1999). These jobs are also less likely than higher-paying, salaried jobs to provide benefits such as medical insurance and retirement plans.

As a consequence of the harsh economic landscape, many working-class young people continue to need their parents' help well after becoming adults. Historically, working-class women and men were significantly more likely than their middle-class counterparts to marry young, often because of a desire to become independent and leave home. More affluent young people, in contrast, delayed marriage to attend college and enhance their employment prospects. Working-class people have also tended to have children earlier than members of higher classes, creating further economic pressures. Many working-class women are employed before they marry, and so young couples may expect that two incomes will enable them to maintain a home. But the demands of a baby can make it difficult to pay for day-to-day expenses. Instead of the happy life they imagined, young couples may begin to feel trapped and anxious. Some couples divorce; others are forced to move back in with their parents, which leads to even more stress.

Past research suggested that communication between working-class husbands and wives regarding personal or emotional matters was sometimes difficult. In one comparative study, middle-class and working-class wives were asked what they valued most in their husbands. The middle-class wives tended to focus on such issues as intimacy, sharing, communication, and the comforts and prestige that their husbands' occupations provided them. Working-class wives were more dismal in their assessments, focusing on the absence of such problems as unemployment, alcoholism, and violence. As one 33-year-old housewife put it, "I guess I can't complain. He's a steady worker; he doesn't drink; he doesn't hit me. That's a lot more than my mother had, and she didn't sit around complaining and feeling sorry for herself, so I sure haven't got the right" (Rubin, 1976, p. 93).

More recent research, however, indicates that such attitudes among working-class couples are weakening. For instance, working-class men and women are significantly more likely to approve of women working outside the home than they were several decades ago (Rubin, 1995). According to the General Social Survey, working-class women in the 1970s were likely to feel that the traditional husband/breadwinner, wife/homemaker roles were the best way for a family to be arranged. By the early 1990s, however, working-class women—who were now likely to be employed outside the home themselves—saw paid employment as a crucial part of a wife's appropriate family role (cited in Cherlin, 1999).

Despite these changing attitudes, working-class families remain perpetually vulnerable to fluctuations in the economy. Sociologist Lillian Rubin (1995) held in-depth interviews with working-class families to examine how the economic downturn of the

1980s and early 1990s had influenced their families and their dreams. The title of her book, *Families on the Fault Line,* suggests a precarious life on the edge of disaster. The families she studied aren't considered officially "poor." Nevertheless, the hope that sustained working-class people through bad times in the 1970s—the belief that if they just worked hard and played by the rules, they'd eventually grab a piece of the American Dream—no longer existed. It's not so much the possibility of falling into poverty that worries them, it's the fear that there's no possibility of ever moving upward.

To psychologically survive in a world of economic instability and powerlessness, many working-class parents begin to define their jobs as meaningless and irrelevant to their core identity. But instead of focusing on the dreariness or the insignificance of their work, they come to view it as a noble act of sacrifice. A bricklayer put it simply: "My job is to work for my family" (Sennett & Cobb, 1972, p. 135).

Defining a job as sacrifice solves the problem of powerlessness in two ways. First, in return for their sacrifice, working-class parents—especially men—can demand a position of power within their own families. Second, framing degrading work as sacrifice allows them to slip the bonds of the disappointing present and orient their lives toward their children's and grandchildren's future, something that gives them a sense of control they can't get through their jobs.

Ironically, framing work as sacrifice can cause other hidden injuries within the family (Sennett & Cobb, 1972). On one hand, working-class parents—like parents of all social classes—want to spend time with their children and show concern for them. On the other hand, they know that the only way they can provide a "good home" for their family is to work longer hours at an unfulfilling job and be absent from home more frequently. Unfortunately, from the perspective of the child, this absence is precisely what constitutes a "bad home."

In addition, it is more difficult for working-class parents to sacrifice "successfully." Upper-class and middle-class parents make sacrifices so that their children will have a life like theirs. Working-class parents sacrifice so that their children will *not* have a life like theirs. Their lives are not a "model" but a "warning." Hence, the sacrifice does not end the conditions that made the parents prey to feelings of shame and inadequacy in the first place. The danger of this type of sacrifice is that if the children do fulfill the parents' wishes and rise above their quality of life, their family may eventually become a burden or an embarrassment to them (Granfield, 2008).

Downwardly Mobile Families

Another group of people whose families are affected by economic insecurities have somewhat different experiences than working-class families. These are the families that have fallen out of the middle class through what sociologists call **downward mobility.**

■ **downward mobility**
Process by which families fall out of the middle class and experience economic insecurity.

According to a national survey conducted by the Pew Research Center, only about a third of U.S. adults say they earn enough money to lead the kind of life they want, and about two thirds worry that good jobs will move overseas and that workers here will be left with jobs that don't pay enough (Kohut, 1999). Many families with healthy incomes are still living close to the financial edge, one layoff or medical emergency away from financial crisis. The rising cost of health care is making it increasingly difficult even for middle-class families to afford insurance coverage (Strom, 2003). Today, one third of uninsured families have incomes over $40,000 a year (Fronstin, 2007).

Median household incomes rose steadily throughout the 1980s and 1990s but have leveled off and even fallen a bit in the mid-2000s (U.S. Bureau of the Census, 2008). After adjusting for inflation, the average hourly wage has dropped from a little over $19 an hour in the early 1970s to about $17 an hour today (cited in Leonhardt, 2007). In 2004, the U.S. Bureau of Labor Statistics reported that the hourly earnings of nonmanagement workers—from nurses and teachers to assembly-line workers—showed the steepest decline since 1991. Many people haven't had raises in years but have seen the cost of living (in particular, of food, energy, and health care) rise steadily (Uchitelle, 2008).

Not only are middle-class jobs paying less than they used to, but there are fewer of them to go around. Many people must accept the growing reality that their middle-class credentials don't protect them against job loss (Uchitelle, 2006a). Corporate downsizing and outsourcing over the past decade have nibbled into stable, white-collar, middle-class occupations. Even solid high-tech companies eliminated thousands of middle-income jobs from their payrolls in the early and mid-2000s because of slowdowns in the personal computer market and the bursting of the Internet bubble. Indeed, the number of U.S. adults with college degrees who were unemployed for more than 6 months tripled between 2001 and 2004 (cited in Greenhouse, 2004).

Some economists and politicians argue that unemployment is not a serious problem and that jobs in the future will be plentiful. However, the types of jobs that will be available may not be the sort that will strengthen people's middle-class status. According to the U.S. Bureau of Labor Statistics, 7 of 10 occupations that are forecast to show the greatest growth between now and 2012 are in low-wage service fields that require little, if any, education or training: retail sales, customer service, food service, cashier, janitor, waitperson, nursing aide, and hospital orderly (cited in Greenhouse, 2004). Most of these jobs pay less than $18,000 a year. By most accounts, high-paying jobs will continue to be in short supply, meaning that many college-educated people will be thwarted in their attempts to earn a comfortable living. It's no wonder that many middle-class U.S. workers feel like they're on a treadmill that constantly threatens to throw them into a less desirable social class.

When someone loses a job, the rapid reduction in income has far-reaching consequences. As you recall from my own story at the beginning of this chapter, it often means moving to inferior housing and leaving behind familiar routines. It means drastically less money for recreation and leisure and more pressures due to insufficient time and finances. The sudden financial strain also causes social dislocation through the loss of familiar friendships and emotional support networks.

Women are particularly vulnerable to downward mobility. Some plunge when they or their partner lose a job. But for most women, the main cause of downward mobility is divorce. Handicapped by a gender-stratified labor market, divorced women rarely have an income equal to that of their former husbands. They are also hurt by a lack of affordable and high-quality child care services and by disproportionate responsibility for child-rearing expenses. What divorced women do earn is thus often not adequate to support a family.

Children are hard hit by downward mobility too. Sudden economic pressures can reduce parents' effectiveness in raising their children (Elder & Eccles, 1995). Not only does such pressure increase the number of hardships that a family must endure, it can also demoralize parents and significantly reduce their confidence. Children's perceptions of their parents, in turn, may also be affected. The parental authority that sprang from financial control disappears. A 15-year-old girl describes the sad transformation of the father she once idolized after he lost his job as a successful show business promoter:

> He just seemed to be getting irrational. He would walk around the house talking to himself and stay up all night, smoking cigarettes in the dark. . . . All I perceived is

that somebody who used to be a figure of strength was behaving strangely: starting to cry at odd times . . . hanging around the house unshaven in his underwear when I would bring dates home. . . . In the absence of any understanding of what was going on, my attitude was one of anger and disgust, like "Why don't you get your act together? What's the matter with you?" (Newman, 1999b, p. 96)

Some children of downwardly mobile families never escape the feeling that failure may be lurking around the corner: "The higher they climb, the more urgently they sense they are about to fall" (Newman, 1999b, p. 142). Their experience of social class during childhood has lifelong consequences—as it does for most children.

POVERTY AND FAMILY LIFE

The economic woes of working-class or downwardly mobile families are difficult, but nowhere is the pain of class stratification more apparent than among the poorest of U.S. families. According to the U.S. Census Bureau (2008), about 7.6 million U.S. families (approximately 10% of all families) are officially poor. Despair and insecurity are everyday features in these families. Acquiring and keeping basic necessities—food, clothing, and shelter—are the daily struggles that provide the inevitable backdrop to family life:

The consequences of family instability in poor neighborhoods are clearly more devastating because the whole institutional structure that surrounds folks at the bottom—the schools, the low-wage work place, the overcrowded labor market, the potholed streets, the unsavory crack dealers on the front stoop—creates more vulnerability in families that have to deal with internal troubles. Support is more problematic, more likely to depend upon resources of relatives and friends who are, in turn, also poor and troubled. (K. Newman, 2005, p. 368)

Poor families face tremendous difficulty accomplishing the tasks families that aren't poor take for granted. Instead, their daily chores, and frustrations, might include:

having to take one's dirty clothing on the bus to the nearest laundromat with three children in tow; being unable to afford to go to the dentist even though the pain is excruciating; not purchasing a simple meal at a restaurant for fear it will disrupt the budget; never being able to go to a movie; having no credit, which in turn makes getting a future credit rating difficult; lacking a typewriter or personal computer on which to improve secretarial skills for a job interview. The list could go on and on. (Rank, 1994, p. 60)

Life on the edge of financial survival is precarious. In general, lower-income families pay higher-than-average prices for basic necessities including for appliances, groceries, insurance, and utilities (Brookings Institution, 2006):

■ Large supermarket chains hesitate to open stores in very poor neighborhoods because of security fears. Hence, residents who are without transportation must rely on small neighborhood grocery stores that charge higher prices for food than larger supermarkets do.

■ Lower-income consumers pay more for furniture and appliances because they are significantly more likely than higher-income households to shop at high-

To poor families without health insurance, sickness or injury means a trip to a crowded clinic; to more affluent families, it means a trip to the comfortable office of a private physician.

priced rent-to-own stores. A $200 television set might end up costing as much as $700 at one of these establishments because of interest.

■ Drivers in lower-income neighborhoods pay between $50 and $1,000 more per year in premiums for car insurance than drivers in higher-income neighborhoods, even when they drive the exact same car.

■ Poor people may also pay more for winter utility bills because of the lack of insulation in poor-quality homes.

Poor people receive less preventive health care than wealthier people and often must endure inadequate treatment in crowded public clinics. According to the U.S. Census Bureau (2007), 31% of poor people have no health insurance, even though they may be eligible for government health insurance (Medicaid). Because of rapidly escalating health care costs and job losses, the number of uninsured people in the United States is increasing, leading some state governments to take measures to stem the crisis. In 2007, California governor Arnold Schwarzenegger proposed a plan that would provide health insurance to the state's 6.5 million uninsured residents. But the plan would have cost $12 billion and has met stiff resistance from business leaders.

Poor, uninsured parents face decisions about the health of their children that more affluent parents never do. When nothing out of the ordinary happens, people are able to manage. But an unexpected event—a sickness, an injury, the breakdown of a major appliance or automobile—can set off a domino effect that imperils everything else. Imagine being a poor single mother with a sick child. One trip to the doctor might cost an entire week's food budget or a month of rent. Dental work or an eye examination is easily sacrificed when other pressing bills need to be paid.

One of the most painful choices facing poor households is sometimes called the "heat-or-eat" dilemma: having to choose between paying the heating bill and buying food. One study of 34,000 people nationwide found that during the cold winter months, families spend less on food and reduce their caloric intake by an average of 10% in order to pay their higher fuel bills (Bhattacharya, DeLeire, Haider, & Currie, 2003). More affluent families can use credit or dip into savings to meet higher winter fuel needs, but poor families don't have access to these resources so their nutritional well-being suffers. A 3-year study in a Boston hospital found that emergency room visits by malnourished children under the age of 6 increased 30% after the coldest months of the year. According to one of the researchers, "parents well know that children freeze before they starve, and in winter some families have to divert their already inadequate food budget to buy fuel to keep the children warm. . . . When we say, 'You have to buy more milk for Johnny,' they say, 'But I've got to pay the bills'" ("Study of Poor Children," 1992, p. A17).

Existing government programs are insufficient to buffer poor families against the cold weather demands on their limited budgets (Bhattacharya et al., 2003). Indeed, in 2005, the federal government denied requests from five states to increase food stamps for low-income families facing higher winter heating bills (Wolf, 2005).

The Working Poor

■ **poverty line**
The minimum amount of money a family needs to survive.

According to the U.S. Census Bureau, the official **poverty line** for a family of four is an income of $20,444 a year. Theoretically, this line identifies the minimum amount of money a family of this size needs to survive. But many economists and sociologists believe that this line is set too low, and that it overestimates the numbers of families earning an income high enough to move them above the official poverty line (thus rendering them ineligible for certain forms of governmental assistance), while underestimating the amount of money families actually need for economic stability and well-being.

Official poverty statistics conceal the people who live on the fringe of poverty, often referred to as the "near poor" or the "working poor." According to the U.S. Bureau of the Census, 39 million people work full time but earn such low income that they are struggling financially (Lalasz, 2005). These are the people who are employed yet face difficulties making ends meet. Their impoverished state is measured not by an income that falls below some official threshold, but by anxiety over debt, lack of savings, and the relentless, dispiriting limitations of their everyday lives (Shipler, 2004). They may be surviving in the present but dread the uncertainty of the future.

The myth that surrounds economic disadvantage in this society is that people struggle financially because they either don't work hard enough, don't care, or lack the skills and abilities to get ahead. The irony is that more than two thirds of low-income people work (Lalasz, 2005). They frequently work long hours, sometimes in more than one job, often sacrificing other aspects of their lives (such as family, education, and recreation) in the interests of economic survival. After years of disappointment and working hard just to barely get by, they either give up on the dream of economic comfort or slip back into poverty and government assistance.

■ TAKING A CLOSER LOOK

The Feminization and Juvenilization of Poverty

■ **feminization of poverty**
The greater likelihood that women, as compared to men, will live in poverty.

The growing rate of poverty among women and children has prompted both social research and public concern. The term **feminization of poverty** was coined in the late 1970s to refer to the greater likelihood that women, as compared to men, will live in poverty (Bianchi, 1999; Pearce, 1978). A little over 14% of U.S. women are poor compared to a little over 11% of men.

The gender gap in poverty is even greater among Blacks and Latino/as (U.S. Bureau of the Census, 2008).

The women at the highest risk of living in poverty are single mothers. As the number of female-headed families has increased, so has the proportion of the poor who live in these families. The poverty rate for families headed by single mothers is 28.3%, compared to 13.2% for families headed by single fathers, and 4.9% for married couple families (DeNavas-Walt, Proctor, & Smith, 2007).

It's often argued that poor women are to blame for their own poverty—not to mention a host of other social problems—because they reject marriage and have children they can't afford. Sociologists Katherine Edin and Maria Kefalas (2005) spent 5 years interviewing 162 poor single mothers who live in poor neighborhoods around Philadelphia. They found little evidence of a rejection of marriage in poor communities. In fact, these women indicated that they valued marriage highly and hoped to be married someday. They saw marriage as sacred, a lifelong commitment. However it was not something they saw happening to them any time soon. To them, marriage was a luxury they aspired to but feared they'd never achieve.

On the other hand, they saw having children as an essential part of a young woman's life and the primary source of identity. Whereas members of higher social classes would likely see an unmarried poor woman with children as proof that the moral fabric of U.S. society is deteriorating, these women felt that having a baby represented an opportunity to prove their worth. With few attractive marital options available to them in these communities—poor, unemployed men usually don't make desirable husbands—they concluded that it was better to have a child outside marriage than to marry rashly only to get divorced sometime later.

Though the connection isn't inevitable, high rates of single parenthood tend to be associated with increased risks of children living in poverty. Children's poverty rates rose fairly steadily between 1970 and the mid-1990s, reaching a peak of 22% in 1993. Children's poverty rates declined a bit over the late 1990s, only to rise again in the early and mid-2000s. Currently, 17.4% of children under age 18 live in poverty, and children under age 6 represent the poorest age group in the nation (20%; DeNavas-Walt et al., 2007). Children's poverty rates vary widely by race (Figure 6.3). In response to these trends, a new term, **juvenilization of poverty** has been coined (Bianchi, 1999; Lichter 1997).

■ **juvenilization of poverty**
The greater likelihood that children, as compared to adults, will live in poverty.

Growing up poor has been linked to a variety of problems in children, such as dropping out of school, low academic achievement, teen pregnancy and childbearing, poor mental and physical health, delinquent behavior, and unemployment in adolescence and early adulthood (Caspi, Wright, Moffitt, & Silva, 1998; Harris & Marmer, 1996). The longer children live in poverty, the worse their cognitive, social, and emotional functioning becomes. In addition, when children grow up in poverty, they are more likely than non-poor children to have low earnings as adults, which in turn reflects lower productivity. It's estimated that this reduced productivity—along with costs of increased crime and health expenditures—costs the U.S. economy half a trillion dollars a year (Holzer, Schanzenbach, Duncan, & Ludwig, 2007).

Poverty affects children at every age, but very young children appear to suffer the most devastating and long-term effects. Recent research suggests that

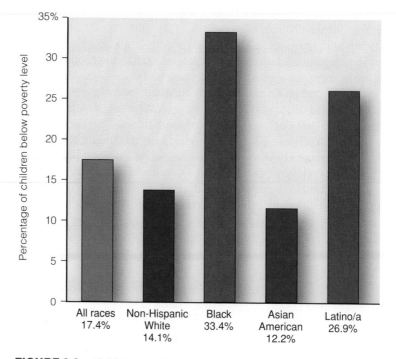

FIGURE 6.3   Child Poverty Rates Among Different Races
Source: DeNavas-Walt, Proctor, & Smith, 2007, table B-2.

economic conditions have the most serious long-term consequences for children during the preschool years (Duncan, Yeung, Brooks-Gunn, & Smith, 1998). Children living in poverty are more likely to be ill-prepared for school, which can set off a disastrous chain of events. They may not have learned basic early skills such as naming colors, sorting, counting, recognizing letters, and knowing the names of everyday objects. Hence, they start school at a disadvantage compared with children who have mastered these skills (Duncan et al., 1998). Later on, this lack of preparation puts them at risk of lower test scores, grade failure, disengagement from school, and higher dropout rates.

Not all poor children suffer from these conditions. Close, positive supervision and emotional support at home can improve social and emotional development, school performance, and self-worth even among the poorest children (Parcel & Menaghan, 1994).

Poverty and Government Policy

In 1935 the U.S. government developed a social welfare system to help people in need—the aged, the poor, the unemployed, the disabled, and the sick. This system is divided into two segments. One segment consists of programs that provide benefits that workers "earn" through employment: Social Security, disability insurance, unemployment insurance, worker's compensation, veterans' payments, pensions, Medicare, and so on. Recipients in these programs are predominantly working and middle class, so benefits are neither stigmatizing nor degrading. When it comes time for federal budget cuts, these programs are usually spared. You may recall the public outrage in response to the Bush administration's announced plan in 2005 to privatize Social Security. Many retired people feared that their benefits would be cut. The plan was quickly dropped.

In contrast, the second—and significantly more controversial—segment of the social welfare system consists primarily of aid to the poor. This segment is what we most commonly associate with the term *welfare.* When budgets need to be trimmed, these programs are usually the first to be cut.

Ironically, the amount of money the government spends on aid to the poor is a fraction of what it spends on assistance programs that serve predominantly middle-class recipients. In 2005, the federal government paid out approximately $40 billion in poverty assistance under the Temporary Assistance to Needy Families and Food Stamp programs. That same year, it spent almost $400 billion on Social Security, unemployment insurance, and Medicare (U.S. Bureau of the Census, 2007).

Over 70 years after its inception, no one is particularly happy with the nation's welfare system. One survey found that more than 70% of U.S. adults believe welfare recipients are abusing the system or have become overly dependent on it. The mere mention of the word "welfare" evokes images of teen pregnancy, unwed mothers, divorce, drug abuse, and unsafe streets (Hays, 2003). Politicians, social critics, and the public at large have a deep, underlying fear that welfare for the poor contributes to the breakdown of family by encouraging women to have more children, extended families to break apart, dependency to be handed down to future generations, single mothers not to marry, and so on.

But the conclusion that welfare *causes* such problems is not supported by the evidence. If it were true that welfare causes or at least perpetuates poverty, you'd expect people living in states with generous welfare payments to show a lower incentive to work and to take a longer amount of time to escape poverty than people living in states with relatively meager welfare payments. Research, however, points out that in the states with more generous payments, women do not spend more time on welfare and are just as likely as women in lower-paying states to seek employment (Vartanian & McNamara, 2000). Furthermore, higher welfare payments actually hasten the escape from poverty for many single-parent families (Butler, 1996).

Does drawing welfare benefits encourage single women to have more babies? Cross-culturally, the answer is "no." Countries that have more generous public assistance programs than we have in the United States—such as Canada and many countries in Scandinavia and western Europe—have lower rates of out-of-wedlock births. Even in the United States, the birthrate of women on welfare is considerably lower than that of the general population (Rank, 1994). In fact, the longer a woman remains on welfare, the less likely she is to give birth. The economic, social, and psychological situations in which women on welfare usually find themselves are not particularly conducive to desiring or having many children. Becoming pregnant and having a child are perceived as making the situation worse, not better, by making it more difficult to ultimately get off welfare—and getting off welfare is something most recipients want. A study by the National Academy of Sciences found that the overwhelming majority of births to single women are unplanned; 70% of births to never married women in general and over 85% of births to unmarried teenagers are unintended (cited in Sandefur, 1996). These figures suggest that most welfare pregnancies are not based on conscious decisions to increase financial benefits.

Family Life on Welfare

In a culture like ours that equates self-worth and success with self-sufficiency, going on public assistance can be a humiliating experience. The psychological strains and stresses simply of being on welfare inevitably influence family relationships. Each type of benefit—housing subsidies, cash assistance, food stamps, Medicaid, and so on—comes with its own set of rules and regulations that recipients must follow if they wish to remain eligible (Dujon, Gradford, & Stevens, 1995). About one quarter of welfare recipients are denied benefits because they fail to comply with welfare rules (Hays, 2003). A woman can be removed from the welfare rolls if she is found to be living with a man without being married to him. If welfare recipients fail to observe child care norms or are believed to use more physical punishment than social workers deem desirable, they can be charged with child neglect or abuse and lose their children to foster care (Gans, 1995).

People who receive public assistance often find they are treated with disdain when they come into contact with the various bureaucrats who act as gatekeepers to government programs (Gilliom, 2001). Surveillance is a big part of the lives of recipients, who fear they could be declared ineligible and have their benefits cut off if they don't yield to caseworkers' demands.

Welfare payments are usually not sufficient to cover ordinary family expenditures. A study of welfare recipients from major urban areas in Arizona, Illinois, Maryland, Pennsylvania, and Texas found that the average amount of benefits for a family of three with no other source of income is between $187 and $430 a month, a figure that falls well short of providing enough money to pay household expenses (Rangarajan & Razafindrakoto, 2004). In one community, the welfare benefits for a family of three are $354 a month, but it costs, on average, $904 per month to purchase day care for two children (Hays, 2003). After covering all her other expenses, one 51-year-old divorced mother of two teenage daughters had to provide food, toiletries, and clothing for her family on what amounted to $4 per person per day. She sums up her life:

> This is probably about the lowest point in my life, and I hope I never reach it again. Because this is where you're just up against a wall. You can't make a move. You can't buy anything that you want for your home. You can't go on a vacation. You can't take a weekend off and go and see things because it costs too much. And it's just such a waste of a life. (quoted in Rank, 1994, p. 52)

Clearly, trying to lead anything close to a proud and normal life while on welfare is extremely difficult. Recipients often have to depend on family, friends, boyfriends, or absent fathers to help make ends meet. Some cut back on their own food intake so they can buy shoes for their children; others hire professional shoplifters to get coats so their children can go to school in the winter (DeParle, 1997).

But rather than being stereotypical "welfare cheats," the vast majority of these individuals bend the rules not as a get-rich-quick scheme but out of financial necessity (Hays, 2003). Many skirt the system by working "off the books" (Economic Roundtable, 2005). One study of 50 welfare mothers in Chicago found that all of them supplemented their welfare checks fraudulently, with either under-the-table work or money from friends and relatives, and none reported this income to the welfare office as they are required to do (Edin & Jencks, 1992). As one welfare recipient put it, "We weren't trying to beat the system. We were just trying to make it" (quoted in Penner, 1995, p. 11).

Moreover, wages earned from employment can cover even less than welfare payments. The costs of *going* to work—for transportation, clothes, and above all child care—are so high that the income of a poor single mother who works full-time is likely to be the same as, or less than, the income of a mother on welfare (Edin & Lein, 1997). So it's not that people on welfare don't want to work. Indeed, most anticipate a boost in self-esteem and social standing from working (Hays, 2003). It's that the available jobs often pay too little, demand too much, and offer few opportunities for advancement (Oliker, 1995). What's more, work income is also less stable than welfare income—employers who offer low-wage jobs can seldom guarantee their workers full-time hours, and the available jobs are often incompatible with parenting. Workers must leave their children in care that may be untrustworthy. Because their jobs rarely offer benefits like sick leave or paid vacation days, it is next to impossible for them to take time off to care for sick children who can't go to school.

Another popular stereotype of welfare parents is that they are neglectful of their children. Most, however, value their children highly. They anticipate them eagerly and believe they can be good parents, even in difficult circumstances (Edin & Kefalas, 2005). In some studies, mothers on welfare speak fondly of the way their children have enriched their lives and the pride they take in their children's accomplishments (Rank, 1994). Like most parents, they worry about their children's well-being and talk about their efforts to do what is best for them. They try to teach their children the importance of education as a means of becoming independent so they won't have to rely on public assistance when they become adults. Of course, most also feel a tremendous amount of frustration over not being able to meet their children's physical, social, and educational needs.

The Ideals and Realities of Welfare Reform

Through the years, state and federal legislators have tried to improve the welfare system, but to no avail. Finally, in 1996, President Clinton signed into law the Personal Responsibility and Work Opportunity Reconciliation Act, an unprecedented welfare reform bill designed to reduce poor people's reliance on government aid and "end welfare as we know it." This law marked the end of the federal government's 60-year commitment to aiding the neediest families.

The new welfare system got rid of the Aid to Families with Dependent Children (AFDC) program, which provided cash assistance directly to poor families with children for an unlimited amount of time. It was replaced with the Temporary Assistance to Needy Families (TANF) program, which imposed work requirements and placed time limits on receiving cash assistance. Instead of giving the money directly to needy families, TANF provides "block grants" to each state and the state then decides how to spend it. In addition, the welfare reform bill slashed the food stamps program and made other cuts that concentrated on legal immigrants, the disabled, and the elderly poor (Corcoran, Danziger, Kalil, & Seefeldt, 2000). The law does require states to provide child care for working mothers, but only for a year after they get off the welfare rolls (Hays, 2003).

In addition to the obvious financial motivation behind this massive effort to cut the welfare rolls, another purpose was to promote marriage, parenting within marriage, and "responsible" fatherhood—that is, paternal support (Carbone, 2000; Curran & Abrams, 2000). To ensure more responsible fatherhood, guidelines now require that mothers comply with measures to identify the father of their children before they can qualify

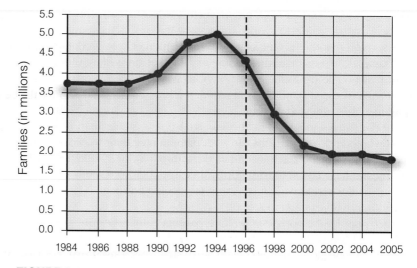

FIGURE 6.4   Temporary Assistance for Needy Families (TANF),*
1984 to 2005

Source: U.S. Bureau of the Census, 2008, table 546.

*Called Aid to Families with Dependent Children prior to 1996.

for benefits. If mothers do not cooperate with paternal identification efforts, states are required to reduce their benefits. States also now have greater authority to collect paternal support from parents who are delinquent in their child support payments.

One of the assumptions behind welfare reform is that making work mandatory will teach welfare recipients important work values and habits and make poor single mothers models of these values for their children. Reformers were motivated by the common belief that all welfare mothers need is a little push "to get them out to work, to keep them from having children they [can't] afford to raise, to get them married and safely embedded in family life" (Hays, 2003, p. 4). As one law professor put it: "welfare reforms are premised on the belief that a working mother as role model is more important for poor children than whatever they may gain from a homebound but publicly supported mother" (quoted in Carbone, 2000, p. 207). The underlying idea is that hard work will lead to the moral and financial rewards of family self-reliance. Thus when it was enacted, welfare reform was more than a set of policies aimed at managing poor people; it served as a symbol of cultural beliefs about how we all should act (Hays, 2003).

Has it worked? Many people hail welfare reform as a great success, focusing principally on two outcomes: the massive reduction of the number of people receiving cash assistance and the increase in employment rates of poor single mothers (Parrott & Sherman, 2006).

The number of families receiving public assistance has dropped dramatically since welfare reforms went into effect (Figure 6.4). Some of the people who left welfare have, in fact, found sustained employment (Duncan & Chase-Lansdale, 2001). However, more than half of the caseload decline in the first decade after welfare reform reflects a decline in the extent to which TANF serves families that are poor enough to qualify for aid rather than to an increase in the number of families who no longer need the assistance. Indeed, in the 1990s, the poverty rate decreased by only 14% (U.S. Bureau of the Census, 2007) and has increased significantly ever since. Moreover, the number of children living in "deep" poverty—that is below *half* the poverty line—has increased substantially in recent years (Parrott & Sherman, 2006).

There has also been a troubling increase in "disconnected families"—poor single mothers who are jobless, receive no public aid, and don't live with others who work or receive cash income support (Fremstad, 2003; Parrott & Sherman, 2006). Members in these families are more likely than those in other poor families to skip meals, be disabled, and have low education levels.

Rather than address the needs of these seriously disadvantaged families, the government has moved in the opposite direction. States are under increasing pressure to reduce the welfare rolls even further. In 2006, the federal government enacted new rules that require states to increase the number of welfare recipients who work or risk having their welfare block grants reduced (Pear, 2006).

The current welfare system can work only if people on welfare have viable employment opportunities, and if those opportunities provide a sufficient wage to lift them out of poverty (McCrate & Smith, 1998). Indeed, one of the best predictors of whether women will exit welfare and stay off it permanently is finding employment within a year (Vartanian & McNamara, 2000). However, many studies of state-run welfare-to-work programs show little or no change at all in unemployment rates and only small increases in earnings, which are due primarily to working longer hours, not earning higher wages. In one study, only 16% of participants in a welfare-to-work program were able to find a job within the mandated time (Brush, 2000). Most women who leave welfare go to work in low-paying jobs that offer no benefits (Corcoran et al., 2000). Only 1 in 4 is employed full-time 5 years after leaving welfare (Cancian & Meyer, 2000). These individuals also switch jobs frequently. Only 17% were employed by the same company for more than 3 years. Most had new employers every 6 to 9 months (Economic Roundtable, 2000).

Because of time limits, millions of these women who do work are forced to accept low wages in menial labor jobs with poor hours, no benefits, and no flexibility (Hays, 2003). A study conducted by the Economic Roundtable (2003) tracked welfare parents in Los Angeles who had entered the labor force between 1998 and 2001. The researchers found that about half had no earnings in 2001, and 78% had earnings that placed them below the poverty line. Other researchers have found that former welfare recipients who work earn on average $400 less a year than they would have received had they stayed on welfare (cited in DeParle, 1999). And more than half the women who leave the welfare rolls when they can support themselves with jobs eventually return to welfare because their jobs end or because they aren't earning enough to make ends meet (Harris, 1996).

It's estimated that, at best, only 30% of the decline in welfare rolls represents "successful" and permanent escape from poverty (Hays, 2003). Rather than pride and self-sufficiency, many families who have left welfare find themselves in greater need of assistance:

> One-half are sometimes without enough money to buy food. One-third have to cut the size of meals. Almost half find themselves unable to pay their rent or utility bills. Many more families are turning to locally funded services, food banks, churches, and other charities for aid. Many of those charities are already overburdened. In some locales, homeless shelters and housing assistance programs are closing their doors to new customers, food banks are running out of food, and other charities are being forced to tighten their eligibility requirements. (p. 227)

A great deal of evidence suggests that the country's poorest families have been driven deeper into poverty by welfare reform. In the first 2 years after reforms went into effect, the poorest 20% of U.S. families lost an average of $577 a year (Center on Budget and Policy Priorities, 1999). Typically, these families had gotten off welfare but had not made up lost benefits with wages. In many cases they still face the same problems they faced while on welfare: violent neighborhoods, bare cupboards, absent fathers, depression, and drugs (DeParle, 1999). Moreover, many parents, while meeting the goals of welfare reform, either have unstable health insurance or have become uninsured (Holl, Slack, & Stevens, 2005). Close to 1 million poor parents nationwide lost their Medicaid health insurance coverage as a consequence of welfare reform. These parents were forced off welfare and had to take low-paying jobs without health benefits. Those who did find jobs that offered insurance were often unable to pay the premiums (cited in Pear, 2000). And it's estimated that about a million additional toddlers and preschoolers are in day care—which in many cases is of poor quality—as a result of welfare revisions that require their mothers to work (Lewin, 2000b).

■ TAKING A CLOSER LOOK ■

Women and Welfare

The reformed welfare system operates under the assumption that most single mothers on welfare are capable of sustained employment. Yet research has found that there are two types of welfare recipients. One group tends to be older and better educated and to have more work experience. These women tend to be short-term recipients who, on average, remain on welfare less than 2 years (Carbone, 2000). People in this group tend to be able to get off welfare on their own.

The second group consists of long-term beneficiaries. Not surprisingly, these women aren't particularly employable. In general, they are not well-educated (many haven't graduated from high school) and have little or no work experience (Carbone, 2000). In short, there is likely to be a significant gap between the skills demanded by employers and those offered by these welfare recipients (Corcoran et al., 2000).

Disabled or battered women are at especially high risk of failing under the new system. Welfare recipients with low literacy skills tend to be placed in low-paying jobs and denied access to further education that could help them secure better jobs (Rivera, 2000). Battering and its consequences can easily delay or derail efforts to enter the labor market. For example, disfiguring or disabling injuries or the need to appear in court to obtain a protective order from the abuser can seriously interfere with a battered woman's ability to attend work or training programs. In one study of 122 women in a job-readiness program designed to help welfare recipients make the transition into the workforce, nearly half had experienced violence in their current or most recent relationship (Brush, 2000).

According to one legal expert, the current system "has the potential—particularly when the economy worsens, time limits expire, and less generous states take a meat-ax to what is left of the protections it offers—to make poor children's material circumstances substantially worse" (Carbone, 2000, p. 207). It is realities like these that make some observers pessimistic about the long-term consequences of this latest overhaul of the welfare system.

Finally, welfare reform may actually help to reshape the image of motherhood—from one of domesticity to one of working parenthood (Carbone, 2000). While some welfare-reliant single mothers express optimism about the benefits of moving from welfare to work, many also express grave concerns about finding adequate and affordable child care for their children and about their own ability to properly supervise them the way full-time mothers can.

Initially, they may have been strongly oriented toward improving the financial well-being of their children and were willing to work long hours and be away from home to do so. But many soon find that they must choose between work and family care. The situation represents an impossible bind. If they put their young children first and decide to stay at home with them, they will lose their benefits; if they abide by welfare regulations and find employment, they lose "quality time" with their children (Scott, Edin, London, & Mazelis, 2001). The public will eventually realize that inadequate day care and after school care or the lack of flexible family leave policies affects poor families as much as middle-class families. Putting so many poor mothers to work may pave the way toward a fundamental rethinking of society's responsibility for children.

Poverty and Housing

It is hard to overestimate the importance of safe, decent, affordable housing in the lives of families. It keeps children in school and adults on the job. It allows upwardly mobile families to save money so they can someday buy a house of their own and keeps downwardly mobile families from having to turn to foster care or homeless shelters (DeParle, 1996). The cost of housing breaks the budgets of low-income families or crowds them into unsafe, dilapidated, and sometimes violent neighborhoods, which are usually some distance from good schools and good jobs.

According to the government, housing is considered "affordable" if it costs 30% of a family's income. The poorest 20% of income earners spends about 78% of their wages on housing. By comparison, the wealthiest 20% of earners spends only 19% of their income on housing (cited in Swartz, 2007). In 2006, the nationwide median housing wage—the minimum amount of money a person would have to make to afford rental housing—was $16.31 an hour, close to 3 times the federal minimum wage at that point and a 6% increase over the 2004 amount. Depending on the state, between 36 and 60% of residents are unable to afford fair market rent for a two-bedroom apartment. Nowhere in the United States does a full-time, minimum-wage job provide enough income to afford adequate housing (National Low Income Housing Coalition, 2006).

As rising wealth at the top end of society drives up housing prices, the poor have been left unable to afford decent housing and are without federal and state programs to help them (Shipler, 2004). So it's not surprising that many families have no place to live. No one knows for sure exactly how many homeless people live in the United States. The National Alliance to End Homelessness (2007) estimates that at a given point in time there are more than 740,000 homeless people in the United States, 44% of whom are unsheltered. But because people move in and out of homelessness or are homeless for a short period of time, it's estimated that somewhere between 2.3 and 3.5 million people experience some type of homelessness over the course of a year. According to a 2006 survey of 27 major American cities, 51% of homeless people are single men, 17% are single women, 30% are families with children, and 2% are children on their own. Of the homeless, 13% are employed and less than a third are substance abusers (U.S. Conference of Mayors, 2006). Families with small children are the fastest-growing segment of the homeless population.

In addition to the "official" homeless, countless thousands of other families are one catastrophe away from homelessness—one fire, one broken water pipe, one collapsed roof, one injury, or one job loss. And the families living doubled or tripled up with strained relatives or friends in cramped apartments are always an argument, fight, or ill-conceived comment away from being kicked back out to the streets.

Many families become homeless because of a specific crisis. Others become homeless when a mother takes her children and moves out of an abusive relationship. What they all have in common, though, is that their move into homelessness is less of a fall than a side step. These are families already living on the edge of survival. Most homeless families are poor well before they become homeless, often living month-to-month until they can no longer sustain a residence.

Homeless parents must deal with a double predicament: They face the disruptive and traumatizing effects of losing a home while simultaneously acknowledging that their capacity to provide protection and support and to respond to their children's needs has been eroded. Studies of homeless parents living in shelters have found that most of them feel that living in the shelter seriously hurts their children. Homeless children are often ridiculed at school or suffer the pressure of keeping their home life a secret (Arrighi 1997). The loss of privacy that comes from parenting in public diminishes a parent's confidence, not to mention his or her relationship with the children. In shelters that are noisy, chaotic, and stressful, there is a lot of wasted time, unsupervised activity, and little opportunity to establish a family routine. One observer described the shelter experience as divided into "time that is mealtime and time that is not mealtime" (quoted in Hausman & Hammen, 1993, p. 360). However, in those shelters that are small, quiet, and orderly, there can be a lot of nurturing, safety, and support, making effective parenting less difficult.

Whatever the conditions at a shelter, when parenting is visible and public, it becomes open to criticism, particularly in such an emotionally fragile environment. Conflict between mothers is a common characteristic of many homeless shelters (Hausman & Hammen, 1993). Mothers may begin to distance themselves from the unruly behaviors of their children in an attempt to avoid blame from other adults. Under such conditions, parents, and ultimately children, can become irritable and demoralized. Homeless families tend to lack the emotional resources that might be drawn on in bad times (Bassuk, Rubin, & Lauriat, 1986). Indeed, a lifetime of disappointing, harmful, and traumatic experiences has taught many homeless mothers to be suspicious of everyone—strangers, acquaintances, and relatives—and reluctant to trust anyone, particularly with the care of children (Browne, 1993). Such isolation contributes to the lonely strain of homelessness and interferes with healthy parent–child relationships.

Unstable housing is particularly hard on children. Poor children whose families do not receive government rent subsidies are more likely to be malnourished and underweight than other children. Some poor families are displaced so often that their children attend half a dozen schools in a single year. The head of foster care in the District of Columbia estimates that as many as half the city's foster children could be reunited with their parents if their families had stable housing (cited in DeParle, 1996).

In addition, homeless children suffer higher rates of depression, anxiety, and behavioral problems than other children. In a comparative study of homeless and housed children, researchers estimated that half of all homeless children demonstrate at least one developmental problem (maladaptive behavior, academic deficiency, emotional problems, and so on), compared to 16% of housed children (Rafferty & Rollins, 1989). Some homeless children are able to succeed despite their desperate conditions, but the vast majority will suffer well into their adulthood. Once again, we see the pervasive and long-lasting effects of social class on family life and people's future prospects.

WHAT DOES IT ALL MEAN?

Economic factors—from the amount of money coming in to the day-to-day management of finances and major purchasing decisions—affect virtually every aspect of family life. When a family doesn't know how it will pay this month's rent or where its next meal is coming from or whether there will be a warm place to sleep that night, that family will have a difficult time being comfortable, happy, and satisfied. When economic foundations are weak, the emotional bonds that tie a family together can easily crumble.

As we've seen in this chapter, the most devastating effects of poverty are felt by the youngest members of society. Experiences with poverty early in life are likely to lead to a series of other disadvantages and eventually culminate in long-term economic and social disadvantages. The current modifications to the welfare system are not likely to improve and may even worsen the economic circumstances or life chances of these children.

Meanwhile, wealth has become increasingly concentrated at the opposite end of the economic spectrum. As the rich get richer, the poorer segments of the population suffer. Even many middle-class people in the United States are experiencing a decline in their standard of living.

Over the years, numerous strategies to reduce poverty and its effects, such as raising the minimum wage, establishing "living wage" policies, and increasing funding for Head Start programs, have been proposed. However, most have failed to receive widespread social or political support. Finally, in 2007, after 10 years of debate, Congress approved a measure that will gradually increase the minimum wage from $5.15 an hour to $7.25 an hour over

2 years. It's unclear, however, whether this increase will do much to close the income gap. In those states that already have a higher minimum wage than the federal level, millions of workers still fall into poverty (Uchitelle, 2006b).

In our strongly individualistic and capitalist culture, it will be difficult to alter attitudes and policies regarding income distribution. But what we may be coming to see is that the indirect costs of poverty (unemployment, nonmarital and early pregnancy, crime, lack of education, and so on) are much greater than are the direct costs of implementing programs to help low-income and poverty-level families.

As you think about the information provided in this chapter, consider these questions:

1. What do you think are the most important ways in which social class influences family life in the United States?

2. How would you characterize your own social class background? Describe the ways you think your class background influenced your childhood. How would your life have been different if you had been born into a different social class?

3. Do you consider the United States to be the "land of opportunity," where people succeed if they try hard enough, or a society that is structured to give some people advantages at the expense of others? Explain.

4. What do you think our society's response to economically disadvantaged families should be? Should we limit government programs to help the poor to force them to become financially independent, or should we expand these programs to help these families? Are these the only two choices?

SUMMARY

■ Stratification is a ranking of entire groups of people that perpetuates unequal rewards and life chances in society. Social class is the primary means of stratification in many societies, including the United States.

■ Social class is more than an economic position; it is a way of life that affects how families experience every facet of their lives.

■ The official U.S. poverty line, the dollar cutoff point that defines the amount of income necessary for subsistence living, may actually be set too low,

thereby underestimating the proportion of families that suffer financially.

■ Nowhere are the stresses of class stratification more apparent than among the poorest of U.S. families where despair and insecurity are features of everyday life.

■ Reforms in the U.S. welfare system over the past decade have reduced the number of families receiving public assistance, but they have also worsened the lives of the nation's poorest families, especially those run by single mothers.

Go to the Online Learning Center at **www.mhhe.com/newman1** to test your knowledge of the chapter concepts and key terms.

KEY TERMS

cultural capital   143

downward mobility   146

feminization of poverty   150

juvenilization of poverty   151

middle-class families   135

new rich   143

poor families   136

poverty line   150

social class   135

social mobility   135

stratification   135

upper-class families   135

working-class families   136

SEE FOR YOURSELF

Even people whose income is well above the poverty line can sometimes find it difficult to make ends meet. Imagine a family of four living in your hometown. Suppose that both parents work, that one child is 7 years old and in elementary school, and that the other is 3 and must be cared for during the day.

Make a list of all the goods and services this family needs to function at a minimum subsistence level—that is, at the poverty line. Be as complete as possible. Consider food, clothing, housing, transportation, medical care, child care, entertainment, and so on.

Estimate the minimum monthly cost of each item. If you currently live on your own and must pay these expenses yourself, use those figures as a starting point (but remember that you must estimate for a family of four). If you live in a dorm or at home, ask your parents (or anyone else who pays bills) what their expenses are for such goods and services. Call the local day care center to see what it charges for child

care. Go to the local supermarket and compute the family food budget. For those expenses that aren't divided on a monthly basis (for example, the purchase of clothing and household appliances), estimate the yearly cost and divide by 12.

Once you have estimated the total monthly expenses, multiply by 12 to get the subsistence budget for the family of four. If your estimate is higher than the government's official poverty line (around $20,444), what sorts of items could you cut out of the budget for the family to be defined as officially poor and therefore eligible for certain government programs? By looking for ways to cut expenses from your minimal subsistence budget, you will get a good sense of what everyday life in poverty looks like.

Describe the quality of life of a hypothetical family that makes too much to be officially poor and too little to sustain a comfortable life. What sorts of things would they be forced to do without that a more affluent family might simply take for granted (for example, annual vacations, pocket money, a second car, eating out once a week)? What would be the impact of poverty on the lives of the children? How will the family's difficulty in meeting its basic subsistence needs translate into access to opportunities (education, jobs, health care) for the children later in life?

Note: In order to shorten the amount of time necessary to complete this exercise, your instructor may have you work in groups of three or four.

Source: This exercise is adapted from M. V. Miller, 1985, and D. Newman, 2006.

7

Love, Sexuality, and Relationship Formation

Do you ever wish we could go back to the good old days, when all people had to do to find a romantic partner was identify someone they found moderately interesting or attractive, nervously approach, and ask that person to go to dinner or a movie or the Senior Prom? If they hit it off, they'd go on more dates and eventually they'd become a couple. This method wasn't foolproof. Indeed, it could be downright painful. And a lot of people never got the hang of it. But there was something gratifying about building a relationship from scratch.

When I asked a class of mine a few years back to describe what students on our campus did on dates, they actually laughed at me. One student rolled her eyes and in the most condescending tone I'd ever heard come out of someone under 20, said "Uh . . . hellooo . . . no one dates around here."

To many single people these days, the old method of dating and courtship seems hopelessly quaint, time consuming, and inefficient. Not surprisingly, many people have turned to new methods to help them meet others:

- Busy professionals who don't have time to develop a relationship the old-fashioned way are "speed dating" (sometimes called "predating"). At organized events, an individual will meet up to 30 potential dates by greeting a new prospect every few minutes, engaging in some small talk, and moving on to the next person when a bell rings. The actual matching process occurs after the event, so people don't have to face rejection in person (Barker, 2002). Speed dating is now a part of popular culture and has been depicted in films such as *Hitch* and *The 40 Year Old Virgin*.

- Personal ads and online dating services, such as Match.com, eCRUSH, and eHarmony, have exploded into a $500 million a year business (Leonhardt, 2006a). Many sites serve the needs of a specific population segment, like Jdate.com (for Jewish singles) and CatholicSingles.com (Rosen, 2006). Countless "niche" sites accommodate individuals with specific needs, such as the hearing impaired, pet lovers, diabetics, people with sexually transmitted diseases, overweight people, or body builders. Each site claims to have the most effective, "scientific," formula for bringing compatible singles together, though one study of a popular site found that for every match that resulted in a marriage, 999 "compatible" matches did not (Thompson, Zimbardo, & Hutchinson, 2005).

- In major urban areas in the northeastern United States, museums, libraries, and bookstores—not the sorts of places that leap to mind when you think of romantic locations for singles to meet—have become trendy hotspots on the contemporary dating scene. These establishments offer a variety of events including formal debates, late-night museum prowls, academic lectures, book readings, even spelling bees, giving young, intelligent singles an opportunity to meet others like them. This new form of dating, dubbed "intellidating," has grown in popularity among urban professionals who've become disillusioned with bars and clubs and would prefer to meet people in a more intellectual and less superficial environment (Faiola, 2007).

Clearly cultural and technological shifts have changed the way people form relationships. But one thing has remained the same: We want closeness and intimacy with someone special. We expect these relationships to provide us with a great deal of joy and recognize that they may serve as a prelude to marriage.

To understand the role of intimate relationships in family life, we need to examine how they develop and what personal and social factors influence them. This chapter looks at the process through which these relationships unfold, paying particular attention to dating, courtship, and mate selection. But first we must look at the broader cultural contexts of love, romance, and sexuality—the defining characteristics of intimate relationships.

THE CULTURAL PROMINENCE OF INTIMACY

Intimacy is the state of being emotionally and affectionately close to another person. It exists in all sorts of relationships, such as those between friends or between parents and children. In this chapter I will focus primarily on the intimacy of romantic and sexual relationships.

■ **intimacy**
The state of being emotionally and affectionately close to another person.

As we've just seen, there's a thriving industry devoted to bringing people together and keeping them together. Add singles' bars, singles' apartment complexes, daytime talk shows, church-based singles groups, and personals sections of newspapers to the mix and you've got the makings of a nationwide obsession with intimacy.

Most of us learn early on that these relationships are the standard against which we judge the quality and happiness of our entire lives. Cultural images and media messages tell us that we can't be truly fulfilled without falling in love, being sexually satisfied, and having a long-term relationship with someone. As one author put it, "as long as you can say 'we,' everything is somehow all right" (Lefkowitz, 2007, p. 100).

Yet dramatic social changes over the past few decades have made relationships confusing and problematic. Young people today become sexually active earlier than ever before. Forms of intimacy once considered unacceptable—heterosexual and homosexual cohabitation, for example—have become more commonplace and acceptable. At the same time, marriages and other long-term relationships are far from permanent. More people are choosing not to marry or are waiting longer to get married. In addition, the darker side of intimacy—physical abuse, sexual violence, and sexually transmitted diseases—is now impossible to ignore.

The intense need for intimacy, coupled with all these potential difficulties, has increased the demands we make on our intimate partners. Most people are inclined to enter a long-term relationship expecting their partner to fulfill all their sexual, emotional, social, intellectual, and economic needs. With this much riding on one person, it's not surprising that so many people spend so much time thinking about how to attract and keep the right partner; how to add spice, vigor, and longevity to a sagging relationship; or how to end a relationship that's not working so the search for a more fulfilling partner can begin.

Romantic Love

To most of us, love is a sentimental, magical emotion that defies logical explanation. We don't really know how or why we fall in love. Most of us would have a difficult time describing the point in time when we first knew we were in love. And for the most part we don't *want* such things explained. Too much analysis defiles the wonderful, mysterious, and at times gleefully irrational essence of the love experience. Who wants to hear about neurotransmitters, scent-signaling pheromones, major histocompatibility complexes, changes in the nerve fibers of the frontal cortex, or the activation of the

(Text continues on page 170.)

Incurably Romantic

crepancy between reality and these cultural images. (quoted in Stehle, 1985, pp. 237–238)

On these pages, we see the images of people with physical or mental handicaps who have been able to overcome significant pain and anguish—not to mention narrowly defined cultural standards of physical appearance—to establish warm, caring, long-lasting romantic relationships. As you examine these photos, note your own responses to the people depicted. How do these couples affect your ideas about intimacy? In what ways are they similar to or different from relationships among able-bodied persons?

A s you are well aware, when it comes to intimate relationships we live in a culture that places tremendous value on physical attractiveness. As one sociologist put it,

> [We are all] surrounded by cultural messages that not only is a beautiful body somehow connected to a beautiful person, but . . . that the notions of love, romance, and sexuality are the province of normal and preferably beautiful bodies and people. Couples in love are conventionally described as "radiant," "lovely," "young," "healthy," and expected to be whole. These are appealing, even romantic notions, and only when we look more closely at the lives of real people do we notice the dis-

hypothalamus that scientists associate with love (Anderson & Middleton, 2006; Kluger, 2008)? Nevertheless, a scholarly examination of love provides us with important insight into common behavior patterns and identifies the role that social forces play in the way we define and experience love.

Webster's Unabridged Dictionary defines love as "attraction or desire for a person who arouses delight or admiration and elicits feelings of tenderness or sympathy." In everyday life, we typically don't use such concepts when we describe love. Indeed, common descriptions of love often include a variety of feelings that can seem more like aching discomfort than an enjoyable emotional experience. The early stages of love are frequently associated with uncertainty, ambivalence, obsessive preoccupation, and jealousy (Hendrick & Hendrick, 1992a). Descriptions of full-blown love can sometimes sound like descriptions of mental disorders—we're "madly" in love, "wild" for a person, or "crazy" about someone. Sometimes love sounds like physical pain, as in this characterization:

> I have trouble concentrating. . . . I experience heart palpitations and rapid breathing. . . . I experience physical sensations—cold hands, butterflies in my stomach, tingling spine. I have insomnia. I can't think of anyone else but my lover. (quoted in Carr, 1988, p. 53)

Sociologists are inclined to use a much more sophisticated description of love:

> Love is a relatively enduring bond where a small number of people are affectionate and emotionally committed to each other, define their collective well-being as a major goal, and feel obliged to provide care and practical assistance for each other. People who love each other also usually share physical contact; they talk to each other frequently and cooperate in some routine tasks of daily life. (Cancian, 1993, p. 205)

Moreover, sociologists are likely to distinguish between different types of love. For instance, **passionate love** refers to the intense, sexually thrilling feelings of attraction that mark the beginning of a relationship. **Companionate love,** on the other hand, refers to the quiet, predictable affection that people experience later in a relationship (Hendrick & Hendrick, 1992b).

What makes one situation between two people who care for each other and revel in each other's company a "friendly relationship" and another a "love relationship"? At one level, the answer lies in the way the two define their own relationship. From a constructionist perspective, it is our subjective interpretation of a specific relationship that defines it as either friendship or love. Maybe you know two people who like to do things together, confide in each other constantly, and are very affectionate toward each other in public. To others, they look for all intents and purposes as if they're in love. Yet they say that they aren't—they're just very close friends. On the other hand, you may know two people who always seem to be at each other's throats—constantly arguing, fighting, and insulting each other. Yet they maintain they're very deeply in love and couldn't live without each other. Sometimes the people in a relationship might themselves have trouble defining it. You probably know of situations in which the two people in a couple have very different definitions of what their relationship is and very different expectations for its future.

With so much room for disagreement and uncertainty, it's easy to see why love relationships don't necessarily develop smoothly. Instead they "ebb and flow, with false

■ **passionate love**
The intense, sexually thrilling feelings of attraction that mark the beginning of a relationship.

■ **companionate love**
The quiet, predictable affection that people experience later in a relationship.

starts and continual negotiations and renegotiations" (Kollock & Blumstein, 1988, p. 481). In the early stages of a relationship, when a clear definition has yet to emerge, a little vagueness may be tolerable or even enticing. Later on, however, ambiguity can become frustrating. Some may tackle the matter boldly and directly by simply asking, "Do you love me?" or "What exactly is going on in this relationship?" Others search for signs and clues of the other person's affections, seeking out the opinions of third parties, or dropping subtle hints in an attempt to draw the other person's feelings into the open.

Cultural Variations in Love

One question that has long interested historians, anthropologists, and sociologists is whether romantic love is a universal emotion and whether long-term relationships require it. For most of human history, love has actually had little to do with marriage. Indeed, it probably seemed inconceivable that people would choose mates on the basis of such a fragile and irrational emotion. Couples were expected to put ties to God, parents, siblings, or other relatives ahead of their feelings for each other. In some cases, public displays of affection between spouses were considered improper, even blasphemous. That's not to say that people didn't fall in love. It's just that rarely in history has love been the main reason for getting married (Coontz, 2005).

■ GOING GLOBAL

What's Love Got to Do With It?

But what about the emotion of love itself? Anthropologists William Jankowiak and Edward Fischer (1992) examined cultural folklore and anthropologists' accounts of 166 societies around the world, seeking indicators of the existence of romantic love. They looked for stories of personal longing, use of love songs in romantic involvement, elopement because of mutual affection, and native accounts of passionate love.

On the basis of these indicators, they found that an overwhelming majority of the societies they studied (about 88%) recognized romantic love as a component in the formation of intimate relationships. One woman who lived in a hunting and gathering society in the Kalahari Desert of Africa differentiated between companionship and romance by contrasting her relationship with her husband and her lover. She used terms like "rich, warm, and secure" to describe her marriage. But in describing her lover she said, "When two people come together their hearts are on fire and their passion is very great" (quoted in Jankowiak & Fischer, 1992, p. 152). The researchers point out, however, that societies vary a lot in how common such passionate feelings are.

In another study (Levine, 1993), college students from 10 countries were asked this question: "Would you marry someone with all the right qualities if you didn't love them?" The researcher predicted that individuals from cultures that emphasized romantic love would be likely to answer "no" to such a question. Indeed, 86% of the U.S. respondents said they wouldn't consider marrying without love; a similar percentage of Brazilian students also said "no." But 75% of Pakistani and Indian students said they would have no problem marrying someone they didn't love.

In Pakistan and India, of course, arranged marriages based on family and economic considerations are still commonplace. In fact, as many as 80% of cultures outside the West employ arranged marriage to some degree (Pasupathi, 2002). To people from these countries, the reason Western marriages frequently fail is the inevitable

In cultures with a tradition of arranged marriage, weddings signify the uniting of two families, not just two individuals.

disappointment that sets in after romantic love wears off (Bumiller, 1992). In response to a question about whether she loved her husband, a 20-year-old married Indian woman once replied:

> That's a very difficult question. I don't know. This whole concept of love is very alien to us. We're more practical. I don't see stars, I don't hear little bells. But he's a very nice guy, I get along with him fine and I think I'm going to enjoy spending my life with him. Is that love? (quoted in Bumiller, 1992, p. 123)

You can see in this comment that this woman is fully aware of the ideal of romantic love—equating it with frivolous experiences like "seeing stars" and "hearing bells." Her perspective is not that romantic love doesn't exist but that it is not, and shouldn't be, the most important force behind a successful marriage.

Many Westerners think of arranged marriages as loveless and oppressive. Such a perception is reinforced by high-profile incidents, such as when a Turkish man living in Germany killed his sister after learning that she had abandoned an arranged marriage to a cousin (Homola, 2006). Yet even though romantic love is not a primary consideration, in most cases love grows in arranged marriages as partners get to know each other. Furthermore, arranged marriages can provide people with significant benefits. For instance, they tend to be more stable than marriages based solely on love. They also strengthen ties with other families, which in turn strengthens the social order of the community (Lee & Stone, 1980; Pasupathi, 2002).

We could also question just how different arranged marriages really are from marriages formed in cultures that place a high value on romantic love. Arguably, some of the innovations in finding mates that I described at the beginning of this chapter hint at an arranged system in which chance meetings are minimized. The difference is that technology, not other family members, plays the critical role in arranging matches. But reliance upon technology to arrange dates may also reflect the frustrations and ineffectiveness of relationship formation in cultures without arranged systems. In cultures where marriages are arranged, couples may experience disappointments and frustrations, but finding a partner and marrying isn't necessarily one of them.

According to some scholars, the presence and importance of romantic love are determined by the broader values and traditions of a given culture. Psychologists Karen Dion and Kenneth Dion (1996) found that romantic love is much more important as a basis for intimate relationships in individualist societies than in collectivist societies that emphasize group obligations. When a society celebrates individual freedom, people's intimate choices are likely to be driven by personal feelings and emotions.

In collectivist societies where romantic love is a less crucial aspect of relationships, people's intimate expectations can seem quite low to us. For example, intimate relationships in Japan are sometimes structured on a very different emotional foundation than we in the West would expect. To some Japanese, the strength of marriage is a matter of patience and low expectations. When asked if he loved his wife of 33 years, one man shared a typical sentiment: "Yeah, so-so, I guess. She's like air or water. You couldn't live without it, but most of the time, you're not conscious of its existence" (quoted in Kristof, 1996c, p. A1).

Ironically, low expectations may help to prevent marital breakups. Indeed, the Japanese divorce rate is slightly more than half that of the United States (U.S. Bureau of the Census, 2008). If two people in a couple discover they don't love each other or have nothing in common, they really don't have much reason for divorce because low emotional involvement is par for the course. Only about a third of the Japanese people in one survey would marry the same person if they had it to do over again (Kristof, 1996c).

The "Feminization" of Love

One question that has occupied the attention of sociologists for decades is whether men and women in the same society differ in their experiences with and expressions of love. Research—not to mention widespread cultural beliefs—suggests that U.S. women generally scrutinize their experiences of love more than men do, leading to more sensitivity and responsiveness to what is going on in their relationships (Holtzworth-Munroe & Jacobson, 1985). Men tend to be less reflective, falling in love more quickly and less intentionally than women. The difference starts early. One study found that during adolescence girls acquire more cultural lessons about romantic love, including the social norms that guide the expression of those feelings, than adolescent boys do (Simon, Eder, & Evans, 1992).

Women also usually experience and express a wider range of emotions in their romantic relationships, such as tenderness, fear, and sadness, and generally seem to be more expressive and affectionate than husbands—a difference that upsets many wives:

> Women tend to complain that their husbands do not care about their emotional lives and do not express their own feelings and thoughts. Women often say that they have to pull things out of their husbands and push them to open up. Men tend to respond either that they are open or that they do not understand what it is their wives want from them. Men often protest that no matter how much they talk it is never enough for their wives. (Thompson & Walker, 1989, p. 846)

■ **feminization of love**
The process by which love comes to be culturally defined in terms of feminine characteristics such as emotional expression, talking about feelings, vulnerability, warmth, and affection.

Perhaps, then, we shouldn't be surprised that the emotion of love itself has become *feminized*. The **feminization of love** means that love is culturally defined in terms of emotional expression, disclosure of feelings, vulnerability, warmth, and affection. We would all agree that these things ought to be present in love relationships, but they are all experiences typically associated with "femininity" in U.S. culture (Cancian, 1993).

Qualities we associate with masculinity—being independent, strong, competent, assertive, and unemotional—run counter to common ideas about love. Hence "masculine" expressions of love lean toward things like practical help, shared physical activities, time spent together, and sex (Cancian, 1993; Cancian & Oliker, 2000). Sociologist Francesca Cancian describes an interview with a 29-year-old man who said he feels especially close to his wife after they have had sex: "I don't talk to her very often, I guess, but somehow I feel we have really communicated after we have made love" (Cancian, 1987, p. 77). For many women, such an attitude is precisely the problem. To them, the only real communication—and therefore the true expression of love—is verbal communication. As one married mother put it:

> It is not enough that he supports us and takes care of us. I appreciate that, but I want him to share things with me. I need for him to tell me his feelings. (Tavris, 1992, p. 251)

In heterosexual relationships, feminized conceptions of love can reinforce men's power over women. The intimate talk about personal concerns and vulnerabilities that we associate with femininity (and love) requires a willingness to see oneself as weak and in need of support, further supporting the idea that men are the stronger, more powerful members of a couple. Furthermore, being responsive to the needs of others leads to giving up some control and, in a sense, being "on call" to provide care whenever it's needed (Cancian, 1993).

The fact that women have more close relationships than men, appear to care about those relationships more, and seem more skilled at expressing feelings doesn't mean that men are distant and unconcerned about love relationships. Indeed, contrary to popular belief, research shows that men and women are actually more similar than different when it comes to providing and responding to emotional support from partners (Bank, 1995; MacGeorge, Graves, Feng, Gillihan, & Burleson, 2004). But the stereotypically feminized definition of love that exists in our culture leads us to believe that women need love more than men do, even though research on the effect of love relationships on physical and psychological well-being shows that men need it at least as much as women do, if not more (Gove, Style, & Hughes, 1990; Umberson, Chen, House, Hopkins, & Slaten, 1996).

SEXUALITY

Sexuality is another crucial element of intimate relationships. Beyond being a procreative necessity, sexuality is often a principal criterion around which people judge the quality of their relationships.

The Biology of Sexuality

Most people, it seems, are inclined to see sexuality as a "natural" biological urge. It's true that our expression of affection for another person has obvious biological components and that human genital equipment is pretty much the same worldwide. So many people simply assume that we're all born with sexual drives that emerge at the appropriate stage of anatomical development.

But if human sexuality were purely biological, it would fall under the kind of strict hormonal control we see in the sexual behavior of other animals. The majority of non-human animals engage in no sexual behavior at all during most of the year. Mating occurs only when the male and female are fertile and such activity can lead to pregnancy. This period of time, known as *estrus,* drives instinctive sexual urges. If you've ever had a pet dog in heat, you know how profoundly its behavior can change during this season.

In humans, as in other mammals, the production of sperm and eggs is controlled by hormones. But human sexuality does not fall completely under hormonal control. We have no limited period of estrus. The average human female is able to conceive about once a month, and the average human adult male is more or less constantly fertile. Furthermore, humans regularly engage in sexual acts that can't lead to pregnancy (for instance, oral sex) or at times when conception is not possible and indeed not desired. They can even engage in sexual activity when they don't necessarily want to—and apparently do so fairly often. In one study of U.S. college students, 81% reported a recent episode in which they experienced ambivalence about engaging in sex with their dating partners, but about half did so anyway (O'Sullivan & Gaines, 1998).

We can conclude that human sexual activity has as much symbolic as biological significance. Our advanced cognitive abilities enable us to become sexually aroused by vivid mental imagery, explicit written descriptions of sex, or simply the sound of a lover's voice. We have sex for a variety of reasons other than procreation. Researchers recently asked a sample of 2,000 college students why they had sex. They came up with a total of 237 reasons that fell roughly into four categories: physical desire, "I wanted to achieve an orgasm"; goal attainment, "I wanted to break up a rival's relationship"; emotions, "I wanted to communicate at a deeper level"; and insecurity, "I wanted to boost my self-esteem" (Meston & Buss, 2007).

If sexuality were a universal biological drive, we'd also expect to see vast similarities across time and location in the ways people experience and express their sexual desires. But people differ dramatically in what they find attractive and arousing. Some people's sexual appetites are insatiable and indiscriminant; others' are highly particular and selective. For some, sex is a pleasurable physical activity that need not be connected to deep emotions; for others, sex is enjoyable only if it occurs within the context of a long-term love relationship.

Culture and Sexuality

You can see that exclusive reliance on a biological explanation for human sexuality falls short. Individual preferences play a big role, but so does culture. Most people in a given society follow the rules and expectations for sexual behavior. Some break them, but none can completely ignore them (Schwartz & Rutter, 1998). Throughout your life you've been receiving cultural messages telling you which sexual desires and behaviors are "normal" and which are "abnormal." These sexual customs and values are passed on by example, through informal and formal teaching and, with increasing frequency, through media images.

The United States, as you surely know, is a society preoccupied with sex and overflowing with cultural images and traditions that emphasize sexuality. Prime-time television shows regularly, and sometimes quite graphically, deal with topics like orgasms, oral sex, impotence, and the visual appearance of one's genitalia. Hard-core pornography is a mouse click away on the Internet. It's the rare consumer product, whether cars or chewing gum, that is marketed without some sexual innuendo or display (Schwartz, 2000).

All this attention is a far cry from the United States in the late 19th and early 20th centuries when sex was something people spoke about only in hushed, secret tones, or avoided entirely. For instance, people started using the terms "white meat" and "dark meat" to describe poultry so that they could avoid saying the names of the body parts "thighs" and "breasts" (Coontz, 1992).

By contrast, today most U.S. adults openly discuss and express opinions about sexual matters and seem to have a relatively matter-of-fact attitude toward sexuality. But this apparent comfort with sexual matters in modern society masks an underlying discomfort. Consider the frequent instances of local communities blocking contraceptive ads on television or parents' groups undermining sex education classes in schools (Schwartz, 2000). The irony is that the culture tacitly encourages early sexual experimentation while overtly forbidding it.

Different families also have their own values and teach widely divergent sexual lessons, even within the same culture. A teenager growing up in a sexually permissive culture but in a family in which sex outside marriage is considered reprehensible may have to suppress feelings of arousal or channel them into other pursuits. Teens raised in a home environment that encourages them to celebrate and act on their sexuality will likely have a much different experience. But neither the culture's nor the family's values unequivocally influence sexuality. Siblings raised in the same home environment can sometimes express their sexuality quite differently.

Cultural expectations regarding sexuality are most notable for their diversity. For example, one study found that 85% of Italians and 89% of Koreans consider sex an important part of their overall lives. However, only 55% of Chinese and 53% of Japanese respondents indicated that sex is important to them (Pfizer, Inc., 2002). In some societies, women have no concept of orgasm; in other societies, they become intensely and unabashedly aroused during sex (Schwartz & Rutter, 1998). In some cultures, sexual contact between people of the same sex is considered a heinous crime punishable by death. In many others, however, it is socially acceptable, at least for certain people at certain times. In ancient Greece, the truest love possible was that between an adult man and a much younger male (Coontz, 2005). Among the Sambia of Papua New Guinea, every adolescent male is expected to engage in sexual relationships with other men as part of his initiation into adulthood; as an adult he's expected to enter a heterosexual marriage.

The acceptability of heterosexual contact outside of marriage varies dramatically from society to society too. In Sweden and the Netherlands, premarital sex is accepted as normal, and both men and women are expected to be sexually experienced when they marry. But in most Islamic societies, virginity at the time of marriage is the norm, especially for women.

Even our ideas about sexual dysfunction are culturally determined. For example, the problem of "abnormal" sexual desire is the number one complaint bringing U.S. clients to sex therapists (Rosellini, 1992). At one end of the spectrum of "abnormality" is a condition called *hypoactive sexual desire disorder,* which the American Psychiatric Association identifies as a deficiency or absence of desire for sexual activity. The afflicted individual is not motivated to seek sexual stimuli and doesn't feel frustrated when deprived of the opportunity for sexual expression. She or he rarely initiates sexual activity and may only engage in it, reluctantly, when it is initiated by a partner. This "disorder" is believed to be about twice as common in women as in men.

At the other end of the spectrum are people, sometimes referred to as "sex addicts," who engage in *compulsive sexual behavior.* They tend to have obsessive thoughts about sex, have frequent sexual encounters, and masturbate compulsively (Gold & Heffner, 1998). Their sexual desire is considered too strong. Although no one knows for sure how many people suffer from this problem, experts estimate the prevalence to be roughly 5% of the adult population (Rosellini, 1992).

Here we have two identifiable sexual disorders that affect millions of people. But what do "too much" and "too little" sexual desire mean? How much sex should a "normal" person want? Obviously, what is considered normal sexual behavior varies widely from culture to culture. A "normal" amount of sexual activity among Chinese married couples, for example, is generally much lower than that among couples in the West, even though approval of pre- and extramarital sex is substantially higher in China (cited in Hatfield & Rapson, 1993).

Even within the same culture, one person's idea of normal sexual desire could easily contrast with another's. Researchers have repeatedly found that spouses have different estimates of the frequency and duration of sexual activity (Rubin, 1990). In a scene from the 1977 film *Annie Hall,* a split screen shows Alvie Singer (Woody Allen) and Annie (Diane Keaton) as unhappy lovers, each discussing the relationship with their respective therapists. Alvie complains that the couple *hardly ever* has sex anymore—only three times a week. On the opposite side of the screen, Annie complains that she feels like they're having sex *constantly*—as much as three times a week (Schwartz & Rutter, 1998).

In sum, sexuality—from what we want to what we do—is more than just biology. Human beings are constantly engaged in complex interactions with others. We all develop our own sexual scripts from the range of experiences we've had. These scripts are limited culturally as well—by what we're taught, what we expect, and what we believe to be permissible and correct.

Sexual Orientation

U.S. culture is characterized by **compulsory heterosexuality**—that is, a culture where heterosexuality is accepted as the normal, taken-for-granted mode of sexual expression. Cultural representations of virtually every aspect of intimate or family life—dating, marriage, childbearing, and so on—presume a world in which men are sexually and affectionately attracted to women, and women to men (Macgillivray, 2000). For instance, adolescent women going to a gynecologist for the first time can expect to receive information on birth control, reflecting the assumption that they will, at some point, have sex with men. In competitive figure skating, the "pairs" competition always consists of women paired with men (Wildman & Davis, 2002). The 2007 film *Blades of Glory* humorously satirized this basic assumption by depicting two men skating with one another in the pairs event.

Heterosexuals are socially privileged because their relationships and lifestyles are affirmed in every facet of the culture. As we saw in Chapter 1, legal marriage is the most obvious area in which social institutions bestow benefits on heterosexuals that are denied to others, such as insurance benefits, property and inheritance laws, and joint

■ **compulsory heterosexuality**
A characteristic of culture wherein heterosexuality is accepted as the normal, taken-for-granted mode of sexual expression.

Although homosexuality has gained more acceptance in society, the public display of same-sex affection can still raise eyebrows.

child custody. Heterosexual privileges include seeing positive media images of people with the same sexual orientation; not having to lie about who you are, what you do, and where you go; not having to worry about being fired from jobs because of your sexual orientation; receiving validation from your religious community; and being able to adopt children (Macgillivray, 2000, p. 304).

In such a culture, homosexuality is likely to be considered an aberration. Despite growing institutional acceptance of homosexuality—as reflected in things like the increasing numbers of gay characters on television and corporate policies granting financial benefits to same-sex partners of employees—public attitudes remain somewhat negative:

- A nationwide study found that although people in the United States seem to be showing increasing tolerance for and acceptance of people of different religions and different racial and ethnic groups, large numbers of people still commonly describe homosexuality as "sick," "immoral," "sinful," "perverted," and "abnormal" (Wolfe, 1998).

- According to the U.S. Defense Department's "Don't Ask, Don't Tell" policy, military personnel can't be asked about their sexual orientation and can't be discharged simply for being gay. However, engaging in sexual conduct with a member of the same sex is grounds for discharge. Gay soldiers in Iraq and Afghanistan reported that the official policy impedes their access to counseling and other support services (Frank, 2004). Even though the majority of military personnel believe that gays and lesbians should be able to serve openly (Zogby International, 2006), the chairman of the Joint Chiefs of Staff recently stated that he felt homosexuality was immoral and therefore supported a ban on gay men and women serving openly in the military (Knowlton, 2007).

■ The Boy Scouts of America prohibits openly gay men from being troop leaders, claiming that they do not provide the sorts of role models they want young scouts exposed to, and in 2000 the United States Supreme Court upheld this policy.

Psychiatrists in the 1950s and 1960s wrote extensively about homosexuals as perverts and degenerates who, with the appropriate therapy, could "learn" to be heterosexual. Their underlying assumption was that homosexuality is a choice, a preference, which is not influenced at all by a person's biological inheritance.

Even today, some religious organizations from a variety of traditions (Orthodox Jews, evangelical Protestants, Mormons, Roman Catholics, and others) are devoted to "converting" homosexuals through treatment counseling (Luo, 2007). One such organization, called Exodus International, proclaims that liberation from homosexuality "is possible through repentance and faith in Jesus Christ as Savior and Lord. We believe such freedom is increasingly experienced as the former homosexual matures through ongoing submissions to the Lordship of Christ and His Church" (quoted in Ponticelli, 1999, p. 157). However, a growing body of literature is providing evidence that homosexuality—indeed, sexual orientation in general—is not a choice but is anatomically or genetically determined.

Biological Influences on Sexual Orientation

In 1995 two scientists at the National Institutes of Health transplanted a single gene into the bodies of male fruit flies that caused them to display "courtship" behaviors with other male fruit flies (Zhang & Odenwald, 1995). Recently a biologist has found that a certain number of male sheep (about 8%) direct all their sexual attention to other male sheep and has concluded that such behavior is hard-wired into their brains before birth (Roselli, Resko, & Stormshak, 2006). Granted, the notion that a fruit fly or a sheep could be "homosexual" in the same sense that a human could be is an overstatement because sexual orientation is a human construction that includes not only physical desires but also psychological imagery and self-identity. Nevertheless, this research adds to the mounting body of evidence that sexual orientation is rooted in biology.

Almost two decades ago, a California neuroscientist performed autopsies on the brains of men and women of known sexual orientation (LeVay, 1991). He found that a tiny region in the center of the brain was substantially smaller among the gay men he examined than among the heterosexual men. Despite the researcher's plea for caution in drawing quick conclusions from his findings—he pointed out that his research couldn't determine whether the observed brain differences were a cause or a consequence of sexual orientation or a consequence of HIV/AIDS (the gay men he studied had all died of AIDS, and the vast majority of the heterosexual men and women had not)—this study became a catalyst for scholarly and not-so-scholarly debate on the origins of human sexual orientation (Ordover, 1996).

Another study found that the male blood relatives of known gay men were substantially more likely to also be homosexual (13.5%) than the sample as a whole (2%). Indeed, the researcher discovered more gay relatives on the maternal side, fueling the contention that homosexuality is passed from generation to generation through women

(Hamer & Coupland, 1994). Some researchers contend that studies like this one point toward a "gay gene."

As interesting as findings like these are, we must interpret them with caution and avoid making too much of any one statistical correlation. The "high" rate (13.5%) of homosexuality among relatives of gay men, for example, means that in over 86% of cases, these relatives were *not* gay.

In addition, a single gene is unlikely to be responsible for any complex human trait. We know, for instance, that genes are responsible for the development of our lungs, larynx, mouth, and the areas of the brain associated with speech. But such complexity can't be collapsed into a single "talking" gene. Similarly, genes determine the development of our penises, vaginas, and brains. But it's a far step from that knowledge to the contention that a single gene determines sexual orientation.

Moreover, these studies really aren't examining the origins of sexual orientation. They're examining the origins of one *type* of sexual orientation: homosexuality. None of these researchers seems interested in explaining the genetic or neurological underpinnings of heterosexuality or, for that matter, bisexuality. For instance, if a certain structure in the brain is small in homosexual men and large in heterosexual men, is it somewhere in between among bisexual men? And no data exist to prove a genetic link or a link based on brain structure with female sexual orientation, whether heterosexual or homosexual.

In short, biology appears to be one factor among many that can help us to understand sexual orientation.

Cultural Influences on Sexual Orientation

Another important factor in determining sexual orientation is culture, which is fundamental to the complex and unpredictable interplay of fantasy, courtship, arousal, and sexual selection that constitute sexuality (Horton, 1995). Your genes may enable you to act in certain ways, but because we are all influenced by culture, your actions necessarily take on specific cultural forms.

Consider the terms we use today—*heterosexual* and *homosexual*—to refer to the ways in which people can classify their sexual orientation. At the time of Plato (roughly the 4th century BCE), people didn't have a notion of two distinctly different sexual appetites allotted to different individuals. They simply saw various ways of enjoying one's pleasure (Foucault, 1990). Terms that encompassed entire sexual identities originated only toward the end of the 19th century when certain behaviors stopped being attributed to particular individuals and came to define certain groups of people (Coontz, 2007). Those who had sexual relations with members of their own sex were now "homosexuals." Those who had sexual relations with people of the opposite sex were a different type, "heterosexuals." Medical writers eventually used these categories to stigmatize same-sex relations as a form of sexual perversion. Men and women could no longer write of their affectionate desire for a loved one of the same sex—as had been commonplace—without causing suspicion (D'Emilio & Freedman, 1988).

Our culture's fondness for either-or sexual categories was challenged in the 1940s when researcher Alfred Kinsey published a report arguing that sexual orientation is not composed of mutually exclusive categories. Kinsey suggested that it in fact lies along a continuum, with "exclusively heterosexual" at one end of the scale and "exclusively homosexual" at the other. An "exclusive heterosexual," for example, is someone who has never had physical or psychosexual responses to individuals of his or her own sex.

In between the two extremes are various gradations of sexuality, suggesting that people could be "bisexual" or "predominantly" heterosexual or homosexual (Figure 7.1). Note that Kinsey and his colleagues recognized that sexual orientation cannot be measured solely in terms of sexual activity. An individual might be sexually aroused by homosexual fantasies but have had only heterosexual physical encounters. Such a person would fall somewhere in the middle of the continuum.

Kinsey and his colleagues found that only 50% of the white males they studied were "exclusively heterosexual" and only 4% were "exclusively homosexual" (Kinsey, Pomeroy, & Martin, 1948). The rest fell somewhere between the two endpoints. In a more recent national survey, more people reported homosexual desire and behavior than reported homosexuality or bisexuality as their main sexual identity (Michael, Gagnon, Laumann, & Kolata, 1994). About 9% of the men surveyed indicated having had sex with a man since puberty, but only 3% identified themselves as gay. Among women, about 4% had had sex with another woman since puberty, but fewer than 2% identified as lesbian.

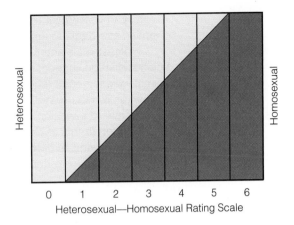

0 - Exclusively heterosexual with no homosexual
1 - Predominantly heterosexual, only incidentally homosexual
2 - Predominantly heterosexual, but more than incidentally homosexual
3 - Equally heterosexual and homosexual
4 - Predominantly homosexual, but more than incidentally heterosexual
5 - Predominantly homosexual, only incidentally heterosexual
6 - Exclusively homosexual with no heterosexual

FIGURE 7.1 Kinsey's Sexual Orientation Scale

Source: The Kinsey Institute, 2007, "Kinsey's heterosexual-homosexual rating scale." www.indiana.edu/~kinsey/research/ak-hhscale.html (accessed March 12, 2007).

■ TAKING A CLOSER LOOK ■

Bisexuality

Although a significant number of people don't fit neatly into an exclusive heterosexual or exclusive homosexual category, relatively few people identify themselves as bisexual. Sociologist Martin Weinberg and his associates (Weinberg, Williams, & Pryor, 2003) note that people who claim a bisexual identity face significantly more hostility even than homosexuals because their identity rejects two recognized categories of sexual orientation:

> While the heterosexual world was said to be completely intolerant of any degree of homosexuality, the reaction of the homosexual world mattered more. Many bisexuals referred to the persistent pressures they experienced to re-label themselves "gay" or "lesbian" and to engage in sexual activity exclusively with the same sex. It was asserted that no one was *really* bisexual, and that calling oneself "bisexual" was a politically incorrect and unauthentic identity. (p. 230)

Weinberg found that people often settled into a bisexual identity many years after experiencing strong sexual attraction to both men and women. Self-proclaimed bisexuals initially face a period of confusion and doubt as they struggle with an identity that doesn't fit into preexisting categories. This period can span years. Eventually, though, they come to see bisexuality as a plausible option and begin to apply the label to themselves.

Homosexuals and heterosexuals alike often consider bisexuality to be a transitional stage. Indeed, the desire to form a permanent, monogamous relationship with someone requires that an individual choose one or the other. Although most of Weinberg, Williams, and Pryor's subjects indicated that they didn't think they were in transition from homosexual to heterosexual (or vice versa), they did acknowledge that at some time in the future they might identify themselves as either homosexual or heterosexual. These expectations may simply reflect the power of a cultural ideology that defines sexual orientation in either-or terms.

Biological or Cultural—Does It Matter?

Although the debate over the origins of sexual orientation is far from settled, let's suppose that sexual orientation is, in fact, biologically determined. What would be the social implications of such a contention? Some people argue that understanding sexual orientation as an innate characteristic beyond personal control, like eye color, will make people more open-minded and more protective of the civil rights of gay, lesbian, and bisexual individuals. For instance, the long-standing concern that homosexuals shouldn't work in occupations involving children (Boy Scout leader, elementary school teacher, child care worker) because of their potentially corrupting influence would disappear because environmental influence would no longer be considered a factor in the development of a child's sexual orientation.

There is some evidence that the explanations people believe about the causes of sexual orientation do affect their attitudes toward homosexuals. A decade ago, a *New York Times*/CBS News poll found that 71% of people who believe homosexuality is "something people choose to be" said they'd object to having a homosexual as a child's elementary school teacher. But only 39% of those who believe homosexuality is "something people cannot change" said they'd object (LeVay, 1996). Incidentally, such negative feelings extended beyond those occupations that offer an opportunity to influence children. People who believe homosexuality is a choice were 4 times more likely to object to gay airplane pilots than people who believe it isn't a choice. More recently, a 2004 Pew Foundation study found that 66% of respondents who believed someone could change their sexual orientation had an unfavorable view of gay people. However, 60% of those who believed sexual orientation was something people can't change had favorable opinions of homosexuals (cited in Chauncey, 2007).

Information about the biological origins of sexual orientation might be used to perpetuate the belief that homosexuality is a "defect" that needs to be fixed, thereby further stigmatizing gays and lesbians. Ideas about biological determinism inevitably carry the threat that we might be encouraged to try manipulating the purported biological cause to adapt it to prevailing social norms. Some scientists have argued that exposure to testosterone during fetal development is a crucial factor in the development of "sex centers" in the brain. If so, prenatal tests such as amniocentesis could, perhaps, "predict" homosexuality. And if this "condition" can be predicted, "prevention" is but a short step away. In 2007, an article in London's *Sunday Times* set off a firestorm of controversy when it raised the possibility that discovering the hormonal causes of homosexuality could someday lead to "preventive treatment" for pregnant women that would reduce or eliminate the chance that the baby would be homosexual (Cloud, 2007b).

Gender and Sexuality

Although contemporary research indicates that the female sex drive is just as strong as the male sex drive, most people assume that men have greater sexual appetites than women. For the first 60 years of the 20th century, sex manuals portrayed female sexuality as nonexistent, weak, or dormant. A woman was expected to be the passive recipient of orgasms given to her by her husband (Groneman, 2000). Even today people assume that women "want" sex primarily within the context of an intimate relationship or within the security of married life and motherhood (Hollway, 1993).

Men are typically depicted as preferring more **recreational sex** (sexual pleasure for its own sake) and women as preferring more **relational sex** (sex within the context of ongoing relationships). In truth, both women and men indicate a preference for relational sex. The vast majority of women and men prefer sex with a regular partner or a spouse (National Opinion Research Center, 1998). The difference is that if relational sex is not available, men are more likely to engage in recreational sex than women are (Schwartz & Rutter, 1998).

Certainly some of women's traditional reluctance to engage in uncommitted, recreational sex stems from its personal and social costs. The **sexual double standard** prevalent in the first half of the 20th century allowed "real" men to have lots of sex with lots of women, while "good" women were to have no sex outside marriage. That seems to have weakened somewhat in recent years, but in some ways it is very much alive (Jackson & Cram, 2003). For young men, sexual desire is framed as "natural and healthy," their ticket to "normal" manhood; for young women, however, sexual desire is "bad" and framed in terms of risk, vulnerability, and dangerous consequences (Tolman, 2006). A review of 30 studies published between 1980 and 2002 found evidence of the continued existence of the sexual double standard, though its intensity varies across social and ethnic groups (Crawford & Popp, 2003). Some scholars have suggested that the intense public concern over teen sexuality is really in response to women's, not men's, increased sexual activity: "Teens are demonized as morally wayward—because women have been admitting to engaging in sex at levels that are increasingly similar to men's" (Schwartz & Rutter, 1998, p. 166).

Studies show that women tend to be regarded more negatively than men if they become sexually active at a young age or have sex within casual relationships (Sprecher, McKinney, & Orbuch, 1987). Consider, for example, how this young college student says he would feel toward a woman who would engage in a one-night stand with him:

> If I met a woman in a bar and had sex with her chances are I wouldn't call her because I wouldn't have any respect for her. Because if she did something like that . . . would I want someone like that for the rest of my life? No, of course not. (quoted in Fromme & Emihovich, 1998, p. 174)

Several of the young men interviewed in this study expressed similar ideas, failing to recognize that they were engaging in exactly the same behaviors that they condemned in women (Fromme & Emihovich, 1998). So ingrained is the double standard in our culture that the inconsistencies and contradictions are hardly noticed. After all, with whom are all these men having sex if women are supposedly not having much sex?

The double standard also affects attitudes toward contraceptive use. Men who come equipped with condoms on a date are considered safe and responsible, but women who are on the pill, have a diaphragm, or provide men with condoms may be seen by others

■ **recreational sex**
Sexual pleasure for its own sake.

■ **relational sex**
Sex within the context of an ongoing relationship.

■ **sexual double standard**
A cultural belief that celebrates men who have lots of sex while punishing women for the same behavior.

as promiscuous. The lingering cultural reluctance to acknowledge women's control over their own sexuality may be to blame for these perceptions:

> One simple way of showing that one is a "nice girl" is to be unprepared for sex—to have given no prior thought to contraception. Both at first sex and with each new partner, a young woman is thus subject to powerful cultural pressures that penalize her for taking responsibility. To use contraception, a woman has to anticipate sexual activity by locating the impetus within herself, rather than in the man who has overcome her hesitancy. (Luker, 2005, p. 491)

College women perceive more negative consequences (such as social disapproval from partners) for women who are "contraceptively prepared" than for women who have unprotected sex (Hynie & Lydon, 1995). Such attitudes are certainly one of the more dangerous outcomes of the double standard of sexuality and perhaps explain the relatively low percentage of sexually active unmarried women—even those with multiple partners—who use condoms consistently (Figure 7.2).

Gender differences in sexuality are further illustrated by comparing lesbian couples and gay male couples. In the 1970s and early 1980s, the gay male community advocated a stereotypically male (that is, recreational) approach to sexuality. By the mid-1980s, however, the specter of HIV/AIDS had brought a noticeable shift toward couplehood and relational sex. Nevertheless, a significant number of gay men still approve of recreational sex and nonmonogamy, even if they are currently in lifetime relationships.

Research suggests that lesbians, like heterosexual women, are inclined to prefer sex in the context of ongoing, committed relationships. Despite the growth in recent years of "lesbian sex clubs," which celebrate anonymous sex, relatively few lesbians approve of recreational or nonmonogamous sex. As a group, lesbians tend to have sex less frequently than married, cohabiting heterosexual couples or gay male couples. They also tend to prize nongenital physical contact such as cuddling, touching, and hugging more than other couples (Nichols, 2005; Peplau, 2003).

But we must be careful in assuming that "having sex" means the same thing to people of all sexual orientations. Does the fact that lesbians indicate a lower frequency of sex than heterosexuals or gay men indicate that they "have less sex"? Perhaps not. Consider this: the average duration of a heterosexual sexual encounter is approximately 8 minutes, punctuated by one partner (typically the man) or both partners achieving orgasm. The average duration of a lesbian sexual episode is quite a bit longer, 30 to 60 minutes on average, and may not result in orgasm on either partner's part (Frye, 1992). How many instances of "having sex" are included in an entire evening's worth of cuddling and hugging? To the extent that a standard heterosexual and male definition is used by everyone, the frequency of "having sex" among lesbians will be underestimated. Indeed, if we simply use achieving orgasm as the event that determines whether an en-

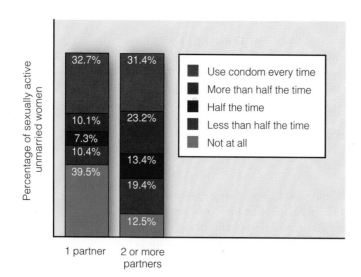

FIGURE 7.2   Condom Use Among Sexually Active Unmarried Women, Ages 15–29

Source: U.S. Bureau of the Census, 2000, table 97.

counter counts as "having sex," then most lesbians (not to mention many heterosexual women) never "have sex."

DATING

Against the cultural backdrop of love and sexuality we can now examine the institutional mechanisms through which people meet potential partners. Every society has its own acceptable means of bringing people together, although the process varies markedly from society to society. In most Western societies, **dating** is the recognized means by which most people move from being single to being coupled. Dating is a somewhat ambiguous phenomenon, blurred by different uses of vocabulary. Terms like "dating," "going out," "going around," "hanging out," "talking," "going steady," and "being involved" often lack clear definition and agreement.

> ■ **dating**
> The recognized means by which most people move from being single to being coupled.

When my older son was 10 he came home from school one day and happily proclaimed that a girl in his class wanted to "go out" with him. But he was in a quandary because it seems he was already "going out" with someone else. What wasn't clear to me was where all these fifth-graders who were going out with each other actually went. So I asked him.

"Oh, we don't go anywhere," he said, matter-of-factly. Nor, it turns out, did he spend any time at school with the girl or even talk to her.

"How do you even know you like each other?" I asked.

"Well . . . she told one of her friends she liked me. Then her friend told one of my friends, who told me. So I told one of my friends I liked her, and he told one of her friends, who told her."

"And that's when the two of you decided you were 'going out'?" I asked, hoping to have finally gotten it.

"I dunno," he said, a little surprised that I'd even ask such a question, "I have no idea what she thinks."

Such a conception of "going out" is a far cry from what most adults would consider dating. Although it's difficult to come up with a definition that would apply across situations—first dates, blind dates, double dates, group dates, formal courtship, dating among divorced or widowed people, and so on—all dating seems to include some degree of companionship, communication, good times, mutual sharing, romantic overtones, and perhaps some kind of sexual contact (Laner, 1989). It is these last two features, romance and sex, that typically distinguish "dating" from casual social outings that take place between people who consider themselves "just friends."

The Social Purposes of Dating

According to many sociologists, an important social function of dating—at least in a heterosexual context—is to allow males and females to interact with and learn about one another. Dating provides an opportunity for exploring romantic intimacy without requiring a rapid escalation toward marriage. It lets individuals learn about the types of people to whom they're attracted. We can think of dating, in this sense, as a sort of rehearsal for future serious relationships.

Indeed, the U.S. dating culture has historically been based on an assumption that dating provides important experiences and valuable lessons that will eventually help people select mates and construct happy marriages. But what exactly *is* the relationship between dating experiences and future marital success and happiness? Sociologist Martin King Whyte (1990) interviewed 459 women in the greater Detroit area to answer this question. The women were from diverse racial and ethnic backgrounds and ranged in age from 18 to 75. All had been married at least once.

Whyte asked them to recall their premarital dating experiences. Contrary to common perceptions, he found that dating variety, length of dating, length of courtship or engagement, and degree of premarital intimacy with a future husband were unrelated to marital success. Women who married their first loves were just as likely to have long-lasting and satisfying marriages as women who had dated a lot of different men before marrying. Similarly, women who married after only a short acquaintance were equally likely to have successful marriages as women who dated their husbands-to-be for years. Marital quality was the same for women who were virgins upon marriage as it was for women who had a variety of sexual partners before marriage.

Apparently dating doesn't really serve as a training ground for marriage, and if you think about it, we really don't have any reason to expect it to. The behaviors that tend to characterize dating—fun, recreation, erotic teasing, and so forth—are not the sorts of activities that necessarily prepare one for the everyday demands of married life.

A Brief History of U.S. Dating

Even a 10-year-old's rather hazy conception of dating assumes that the participants are solely responsible for deciding whether or not to "go out" with each other. Parents, relatives, or peers may influence these decisions, but they usually don't directly arrange dating relationships.

The United States has never had a tradition of "arranged relationships" or parent-dominated courtship. Eligible males and females, even as early as colonial times, have taken the initiative to get to know each other, and the decision to marry was always left to them, even if that decision was ultimately subject to parental approval (Whyte, 1992). Later, when large numbers of European immigrants arrived either as single individuals or as nuclear families, ties to extended families—and with them, ties to traditions of arranged relationships—inevitably weakened (Murstein, 1974).

Although singles in the United States have always had a lot of choice in whom to date, dating was (and still is) controlled by social norms. Historical research into U.S. dating practices provides a fascinating glimpse into the ways many young persons in the past sought intimacy.

Bundling

In the 18th century most relationships probably began in a rather informal way. Unmarried individuals had many opportunities to interact in mixed-sex groups (Cate & Lloyd, 1992). These young men and women had typically grown up together in small communities where there were few strangers, so they knew a lot about one another. Even close physical contact was not unheard of, as evidenced by the colonial practice of bundling among middle- and upper-class whites.

■ **bundling**
An 18th-century practice in which an unmarried woman and an unmarried man, fully clothed, slept together in the same bed.

In **bundling,** an unmarried woman and an unmarried man, fully clothed, slept in the same bed together (Rothman, 1984). Mothers (and daughters) may have favored the practice, perhaps because it was a ritual over which women had significant control. It was up to the young woman to permit or deny access to her bed. In a letter from the late 18th century, one man noted that it was "not the fashion to bundle with any chap who might call on a girl, but that it was a special factor, granted only to a favorite lover" (quoted in Rothman, 1984, pp. 47–48).

Although lying in bed together was approved by parents, sexual activity was not. Parents devised a variety of techniques to inhibit sexual contact:

> a wooden board might be placed in the middle of the bed; the young girl might be encased in a type of long laundry bag up to her armpits; or her garments might be sewn together at strategic points. (Murstein, 1974, p. 317)

Indeed, when we consider that homes during this time didn't usually have separate bedrooms for privacy, it would have been difficult to accomplish much sexual activity in the same room as, or in close proximity to, the woman's parents and siblings. Difficult, but apparently not impossible. During the latter part of the 18th century, a period that has been called the "heyday of bundling," premarital conception was quite high, for instance, 30% in the 1770s (Cate & Lloyd, 1992; Rothman, 1984).

Bundling disappeared after 1800, in part because women's roles were being significantly redefined. Prior to 1800, women had tended to be viewed as "especially sexual" persons, but in the 19th century they came to be seen as "sexually passionless by nature" (Rothman, 1984, p. 48). Gender ideologies that emerged during the 19th century emphasized the differences between men and women, and the sexes became segregated in virtually every aspect of their lives (Rothman, 1984). These shifts had profound implications for courtship practices.

Calling and Keeping Company

The new gender separation that emerged in the 19th century meant that men and women were not able to socialize as freely as they had before. Courtship became more formal, and certain customs and traditions (such as the engagement ring, the formal wedding ceremony, expensive gifts) became common (Rothman, 1984). A highly ritualized system of dating and courtship known as **calling** emerged during the latter part of the 19th century, especially among the middle and upper classes. Young people still could meet in a variety of ways—at community or church socials, at fairs and dances, informally on the street or in school, or through introductions by friends or relatives (Whyte, 1992). But when one or both parties wished to pursue a relationship, the young man was required to visit the young woman at her home, usually during daylight hours. The process entailed many specific guidelines:

■ **calling**
A highly ritualized system of dating and courtship.

> When a girl reached the proper age or had her first "season" (depending on her family's social level), she became eligible to receive male callers. At first her mother or guardian invited young men to call; in subsequent seasons the young lady . . . could bestow an invitation to call upon any unmarried man to whom she had been properly introduced. . . . Other young men . . . could be brought to call by friends or relatives of the girl's family, subject to her prior permission. . . . The call itself was a complicated event. . . . [R]ules governed everything: the proper amount of time between invitation and visit (two weeks or less); whether or not refreshments should be served . . . ; chaperonage (the first call must be made on mother and daughter . . .); appropriate topics of conversation (the man's interests, but never too personal); how leave should be taken (on no account should the woman accompany [her caller] to the door nor stand talking while he struggles with his coat). (Bailey, 1988, pp. 15–16)

During initial visits the mother remained present in the room at all times; later on she might hover in an adjacent room. With supervision so tight, anything resembling recreational enjoyment or romance was next to impossible.

Everyone understood that calling was a means by which to examine potential marriage partners and test their suitability, breeding, and background (Bailey, 1988). It enabled the middle and upper classes to protect themselves from what many at the time considered the "intrusions" of urban life, and to screen out the effects of social and geographical mobility that were reaching unprecedented levels at the turn of the 20th century. It also allowed parents to exert some degree of control over their children's relationships without going so far as to actually arrange them.

The courtship process didn't end with calling. If the relationship deepened sufficiently, it might progress to *keeping company,* an early version of going steady (Whyte, 1992). Visits would still take place in the young woman's home, but now those visits were limited to one man rather than a host of suitors, they more frequently took place at night rather than in the afternoon, and they sometimes continued after the young woman's parents had retired to bed.

Like couples in previous generations, young people at the end of the 1800s did find time to be alone. Premarital sex and premarital births were not uncommon. According to one study, 13% of U.S. women born before 1890 and 26% born between 1890 and 1899 engaged in premarital intercourse (Terman, 1938). The premarital pregnancy rate increased from 10% in the mid-19th century to 23% in the decades between 1880 and 1910 (D'Emilio & Freedman, 1988).

Dating and Going Steady

The formal tradition of calling began to disappear in the early 20th century, to be replaced by what we recognize more easily as a form of dating. Economic and educational innovations enabled young people to interact with the opposite sex away from the watchful eyes of parents (Coontz, 1992). Compulsory schooling in public, coeducational institutions provided an arena where young people could see each other every day. The expansion of commercial recreation in the form of movie theaters, dance halls, amusement parks, and so on gave young people new places to meet and congregate.

In addition, growing affluence and the shift from an agricultural- to an industrial-based economy meant that more and more young people had leisure time on their hands. These trends coincided with part-time and after-school employment, which provided young people with spending money that didn't have to be turned over to the family. By the 1920s and 1930s autonomous dating among young people had become a common feature of America's interpersonal landscape (Gordon, 1981).

Technology also played a prominent role in the growth of the institution of dating. The innovation that perhaps had the most direct and long-lasting effect was the automobile. Cars were a means of transportation away from home, and they also provided a somewhat private space for romantic and sexual activity (Whyte, 1992). The advent of the drive-in movie theater in the early 1930s coincided with the growing role cars played in young people's intimate lives. In later years, the borrowed family car was replaced by cars (and then vans) owned by young people themselves. One observer in the early 20th century called the car "a house of prostitution on wheels" (quoted in Coontz, 2005, p. 200).

By the 1920s and 1930s dating had pretty much moved out of the home and into the public sphere. In the process, family supervision was replaced with peer supervision and judgment. Dating now occurred in places that were virtually off-limits to parents, such as private parties and dance halls. In most communities young people identified secluded areas (sometimes referred to as "lovers' lanes") where they could escape the surveillance of peers as well as adults. Nine of 10 U.S. college women in the 1920s reported engaging in "petting," and about half had sex before marriage (Coontz, 2005).

The gender roles associated with dating and courtship changed too. For one thing, women came to have less control over the process than they had previously. Dating, unlike calling, required money, which was the man's responsibility. Although men now had a greater financial burden, control over economic resources also gave them greater power in interactions with women (Cate & Lloyd, 1992). Consequently, the initiative shifted from the woman to the man. He asked her out rather than waiting for an invitation to call, and finances and transportation were his responsibility. In exchange, she was expected to provide the pleasure of her company and maybe some romance and intimacy. Although women could withhold affection and thereby exercise some control over the event, the absence of parental oversight outside the safe confines of their own home placed women in a more vulnerable position than during the era of calling.

Greater privacy and autonomy promoted romantic and sexual experimentation too, perpetuating the sexual double standard. Men were expected to be the sexual aggressors, and the "success" or "failure" of their date could often be measured by how much intimacy they were able to achieve. One dating manual for girls in the 1940s stated that the average young man "will go as far as you will let him go" (quoted in Coontz, 2005, p. 209). Women who "went too far" risked destroying their reputations and their ability to attract other desirable men. They bore the responsibility of setting limits and therefore had to walk a fine line between being too unfriendly and too friendly (Whyte, 1992).

One of the key features of the modern form of dating, which emerged during the 1930s and 1940s and continues today, is a primary concern with enjoyment rather than selection of a marital partner. Starting in the 1930s and 1940s, dating was viewed as a necessary first step toward marriage, but that wasn't its primary purpose. Both young men and young women were encouraged to "play the field," and the frequency of dating was often a barometer of popularity.

By the 1950s an intermediate phase between dating and marriage developed: *going steady*. It was considerably different from the turn-of-the-century notion of "keeping steady company," which was almost always a prelude to engagement. Going steady simply entailed a recognizable commitment on the part of both people to date each other exclusively for a time. Few steady couples expected to marry each other, although they often acted as if they were married, typically by exchanging some symbolic token of commitment such as a class ring or school sweater, which often led to heightened expectations regarding intimacy (Bailey, 1988). Not surprisingly, many adults feared that going steady would inevitably lead to more serious sexuality between young people. Some dating manuals of the 1950s even argued that a young woman was better off dating a series of strangers than having a steady boyfriend (Bailey, 1988). Teenagers, on the other hand, simply viewed going steady as a form of "social security"—guaranteeing a date for weekends and major social functions.

These patterns of dating and going steady from the 1950s persisted well into the 1970s and 1980s (Cate & Lloyd, 1992). On first dates, in particular, traditional gender roles persisted:

> On a first date . . . a man is supposed to control the public domain (make plans and transport the date) as well as the physical and economic resources (car and money). Women's control and resources (beauty, sexuality, and charm) are supposed to be in the private sphere. (Rose & Frieze, 1989, p. 266)

However, some important changes did occur. For instance, opportunities for informal mixed-sex interaction became more plentiful in the 1970s and 1980s. The development of a relationship through a series of recognizable stages also became less structured, and cohabitation emerged as a more common stage in the courtship process (Rice, 1990, cited in Cate & Lloyd, 1992). Indeed, dating came to be defined more in terms of immediate gratification than choosing a life-long partner.

Strict gender roles also began to weaken a bit. It became more acceptable for girls and women to initiate dates than in previous decades, and they were encouraged to pay their own way to avoid the presumption of sexual activity. Although such a change didn't necessarily point to a major, society-wide power shift in dating relationships, it did suggest that the intimate environment young people faced wasn't as gender imbalanced as it once had been.

Contemporary Dating and the Persistent Double Standard

Sexual double standards don't die easily. Considering what we already know about gender differences in sexuality, we shouldn't be surprised that men and women still evaluate contemporary dating experiences differently. Researchers have found that men tend to perceive sexually suggestive behavior on the part of a dating partner (for example, leaning close when sitting together, repeated touching) as an indicator that things are moving toward more intense sexual activity, whereas women are more likely to be uncomfortable with men's sexually suggestive behavior. Men also tend to see rejection of their sexual advances as a sign of a "bad date" (Alksnis, Desmarais, & Wood, 1996).

Disagreement over signals of sexual desire is one of the most notable problems in contemporary dating. One study found that 53% of female high school students had been in a dating situation in which they believed a boy overestimated the level of sexual intimacy the young woman desired; 45% of male students had been in situations where they felt girls underestimated the young man's level of desired sexual intimacy (Patton & Mannison, 1995).

Indeed, young women consistently report that the thing they dislike most about dating situations is unwanted pressure to have sex (Reinholtz, Muehlenhard, Phelps, & Satterfield, 1995). According to one study, 40% of teenage girls know someone who has been pressured into having sex (cited in Prah, 2006). And almost a quarter of college women in another study reported one or more experiences of unwanted sex in a dating situation (Flack et al., 2007).

Even more young women, perhaps more than half the population, engage in unwanted sexual activity for reasons other than pressure from a dating partner, such as general peer pressure; fear of appearing shy, afraid, unfeminine, or inexperienced; and a desire to be more popular. This sort of pressure doesn't come from a dating partner but from the person's own expectations about how she should behave sexually (Reinholtz et al., 1995).

■ TAKING A CLOSER LOOK

The Hook-Up

Because contemporary dating can be fraught with tension and misunderstanding, larger and larger numbers of young people are eschewing it altogether. In one recent survey, over half the respondents who had been in college for 2 years had been on fewer than five dates during that time; and 21% of the men and 32% of the women hadn't been on a single date. Young people are much more likely to go out in groups than to go on one-on-one dates (Rackl & Herrmann, 2005). While not dead, traditional dating seems to be on life-support.

Among college students, traditional dating has seemingly been replaced by *hooking up,* in which two people hang out in a dorm room or meet at a party, go somewhere private, and engage in some form of sexual behavior, which can range from kissing to intercourse (England & Thomas, 2007). Alcohol is usually involved, but intimacy and romance rarely are. In fact, romance seems to be out of the picture entirely, at least initially.

Hooking up has become a principal path into serious relationships, sometimes preceded by friendship and "hanging out" (England & Thomas, 2007). The traditional dating that does occur often takes place *after* a couple has defined the relationship as sexually exclusive. As one male college student put it:

> A lot of my guy friends aren't looking for relationships . . . but when they meet those girls, it's often been within the group of friends. . . . And then . . . you try to hook up with them. And then you can start dating. (quoted in England & Thomas, 2007, p. 155)

Though common on college campuses, hook-ups have not created a gender-balanced sexual landscape. Indeed, many vestiges of the traditional sexual double standard still exist in the hook-up culture. For instance, women are less likely than men to see hook-ups as purely casual sex and more interested in turning them into long-term relationships. And women still risk getting a bad reputation for hooking up with too many people, leading some to argue that equal opportunities for women have advanced more quickly in the educational and occupational worlds than in the college sex scene (England & Thomas, 2007).

Violence in Dating Relationships

The pressures, ambiguities, and conflicting expectations that surround contemporary dating and hooking up can sometimes be dangerous. According to the Centers for Disease Control (2006a), 1 in 11 adolescents report being physically abused in a dating relationship. When we add in verbal and emotional abuse, the figure grows to 1 in 4. And 1 in 5 high school girls has been hit, slapped, or shoved by a dating partner (Silverman, Raj, Mucci, & Hathaway, 2001). Nearly 60% of teens in one survey said they knew a fellow teen who had been physically, emotionally, or sexually abused in a dating relationship (cited in Hurst, 2005). Dating violence crosses lines of race, ethnicity, age, class, and sexual orientation (Levy, 1991).

Perhaps the most pernicious form of dating violence is rape and sexual assault. According to the National Crime Victimization Survey, an annual assessment of crime victimization carried out by the U.S. Bureau of Justice Statistics (2006), close to 210,000 women over the age of 12 report being raped or sexually assaulted annually, more than double the roughly 94,000 incidents of forcible rape that are officially reported to the police each year (U.S. Bureau of the Census, 2008). In 65% of rapes and sexual assaults, the victim knew the attacker (U.S. Bureau of Justice Statistics, 2006). On college campuses, where about 3% of college women experience a completed or attempted rape during a typical college year, 90% of the victims know their attackers (U.S. Bureau of Justice Statistics, 2001).

Cultural norms and beliefs about male sexuality influence our understanding of rape when it occurs in dating relationships. One such belief is that young men's sexual urges are uncontrollable. Men are frequently portrayed as overwhelmingly sexual beings who, once aroused, are compelled by forces beyond their control to seek sexual gratification. Thus sexual coercion and violence are rendered inevitable.

Rape in dating situations is viewed less as an act of deviance and more an act of excessive conformity to cultural expectations; less an act by abnormally brutal individuals and more an act by "normal" men behaving in ways they think are appropriate. As one author wrote two decades ago, rape is the "all-American crime," demonstrating precisely those characteristics traditionally regarded as desirable in men: strength, power, domination, and control (Griffin, 1989).

Related to this belief in uncontrollable male sexuality is the conviction that women are ultimately responsible for men's sexual behavior. That is, women "do something to" men that arouses their sexuality, and men cannot resist. A woman who is raped by a dating partner is therefore considered responsible for failing to control the man's behavior (Reinholtz et al., 1995).

One explanation for the widespread tendency to hold women responsible is the common definition of rape that focuses on the sexual component, penile-vaginal penetration, rather than on the violent context within which the act takes place. Conceiving of rape purely as a sexual act requires that information about the intimate circumstances of the act and about the relationship between the people involved be taken into consideration, all of which tends to put female rape victims at a disadvantage if they file charges. Victims must provide some evidence that they were "unwilling" and tried to resist. No other crime requires that the victim prove lack of consent. People aren't asked whether they agreed to have their car stolen or whether they did something to provoke being robbed.

To make matters worse, different states define consent differently. In Connecticut and Kansas, for example, a woman may withdraw her consent to have sex at any time and if the man continues, he is committing rape. However, in North Carolina and Maryland, once a woman gives consent, she can no longer rescind it. Such an understanding of consent rests on the belief that at a certain point during arousal, a man loses the ability to stop (Lee-St. John, 2007b).

Research consistently shows that observers attribute more blame to victims and minimize the seriousness of the assault when the perpetrator is a dating or steady partner (Bell, Kuriloff, & Lottes, 1994). One study of convicted rapists found that those who assaulted strangers received longer prison sentences than rapists who were acquaintances or partners of their victims, regardless of the amount of force used or the physical injury to the victim (McCormick, Maric, Seto, & Barbaree, 1998).

Many people also regard women as partly or wholly responsible for being victimized when they purportedly place themselves at risk by getting drunk at parties, acting seductively, wearing provocative clothing, or telling dirty jokes. In one study, male and female high school students were given a list of statements and asked to indicate the extent to which they agreed with them (Kershner, 1996). Of the male and female subjects, 46% felt that women encourage rape by the way they dress, and 53% said they felt that some women provoke men into raping them. Moreover, 31% agreed that many women falsely report rapes, and 35% felt the victim should be required to prove her innocence during a rape trial. Research has linked such attitudes to an increased likelihood of blaming rape victims for the assault (Frese, Moya, & Megías, 2004) as well as a heightened risk of rape and sexual assault on college campuses (Ching & Burke, 1999).

The crucial consequence of these attitudes is that women must bear most, if not all, of the responsibility for *preventing* rape. They're the ones who must monitor what they wear, how they act, what they say, where they go, and so on. Without a fundamental restructuring of society and of the cultural expectations that surround intimacy, no significant reduction in sexual violence in dating situations is likely to occur. We would have to transform male-female relationships and childhood socialization, override the cultural beliefs and images that perpetuate certain sexual attitudes, and institute a more equitable sharing of political and economic power. Until that time arrives, the most practical response may be to clarify the fuzzy boundary between seduction and coercion, helping men and women understand the conflicting values and expectations they bring to dating relationships.

THEORIES OF ATTRACTION AND RELATIONSHIP DEVELOPMENT

Social theorists have developed several ways of explaining patterns of attraction and relationship development. Three well-known models are the sociobiological model, the stage model, and the social exchange model. Unfortunately, their cold, scientific language contradicts our culture's deeply held romantic visions of how intimate relationships begin and grow. But theories provide important insights into the possible ways relationships develop. Although many of us like to think our love experiences are unique, theories can reveal patterns in the ways couples interact. We can begin to see that while our experiences are deeply personal, they are also shaped by social forces.

The Sociobiological Model of Attraction

To some scholars, most notably sociobiologists (also called evolutionary psychologists), attraction is less a matter of choice than of fulfilling our genetic destiny. They argue that all species must evolve efficient ways to pass on their genetic material through successful reproduction (DeLamater & Hyde, 1998; van den Berghe, 1979).

Different strategies require different levels of **parental investment**—the relative contribution parents make to the genetic fitness of offspring. Some species, like most fish, have evolved a strategy in which parental investment in offspring is quite low. Female fish produce and lay thousands of eggs at a time. Males produce billions of sperm, which they spread over the eggs that have been laid. In this strategy, males and females don't have to "pair up" to raise their offspring. Thousands of eggs are fertilized, but most die or are eaten by predators. Only a tiny percentage survive and grow to adulthood, but they are enough to allow the species to continue. Other species, like humans, invest a great deal more effort in each fertilized egg. Both men and women gain an evolutionary advantage, as does the entire species, by producing as many healthy offspring as possible and ensuring that enough of them live long enough to perpetuate the gene pool.

Some sociobiologists hypothesize that to maximize the chances of species survival, men and women have evolved different mate-selection strategies, based on biological differences in the reproductive process (Buss, 1994). Compared to some other animals, human females make an enormously high investment in the reproduction process. They produce very few eggs, perhaps between 12 and 15 a year. A single act of sexual intercourse can close off the woman's other mating opportunities for at least 9 months.

■ **parental investment**
The relative contribution mothers and fathers make to the genetic fitness of their offspring.

While pregnant, she obviously can't become pregnant again. Women also bear exclusive responsibility for lactation, which can last up to 3 or 4 years after the child is born.

Human offspring take a long time to mature in the mother's womb and are completely helpless at birth. The large size of human babies' heads and the small size of the mother's pelvis (a consequence of walking upright) means human babies must be born at a much earlier stage of development than other animal babies. A day-old human can't get up and gallop away like a newborn colt. Human babies need a great deal of supervision and care to ensure their survival until they are independent enough to survive on their own. From the perspective of species survival, babies are a scarce and precious resource.

As a result, women are generally more interested in long-term rather than short-term mating strategies. In our evolutionary past, women may have had to be extremely selective in their mating and "stingy" in offering their reproductive resources. Their taste for sex within the context of an ongoing relationship and the greater significance for them of each sexual act are thought, in the sociobiological model, to be consistent with women's high reproductive investment.

The picture is strikingly different for men. They have just as much interest in species survival as women do, but their biological investment in the process is not that much higher than that of a male flounder. To put it crudely, sperm are plentiful and cheap relative to eggs. One man can fertilize as many eggs as his stamina and the sexual availability of ovulating women will allow. The most prolific human parent, according to *The Guinness Book of World Records,* was the 18th-century emperor of Morocco, Moulay Ismail, who reportedly fathered more than 1,000 children. A single act of sexual intercourse for a man requires minimal investment. Once he "deposits" his sperm, he is free—in a physiological, not an interpersonal or moral, sense—to do anything he wants, even impregnate other women. If so inclined, he could walk away from a casual coupling without any biologically necessary obligations to the resulting offspring.

According to some sociobiologists, men's apparent inclination for recreational sex and their desire for a variety of partners are consistent with their evolved reproductive strategy. Their sexual interest is more easily aroused than women's because sex has fewer biological costs for them. Some sociobiologists cite the fact that, worldwide, prostitution is a service overwhelmingly sought by males rather than females as evidence of men's biologically based sexual strategies.

Some sociobiologists also argue that because of gender differences in reproductive investment, men and women are genetically programmed to desire different traits in a mate. They claim that women's reproductive need for protection and stability helped them evolve a preference for mates capable of acquiring resources, and willing and able to support and protect their mates and their children (Hatfield & Rapson, 1993). A study by British and Japanese psychologists found that women's preferences in men change during their menstrual cycle. Most of the time they prefer slightly feminized male facial shapes. But when they are ovulating (that is, when chances of conception are highest), they prefer more rugged, masculine features, which, according to sociobiological thinking, are associated with reproductive success. The researchers also noted that women's general distaste for the way men smell diminishes when their fertility is at its peak (Penton-Voak et al., 1999).

Following this logic, men can afford to be less choosy. Because of their low level of investment in the reproductive process, they have evolved a powerful desire for engaging in sexual encounters with a wide array of partners. In the interests of reproducing offspring with the highest likelihood of survival, they are attracted to women who show visible signs of fertility: physical attractiveness, health, and youth (DeLamater & Hyde, 1998). One study of 1,500 college students in the United States, Russia, and Japan found that in all these cultures men rated physical attractiveness as more important than did women. In all cultures, women rated intelligence; ambition; potential for success; money, status, and position; kindness and understanding; and expressiveness as more important than did men (Hatfield & Sprecher, 1995).

In sum, according to this sociobiological argument, sexual tendencies in humans evolved because a certain kind of sexual partnership and division of labor maximized the probability of survival for individuals, groups, and ultimately the species. However, we have no way of proving unequivocally that these tendencies stem exclusively or even primarily from biological imperatives. Historically, norms and laws were designed to protect men's sexual property; namely, women. Even today, sexually promiscuous women are substantially more likely to be called derogatory names than sexually promiscuous men. Given such a cultural context, we should expect men and women to show different sexual proclivities.

Furthermore, if the sociobiological model is accurate, you'd expect that men's and women's preferences in partners and mates would remain the same even as social conditions change. One study, however, found that people's mate preferences in the United States have changed over time (Buss, Shackelford, Kirkpatrick, & Larsen, 2001). Men today place greater importance on finding a mate with good financial prospects than they did in the past. Other research suggests that women's romantic preferences also change as their social and economic position improves. In societies in which women are economically independent, women tend to focus more on sex appeal than on the ability to be a good provider in choosing sexual partners (Gangestad, 1993). Thus the role of biology in attraction and mate selection is still a question mark.

The Stage Model of Relationship Formation

Although some sociologists insist that biological factors play an important role in human behavior (e.g., Massey, 2000), most argue that relationship development is about social and interpersonal processes rather than innate biological drives. In this view, even the most personal elements, such as who we initially find attractive, are affected by social forces.

According to sociologist Ira Reiss (1960), once mutual attraction takes place, emotional attachment develops in a series of stages: rapport, self-disclosure, and mutual dependency and need fulfillment. Before we will disclose intimate information about ourselves, we must first achieve a certain level of rapport and compatibility with that person. Let's look at each stage.

Attraction and Initiation

Before any relationship can develop, two people must overcome a number of cultural barriers. The perception that someone we're interested in is "out of our league"—meaning too attractive, too rich, too popular, and so on—is strongly influenced by cultural ideals of attractiveness. Gendered patterns of communication also can interfere with relationship formation. If a woman feels uncomfortable approaching someone and initiating a date, she must try to make her interest known indirectly and discreetly. Because her cues are so subtle, the object of her desire might misinterpret her behavior as a lack of interest. Men's reluctance to approach women due to their fear of rejection can likewise be misinterpreted by women as a lack of interest (Vorauer & Ratner, 1996).

Social psychologists have long argued that (mutual) attraction is a critical factor in determining whether a romantic relationship develops (Murstein, 1987). Unless there is some initial attraction, a relationship is unlikely to develop. Interestingly, the growing popularity of online relationships may be altering this dynamic in significant ways (Cooper & Sportolari, 1997). Physical attributes, so critical in real-life interactions, are often not evident (or verifiable) online, which can lead to the development of relationships that otherwise might never have gotten off the ground. Online attraction has the potential to rely more heavily on other factors, such as rapport and similarity. Whether a relationship begun online can override the possible lack of physical attraction when the couple finally meets face-to-face is not clear.

Rapport

■ **rapport**
A general sense of compatibility in the early stages of a relationship.

When two people first start forming a relationship, their interactions tend to be somewhat superficial. Nevertheless, they attempt to establish **rapport,** a general sense of compatibility (for example, "My favorite ice cream flavor is Vanilla Swiss Almond, I like to play tennis, and my favorite music group is the Black Eyed Peas").

At this stage, our interactions may be complicated by our deliberate attempts to manipulate information about ourselves. We may try to present values, opinions, and biographical information we think the other person will find appealing and avoid saying or doing things that will upset, anger, or repel the other person. We want to present idealized images of ourselves and at the same time accept the idealized image we're getting of the other person.

Intimate Self-Disclosure

■ **intimate self-disclosure**
A willingness to go beyond providing basic background information to reveal some very personal facts, thoughts, and feelings.

As people grow more comfortable with and trusting of each other, their disclosures become more intimate and revealing and, therefore, more risky. This next stage of relationship development is characterized by **intimate self-disclosure,** a willingness to go beyond providing basic background information to reveal some very personal facts, thoughts, and feelings. These disclosures can include problematic events in our past, the depth of our feelings toward the other person, our fears and vulnerabilities, and so on. They not only convey information, they are symbolic gestures meant to tell the other person, "I feel close enough to you to share this with you. I trust you not to laugh, belittle, devalue, or fear what I am going to tell you." Research has shown that the greater the level of self-disclosure between partners, the greater their satisfaction in the relationship (Altman & Taylor, 1973; Hendrick, 1981).

Self-disclosure is governed by a clear set of social norms and expectations. One important, but often unspoken, one is that the intimate self-disclosure should be reciprocated (Derlega, Harris, & Chaikin, 1973). We provide more and more intimate facts about ourselves in hopes that our partner will do the same. When people complain about communication problems in their relationships, they are usually referring to an imbalance in the nature and amount of information that partners are sharing. Often we go through a great deal of strategic maneuvering before first disclosing to our partners how we feel about them. But once we do, we expect similar levels of disclosure from our partners (Cunningham, Strassberg, & Haan, 1986). When they don't reciprocate, we are forced to acknowledge that our definition of the relationship does not conform to theirs.

So you can see that self-disclosure is a potentially hazardous stage in development of a relationship. When our partners don't disclose enough, we don't know what they're truly feeling. But we don't want to appear pushy by constantly asking for feelings and reassurances, so we sometimes resign ourselves to quiet suffering. In the absence of clear information, we frequently let our imagination run wild. We find ourselves attributing feelings that we think our partner has. We scrutinize every sentence, every gesture for some tiny morsel of information that will tell us what this other person is feeling.

Of course, disclosing too much, too quickly can also be problematic. Those who tell everyone, even complete strangers, every intimate detail of their lives and feelings have not learned about the importance of timing self-disclosure. The recipient of prematurely personal disclosures usually feels quite uncomfortable in the role.

Mutual Dependency and Need Fulfillment

When a relationship endures beyond the point of shared self-disclosures and partners begin to interpret their level of commitment as serious, they enter the next stage: **mutual dependency and need fulfillment** (Reiss, 1960). Eventually the everyday lives of the partners become intertwined. We get used to the other person being an audience for our jokes, a confidante for the expression of our fears and wishes, and a partner for our sexual experiences (Reiss & Lee, 1988). As a relationship progresses to this point, we begin to rely on our partner to satisfy our psychological and physical needs. These needs can be as basic as sexual appetites but also may include the desire for someone with whom we can share feelings, someone who can take care of us and whom we can take care of, and someone who will reinforce our own sense of worth and identity (Brehm, 1992).

> ■ **mutual dependency and need fulfillment**
> A relationship that endures beyond the point of shared self-disclosures and partners begin to interpret their level of commitment as serious.

From this stage model we can see that establishing and maintaining an intimate relationship is no easy feat. To get to the last stage of Reiss's model, many couples must endure conflicts, disappointments, and ambivalent feelings. Reiss viewed his model as a wheel, with rapport, self-disclosure, and dependency and need fulfillment as the spokes. As couples pass through each stage, or spoke, the relationship deepens and so, too, does their rapport, intimacy, and dependency—each one reinforcing the other.

At some point, couples may decide to formalize their commitment through marriage or some other "permanent" living arrangement. But not all relationships endure. In fact, most don't. As you may already know, ending a relationship with someone you've shared your deepest hopes and fears with, someone on whom you've come to depend, can be extremely difficult, even traumatic. If the breakup is not mutual, one person is left to come to terms with feelings of inadequacy and failure.

The Social Exchange Model

The stage model identifies the steps in a process of relationship development. The social exchange approach tries to explain why we are attracted to some people and not others (Blau, 1964; Emerson, 1962; Homans, 1961; Rubin, 1973; Thibaut & Kelley, 1959). One reason is that we evaluate our own qualities, such as economic standing and physical attractiveness, and seek partners whose assets match them.

The exchange approach also explains why we pursue some relationships and avoid others. Intimate relationships provide obvious rewards including love, sexual gratification, warmth, desirable characteristics of the partner, and companionship. But they present certain costs as well: the time and effort spent trying to maintain the relationship, undesirable characteristics of the partner, and interpersonal conflict.

Like sociobiologists, economist Gary Becker (1981) argues that men and women look for different things in a relationship. However, he focuses less on unseen genetic urges and more on the cultural capital individuals have at their disposal and the demands of the relationship marketplace. According to Becker, relationships develop when the arrangement is mutually beneficial to the parties, with benefits being greatest when each is able to contribute to the relationship what he or she does best. So, if women are more "skilled" at household labor and child care, and men are more "skilled" at earning money, both will benefit if the wife specializes in housework and the husband specializes in paid work. In such a traditional environment, women are compelled to search for "good providers," and men are likely to search for "good homemakers."

Since Becker first presented these ideas, the cultural climate has changed dramatically. People's preferences are less likely than perhaps they were in the past to be confined to specific specialized skills or traits. Today both men and women are likely to prefer a mate who is gainfully employed (South, 1991). Nevertheless, the assumption of the social exchange perspective that people seek out others whom they perceive as potentially rewarding remains valid.

Expectations

In addition to taking into account costs and benefits, the social exchange perspective also considers people's preferences and expectations. These shed light on the curious and sometimes inexplicable things people do in their intimate relationships. Surely you've seen people who remain in relationships that to outside observers seem undesirable or unrewarding. Why would they stay if, as social exchange theorists argue, people form and maintain relationships only so long as they're profitable?

The person's expectations and perceptions of alternatives may play a role. For example, if a woman receives certain necessary resources (such as financial support) from her obnoxious, beer-swilling partner and feels that she can't get those resources elsewhere, she may stay in the relationship out of necessity. If a man has had a history of bad relationships, his expectations may be quite low to begin with, so it wouldn't take much to exceed them. He may be satisfied in a relationship that others would find intolerable.

Availability of Partners

Our evaluations of the relationships we are forming are also influenced by larger social or "market" conditions. Relationship opportunities vary by age, race, and educational attainment (South & Lloyd, 1992). In addition, because you must have some contact with someone before you can fall in love and begin a relationship, clearly where you live will also limit your pool of prospective partners (Lichter, LeClere, & McLaughlin, 1991). In South Korea the traditional preference for sons has created a disproportionate number of unmarried men fighting over a shrinking pool of marriageable women. Consequently, more men are seeking wives in other countries. About 14% of all marriages in South Korea involve men marrying foreigners; that's more than triple the rate just 5 years ago (Onishi, 2007).

Marriage rates can also be affected by the overall supply of men and women of marriageable age with desirable economic and social characteristics (Lichter et al., 1991). Thus the shortage of marriageable, well-educated, and employed black men may account for the marriage rate among African Americans being lower than for other groups. This explanation of mate selection suggests that improving the socioeconomic status of black men could increase the number of potential marriage partners and have a stabilizing effect on black families.

Perhaps you disagree with this contention. Don't people who face a shortage of attractive potential partners simply lower their standards a bit? This question was addressed by sociologist Dan Lichter and his colleagues (Lichter, Anderson, & Hayward, 1995). They found that a favorable marriage market—that is, lots of possibilities—indeed increases the likelihood of marrying someone with a good education and a good job. However, they also found that people will forgo relationships entirely in an unfavorable market—that is, when no suitable mates are available.

WHAT DOES IT ALL MEAN?

Trying to shed light on something so precious and so personal as love relationships has several inherent dangers. One is that on close inspection the dark side of intimacy will appear. We've seen in this chapter that intimacy often includes conflict and even exploitation. Such facts fly in the face of popular images of intimacy and shake the foundation of what is culturally and personally valuable: our love relationships.

Another danger is that the attempt to intellectually examine intimacy will appear cold and emotionless. Who among us wants to equate love with a marketplace where people seek to maximize benefits and minimize costs through negotiation, bargaining, and comparison shopping? These concepts conflict with our deeply held, romantic visions of what love relationships are or should be. The fact that we desire, establish, and maintain intimacy with others only because we find it profitable to do so, or that nonromantic factors such as race, class, religion, and geography determine, to some degree, whom we find attractive is a bitter pill most of us would prefer not to swallow. The idealized image of love in U.S. culture largely denies control and rationality. We're "swept off our feet," we're "carried away," or love "puts a spell on us."

Yet we're all aware, at least at some level, that these nonromantic factors are important and that many of them influence our intimate choices. We secretly express doubt over the staying power of a relationship between two people who love each other very much but who have no visible means of support and no future prospects. "Starry-eyed romance" may make for enjoyable novels, but it may not be enough to sustain a relationship through the practical demands of day-to-day family life. As you think about what you've read in this chapter, consider the following questions:

1. Does dating exist at your school? Describe the most common ways that people develop intimate, long-term relationships on your campus? How are these processes different from or similar to the ways relationships were formed in your high school?

2. How do you think men and women differ in their approaches to intimate relationships? Do you think the sexual double standard still exists?

3. What are the relative advantages and disadvantages of a system of relationship formation based on love compared to a system based on family arrangement?

4. The social exchange perspective argues that we are drawn to relationships that provide us with the most benefits and the fewest costs. In general, when it comes to intimate relationships, do you think we are more inclined to be *selfish* (consciously aware of our own costs and benefits) or *selfless* (altruistic)?

SUMMARY

- Although love exists everywhere, it is not experienced in the same way in all cultures. The role that love plays in people's intimate lives is determined by the nature of the culture in which they live.

- In this society, love has become a "feminized" emotion, making it incompatible with such socially valued traits as power, independence, and control. Consequently, men and women tend to express love differently although they are equally capable of loving.

- Human sexuality is more than just a biological drive. Its expression is subject to strong societal norms. Hence, the way it is experienced by individuals varies from culture to culture and among different groups within the same culture.

- Unlike societies in which relationships are arranged by families, U.S. society recognizes dating as the means by which most people move from being single to being coupled.

- Dating is not a matter of completely free choice, however. Parental influence, cultural conceptions of gender, concerns over social class, and other societal constraints may determine who dates whom. Over the years the nature of dating has been changed by economic, educational, and technological changes in society.

- According to recent research, most dating relationships may be marked by some form of coercion, violence, or sexual assault.

- Attempts to identify the biological underpinnings of our intimate relationships remain controversial. More useful at this point are the stage model and the social exchange model. They attempt to explain how people become attracted to each other and why they stay together. Relationships appear to develop in stages, and they are influenced by partners' expectations and availability.

Go to the Online Learning Center at **www.mhhe.com/newman1** to test your knowledge of the chapter concepts and key terms.

KEY TERMS

bundling   186

calling   187

companionate love   170

compulsory heterosexuality   177

dating   185

feminization of love   174

intimacy   167

intimate self-disclosure   196

mutual dependency and need fulfillment   197

parental investment   193

passionate love   170

rapport   196

recreational sex   183

relational sex   183

sexual double standard   183

SEE FOR YOURSELF

The formal purpose of a university is to provide students with a quality education that will prepare them for their careers. But universities also informally provide students with countless lessons about friendship, intimacy, sexuality, and so on—lessons they will carry with them for the rest of their lives.

To delve deeper into the role that colleges play in creating and reinforcing expectations regarding intimacy, consider *all* the ways people meet, become attracted to, and establish intimate relationships with others on your campus. This task will require you to observe as well as speak to other students and staff members to gather information. *Do not rely solely on your personal experiences.*

What are the *institutional* (that is, structural) mechanisms that are designed explicitly to bring people together (university-sponsored social events, fraternity and sorority parties, and so on)? Have some places in the surrounding community (bars, restaurants, coffee houses, and so on) gained a reputation for being good spots to "meet people"? Does your campus newspaper or local newspaper have a "personals" section? How do people on your campus feel about the effectiveness of these mechanisms in forming and sustaining long-term intimate relationships? What are some of the barriers that impede their effectiveness?

Describe the campus programs that are available to help students deal with the *problems* of intimacy (for example, awareness programs about sexually transmitted diseases, sexual assault support networks, contraceptive availability, pregnancy testing, and abortion information). Talk to the people who run these programs and ask them what the programs offer and how effective they think they are. Try to find out how many students use these services in a given month.

What do your observations and the information you've gathered tell us about broader beliefs about gender and intimacy. Do they tend to reinforce or contradict traditional gender expectations? What do they tell us about the pervasiveness of gender ideologies in everyday campus life?

Now think about other social factors at work. How does the process of relationship formation here differ along racial/ethnic, social class, or sexual orientation lines? Do the programs on campus segregate students, or do they actively seek to integrate students from different social backgrounds?

More generally, what should be the university's role in creating or enhancing students' intimate experiences? What are the regulations your university imposes on students' intimate lives? Should universities restrict these behaviors at all? Should they be liable for any harm that these relationships might cause (for example, sexual violence)?

8

Marriage and Cohabitation

Weddings are perhaps our most treasured intimate ritual. The ceremony itself has long been recognized as the epitome of relationship commitment, the most desirable and the most recognizable public declaration of love and devotion. Americans spend more than $50 billion a year on weddings (Cloud, 2007a). In romantic Western fairy tales, marriage is the ultimate goal, and the stories typically end with a majestic wedding. Many of us learn, from a very young age, that someday, if we're lucky, we'll find that special someone and have a grand wedding.

The esteemed position of weddings is reflected in their presence in popular media. Hundreds of Web sites and dozens of magazines provide help in planning every conceivable aspect of a wedding. You cannot pick up an edition of *People* or *Us* magazine without finding a breathless description of some celebrity's lavish wedding.

Weddings—some sweet and poignant, others humorously disastrous—are also a staple of the film industry. Consider some box office successes of the past decade or so: *Father of the Bride* and *Father of the Bride II, Three Weddings and a Funeral, My Best Friend's Wedding, The Wedding Singer, Muriel's Wedding, The Wedding Banquet, Polish Wedding, Runaway Bride, My Big Fat Greek Wedding, The Bachelor, The Wedding Planner, The In-Laws, American Pie: The Wedding, Wedding Crashers, The Wedding Date,* and *27 Dresses.* The Internet Movie Database Web site lists 900 movie titles that contain the words "wedding," "bride," or "groom," and more than 700 that contain some variant of "marriage."

Weddings retain an unquestionably revered place in our culture, but a darker side also exists. A film critic, writing about yet another movie that focused on a wedding, put it this way:

> Say what you will about the institution of marriage, but without it the possibilities of romantic comedy would be impoverished. Not only is the fantasy of everlasting love capable of melting the most cynical heart, but weddings, with their ridiculous formal wear, pretentious catered food, free liquor and cheap sentiment, also overflow with potential for comic disaster. (Scott, 2001, p. 1)

Indeed, lurking behind the romance of weddings are some common negative images of the ensuing marriage: the nagging wife; the beer-swilling, television-addicted, couch potato husband; the domestic grind; the boring or nonexistent sex life; the "ball and chain"; the possessiveness, deceit, and suspicion. Even popular jokes like these depict the disagreeable side of marriage:

- Marriage is a three ring circus: engagement *ring,* wedding *ring,* suffe*ring.*
- Marriage is not a word, it's a sentence—a life sentence.
- Marriage is a great institution, but I'm not ready to live in an institution.
- I don't worry about terrorism. I was married for 2 years.

Our love-hate relationship with marriage is also reflected in the different ways men and women approach it. Consider the common ritual of the prewedding bachelor party, which has traditionally symbolized the groom's last precious hours of freedom before settling down to married life. Strippers, exotic dancers, and various sorts of pornography are not uncommon. The wedding is often seen more for what it is ending—the carefree life of bachelorhood—than for what it is beginning. Notice how such a ritual portrays marriage not as fulfilling but as constrictive, more like a prison than a paradise.

In contrast, a woman's wedding shower is usually a gift giving, happy affair that reinforces the "goodness" of getting married. Despite the occasional gag gifts such as edible underwear and odd sex toys, the atmosphere is usually one of eager anticipation. You don't hear many women at wedding showers bemoaning the bride-to-be's impending loss of freedom.

Despite its sometimes negative portrayal and public concern over the weakening of social norms that define people's behavior within it (Cherlin, 2007), marriage remains the pinnacle of committed intimacy in the United States. It's no surprise then that even though a decreasing percentage of the population is married, most unmarried men and women say they want to marry (Pew Research Center, 2007). Even those people who don't want to marry will likely experience living in a long-term committed relationship at some point in their lives.

In this chapter we take a close look at life in couples. We'll examine these relationships both as intensely personal experiences of individuals and as a social institution, which we can only fully understand in its cultural context. Then we'll compare marriages to other types of long-term relationships to see how different and how similar they are.

SOCIETAL INFLUENCES ON INTIMATE RELATIONSHIPS

Intimate relationships are universal; we find them in every human society. However, people's attitudes toward and experiences in relationships are clearly shaped by specific historical and cultural forces. We saw this influence with regard to dating in Chapter 7. As couples of all sorts—heterosexual or homosexual, unmarried or married—move into more committed, long-term relationships, they continue to be influenced by culturally prescribed norms.

Exogamy and Endogamy

Long before we settle into a long-term relationship, powerful social norms are at work, influencing whom we are likely to end up with. Two important social rules that limit the field of eligible partners are exogamy and endogamy.

At any given point in time, each one of us is a member of many groups simultaneously. We belong to a particular family, a friendship group, a set of coworkers, a religion, a race, an ethnicity, an age group, a social class, and so on. Entering into intimate relationships with fellow members of some of these groups is considered inappropriate. So society follows a set of customs referred to as **exogamy** rules, which require that an individual form a long-term romantic relationship with someone *outside* certain social groups to which he or she belongs.

In almost all societies, exogamy rules define marrying or having sex with people in one's own immediate family (siblings, parents, and children) as incest. These rules prohibit unions between people who are closely related genetically, thereby reducing the chance that offspring will inherit two copies of a defective gene. Exogamy prohibitions often extend to certain relatives outside the nuclear family too, such as cousins, grandparents, aunts, uncles, and, in some societies, stepsiblings. In the United States, 24 states completely prohibit first cousins to marry, and 6 others allow it under certain circumstances, such as when both partners are over 65 or when one is unable to reproduce (National Conference of State Legislatures, 2007). Informally, opposition to relationships between coworkers or, on college campuses, between people who live in the

■ **exogamy**
Rules that require an individual to form a long-term romantic relationship with someone *outside* certain social groups to which he or she belongs.

same dormitory (called "dorm-cest") illustrate a common belief that relationships work best when they occur between people who aren't in constant close proximity.

■ GOING GLOBAL

Marital Restrictions Around the World

The rules of exogamy are applied differently in different cultures. In South Korea, for example, people are strongly discouraged from marrying someone with the same surname, not a trivial rule considering that 55% of the population is named Kim, Park, Lee, Choi, or Chong. This rule originated centuries ago as a way of preventing marriages between members of the same clan. It is not as stringent as it once was, and various groups routinely lobby the government to rescind it. However, most single people still try to avoid lovers with the same name. As one college student put it, "When I'm introduced to someone, I very casually ask what her name is, and if I find out that it's the same as mine, it puts a mark against her right there" (WuDunn, 1996, p. A4).

One of the advantages of exogamy rules is that they encourage alliances between groups larger than the primary family. The Temiar of Malaysia, for example, forbid marriage between two people of the same village, though in practice many people still form such unions ("Temiar Marriage and Family," 2007).

In other places, the violation of this restriction can lead to severe sanctions. In 2003 a young Indian couple was beaten to death by members of their own families for being lovers. In their community, it was considered incest for two people from the same village to fall in love. A resident of the village said, "In our society all the families living in a village are all sons and daughters of the whole village. We are like brothers and sisters. The marriage of brothers and sisters is not accepted" (quoted in Waldman, 2003, p. A4).

■ **endogamy**
Rules that limit intimate choices to people within one's social group, principally race, ethnicity, religion, and social class.

Less formal, but just as powerful, are the rules of **endogamy,** which limit intimate choices to people *within* one's social group, however that group is defined. The vast majority of marriages in the United States occur between people from the same religion, ethnoracial group, social class, and age group. Patterns of school and residential segregation increase the likelihood that people of similar backgrounds will come into contact. These similar backgrounds, in turn, increase the likelihood that the two people will share common beliefs, values, and experiences. But more important from a sociological point of view, rules of endogamy reflect our society's traditional distaste for relationships that cross group boundaries.

Religion

Although the traditional endogamy rules that once obligated people to marry within their faith have faded over the years, most religions still actively discourage interfaith marriages. Their concern is that such marriages may weaken people's religious beliefs and values, lead to raising children in a different faith, or take religion out of the family entirely. Religious leaders often worry about the bigger problem of maintaining their religious identity within a diverse and complex society.

Approximately 80 to 90% of U.S. adults marry someone of the same religion (Kalmijn, 1991), although sociologists note that these figures may overestimate religious endogamy because some spouses originally come from a different faith but convert to their

partners' religion before or shortly after marrying. Nevertheless, the high rate of religious endogamy reflects the influence
of religion on individuals' behaviors and expectations—even
(or especially) taking into account that some spouses feel it's
important enough that they're willing to convert. For very religious individuals, marrying someone of a different faith or
even no faith would be unthinkable; they'd probably not find
those individuals attractive in the first place.

Race and Ethnicity

Similarly, most U.S. marriages are racially or ethnically endoga-
mous. Marriages that cross racial or ethnic lines have become
more common in U.S. society over the past few decades, however. In 1970 there were 300,000 interracial married couples (or
about 0.7% of all marriages). Today there are 2.3 million interracial couples, constituting almost 4% of all U.S. marriages.
In addition, marriages between Latino/as and non-Latino/as
(regardless of race) increased from 1.7% of all married couples
in 1980 to 3.7% today (Figure 8.1). About 27% of Latino/as marry
someone of a different ethnic group, a rate that has been fairly
stable since the 1980s (U.S. Bureau of the Census, 2007).

The strength of racial and ethnic endogamy rules varies from group to group. Today, Native Americans have the
highest rate of intermarriage (over 56% for both men and
women), whereas non-Latino whites have the lowest (around
2%) (Jacobs & Labov, 2002). Most scholars have attributed
high rates of intermarriage in certain groups to the process of
assimilation, whereby minority identity gradually dissolves as
individuals adjust to the practices of the dominant culture.

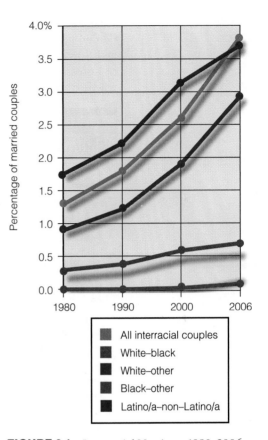

FIGURE 8.1   Interracial Marriage, 1980–2006
Source: U.S. Bureau of the Census, 2008, table 59.

Intermarriage rates for all groups are affected by a variety
of social factors, such as social class, opportunities to interact with members of other
ethnoracial groups, and increasing numbers of newly arrived immigrants, especially
from Asia and Latin America (Qian & Lichter, 2007). Intermarriage is more common
among people with college educations than among people who didn't go to college.
Clearly, college facilitates contact between people from different groups (Jacobs &
Labov, 2002). Similarly, military service creates occasions for personnel to meet, fall in
love with, and marry people from diverse backgrounds either in their own units or on
the base. Not surprisingly, intermarriage rates are higher in the military than they are in
the general population (Jacobson & Heaton, 2003).

Moreover, intermarriage is not uniform from one region to another. The highest rates
of interracial marriage (close to 10% of all marriages) are found in the West, where racial
attitudes in general tend to be more tolerant than in other parts of the country. Rates in
the South, Northeast, and Midwest are only around 4% (Lee & Edmonston, 2005).

Where ethnic communities are strong and concentrated, rules of endogamy tend to
be powerful impediments to intermarriage. Strong communities provide a large supply
of ethnically similar marital candidates. Ethnic institutions in these communities (social
clubs, churches, synagogues, and so on) often actively discourage intermarriage. Gos-
sip and ostracism from within the community can sometimes be enough to discourage
people from choosing a mate from outside the group. But where these community

structures and social networks are weak, personal interests and desires can easily override group constraints. One study found that intermarriage among Chinese Americans and Korean Americans is significantly higher in Hawaii, which has no large Chinese or Korean communities exerting control over marital choice, than it is in Los Angeles, where ethnic communities are strong (Kitano, Yeung, Chai, & Hatanaka, 1984).

■ TAKING A CLOSER LOOK

Interracial Relationships Through History

The issue of ethnoracial endogamy has always been an especially emotional one in U.S. society. The first law against interracial marriage was enacted in Maryland in 1661, prohibiting whites from marrying Native Americans or African slaves. Over the next 300 years or so, 38 more states put such laws on the books, expanding their coverage to include Chinese, Japanese, and Filipino Americans. It was believed that a mixing of the races (then referred to as "mongrelization") would destroy the racial purity (and superiority) of whites. The irony, of course, is that racial mixing had been taking place since the very beginning of this country, much of it through white slave owners raping black slaves.

Legal sanctions against interracial marriage persisted well into the 20th century. The gruesome murder in 1955 of Emmett Till, a black youth who was thought to have flirted openly with a white woman, brought to light the deepseated feelings that some people harbored over even the suggestion of interracial intimacy. In 1958, when white Richard Loving and his new wife, black Mildred Jeter Loving, moved to their new home in Virginia, a sheriff and two

In 1958, Mildred and Richard Loving were arrested for violating Virginia's law prohibiting interracial marriage.

deputies acting on an anonymous tip arrived to arrest them for violating a state law that prohibited interracial marriages (the couple received their marriage certificate in Washington, D.C.). The Lovings were sentenced to 1 year in jail but then learned that the judge would suspend the sentence if they left the state and promised not to return for 25 years. They agreed, but after leaving town filed suit. In 1967 the U.S. Supreme Court ruled in their favor, concluding that using racial classifications to restrict freedom to marry was unconstitutional. Sixteen states, mostly in the South, had their interracial marriage prohibition laws struck down with this ruling.

Fifty years later, people are no longer banished for marrying someone of a different race. For the most part, interracial intimacy has never been more positively received (Kennedy, 2002). Nevertheless, even though attitudes are becoming more tolerant, discomfort with interracial relationships still lingers. South Carolina and Alabama had laws against interracial marriage on the books until the mid-1990s. Even today, rural judges can sometimes make it difficult for interracial couples to marry (B. Staples, 1999).

People in interracial relationships often cite racism as the most difficult problem they face, both before and after marriage (Rosenblatt, Karis, & Powell, 1995). About half the black-white couples in one study felt that biracial marriage makes things harder for them, and about two thirds reported that their parents had a problem with the relationship, at least initially (Fears & Deane, 2001). Many U.S. couples, especially black-white relationships, still experience a lack of family support when choosing to marry someone of a different race (Lewis & Yancey, 1997). Everyday activities may require more time and effort for interracial couples. For instance, when planning vacations, many interracial couples do extensive research of potential leisure destinations to see how accepting they are of relationships like theirs (Hibbler & Shinew, 2005).

Social Class and Education

If we based our ideas about the formation of romantic relationships on what we see in movies, we might be tempted to conclude that divisions based on social class and educational attainment don't matter or perhaps don't exist at all. Films like *Titanic, Good Will Hunting, The Wedding Planner, Maid in Manhattan, Working Girl, Pretty Woman, Fools Rush In, Love Story,* and *Sweet Home Alabama* send the message that when it comes to love, we're all really alike. In these stories the power of love is strong enough to blow away differences in schooling, pedigree, resources, and tastes. When it comes to love, Hollywood's United States is a classless society.

In reality, however, class and education are powerful factors in marriage. As we saw in Chapter 6, members of the upper classes face strong pressures to choose marital partners of similar social standing (Kalmijn, 1998). Even if two people from different races or religions marry, chances are they will have similar socioeconomic backgrounds. Certainly some people do marry a person from a different social class, but the class tends to be an adjacent one—for instance, an upper-class woman marrying a middle-class man. Cinderella-like marriages between people of vastly different class rankings are quite rare. Similarly, highly educated people tend to marry other highly educated people (Zernike, 2007).

Individuals of similar social status are more likely to participate in activities in which they come into contact with people who share their values, tastes, goals, expectations, and background (Kalmijn & Flap, 2001). Our education system plays a particularly important role in bringing people from similar class backgrounds together. The proportion of married couples that share the same level of schooling is the highest it's been in 40 years. The odds of someone with only a high school education marrying a college graduate have been decreasing since the 1970s (Schwartz & Mare, 2005).

Moreover, neighborhoods and neighborhood schools tend to be made up of people from similar social classes. College often continues class segregation. People from upper-class backgrounds are considerably more likely to attend costly private schools, whereas those from the middle class are most likely to enroll in state universities, and those from the working class are most likely to enroll in community colleges. These structural conditions increase the odds that the people college students meet and form intimate relationships with will come from a similar class background.

Age

In many societies, husbands are older than their wives, sometimes considerably older (see Chapter 3). In contrast, U.S. marriages tend to be age-endogamous. Husbands and wives have always been fairly close in age. In fact, about 32% of U.S. marriages consist of couples who are within 1 year of each other in age; in fewer than 10% of all marriages is one spouse 10 or more years older (U.S. Bureau of the Census, 2000). When age discrepancies in U.S. marriages do exist, it is almost always men who are older. Only about 12% of all marriages consist of wives who are 2 or more years older than their husbands (U.S. Bureau of the Census, 2000).

Social Expectations

Rules of exogamy and endogamy help determine who marries whom. But even after relationships form, cultural forces continue to exert influence on couples' lives, affecting what they expect of each other.

The Expectation of Interdependence

■ **interdependence**
The degree to which partners rely on each other to provide needed resources such as affection, companionship, sex, and money.

Sociologists maintain that the key feature of long-term intimate relationships is **interdependence,** the degree to which partners rely on each other to provide affection, companionship, sex, money, and so on (Berscheid & Peplau, 1983; Scanzoni, Polonko, Teachman, & Thompson, 1989).

Traditionally, middle- and upper-class wives tended to be economically dependent on their husbands because women were less likely than men to work outside the home. In return, wives usually managed the household, the children, the couple's social life, and the emotional quality of the marriage. Although both men and women were likely to depend on and benefit from the exchange, some sociologists argue that women's economic dependence, which made it difficult for them to survive outside marriage on their own, is mainly what stabilized marriages (Nock, 1999; Popenoe, 1999). As women have gained greater economic independence and more couples have become dual earners, economic interdependence is becoming a less common reason for two people to stay married.

Some people fear that the declining expectation of interdependence reduces interest in marriage and leads to higher divorce rates. But studies show that economic interdependence is still likely to exist in contemporary relationships, including those in which both partners work outside the home. Each partner comes to rely on the other's income to provide the higher standard of living it affords. Furthermore, commitment in relationships consists of more than just economic interdependence. Couples tend to depend on each other for everything from practical assistance to emotional support. Often, this sort of interdependence leads to what social scientists call specialization— each partner developing some skills and neglecting others "because each can count on the other to take responsibility for some of the work involved in making a home or living" (Waite & Gallagher, 2000, p. 26).

The Expectation of Equity

Nowadays, most people enter long-term relationships, whether marital or cohabiting, with certain expectations about **equity** (that is, fairness) and the balance of power. According to the social exchange model, in forming relationships we are motivated to maximize our benefits and minimize our costs.

> ■ **equity**
> The level of perceived fairness or justice that exists in a relationship.

But judgments of how much "profit" is to be derived from a relationship and how well it compares to past experiences and perceived alternatives are not made by one partner alone. Each person is simultaneously interested in maximizing rewards and minimizing costs. Once established, relationships work best when the exchange is fair, or equitable; that is, when both partners derive benefits from the relationship proportional to what they invest in it. The presence or absence of such interpersonal equity has profound effects on the satisfaction felt by individuals as well as the stability of the relationship itself (Hatfield, Traupmann, Sprecher, Utne, & Hay, 1985; Utne, Hatfield, Traupmann, & Greenberger, 1984). Indeed, research shows that the happiest couples are those in which partners provide each other with many rewarding experiences and few costly ones (Birchler et al., 1975; Rusbult, 1983; Vincent et al., 1975).

In the context of relationships, investments are not only financial. An **investment** can be anything someone has to offer to the relationship, such as time, money, interest, or personal characteristics like good looks or a sense of humor (Brown, 1986). Investments are important because they create feelings of entitlement or deservedness. When friends say to you, "You deserve better than her" or "You're entitled to some happiness," they're making an implicit statement about equity: "Given what you have invested or what you have to offer, in all fairness you should be receiving greater benefits."

> ■ **investment**
> Anything that a person can offer to a relationship, such as time, money, interest, or personal characteristics, that creates feelings of entitlement or deservedness.

As you might suspect, not every relationship is perfectly equitable. When things become disproportional, feelings of unfairness can result. In general there are two types of inequity: *underbenefited inequity* (that is, you feel you are not getting out of the relationship what you feel you deserve) and *overbenefited inequity* (that is, you feel you are getting too much for what you have to offer). Each kind of inequity can threaten the stability of the relationship, though underbenefited inequity leads to more distress (VanYperen & Buunk, 1990) and is especially likely to create feelings of depression (Longmore & Demaris, 1997).

■ TAKING A CLOSER LOOK

Overcoming Inequity

Social psychologist Elaine Hatfield and her colleagues (Hatfield, Walster, & Traupmann, 1978) interviewed 537 college men and women who were dating someone. She asked them whether they expected to be with their partners in 1 year and in 5 years. Those who felt their relationships were perfectly equitable were much more likely than others to think the relationships would last. Interestingly, the overbenefited participants were just as doubtful as underbenefited participants about the future prospects of their relationships. Presumably, the underbenefited individuals felt they would do better in the future, and the overbenefited individuals didn't expect their luck to last. Incidentally, a follow-up study 3 months later indicated that the equitable relationships were, in fact, more likely to still be intact.

Both types of inequity are uncomfortable and motivate individuals to restore either actual or psychological equity (Brehm, 1992). Underbenefited partners may attempt to reduce their investments in the relationship or demand more from their partner. For example, if you feel you're being underbenefited, you may decide not to do as many favors for your partner or you may stop showing affection. If that fails, you may start to demand more benefits or more investments from your partner: "Do you think you could start showing some appreciation for all that I do for you around here?" Overbenefited partners, on the other hand, may feel guilty and try to increase their contributions (such as taking more responsibility for planning social events) or increase the benefits they offer their partner (such as showering him or her with gifts).

The problem with these strategies is that they may backfire. Your reduction of contributions to the relationship may be met by a similar reduction on the part of your partner. Or your partner may take advantage of your attempts to increase his or her benefits. Hence, individuals will often resort to attempts to restore equity psychologically, convincing themselves that, although it seems otherwise, equity does in fact exist (Brehm, 1992). If you are the underbenefited partner, you may talk yourself into believing that your partner is a special person who deserves more than you do. Perhaps she or he has had terrible experiences in the past and deserves to be treated well in this relationship. On the other hand, if you are the overbenefited partner, you may convince yourself that, because of some particularly noble quality you possess, you truly deserve the favorable inequity.

Inequity is fairly obvious when the imbalances involve things that are easy to see: financial contributions to the relationship or the performance of certain chores around the house. But an imbalance in feelings—in emotional investment—is more difficult to identify. We all know of relationships in which one partner seems to be more in love than the other partner. Such imbalances in emotional attachment have the potential of creating serious and potentially dangerous power differences in relationships. The person who loves less or does not express unconditional affection has the upper hand in the relationship because the partner will presumably suffer more if the relationship should end (Blau, 1964). Hence, the individual who loves less can dictate the terms of the relationship and can, if so inclined, exploit the other by making heavy demands. The partner who loves more has greater interest in maintaining the relationship and may be forced to put up with a lot to do so.

principle of least interest Power in a relationship rests with the partner who loves less and has the least interest in continuing it.

Such a situation implies a rather depressing reality about intimate relationships. The less-dependent partner—that is, the one who has more alternatives outside the relationship—has the greater power in it because that person can more easily abandon the relationship. This phenomenon, referred to as the **principle of least interest,** suggests that control over the relationship rests with the partner who has the least interest in continuing it. This person is able to dictate the conditions of the relationship, make demands of the other, and even exploit that person's dependence if he or she is so inclined.

The Expectation of Commitment

To understand the true nature of enduring relationships, we need to view expectations surrounding interdependence and equity within a broader context. After all, why do we make investments in our relationships? How can individuals justify continuing in what, objectively, appears to be an inequitable arrangement? Why would an individual become economically or emotionally dependent on a relationship if the option to be more independent exists elsewhere?

The answer to these questions is that enduring relationships require a certain degree of commitment. **Commitment** is personal dedication to the relationship, a desire to maintain and improve it for the benefit on both parties (Stanley & Markman, 1992). In our culture, we expect couples to express commitment and concern for each other, and to come to the other's defense when threatened. What characterizes a committed relationship is genuine concern for the partner's well-being, not just one's own (Stanley & Markman, 1992). Committed partners worry about each other and feel responsible for each other (Waite & Gallagher, 2000). Here's how one wife describes what commitment means to her:

> We are responsible for each other . . . for each other's health, each other's well-being, mental health, financial stability. . . . [W]e are each other's keeper. . . . [W]e have a responsibility to go to a fair amount of trouble in order to make sure that we stay together and we continue to be responsible for each other. (quoted in Waite & Gallagher, 2000, p. 19)

When you're committed to a relationship or a partner, you are more likely to make sacrifices for the relationship and to invest in it. In a highly committed relationship, partners are willing to tolerate a certain amount of powerlessness or momentary inequity because they believe that things will balance out in the long run (Clark & Mills, 1979). A husband may be willing to forgo his own educational plans so his wife can pursue an advanced degree because, in the long term, he expects to benefit from her higher income.

The Expectation of Permanence

Another cultural expectation that characterizes long-term intimate relationships is that of permanence. Despite the high rate of divorce in the United States, most couples still marry with the expectation that they will be married forever. Although cohabiting relationships are often shorter than marriages, many cohabitors still expect that their relationships will be permanent.

Expectations of permanence vary widely among different social groups. Conservative religious groups, such as fundamentalist Christians, are morally opposed to divorce and feel it is better to stay in an unsatisfying marriage than to divorce. Others, however, feel that permanence, simply for the sake of permanence, is not necessarily desirable.

The Expectation of Sexual Access

In the United States, another distinguishing feature of long-term, intimate relationships is the expectation of sexual access. Traditionally, heterosexual marriages have been created by establishing sexual ties; thus the first act of sexual intercourse on the wedding

■ **commitment**
Personal dedication to a relationship; a desire to maintain and improve it for the benefit of both partners.

night symbolically ratifies the marriage. If two people who are legally married have never had sexual intercourse, they are said not to have "consummated" the marriage. Such a situation used to be grounds for **annulment**—a declaration that a marriage is null and void because a key term of the marriage contract had not been put into effect.

For generations, most men probably had some sexual experience before marriage, but for women marriage usually meant their initiation into an adult sexual relationship (see Chapter 7 for a discussion of the sexual double standard). Even for those people who did have some sexual experience before marriage, there was a big difference between "the guilty, if passionate, tumblings in the back seat of a car, the corner of a park, or the living room couch and the luxury of a bed of their own, unconstrained by concerns about time or parents" (Rubin, 1990, p. 161).

Today, however, marriage is likely to follow a period of sexual exploration with a variety of partners and is just as likely to be the continuation of an already existing sexual relationship as the beginning of a new one. Nevertheless, spouses and other long-term partners still expect to have relatively unimpeded sexual access to one another. The two people may have different levels of desire or different levels of adventurousness, but they know they will be able to have sex with their partner without the anxiety and auditioning that often characterizes sexual behavior in casual relationships.

Because of sexual access, married couples and long-term cohabitors have sex more frequently than single people (Laumann, Gagnon, Michael, & Michaels, 1994). But frequency declines precipitously after the early years of a relationship (C. Liu, 2000), and every year thereafter sex gets a little rarer:

> There is an old saying that if a couple puts a penny in a jar for every time they have sex in the first year of marriage and then takes a penny out of the jar for every time they have sex the rest of the marriage, the pair will never empty out the jar. (Schwartz & Rutter, 1998, p. 132)

Aside from biological aging and diminished health, a reason typically cited for this decline is habituation or, to put it less delicately, boredom (Call, Sprecher, & Schwartz, 1995). Once the novelty and uncertainty disappear, sex becomes mundane. Both men and women can become bored by predictability (Schwartz & Rutter, 1998). Furthermore, the distractions of daily life, which multiply exponentially if children are around, can also reduce desire and energy.

The Expectation of Sexual Exclusivity

An expectation of sexual access is usually accompanied by an expectation of sexual exclusivity, which is apparent in the kind of sexual possessiveness that frequently characterizes long-term relationships. In U.S. society, marriage is considered a contract for exclusive sexual rights between two spouses (Collins, 1992).

This expectation of sexual exclusivity has historically applied more to women than to men. In traditional societies, a woman's body was the sexual property of her husband (which explains why more emphasis was placed on the bride's being a virgin at marriage than the groom). A husband's property rights over his wife were threatened if she had intercourse with another man. Under English common law, a man was legally incapable of committing adultery. Indeed, the offense of adultery was not the sexual betrayal of one partner by the other but the wife's engaging in acts that could taint the husband's bloodlines (Stoddard, 1992). In contemporary Pakistan, rape laws include a section stating that a woman must have four male witnesses to prove a rape. If she fails to provide proof, she faces the charge of adultery (Masood, 2006).

The vast majority of individuals in the United States, about 9 out of 10 in one national survey, believe that extramarital sex is morally wrong (Laumann et al., 1994). Most people believe that it is both the cause and consequence of marital deterioration (Previti & Amato, 2004). As with the ideal of permanence, however, such attitudes reflect an expectation, not necessarily the reality. When sociologist Edward Laumann and his colleagues (1994) asked married individuals "Have you ever had sex with someone other than your husband or wife while you were married?" about 25% of men and 15% of women answered "yes." The researchers also found a slight tendency for cohabitors to report affairs more often than married persons, even when the duration of the relationship was the same.

Interestingly, for heterosexual couples, extramarital affairs are defined almost exclusively by sexual infidelity. Emotional infidelity seems to be of less concern. Among gay couples, fidelity is defined more in terms of emotional commitment and betrayal (McWhirter, 1984, cited in Steen & Schwartz, 1995).

Technology is also changing the definition of infidelity. The Internet affords individuals the opportunity to talk to, flirt with, or seduce virtually anyone, no matter how distant. It is possible for someone to sexually connect with another person via the Internet every way but physically and therefore still feel completely faithful to one's partner. There may be a greater tendency to self-disclose and experiment on the Internet than one would in real life because online communication offers a sense of anonymity and security. But some therapists insist that online affairs can be as threatening to a relationship as real-life ones (Greenfield, 1999).

The Expectation of Being a "Couple"

One of the major expectations surrounding long-term relationships is that the people in them behave like a couple. In our culture, for instance, we typically expect married couples to live together and spend time together, to pool financial resources, to entertain other couples, and so forth. Imagine a newlywed couple in which the husband wants to continue hanging out with his old single friends. To the wife (and others), such actions might lead to questions about his commitment to the relationship, and even his desire to be married in the first place.

Being a couple implies something far more important than simply acting the part; it means feeling and thinking like a couple. In other words, it includes the expectation that the two people will create a new *identity* as a couple. It means thinking less in terms of "me and mine" and more in terms of "we and ours." For many individuals, one of the difficult challenges of entering a long-term relationship is balancing their new "couple" identity with their old "individual" identity. Such a balancing act is especially difficult in marriages, where institutionalized expectations encourage, and sometimes even require, a person to abandon his or her identity as a single person.

As relationships progress, couples construct this new couple identity for themselves and, through interaction with each other, reinforce it (Berger & Kellner, 1964). Third parties also play an important role in reinforcing the couple's new identity. Whether outsiders approve of the relationship ("You two make a lovely couple") or disapprove of it ("I think you can do better"), on some level they are validating the couple by responding to them as a couple, acknowledging that a "couple" entity even exists (Berger &

Kellner, 1964). Such external validation is important to developing intimate relationships. Sometimes partners don't even consider themselves a couple until they are publicly recognized as such by their friends and relatives.

Once others recognize two people as "coupled," they are likely to impose a new and complex set of expectations. The couple might be issued joint invitations to social gatherings, be expected to accompany each other to public events, or be assumed to know each other's whereabouts at all times.

The power that these expectations have over how we act and think reinforces the contention that personal relationships always develop within a social context. As much as we would like to believe otherwise, intimacy—even love—is not just a phenomenon that occurs between two people. Third parties, especially parents, peers, and children (indeed, anyone who has a vested interest in the couple's well-being), can have a significant role in shaping their relationship.

Even the most private aspects of the couple's interactions, such as their sexual activities, can be subjected to third-party influences (Laumann et al., 1994). Childless married couples often feel pressured to have children, and children may actively discourage their single parents from dating and becoming sexually intimate with persons they deem unacceptable.

THE PRIVATE CULTURE OF COUPLED LIFE

I f all relationships are governed similarly by a culture's rules and expectations, it would seem that all couples, at least those within a given culture, would be pretty similar. But, of course, this isn't the case. As you're well aware, no two relationships are ever exactly alike.

It's true that we all enter a relationship with a set of religious beliefs, ethnic traditions, and community norms that shape our desires and give us an idea about what to expect. We also bring with us information from our parents', relatives', and friends' relationships as well as the images of relationships we see in the media. Despite possible similarities, however, no two people's ideas, experiences, and expectations are identical. Thus each couple faces the task of forging its own unique relationship while at the same time conforming to broader social norms.

> ■ **private culture**
> A couple's unique way of dealing with the demands of everyday life, such as how important decisions will be made, what are appropriate expressions of sexuality, how the individuals will communicate with one another, and how household labor will be allocated.

Over time, couples create a unique pattern of interaction, a set of habits, rules, and shared reality. They develop a sort of **private culture**—their own particular way of dealing with the demands of everyday life, such as how important decisions will be made, what are appropriate expressions of sexuality, and how household labor will be allocated (Blumstein & Kollock, 1988). The private culture includes things as mundane as a weekly dinner schedule or a Sunday morning ritual of breakfast and newspaper reading in bed, or as serious as the distribution of power and the handling of household finances. Some rituals and habits disappear as the composition of the family changes (for instance, with the arrival of children); others persist and are passed on to future generations.

The private culture of marriages and other enduring intimate relationships creates for individuals a sense of order and connection (Berger & Kellner, 1964). Committed, intimate relationships validate the participants and the world they live in. This sense of order is key to our sense of well-being. Sociologists have long recognized that people who lack such connections can feel profoundly alienated (Durkheim, 1897/1951). Simply being married or in a committed relationship doesn't make someone impervious to these negative feelings. Undoubtedly, some married persons feel alienated and distant from their spouses.

Communication Styles

From a constructionist perspective, communication patterns are essential to establishing a shared reality and private culture and ultimately to building a successful relationship (Berger & Kellner, 1964). Partners continually define and redefine their relationship through communication. They look to their interactions with each other for confirming evidence that the partner understands and accepts them (Weger, 2005).

For decades social scientists have tried to explain why relationships succeed or fail by looking at factors like income, education, age at marriage, and the age difference between partners. Many now believe that these factors may be less important than the communication that occurs between partners: not only how they converse but how they interpret each other's words and actions. It's not simply a lack of money that causes problems in a relationship; it's how the couple negotiates and talks to each other about their financial difficulties (Fitzpatrick, 1988). Research evidence consistently shows that the way partners communicate when trying to support one another or when trying to resolve problems is closely related to relationship satisfaction (Cohan & Kleinbaum, 2002). Indeed, married couples seeking divorce frequently cite "communication problems" as a reason for the breakup (Kincaid & Caldwell, 1995).

There is no single recipe for communication and, therefore, marital success. What works for some couples may not work for others, as sociologists John Cuber and Peggy Harroff (1965) found almost 50 years ago. They conducted extensive interviews with more than 400 upper-middle-class husbands and wives between the ages of 35 and 50 to uncover the patterns of communication that emerge in enduring marriages. All their respondents had been married at least 10 years, and all claimed they had never considered divorce or separation. In other words, these couples were not in any sort of crisis.

Cuber and Harroff found that stable couples are quite diverse. They identified five different types of marriage based on different patterns of communication:

■ *Conflict-habituated marriages* are marked by a pervasive and constant air of tension. These are the couples who seem to constantly fight and argue. Simply being in each other's company is enough to trigger an argument. To the outside observer, such conflict would appear to characterize a marriage doomed to failure. But these couples had no intention of ending their relationship. The conflict-habituated way of interacting could last a lifetime.

■ *Devitalized marriages* are those of couples who were once deeply in love but who have drifted apart over the years. Communication is minimal and usually devoted to specific tasks or problems. Most of the time they spend together is "duty" time: entertaining guests, spending time with the children, pursuing community activities. They realize their marriage isn't what it used to be but remain together out of a sense of obligation and loyalty.

■ *Passive-congenial marriages* look, for all intents and purposes, like devitalized marriages, except they have been this way from the start. The couple rarely argues, but they also have no expectation of love or passion. The marriage provides stability for the couple so they can direct their energies elsewhere. They define their lack of intense involvement as the way they want their marriage to be.

- *Vital marriages* conform most closely to the ideal image of what marital communication should be. These are spouses who truly share intimacy in all important aspects of their lives. Their primary satisfaction in life is derived from the time they spend with each other, although they do not lose their separate identities.

- *Total marriages* differ from vital marriages in the degree to which couples share time with each other. In a total marriage, the spouses are completely absorbed in each other's lives; they may even work together. Twenty-four hours a day in each other's company is still not enough. Privacy from each other is a foreign concept.

Although Cuber and Harroff's typology of marital communication patterns was based only on upper-middle-class couples and therefore may not be applicable to all marriages, it shows us that stable (or successful) relationships needn't always be the picture of happiness. As long as both partners in the relationship agree that a particular pattern of communication suits them, things are fine. Trouble can arise, though, when individuals expect different sorts of conversations and responses from their partners. One factor that can cause different expectations is gender.

Gender, Intimacy, and Communication

Some of the most popular books on intimate relationships in the past decade or so, such as John Gray's *Men Are From Mars, Women Are From Venus* and Deborah Tannen's *You Just Don't Understand,* focus on the different ways that men and women communicate. To state that men and women are from different planets, even in jest, obviously overstates the effect that gender can have on intimate communication. When it comes to the way they communicate, men and women are more alike than different. Nonetheless, gender undoubtedly influences the way people interact in relationships. For heterosexual couples, gender can pose significant challenges if men and women bring different understandings and communicative experiences to the relationship. Even for same-sex couples, gender can shape communication and lead to problems.

Communication in Heterosexual Relationships

Research on gender differences in communication have consistently shown that women's and men's conversational patterns differ in many ways. For example, studies over the years have found the following (Maltz & Borker, 1982; Noller, 1993; Parlee, 1989):

- Women tend to ask more questions.
- Women use more positive minimal responses, such as "mm hmms."
- Men tend to interrupt more.
- Women are more likely to use modifiers and hedges such as "sort of," "kind of," and "I guess."
- Women are more likely to use tag questions at the end of declarative sentences such as "It's cold outside, *isn't it?*"
- Men are more likely to change the topic of conversation.
- Men are more likely to want to problem solve; women are more likely to want to listen.
- Men are less open and less likely to engage in intimate self-disclosure.

Such differences can have important implications for the way private cultures develop in long-term relationships:

> Women feel it is essential to keep conversation going, which they do by encouraging other speakers, filling silences, and asking questions. Men, on the other hand, view such supportive devices as weak, and prefer to use strong tactics such as making statements and interrupting other speakers. Gendered patterns of decision making and problem solving stem from these broader views of the purpose of communication. Women seek consensus in making decisions, because their primary objective is to maintain the emotional link between partners. Men seek to make decisions more expeditiously, with the more powerful person deciding the outcome. In responding to others' concerns or problems, men are likely to suggest solutions or possible actions, whereas women are more likely to express sympathy by sharing similar feelings or experiences, thus creating the intimacy that is women's goal in conversation. (Steen & Schwartz, 1995, pp. 310–311)

In everyday conversation, but especially during arguments, these differences can hinder effective communication and, as a result, interfere with the sense of connection in a relationship. For example, if a man "clams up," interrupts, or changes topics frequently in conversation, it may appear to his partner that he isn't paying attention, even if he is (Noller, 1993). During conflict, gendered patterns of interaction can result in what has been termed the demand–withdraw pattern, in which one partner's (usually the woman's) attempts to confront a problem are met with the other partner's (usually the man's) attempts to avoid the discussion (Weger, 2005). If the key to successful relationships is clear communication, such gender differences can pose a serious barrier.

Communication in Homosexual Relationships

In heterosexual relationships it is the gender *difference* in conversation patterns that may hinder communication, but in homosexual relationships, gender *similarity* can be just as problematic. As one therapist notes:

> It was always the woman who has a glimmer for thirty seconds of how wonderful intimacy feels, how close it feels, and then the guy jumps up and wants a cup of coffee or wants to do this or wants to do that. . . . You put two women together who know what it is they're after, and it's hard to resist them wanting a constant peak experience. (quoted in Weston, 1991, p. 152)

Lesbian partners sometimes experience difficulty solving problems because their approach is too similar. "If both women are committed to reaching complete consensus, discussions may go on interminably, erupting in anger when frustrated partners cannot reach mutual agreement" (Steen & Schwartz, 1995, p. 316).

The opposite problem can arise for gay men who may have acquired more traditional male communication patterns:

> It was much different in the beginning of the relationship, because we didn't realize how much we didn't communicate. You tend to overlook familiar things and they don't come out. We were ignorant—or afraid—about how to discuss things. (quoted in Blumstein & Schwartz, 1983, p. 542)

Interestingly, many same-sex couples actually experience communication dynamics very similar to those of heterosexual couples, especially with regard to relationship maintenance behaviors (Haas & Stafford, 2005). But they may also face similar difficulties. That is, one partner is likely to be more open and work harder to keep the "conversation" going while the other is more withdrawn.

Power in Couples

Clearly then, gender is important, but it's not the only factor shaping communication patterns in the private culture of long-term relationships. Sociologist Cathryn Johnson (1994) conducted an experiment in which men and women were instructed to play either a managerial role or an employee role in a fictitious office setting. She found that positions of authority were far more important than gender in understanding conversational patterns. Subordinates exhibited more conversational support and were less assertive than those in the manager role, regardless of gender.

When we examine conversational patterns and dynamics in intimate relationships more closely, we find that the person in power—no matter the gender—tends to dictate the nature and direction of communication. Sociologists Peter Kollock, Phil Blumstein, and Pepper Schwartz (1985) examined taped conversations between intimate partners in heterosexual, gay male, and lesbian couples to see whether positions of power influenced people's conversational behavior. They were particularly interested in such conversational norm violations as interrupting, talking over the other person, and monopolizing the conversation. They found that regardless of the gender composition of the couple, people in positions of power (that is, who earned more money and who were more responsible for making important decisions) interrupted more, overlapped their partners more, and talked for longer periods of uninterrupted time than the partners with less power. In other words, power can create a conversational division of labor. Because men tend to be more powerful in relationships than women, they do tend to dominate conversations. But these differences stem from being more socially powerful, not simply from being male.

Power is important in the context of intimate relationships not just because it provides conversational privileges to some people and not others. Power can affect all aspects of the private culture. Being part of a couple requires many decisions and choices. When two people fall in love and want to spend their lives together, they must choose whether to maintain separate residences or live together. If they decide to live together, they must decide where to live, how to decorate the home, and who will be responsible for certain domestic tasks. They must make decisions about how their respective careers will influence family life, whether to have children, how to discipline them, and so on. The way they make all these decisions—from the trivial ones like what to have for dinner to the important ones like whether to accept a job transfer to another state—depends on the way they structure relationships of power and authority.

The expression of power in intimate relationships certainly emerges from the interactions and personalities of the specific individuals. But we also must not forget that couples are embedded in a social system that perpetuates unequal rewards and life chances in society. In a society stratified along gender lines, for example, women will continue to have limited opportunities to claim legitimate power in the larger society. These variations in social power can play out in interesting ways within couples' lives.

Power arrangements that were once taken for granted, such as who's going to sacrifice a career to stay at home and raise children, are now more likely than ever to be the product of decisions arrived at by partners through open negotiation. At the very least, people entering into long-term relationships are starting to acknowledge that not every woman wants or expects to have children and take care of the household and not every man wants to be a primary breadwinner. More and more women are in the paid labor force and are therefore less dependent economically on their husbands than they once were (see Chapter 9 for more detail). Only in 22% of married couples is just the husband employed (U.S. Bureau of the Census, 2008). In addition, an increasing number of employed wives are now primary breadwinners. In one study of dual-earner couples, 20 to 25% of wives earned more than their husbands (Winkler, 1998). Most important, gender norms are changing, and more and more couples today are trying to establish relationships in which power is balanced (Schwartz, 2007).

Yet most heterosexual relationships in the United States continue to be dominated by male partners, in part because resources are still unequally distributed by gender and because gendered norms are deeply entrenched in society. Because of their historical position in society, men are less likely to see gender inequality as unjust or to see change as necessary. Indeed, most men do not see gender inequality in their relationships or in society at large as their fault or their problem; it's a "women's issue." Like most people whose interests are supported by the way society is structured, men are largely unaware of the small and large advantages that society and prevailing family ideology provide them (Goode, 1981).

Even couples who identify their relationships as equal and their roles as nongendered may show traditional male-dominant patterns. Sometimes couples are derailed from the goal of an equal marriage because of the realities of raising children and the need to maximize the male partner's income (Schwartz, 2007). One study found that among egalitarian couples wives were more likely than husbands to accommodate their partners' desires and needs, worry about upsetting their partners, do what their partners wanted, and try to fit their lives around their partners' schedules (Kudson-Martin & Mahoney, 1998). Studies like this one are important because they show us that even though women have gained ground economically, traditional gender expectations continue to exert powerful influence over people's family experiences.

MARRIAGE AND COHABITATION

Think about the expectations that have traditionally accompanied marriage:

- It's something all adults should do.
- It's a relationship available only to one man and one woman.
- It's supposed to last forever.
- It means couples will have (or at least will want to have) children.
- It provides clear roles of wives/mothers and husbands/fathers.

If you were to judge the health of contemporary marriage by how closely it meets these expectations, you might conclude that marriage is in serious trouble. Here are some facts about marriage today:

- More and more adults are choosing not to marry, and those who do marry are waiting longer.
- Same-sex couples continue to fight for their right to legally marry.

- More and more couples are choosing to delay childbearing or to remain childless.
- Traditional gender roles in marriage are significantly less common than they were even 20 years ago.

However, for all the rhetoric about its fragile state (see Chapter 2), marriage remains an enduring component of intimate, family life. Most U.S. adults continue to hold it in higher esteem than is the case in other Western societies (Figure 8.2). Indeed, by the time they reach their 70s, about 97% of the U.S. population has been married at least once (U.S. Bureau of the Census, 2008). Compared to some countries, we're practically marriage fanatics. In Sweden, where tax laws don't privilege married couples as they do in the United States and where bearing children outside of marriage is more acceptable, 40% of adults are unmarried cohabitors, compared to about 5% here (Masci, 2004; U.S. Bureau of the Census, 2007).

All enduring relationships, whether same-sex or heterosexual, married or unmarried, are likely to have some common features: patterns of exogamy and endogamy, expectations regarding couplehood, and patterns of communication and power. Some sociologists have even argued that because all close relationships have similar characteristics and require similar behaviors from their members, there's nothing particularly unique or special about marriage. They argue that it makes more sense to talk about and study "sexually based primary relationships," regardless of legal status (Scanzoni et al., 1989).

But are marriages really like any other committed intimate relationships? Is there nothing special about marriage? If there isn't, the fight to ensure that same-sex couples have the right to marry may be unnecessary, except on symbolic grounds. In this section, we'll examine the differences between two similar relationships—cohabitation and marriage—and the implications for persons in these unions.

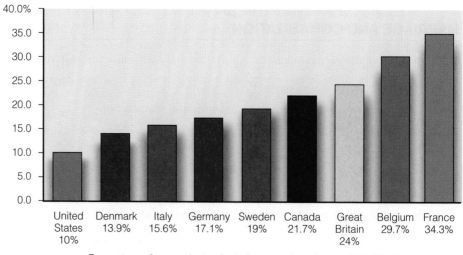

Percentage of respondents who believe marriage is an outdated institution

FIGURE 8.2   Is Marriage an Outdated Institution?
Source: World Values Survey, 2007.

Cohabitation Versus Marriage

In Chapter 2 we saw that unmarried cohabitation is becoming more popular. Whether they cohabit as a way of testing their compatibility before marriage or as a permanent alternative to marriage, unmarried cohabiting couples now make up about 5% of all U.S. households, a 50% increase over the proportion a decade earlier (Masci, 2004; U.S. Bureau of the Census, 2007). Most of the decline in marriage rates we've seen in the past few decades is attributable to the rise in nonmarital cohabitation (Seltzer, 2007). Cohabitation is especially prevalent among people who are divorced or separated. Most cohabiting relationships are short-lived, however, typically lasting for about a year or so until they either end or transform into marriage (Waite, 2000a).

According to one researcher, societies experience the acceptance of cohabitation in a series of stages. In stage one, cohabitation is a fringe, almost experimental, activity practiced by relatively few people. In the second stage, it is accepted as a testing ground for marriage. In stage three, it becomes an acceptable alternative to marriage. Finally, in stage four it becomes identical to marriage (Kiernan, 2002). The United States seems to be between stages two and three (Smock & Gupta, 2002).

Clearly, we haven't reached a point where cohabitation is considered the same as marriage, whether in a legal sense or in terms of how others value it. But how different is it? For decades, sociologists have been interested in how cohabitation compares to marriage. In terms of everyday relationship issues like sexual activity, decision making, parenting, and concerns about employment, cohabitors look a lot like married couples (Scanzoni, 2000). But beyond the obvious differences in legal status and promises of lifelong commitment, cohabiting relationships differ from marriages in several ways. The following are among the most significant and noteworthy findings.

- Cohabitors report significantly lower satisfaction and happiness with their relationships than spouses do (Booth & Johnson, 1988; Nock, 1995).

- Cohabitors are almost twice as likely as spouses to report that they believed their relationship was in trouble over the past year, even after controlling for age of the partners and duration of the relationship (Bumpass, Sweet, & Cherlin, 1991).

- Male cohabitors are much more likely than husbands to say they overbenefit in their relationships, although men in both types of relationships view themselves as benefiting more from the relationship than do women (Kollock, Blumstein, & Schwartz, 1994).

- Cohabitors report having poorer relationships with their parents (Nock, 1995), face more social disapproval, and receive less social support than married couples (Seltzer, 2007).

- Young adults become more tolerant of divorce as a result of cohabiting, no matter what their initial views were (cited in Seltzer, 2007).

- Spouses who cohabited prior to marriage have higher rates of separation and divorce than spouses who didn't cohabit before marriage (Cohan & Kleinbaum, 2002).

Some research suggests that cohabitors actually look more like single people than married ones in terms of such things as childbearing intentions, schooling, homeownership, and employment (Smock, 2000). However, we must realize that such findings may depend on the type of cohabitors being studied. Cohabitors who plan to marry each other in the future may look more like married couples; those who don't intend to marry may look more like single persons (Brown & Booth, 1996).

Overall, it does appear that cohabitation is different from marriage on several important counts. Such differences don't necessarily mean that married and cohabiting relationships operate on fundamentally different rules and principles, only that they acknowledge them to different degrees. In other words, many relationship expectations regarding, for example, sexual exclusivity or gender roles may apply to both types of relationships. Ironically, violating rules in a cohabiting relationship where such rules might not be as obvious can actually be more disruptive than any comparable violation in marriage. Comparing cohabitors and married couples, sociologists Julie Brines and Kara Joyner (1999) noted that the idea of cohabitation initially attracts some people because it appears to be more flexible and experimental than marriage: "In short, it bespeaks few 'rules'" (p. 350). In fact, though, they found that cohabitors were more likely than married couples to end their relationship when women earned more than their male partners; that is, when a traditional social norm regarding the male bread-winner role had been violated.

Unique Aspects of Marriage

Are we to conclude, then, that marriage is like cohabitation only more so? Probably not. A variety of cultural and structural features of marriage distinguish it from other relationships and provide it with the high levels of recognition and cultural importance it currently enjoys.

The Marriage Contract

The legendary actress Katherine Hepburn once said: "It's bloody impractical to love, honor, and obey. If it weren't, you wouldn't have to sign a contract" (quoted in Ingraham, 1999). In some sense, she was right, of course. The legal contract that binds spouses in marriage adds formality to the union, as well as a set of rights and obligations. It can also make termination of the marriage difficult and complicated.

By contrast, no state has determined all the "contractual" rights and duties of cohabitors. In some sense, the lack of a clearly defined contract might make termination of the relationship easier, but it is also likely to inhibit the investments in the relationship that might bring couples closer together (Brines & Joyner, 1999). Cohabitors could create such investments if they choose to—for example, by pooling incomes and signing written agreements that would make their relationship more comparable to marriage—but few do.

Increasingly, though, marriages also have become less subject to regulations by the state. Some traditional provisions of the marriage contract—such as that husbands were legal heads of households responsible for financial support and that wives were responsible for housework and child rearing—have been eliminated. In addition, many companies now grant unmarried cohabiting employees the same rights and benefits as married employees. In this sense, the legal contract has probably become a less distinguishing aspect of marriage.

Indeed, some scholars have insisted that the idea of a contract is no longer appropriate for describing marital arrangements. Law professor Margaret Brinig (2000) suggests that while husband–wife (and parent–child) relationships are bound by a contract, a legally enforceable agreement, this contract is really only relevant when entering into family arrangements (marriage, adoption) or exiting them (separation, divorce, termination of parental rights). A contract "does not have the right concepts or language to treat love, trust, faithfulness, and sympathy, which more than any other terms describe the essentials of family" (p. 30).

Brinig (2000) proposes that the term "covenant" replace the more traditional idea of the marriage contract:

> Covenants are those agreements enforced not by law so much as by individuals and their social organizations. Though rich in religious provenance . . . "covenant" refers to the solemn vows that create and characterize the family. Enforcement stems from that solemnity and from the values of the family members. Thus, while some covenants draw power from religious values, today we find families whose covenants derive most of their power from the family members' mutual commitment to one another and to the preservation and protection of the family itself. (p. 1)

The covenant between husbands and wives implies unconditional love and permanence. Of course, such a covenant could exist between cohabiting partners too, but persons in marriage covenants are "bound not only to each other but also to some third party, to God or to the community or both" (pp. 6–7). The covenant implies duties and obligations that reflect the needs of the wider community in a way that nonmarital relationships do not.

The Wedding Ceremony

One of the obvious ways that legally married couples differ from other couples is that they are expected to engage in a public wedding ceremony. Although "commitment ceremonies" are becoming increasingly popular among same-sex couples who can't legally marry, they're not required or expected to have them. These ceremonies can look just like weddings and have the same social purpose: to provide friends and family members with an opportunity to bear witness to the couples' love and commitment (Haldeman, 1998). But commitment ceremonies remain purely symbolic and lack legal recognition.

Weddings vary in innumerable ways across different social classes, religions, and ethnoracial groups but usually include some common roles, rituals, and images. Whether they're religious or secular, large or small, formal or informal, in a cathedral or on a beach, a first marriage or a remarriage, most weddings include:

- a supporting cast of bride's maids, groomsmen, flower children, ring bearers, ushers, and musicians
- an authoritative figure—usually a justice of the peace or a clergy person—who will pronounce the marriage valid and legal
- an audience of encouraging witnesses
- the exchange of vows and rings between spouses and a kiss that seals the deal
- some sort of celebratory reception afterward that usually includes testimonial speeches and toasts, the cutting of the cake and the mashing of it into the new spouse's face to the laughs and cheers of onlookers, the newlyweds' first dance, the throwing of the bouquet and the flinging of the garter, the vandalizing of the bride and groom's car, and ultimately the couple's getaway

The symbolic importance of the wedding ceremony is undeniable:

> At the time of their wedding, their kin and friends, along with the state and often the church or synagogue, bestow on the couple a type of approval, honor, and esteem that is unique and obtainable by no other discernible means. What is more, that esteem follows them beyond the wedding, because whenever they happen to make known their marital status, strangers immediately accord them the respect appropriately due that position. (Scanzoni, 2000, p. 58)

Wedding ceremonies also reaffirm the primacy of heterosexuality found in U.S. society. Sociologist Chrys Ingraham (1999) argues that weddings are a prime means by which the heterosexual standard is sustained: "Weddings are one of the major events that signal readiness and prepare heterosexuals for membership in marriage as an organized practice for the institution of heterosexuality" (p. 4).

The Institutionalized Nature of Marriage

Finally, we can't ignore the fact that marriage is far more institutionalized than even the most serious cohabiting or dating relationships. Other types of arrangements are still treated as "makeshift or temporary, however long they last" (Coontz, 2005, p. 309). Marriage remains a patterned way of life that includes a set of commonly known roles, statuses, and expectations.

Because marriage is an institutionalized form of intimacy, we can anticipate what it will be like long before we actually marry. There is no longer clear agreement on what it means to be a wife or husband, but as sociologist Steven Nock (1995) claims, "there are clearly traditional standards of propriety and decorum associated with one's relationships with married individuals" (p. 56). By contrast, what it means to be a "cohabiting" person is much less clear. Consider the fact that the English language lacks any term to describe one's cohabiting partner. "Significant other," "life partner," "lover," or "intimate roommate" just don't capture the nature of this type of relationship. In contrast, telling someone, "This is my wife (or husband)" immediately conveys a world of information about the couple's relationship and will evoke a set of expectations on the part of others, whether or not the couple consciously attempts to live up to these expectations:

> A wife should spend weekends with the family, not friends; a husband can give his pregnant wife (but not his pregnant sister) his insurance benefits; a man or a woman should put . . . [his or her] spouse first before the demands of parents, friends, or other family members; married people should support each other financially as well as emotionally. (Waite & Gallagher, 2000, p. 20)

Another implication of living in a highly institutionalized relationship such as marriage is that it integrates the partners firmly within the social networks of other married couples. These networks, especially those between parents and adult children, can represent an important source of support for the couple. Cohabiting couples tend to receive less approval and support (emotional and economic) from family than do married couples, which can adversely affect the relationship (Nock, 1995).

The law provides further support for the institution of marriage. By contrast, cohabitors are in a position of "legal insecurity" (Seff, 1995), which can have long-term economic disadvantages. You may have relied on your partner for financial support for many years, but if the relationship breaks up, you may have no clear right to support payments (whereas a spouse would automatically be entitled to such support). You may also have no clear right to share in the assets your partner may have accumulated during your relationship (whereas in a marriage such assets may be considered community property). Likewise, if your partner becomes ill and unable to make medical decisions for him- or herself, you have no legal right to make decisions for him or her. In these situations, married partners have greater opportunities to protect their financial assets.

The Marriage "Benefit"

If marriage, more than cohabitation, fosters a sense of meaning, generates greater social support, and provides greater legal protection, it seems reasonable to expect that marriage would have positive effects on the well-being of individuals. Indeed, married people, on average, are better off physically, emotionally, and economically than single or divorced people (Coontz, 2005).

Health Benefits

According to the Centers for Disease Control, married people enjoy a wider range of health benefits compared to single, divorced, cohabiting, and widowed people (Figure 8.3). Marriage also seems related positively to mental health. Research indicates that becoming married is associated with lower levels of stress and depression, especially for those who believe in the desirability and importance of marriage. In contrast, separating and divorcing is associated with greater depression, especially for persons who believe most strongly in the permanence of marriage (Simon & Marcussen, 1999). Indeed, some researchers fear that recent trends away from marriage (like higher rates of divorce, cohabitation, and singlehood) will have negative consequences for the health and well-being of more and more older people who will enter their retirement years unmarried (Pienta, Hayward, & Jenkins, 2000).

One way marriage benefits health may be by providing individuals with someone who monitors their health and discourages risky and unhealthy behaviors. In addition, good marriages provide people with a sense of being cared for, loved, and valued as a person. Marriage also increases material well-being, as you'll see shortly, leading to better medical care, better diet, and safer neighborhoods for married persons than for unmarried persons.

But marriage in and of itself may not be what creates these physical or psychological benefits; the quality of the relationship may be far more important. Having a stable relationship with someone whom you can confide in and count on for understanding and help can serve as a buffer against physical problems and emotional distress. Researchers at the University of North Carolina have found that warm interactions, such as frequent hugging, can dramatically reduce blood pressure (cited in Mahoney, 2006). Obviously, such behavior and the health benefits that result can occur in any long-term committed relationship. Indeed, now that same-sex couples in Great Britain can enter legally recognized civil unions, researchers there predict a trend toward lower rates of heart disease among gays and lesbians in these relationships akin to those found among heterosexual spouses ("Healthier Hearts Through Marriage," 2006).

Of course the purported health benefits of marriage don't mean that everyone should rush out and find a spouse so he or she can live longer. Marrying simply for

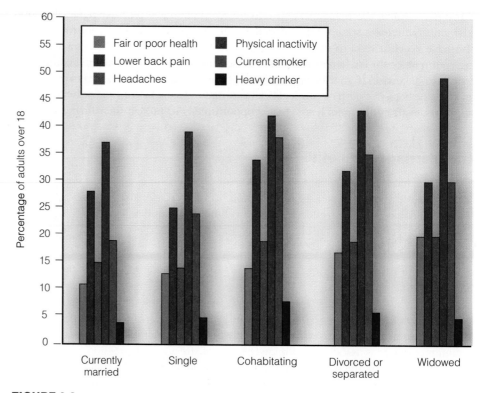

FIGURE 8.3 Marital Status and Health
Source: Data from Schoenborn, 2004, tables 4, 6, & 8.

the sake of reducing health risks would undoubtedly result in a number of bad marriages, which would not confer many benefits on the partners. The key to marriage's health benefits appears to be whether the relationship is supportive and interactions are positive. Individuals in problematic and unsupportive marriages, characterized by neglect, conflict, or abuse, tend to experience greater psychological distress than those in more supportive relationships (Gove et al., 1990; Horwitz, McLaughlin, & White, 1997).

Economic Benefits

When the late model Anna Nicole Smith married billionaire J. Howard Marshall II in 1994, virtually everyone in the country assumed she married him for money. She was 27 at the time; he was 90. But Smith insisted otherwise:

> "I'm very much in love," Smith told an interviewer, flashing her asteroid-size 22-carat engagement diamond and her diamond-dusted wedding band. . . . "I could have married him four years ago if I'd just wanted to get rich." (quoted in Ingraham, 1999, p. 109)

Of course, imagine how shocked we'd be if Smith, or any bride or groom to be, bluntly stated that he or she was marrying for "money." People getting married generally downplay the impact that marriage will have on their standard of living. In 1994, only 17% of adults interviewed for the General Social Survey agreed that the main advantage of marriage is financial security. Individuals are more likely to view the benefits of marriage in terms of overall happiness, emotional security, and an improved sex life than in terms of economic benefits (South, 1992). Interestingly, however, economically disadvantaged groups (for example, Latina and black women) and older people seem to have a more realistic picture of the role that economics plays in a marriage.

Marriage in many other societies is recognized openly as an economic arrangement, a contract between families. Marriages are important in such settings not because they are personally fulfilling to partners who are in love with each other but because they provide economic links between kin groups. In societies that have an elaborate and highly structured stratification system, such as India and Pakistan, a family's social status is extremely important in determining who is eligible to marry whom. Marriages are usually arranged from within the same caste, although the ideal situation is that the man's family be of slightly higher status than the woman's. Under such circumstances little thought is given to the desires or shared affections of the partners.

Although people raised in the United States tend to emphasize the importance of love rather than money, and to resist the idea that marriage is economic in nature, marriage clearly has economic advantages. Sometimes those advantages are built into the law. The General Accounting Office has counted 1,138 statutory provisions in which marital status is a factor in determining whether someone is eligible for certain benefits, rights, and privileges (Congressional Budget Office, 2004).

Politicians have frequently worked to increase the economic benefits of marriage. The Tax Relief Act of 2001 reduced some, though not all, of the economic burden on dual-earner married couples by increasing the standard deduction for people filing joint federal income tax returns (Sahadi, 2006). Up to that point a husband and wife who both worked and made similar incomes would have had to pay significantly more in taxes than if they were single people filing separately. This tax disadvantage wasn't noticeable when it was common for one spouse to work and the other to stay at home. But as more wives entered the workforce and started earning salaries similar to men's, the number of married people paying more than their share of taxes jumped. The law has had a noticeable positive effect on the tax burden of married couples; a single person earning $50,000 a year in 2005 paid 35% more in taxes than a married couple earning that amount (cited in DePaulo, 2006).

The economic benefit of marriage takes shape in a variety of other less obvious ways (Wilmoth & Koso, 1997):

- The division of labor in marriages allows each spouse to specialize in specific skills and tasks. In time, this specialization can become efficient and productive.

- Married couples benefit because they are able to share resources, such as housing, food, and utilities, which minimizes the cost of living and provides insurance against unemployment or an unexpected illness.

- Marriage broadens social support systems and increases participation in other social institutions. Connections established in these activities can lead to additional opportunities and benefits.

- Married couples usually have access to health or life insurance benefits through a spouse's employment.

Marital status is also related to wages. When you look at wealth among older couples—those who have been together long enough to feel the economic effects of marriage—married individuals have significantly higher median incomes and net worth than older widowed, divorced, or never married adults (Seigel, 1993). Gender can have a role to play here. Married men have higher incomes, educational attainments, and labor force attachments than unmarried men (Nock, 1998a). Some argue that these differences exist because married men are more productive and have spouses who can take over household tasks, freeing their time and energy for work. Marriage may also increase men's incentives to perform well at work so they can successfully meet their family obligations (Waite, 2000b).

Another economic advantage stems from the fact that marriages tend to last longer than other types of relationships. In the early years of a relationship, cohabitors may not differ much from married couples in terms of combined earnings. In fact, women's earnings in the early years of a cohabiting relationship are much more likely to approximate their partners', and they are more likely than married women to earn more than their partners do (Brines & Joyner, 1999). As couples age, however, the balance of economic benefits shifts in favor of married couples.

Though all this evidence of a marriage benefit seems clear, we must be cautious in how we interpret it. Individuals with more desirable resources (for example, good health and high income) are more attractive as mates in the first place and are therefore more likely than those without such resources to marry. Hence, it is difficult to determine whether marriage itself leads to these benefits or whether already advantaged individuals are more likely to be married.

The Marriage "Problem"

Given all the publicity these sorts of marital benefits receive in the culture, it's not surprising that the government, not to mention researchers, pundits, and the general public, feel that stronger support for marriage could solve many of society's woes—including welfare dependency, the federal deficit, antisocial behavior, and public incivility (Flanders, 1996; Ingraham, 1999)—and increase disadvantaged people's economic self-sufficiency (Lichter, Graefe, & Brown, 2003). But we shouldn't regard marriage as a cure-all for people's problems, particularly poor, unwed mothers. For one thing, it's not as if there is a pool of financially stable men looking to marry poor, single mothers. One study did find that poverty can be reduced for those single mothers who marry and stay married. However, for single mothers who marry but later divorce, which is not uncommon, poverty is worse than it would have been if they never got married in the first place. Nor can marriage alone offset the long-term negative effects associated with unwed childbearing (Lichter et al., 2003).

Others argue that the elevation of marriage to its exalted status in society has led people to expect too much from their spouses. The growing belief over the last century that people can receive all their emotional sustenance and fulfillment from their spouse has created an increased sense of isolation. The proportion of U.S. adults who depend solely on a spouse for important conversations and have no one else to turn to has doubled in the last two decades. As one author put it, "we can strengthen our marriages the most by not expecting them to be the sole refuge from the pressures of the modern work force" (Coontz, 2006, p. A23).

Furthermore, not everyone believes that the future stability of society depends on strengthening the institution of marriage. They argue that the traditional structure of marriage has overwhelming emotional, psychological, and economic costs for women. Women may be more attracted to marriage than men, but they end up getting less out of it. Women experience more legal, social, and personal changes when they become wives than men do when they become husbands. Women still make more concessions and adjustments to their lives upon marriage than men do. Married couples are more likely to relocate because of the husband's career than the wife's, and wives are more likely than husbands to leave the workforce upon the birth of a child. In traditional marriages, wives tend to be known more for their husbands' accomplishments than for their own.

Consider, also, the common practice of wives giving up their last names when they marry, something the majority of women still do (Scheuble & Johnson, 2005). Usually a woman can take her new husband's surname simply by checking a box on the marriage license. If a man wants to take his wife's surname, he has to petition the court, announce his intent in a newspaper to make sure no one objects, and pay hundreds of dollars in fees ("Gender-Neutral Name Game," 2007). Deviation from the name changing norm can be met with hostility, as is evident in the following letter to Ann Landers:

> Dear Ann: When our son married, he informed us he and his wife were going to use a hyphenated name: "John and Jane Smith-Jones." . . . My husband and I were very upset. Our name should be good enough for her by itself. I refuse to recognize my son's new name and have told him so. This has caused a rift in our relationship. . . . His wife is a control freak. (Landers, 1993)

Is there any validity to the feminist arguments that marriage hurts women? Let's take a closer look at the marital benefits described earlier. The relationship between marital status and wages is different for women than it is for men and may even vary along racial lines. Childless black women, for example, earn substantially more if they're married than if they're single, but this advantage shrinks with each child they have. Among white married women, only those who are childless enjoy increased wages. Once white women become mothers, marriage actually decreases their earnings because many mothers choose or are forced to reduce their hours at work (Blaisure & Allen, 2000).

And what about the health benefits of marriage? Over two decades ago, sociologist Jessie Bernard (1982) made the startling claim that marriage was good for men but made women sick. She based her claim on research showing that husbands seem to enjoy greater health benefits than wives. Research on this topic continues to reveal that married women experience higher rates of some types of mental and physical illness and distress than married men (Figure 8.4).

One explanation for the different effect that marriage has on men's and women's health concerns the types of roles women play in marriage and society (Gove, 1980). Women's increased labor force participation has not been matched by men's increased involvement in the home

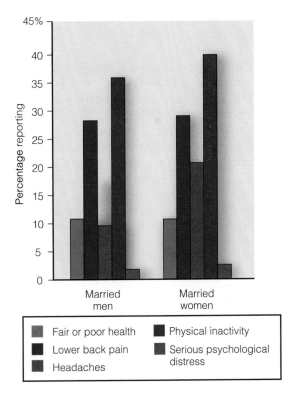

FIGURE 8.4 Gender and Health Among Married Men and Women

Source: Data from Schoenborn, 2004, tables 4, 6, & 8.

(Hochschild & Machung, 1989). For the most part, women are expected to take primary responsibility for household work once they get married, even if they work full time outside the home (see Chapter 9 for more detail). Such a heavy burden, especially when women enter a marriage expecting that the division of labor will be more balanced, can lead to psychological distress. Indeed, wives experience less depression when their husbands contribute significantly around the house (Glass & Fujimoto, 1994).

Interestingly, economically independent women who remain unmarried may not necessarily forgo the noneconomic benefits of marriage. Research suggests that the health benefits that married women experience are often the result of their greater economic resources (provided by their husbands' income), which affords them safer living conditions, better health insurance plans, and so on (Lillard & Waite, 1995). Men, on the other hand, appear to benefit from simply living with a spouse who encourages them to look after their health needs.

It might appear that marriage does have more benefits for men than for women, especially women who could be economically self-sufficient. Even so, the majority of U.S. women and men find marriage to be a source of benefits unavailable anywhere else.

WHAT DOES IT ALL MEAN?

Marriage is a series of contradictions. It is both revered and ridiculed. It is considered by many to be the key to a strong society, but it is also relentlessly criticized as weak and ineffectual. It is dynamic and changing in some ways, but static and traditional in others. It is an intensely private relationship, but it is shaped by broad social forces such as the law, economics, religion, and culture. Many single men resist it and many single women long for it, but men seem to benefit from it the most. It represents the summit of our romantic hopes, but also the pit of our intimate fears.

Clearly there is no fail-safe path to a successful marriage. It would be nice to end this chapter with a checklist of actions, beliefs, and perceptions that would guarantee a satisfying relationship, but no such list exists. For all marriage's popularity and commonality, for all the prior expectations people bring with them when they get married, and for all the influence social and cultural forces have on it, each marriage must be constructed from scratch by the people involved.

At the same time, we're at a point in history when people can't even agree whether marriage is a good or bad thing. Research shows that marriage rates are declining in the United States, but marriage as an institution seems to matter to people more than ever. Surely people who legally marry enjoy numerous benefits. So many, in fact, that politicians of all stripes continue to assume that marriage can be the solution to many of our most pressing individual and social problems. But others do just fine without marriage.

So we're left to ponder the question of whether people's need to feel connected to another person in an ongoing, committed relationship ought to be satisfied only in the context of a legally recognized marriage. Although more and more couples are exploring various types of living arrangements such as cohabitation, most still want some kind of formal recognition of their love for each other. Such a desire is not surprising in a society like ours, which values romance so highly and continues to privilege marriage above all other relationships. Perhaps, in addition to "strengthening" marriage, we as a society should also focus on increasing the socioeconomic and psychological well-being of cohabitors and individuals who do not or, because of legal restrictions, cannot enjoy the benefits of marriage.

As you examine the information covered in this chapter, consider the following questions:

1. Think of the most recent intimate relationship you've been in (if you're in one now, think of that one). How would you characterize the balance of power between you and your partner? Consider the ways in which you and your partner communicated. To what extent did gender and power influence the way you solved problems or dealt with conflict?

2. In this chapter you learned about some of the controversies associated with marriages that cross certain social boundaries, especially religious and ethnoracial boundaries. When people form relationships, should they *only* consider their own feelings of attraction for another person, or do they have a larger responsibility to their religious or ethnoracial community to find partners from within those groups?

3. We've seen that problems arise in relationships when they are inequitable (unfair). Do you think it's appropriate for people to constantly weigh the costs and benefits of a relationship to ensure that it is equitable? Can you think of problems that could arise in couples that seek perfect equity?

4. Do you believe that increasing rates of cohabitation pose a serious threat to the well-being of marriage in this society? Would you personally consider cohabiting, either as an alternative to marriage or as a preliminary to marriage? Explain.

5. Few people would be in favor of penalizing people who marry, but do you think it's the responsibility of the federal government to promote marriage through official laws and policies that provide significant benefits to married couples?

SUMMARY

- Mate selection is strongly influenced by cultural rules of endogamy and exogamy. Although we are not supposed to marry close relatives, we tend to find partners among people who resemble us in terms of religion, social class, race, and ethnicity.

- Modern relationships are more flexible than ever before, but they are still governed by expectations of interdependence, equity, commitment, permanence, sexual access, and sexual exclusivity. Couples still feel pressured to be "coupled"—that is, to act and think like a couple.

- To some degree, each relationship is unique and is characterized by a private culture that arises from a couple's interactions and communication. But social forces always influence these interactions, even the most personal and private ones, such as communication and sex.

- Power, a part of all intimate relationships, is reflected in couples' communication and interactions. Despite women's increased economic role, in intimate relationships men continue to have more power.

- Cohabitation and marriage vary in several important ways. The institutionalized nature of marriage appears to bestow both health and economic benefits on many individuals, though this evidence must be interpreted with caution.

Go to the Online Learning Center at **www.mhhe.com/newman1** to test your knowledge of the chapter concepts and key terms.

KEY TERMS

SEE FOR YOURSELF

For any intimate relationship to survive, couples must communicate frequently and openly about a wide range of issues and concerns. But couple communication involves much more than simply negotiating schedules and expressing one's feelings. Communication in intimate relationships also contains underlying messages about respect, authority, and power.

To explore this "hidden language" in couple communication, ask any two couples you know to tape-record their conversation for 15 minutes. Try to choose two different types of couples (e.g., dating along with married or cohabiting, heterosexual along with homosexual, affluent along with working class, dual-earner along with single-earner). Ask them to choose a time when they're likely to be engaged in a casual discussion about their day (e.g., when they're making or eating dinner together) and to simply leave the recorder running. Assure them that it's fine if they are not talking about anything really important. It's best, in fact, if they are simply conversing about the mundane aspect of their day.

Listen to each tape and record the following data for each person. You will probably have to listen several times to each conversation to pick up on these details, which we usually pay no conscious attention to.

- How many questions did each partner ask?
- How many times did each partner *not* answer a question?
- How many times did each partner interrupt the other?
- How many times did each partner change the topic of the conversation?

Next, answer the following questions about each couple's interaction:

- Which partner seemed to work harder to keep the conversation going?
- Which partner tended to ignore the other person more?
- Which partner did most of the talking?

Compare your results to those of other students in the class. Consider what you know about these couples (Do they both work outside the home? Have they been together a long time?). Look for the following patterns in your data.

- Who tends to do more to keep the conversation going, men or women? Who asks more questions?

- Could you detect gender differences in who is more likely *not* to answer questions, ignore their partner, use more silence, interrupt and change the topic?

- Do communication patterns differ when both partners work outside the home versus when one does and the other doesn't?

- Are the patterns observed among heterosexual couples different from those of same-sex couples?

- Are the patterns observed among dating couples different from those of cohabiting or married couples?

- Do you notice any variations among couples of different social classes or racial/ethnic groups?

Discuss how consistent your data are with findings discussed in this chapter. What might account for any differences? Reflect on what you've learned about couple communication through this exercise. Did anything surprise you? How do you think your own communication is influenced by your gender, status, race, and so on?

9

Work and Family

Norah Vincent is a female journalist who wanted to know what life was really like for men. With the help of a makeup artist, a personal trainer, and a voice coach, she embarked on an 18-month odyssey, observing and participating in the world of men as a man named "Ned." She joined a men's bowling league, went to strip clubs, and participated in a men's therapy group.

But Norah realized that to fully understand the world of men, she had to go where the money was and infiltrate the workplace. So, posing as Ned, she applied for several jobs. After interviewing for some entry-level sales positions, Norah/Ned noticed how different—and advantageous—it was to be a male job candidate:

> I was walking taller in my dress clothes. I felt entitled to respect, to command it and get it. . . . For the first time in my journey as Ned I felt male privilege descend on me like an insulating cape. . . . I spoke more slowly, with what seemed to me to be an absurd authority. . . . [I]n Ned's interviews, people didn't expect him to make nice. They expected him to brag about himself, to be smugly charming and steadfast. . . . [E]ven when I said things that were inappropriate, somehow even they managed to work themselves to my advantage. . . . Ned was offered every job for which he applied. (Vincent, 2006, pp. 187–191)

All societies have clear conceptions about what men and women are obligated to do or what they're entitled to, particularly when it comes to meeting the financial needs of a family. Gender and work are tightly intertwined. That is, earning capacity and professional credibility have always been linked in some way to gender. In the past, women had few opportunities to enter prestigious occupations, own property, or be financially independent. That's still the case in many countries around the world.

In U.S. society today, the traditional barriers to financial stability are no longer as impenetrable as they once were. U.S. women don't have to go undercover as men, like Norah Vincent did, to find employment and successfully support their families. Yet they still lag behind men economically and politically and continue to encounter frustrating cultural obstacles and closed doors. Ironically, when women do attain some degree of economic stability and social power, it's usually by drifting away from their traditional feminine family roles and entering historically male realms of occupational life.

In this chapter we'll examine the ways that the different work experiences of women and men, both inside and outside the home, influence family life. The intersection of work, gender, and family is centrally important in a society in which, as in ours, both men and women are expected to make familial as well as economic contributions.

TWO WORLDS? WORK AND FAMILY

Until the mid-19th century, the U.S. economy was predominantly agricultural. Most people's lives centered around the farm, and husbands and wives were partners not only in making a home but in making a living (Vanek, 1980). The word *housework*—activities distinct from work done in other places—was not even part of the language. Research suggests men and women were responsible for different tasks and that they were by no means equal, but they worked together:

> In the division of responsibility, women got the bulk of internal domestic chores. Normally, they took care of the house—including the preparation of food, cloth, can-

dles and soap—and supervised farm animals and kitchen garden, while husbands did the plowing, planting, and harvesting. Yet interaction never stopped. Husbands helped at the spinning and weaving when farm work was done. In the southern colonies, wives hoed and female servants worked in the fields. Male apprentices often found themselves doing household chores. Female servants spent as much time in the workshop as in the household. Mothers taught young children their letters, while fathers tended to take over the educational process as offspring grew older. Wives routinely developed competency in their husband's [sic] businesses; they could and did inherit them when death demanded it. (Kessler-Harris, 1982, p. 7)

With the advent of industrialization, though, things began to change. New forms of mass production technology and the promise of new financial opportunities and a good living drew people away from the farms and into cities and factories where they could earn wages in exchange for their work. "Work" was now paid activity undertaken in a "workplace" away from the home (Runté & Mills, 2004). For the first time in U.S. history, the family economy was based outside the household, and the majority of families depended on wage labor for their financial support. Instead of being self-sufficient, people now operated under the rules and regulations of factory owners, who were likely to believe that family responsibilities were incompatible with productivity (Glass, 2000).

Contrary to popular belief, many of the first factory workers were women. But as factory work came to be seen less as a peripheral activity and more as the primary feature of the new economy, men began to take control of this new source of income, power, and prestige (Haas, 1995). In addition, industrialization relieved men of many of their domestic duties, and women no longer found themselves engaged in the day-to-day supervision of the family's business as they had once been. Instead, women were consigned to menial and powerless positions in the workforce and to the only domestic responsibilities that remained: caring for and nurturing children and running the household.

This shift redefined motherhood, making women the emotional center of family life (Coontz, 2007). Because the kind of work women now did was either low paid (when outside the home) or remained unpaid (when inside the home), and because salable goods were no longer being produced at home, women's work became devalued in the emerging industrial economy (Hareven, 1992).

Looking at these changes from men's point of view, we can see that industrialization had a profound effect on their lives too. It's been estimated that in hunting and gathering societies, men provided only about a fifth of the resources needed for their family's subsistence and women provided the rest (Boulding, 1976). In colonial times, as well, women were as important as men in providing for their families. They ran inns and taverns, managed shops and stores, and sometimes even worked in the fields (Bernard, 1981). Industrialization created new roles for men: "primary breadwinner" and "good provider." Men were now almost solely responsible, at least in the eyes of the community, for their family's economic well-being.

The Ideology of Separate Spheres

The divergence between men's and women's labor in the late 19th century resulted in the **ideology of separate spheres**: the widespread belief that women's place *should be* in the home (the private sphere) and men's *should be* in the work world outside the

■ **ideology of separate spheres**
The widespread belief that women's place *should be* in the home (the private sphere) and men's *should be* in the work world outside the home (the public sphere).

home (the public sphere). This expectation was rationalized by the notion that men and women were naturally predisposed to different pursuits. Women were assumed to be inherently nurturing, demure, and sacrificial, a perfect fit for their restricted domestic roles. Women's "natural" weakness and frailty were assumed to make them ill-suited to the dog-eat-dog life of the competitive labor force, and to justify their limited job opportunities. Those who did work outside the home were paid significantly less than men and were confined to "female" jobs (Cowan, 1987).

In the 19th century, this belief system was linked to the idea that to be truly feminine or womanly, women had to devote themselves entirely to home and family. Thus the ideal, glorified role for women focused entirely on the more limited and less socially valued domestic role.

The ideal image of men, on the other hand, was of the rugged individual whose virtue came from self-reliance, power, and mastery of his job and family. Men were thought to be naturally strict, aggressive, calculating, rational, and bold—a perfect fit for the demands of the marketplace.

Discounting Women's Work in Industrial Society

The reality of family life in the United States has never quite fit the image painted by the ideology of separate spheres, however. Even in the 19th century, men weren't the only ones who left their homes each day to work in factories. Women were a substantial presence in the industrial labor force. By 1900, one fifth of U.S. women worked outside the home (Staggenborg, 1998). But the experiences of working women varied along class and race lines. For middle- and upper-class white women, few professions other than teaching and nursing were available, and these jobs paid poorly.

In contrast, poor and working-class women labored mostly in low-paid, unskilled jobs in clothing factories, canning plants, or other industries in which working conditions were often dangerous and exploitive. Female factory workers often faced an exhausting pace of work and serious health risks, sometimes for 14 hours a day. Some were forced to pay "rental fees" for the machines and equipment they used on the job (Staggenborg, 1998).

The conditions for women of color were especially bad. Under slavery, black women, like black men, reaped no benefits at all from their labor. After slavery, black female domestic servants were often forced to leave their own families and live in their employer's home, where they were expected to be available around the clock, and most had little choice. Throughout history, black women have rarely had the luxury of being stay-at-home spouses and parents. In 1880, 73% of black single women and 35% of black married women reported holding paid jobs. Only 23% of white single women and 7% of white married women reported being in the paid labor force at that time (cited in Kessler-Harris, 1982).

Women of color and poor white women were excluded from the luxury of keeping their spheres separate. Ironically, the privileged, upper-class women who could afford to embrace the separate spheres ideology were able to do so only because they used other women as servants to do much of the household labor (Boydston, 2001).

The doctrine of separate spheres has been weakened from time to time by larger historical, political, and economic needs. During World War II, for example, the government initiated a massive public relations program designed to lure women out of their homes and into factories where they would take up the productive work of men who had gone off to fight in the war. Government motivational films depicted child care centers as nurturing environments where children would flourish while their mothers worked, and in 1942, the Lanham Act was passed, allowing the federal government to establish and fund child care centers. Between 1940 and 1945 the female labor force increased more than 50%. Six million women, represented by the icon of "Rosie the Riveter," worked in the manufacturing plants that produced weapons and munitions during the war. Three fourths of these new workers were married, and a majority had children (Coontz, 1992).

After the war ended, however, the message changed dramatically. Child care centers were depicted as horrible, dangerous places. Working mothers were labeled as selfish and irresponsible. Practically overnight, the political atmosphere had been transformed and with it the perception of women's appropriate place in the family and in the economy. Although many women remained in the labor force, especially those who had moved into higher-paying jobs during the war, others quit their jobs or were laid off (Kessler-Harris, 1982). Those who quit, not surprisingly, tended to be young married women, many of whom were, or were soon to be, young mothers.

The years right after the war represented the heyday of the separate spheres ideology. Media messages heavily emphasized women's obligations to take their rightful position on the domestic front. Men began to pursue advanced educational opportunities during this period, but few women entered college. Of those who did, 2 out of 3 dropped out before graduating. Most women left because they feared a college education would hurt their marriage chances (Mintz & Kellogg, 1988) or because they had already married and chose to abandon their educational pursuits to turn their attention to raising a family (Weiss, 2000). The ideology of separate spheres seemed to have returned in full force.

During World War II, federally funded day care centers served the needs of mothers who were encouraged by the government to fill the factory jobs vacated by men fighting overseas.

Taking Stock of Separate Spheres Today

Since the 1950s, the boundary separating men's and women's spheres has steadily eroded. Prior to 1960, about a third of female high school graduates enrolled in college (compared to over half of male graduates). By 2004, more women (70.4%) were enrolled in college than men (66.5%; U.S. Bureau of the Census, 2008). In 1950 a little over 30% of adult women were in the paid labor force; today close to 60% of all women over age 25 work outside the home (U.S. Bureau of the Census, 2007). At the same time, men's labor force participation has declined from about 87% of all men in 1950 to about 75% today. About half of all people in the paid labor force today are women, compared to a little less than 32% in 1950. Furthermore, 68% of married mothers, 73% of single mothers, and 80% of divorced, separated, or widowed mothers are employed (Figure 9.1).

Despite these trends, the separate spheres ideology has not completely disappeared. When we examine the percentage of women employed full time, year round, gender differences become apparent. Employed men, on average, work almost an hour more each day than employed women (U.S. Bureau of the Census, 2008), and about 26% of

FIGURE 9.1

Working Mothers, 1960 to 2005

Source: U.S. Bureau of the Census, 1994, table 626; 2008, table 580.

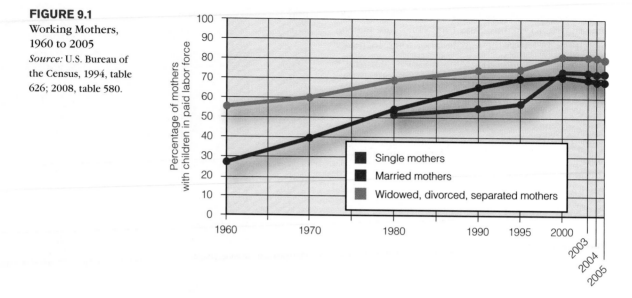

employed women work mostly part time, compared to a little over 10% of employed men (U.S. Bureau of Labor Statistics, 2005a). If you include those who stay at home full time, 2 of every 3 mothers between ages 25 and 45 work less than 40 hours a week in the paid labor force (cited in Glazer, 2003). Women's work decisions appear to be grounded in a slightly evolved separate spheres ideology: it's appropriate for women to work outside the home, but they're not expected to devote themselves fully to their jobs the way men are.

In addition, many U.S. adults still perceive domestic work as women's sphere and outside employment as men's sphere:

> When it comes to marriage and family life, Americans are . . . ambivalent about women's roles, wanting them to be generous self-sacrificing mothers even if they are also expected to be dedicated professionals. Although women are encouraged to go to college and pursue their careers as never before, they are still held accountable for what was once called "women's work." If their houses are a mess, or if their children are unkempt, women . . . are still subject to blame. (Coltrane, 1996b, p. 26)

In some corners of U.S. society, calls can be heard for a return to the traditional male breadwinner–female homemaker division of labor. But how likely is it that vast numbers of women in the United States will willingly withdraw from paid employment and happily return to the domestic sphere? A growing number are now the primary source of financial support in their families, and it isn't just money that motivates them. One national poll found that only about a third of working women said they'd prefer to stay home even if money were no object; they value the respect, esteem, and friendship networks their jobs provide (cited in Coontz, 1997). Women are just as likely as men to feel successful in their work lives and their family lives, as well as in balancing the two.

Gender in the Workplace

Although women and men are now both present in the workplace, traditional gender ideologies still affect their experiences there. Employers as well as the public at large still believe women and men are naturally inclined to behave in certain ways at home and in the workplace (Reskin & Hartmann, 1986). Those beliefs translate into unequal rewards for women and men who work outside the home.

Discrimination Built Into the System

Think for a moment about what you have to do to be considered a good worker by your boss. Obviously you have to show competence and a deep, serious commitment to the company. But how do you show such commitment? You probably have to be willing to work extra hours, travel to faraway business meetings or professional conferences, attend special training programs, work unpopular shifts, entertain out-of-town clients on weekends, and relocate if necessary—all of which illustrate a commitment to the job over family obligations. In the 1989 film *Parenthood,* a boss tells a forlorn employee (played by Steve Martin) that he lost out on a promotion to someone less qualified because the other guy had no family obligations:

> Phil has just brought in three brand-new, multimillion-dollar clients. He has spent the last month wining and dining these guys. . . . He doesn't tell me about problems with his kids. I'm not even sure if he has kids. If this man's [penis] fell off, he would still show up for work. He is an animal. That's what dazzles, not the work.

Although women and men can both be successful workers, when jobs require extra time and commitment, women find it much harder than men to conform to the "ideal worker" mold (Williams, 2000). Because women, especially mothers, still tend to have the lion's share of responsibilities at home, they have more difficulty demonstrating to their bosses that they are good, committed employees. Consider these recent cases (J. C. Williams, 2006):

■ A bus driver was fired when she arrived 3 minutes late because her son had a severe asthma attack.

■ A packer was fired when she left work after receiving a call that her daughter was in the emergency room with a head injury.

■ A divorced mother lost her job as a janitor when she missed a day of work because her mentally handicapped son's babysitter didn't show up.

By hiring, rewarding, and promoting those workers who successfully separate work from family responsibilities, most workplaces operate as if the male provider–female homemaker model were still the norm.

Let's think about this in another way. Imagine that you're a boss who's just been told that your best employee, Chris, is engaged to be married. How will you respond?

If Chris is a man, chances are his impending marriage will be seen as a "stabilizing" influence. Job security will now be extremely important to him, perhaps making him an even more dependable worker. He might even need a raise because fatherhood is probably looming not far down the road. You'd be unlikely to think that these new family responsibilities will somehow prevent Chris from devoting himself entirely to his job. On the contrary, it's likely that family obligations will motivate him to work even harder and longer so he can support his family. Indeed, if his new wife has a job in another town, it's doubtful that Chris will give up his job and relocate so she can pursue her career.

Now suppose Chris is a woman. Chances are her upcoming marriage will seem a potential impediment to career mobility. You might begin to question whether she'll be able to remain fully committed to the job. Will she move if her husband finds a good job somewhere else? Research indicates that when couples decide that one partner has to stop working, it's usually the woman (Porter, 2006). Perhaps you begin to wonder how long it will be before Chris becomes pregnant and seeks maternity leave or quits altogether. Rather than making her a more dependable worker, marriage may actually make her seem less dependable, less stable, and less invested in the company.

Even an ideal worker might be discriminated against by an employer who assumes that she will be less productive because of her family responsibilities or will become pregnant and quit work. Mothers are at particular risk for facing such workplace discrimination, especially those in low-wage positions. One study found that women without children are more likely than mothers to be seen by their employers as committed to the job and more likely to be promoted (Deam, 2006).

Because they're not assumed to be the "primary" parent, fathers rarely suffer the same sort of workplace discrimination that mothers face. Not surprisingly, married men earn 10 to 40% more than comparable unmarried men (Ginther & Zavodny, 2001). These differences may be the direct result of employer discrimination or come from the fact that men with high earnings are more likely to get married. But it's also possible that these differences are a more subtle consequence of a pervasive ideology that underlies our beliefs about gender, family, and the workplace.

Women in traditionally male occupations (e.g., law, medicine, and engineering) carry extra burdens as they try to adjust to others' workplace expectations and overcome their prejudices. When college students were asked to evaluate two highly qualified candidates for a job in engineering—one had more education; the other had more work experience—they preferred the more educated candidate 75% of the time. But when the more educated candidate had a female name, she was picked only 48% of the time (cited in Angier & Chang, 2005).

The Wage Gap

The 1963 Equal Pay Act guaranteed women equal pay for equal work, and Title VII of the 1964 Civil Rights Act banned job discrimination on the basis of sex (as well as race, religion, and national origin), but women continue to face a **wage gap.** Their earning power, and thus their ability to financially support their families, consistently lags behind men's. In 2005 the average earnings for all U.S. men working full-time, year-round was $42,743. All women working full-time, year-round earned an average salary of $32,903 per year (DeNavas-Walt et al., 2007). To put it another way, for every dollar a U.S. man earns, a woman earns only about 77 cents.

These figures are clearly an improvement over past wage differences (Figure 9.2). Advances in work experience and job-related skills have enabled some women, particularly middle- and upper-class women, to improve their income levels relative to men's. But some sociologists argue that any narrowing of the wage gap recently is not because women's earning power has improved but because men's has worsened. Between 2002 and 2004, women's earnings dropped 1%. During that same period, men's earnings dropped 2.3% (National Committee on Pay Equity, 2006).

The wage gap is not uniform across all groups. Latino and black men tend to earn less, on average, than other men, so the wage gap between men and women is narrower in these groups than it is among whites and Asian Americans (U.S. Bureau of the Census, 2008).

Mothers are particularly susceptible to the wage gap. Research suggests that compared to women without children, mothers looking for work are offered lower starting salaries (cited in Aloi, 2005). One study that charted the work experiences of more

■ **wage gap**
A persistent difference in the amount of money women earn compared to men, regardless of the occupation.

than 5,000 women over a 10-year period found that mothers' wages dropped by 7% per child (Budig & England, 2001). These wage "penalties" are larger for married mothers than for unmarried mothers. The researchers concluded that only about one third of this penalty is attributable to deficiencies in past work experience or lack of seniority. They suggest that the bulk of it results from the effects of motherhood on productivity, extended leaves of absence, or employer discrimination.

Among mothers who graduated from college in 1993, more than one third were either out of the workforce entirely or had switched to part-time work 10 years later, compared to only 4% of men (Dey & Hill, 2007). As a consequence, these women lose significant amounts of their income, paying what one writer calls a cumulative "mommy tax" (Crittenden, 2001). Over the span of her working life, a college-educated woman can lose up to $1 million in wages given up in the interests of caring for others. In addition to a loss in wages, the "mommy tax" also includes a loss of benefits, promotions, and raises.

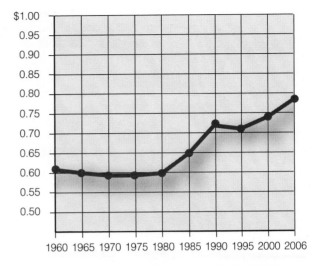

FIGURE 9.2   Male-to-Female Earnings Ratio, 1960 to 2006

Source: DeNavas-Walt, Proctor, & Smith, 2007, table A-2.

Brand new mothers face other obstacles. Highly paid professional women who return to work after giving birth are likely to find support for pumping their breast milk into bottles to be taken home at the end of the day: about one third of large corporations now provide "lactation rooms" for such activities. But lower-income mothers working in factories or restaurants find that pumping is either discouraged or impossible. Some are forced to choose between feeding their babies and earning a living. Most pediatricians agree that breast-fed babies have fewer health problems down the line than babies who aren't breast-fed, so such limitations can have long-term health disadvantages. To date, 12 states have had to enact laws protecting the rights of mothers to "pump" on the job (Kantor, 2006).

The gender wage gap is not an exclusively U.S. phenomenon. To varying degrees, in every country around the world men earn more than women. Worldwide, women still average slightly less than 78% of the wages given to men for the same work, a gap that refuses to close in even the most developed countries (Lopez-Claros & Zahidi, 2005).

Why does the U.S. wage gap persist? One reason, of course, is occupational segregation and the types of jobs women are most likely to have. A study of workers in major U.S. cities found that women in female-dominated jobs earn the lowest wages (less than $6.95 per hour) whereas men in male-dominated jobs earn the highest wages ($11.60 per hour; Cohen & Huffman, 2003). For five of the "most female" jobs in the United States (that is, those that are around 95% female)—preschool teacher, teacher's assistant, secretary, child care worker, and dental assistant—the average weekly salary is $457. For five of the "most male" jobs (those around 95% male)—airplane pilot, firefighter, aircraft engine mechanic, plumber, and steel worker—the average weekly salary is $940 (U.S. Department of Labor, 2006).

Even in the same occupations, men's and women's earnings diverge. Women have made substantial inroads into previously male professions such as law and medicine. In 1983 about 15% of attorneys and 16% of physicians in the United States were women;

The entertainment industry is notorious for its grueling hours and seemingly family unfriendly environment. But the profession is a surprisingly good fit for female TV writers. These women work flexible hours and sometimes bring their children to the studio.

by 2006 those figures had doubled (U.S. Bureau of the Census, 2008). Yet even in these occupations, women's pay lags behind men's. Women tend to earn less than men in traditionally female occupations as well (Figure 9.3).

Some economists and policymakers argue that the wage gap is essentially an institutional by-product that exists because men on the whole have more work experience and training, work more hours per year, and are more likely to work a full-time schedule than women (U.S. General Accounting Office, 2003). As we saw earlier, more employed women work part time than employed men. Not only do part-time workers earn less, but during hard times, they are usually the first ones pushed out of employment—not because they're women but because their jobs are the most expendable.

However, sex differences in education, labor force experience, and seniority, factors that might justify discrepancies in salary, account for less than 15% of the wage gap between men and women (National Committee on Pay Equity, 1999). The average income of female workers in the United States is significantly lower than that of men with the same level of education or training. Women with a bachelor's degree can expect to earn only a little more than men with just a high school diploma (median annual earnings of $40,684 for college-educated women compared to $35,248 for high school–educated men). Similarly, women with doctoral degrees (mean annual earnings of $66,411) earn less than men with bachelor's degrees (mean annual earnings of $67,980; U.S. Bureau of the Census, 2008). Indeed, the pay gap between men and women has actually widened recently for women with college degrees. Some econo-

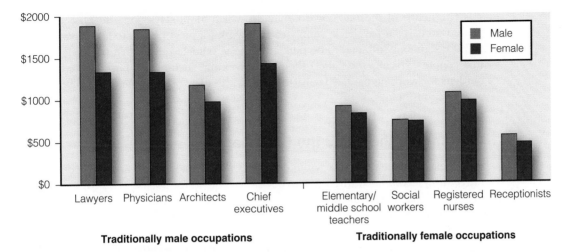

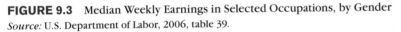

FIGURE 9.3   Median Weekly Earnings in Selected Occupations, by Gender
Source: U.S. Department of Labor, 2006, table 39.

mists attribute this trend to a sharp increase in highly educated mothers who choose to stay home with young children; others point to lingering workplace discrimination, which keeps women from reaching the upper echelons of their professions (Dey & Hill, 2007; Leonhardt, 2006b).

DUAL-EARNER HOUSEHOLDS

Despite the persistent wage gap, women remain committed to the idea of participating in the workforce. In 2005 about 65% of married-couple households with at least one child under the age of 18 had two working parents. That figure was up from 39% in 1970 (Coontz, 2005; U.S. Bureau of the Census, 2008). The number of dual-earner families has actually declined slightly in recent years, leading some to conclude that we're experiencing a rebirth of traditional, male-breadwinner families as more women forgo work to devote time to their families. But this small trend may actually have more to do with economic downturns and a lack of employment opportunities for men and women alike than with some kind of major cultural shift (C. Williams, 2006). Even those professional women who drop out of the workforce average only about 2 years away from their jobs before financial need leads them to return (Hewlett & Luce, 2005). Furthermore, the decline in women's labor force participation has been about the same for mothers as for women without children, undercutting the conclusion that women are "opting out" of the workforce to spend time with their children (Boushey, 2005).

One obvious reason dual-earner families are so common is that the financial demands of modern living—shrinking incomes, increasing cost of housing and health care, and so on—have made it nearly impossible for most couples to survive on a single income. Since the mid-1970s, the amount of an average family budget earmarked for mortgage payments has increased 69%. The cost of sending a child to college, when adjusted for inflation, is double what it was a generation ago (cited in Tyagi, 2004). But incomes have not risen proportionately. In fact, in constant dollars, median household incomes have dropped since 1999 (U.S. Bureau of the Census, 2008).

The image of the traditional family, in which Mom stays home to raise the kids while Dad earns a paycheck, simply cannot work for most people today. Nevertheless, social institutions still tend to be built around the outdated belief that only one partner in a couple (typically the father) should be working. Such beliefs have created serious burdens for working parents trying to balance the demands of their families with their work responsibilities.

Working Mothers and the Guilt Gap

Sociologist Kathleen Gerson wrote *Hard Choices: How Women Decide About Work, Career and Motherhood* in 1985. The book, a classic in the sociology of work and family, focuses on how women struggle to balance their work and family commitments. Drawing on the life histories of working- and middle-class women, Gerson paints a vivid picture of the complex and competing forces women face: their aspirations, their commitment to motherhood, their beliefs about children, and their perception of their place in their families and in society.

The experiences of the women in Gerson's study were quite diverse. Some of these women entered adulthood wanting to become mothers and homemakers; others began adulthood with ambivalence or downright animosity toward motherhood. Some continued on these early paths; others veered off, experiencing a dramatic change in their family plans and desires. But all faced tough decisions about how to balance work and family. More than two decades later, the choices for women remain hard.

Such difficulty stems from powerful and sometimes conflicting social pressures and cultural ambivalence regarding how mothers ought to behave. At one extreme is the image of the traditional mother who stays at home with the kids and devotes all her energy to her family. At the other extreme is the image of the "supermom," effortlessly juggling the demands of home and work. She has a briefcase under one arm, a cell phone in one hand, a baby in the other, and a smile on her face.

The cultural ambivalence derives from the fact that although both images are considered socially acceptable, both are also indicted for their failings. Add to the mix the fact that U.S. culture seems suspicious of childless career women, and you can see how an adult woman faces a no-win situation (Hays, 1996). If she voluntarily remains childless, some will accuse her of being cold, selfish, and unwomanly. If she is a mother who works hard at her job, some will accuse her of neglecting her children. If she has children, is employed, but puts her kids before her job, some will judge her to be uncommitted to her work. And if she is a full-time homemaker, some will call her an unproductive throwback to the 1950s, content with her subordinate status in the family.

These images lead many women to *feel* less than adequate. It's difficult for a stay-at-home mother to be happy and fulfilled when she keeps hearing that she is mindless and bored. It's difficult for a working mother to ably juggle her roles when she hears that she is shortchanging her children and must dedicate *all* her energy in *both* directions to be considered successful:

> The Working Moms look down on the Stay-at-Home Moms: *What on earth do they do all day? How can they be so dependent?* The Stay-at-Home Moms feel sorry for the Working Moms: *Do they know what they're missing?* . . . Why does having children, while bringing out our most loving, effusively maternal selves, simultaneously ignite our fears and turn us against one another? (Cheever, 2006, pp. 38, 41)

It's not surprising that many employed mothers feel guilty and many stay-at-home mothers feel isolated and invisible to the larger society. Employed mothers can come up with lots of compelling reasons why it's good and right to have a job and career; and traditional mothers can come up with equally compelling reasons why it's good and right to stay home (Hays, 1996).

Because of the lingering notion of separate spheres, men have historically been able to feel they are fulfilling their family obligations by simply being financial providers. An employed man may have to explain to people why he's chosen a particular career, but he rarely, if ever, has to explain or justify *why* he is working in the first place. Most people would interpret his long hours at work as an understandable sacrifice made for his family's sake.

In contrast, women's employment is still sometimes perceived as optional (for earning "pin money") or, worse, as potentially damaging to family life. Even though women work for the same reasons men work—because they need the money—and bring home paychecks that cover a major chunk of the family's bills (Warren & Tyagi, 2007), women have traditionally had to justify why working outside the home is not an abandonment of their family duties. You'd be hard-pressed to find many journalists and scholars fearfully describing the perilous effects of men's outside employment on the family. But a mountain of articles and editorials in popular magazines, newspapers, and academic journals over the years focuses on the difficulties women have in juggling the demands of work and family and on the negative effects of mothers' employment on their children's well-being. Newspaper accounts of studies showing that children who spend time in day care have more behavioral problems than children who don't—even if the effect is slight—perpetuate the idea that mothers' labor force choices are potentially dangerous (Carey, 2007b).

Despite these concerns, most research shows that wives' and mothers' employment actually has very little negative impact on their family's well-being (Bianchi, 2000). Most U.S. adults believe that working mothers are just as capable of establishing warm relationships with their children as mothers who don't work outside the home. Nevertheless, popular images die hard, and so it's not surprising that some married women with children don't feel completely self-confident in their choice to enter or remain in the paid labor force. Men, on the other hand, rarely spend as much time worrying about the effect their work will have on their children as mothers do. This gender difference in worrying is referred to by some as the **guilt gap** (Hays, 1996).

Some men do make sacrifices regarding their careers or their families, but in general men don't face the same kind of cultural pressures and hard choices that women continue to face. In fact, men's choice, for the most part, is no choice at all. Men are still expected to attach primary importance to their careers, so they seldom feel stress over sacrificing family time for their jobs. The stress some men do feel over balancing their careers and their family commitments can be tempered by the knowledge that they are conforming to cultural expectations when they devote most of their time to work.

■ **guilt gap**
Gender difference in the amount of concern men and women express over the effect their employment will have on their children.

Men's Changing Commitments to Work and Family

Men's lives aren't completely stress-free, however. Overall, women may earn less than men, but working wives today still make substantial contributions to their household's income. In 30% of all households, working wives actually earn more than their husbands (Coontz, 2005). The previously unchallenged belief in the superiority of the male "good provider" has been replaced by uncertainty over men's proper place in society.

It's no longer obvious what goals men should pursue and how much energy they should devote to pursuing them. Compared to their own fathers, many men today feel less powerful and less confident about making a living (Faludi, 1999).

■ TAKING A CLOSER LOOK

Is the Male Breadwinner Role Disappearing?

Men today are facing new choices about how to structure their lives and uncertainty about their role as breadwinner. Sociologist Kathleen Gerson (1993) interviewed 138 men ranging in age from the late 20s to the mid-40s. These men came from diverse social and occupational backgrounds. Less than half remained committed to the traditional male breadwinner role and expected women to occupy the traditional female homemaker role. These men felt that changes in women's lives had not, or should not, change men's traditional status as dominant breadwinner.

But the remainder of the men Gerson interviewed rejected the traditional male breadwinner role. Of these men, the largest group, about 46% (or 24% of the total sample), cited freedom from the breadwinner role as a reason to renounce marriage and parenthood. They felt they had much to lose and little to gain by getting married. Many had negative experiences with other people's children, which convinced them that parenthood was not something they wished to pursue either. Fearing that becoming responsible for a family would rob them of the option to pursue unpredictable careers or nontraditional jobs, these men rejected the domestic and work commitments that constitute the traditional definition of male success and turned away from family altogether. Those who had already fathered children were quite uninvolved in their lives.

Other men Gerson interviewed—about 39% of those who turned away from the breadwinner role (21% of the total sample)—simply didn't think or plan for the future at all. But about 15% of this nontraditional group saw the decrease in breadwinning responsibilities as an opportunity to embrace a more nurturing parent role and construct a marriage based on equality and fairness. As one man put it, "I just could not see myself being attracted to somebody who was not gonna have their own career, and have the same kind of interest and passion about what they want to do as I had about my career" (quoted in Gerson, 1993, pp. 65–66). They hoped that an employed spouse would lessen their own economic burden and give them the freedom to seek personal fulfillment and not just job security at work. They wouldn't have to worry about earning a big paycheck. These men also showed a deep emotional attachment to their children and devoted much of their time at home to their care. They showed a willingness to parent not seen in their fathers' or grandfathers' generations.

Although still statistically in the minority, such attachments are becoming more socially acceptable. Sociologist Rosanna Hertz (1999) studied a group of family-focused fathers in dual-earner marriages. What made these men interesting was that most of them had spent part of their adulthood focused primarily or exclusively on their careers. So what happened to change their perspectives?

Hertz found that some of the men made a very conscious decision to put their families above their work commitments, but some came to that decision indirectly. The latter tended to be working-class men who found themselves without a job or underemployed after they were "downsized" from their jobs. Their wives, by necessity, worked full time or overtime while the fathers were forced to assume many of the child care responsibilities. Because they were committed to keeping the family central to their lives, these fathers stepped up their involvement and were able to master the parenting role.

The other group of men in Hertz's study were committed to a "new parenting" approach, one in which family is organized around children and both parents are full participants. But social class was at work here too. These men tended to hold managerial and professional positions, so they were able to negotiate flexible hours or reduced workweeks in order to spend more time with their families. They were similar to those studied by sociologists Penny Becker and Phyllis Moen (1999), who found that some professional men in their study intentionally placed limits on the number of hours they worked and reduced their expectations for career advancement in order to be more involved with their families. Their decisions were usually prompted by a desire to spend more time with their children and to be more involved than their fathers had been.

Work Expectations in Same-Sex Couples

In gay and lesbian households, domestic and breadwinning responsibilities cannot be automatically based on gender; they must be negotiated. The issue is not who has the gender-based right to work or, conversely, the obligation not to work. Instead, the issue is how the relationship and the household can be kept together given the career demands on *both* partners. The vast majority of same-sex couples emphasize sharing and fairness and believe that both partners in the relationship should be employed (Blumstein & Schwartz, 1983). Few consider either not working or supporting someone who chooses not to work. The reasons for their feelings about this issue provide insight into the meaning of work for both men and women, regardless of sexual orientation.

For gay men, as for all men, work remains a key aspect of self-respect. Unlike some heterosexual men though, gay men don't feel obligated to support their partners financially. Instead, each partner is expected to work because that is what it means to be a man (Blumstein & Schwartz, 1983). Few gay men are interested in being full-time homemakers. Sociologist Christopher Carrington (1999) describes one gay couple, Rich and Bill, who have a fairly unequal division of labor. Although Bill performs most of the domestic work, his partner goes to great lengths to clarify for the researcher that Bill's not "just a housewife." When asked how he would feel about Bill's becoming a full-time homemaker, Rich responds:

> I wouldn't like it at all. I don't see how that could be fair, for one person to contribute everything and the other to give little or nothing to the relationship. Plus, what about one's self-respect? I don't see how one could live with oneself by not doing something for a living. I would not be comfortable at all telling people that Bill is just a housewife." (quoted in Carrington, 1999, p. 54)

For many lesbians, work means the ability to avoid being dependent on others and being cast into the stereotypical homemaker role. But lesbians don't expect to be the head of a household in the same way a husband expects to enter the breadwinner role in a traditional heterosexual marriage. Although they understand the importance of earning their own living, rarely do these women think they will have to either support, or be supported by, another person. They are likely to see themselves as "workers," not "providers" or "dependents" (Blumstein & Schwartz, 1983).

Family Friendly Workplaces

Many dual-earner U.S. families, especially those with young children, continue to struggle with lack of support from employers, government, and businesses. They face difficulty trying to fit in all the tasks that used to be performed by stay-at-home mothers and trying to find dependable day care at the same time that they are trying to earn enough money to make ends meet.

Many experts feel that the single most important step U.S. society could take to help working families would be to help them deal with child care demands. As recently as 1990, only 52% of the nation's largest companies had some form of maternity leave guaranteeing that an employee could take vacation or sick time upon the birth or adoption of a child and not lose her or his job (Aldous & Dumon, 1990). In 1993 President Clinton signed into law the Family and Medical Leave Act (FMLA), which guarantees some workers up to 12 weeks of *unpaid* sick leave per year for the birth or adoption of a child or to care for a sick child, parent, or spouse. However, FMLA has some important restrictions that seriously limit its usefulness to the entire working population:

- The law covers only workers who have been employed continuously for at least 1 year and who have worked a total of at least 1,250 hours (or about 25 hours a week). As a result, temporary or part-time workers are not eligible.
- The law exempts companies with fewer than 50 workers.
- The law allows an employer to deny leave to a "key" employee—that is, one who is in the highest-paid 10% of its workforce—if allowing that person to take the leave would create "substantial and grievous injury" to the business's operations.

Currently, only 54% of U.S. workers are eligible for FMLA benefits. In 2005, 17% of eligible employees actually took leave (U.S. Department of Labor, 2007). Over three quarters of the eligible employees who don't take unpaid leave are parents who need the time off but don't take it because they can't afford to go without a paycheck (National Partnership for Women & Families, 2006). In fact, 9% of employees who take unpaid leave under FMLA end up going on public assistance to make up for the lost wages (National Partnership for Women and Families, 2005). Even with FMLA, the number of workers who end up suing their employers for mistreatment on account of their family responsibilities has increased more than 300% since the mid-1990s (Press, 2007).

■ GOING GLOBAL ████████████████████████████

Family Leave Policies Around the World

Although FMLA represents an improvement over past conditions, the United States still lags behind other countries in terms of government support for dual-earner families. According to a Harvard University study of 168 countries, 163 guarantee paid leave to women in connection to childbirth, and 45 guarantee paid paternity leave. The majority of these countries provide 100% wage replacement for at least some of the guaranteed leave. Only Lesotho, Papua New Guinea, Swaziland, Australia, and the United States offer no paid family leave. In addition, 139 countries provide paid leave for workers to care for family members with short- or long-term illnesses (Heymann, Earle, Simmons, Breslow, & Kuehnhoff, 2004).

Consider the policies of a few other industrialized nations (Bell-Rowbotham & Lero, 2001; "Parental Leave," 2007):

■ In France, mothers receive 16 weeks off work at 84% pay for the first and second children, and 24 weeks off at the same rate of pay for the third and subsequent children. They also receive up to 3 years of unpaid leave with job protection.

■ In Norway, parents can take 42 weeks of leave at 100% pay or 52 weeks at 80%. Fathers are entitled to 4 weeks of this leave. Parents can also combine part-time work and partial parental benefits. For example, one parent could take full leave at 100% pay for 42 weeks and the other could combine 80% work and 20% leave for nearly 2 years.

■ In the United Kingdom, parents receive 18 weeks of maternity leave at 90% of their salary and 12 weeks at a flat rate. They can also take up to 40 weeks of unpaid family leave.

■ In Bulgaria, mothers receive 45 days of sick leave at 100% pay *prior* to the date their child is due to be born. Then, after the child is born, they are entitled to 2 years of paid leave, and 1 additional year of unpaid leave. The employer is required to restore the mother to the same position upon return to work. In addition, pregnant women and single mothers cannot be fired.

To make matters worse, relatively few private employers go beyond the minimum unpaid leave policies mandated by FMLA. Just 12% of U.S. companies offer *paid* maternity leave to their employees, and only one state, California, guarantees paid family leave (although for no more than 6 weeks) for public sector employees (National Partnership for Women and Families, 2005).

This reluctance to provide financial protection to employees with family obligations doesn't mean that employers are completely insensitive to their workers' needs. Each year the number of employers who offer some type of "family friendly" work policy grows. In some cases (often at very large companies) you can now choose to work part time, share a job with another worker, work some of your hours at home, or work on a flexible schedule.

Now you might expect workers to be rushing to take advantage of these opportunities. But a study of 188 companies found that, when flexible hours were available, fewer than 5% of employees made use of part-time shifts, and fewer than 3% chose to work some hours at home (Hochschild, 1997). Yet the majority of nearly 10,000 husbands and wives surveyed for the National Study of Families and Households study said they were not working the schedule they preferred (Clarkberg & Moen, 2001). Two thirds felt that they were working too much. Many working parents say they want to spend more time with their families and less time at work, but relatively few are taking advantage of opportunities to do so.

Some individuals may invest more time and energy at their work because there is so little emotional pull from family. Women in one study felt their emotional needs were met in the workplace, not at home. Some had older children or were childless, but even women with young children sometimes felt that growing up with a working mother had made their children so independent they didn't need much emotional investment from their mother (Philipson, 2000).

In her study of a *Fortune 500* public relations company, sociologist Arlie Russell Hochschild (1997) uncovered a different reason behind some individuals' reluctance to work less and spend more time with family. In this company, work had become a sort of refuge. Some of the male and female workers Hochschild interviewed told her that they come to work early and stay late just to get away from the house. At work they can relax, have a cup of coffee, and share jokes and stories with friends without the hectic anxiety that characterizes modern home life. Not surprisingly, they are perfectly willing to flee a world of unrelenting demands, unresolved quarrels, and unwashed laundry for a world of relative harmony, companionship, and understanding.

Although Hochschild suggests these patterns reflect a recent tendency to see home as work and work as home, others say there have always been individuals who find greater fulfillment at work than at home (Maume & Bellas, 2001). In addition, new management techniques have transformed some workplaces into more appreciative, more personal sorts of places.

Ironically, after decades of companies enacting "family friendly" initiatives, single and childless workers are beginning to speak out against them. They feel that workers with few family obligations are footing the bill for these policies (Hegtvedt, Clay-Warner, & Ferrigno, 2002). According to one study, over half of childless, single employees believe they're being taken advantage of by their married and child-rearing coworkers (cited in Bradley, 2006). Compared to other employees, single, childless workers say they receive fewer benefits, work longer hours, and have less flexible vacation time. As one psychologist puts it:

> I think one of the biggest issues is that people assume that if you're single, you don't have a life. You don't have anything to do with your time, or you don't have anything that qualifies as being as important as what married people have to do. It's just assumed that you will do whatever the rest of the workforce doesn't want to do. (quoted in Bradley, 2006, p. 13)

The search for balance between work and family remains a struggle for many U.S. families. Most social and policy research suggests that the solution lies not in individual adjustments and accommodations but in collective ones, such as greater corporate involvement and response to workers' needs.

Coping Strategies of Dual-Earner Households

Clearly, couples who want to work and remain committed to their families are subject, to some degree, to the whims of the workplace. For instance, as the economy has become more global, more companies require around-the-clock shifts to meet the demands of international customers in different time zones. Many dual-earner and dual-career couples have had to reconstruct their lifestyles to adapt to these and other demands.

Time Adjustments

Given a choice, many men and women say they would prefer more flexibility at work so they can spend more time at home (Gerson & Jacobs, 2007). Because of contemporary economic realities, however, many couples and single parents find they must instead make trade-offs to try to balance their work and family lives. Some parents end up working longer hours to earn enough money to support the family. For dual-earner couples with kids under 18, the combined hours at work for both partners grew from 81 hours a week in 1977 to 91 hours in 2002 ("The Case for Staying Home," 2004). Some employers demand long work hours or explicitly reward employees who put in long hours, thereby pressuring individuals to work longer and harder to ensure job security or promotions (Clarkberg & Moen, 2001; Golden, 1998).

The unfortunate consequence of working more hours—either by choice or necessity—is that people may "downsize" their ideas about how much care a child or a partner really needs from them (Hochschild, 1997). Families learn to make do with less time, less attention, and less support at home than they once imagined possible. Sociologists have found that when one or both spouses work long hours (more than 45 hours a week), their quality of life is reduced (Moen & Yu, 2000).

Other couples make trade-offs in the opposite direction by reducing their time at work or by forgoing opportunities for advancement (Becker & Moen, 1999). Often such scaling back occurs while couples have young children at home and family demands are most intense. Although women are more likely than men to scale back their work hours (Gerson & Jacobs, 2007), husbands too sometimes make very conscious decisions to be more involved in family (Becker & Moen, 1999).

Shift Work

About 42% of full-time wage and salary workers work nontraditional shifts (evening shift, night shift, employer-arranged irregular schedules, or rotating shifts) or flexible schedules (U.S. Bureau of Labor Statistics, 2005b). In addition, one half of dual-earner couples consist of spouses who work different shifts (cited in S. Greenhouse, 2000).

Young, middle-class couples might perceive shift work as an attractive alternative for the flexibility it offers. For working-class families, however, shift work is likely to be an arrangement over which workers have little control. Parents earning the lowest incomes are the ones who are more likely to be assigned to work on weekends and on unstable or rotating schedules.

Although shift or flexible work is attractive to some couples, it can reduce marital happiness and the amount of interaction that occurs between partners, increase sexual and household problems, and ultimately increase the likelihood of divorce (White & Keith, 1990). Furthermore, relatively few child care centers operate 24 hours a day or on weekends. Most couples must either rely on friends and relatives for child care or work opposite shifts, sacrificing time together so that one of them can be with the children (Hays, 1995).

Such tension is not inevitable. One study found that individuals working on the weekends were more likely than individuals in Monday–Friday jobs to experience family conflict, lack of balance between work and family, and worker burnout. However, working night shifts and rotating shifts posed no problems for workers or their families (Fenwick & Tausig, 2001). The researchers also found that when individuals have choices over their work schedules, shift work does not pose serious health or family problems.

Coping Strategies in Single-Parent Families

The coping strategies of dual-earner families simply can't apply to single-parent families. In these households, there is no partner to work a nonstandard shift. Although it may be possible for single parents to reduce their hours at work, most, especially those headed by women, do not have the financial resources or job status to scale back in this way (Golden, 2001). In fact, for poor single parents, striking the balance between work and family usually means working more, not fewer, hours. They may have to find part-time jobs in addition to their full-time jobs, such as cleaning homes, babysitting in their homes, waitressing in the evening, and so on to make ends meet. Such jobs provide few or no benefits. "Making good money without benefits might be doable without a child, but having a child can dramatically change one's financial situation from independence to welfare dependence in a matter of months" (Hertz, 1999, p. 25). When jobs lack benefits, these women typically are forced to turn to government assistance such as Medicaid.

To complicate matters even further, working multiple jobs requires even more child care. Thus, a major coping strategy for these single, employed mothers was building and nurturing an informal but extensive social support system of friends, neighbors, and nearby relatives.

Single mothers who are able to scale back are usually professional women (Hertz, 1999). For these women, working less requires years of planning *before* the child arrives, such as saving money and amassing sick leave to offset some of the costs of cutting back their hours. Some of these women are also able to arrange flexible hours or shorter workweeks.

THE DOMESTIC DIVISION OF LABOR

Work performed for wages, no matter how menial, is always regarded as *real* work. But work performed within the home is generally invisible, and therefore excluded from typical definitions of "work." Sometimes the invisibility of domestic work is purposeful, as it is for the following individual:

> I just want to get [the laundry] done, and out of the way, before Andrea gets home. . . . I just don't want her to have to deal with it. I really like us to be able to have quality time when she gets here. She has enough pressure to deal with at work, so I try to keep this kind of stuff out of her way. (quoted in Carrington, 1999, pp. 203–204)

But the invisibility of domestic work is more likely to stem from two more important sources: the prevailing notion that housework is really a "labor of love" and not work at all, and the fact that it is unpaid. When you actually detail what has to happen within any given household to make it run smoothly, it is startling to see just how much work there is. Consider all the unpaid labor (excluding child care work) that goes into keeping a household going (Carrington, 1999):

- *Feeding work:* planning meals, learning about foods, buying food, preparing the meals, cleaning after meals, and so on.

- *Housework:* Cleaning house, caring for clothing and linen, caring for pets and plants, managing household paperwork and financial work, dealing with nonkin (e.g., deliveries, service workers), scheduling and monitoring home repairs and maintenance, and so on.

- *Kin work:* visiting relatives, writing and sending cards and letters, making phone calls, and purchasing gifts (along with all the forethought and decision making that goes into these tasks).

- *Consumption work:* visiting stores, reading about products and services, ordering materials, comparison shopping, monitoring performance of products and services, record-keeping and organizing manuals and instructions, managing money, and so on.

Notice that each one of these categories of domestic work includes multiple tasks. For instance, planning meals includes knowing family members' food preferences and nutritional needs, keeping track of everyone's schedules to know when the family can sit down to eat, and so forth. When we add in all the different types of work that are part of child care—supervision, direct care and interaction, being "on call"—the list of domestic tasks grows even more.

Many sociologists and economists point out that domestic labor is invaluable to the entire economic system (Gerencher, 2001). However, the people who perform the majority of domestic work—that is, women—earn no money for providing these services. Mothers also provide an important service to society by physically and emotionally nurturing the next generation of workers. If a woman were to be paid the minimum going rate for all her labor as mother and housekeeper—child care, transportation, errands, cleaning, laundry, cooking, bill paying, grocery shopping—her yearly salary would be larger than the average salary of male full-time workers. One recent study found that if we apply average hourly wage rates to the average daily amounts of child care mothers of children under age 12 provide, a low-end estimate of the monetary value of this work is about $33,000 a year (Folbre & Yoon, 2006). A decade ago, women's unpaid work around the world was valued at $11 trillion, compared to the official global output that year of $23 trillion (Human Development Report, 1995). If domestic work were paid, women would no doubt be the major breadwinners worldwide.

In fairness, women who are full-time homemakers are not completely suppressed economically. They are, after all, entitled to support from their husbands' wages and have a share of the property, whether the marriage survives or not. However, domestic labor does not afford the prestige it might because societal power and family power are usually a function of who earns the money. It's not that homemakers don't work; it's that they work invisibly outside the mainstream economy, in which work is strictly defined as activity someone is paid to do (Ciancanelli & Berch, 1987; Voyandoff, 1990).

Furthermore, defining unpaid household labor and child rearing as "women's work" upholds male privilege in society. Free of such obligations, men are able to enjoy more leisure time and take advantage of the opportunity to pursue their own careers and interests. Women burdened with domestic responsibilities have less time and energy to devote to their careers. Research shows that the more housework employed women do, the lower their wages (cited in Glazer, 2006). Hence, the division of labor in the home reinforces the division of labor in the workforce, further solidifying the gender-based power structure of U.S. society.

As we saw earlier, some men do aim for a better balance between work and family responsibilities. But in general their involvement in domestic work has not kept pace with women's increasing commitment to paid employment. Some sociologists have referred to this situation as a "stalled revolution" (Hochschild & Machung, 1989). It contributes to the sluggishness of the movement toward gender equity both inside and outside the home (Arrighi & Maume, 2000). For instance, many wives choose to quit their jobs rather than continue to argue with their husbands about who should do what around the house. So men's reluctance to take on more of the daily household tasks can indirectly contribute to the disruption of women's tenure in the job market and reduce their earnings (Corcoran & Duncan, 1979).

Even where wives have prestigious careers, domestic matters are typically assumed to be outside the repertoire of male responsibilities, and not only in the United States. In Mexico, for example, women have entered the workforce and universities in unprecedented numbers in the past several decades; the percentage of women in the paid labor force has doubled since 1970. However, their place in the family has changed little. Statistics show that less than half of working men pitch in at all around the house, compared to 94% of working women. In 2000, thousands of Mexican housewives went on a day-long strike against housework to protest the imbalance and highlight their contribution to society. For one woman the day of the protest was the first time in *23 years* that she didn't get up at 6:00 a.m. to fix her husband's meals for the day (Sheridan, 2000).

Time Doing Housework

Estimates of the amount of time people spend on domestic work vary depending on the method of data collection used: self-reports or spousal estimates (Lee & Waite, 2005). But regardless of what method is used, gender gaps in housework prevail (Figure 9.4). In addition, employed women spend almost an hour a day more than men caring for young children (U.S. Bureau of Labor Statistics, 2004). Thus although the ratio of women's to men's hours doing domestic work has narrowed, it's not because men are doing substantially more but because women are doing less (Bianchi, Milkie, Sayer, & Robinson, 2000).

Moreover, the housework husbands do tends to be quite different from the work their wives do. Women do more of the core housework chores than men, the tasks that have to be done regularly or daily, such as housecleaning, cooking, and meal cleanup. By contrast, men tend to do more outdoor chores and home repairs, tasks that are typically infrequent, irregular, or optional (Lee & Waite, 2005).

Two decades ago, sociologists Arlie Hochschild and Anne Machung (1989) pointed out that because of this persistent gender imbalance, the average U.S. working wife routinely works two shifts—one at the office and one at home. More recently, Michele Bolton (2000)

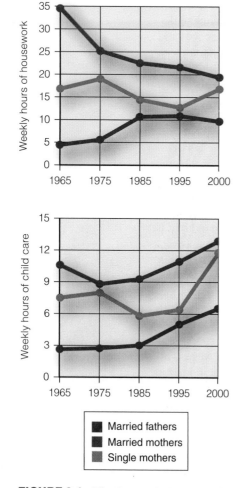

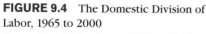

FIGURE 9.4 The Domestic Division of Labor, 1965 to 2000

Source: Bianchi, Robinson, & Milkie, 2006, tables 4.1 and 5.1.

has suggested that many women actually work a *third* shift—a relentless, psychologically draining period of rehashing the events of the day:

> Most of the women I interviewed . . . seemed to use their private, quiet time—in the car, in the shower, before falling asleep at night—as a psychological third shift after finishing the actual first and second shifts that made their days too busy to fully think through their actions and choices. (p. 2)

From a structural functionalist perspective, traditional gender disparities in household responsibilities may actually reflect a fair, functional, interdependent division of labor that maximizes benefits for the entire family. If this were the case, you would expect households in which both partners work full time to distribute domestic labor equally, right? Evidence does indicate that husbands perform more of the mundane household tasks traditionally performed by wives when their wives have a long history of extensive work in the paid labor force (Pittman & Blanchard, 1996). However, in general, the gender discrepancy in household responsibilities does not diminish all that much as a result of women's full-time employment.

Women employed outside the home continue to be primarily responsible for the upkeep of the household (Bianchi et al., 2006). Interestingly, this discrepancy holds even among couples who profess egalitarian, nonsexist values. Husbands who say that all the housework should be shared equally still spend significantly less time doing it than their wives do (Blumstein & Schwartz, 1983). However, compared to other husbands, those with more egalitarian attitudes who are married to women with similar attitudes do perform more housework (Greenstein, 1996a).

Rates of housework are not uniform across all groups. Race and ethnicity can play an important role in the domestic division of labor. Asian and Latino men tend to do less domestic work than other men (John, Shelton, & Luschen, 1995). This tendency is particularly pronounced in ethnic neighborhoods in which the high proportion of recent immigrants ensures a steady flow of people with traditional views about gendered family roles. In contrast, despite stereotypes about black men abandoning their family obligations, they are actually *more* likely than white, Asian, or Latino men to be intimately involved in domestic work and child rearing (Taylor, 2007). Black men employed full time may actually spend *more* time doing household labor than unemployed black men, indicating that when men are attached to the provider role they are also committed to their family obligations (Shelton & John, 1993).

Social class has a mixed effect on the gender-based division of domestic labor. One stereotype is that working-class men are less "enlightened" and therefore do proportionately less domestic work than middle-class men. Stereotypically, the macho factory worker whose masculinity is threatened by doing laundry and cleaning the bathroom is contrasted with the "yuppie" father happily cooking meals and pushing a stroller in the park. But research shows that class has little to do with how much housework husbands perform (Wright, Shire, Hwang, Dolan, & Baxter, 1992).

Furthermore, men's economic standing relative to their spouse's doesn't appear to affect how much housework they do, although the reasons behind their involvement may vary. When women earn more than men, couples sometimes resort to a traditional division of family power in order to reinforce the gender differences that could be undermined by the switching of traditional economic roles. Men who experience challenges to their masculine identity on the job (e.g., low pay, lack of autonomy,

Hectic schedules in dual-earner families often result in less getting done around the house.

subordinate status) are especially reluctant to engage in what they consider "feminine" household tasks because doing so would threaten their masculinity even more (Arrighi & Maume, 2000). Men who have suffered through prolonged joblessness are prone to entirely disavow housework, the performance of which would be further evidence of their "failure" at the male provider role (Brines, 1994).

At the same time, though, there is some evidence that men's education level, a component of social class, is associated with involvement in their children's lives. College-educated men spend more time eating with their children, diapering them, bathing them, talking to them, and helping them with their homework than less-educated men. These differences based on education apply to resident as well as nonresident fathers (Martinez, Chandra, Abma, Jones, & Mosher, 2006).

For those couples who do share household tasks, the arrival of children often signals a return to a more traditional division of household labor (Cowan & Cowan, 2000; Schwartz, 2007). In fact, employed men may actually *increase* their time at work upon becoming parents while women significantly decrease theirs (Shelton, 1992).

Men are likely to further decrease their share of housework as the number of children in the household increases (Greenstein, 1996a). In other words, having children often means more work *inside* the house for women and more work *outside* the house for men.

Many women whose husbands make significant contributions to household work and child care report frustration over the fact that they are still "household managers" who are ultimately responsible for planning and initiating household activities (Coltrane, 1996b). Some women have found that if they want their husbands to do certain household tasks, they must prepare itemized lists every time they leave the house, spelling out exactly what needs to be done (Hays, 1996). Others give up trying, concluding that it's easier just to do the job themselves.

Women's Work, Men's Help

Rather than defining the work they do around the house as an ordinary, expected aspect of their family responsibilities, many men may define it as "help"—implying that they're assisting the person who's usually responsible for such tasks.

Even men who assume major responsibility for planning and initiating housework and child care tend to define their role as "helper" (Coltrane, 1989). The tendency of some fathers to refer to their child care behavior as "babysitting" is noteworthy because it verbally aligns them not with the general category of parents for whom taking care of children is a taken-for-granted element of their family role, but with outsiders who periodically care for other people's children. Mothers rarely refer to the time they spend with their own children as "babysitting."

Let's take a closer look at the concept of "help." A key social element of "help"—as distinct from "work"—is that it obligates the person receiving assistance to express gratitude or at a minimum acknowledge it (Hochschild & Machung, 1989). A husband who does the laundry, dusts the furniture, and washes the dishes may feel that he is providing more help than his wife could reasonably expect from a man. Given such a frame of reference, his domestic tasks are something extra—a helpful gift—and his wife should feel grateful. However, if the wife is still responsible for 70% of the domestic work in addition to her full-time job, she may perceive her husband's contribution as barely being what she deserves—not something extra and certainly not a gift.

He may see her failure to thank him for watching the baby a few hours each afternoon as a lack of appreciation for "all he's done." She thinks he's just done what he should do as a parent and therefore she's not obliged to express any special appreciation. She may even resent him for demanding that she acknowledge his domestic contributions, which, relative to her ordinary responsibilities, are probably quite small.

Perceptions of Inequity

Imbalances and inequalities exist in most families. However, actual, objective inequity in domestic responsibilities is less important than the *perception* of inequity. As you might expect, men in general are less likely than women to perceive the unequal distribution of household labor as unfair. A national survey found that almost 60% of women felt they did more than their fair share of housework, compared to 16% of men (National Opinion Research Center, 2006).

Gender Ideology and Domestic Work

Under what circumstances do perceptions of inequity arise? People's perceptions are, in part, contingent on their beliefs and ideologies about gender. In general, husbands with egalitarian gender ideologies tend to see the typical gender-based division of domestic work responsibilities as more unfair to their wives than do husbands with traditional ideologies (DeMaris & Longmore, 1996).

Wives with a "traditional" gender ideology are likely to value stability and harmony in their relationships, but "egalitarian" wives might be more concerned with independence and autonomy (Greenstein, 1996b). If a wife truly believes that married women—no matter what their employment status—are *supposed* to do most of the housework, she will probably view inequalities as legitimate and not see them as unfair. On the other hand, a wife who enters marriage expecting her husband to share in the household work will perceive the inequalities as unfair because her expectations are being violated. Such unmet expectations are likely to increase marital discord (Barnett & Baruch, 1987). Indeed, there is some evidence that traditionally minded women who do most of the housework are actually happier with their marriages than "feminist" women (O'Rourke, 2006).

One obvious source of ideas about gender and domestic responsibilities is culture. Most gender differences are culturally learned. However, gender differences in domestic work aren't just reflections of culturally learned patterns. If women were taught to believe that doing household chores was part of being a woman, gender differences in domestic work responsibilities would be noticeable in all types of household arrangements. But although the amount of domestic work that men do is quite similar whether they are married, cohabiting, or single, the amount that women do fluctuates considerably (South & Spitze, 1994). Single women do about the same amount of housework as single men. Significant differences between women and men exist only among married and cohabiting couples and are especially pronounced among couples with children.

Such differences in contributions to domestic work based on marital status apparently reflect different expectations of how one should "do gender" (see Chapter 4). One study found that women in their second marriages contribute significantly less time to housework than women in first marriages. Men's housework time was uniformly low across all types of relationships (Sullivan, 1997). The women in second relationships may have started their first relationship under one set of norms and reexamined those norms prior to the second relationship. In another study, a majority of divorced women said they'd left their first marriage because of inequitable treatment (Schwartz, 1994). So a woman who perceived the domestic division of labor in her first marriage to be unfair might be inclined to seek a more equal division in subsequent relationships.

Social Exchange and Household Inequity

The social exchange perspective may also shed some light on how men and women perceive domestic arrangements. This perspective argues that people can feel deprived without feeling dissatisfied if they conclude that they are getting what they deserve out of their relationships. People with few outside alternatives tend to have lower expectations of a relationship because they stand to lose more from its disruption than people who have more options available to them (Lennon & Rosenfield, 1994).

Thus, women who have fewer alternatives to marriage and fewer available economic resources are more likely to view an unequal division of domestic work as fair. If wives have low wages and sense a high risk of divorce in their marriages, they may lower their expectations and feel grateful for whatever household chores their husbands do (Hochschild & Machung, 1989). On the other hand, women who are self-sufficient and who perceive available alternatives to their marriage are less dependent on their spouses and are less fearful of divorce. Hence, they are more likely to view unequal domestic work as unfair. These women tend to be more distressed and depressed by an unequal division of household labor than women who accept inequality as fair (Lennon & Rosenfield, 1994).

Perceived responsibility for the "breadwinner" role can also be a critical justification for the unequal distribution of domestic labor (Ferree, 1991). What's important is not just the actual income difference between partners but the meaning attached to that difference. A wife may earn more than her husband, but her earning power may not have an impact on her feelings of inequity over household responsibilities if she and he don't perceive her as being *responsible* for breadwinning as well (Potuchek, 1997). Those wives who do believe they are the family breadwinner are likely to feel entitled to more assistance around the house and therefore perceive greater inequity if their husbands don't contribute their fair share.

WHAT DOES IT ALL MEAN?

Men's participation in household tasks has increased only slightly over the years, despite their growing attachment to fatherhood and the dramatic increase in employment outside the home among married women. But as the gender attitudes of men and women gradually become more egalitarian, both sexes may begin to expect men to do more domestic work. Whether these expectations eventually translate into actual behavior may depend on things like the relative power of the partners, as indicated by differences in education, earnings, and so on.

What seems quite clear is that, both in fact and as an ideal, the traditional division of labor that assigned wage-earning responsibilities to men and unpaid domestic work to women is weakening. Women are in the labor force to stay. Yet at the beginning of the 21st century, women still aren't able to share equally in providing the family income because of persistent inequalities in the labor market and men's persistent lack of interest and full participation in domestic work.

Nevertheless, men's and women's interests are beginning to converge. Women, in some respects, have become more career-oriented but remain committed to family; men, in some respects, have become more family-oriented yet still find their primary source of identity in their careers.

Unfortunately, these changes have not been matched by changes in the workplace. Many U.S. employers continue to value a workaholic ethic that leaves little time for family life. Couples that equitably share work and domestic responsibilities still face a culture that doesn't quite know what to do with them. These couples may shrug off or angrily reject others' disapproval, but they are often called on to justify their nontraditional division of labor. Why is *he* in the grocery store or in the park with his 3-year-old in the middle of the day? Why are they moving to another city to accommodate *her* career?

As a society, we face the crucial task of integrating family and work as smoothly and effectively as possible without sacrificing too much of either. We can resist the social changes that are uniting the once "separate" spheres of work and family, or we can accept these changes and work with them. We can encourage men to sacrifice their family lives to fit into the rigid structure of the conventional workplace and encourage women to sacrifice their careers to meet their family responsibilities, or we can learn to value family caretaking and economic productivity in equal degrees. Piecemeal adjustments on the part of individual workers and couples will not be enough. What are needed are adjustments in institutional support systems—for example, the ability to work flexible hours or shorter workweeks, benefits for part-time workers—so men can feel free to act on their emerging interest in family life without fearing a risk to their careers and women can feel free to pursue their careers without fearing they are placing their families at risk.

As you think back on the information presented in this chapter, consider these questions:

1. How useful is the concept of "separate spheres" today? Are there advantages to separating work and family along gender lines? What are the problems with such a separation?

2. What does it mean to say that the U.S. workplace is based on a male prototype of the ideal worker? Describe the ways that *both* men and women suffer from the expectations associated with this ideal.

3. Assess the value of "family friendly" workplace policies. Do you think employees with children ought to be given special benefits and privileges so they can devote more time to their families?

4. Should the government go beyond the Family and Medical Leave Act to mandate *paid* leave for employees who are having or adopting babies or who have to take care of sick children? If such an expansion meant that your taxes would be raised, would you support it?

5. Although women are making significant strides toward equality with men in other parts of society, household work still tends to be divided along traditional gender lines. Why do you think this is the case? What is the significance of men defining their household work as "help"?

SUMMARY

- The contemporary belief that work life and family life are separate spheres emerged with industrialization in the 19th century. Along with this shift came an expectation that family life was women's domain and work life was men's domain. However, the notion of "separate spheres" has never applied equally to members of different classes and different ethnic groups.

- Work and family are never completely separate. Nevertheless, the ideology of separate spheres was, and continues to be, a powerful force in economics and politics. Consequently, women's experiences in the labor force—from the jobs they occupy to the wages they earn—are still tied to broader cultural assumptions about gender.

- Lingering notions of separate spheres shape the way men and women today perceive the balance between their family lives and their work lives.

- Recent decades have witnessed a dramatic increase in dual-earner families. This change has placed unprecedented demands on the workplace to accommodate employees with family obligations and on families to find ways of tending to their needs when time at home is limited.

- The growing presence of women in the paid labor force has not been accompanied by a substantial increase in the responsibility men take for household work. An inequitable division of household labor continues to be a source of strain for many families.

Go to the Online Learning Center at **www.mhhe.com/newman1** to test your knowledge of the chapter concepts and key terms.

KEY TERMS

guilt gap   249

ideology of separate spheres   239

wage gap   244

SEE FOR YOURSELF

The intersection of gender, family, and work is where we see most clearly how expectations and beliefs can be translated into action. Try to locate at least one of each of the following types of couples in which both partners work full time outside the home:

- Cohabiting heterosexual
- Cohabiting homosexual
- Married without children
- Married with at least one child living at home

Ask each person in each couple to provide the following information. Try to make sure that partners are *not* in each other's presence when making their lists:

1. Make a list of all the household chores that need to be done during the course of a typical week. Be as specific and exhaustive as possible (for example, "cleaning windows," "dusting," and "vacuuming," rather than "cleaning the house"; "buying groceries," "cooking dinner," and "doing dishes" rather than "meal preparation").

2. Indicate which person has primary responsibility for each of the tasks you identified in Question 1 using the following categories:

   1 = I am primarily responsible.

   2 = We share this task more or less equally.

   3 = My partner is primarily responsible.

3. Estimate the amount of time per week that you spend on each task.

4. Indicate how many hours you work *outside the home* during a typical week.

Compare responses of the following groups to see if you can find any differences in the time people spend doing housework and the number of tasks for which they are responsible:

- Men versus women
- Younger versus older couples
- Married versus cohabiting couples
- Couples with children at home versus couples without children at home
- Married versus remarried couples
- Heterosexual versus homosexual couples

Do the women still bear the primary responsibility for housework? Are household responsibilities more equitably split within certain types of couples? If partners within the same couple had different ideas about domestic responsibilities or different estimates of time spent on housework, to what can you attribute this lack of agreement? Is the amount of time a person spends working outside the home related to the amount of household work they do? Describe the tensions men and women experience when trying to balance work and home responsibilities.

10

Entering Parenthood

If a Hmong woman in Laos experiences problems becoming pregnant, she may consult a shaman, who will ask her to sacrifice a dog, cat, chicken, or sheep. After the animal's throat is cut, the shaman strings a rope bridge from the doorpost to the bed, over which the soul of the couple's future baby can travel to earth, free of the malevolent spirit that had detained it.

Once pregnant, the Hmong woman can ensure the health of her baby by paying close attention to what she eats. If she craves ginger but doesn't eat any, the child will be born with an extra finger or toe. If she craves eggs but doesn't eat them, the child will be born with a lumpy head.

A long or painful labor can be eased by drinking water in which a key has been boiled to unlock the birth canal (Fadiman, 1997). When a Hmong woman gives birth, she squats on the dirt floor in the center of her one-room house. But the newborn doesn't get dirty because the mother never lets it actually touch the floor. Instead, she delivers the baby into her own hands, reaching between her legs to ease out the head and then letting the rest of the body slip out onto her forearms (Fadiman, 1997). No birth attendant is present. If the mother becomes thirsty during labor, her husband can bring her a cup of hot water, but he is forbidden to look at her body. Because the Hmong believe that moaning and screaming can disrupt the birth, she labors in silence, except for an occasional prayer to her ancestors.

If the infant is a girl, the father buries the placenta under the parents' bed; if it's a boy, the placenta is buried in a place of greater honor, near a central wooden pillar that holds up the roof of the house. The placenta is always buried with the smooth side, the side that faced the baby in the womb, upward. Otherwise, the baby will vomit after nursing. If the baby develops spots on its face, it means ants are attacking the placenta and so boiling water is poured down the hole (Fadiman, 1997).

Although most Hmong families are extremely poor, the amount of love, care, and attention parents heap on their infants is, by Western standards, astounding. A newborn baby is never apart from its mother, sleeping in her arms all night and riding on her back all day. Hmong children are almost never beaten because it's believed that an evil spirit who witnesses such mistreatment might assume the child is unwanted and take him or her. Research indicates that Hmong mothers are more sensitive, more accepting, and more responsive to their children's signals than are U.S. parents. They hold and touch their babies much more frequently (cited in Fadiman, 1997). So, although their childbirth practices might strike the Western observer as potentially dangerous, the Hmong actually seem to be better parents than we are.

It's hard to imagine an experience more universal than having and raising children. Reproduction is the essence of life—human and otherwise. Yet parenthood can hardly be separated from cultural norms, values, and definitions. Furthermore, although we live in a society that places enormous value on children and in which the vast majority of adults want to have them, becoming and being a parent are seldom problem-free experiences. In this chapter, we'll discuss some of the important issues associated with parenthood, including the cultural value of parenthood, the social construction of childbirth, and the relationship between gender and parenthood.

THE CULTURAL IMPORTANCE OF PARENTHOOD

One of the cornerstones of family life in U.S. society is the belief that married couples should reproduce or should at least want to reproduce. Most people marry with the expectation that they will have children, and they become parents because parenthood brings significant social approval. Having children is not only considered desirable, it is seen as normal and taken for granted. It's often said that weddings create couples, but childbearing makes a family (Gillis, 1996). People learn that having children proves their worth and gives them the status of mature adults.

This cultural value, what sociologists refer to as **pronatalism,** has its roots in a Judeo-Christian tradition that depicts children as "blessings" and childlessness as a curse or punishment (Miall, 1989). The Bible encourages people to "be fruitful and multiply." These norms—coupled with pro-birth governmental policies such as income tax deductions for each child—encourage reproduction and reinforce the belief that parenthood is a vital feature of society.

■ **pronatalism**
A cultural belief that married couples should reproduce or should want to reproduce.

All societies, regardless of their economic or political systems, value childbearing, but in different ways. In agricultural societies, having children is a good thing because children directly contribute to the family's economic potential. In industrial and post-industrial societies, children provide their parents with psychological benefits, serving as an object and source of affection and love, and a way to avoid loneliness (Jones & Brayfield, 1997).

Comparatively speaking, the United States is not as pronatalist as societies in which women's status and social position are determined almost exclusively by their reproductive capacities and mothering. The percentages of U.S. households with at least one child under age 18 have steadily declined since 1960 (National Marriage Project, 2005). As you can see in Figure 10.1, people also are waiting longer to have children.

Nevertheless, the United States continues to embrace certain pronatalist beliefs and practices. The culture still portrays having children as important to self-fulfillment and necessary for the future survival of the society. Eighty-five percent of the respondents to the 2002 General Social Survey agreed or strongly agreed that watching children grow up is one of life's greatest joys (National Opinion Research Center, 2006).

Adoption and the Primacy of Genetic Parenthood

In most cultures, the biological, genetic bond between parents and children is considered of paramount importance, forming the basis of "real" families (Fuscaldo, 2005; Wegar, 2000). "He's got your eyes" or "She has her Grandma's mouth" are the sorts of things most new parents hear frequently as friends and relatives try to establish genetic links through physical resemblances. Physicians seeing a child for

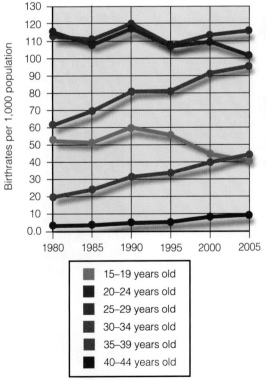

FIGURE 10.1   Birthrates by Age of Mother, 1980 to 2005
Source: U.S. Bureau of the Census, 2008, table 79.

the first time often ask about family health history, presuming a biological connection between parent and child.

So it's not surprising that in a culture where people tend to associate parenthood with procreation and blood links, adoption is sometimes considered a lesser form of parenting (Fisher, 2003). Community attitudes toward adoption have improved over the last decade as the number of people who have adopted a child, placed a child for adoption, or know someone who's been adopted has increased (Evan B. Donaldson Adoption Institute, 2002). Some research shows that adoptive parents actually invest more time and financial resources in their children than do biological parents (Hamilton, Cheng, & Powell, 2007). Nevertheless, some still fear that adopted children will always lack a crucial piece of their identity. As one adoptee put it:

> I seem to have a compelling need to know my own story. It is a story that I should not be excluded from since it is at least partly mine, and it seems vaguely tragic and somehow unjust that it remains unknown to me. (R. S. Anderson, 1988, quoted in Grotevant, Dunbar, Kohler, & Lash Esau, 2000, p. 379)

Indeed, this theme provides the backdrop for the many moving stories we hear about adoptees searching for their biological roots. These experiences appeal to the cultural notion that our "real" identity is linked to shared genes.

Research suggests that adopted children, especially those placed after infancy, are more likely than those raised by their biological parents to experience difficulties in intellectual development, identity formation, and the ability to establish attachments with others as they get older (Nickman, 2005). Using data from the National Longitudinal Study of Youth, sociologist William Feigelman (1997) compared children raised in adopted homes with those from intact biological families and "attenuated nuclear families" such as foster, divorced, or stepfamilies. Adoptees were similar to children from

Adopted families are often indistinguishable from biological families.

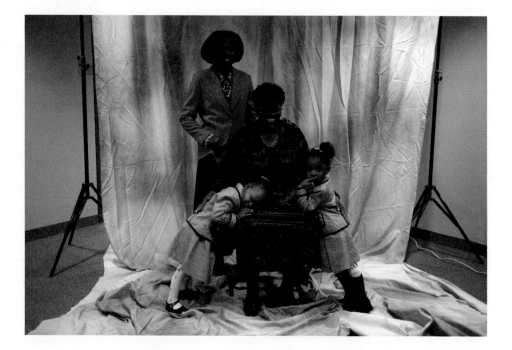

attenuated families in their tendency to have higher rates of delinquency, youth crime, and alcohol and drug use during adolescence than children from intact biological families. As adults, they were more likely to report lower levels of marital satisfaction.

We must interpret such findings with caution, however. There is tremendous variation among the 1.6 million or so U.S. children under 18 who are adopted (U.S. Bureau of the Census, 2007). Some are adopted by their stepparents, others by strangers. Some are infants when adopted, others are adolescents. Some are physically and mentally healthy, others may have mild or severe disabilities or be at genetic risk of developing problems. Some are placed in families with other adopted children, some enter homes where they are the only child or perhaps the only adopted child among siblings. Some children have been institutionalized for lengthy periods prior to adoption, some have stayed in a number of foster homes, and others spend no time in institutionalized care. Some adoptions are international or transracial, others take place among people of the same nationality or race (Grotevant, Ross, Marchel, & McRoy, 1999). In short, many factors can explain the problems some adolescent adoptees face, but few studies have controlled for these.

Furthermore, the vast majority of adopted children do quite well and are raised in nurturing, economically stable homes. The median income of households with adopted children is $56,138, compared to $48,200 in households with only biological children (U.S. Bureau of the Census, 2007). Adoptive parents must devote a great deal of effort to becoming parents. They *want* to be parents. By contrast, some biological parents conceive by accident and may see parenthood as the least bad of the various bad options available to them (Bartholet, 1993).

Yet the cultural primacy of biological over adoptive parenthood lies at the heart of the growing movement to give adoptees full access to their birth records. In the United States, currently only five states allow adult adopted persons to receive or even look at a copy of their original birth certificate (Figure 10.2). The practice of "closed" adoptions grew in part from a concern that if an adopted child knew his or her biological parent(s), this genetic connection would be so powerful it would weaken attachments to his or her adoptive parents (Gross & Sussman, 1997). The move to open adoptions sends the message that the biological parent is an essential part of an adopted child's life, regardless of whether that parent has any emotional, financial, or social connection to the child.

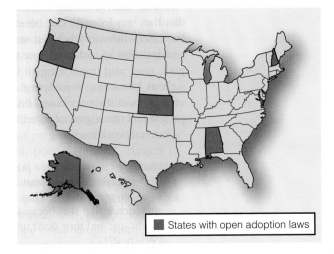

■ States with open adoption laws

FIGURE 10.2 States With Open Adoption Laws
Source: Adopting.org, 2006.

Infertility

The power of pronatalism is also illustrated in the societal response to **infertility**, the inability of couples who want genetically related children to have them. According to the Centers for Disease Control and Prevention, 7.4% of married women between 15 and 44 (about 2.1 million) are infertile (defined as having not used contraception and not become pregnant for at least 12 months). This figure doesn't include women who are surgically sterile (Chandra, Martinez, Mosher, Abma, & Jones, 2005).

■ **infertility**
Couples who want genetically related children but are unable to have them.

advances in medical technology in the 20th century, affluent women were beginning to believe that they had a right to avoid it if at all possible. Initially, women were put to sleep with chloroform or ether throughout labor and delivery. Eventually, localized anesthetics that alleviated pain but allowed women to remain conscious throughout the delivery became popular.

■ **medicalization of childbirth**
The process by which labor and delivery moved from the home to the hospital, carried out under the supervision of medical professionals.

The **medicalization of childbirth** increased women's dependence on the predominantly male medical profession (Cahill, 2001). Little interest was given to the mother's well-being or self-esteem. Typically she was placed in a position with her legs widespread in the air and her genitals exposed. Once labor began, doctors commonly resorted to invasive procedures such as the use of forceps and suction. Episiotomies, incisions that increase the size of the vaginal opening to give the baby more room to emerge, became a common part of the birthing process.

Today the vast majority of women giving birth experience some kind of medical intervention, such as electronic fetal monitoring, epidural or spinal pain medication, urinary catheters, or drugs to speed up labor (Childbirth Connection, 2006). Some researchers estimate that episiotomies, a cut in the muscle between the vagina and the anus to widen the birth canal, are used in close to half of all low-risk U.S. births, and cesarean sections are performed in almost a third of all births, a 50% increase over the past 10 years (Allen & Hanson, 2005; Martin, Hamilton, Menacker, Sutton, & Mathews, 2005; Yabroff, 2008). Some states have even gone so far as to enact laws prohibiting midwifery by people who are not certified health care workers. In Indiana, a midwife was charged with a felony punishable by up to 8 years in prison for assisting with a home birth (Liptak, 2006). Clearly, medicalization means that the doctor, not the mother, delivers the baby.

As early as the 1950s, concern was growing over the possibility that babies might be harmed in some way by the use of drugs and other invasive procedures during delivery. Women were also beginning to complain about the dehumanizing conditions of hospital delivery wards. As one mother of three wrote in the 1950s:

> Women are herded like sheep through the obstetrical assembly line, are drugged and strapped on tables while their babies are forceps-delivered. Obstetricians today are businessmen who run baby factories. Modern painkillers and methods are used for the convenience of the doctor, not to spare the mother. (quoted in Gillis, 1996, p. 173)

"Natural" childbirth, without the aid of anesthetics, became popular in the 1960s and 1970s and restored women to a more central role in the birth process. Expectant mothers, and their sometimes reluctant husbands, were encouraged to attend childbirth classes to learn special breathing techniques that could ease the delivery without resorting to drugs.

One of the major changes in the process of childbirth over the past 30 years is the growing role of fathers. In the past, every effort was made to keep men as far away from the painful, messy, and sometimes lethal birthing process as possible. A father's participation was usually confined to driving his wife to the hospital and pacing the waiting room until someone came to tell him his baby had been born.

Today, however, fathers are expected to be present during the delivery, and about 90% of fathers are (Griswold, 1993), although most are passive, sometimes queasy witnesses or cameramen, not active participants. Nevertheless, fathers who choose not to be involved risk being labeled insensitive and uncaring.

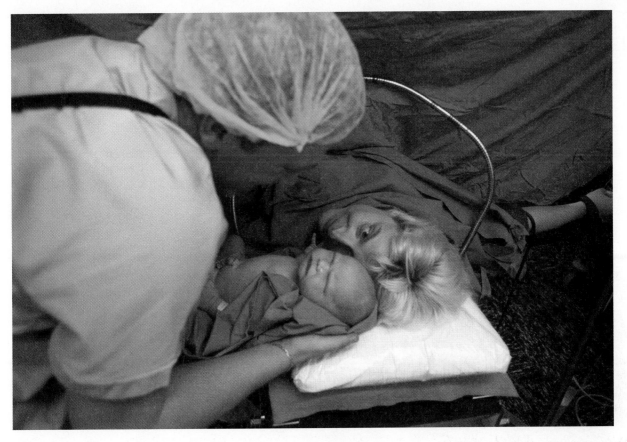

It's now common for fathers to be present at the birth of their babies, though their actual participation in the birth process is usually minimal.

The popularity of natural childbirth—less medical intervention, more maternal contact with the newborn right after birth, and so on—has been accompanied by a nostalgic desire to return to a simpler, less medicalized childbirth experience. Many hospitals today are turning their cold and sterile "delivery" rooms into homelike, reassuring "birthing" suites. The goal is to re-create the benefits of the cozy home birth of the 19th century in a safe hospital setting. Most of these rooms are large enough so that the baby and the father can sleep there as well. In addition, some expectant couples are now choosing to give birth at home (albeit under medical supervision) with relatives, friends, and other children in attendance.

The Social Transition to Parenthood

Becoming a parent is more than just giving birth; it means entering a social role that represents a significant shift in a person's life and identity. Whether the parent is single or married, rich or poor, heterosexual or homosexual; whether the birth is planned or unplanned; or whether the child arrives by birth or adoption, few transitions are more life altering than that from nonparent to parent.

For many parents a child is a tangible symbol of the love they share for each other (Neal, Groat, & Wicks, 1989). Children often give parents a sense of meaning and purpose and an enormous feeling of pride. Most people are genuinely thrilled when they become parents (Cowan & Cowan, 2000). Children also expand their parents' social

(Text continues on page 282.)

How to Give Birth

Perhaps there is no more universal human experience than childbirth. In every society, in every historical era, women have given birth to babies. But just because it happens everywhere doesn't mean it looks the same or is experienced in the same way everywhere. People in different cultures, different ethnoracial groups, different social classes, even different geographical areas in the same society may have very different ideas about the best way to give birth.

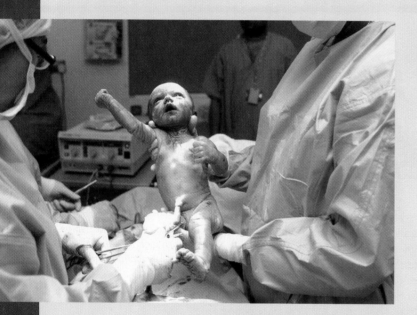

In most Western societies, childbirth is almost always a medical procedure overseen by doctors and nurses. We usually associate hospital births with cleanliness, safety, and pain minimization . . .

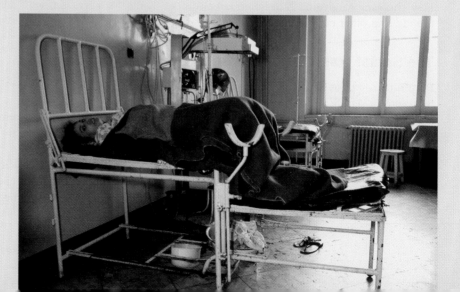

. . . but in some countries hospital births can be quite dangerous. This woman is awaiting delivery in an Albanian hospital.

The natural childbirth movement, which became popular in the 1970s, has led some expectant mothers to eschew the medical establishment altogether. Here a midwife helps a mother give birth at the Farm, a cooperative community near Summertown, Tennessee.

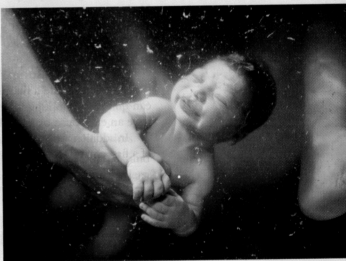

In many cultures, women give birth by themselves, unattended by doctors, nurses, or midwives.

To minimize pain and create a less traumatic birth experience for the baby, some mothers choose "water-births." However, critics argue that the procedure poses risks to the infant such as infection and water inhalation.

11

Childhood and Adolescence

Images of Childhood

The Social Complexities of Raising Children

Entering Adolescence

Children of War

We usually associate the loss of childhood innocence with children's increased, and some would say alarming, exposure to adult images and information in the media or on the Internet. Or we fret about children "growing up too quickly" because their parents push them out of carefree childhood and into an environment saturated by concerns over achievement, competition, and future success.

Yet across the globe, the loss of childhood innocence means something far more immediate and tangible. In war torn countries near and far, children experience violence and tragedy not in cartoonish video games but in their everyday lives. Sometimes they bear witness to battles that play out on their doorsteps; other times, children themselves are forced into military service. According to the United Nations (2007), more than 250,000 children have been exploited as child soldiers and are taking part in armed conflicts in places such as the Sudan, Colombia, Myanmar, Iraq, and Afghanistan. We can only speculate about the effect these sorts of experiences will have on these children as they grow and develop.

Ethiopian refugees at the Ban Mundule Camp.

A boy in Darfur walks by a truck full of rebel fighters from the Sudanese Liberation Army.

(Text continues on page 306.)

Chechen children play war games near Grozny following a Russian Army offensive on the city.

A U.S. soldier interacts with Iraqi children in Baghdad.

A young soldier in the Popular Front for the Liberation of Palestine.

A boy in Unadilla, New York, says a final goodbye to his brother, who was killed in Iraq.

12

Adulthood and Later Life

The Transition to Adulthood

- Defining Adulthood

- Delayed Adulthood

Becoming a Grandparent

- Cultural Expectations of Grandparents

- Ethnoracial Differences in Grandparenting

Later Life

- The "Graying" of the United States

- Widowhood

- Culture and the Elderly

- Intergenerational Obligations

Throughout this chapter we've seen the importance of how a society defines childhood and adolescence. One way to glimpse these definitions is by analyzing media images. The media often reveal a society's unspoken, shared understandings and assumptions about who children and adolescents are, and who we want them to be. Because multiple definitions of childhood and adolescence can and do exist simultaneously, we often find contradictory messages or a discrepancy between what we say we want and what we actually expect from our youth. For instance, although we say young children should be shielded

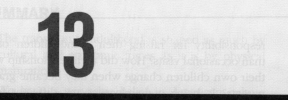

Intimate Violence

The Culture of Intimate Violence in the United States

Violence Between Intimate Partners

    Gender and Intimate Violence

    Explanations of Intimate Partner Violence

    Escape From Abusive Relationships

    Power and Violence in Gay Male and Lesbian Households

Child Abuse

    Child Mistreatment Across Cultures

    The Emergence of Child Abuse as a Social Problem

    Explanations of Child Abuse

    Privacy, Parental Rights, and State Intervention

    Corporal Punishment

Elder Abuse

The past few years have been awash in highly publicized cases of intimate violence. Hardly a week goes by without some famous celebrity being accused of beating a spouse or mistreating a child or having their violent outbursts caught on YouTube or TMZ. What is perhaps even more disturbing than these high-profile cases is the sheer volume of incidents that most of us never hear about—those local stories that don't make the national news and remain tucked away in the back sections of newspapers. The following is just a sampling of domestic violence incidents reported in one newspaper during the first 4 months of a single year:

- January 1: A 38-year-old mother of three was charged with reckless endangerment in the death of her 10-month-old daughter, who was found with a fractured skull, fractured leg, and multiple blunt-force traumas.
- January 5: A 49-year-old man was charged with assault and attempted murder after he threw rubbing alcohol on his wife and set her on fire.
- January 6: A 22-year-old mother was arrested and charged with murder for throwing her newborn girl out of a third-story window into an alley.
- February 12: A 35-year-old man who spent 16 months in prison for killing a baby in 1985 was taken into custody on charges that he fractured the skull of his girlfriend's 5-month-old son.
- February 22: A pregnant mother and her boyfriend were each charged with seven counts of aggravated assault and endangering the welfare of a child after all seven of her children were found with bruises and welts.
- March 7: A 26-year-old man was arrested after a rampage in which he beat his five young children. Two of the children—ages 3 and 4—suffered broken legs.
- March 27: A 23-year-old man was charged with kidnapping and murdering his fiancée just days after she had obtained a court order of protection against him.
- March 31: A 27-year-old woman was charged with murder after taking her 5-year-old son—his bruised body already lifeless from weeks of starvation and abuse—to a nearby hospital.
- April 2: A 33-year-old woman was arrested on charges that she severely burned her 7-year-old daughter by forcing her to sit on a radiator as punishment for fighting with her siblings.
- April 10: A 28-year-old woman was charged with attempted murder for trying to strangle her 8-year-old daughter on a busy sidewalk while another woman tried to shield them from view.
- April 11: A 22-year-old man was charged in the beating death of his girlfriend's 3-year-old son. The boy died from stomach wounds, blunt trauma, and internal bleeding.
- April 21: A 33-year-old man was charged with attempted murder for beating his girlfriend's 14-month-old son into unconsciousness.

We can only imagine how many other cases took place during that period, which either didn't result in debilitating injury or death or simply never came to the attention of the police or the press. Had a different 4-month period in a different year or a newspaper from a different major city been examined, there's a good chance we'd see a similar array of tragic stories.

In this chapter we will take a close look at the nature, prevalence, causes, and consequences of intimate violence and abuse. Given such a broad and emotionally volatile topic, it is impossible to cover every aspect or acknowledge every opinion. For instance, perhaps the most prevalent and taken-for-granted form of intimate violence occurs between siblings, but such violence rarely escalates to the point of life-threatening injury. So we will limit our focus to three types of violence: spouse or intimate partner abuse, child abuse, and elder abuse. Further, although violence between intimates usually includes emotional, psychological, and sometimes financial maltreatment as well, we will pay particular attention to its physical dimension. Finally, terms like *intimate violence, domestic violence,* and *family violence* will be used interchangeably to refer to acts of violence and aggression that take place between people related by blood or romantically involved.

THE CULTURE OF INTIMATE VIOLENCE IN THE UNITED STATES

No one would deny that the United States is a violent society. Rates of violent crime here have risen in recent years (Eggen, 2007) and exceed those of any other industrialized nation (Figure 13.1). Violence is in our streets, our schools, our movies, our television shows, our computer/video games, our toy stores, our spectator sports, and our government.

What may be surprising, however, is that the majority of violent acts in the United States occur between people who know each other. According to the U.S. Bureau of Justice Statistics (2006), only 46.8% of assaults, 34.7% of rapes, and 34.4% of sexual assaults involve strangers. The rest occur between acquaintances, friends, romantic partners, and family members.

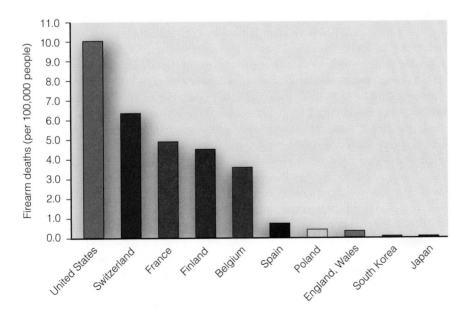

FIGURE 13.1 Firearm Deaths in Selected Countries
Source: Begley, 2007.

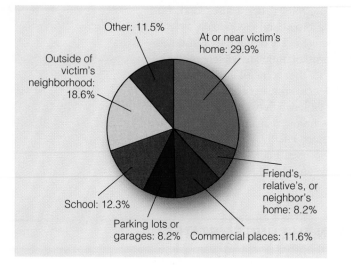

FIGURE 13.2   The Location of Violent Crime in the United States
Source: U.S. Bureau of the Census, 2008, table 316.

Certainly most of us are reluctant to label U.S. families violent. "Violence" and "families" are words that don't seem to naturally go together. One of the most enduring popular images of family is that it is a "safe haven"—the one place in society to which we ought to be able to escape when life becomes overwhelming. Family is not a place where you'd expect to get screamed at, emotionally belittled, punched in the face, raped, or threatened with death simply because you came home too late, got a C on a calculus test, said the wrong thing at the wrong time, or just happened to be there. But that is precisely what awaits a large number of people in this country, especially children and women.

The tragic truth is that, outside of wars and riots, the home is the single most violent location in U.S. society (Figure 13.2). Violence happens in rich homes and poor homes, black homes and white homes, heterosexual homes and homosexual homes, rural homes and urban homes.

As recently as 50 years ago, most U.S. adults saw violence between intimates as an unfortunate, but nonetheless "understandable" part of family life. In the popular 1950s sitcom *The Honeymooners,* Ralph Kramden (played by Jackie Gleason) would routinely threaten to punch his wife so hard he would send her "to the moon." Such scenes never failed to elicit laughs from the audience.

At the same time, though, intimate violence has never been something a family wanted to publicize. It was typically considered a secret that was better kept out of sight. Because it remained so well hidden, particularly among the middle and upper classes, the public didn't believe such behaviors constituted a serious social problem. Instead, family violence was thought to be characteristic of those segments of the population unable to keep their private lives private, namely, poor and minority families.

The hidden, private nature of domestic violence prevented the vast majority of victims from seeking help. Indeed, they had little choice but to keep their experiences to themselves. They couldn't call for help because there wasn't any help available.

Since the 1970s, however, we have witnessed a marked change in public conceptions of domestic violence. Child abuse, spouse abuse, elder abuse, and other forms of intimate violence have been publicly redefined. Although still cloaked in secrecy, domestic violence no longer has the sort of tacit approval and look-the-other-way tolerance it once enjoyed from police, courts, and the public at large. The 1994 Violence Against Women Act, which was reauthorized in 2006, provides billions of dollars to help victims of domestic violence. Today, every major city has shelters for battered women and self-help groups for victims and former abusers. Hospitals sponsor special treatment programs concerned with abused and neglected children. The Internet offers hundreds of Web sites devoted to helping people cope with domestic violence.

Families themselves are no longer the harsh little dictatorships they once were, in which parents, especially fathers, ruled with iron fists. Children now have recognized rights. Women are no longer expected to be docile and subservient. They are now likely to enter marriage assuming they will have a high degree of autonomy and sufficient opportunity to assert themselves educationally and professionally (Pleck, 1987). Few people would dare argue that wife battering is justifiable when wives disobey their husbands or that regular beatings are the best way to raise a child.

Despite the very real changes that have taken place in society, old attitudes die hard. Intimate violence remains part of the cultural landscape. How many times have you heard a parent "playfully" threaten a child by saying, "You're cruisin' for a bruisin'?" Several years ago, after his college football team lost a heartbreaking game, Penn State head coach Joe Paterno "jokingly" told reporters, "I'm going to go home and beat my wife" (quoted in Nack & Munson, 1995). I don't think parents who say such things really want to bruise their children, and to my knowledge Coach Paterno didn't, in fact, go home and beat his wife that day. But such statements, even though they shouldn't be taken literally, do show that those old attitudes toward intimate violence are far from extinct.

VIOLENCE BETWEEN INTIMATE PARTNERS

Statistics on intimate partner abuse indicate that it is a widespread problem, although it has declined somewhat in recent years. According to the U.S. Bureau of Justice Statistics (Catalano, 2006), more than 625,000 nonlethal violent acts (including rape, sexual assault, robbery, aggravated assault, and simple assault) were committed by current spouses, former spouses, boyfriends, or girlfriends in 2004 (the most recent year for which such figures were available).

Other studies place the prevalence rate for intimate partner violence significantly higher. For instance, the National Violence Against Women Survey of 16,000 women and men across the country found that nearly 25% of surveyed women and 7.6% of men said they'd been raped or physically assaulted by a spouse, partner, or date at some point in their lifetimes. Within the previous 12 months, 1.5% of women and 0.9% of men reported being raped or physically assaulted. According to these estimates, about 1.5 million women and more than 800,000 men are assaulted by an intimate partner annually in the United States, well above the official Bureau of Justice Statistics figures. If we add relatively minor acts of violence such as pushing, grabbing, shoving, and slapping, the figures would rise to more than 3 million incidents for men and more than 5 million for women (Tjaden & Thoennes, 2000).

Exact statistics about the prevalence of spousal or partner violence are difficult to collect, like those for all forms of intimate violence, because it is concealed and private, occurring beyond the watchful eyes of relatives, neighbors, and strangers. Even with the more stringent rules for police reporting of domestic calls that have been instituted in the past decade or two, most incidents are never reported; others are dismissed as accidents. Furthermore, definitions of abuse and reporting practices vary from state to state. Given the shame and stigma associated with such violence, we can assume that the reported figures on assault are probably *under*estimates of the actual incidence of violence between intimates.

In addition, not all acts of intimate violence are the same. The Centers for Disease Control and Prevention (2006b) identify four types of intimate violence: physical violence, sexual violence, psychological abuse, and stalking. Each type can have different motivations. For example, physical violence between partners may be mutual and occur only in the context of specific arguments, it may be one-sided and motivated by the desire to terrorize or control the other partner, or it may occur in self-defense (Johnson & Ferraro, 2005).

Although all forms of violence between intimate partners are serious and deserving of attention, we cannot get a clear picture of the nature of spousal and partner violence when they are combined into one category. For example, reported research can be somewhat misleading if incidents of violence motivated by a desire to humiliate are lumped together with incidents of self-defense.

Gender and Intimate Violence

These distinctions may shed light on one of the most contentious debates between researchers studying intimate partner violence: whether men or women are equally likely to be victims. Certainly women sometimes abuse their male partners. In some cities around the country, a quarter of arrests for domestic violence are of women (cited in Goldberg, 1999). But the motivation behind the violence is likely to be different for male and female perpetrators. Female intimate violence is often retaliatory (Kurz, 1989). In fact, close to half of women who are arrested for killing their spouses were acting in self-defense (Langan & Dawson, 1995). Furthermore, because violence committed by men tends to be more severe and more difficult to escape than violence committed by women, women clearly are the disproportionate victims of the most dangerous and life-threatening forms of intimate violence. Twice as many women as men sustain injuries when victimized by a partner (Tjaden & Thoennes, 2000).

In 2004, about 1,500 murders were attributed to intimate partners and three quarters of the victims were women. Overall, about 30% of all female murder victims were killed by an intimate partner (Catalano, 2006). One study found that almost half the women murdered by their intimate partners had visited the emergency room within 2 years of being killed (Crandall, Nathens, Kernic, Holt, & Rivara, 2004).

Women don't just suffer disproportionate physical consequences. Female victims of intimate violence are also more likely than male victims to suffer psychologically (e.g., from depression, anxiety, or low self-esteem) and socially (such as by isolation from friends). The economic costs can be steep as well. It's estimated that intimate violence costs about $4.1 billion in direct costs (that is, medical and mental health care) and $1.8 billion in indirect costs (lost productivity) each year. Women who experience severe forms of abuse are also more likely than women who experience less serious forms of abuse to lose their jobs or to go on public assistance (Centers for Disease Control and Prevention, 2006b).

■ GOING GLOBAL

Spousal Violence Across Cultures

When we examine *all* forms of family violence, it appears that most people around the world have either been the victim of, the perpetrator of, or a witness to violence within their families (Levinson, 1989). According to the World Health Organization, women worldwide—whether they live in the developed or developing world—face the greatest threat of violence *in their own homes* (Garcia-Moreno, Jansen, Ellsberg, Heise, & Watts, 2006). A recent study of intimate violence in developing countries found that about one third of women in Egypt and Nicaragua and close to one half of women in Peru, Colombia, and Zambia have been beaten by their spouses or partners (Kishor & Johnson, 2004).

In those cultures in which men's dominance is considered legitimate, husbands control their wives and use violence to maintain that control when they believe it is necessary. In South Korea, for instance, more than one third of women report being physically abused by their husbands (UNICEF, 2000). Although things are changing, especially among young, better-educated couples in large cities, and most people say that beating is wrong, violence continues to be a "normal" part of Korean family life. One man, when asked if he had ever beaten his wife, replied:

> I was married at 28 and I'm 52 now. How could I have been married all these years and not beaten my wife? For me it's better to release that anger and get it over with. Otherwise, I just get sick inside. . . . Of course, you have to apologize afterward. (quoted in Kristof, 1996a, p. A4)

Korean women's attitudes also support men's authority and right to beat their wives:

> Of course my husband beats me. But it was my fault because I scolded him. Maybe there are some cases where it's just the man's fault, but ultimately the woman is to blame, because if she won't argue with her husband, he probably won't beat her. I told [my daughter], "if he hits you, just sit back and take it." (quoted in Kristof, 1996a, p. A4)

In South Africa, it's estimated that nearly 70% of marriages involve some type of violence (Dangor, Hoff, & Scott, 1998). In that culture, with its legacy of apartheid, black women in particular have had to bear the brunt of such violence. As you can see in the following quotes, these women are often acutely aware of their vulnerability:

■ "Black women are the worst off because they're the wrong color and the wrong sex."

■ "[There's] a lack of respect for women—men want to prove their superiority and show us that we are objects of manipulation to suit their needs."

■ "Men like being in control, and abusing women gives them power." (quoted in Dangor et al., 1998, p. 134)

In the Central American country of Belize, men have historically exercised almost complete economic and political power over women. In families, they have always exerted their authority and control through physical battering. Husbands frequently beat their wives with anything they can get hold of: guns, knives, crowbars, machetes, electric wire, bottles, mop handles, rocks, boards, rope, and so forth. These violent acts go unacknowledged by the community and unreported to the police and are rarely discussed among friends and families (McClaurin, 1996). Despite the fact that local papers periodically run stories of women mutilated, burned, and murdered by their husbands or partners, wife battering doesn't warrant any mention in the country's official crime documents.

Women's dependence is so deep in Belize that they are usually willing to accept abuse and tolerate offensive behavior in exchange for economic security. Over the past two decades, however, frustrated Belizean women formed several organizations aimed at increasing women's status, decreasing their dependence, and ending domestic violence. Their efforts came to fruition in 1993 with passage of the Domestic Violence Bill, which gives women the ability to acquire legal restraining orders against their husbands and grants police the power to make arrests in domestic disputes.

Explanations of Intimate Partner Violence

Trying to figure out why intimate partner violence occurs is not a simple task. It's tempting to see such violence in purely individualistic terms: People who beat their partners are cruel individuals incapable of controlling their rage or who gain some sort of pathological pleasure and feeling of power by inflicting pain on their partners.

Alcohol is often cited as a key culprit in intimate partner violence. To some researchers, the relationship between alcohol and violence is undeniable: "Just as high alcohol intake leads to cirrhosis of the liver, brain damage, and heart failure, so does high alcohol intake lead to violence in the family" (Flanzer, 1993, p. 171).

However, the contention that alcohol or other drugs such as cocaine and crack directly and inevitably produce violent and abusive behavior has little scientific support. Evidence from laboratory studies and blood tests of men arrested for wife beating indicates that although alcohol and drugs may be an immediate antecedent to some acts of violence, they are far from being a necessary or sufficient cause of domestic violence. One study of men charged with assaulting their partners found that about a third of them had been using drugs (cited in Logan, Walker, Staton, & Leukefeld, 2001). Findings from another study of 5,159 couples nationwide revealed that alcohol is involved in only about 25% of instances of wife abuse (Kanter & Straus, 1990), which means the vast majority of cases (75%) take place when neither person has been drinking. Furthermore, about 80% of men who are defined as heavy or binge drinkers *do not* beat their wives at all. Hence, although the stereotype of the violent, drunken husband has a kernel of truth, we cannot explain domestic violence as simply the result of alcohol.

Attributing intimate abuse to mentally defective, high, or drunken men might be psychologically comforting to the public at large, but we can only truly understand such violence as the complex product of psychological, interpersonal, societal, historical, and cultural forces. Each act of domestic violence brings these forces together. As one sociologist puts it, "Compressed into one assault are our deepest human emotions, our sense of self, our power, and our hopes and fears about love and intimacy, as well as the social construction of marriage and its place within the larger society" (Yllo, 1993, p. 47). In short, intimate partner violence is best understood by going beyond individual-level explanations to an examination of the sociocultural environment in which it takes place.

The Social Organization of Families

Families have many characteristics that promote warmth and intimacy, but those very factors can increase the probability of conflict and violence as well. For instance, we spend a lot of time with family members, and we interact with them across a wide range of situations. These interactions can certainly enhance the affection we feel toward our loved ones. At the same time, though, they can be intense. Emotions run deep. It's ironic that the people whom we can care about the most are also the ones who can make us the angriest. The anger we may feel toward a stranger or an acquaintance never approaches the intensity of the anger we feel toward a spouse or, for that matter, toward a sibling or a child.

Moreover, we usually know more about family members than we know about other individuals in our lives. We know their likes and dislikes, their fears and their desires. And they know these things about us too. If someone in your family insults you, you know immediately what you can say to get even. Intimate partners usually know the "buttons" they can push to hurt or infuriate each other. Arguments can escalate into violence when one partner focuses on the other's vulnerabilities and insecurities.

Long periods of intense contact with people about whom you know virtually everything can elevate even trivial matters into conflict situations. In many couples, everyday decisions occur in a context of winning and losing. Hence, some of the most serious conflicts begin over seemingly insignificant issues, like what program to watch on television or what restaurant to go to for dinner.

Finally, family life contains endless sources of stress. For one thing, we expect a lot from our families: emotional and financial support, warmth, comfort, and intimacy. When these expectations aren't fulfilled, stress levels escalate. Moreover, common events in a relationship—the birth and raising of a child, finances, employment transitions (voluntary or involuntary), illness, old age, death, and so on—can increase stress. Research indicates that the likelihood of intimate violence increases with the number of stressful events a family experiences. Indeed, stressful life circumstances are the hallmark of violent families (Gelles & Straus, 1988).

Power and Family Inequality

Focusing exclusively on the role that family structure plays in intimate violence can obscure the role of gender and power. As we saw in Chapter 4, coupled life can be characterized by significant inequality. The more resources a person controls, whether personal, social, emotional, or financial, the more influence he or she has over the relationship.

Power, power confrontations, and perceived threats to dominance and authority are underlying issues in almost all acts of intimate violence (Gelles & Straus, 1988). Research has consistently shown that the balance of power within couples has a noticeable effect on domestic violence. Sociologists Murray Straus, Richard Gelles, and Suzanne Steinmetz (1980) found that the level of violence against wives is lowest among couples who follow a pattern of egalitarian decision making and highest where decision making is dominated by one or the other partner.

In male-dominated households, husbands sometimes turn to violence to maintain the subordination of their wives. But why would the rate of spouse abuse be high in families when *wives* tend to have the most say over decisions? Husbands in these families may be lashing out violently when they feel their masculinity is under attack. In other words, husbands may use violence as a final resort to gain control when other resources are insufficient or lacking. In an achievement-oriented society, husbands who lack the financial, occupational, and educational resources necessary to establish household dominance may turn to violence or coercion to reestablish their power (Yllo & Straus, 1990).

Men have traditionally maintained their edge in family resources through their advantages in the workplace. The effect of men's employment on violence was demonstrated in a study of 12,000 adult Canadian women (MacMillan & Gartner, 1999). The researchers found that wives' exposure to spousal violence had little to do with whether or not they were employed. When their husbands were unemployed, however, employed wives' risk of being victimized increased significantly. Not only were these women at greater risk of physical violence, but they also were subjected to greater "coercive control," such as when a husband expresses jealousy and doesn't want his wife to talk to other men, tries to limit her contact with family and friends, insists on knowing with whom and where she is at all times, and prevents her from knowing about or having access to the family income.

Power and Structural Inequality

The forces of power operate at the societal level as well as the relationship level. In most societies, economic and social structures continue to support male domination, which is revealed in the relatively low positions women hold in the workplace, schools, politics, and other social institutions (Yllo & Straus, 1990). In the most extreme male-dominated societies, men blatantly classify and treat women as possessions. Globally, male dominance has a long history. Roman law, for instance, justified a husband's killing his wife for reasons such as adultery, wine drinking, and other so-called inappropriate behaviors (Steinmetz, Clavan, & Stein, 1990).

In the United States, too, male dominance is part of a centuries-old legacy of intimate violence. Early American law provided that upon marriage a husband acquired rights to his wife's person, the value of her paid and unpaid labor, and most property she brought into the marriage. The wife was obliged to obey and serve her husband. Her legal identity "merged" into his so that she was unable to enter into contracts without his approval. The husband, in turn, was responsible for his wife's conduct. As master of the household, he could subject her to corporal punishment or "chastisement" as long as he didn't inflict permanent injury (Siegel, 1996). Rape was considered a crime against men, or more accurately, against men's property (Siegel, 2004).

Just prior to the Civil War, corporal punishment became the subject of widespread controversy, and campaigns against it began to develop. These movements coincided with early movements for women's rights. Over time, the U.S. legal system did respond. In 1871 an Alabama court declared that a husband no longer had the privilege of beating his wife:

> The wife is not to be considered as the husband's slave. And the privilege, ancient though it be, to beat her with a stick, to pull her hair, choke her, spit in her face or kick her about the floor, or to inflict upon her like indignities, is not now acknowledged by our law. (quoted in Siegel, 1996, pp. 2121–2122)

This privilege had such a long tradition in married life that it didn't die easily. The legal system continued to treat wife beating differently from other violent crimes, intervening only intermittently in cases of marital violence. To protect male authority and the privacy of families, courts granted most men formal or informal immunity from prosecution, implying that it was easier for a wife to forgive her husband's impulsive violence than for a husband to suffer the loss of his power and the damage to his reputation that would occur when his behavior was scrutinized by public officials.

At the beginning of the 20th century, judges, clergy, and social workers routinely urged troubled couples to reconcile and preserve the marriage. Battered wives were discouraged from filing charges against their husbands, advised to accept responsibility for their role in provoking the violence, and encouraged to remain in the relationship and rebuild it rather than separate or divorce (Pleck, 1987; Siegel, 1996). Physical violence in the home was not viewed as criminal conduct; it was viewed as an expression of emotions that, through counseling, needed to be re-channeled into the marriage. Such a "therapeutic" framework regulated marital violence for much of the 20th century.

Not until the late 1970s did the feminist movement mount a significant challenge to male primacy and authority. Since then, many reforms have been secured, such as shelters for battered women and their children, new arrest procedures, and federal legislation that makes gender-motivated assaults a civil rights violation and prevents people convicted of domestic violence from purchasing handguns.

But the tradition of male dominance persists. For instance, the laws relating to rape in many states in this country, and in most countries around the world, include what is commonly known as "the marital rape exemption." These laws typically define rape as "the forcible penetration of the body of a woman, *not the wife of the perpetrator,*" making rape in marriage a legal impossibility (Russell, 1998, p. 71). Most states have narrowed the marital rape exemption (Denno, 2003), but only 17 states punish marital rape as they do other rape cases. Thirty-three states sometimes exempt husbands from rape prosecutions, usually when the degree of violence is minimal or when the couple is not living apart or separated at the time of the incident. Four states—Connecticut, Iowa, Minnesota, and West Virginia—extend these privileges to unmarried cohabitors (Bergen, 1999). With rare exception, courts have validated state laws protecting marital rape (Hasday, 2000).

When the American Law Institute (ALI), an organization devoted to clarifying and simplifying the law through legislative reform, revised the Model Penal Code provisions on rape about a decade ago, it decided to preserve language that exempted husbands from rape charges in hopes of protecting family privacy:

> The problem with abandoning the [marital] immunity in many . . . situations is that the law of rape, if applied to spouses, would thrust the prospect of criminal sanctions into the ongoing process of adjustment in the marital relationship. . . . Retaining the spousal exclusion avoids this unwarranted intrusion of the penal law into the life of the family. (quoted in Siegel, 1996, p. 2174)

The Model Penal Code even went beyond marriage, specifying that lesser felony charges could apply when the victim was the defendant's "voluntary social companion" and had "previously permitted him sexual liberties" (quoted in Denno, 2003, p. 210).

Legal definitions like these are based on the assumption that violence is a private matter between intimate partners. However, focusing instead on the power structure of society enables us to see that marital rape—not to mention battering, economic abuse, coercion, intimidation, and emotional abuse—is not simply a "family problem" isolated from the rest of society. It is the manifestation of a social system in which male domination and control are built into the very structure of society.

Such sociological explanations make intuitive sense, but, for the most part, they have not been tested empirically. One exception is a study by sociologists Kersti Yllo and Murray Straus (1990), who examined the relationship between the structural inequality of women and wife beating. They ranked all 50 states in terms of women's status as a group relative to men's, taking into consideration four social institutions: economics, education, politics, and the law.

Yllo and Straus found that wife beating is highest in those states where economic, educational, political, and legal inequality are greatest. As the overall status of women improved, violence declined—but only to a point. Surprisingly, in those states in which the status of women is highest, the rate of wife beating is also quite high.

The researchers suggest that two different processes are at work. When social inequality is high, more coercion is needed to maintain an unbalanced system. Thus force is used to keep wives "in their place" in those states in which women have the lowest status. But rapid changes in gender roles and shifts in the balance of power between the sexes, found in states in which women's status is high, may contribute to increased marital conflict because of the threat these changes pose to men.

Even though these forces provide a fertile social environment for violence, they don't make it inevitable. After all, most husbands who live in this violent, male-dominated society don't abuse their wives. Nevertheless, if a significant percentage of people do beat their partners because they feel that such behavior is appropriate given their position in society and in their families, then we would be wrong to conclude that abusers are simply psychotic, deranged, "sick" individuals. Rather, they are people who believe that dominance is their birthright.

Privacy

Even though some in the United States may accept the principle of male dominance, most of us are genuinely horrified at the thought of a person beating or killing a partner—or, for that matter, a parent killing or beating his or her child. At the same time, we also dislike the thought of the state intervening in the private affairs of families. An eminent anthropologist once observed that among the societies she had studied, violence between intimates tended not to occur when families lived communally. Only when the walls of separate houses went up did the hitting start (cited in Gelles & Straus, 1988).

In U.S. society, people who are socially isolated from neighbors and relatives are more likely to be violent against family members. Conversely, when families are well integrated into their communities and belong to groups and associations, violence becomes less likely (Gelles, 1995).

The cultural value of family privacy has helped to reinforce a perception that intimate partner violence is somehow less bothersome and more tolerable than other types of violence. Even when violence between spouses occurs in public, it is often perceived as a private matter. Psychologists Lance Shotland and Margaret Straw (1976) performed an intriguing experiment by staging what appeared to be a heated altercation between a man and a woman as they emerged from an elevator. The researchers set up two scenarios that were identical except for one important detail. In the first, the woman, who is the object of the man's verbal and physical threats, shouts, "Get away from me! I don't even know you!" In the second (with identical actors and identical behaviors), she says, "Get away from me! I don't know why I ever married you!" In the first situation, involving apparent strangers, 65% of the bystanders attempted to stop the fight. In the second situation, involving apparent spouses, bystanders intervened only 19% of the time. Clearly, the second case was defined by observers as a domestic dispute, conjuring up a set of norms that stopped them from getting involved in the private affairs of a married couple.

The family privacy so valued in the 21st century has diminished the influence of neighborhoods, extended kin, and other informal networks in protecting people against violence from intimates. Although more and more urban neighborhoods band together to organize crime watch groups to prevent street crime or patrols to watch out for local teens who might get into trouble, such organizations rarely, if ever, address the violence that occurs off the streets, in the private confines of neighborhood homes (Mannon, 1997a).

■ **masochism thesis**
A psychological explanation, popular in the 1950s and 1960s, that claimed women stayed in abusive relationships because they derived pleasure from being humiliated and hurt.

Escape From Abusive Relationships

One question that has captured the attention of many family researchers is, Why do victims stay in abusive relationships? Because most victims of serious abuse are female, the preponderance of attention has focused on battered women. During the 1960s the **masochism thesis**—that women derived pleasure from being humiliated and hurt—

was the predominant reason offered by psychiatrists (Saul, 1972). Even today, many psychiatrists believe masochism, now renamed *self-defeating personality disorder,* should be a "legitimate" medical explanation for women who stay in abusive relationships. Other contemporary explanations focus on character flaws, such as weak will or abnormal emotional attachment.

A substantial proportion of the public subscribes to various stereotypes about battered women and the nature of domestic violence. In one study of 216 predominantly white registered voters, more than a third believed that a battered woman is at least partially responsible for the beatings she suffers and that if she remains in the relationship she must be either masochistic or emotionally disturbed. Nearly two thirds believed that battered women can "simply leave" a relationship when it becomes abusive. Interestingly, women were more likely than men to subscribe to these stereotypes (Ewing & Aubrey, 1987).

These explanations and attitudes focus solely on the victim while paying little attention to her social situation. Many battered women, or men for that matter, end up staying in abusive relationships not because they are masochistic or weak willed but because they come to believe that there are worse things than being beaten. For example, they might fear that if they are unsuccessful in escaping from the relationship, the violence might get worse. In addition, they may be concerned for the well-being of children or possible retaliation against parents or other close relatives. Others worry about the batterer's pursuing them after they leave. Research shows there are approximately 200,000 cases of "stalking" in the United States each year, and 90% of U.S. women killed by estranged husbands or boyfriends were stalked prior to their murders (Moore, 2003).

According to social exchange theory, one of the most powerful reasons women stay in abusive relationships is dependence. That is, an individual will be inclined to stay in a relationship—even a bad or abusive one—if she believes she has no other options. As one woman put it, "I had no place to go and no help. . . . I need to take care of my family" (quoted in Baker, 1997, p. 61). Indeed, the greatest obstacle to escaping an abusive relationship is the victim's lack of access to money so that she can support herself and her children. As one author put it, "given a choice between watching her children go hungry and homeless, a battered woman will often remain with or return to an abusive relationship so that her children will have food to eat and a place to live" (Moore, 2003, p. 475).

Some women in abusive relationships develop beliefs that help them accept the fact that they are staying in a situation generally condemned by society. Kathleen Ferraro and John Johnson (1983) were participant observers at a shelter for battered women in the Southwest. They gathered information from 120 women, ranging in age from 17 to 68, who came to the shelter over the span of a year. Some women had convinced themselves that they must endure the abuse while helping their "troubled" partners return to their "normal," nonabusive selves. Others claimed their abusive partners were "sick" and that their actions were beyond their control; in other words, their partners were also victims. Finally, many women blamed themselves, taking the responsibility away from their spouses.

The perception that battered women who stay in violent relationships simply sit back and take the abuse, thinking they somehow deserve it, is inaccurate. One study of 1,000 battered and formerly battered women nationwide found that they tried a number of active strategies to end the violence directed against them (Bowker, 1993). They tried to talk men out of beating them, extracted promises that the men wouldn't batter them

IT'S HARD TO CONFRONT A FRIEND WHO ABUSES HIS WIFE. BUT NOT NEARLY AS HARD AS BEING HIS WIFE.

THERE'S **NO** EXCUSE

Ad Council

Family Violence Prevention Fund

for Domestic Violence.

In recent years, organizations around the country have embarked on a massive information campaign to make the public more aware of the horrors of domestic violence.

anymore, avoided their abuser physically or avoided certain volatile topics, hid or ran away, and even fought back physically. Many of these individual strategies had limited effectiveness, however, and most of these battered women eventually turned to people outside the relationship for informal support, advice, and sheltering. From these informal sources, the women generally progressed to organizations in the community, such as police, social service and counseling agencies, women's groups, and battered women's shelters. Some of these women were able, eventually, to end the violence; others weren't. The study points out that most women actively try to end their victimization.

Institutional Impediments to Escaping Abuse

One of the reasons so many battered women are unable to get out of abusive relationships is that the social organizations and institutions designed to help them have traditionally been ineffective. Throughout the years, hospitals, police departments, and courts have been notoriously unsympathetic to the plight of battered women.

As recently as 20 years ago, emergency room workers routinely interviewed battered wives about their injuries with their husbands present. But things are changing. For example, many communities have created sexual assault nurse-examiner programs in which specially trained nurses provide 24-hour-a-day, first-response care to sexual assault victims in both hospital and nonhospital settings (Campbell & Wasco, 2005). Such programs provide more sympathetic institutional responses to rape victims and increase the likelihood that the crimes will be reported. Nevertheless, women are still reluctant to tell attending emergency room doctors that they are victims of domestic abuse (Rhodes et al., 2006).

Police departments, in particular, have traditionally been reluctant to get too involved in domestic disputes. In the famous O. J. Simpson case in 1996, police were called to his home on at least nine occasions because of his physical abuse of his wife, Nicole. In the recent past, many police departments had informal arrest policies called "stitch rules," which specified how serious an injury a victim had to sustain, measured by how many surgical stitches are required, to justify an arrest of the assailant (Gillespie, 1989). Contemporary research confirms that police still tend to treat men who beat their spouses less punitively than other violent offenders. In one study, police made arrests in 13% of male-on-female spousal assault cases but in 28% of other assault cases (Fyfe, Klinger, & Flavin, 1997).

It's no surprise that many battered women are reluctant to go to the police, and this unwillingness is especially powerful for those who are already in a vulnerable situation.

For instance, battered immigrant or refugee women often encounter language barriers, cultural differences, and discrimination that can deter them from seeking help from the police. They may fear that contacting the police would hurt family honor and their own personal reputations within the community (Wolf, Ly, Hobart, & Kernic, 2003). Their reluctance also may be a result of the belief that contacting the police will just increase the violence, or their perception that the police would be unsympathetic and unresponsive anyway. Indeed, some evidence suggests that police often view intimate violence as part of the immigrant culture, leading officers to conclude that it's not a crime if the victim is an immigrant (Ammar, Orloff, Dutton, & Aguilar-Hass, 2005).

The courts, too, have historically treated spousal violence less seriously than other crimes, making it even more difficult for women to seek help. In 1978, for instance, an Indiana prosecutor refused to prosecute for murder a man who beat and kicked his ex-wife to death in the presence of a witness and then raped her as she lay dying. Filing a manslaughter charge instead, the prosecutor said, "He didn't mean to kill her. He just meant to give her a good thumping" (quoted in Jones, 1980, p. 308).

Today, however, as a result of the battered women's movement and other advocates who have worked hard to educate the public about domestic violence, police departments and courts have become somewhat more responsive to the needs of abuse victims. For one thing, most police departments around the country have replaced their unspoken "hands-off" approach to domestic violence with mandatory arrest policies or "no drop" rules, whereby victims can't drop charges against their batterers. Many police departments now have special domestic violence units to better serve victims and hold perpetrators more accountable. There are now about 300 "domestic violence courts" in 23 states in which victims are provided with an advocate and a team of prosecutors that see each case from beginning to end, dealing with criminal charges, protection orders, and custody matters as they arise (Gettelman, 2005). In addition, the Federal Office on Violence Against Women has provided funding for 15 "family justice centers" around the country, which provide one-stop help for victims, including legal, medical, and social services (Prah, 2006).

These changes have improved the situation for many battered women around the country, but they've also changed the cultural notions of what battered women should do to avoid further violence. Victims are now expected to get away and stay away from their abusers. Those who don't or can't leave violate this new cultural expectation and may find that others blame them for not preventing further violence. Few people nowadays think that victims who stay in relationships enjoy the abuse. But at the same time, many people believe that the "victim not leaving" is the primary reason intimate violence continues to be a problem. Such an attitude is reflected in statements like this one: "If a man hits you once, it's his fault. And if he hits you twice, it's your fault" (quoted in Berns, 2004, p. 18).

To many battered women, these new expectations seem overly narrow and unrealistic. Consider, for example, the current welfare system (see Chapter 6). In the past, as many as two thirds of women who received welfare payments had abuse in their backgrounds, suggesting that welfare may have been an escape route for many battered women with children (Gordon, 1997). Today, however, the inadequacy and unpredictability of the revised welfare system may force many of these women to stay in relationships with men who abuse them or their children. Battered women often have difficulty complying with the work requirements of the current system. A battered woman may be forced to choose between the welfare money her family needs and the physical safety of both herself and her children. Those who manage to leave often have no transportation, no home, no bank account, and no job. If government assistance is not available, they may be forced to remain in or return to a dangerous situation (Moore, 2003).

The situation is so bad that some states, though not all, have enacted provisions called Family Violence Options, which exempt battered women who meet the criteria from work requirements and lifetime welfare benefit limits. Critics, however, argue that these provisions are insufficient because states have limits on how many exemptions they can grant (Moore, 2003).

Sometimes the resources in place to assist battered women are simply inadequate. In rural areas with no public transportation, shelters exist but may be inaccessible to women who live miles away and don't own a car. In small towns, confidentiality is virtually impossible. The fact that people tend to know one another can dissuade a woman from calling a local sheriff's office for help because the person answering could easily be a friend or relative of her abusive partner.

The problem of inadequate resources is not limited to sparsely populated rural areas, however. Some major cities don't have enough spaces to accommodate all abuse victims. One study found that 4,000 battered women were turned away from emergency shelters in New York in 2004 (cited in Colangelo, 2005). These women either have to remain in the relationship or agree to be bused far away where shelter is available. This remedy may get them out of harm's way, but it may also wreck their work lives, isolate them from family and friends, endanger welfare checks, and disrupt their children's schooling.

Women Who Kill Their Abusers

There comes a time for some battered women when they realize they can't escape the situation, can't make the violence stop, and can no longer explain it away. Seeing no way out, they resort to more drastic, violent measures. Law enforcement statistics estimate that more than 1,000 women a year kill their abusive husbands or boyfriends (cited in Huss, Tomkins, Garbin, Schopp, & Kilian, 2006).

Some battered women's advocacy organizations claim there are thousands of women in prisons nationwide who were convicted of killing an abusive partner. These cases present dilemmas for the legal system. Some people feel that charging these women with murder is unfair (Kaser-Boyd, 2004) because their acts typically occur after they have endured frequent physical attacks, sexual coercion or rape, psychological humiliation, and perhaps even death threats. Most are making a "last ditch" effort to get out of a situation they perceive as life threatening.

Battered women who kill their abusers have traditionally had trouble claiming self-defense. First, a finding of self-defense requires that the defendant had reason to believe that death or grievous bodily injury was imminent *at the time of the killing* (Schuller & Vidmar, 1992). Battered women, however, often develop a keen ability to predict attack from a long history of observing their abuser's actions. Hence, many kill their abusive partners before the situation reaches the precise point at which the court could consider it life threatening. Furthermore, because of fear, women are likely to wait until a time when their partner is least dangerous and most vulnerable. One study found that in two thirds of the cases reviewed, the woman had committed the killing outside a direct confrontation, when no "imminent" threat seemed apparent to an observer. Commonly, the man was walking away or was asleep (Ewing, 1987).

Second, in some states self-defense stipulates that people in dangerous situations first have a "duty to retreat." That is, as an alternative to using force, they must first attempt to escape from the situation. Only when no such opportunity exists can they legally use lethal force. With regard to domestic violence cases, for many judges, attorneys, and juries the "duty to retreat" has become a duty to leave a relationship in which violence has been occurring for a long time. During the course of the trial, prosecutors usually ask, "Why didn't the woman leave, if she was really being abused?" (Roberts, 1996). Such a question implies either that she hadn't really been beaten (therefore nullifying the self-defense claim) or, if she were, that she could and should have "retreated," thereby putting an end to the violence.

Finally, self-defense requires that the victim respond with "proportional" force. For example, shooting someone you find rummaging through your garbage can is not usually considered self-defense. Historically, in domestic violence cases, courts have ruled that a woman cannot use lethal force against a man who slaps her around or is psychologically abusive. But because of the differences in physical strength between a woman and her male abuser, hitting back with proportional force is not easy for a woman. Hence, the force she is likely to use will probably involve a deadly weapon.

■ TAKING A CLOSER LOOK

The Battered Woman Syndrome

Because of activism by feminists in the battered women's movement, the legal treatment of women who kill their abusers has changed in the past few decades. In the late 1970s, forensic psychologist Lenore Walker (1979) identified the essential characteristics of what has become known as the **battered woman syndrome** (BWS). According to Walker, BWS is a state of mind that occurs when a woman's exposure to long-term physical and mental abuse makes her feel psychologically trapped in a relationship. This syndrome affects her judgment in such a way as to make her believe she is in imminent danger and that the use of force is the only way to escape.

The court's acceptance of BWS as a legitimate defense marked a major turning point in the judicial treatment of battered women. It helped shift the focus from the defendant to the person responsible for the victimization and helped overcome bias among the many judges who refused to recognize that self-defense laws apply to battered women. Now a long history of abuse could in itself constitute a reasonable expectation of attack. Since the initial use of BWS, hundreds of battered women in prison for killing or assaulting their abusive partners have been granted clemency (cited in Gross, 1997a). But the use of BWS is not always successful. In 2006, the governor of Michigan denied clemency petitions of 20 female prisoners. Most were sentenced to life in prison in the 1980s, before the Michigan Court of Appeals ruled that expert testimony about BWS was permissible (Associated Press State & Local Wire, 2006).

Not everyone thinks the use of BWS as a criminal defense is a good thing. Some critics argue that it is a setback for the women's movement because it depicts battered women as psychologically impaired and helpless rather than as rational individuals responding to perceived danger (Bowker, 1993; Downs, 1996). They point to the most famous case—or infamous, depending on your perspective—of the use of the battered woman syndrome defense, that of Lorena Bobbitt. In 1993 Bobbitt was acquitted of charges that she maliciously

■ **battered woman syndrome**
A state of mind that occurs when a woman's exposure to long-term physical and mental abuse makes her feel psychologically trapped in a relationship.

wounded her husband John when she cut off his penis with a kitchen knife while he was asleep. The jury decided that Ms. Bobbitt was not responsible for her actions because a history of physical, psychological, and sexual abuse by her husband had rendered her temporarily insane. Instead of focusing public attention on the society-wide problem of domestic violence, this case simply became a sensational news story about an individual woman who had "gone crazy" and was unable to control her actions.

In sum, the decision to stay in an abusive relationship or to use lethal force to end the abuse is the result not of irrationality or mental dysfunction but of rational choices women make in response to an array of conditions, including fear of and harassment by the abuser, the complex everyday realities of dependence, and the lack of institutional support (Baker, 1997). When we encourage battered women to leave abusive situations, we mean to be helpful, of course. However, without adequate institutional support, often all we accomplish is making these women feel guilty about their already difficult and dangerous decision to stay.

Power and Violence in Gay Male and Lesbian Households

Although domestic violence between heterosexual partners gets most of the attention, same-sex couples are not immune to the problem. Indeed, same-sex intimate violence is widespread. It's estimated that between 42 and 79% of gay men and 25 to 50% of lesbians have experienced some type of intimate violence (cited in Burke & Owen, 2006).

The causes of domestic violence are much the same as they are in other types of relationships. For example, although most gay and lesbian couples embrace the ideal of equal power in their relationships, inequality is not uncommon. Power differences may not automatically generate violence, but they are associated with a higher likelihood of physical aggression and psychological abuse (Elliot, 1996).

Furthermore, stress, which is a major contributor to violence in heterosexual couples, is prevalent in same-sex relationships too. This stress can come from sources heterosexual couples typically don't have to face. For instance, many gay and lesbian couples must deal with neighbors and extended family who disapprove of their relationship. They must struggle to create and sustain intimate ties without the legal protection of marriage, while protecting themselves and perhaps their children from antigay violence and harassment. Employment and housing discrimination can create further financial stress in these households.

And there are other important differences between same-sex and heterosexual intimate violence. For instance, "outing" a partner is a common threat for gay people in abusive relationships. For victims who want to keep their sexual orientation quiet, such a threat can create serious fears about the loss of a job or estrangement from one's family. Same-sex violence can also be complicated by HIV/AIDS. Though HIV is by no means exclusively a gay disease, there have been some reported cases of individuals deliberately infecting a partner to prevent the victim from leaving the relationship. Others have threatened to reveal a partner's HIV status to parents, employers, or friends (Burke & Owen, 2006). Moreover, some people experience sexual, physical, or verbal abuse as a direct consequence of asking their partners to use safer protection during sex (Heintz & Melendez, 2006).

For the most part, same-sex intimate violence remains invisible to the public, making it especially difficult for victims to get help. Battered gay men, for example, cannot get sympathy for being the victims of sexism and male dominance, as battered hetero-sexual women sometimes do. Indeed, many gay male victims themselves believe that battering is something that happens only to women and are extremely uncomfortable identifying themselves as battered (Letellier, 1996). A "real man," regardless of sexual orientation, is supposed to be able to protect himself in any situation.

Gay male victims of intimate violence often try to protect themselves when being beaten by striking back at their partners. Such retaliation, whether effective or futile, enables these men to characterize the violence as "mutual combat," an explanation imply-ing that both men are equally capable of and willing to commit violence. Unfortunately, this characterization suggests that the violence is a "relationship problem" for which they are both responsible, and not an act of aggression inflicted by one partner on the other. In fact, police officers often assume that if two men are involved, they're of equal strength and can handle themselves without their intervention (Burke & Owen, 2006).

Battered gay men and lesbians have an especially difficult time escaping violence and getting help because of the denigration and animosity directed toward homosexuals in the larger society and the gay community's failure to acknowledge domestic violence as a serious problem. Consequently, battered homosexual partners are even less likely than battered heterosexual wives to tell anyone about the abuse, putting themselves at risk for more severe and more frequent violence. Resources available to assist them are few and far between.

CHILD ABUSE

According to the U.S. Bureau of the Census (2008), there were about 900,000 sub-stantiated cases of child abuse and/or neglect in 2005 (a substantiated case is one in which an investigation has determined that there is sufficient evidence to con-clude that maltreatment occurred or that the child is at risk of maltreatment). Because the vast majority of child abuse incidents involve victims who can't protect themselves and remain hidden from the police and social service agencies, many researchers think the actual figure is much higher. If we take violence against children to mean *any* act of phys-ical aggression directed by an adult toward a child, including spanking and slapping, perhaps as many as 9 of every 10 U.S. children under the age of 3 have been the object of violence at the hands of their parents or caretakers (Straus & Gelles, 1990).

Because of the relative size of victims and abusers, child abuse can sometimes be fatal. About 1,500 children died of abuse or neglect in 2004, and 90% of the victims were killed by parents, unmar-ried partners of parents, or other relatives. Over 80% of them were younger than age 4 (Administra-tion for Children and Families, 2006b).

Aside from physical violence and neglect, another type of child abuse that has received a lot of public attention recently is sexual abuse. Although sexual abuse represented only about 1 of every 10 cases of substantiated child abuse or neglect, two thirds of all sexual assault cases reported to law enforcement agencies involve children (Figure 13.3). Definitions of child sexual

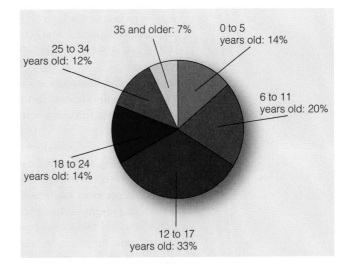

FIGURE 13.3　Sexual Assaults by Age of Victim
Source: Snyder, 2000, table 1.

abuse vary widely, but they usually include intrusive acts (e.g., oral, genital, or anal penetration), genital contact without penetration, and other sexual acts, such as genital exposure or fondling breasts or buttocks (Sedlack & Broadhurst, 1996; Winton & Mara, 2001). One study found that about 12% of prepubescent girls are victims of sexual abuse involving genital fondling or vaginal, oral, or anal penetration by an older person (Browning & Laumann, 1997). In more than 92% of these cases, the abusers were older males. Girls are about 3 times more likely to be victims of sexual abuse than boys (Sedlack & Broadhurst, 1996), and whereas girls are likely to be abused by adults, boys tend to be abused by adolescents. About 50% of cases of child sexual abuse include acts by parents or parent substitutes (Sedlack & Broadhurst, 1996).

Child Mistreatment Across Cultures

Around the world, most acts of direct violence against children are carried out by their parents or other adult caretakers. Anthropologist David Levinson (1989) studied 90 small-scale and folk societies in all major cultural regions of the world to determine the extent to which violence against children is present in family life worldwide. About 74% of the societies he examined used physical punishment of children. Such punishment included slapping, spanking, hitting, beating, scalding, burning, pushing, and pinching.

In most societies where physical punishment of children is used, it is infrequent. But parents in some cultures, such as the Goajiro of Colombia, rely on physical punishment as their major method of child rearing:

> There are punishments of various kinds. Some . . . consist of striking the child, and these are the most frequent. They slap them on the mouth when they are insolent when given an order or when they give a sharp answer to the father or mother. They are punched and kicked or are whipped with lassos or riding whips, with twigs from woods or cudgels; but the mother generally beats them with a bunch of nettles when they commit any kind of naughtiness. . . . Another quite common form of punishment is to take the child and put him into a mesh bag of agave fiber, sling it on one of the high branches on [a bough-covered shelter] and rotate it until the child is nauseated and vomits, becoming unconscious. He is then lowered and left on the ground until he recovers. (quoted in Levinson, 1989, p. 28)

Ironically, the children most at risk for maltreatment worldwide are those who are most frail: the sick, malnourished, deformed, and unwanted. In many societies, including the United States, stepchildren are also particularly vulnerable to physical abuse (Kobrin, 1991).

On the other hand, children in extended family households that contain many relatives are less likely to be physically punished than children in single-parent or nuclear family households (Levinson, 1989). When child rearing is shared within a supportive community, chances of maltreatment are diminished. Such networks not only scrutinize the actions of parents and enforce standards of child care, they also provide assistance with child-rearing tasks and responsibilities that can reduce parental stress. Among rural Hawaiians, for instance, relatives don't hesitate to yell from one house to the next that a spanking has gone on long enough or is too severe for what the child has done (Kobrin, 1991).

It's important to remember that the abusive nature of a particular parental behavior lies not in the act itself but in the way it is defined by a particular culture. What we in the United States consider to be the "healthy" practice of isolating small children in beds and rooms of their own at night would be considered abusive by members of societies in which parents form close bonds with their children by sleeping with them in the same bed. In a few areas of Turkey, mothers routinely kiss the genitals of their young children when they're playing or when their diapers are being changed, an act that would be considered sexual abuse in this country (Olson, 1981).

■ GOING GLOBAL

Mother Love and Child Death in Northeast Brazil

Even something as universally abhorrent as a parent causing the death of a child can be interpreted quite differently in different cultures. In one region of northeastern Brazil, for example, mothers show such extreme neglect for some of their children that the infants eventually die. When we look at the situation more closely, however, this apparently harsh treatment makes cultural sense (Scheper-Hughes, 1989). This area is extremely poor with a very high rate of infant and child mortality. Children are most often raised in single-parent households, and mothers commonly leave babies at home alone when they go to work. The high rate of infant death has led to a pattern of nurturing in which infants are divided into two groups: those who are healthy and have a good chance of surviving, and those who are sickly and have little chance of surviving. The latter group are children who are born weak, small, and passive. They suffer frequent respiratory infections and other common ailments of infancy. People in this region say that such children are born "wanting to die."

The children who are considered survivors are nurtured and cared for quite well. The others, however, are purposely neglected. If they develop acute symptoms like convulsions or very high fevers, food is withheld and they are simply left alone to die. Some die even before they have shown any life-threatening symptoms. Their death is seen as a way of letting nature take its course.

In this area of Brazil, being a good mother means learning when to let go of a child who shows it "wants" to die. Although this emotional detachment contributes to the already high infant mortality rate, it is not seen as abusive within that culture. Instead, it is considered a practical recognition that not all of a mother's children will live. Under desperate economic conditions, selective neglect is a survival strategy that "weeds out" the weakest infants in order to enhance the life chances of healthier siblings and future children.

Poor economic conditions can also influence the treatment of children in industrialized countries. Until recently, child abuse and neglect as we understand them in the West didn't constitute a serious social problem in Japan. Japanese parents rarely inflicted physical punishment on their children. In 1990 there were only about 1,100 reported cases of child abuse. However, over the past decade or so, a period marked by deteriorating social and economic conditions, there has been a 17-fold increase in the number of reported child abuse cases in Japan ("Child Abuse Cases," 2001). Some observers now feel that child abuse is as prevalent in Japan as it is in the United States (Kitamura & Kijima, 1999).

The Emergence of Child Abuse as a Social Problem

In the distant past, Roman law and English common law granted parents limitless power over their children, who had no legal right to protection against parental mistreatment. U.S. parents in the 18th and 19th centuries had the right to impose any punishment deemed necessary for the child's upbringing. Terms like *child abuse, child battering,* and *child neglect* didn't exist; they appeared in our collective vocabulary only within the past four decades or so (Johnson, 1995). Indeed, the United States had no child abuse laws until the early 1960s (Pfohl, 1977).

In 1962, an article titled "The Battered-Child Syndrome" (Kempe, Silverman, Steele, Droegumueller, & Silver, 1962) was published in the *Journal of the American Medical Association,* accompanied by an official editorial asserting the grave nature of this "new" medical problem. The features of the **battered child syndrome** included traumatic head injuries and fractures of the long bones, inflicted most commonly upon children under the age of 3. The media paid a great deal of attention to this article. By 1967 every state in the country had recognized the problem and quickly passed legislation calling for its control and punishment.

There had been a few attempts to draw attention to the problem of child battering in the late 19th and early 20th centuries, but none of these had the backing of groups powerful enough to convince the public that parents who purposely inflict injury upon their children should be punished and perhaps even lose custody of their children. Early efforts to fight child abuse generally resulted in institutionalizing beaten or neglected children for their protection rather than punishing violent parents.

The fact that the 1962 article had the backing of the powerful medical profession gave it credibility. However, according to sociologist Stephen Pfohl (1977), medical professionals, who would be the people most likely to see and report the devastating effects of parental violence, were actually unaware of the problem until they were forced to recognize it by a relatively obscure subspecialty: pediatric radiology (the interpretation of children's x-rays).

Pfohl argues that pediatric radiologists were not particularly heroic; they were near the bottom of the medical prestige hierarchy. But unlike other medical specialists, they had more to gain than to lose by publicly recognizing the problem of child abuse. The discovery of the battered child syndrome allowed them to work in the higher-status domain of the more prestigious specialties. Furthermore, pediatric radiologists looked at children's x-rays, not at the children themselves. The fact that they didn't see patients face-to-face freed them from the restraints of psychological denial and confidentiality that may have inhibited the diagnostic judgment of other medical professionals.

But medical professionals didn't uncover the problem of child abuse alone. Newspapers, magazines, and television also helped to expand the concern. By 1976, the issue had grown to encompass a much broader array of conditions that threatened the health and well-being of children (Best, 1993). The more general term, *child abuse and neglect,* replaced the narrower concept of the *battered child.* Maltreated children could be abused emotionally, verbally, psychologically, or nutritionally as well as physically by their parents. Child abuse was now much more than a medical problem to be treated by physicians.

New state laws have expanded the official domain of child abuse. Since 1994, all but five states have enacted laws that, to varying degrees, require health practitioners to report cases of suspected domestic violence (Hyman, Schillinger, & Lo, 1995). Nurses, teachers, social workers, and law enforcement officers, in addition to physicians, are

■ **battered child syndrome** A condition first identified in the early 1960s that included traumatic head injuries and fractures of the long bones, inflicted most commonly upon children under the age of 3.

now obligated to report their suspicions. Child protection workers have been granted extraordinary powers to investigate cases and to separate children from their parents. Needless to say, child abuse in recent years has become well-recognized as a social problem.

One of the most important actions taken in the fight to detect and prevent child abuse has been the formation of Child Death Review Teams composed of a coroner and representatives from medicine, law enforcement, public health, social services, education, child protective services, and mental health. The first such group was formed in Los Angeles County, California, in 1978. Since then, all 50 states and the District of Columbia have established Child Death Review Teams. These groups review the causes and circumstances of each child's death to find hazards that may place other children at risk from neglect, abuse, and violence. They then make recommendations to counties and states on effective strategies to prevent future fatalities (Injury Prevention Web, 2000).

The state's interest in child abuse extends beyond physical injury and death today. Indeed, the term *child abuse* itself is now such a fundamental part of the culture that it applies to a variety of acts, such as failing to pay child support, exhibiting unusual religious fervor, smoking in the presence of children, kidnapping by parents, exposing children to explicit rock lyrics, even circumcising boys (Best, 1993). Child abusers are no longer just parents and guardians; now other relatives, teachers, medical personnel, and even other children are potential offenders.

Explanations of Child Abuse

As discussed in Chapter 10, pronatalist ideals form the foundation of U.S. family life. We simply assume in this culture that "normal" people will have, or at least want to have, children. Why, then, in a social environment that idealizes children, would we find such consistently high rates of child abuse, maltreatment, and neglect?

Like popular theories of intimate partner violence, common explanations of child abuse tend to focus on characteristics of individual abusers. Many people assume that parents who beat their children are alcohol or drug abusers or have some personality or psychiatric defect that renders them incapable of controlling their rage. Abusive parents are sometimes characterized as psychologically immature and unable to see their children as children. Therefore, the parents may expect more responsibility and control from their children than the parents themselves are capable of showing, leading to disappointment, anger, and violence. Most experts agree, however, that such characteristics actually account for only a very small percentage of child abuse cases.

A parent's financial situation would also seem to have something to do with child abuse. Existing data indicate that cases of child abuse are more likely to be reported among parents who have low income, low educational attainment, and long-term dependence on public assistance. According to one study, children from families with incomes of less than $15,000 a year are 22 times more likely to be maltreated and 44 times more likely to be neglected than children from families with annual incomes over $30,000 (Child Welfare League of America, 2006). In fact, any purported racial differences in domestic violence tend to disappear when parents' social class standing is taken into consideration (Cazenave & Straus, 1990).

We must be cautious about drawing the conclusion that child abuse is confined to lower-class parents. Wealthier parents might very well be better able to hide abuse because they are more likely to live in private homes and are less likely to use public services for health care or transportation, where their actions can be scrutinized by others. Furthermore, doctors, school officials, day care workers, and other professionals who deal with children directly are likely to perceive a child's suspicious injuries differently depending on whether the parents are upper class or lower class. Indeed, some studies have found that medical practitioners are more likely to label an injured child "abused" if the parents are perceived as working class than if they're perceived as middle class (cited in Gelles & Straus, 1988).

Unemployment, often associated with other risk factors such as low self-esteem, stress, and depression, is frequently associated with child abuse (Gillham et al., 1997). Unemployed people also spend more time at home, increasing their interactions with children. Certainly the resulting tension and frustration can increase the likelihood of child abuse as well as other forms of domestic violence.

It may come as some surprise that aside from sexual abuse, women are actually more likely than men to neglect, physically abuse, or emotionally abuse their children (cited in Winton & Mara, 2001). About 58% of all perpetrators of child abuse and neglect are women (Administration for Children and Families, 2006b). Women's increased likelihood of abusing and neglecting children is most likely the result of their typical family roles. Simply put, women have more opportunity to abuse because they tend to spend more time with children, often isolated from other adults. They usually also are responsible for the arduous and frustrating aspects of child rearing, including disciplining children.

An individual-level factor that has become one of the most popular explanations of child abuse is the so-called **cycle of violence,** the tendency for people who are abused as children to grow up to be abusing parents and violent spouses themselves. Research suggests that childhood exposure to abuse or neglect doesn't guarantee that people will become violent as adults. For instance, one study found that 30% of individuals who were abused as children grew up to become abusers as adults, compared to only 5% of people who weren't abused as children growing up to become abusers. This finding shows a significant increase in the likelihood of becoming an abuser for those who were victimized as children, but it also shows that 70%—over two thirds—of abuse victims *don't* become abusers in adulthood (Kaufman & Zigler, 1987).

Other research has shown a relationship between childhood abuse and juvenile or adult violence of various types. In a study conducted by the National Institute of Justice, 1,575 individuals were followed from childhood to adulthood (Widom & Maxfield, 2001). Of these, 908 individuals had experienced substantiated cases of childhood abuse or neglect between 1967 and 1971. The remaining 667 individuals had not officially been abused or neglected and served as the control group in the study. This latter group and the group of individuals who had been abused were matched in terms of sex, age, family socioeconomic status, and race. Criminal records for both groups were then reviewed over a 25-year period.

The study found that although the majority of individuals in both groups had not been involved in juvenile or adult crimes, being abused or neglected as a child increased the likelihood of juvenile arrest by 59%, adult arrest by 28%, and arrest for violent crime by 30%. Furthermore, the individuals who had been abused and neglected as children were younger when first arrested, had committed nearly double the number of offenses, and had been arrested more often than those in the control group. Interestingly, men tended to have higher rates of criminality overall, but the effect of childhood abuse and neglect on women was far stronger. Compared to the control group, those who had been abused and neglected as girls were 73% more likely to have been arrested for various offenses. Another important finding from this study was that individuals who were

■ **cycle of violence**
The tendency for people who are abused as children to grow up to be abusing parents and violent spouses themselves.

neglected as children, but not physically abused, were more likely to develop violent criminal behavior than those in the control group.

Other studies suggest that children don't necessarily have to be directly victimized to feel the lasting effects of abuse. Those who *observe* their parents hitting each other may also have an increased likelihood of becoming violent adults. According to Gelles and Straus (1988), seeing such violence teaches a child three things:

- Those who love you are also those who hit you, and those you love are people you can hit.
- Hitting those you love is "morally right."
- If other means of getting your way, dealing with stress, or expressing yourself don't work, violence is permissible.

Although these personal factors may explain the violent outbursts of some individual parents, they do little to explain why child abuse exists as a societal phenomenon and why it is so difficult to stop. To address these issues, we must turn to broader social and cultural conditions.

Privacy, Parental Rights, and State Intervention

On the night of April 18, 1993, Amanda Wallace and her two sons, 3-year-old Joseph and 1-year-old Joshua, were visiting relatives. Ms. Wallace began raving that Joseph was nothing but trouble and threatened to kill him with a knife. The boy's grandmother offered to keep him overnight, but Ms. Wallace refused. At about 1:30 a.m. she stuffed a sock in Joseph's mouth and secured it with duct tape. She wrapped an extension cord around Joseph's neck several times. She carried him into the living room where she looped the cord around the metal crank arm over the door and, as he waved goodbye, hung him (Ingrassia & McCormick, 1994).

Amanda Wallace had been a ward of the state since the age of 8. Between 1976 and 1989, when Joseph was born, she had swallowed broken glass and batteries and had attempted to disembowel herself. When pregnant with Joseph, she repeatedly stuck soda bottles into her vagina, claiming the baby wasn't hers. When Joseph was born, a psychiatrist who had examined Amanda warned that she "should never have custody of this or any other baby."

When Joseph was 11 months old, he was removed from his mother because of suspected child abuse, but an assistant public defender persuaded a juvenile court judge to return Joseph to Amanda. Over the next 2 years, caseworkers removed Joseph from the home two more times following his mother's suicide attempts. A Department of Children and Family Services report recommended that he be sent back to his mother, citing the fact that she had gotten an apartment and had entered counseling. The last time Joseph was returned to his mother, 2 months before his death, the judge ignored Amanda's turbulent history, saying to her, "It sounds like you're doing O.K. Good luck."

Each time, the state had determined that in the interests of protecting the mother's right to control her own affairs, it would be best if the child were returned to her. The sanctity of the family, state officials concluded, was paramount, no matter how undesirable the situation might appear to outside observers.

The vast majority of cases of child abuse aren't nearly as horrific as this one. Yet even here, where the evidence *against* placing this child with his mother would seem incontrovertible, the decision was still made to do so—on three separate occasions. Overall, about 70% of children who are placed in foster care are eventually reunited with their parents (National Court-Appointed Special Advocate Association, 2000). In many cases, such placement may not be completely safe. It's estimated that children who were identified as abuse victims in the past are 60% more likely to be maltreated than children who were not victimized previously (National Court-Appointed Special Advocate Association, 2006).

Most modern child abuse laws are designed not to protect children but to uphold the family's integrity—that is, keep the family intact by giving abusive parents multiple opportunities to change their ways and retain custody. As these laws read, parents must be given every reasonable opportunity to resolve their problems before a child is removed permanently from the home. Children are not entitled to be free from all harm, just from serious harm. Indeed, in 1989 the U.S. Supreme Court ruled that the state had no constitutional duty to protect abused children against violence at the hands of their parents ("Can't Sue," 1989).

However, the long-held premise that keeping families intact is the best policy has weakened. More and more parents are being arrested for child abuse and neglect, and many cities and states now favor child protection over family preservation (Swarns, 1997). Some child welfare and law enforcement officials across the country have been doing everything possible to delay or avoid returning children to potentially abusive or neglectful families. As a result, more children are spending longer periods of time in foster care. Between 1987 and 2003, the population of children in foster care increased from 300,000 to 523,000. These children stay in foster homes for an average of 33 months (National Court-Appointed Special Advocate Association, 2000, 2006).

Solutions to the problem of child abuse are complex when weighing the value of parental rights and the desire to keep families intact against the safety of individual family members. On one side are situations like the murder of Joseph Wallace, in which state intervention is considered too slow or insufficient to prevent serious harm to a child in danger. In these cases, if families are allowed to function as they see fit or if the authorities are hesitant to violate parental rights and family autonomy, some individual members will suffer. To make matters worse, because child abuse—as well as other types of intimate violence—overwhelmingly occurs in private and the victims are typically helpless to seek aid themselves, untold numbers of children face life-threatening danger in their own homes.

On the other side, however, are those situations in which state intervention is considered to be too quick or overzealous, causing unnecessary harm to families. By its very nature, intimate violence thrives on privacy. So to encourage ordinary members of the community to report cases of suspected abuse, most states let the accusers remain anonymous.

Research indicates that perhaps as many as two thirds of investigated child abuse reports are either false or unsubstantiated (Besharov & Laumann-Billings, 2006). Some false accusations are intentionally false; others may be based on honest mistakes or exaggerated concerns. Authorities in the field say that most baseless complaints come from warring family members, especially ex-spouses looking for revenge or seeking to gain custody of children.

Some states have tried (so far unsuccessfully) to bar social service officials from beginning a child abuse investigation based on an anonymous report. Other states across the nation have been successful in passing laws that make false reports of domestic violence a crime. Such attempts, designed to protect the rights of people falsely accused,

Washington County Sheriff Department

Name Devlin, Michael John
Address 491 S. Holmes APHD St. Louis
D.O.B. | Hair | Eyes | Weight | Build | Age
Month 11
Day 19
Year 65 | Bro | Blu | 240 | 604 | 41
Charge Kidnapping/Armed Criminal Action Forcible Sodomy X3/A# Murder
Date Of Arrest Attempt Forcible Sodomy

05/21/2007

In 2007 Michael Devlin was arrested for kidnapping two boys and living with them in Kirkwood, Missouri. One of the boys was in captivity for almost 5 years. Neighbors didn't report anything when they noticed the boys not going to school because they didn't want to get involved in private "family matters."

will unfortunately have a chilling effect on well-meaning relatives or neighbors. They might not come forward to report real abuse if the government doesn't shield their identities. Therefore, the cloak of privacy may drop over family violence once again.

Corporal Punishment

No one wants to see children hurt, abused, or killed. At the same time, though, the U.S. public generally approves of nonabusive, disciplinary violence: **corporal punishment.** About 300,000 U.S. children receive some form of corporal punishment in their schools each year, usually a swat with a wooden paddle (cited in Lyman, 2006). Such treatment is even more common and acceptable when it occurs in families. Although less than 10% of the 2,000 parents in a recent study actually admitted to spanking their children (Barkin, Scheindlin, Ip, Richardson, & Finch, 2007), in a separate nationwide survey more than 75% of U.S. adults agreed that it's sometimes necessary for a parent to discipline a child with a "good, hard spanking" (National Opinion Research Center, 2006). In other words, hitting one's children is still considered acceptable and effective "when necessary."

"When necessary" is usually taken to mean when the child continually misbehaves after being told to stop or does something potentially dangerous. The most famous and popular baby advice book over the past half century, Benjamin Spock's *Baby and Child Care* (2004), doesn't advocate corporal punishment. However, it states that corporal punishment should be avoided "whenever possible," implying that sometimes it's not possible to avoid hitting children. Indeed, most advice books say that corporal punishment ought to be used under certain circumstances.

■ **corporal punishment**
Nonabusive disciplinary violence inflicted on children either by school officials or parents.

(Text continues on page 378.)

Spanking

Sociologists are quick to point out that "child abuse" is not a feature inherent to particular violent acts; rather, abuse is a definition conveyed upon those acts by others. The very same behavior could be considered abusive by some and perfectly appropriate, even desirable, by others. Do you think spanking is a form of abuse? Does it matter who is doing it to whom, when it is done, how it is done, or the motivation behind it?

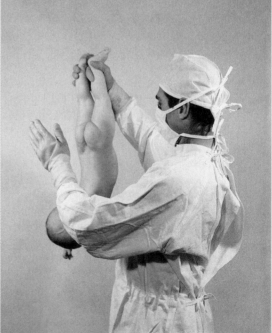

Is this abusive? In the early 20th century, spanking was a common, almost universal, component of parent–child interaction. Parents had the right to discipline their children in virtually any way they saw fit.

Is this abusive? In 1938 Tom Bradley, 16, pulled an emergency cord in a New York subway train. The court ordered that he be "spanked" by his mother as punishment.

Is this abusive? Doctors commonly "spank" newborn babies to get them to cry so that fluids can be cleared out of their lungs.

Is this abusive? In the 1963 film McLintock!, *a character played by John Wayne "spanks" his wife, much to the delight of onlookers.*

Is this abusive? A woman "spanks" a submissive partner at La Nouvelle Justine, a French bistro with a sadomasochistic theme.

Parents who spank their children may consider the tactic useful and effective, but it can look very different from the perspective of a small child.

14

Divorce and Remarriage

Just Heard About
Your Divorce

to cooperate fully in raising the child (Maccoby & Mnookin, 1992). More commonly, parents continue to fight with each other or develop a pattern of "parallel parenting," wherein the child is shared but the parents don't cooperate at all (Furstenberg & Nord, 1985). In fact, any benefits of joint custody can quickly disappear when parents continue to fight (Lee, 2002).

Opponents of joint physical custody argue that it undermines the continuity and stability that are essential to the child's adjustment. Shuffling back and forth between two parents and two households with different authority figures and different values can be confusing and unsettling. In addition, the demands of joint custody may restrict the mobility of a parent. He or she may have to forgo career advancement if it means moving to another city or accepting changes that would otherwise interfere with the shared parenting arrangement.

Research on the effects of joint custody is mixed. An analysis of 33 studies comparing the effects of joint and sole custody arrangements on children's well-being did find that children in joint custody situations showed fewer behavioral and emotional problems, had higher self-esteem, better family relationships, and better school performance than children in sole custody situations (Bauserman, 2002). Furthermore, mothers in joint custody arrangements tend to report better relationships with their former spouses, better interactions with them involving child-rearing decisions, and greater levels of emotional support for parenting than mothers with sole custody (Arditti & Madden-Derdich, 1997).

Some children in joint custody arrangements seem to appreciate the contact with both parents and the change of pace it allows. Others, however, report feeling torn by the arrangement, especially as they get older. Joint custody does tend to cause more problems for families when the arrangement is mandated by the state than when both parents agree it would be the best situation for the child. Because of these problems, some states (for instance, California) have removed the legal preference for joint custody. It seems, then, that children and parents would be better served through policies that make joint custody an available option to those who want it, rather than a legal presumption (Flynn, 1991).

In short, we have no evidence to suggest that joint custody is always best for children, but neither do we have evidence that it is more harmful than traditional sole custody.

The Father Role After Divorce

Despite growing interest in joint custody, maternal physical custody continues to be the most common arrangement. In the typical scenario, the father is required to pay child support and receives some visitation rights in return, usually the opportunity to take the child out of the mother's home for a few days each week or month. However, this arrangement seldom works perfectly. Some divorced mothers complain that they do not receive the child support payments mandated by the divorce courts. Noncustodial fathers often complain that their visitation rights are inadequate to begin with or are abused by the mother. Society as a whole, which is redefining the father's role in family life, frets that children of divorce growing up without a father's support and influence will suffer long-term harm. We therefore struggle to develop policies that will keep fathers involved—at least financially. But should we insist on fathers' obligations without also protecting some of their rights? Many divorced fathers don't think so.

Child Support Policies

As you've seen, women and children tend to be economically disadvantaged by divorce. One of the key reasons is the inadequacy of court-ordered child support payments. Even more problematic is the failure on the part of many noncustodial parents to pay court-ordered child support. In 64% of divorces in which mothers have sole physical custody, fathers are required to pay child support (Grall, 2006). Of these, only 45% of noncustodial fathers pay the full amount, 32% pay a partial amount, and 23% pay nothing. Hence, more than half of divorced mothers with sole custody of children don't receive the total financial assistance they have been awarded. Award rates are especially low for African American and Latina women, who are likely to suffer from higher poverty rates to begin with (Grall, 2006). Although custodial mothers suffer economically more than custodial fathers, noncustodial mothers are actually more delinquent in paying child support than are noncustodial fathers, in part because they already have lower incomes.

One of the key problems has always been the ineffectiveness or lack of enforcement procedures in child support cases. Growing concern over unpaid child support led the Department of Health and Human Services to expand the powers of the federal Office of Child-Support Enforcement (OCSE) in the mid-1990s. This agency oversees all states and territories and provides custodial parents with a number of services, such as locating noncustodial parents, establishing paternity, and collecting support payments (Klawitter, 1994). With the help of a national database, officials can reach across state lines to seize "deadbeat" parents' property (homes, cars, and so forth), garnish wages directly from paychecks, and secure money directly from a checking account even if located in another state. In 1997 the federal government began operating a computer directory showing every person newly hired by every employer in the country, so that investigators can track down noncustodial parents who move from state to state while owing money to their children.

This approach may have a lot of appeal, but simply forcing noncustodial parents to pay the child support they owe may not be the sole solution to the economic problems associated with divorce. Low-income custodial mothers tend to be associated with low-income noncustodial fathers, who may struggle to provide even for themselves (Nelson, 2004). Indeed, the amount of child support awarded to low-income women is lower than that for other women and remains low relative to the costs of raising children (Klawitter, 1994). Stricter support policies may eventually narrow the differences in award rates for custodial mothers at various income levels, but they are unlikely to significantly alter the poverty rates of low-income women.

Absent Fathers

Financial support isn't the only thing missing from the lives of many children whose parents are divorced. With heightened attention now paid to fatherhood in general (see Chapter 10), sociologists have become increasingly interested in the role that noncustodial fathers play in their children's lives. Some research indicates that noncustodial fathers rarely see their children regularly or maintain chose relationships with them (Furstenberg & Harris, 1992). One study found that 75% of noncustodial fathers never attend their child's school events, 85% never help them with homework, and 65% never take their children on vacations (Teachman, 1991), and the contact they do have with their children often diminishes over time (Manning & Smock, 1999).

role remains unclear. Step-relatives are more like in-laws than kin. In fact, in France the same term *beau-parent* means both stepparent and "parent-in-law."

The guidelines and norms are much less clear for stepparents than they are for parents, and stepparents themselves tend to be more uncertain about their roles than are other members of the family (Fine, Coleman, & Ganong, 1998). One obvious illustration of this lack of clarity has to do with how children refer to their stepparents. *Step-dad* sounds too awkward and indeed is quite rare. Some children use the term *Dad,* but many others use the first name, which suggests a relationship somewhere between parent and stranger. Not using the term *Dad* or *Mom* for a stepparent implies that children aren't granting stepparents the rights and obligations typically associated with parenthood.

After a divorce, newly single parents and their children establish, often with some difficulty, new rules, routines, and schedules. They create a system with shared histories, intensive relationships, and agreed-upon roles. When a stepparent enters the former single-parent household, the entire system may be thrown out of balance. He or she may be seen as an outsider, or worse, as an intruder. Rules and habits have to change, and for a time, confusion, resentment, and hostility may be the norm. Although conflict is common in all types of families, issues like favoritism, divided loyalties, the right to discipline, and financial responsibility are particularly likely to occur in stepfamilies. Indeed, studies have found that remarried couples disagree more than couples in first marriages, and that most of their disagreements center around issues related to the stepchildren (Hobart, 1991).

The friction and disruption found in stepfamilies decrease the odds of building durable, intimate bonds. Sadly, some evidence suggests that stepfathers' relationships with stepchildren tend to deteriorate over time (cited in Coleman et al., 2000). One economist even found that mothers spend less money on their stepchildren's education, health care, and food than biological mothers (cited in Lewin, 2000a). Many studies show that the well-being of children in stepfamilies isn't all that much better than that of children in single-parent households (Cherlin & Furstenberg, 1994). In fact, some people who counsel children of multiple divorces say that the trauma of forming a new stepfamily, with a stranger intruding on their time with their parent, can be harder on children than a prior or subsequent breakup (Chira, 1995).

However, remarriage can improve the financial well-being of children whose parents had divorced. About 21% of children who live with their biological mother and a step or adoptive father fall below the poverty line compared to 37% of children in single-mother households (Kreider & Fields, 2005). In addition, a stepparent adds a second adult to the household who can interact with the child, serve as a role model, and take some of the burden off the custodial parent.

Despite the difficulties posed when stepfamilies are created, most stepparents manage to build strong, durable, and loving relationships with their partner's children. The majority of stepparents and children in one national survey described their households as "relaxed" and "close." And most children in stepfamilies are doing quite well psychologically (cited in Coontz, 1997). In fact, the biggest source of problems for kids in stepfamilies may actually be parental conflict left over from the first marriage (Rutter, 1997).

The success of remarriages and stepfamilies depends in large part on the nature of the divorce itself. Adults and children who welcomed a divorce or defined it as basically a "good thing" are more likely to approach remarriage with eagerness and to see it as a chance for a new start than those who regret the divorce and see it as something that should have been avoided.

But what works well for divorced spouses may not always work so well for stepfamilies. A stepparent might feel threatened by the continuing intimacy maintained by the ex-spouses. Likewise, children may resent changes in routines initiated by the stepparent.

Ironically, the most conducive postdivorce environment for a stepfamily may be a total lack of contact between former spouses. With no ex-spouses present, stepparents can more easily adopt stepchildren. Defining parental roles is less of a problem because the noncustodial biological parent is out of the picture, and the stepparent can serve as a replacement or substitute parent. Thus the newly formed family can more closely approximate a nuclear family. However, what works well for the stepfamily may not necessarily be in the children's best interest because having a good relationship with both one's biological father and stepfather seems to be associated with more positive outcomes (White & Gilbreth, 2001).

It seems that stepfamilies can never function quite like first-marriage nuclear families. Family relationships and, as a result, the emotional life of the family are both more complicated (Rutter, 1997). The extensive kin connections established in first marriages cannot be overlooked or ignored. Hence, stepfamilies have to remain more flexible and open than nuclear families (Ganong & Coleman, 1994).

As you can see, the high levels of conflict within some stepfamilies are not simply an outgrowth of the spouses' psychological inability to sustain intimate relationships, as some analysts have claimed. The fact that remarriages are not fully institutionalized makes them susceptible to difficulty. The lack of clear role definitions, the absence of established societal norms, and the increased complexity of the family structure all increase the likelihood of tension and turmoil. Perhaps in the future our culture will develop standard ways of defining and coping with remarriage.

WHAT DOES IT ALL MEAN?

Throughout history, some couples have sought escape from bad marriages. But as long as the community was able to cite the flaws of the individuals involved as the source of the marital problems—one or the other partner was abusive; one or the other partner was unfaithful; one or the other was incapable of sustaining emotional commitment; or, in later years, these two individuals were simply incompatible—the sanctity of marriage remained intact.

Even though divorce is a tragic private experience, it is not solely a personal matter. If the only causes of divorce were simply individual unhappiness and mistreatment, we wouldn't see differences in *rates* of divorce over time, between groups, or across cultures. Divorce rates are the product of long-term social and economic changes, not a breakdown of personal values.

Legal restrictions or moral warnings are not likely to alter historical trends that have been building for so long. Divorce is here to stay. As long as we live in a society that grants individuals the freedom to choose whom to marry, people will from time to time make bad choices. Perhaps, then, the solution to the "divorce problem" lies not so much in increasing legal and economic sanctions against it, restigmatizing it, or restricting access to it, but in helping people to have more realistic marital expectations and to learn better methods for dealing with conflict before, during and, if need be, after their marriages.

And what about children? Divorce is no picnic, but it needn't be disastrous either. If we could just figure out why some kids do well and others don't, perhaps we could create programs or policies that would help minimize the damage. Unfortunately, clear answers to this sensitive question remain elusive.

Or, even more radically, maybe the answer lies in not perceiving divorce as a problem in the first place. Our society would have to acknowledge that, although a long-lasting marriage is something all couples should strive for, a certain proportion of marriages will always end in divorce. Instead of punishing divorced people and making their lives, and their children's lives, more difficult, we might consider aiding parents in their transition from marriage to singlehood, and children in their transition from two live-in parents to one—and then, if remarriage occurs, give stepfamilies room to establish working relationships.

As you think about the information presented in this chapter, consider the following questions:

1. It's tempting to equate low divorce rates with high rates of marital satisfaction. Explain why such a conclusion may not be warranted. How might high rates of divorce reflect positively on the institution of family?

2. One of the most pressing concerns about divorce in the United States is its effect on children. Describe the different factors that can explain why children may have problems after their parents' divorce. What role do you think gender should play in child custody and child support policies?

3. Do you think it's in society's best interest to make divorce more difficult? Explain why or why not. What would be the problems or advantages of making divorce *easier* to obtain?

4. Do you agree that remarriage is an incomplete institution? Explain. Can you think of any policy changes that could relieve some of the stress of stepfamilies? Should stepparents have the same legal rights that original (biological/adoptive) parents have?

SUMMARY

■ Although divorce is more common and acceptable in some societies than in others, virtually all societies have provisions for dissolving marriages. Nevertheless, no society places a positive value on divorce.

■ In the United States, the prevalence of divorce varies among racial, ethnic, and religious groups.

■ Changes in divorce laws over the past three decades have made it easier for people in unsatisfying marriages to end them. However, no-fault divorce laws have had disastrous effects on some women and children, who are likely to suffer financially as a result of divorce. As a result, some states have attempted to make divorces more difficult to obtain.

■ The individual experience of divorce is a process that can extend for months, even years, beginning well before the actual separation and continuing far beyond the time when the divorce becomes final.

■ Most of the societal concern over high divorce rates focuses on the impact on children. However, the bulk of research suggests that the problems children experience after a divorce are caused not by the breakup but by the conflict between the parents. In fact, children who grow up in intact but conflict-ridden families may suffer more than children whose parents divorce but maintain a friendly relationship.

■ Although mothers still retain custody of children in the vast majority of divorce cases, joint custody and paternal custody are becoming more common. Child support policies remain inadequate to meet the economic needs of children in single-parent families.

■ The large number of remarriages and stepfamilies challenges traditional notions of what a family is. These families create complex roles, alliances, and loyalties, which can make adjustment difficult, especially for children.

Go to the Online Learning Center at **www.mhhe.com/newman1** to test your knowledge of the chapter concepts and key terms.

KEY TERMS

bilateral no-fault divorce 393	joint custody 407	physical custody 404
displaced homemakers 394	legal custody 404	sole custody 405
incomplete institution 412	no-fault divorce 392	unilateral no-fault divorce 393

SEE FOR YOURSELF

We've seen in this chapter that divorce and remarriage have become a common part of everyday family life in this society. Nevertheless, stepfamilies still face many unique dilemmas and challenges.

To gain insight into these issues, interview a variety of people who grew up or currently live in stepfamilies. Try to speak to both stepsons and stepdaughters, although they need not be from the same family. See if you can also talk to people from various social class, racial, and religious backgrounds. Try to talk to children who still live at home as well as grown children who live on their own.

First, to get some background information, ask your respondents the following questions:

- When did your parents divorce? How old were you at the time?

- When did one or both of your parents remarry?

- How long did you live in a single-parent household after the divorce?

- How many siblings, step-siblings, and/or half-siblings do you have? What are their sexes and ages?

- How did your living arrangements change upon remarriage? Did you remain in the home you lived in before the divorce, move into a stepparent's home, or move into a new "neutral" home?

Next, ask some questions about your respondents' initial reactions to the new stepparent situation:

- How did you feel toward your new stepparent when you first met him or her? Would you characterize your response as mostly positive or mostly negative? If negative, would you characterize your

feelings as hostile, confused, or resentful? If there were step-siblings, how did you feel about them initially? How have your feelings toward your stepparent and step-siblings changed since your first met them?

- Did the new living situation confirm or contradict your expectations of what life would be like after a remarriage?

- When your parent first remarried, what term did you use to refer to your new stepparent? What about now? Are you comfortable calling this person Dad or Mom?

- Describe as best you can the role your new stepparent played (or continues to play) in the following everyday family matters?

  Parental discipline

  Financial support

  Social support

  Leisure time activities

After you complete your interviews, see if you can identify any common problems people have in adjusting to stepfamilies. Compare responses to see if you can detect differences between people whose stepparent is of the same sex and those whose stepparent is of the opposite sex. Are there differences between those who were relatively young and those who were older when remarriage occurred? Did you find any class, race, or religious differences?

What conclusions can you draw from your interviews about the nature of stepfamilies and their place in the larger society?

15

Change, Stability, and Future Families

Margaret Atwood's best-selling novel, *The Handmaid's Tale* (1985), takes place in the not-too-distant future society of "Gilead." A brutal fundamentalist regime has closed all universities. "Enemies" of the state—homosexuals, religious "heretics," people who speak freely, doctors who've performed abortions—are routinely executed. A regular police force completely controls people's lives, and a secret organization of faceless spies called the "Eyes" monitor citizens' activities.

Women have been systematically deprived of any power or autonomy and forbidden to read or have access to their credit cards or bank accounts. Following an environmental disaster that has left most women infertile, those few who still have "viable ovaries" are rounded up and assigned to high-level government and military officials for breeding purposes. These women, known as Handmaids, have become faceless reproducers, wearing long red cloaks, red gloves, and white winged hats that hide their bodies and faces. Poor women who cannot bear children have become either "Marthas" (domestic servants) or "unwomen," who are shipped to a far-off place called the Colonies. Infertile women lucky enough to be married to powerful men, known as Commander's Wives, retain their position as upper-class housewives.

Handmaids occupy a curiously paradoxical role in Gilead. Because the future of society lies in their ability to reproduce, others must show them respect, but their ostensibly high status is purely symbolic. They have no authority in the household or in society. They are forbidden to marry. They are treated exclusively as reproductive "machines" with no human feelings or identity. For instance, the story's narrator is a Handmaid named Offred, or "of Fred," meaning she belongs to a Commander named Fred.

After a child is born, it is immediately given over to the Commander's wife. After a few months of breast-feeding, the Handmaid is transferred to another household to become impregnated by a different Commander, thereby maximizing genetic variety as much as possible. Handmaids have no parental rights, no legally or socially recognized relationship to the children they've borne. They are not considered part of any family. Nor are they considered sexual beings.

Intimacy and emotional commitment—what we would consider the cornerstones of family life—no longer exist in Gilead. Indeed, the institution of family as we know it has been destroyed.

Atwood's portrayal is not meant to be a realistic prediction of the future. Instead, it is speculative fiction, a cautionary tale of what would be the most extreme outcome if some current trends, particularly those regarding societal attitudes about women's place in families and in society, were to continue. As Atwood told an interviewer, "There is nothing in *The Handmaid's Tale,* with the exception of maybe one scene, that has not happened at some point in history . . . I didn't invent a lot" (quoted in Davidson, 1986, p. 24).

The Handmaid's Tale illustrates the theme of this final chapter—that the future is never completely separate from the past or the present. It is a continuation and an extension of the events and trends that precede it. Of course, trying to document and anticipate the events and trends that will affect people's family experiences 100, 50, or even 10 years from now is quite difficult. Simply knowing about our past and the present is never enough to enable us to project into the future with complete certainty. A sudden downturn in the economy, a lethal epidemic, a natural disaster, a protracted war, or a dramatic shift in political leadership could wreak unanticipated havoc on people's family lives.

Yet underlying any discussion of future families is the notion of *change.* At the individual level, families are always changing, gaining and losing members through births, deaths, marriages, divorces, or migration. But families can be reshaped by changes that occur at the cultural or institutional level too. In this final chapter, we explore some of these broader patterns of family change and their sources. I describe current trends, make some tentative projections about what families may look like in the future, and discuss society's role in influencing these changes through public policy.

SOCIAL CHANGE

Part of the difficulty in talking about families in the future is that the present is so fleeting. Change is the preeminent characteristic of modern human societies, whether it occurs in our personal relationships, in our cultural norms and values, or in our social institutions. No doubt, the world in which you are living at this precise moment is, in many ways, different from the one I experienced when I was writing this book.

Over the last half of the 20th and the beginning of the 21st century, we've seen divorce rates drop, skyrocket, stabilize, and go down. People are waiting longer to get married and then, once they do marry, are having fewer children. Cultural concerns over gender equality have altered the way men and women relate to each other inside and outside families. Social and sexual rules that once seemed eternal have disintegrated: Unmarried couples now live together openly, unmarried women routinely have and keep their babies, and remaining single and remaining childless have become acceptable lifestyle options (Teachman, Tedrow, & Crowder, 2000).

Fifty years ago, few people questioned the "supremacy" of the female homemaker–male breadwinner family structure. Functionalist sociologists wrote about how this family type was ideally suited to meet the needs of individuals and social institutions (Gerson, 2000). Today, less than one quarter of U.S. families fit this pattern (U.S. Bureau of the Census, 2008). More households contain single people living alone than households with married parents and children (DePaulo, 2006). The majority of families today are either dual-earner, single-parent, childless, blended, or empty-nest. Mothers are less likely to be the primary caretakers of their children than they were 50 years ago, forcing them to depend on others—paid caregivers, friends, spouses, other relatives, teachers—to fulfill the traditional mother role. In many ways, today's U.S. families bear little resemblance to the cultural ideal that existed just a generation ago.

People just beginning their families today face tough decisions about issues that past generations simply took for granted:

> In place of compulsory marriage are questions about whether and when to get married or stay married. In place of separate spheres are conflicts between the paid work of supporting family members and the unpaid work of caring for them. In place of full-time mothering and distant but steady fatherhood are tensions between the need to care for others and the need for autonomy and personal achievement. (Gerson, 2000, p. 183)

These new family dilemmas and contradictions are unsettling, but they are simply a result of other types of social change.

Sources of Social Change

Although individual families may undergo rapid, sudden changes in their structure and dynamics due to death, illness, divorce, job loss, and so on, changes in the *institution* of family tend to occur gradually over time in response to changes that occur in other

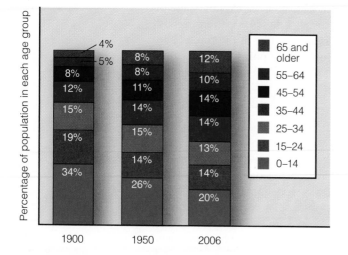

FIGURE 15.1   Age Distribution of U.S. Population, 1900 to 2006

Source: U.S. Bureau of the Census, 1999, table 1413; 2008, table 7.

areas of society. Indeed, we can understand long-term family change only in the context of broad social changes in other institutions. Demographic shifts in the shape and size of the population, technological innovation, and cultural, institutional, and economic trends often force families to alter the way they do things. For instance, feminism is often identified as the major reason for family change over the past several decades. But the feminist movement has been able to transform women's lives only because new economic options became available. Most women—and men, for that matter—are now able to live on their own financially and thus are not compelled solely by economic need to get married or stay married (Gerson, 2000).

Population Pressures

The age distribution of the U.S. population has shifted over the course of the 20th and 21st centuries (Figure 15.1). Such alterations can create change in society as well as in individual families. For instance, the passing of the massive baby boom generation—those U.S. residents born between 1946 and 1964—through the life course has been described metaphorically as "a pig in a python." If you've ever seen one of those nature films of snakes digesting small animals, you know how apt the metaphor is. In 1980 the largest age group in the United States consisted of people between 20 and 24 years of age. In 1990 the largest group was 30- to 34-year-olds. In 2005 it was people between 40 and 44 and in 2010, it will be 45- to 49-year-olds (U.S. Bureau of the Census, 2008). As this generation ages, it stretches the parameters of the relevant social institutions at each successive life stage. Baby boomers packed hospital nurseries as infants; school classrooms as children; and college campuses, employment lines, and the housing market as young adults (Light, 1988). The drastic increase in divorce during the 1970s can be attributed in part to an increase in marriages of short duration initiated by individuals in the baby boom generation (Teachman et al., 2000).

This trend will continue into the foreseeable future. Over the next 20 years, the size of the aged population is projected to double, so that by the year 2030, about 1 in 5 persons in the United States will be 65 or older (U.S. Bureau of the Census, 2008). As the baby boomers reach the so-called golden years, those institutions concerned with later life—pension plans, Social Security, medical and social care—will be seriously stressed.

Because of its size, the baby boom cohort's mark on families has been especially influential. That generation was the first to redefine families to include a variety of living arrangements: cohabitation, domestic partnerships, and never-married women with dependent children (Wattenberg, 1986). It was also the first to expect paid work to be a central feature of women's lives. And it was the first to grow up with effective birth control, making delayed childbearing and voluntary childlessness possible.

Since the appearance of the baby boomers, succeeding generations have also changed society and family life. Children born between 1980 and the late 1990s—referred to as the Millennium Generation—represent a sizable generation in their own right. Between 1985 and 2004, the number of school-age children in the United States increased by nearly 10 million (U.S. Bureau of the Census, 2007), and school districts around the country have had to deal with overcrowded classrooms as these individuals entered the educational system. Political pressure from their parents has led to an increase in instructional staff, the building of new schools, increased scrutiny of television programs for children, and heightened concern over the effect of advertising on children.

Technological Innovation

Sometimes social change is spurred by scientific discoveries and technological inventions. The discovery of fire and electricity changed the nature of human lives and cultures for all time. The invention of the internal combustion engine, television, telecommunications, and the microchip were instrumental in determining the course of history in the 20th century. Scientific developments like improved knowledge of disease processes, medical care, nutrition, and water quality have all helped to reduce illness and increase life expectancy.

We saw in Chapter 9 that by separating economic production from home life, industrialization in the 19th century had a powerful effect on family dynamics and gender roles. Along with these trends came other important changes: Both men and women began acquiring more formal education as access to schools increased and new labor force skills became necessary. Industrialization created greater access to wealth and thereby increased the size of the middle class. Members of the middle class also gained more leisure time, which could be devoted to pursuits such as volunteer work. Birthrates declined, in part because the large number of children who were useful and necessary in a farm-based economy became an economic burden in a more technologically advanced one (Staggenborg, 1998; Zelizer, 1985).

Technological innovations increase the moral choices individuals and families must make. The growing availability of birth control and reproductive technologies, for instance, has given women greater choice over whether and when they will have children. In 2006 the Food and Drug Administration approved the over-the-counter sale of the "morning after" pill, an emergency contraceptive drug that will significantly reduce the likelihood of pregnancy if taken within 72 hours of unprotected sex. The existence of this drug adds another layer of choice to people's reproductive behaviors and may influence the way people approach their intimate sex lives.

Another technology with significant implications for childbearing is genetic engineering. Prenatal diagnostic tests can now determine the presence of a host of genetic conditions and tendencies, from debilitating and sometimes fatal diseases like cystic fibrosis or Tay-Sachs, to certain physical traits and perhaps even intelligence (Harmon, 2006, 2007). The availability of such tests has created ethical dilemmas regarding the degree to which parents can or should intervene in the genetic makeup of their children. For some parents, this may mean "creating" a child with the healthiest traits and the most desirable physical qualities. This, of course, raises the question of what parents can or should do with fetuses that carry undesirable or "defective" genes; about 90% of pregnant women who learn their fetuses carry the chromosome that causes Down syndrome choose an abortion (Harmon, 2007).

Unless prospective parents can rely on tolerance and respect for children who have chronic illnesses or who may be physically or mentally handicapped, the pressure to view reproduction as a process in which the "right" products have the societal stamp of approval and the "wrong" ones should be discarded will be difficult to resist. Indeed,

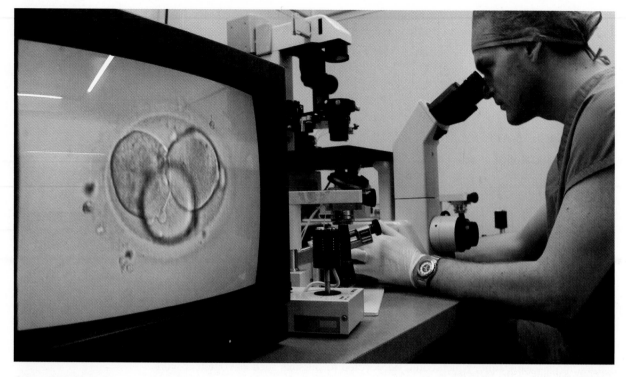

Advances in reproductive technologies have increased the opportunities for individuals and couples to have children; at the same time, though, they have raised some troubling cultural and legal issues.

as long as we assign high social and economic status to those who meet society's prevailing standards of attractiveness and achievement, many middle-class and upper-class parents may feel compelled to have only children whose genes increase the likelihood for interpersonal and economic success. At the other end will be working-class and poor families who cannot afford genetic testing or in vitro therapy. They are more likely to bear children whose genetic shortcomings doom them to unemployment or, at best, precarious and low-paying employment. Hence, some genetic disabilities virtually eliminated in the middle and upper classes could persist in the lower classes. Given today's social attitudes and the persistent gap between the rich and poor, it is not far-fetched to project that socioeconomic inequality could help to create a true genetic underclass in the future.

But the desire on the part of parents to "create" a child with certain characteristics doesn't always mean that all parents would want a "perfect" child. Some parents, with traits such as deafness or dwarfism, are opting for prenatal genetic testing not to weed out some genetic flaw but to ensure that their offspring stay in their cultural world by sharing the condition they have. As one deaf mother put it, "a hearing baby would be a blessing, but a deaf baby would be a special blessing" (quoted in Sanghavi, 2006, p. 5).

Technology also raises moral issues regarding the end of life. Advances in medical technology, prenatal care, hygiene, and nutrition have not only increased life expectancy but also delayed the onset of serious disease. Researchers have found that heart disease, lung disease, arthritis, and other ailments now occur, on average, 10 to 25 years later than they used to. People even look different. U.S. men are nearly 3 inches taller and 50 pounds heavier than they were 100 years ago (cited in Kolata, 2006). With the help of respirators and other advanced life-support equipment, frail people can now be kept alive long after their brains have ceased functioning.

Perhaps, sometime in the future, death from disease in the developed world will become a matter of choice. Several years ago, scientists discovered a gene mutation in fruit flies that doubles their life span. The same long-life gene exists in humans, leading some researchers to predict that future drug therapies could allow humans to double their life span, to about 150 years (Recer, 2000). Imagine how such developments would alter our ideas about old age and the life course. For instance, scientists found that female fruit flies with this mutation could reproduce throughout their lives, laying nearly double the normal number of eggs. In humans, such an effect could result in a much more extended childbearing period, or perhaps some women would delay childbearing until age 100 or older. Maybe you'll be sitting down to dinner in the year 2100 with your great-great-great grandchildren!

Society can sometimes be slow to adjust to the changes brought about by scientific and technological innovation. Artificial insemination, in vitro fertilization, surrogate motherhood, and other medical advances in the area of infertility treatment have increased the number of infertile couples who can now have children. Yet these technological developments were changing the face of parenthood well before society began to recognize and address the ethical, moral, and legal issues they raised. For instance, in divorce cases, legal battles sometimes rage over which partner is entitled to custody of frozen embryos conceived in a laboratory.

Electronic and telecommunications advances also have undeniable consequences for family life. In the early to mid-20th century, telephones and televisions reduced the time family members once spent interacting with each other and with their neighbors. More recently, satellite dish TVs, personal computers, home entertainment systems, and handheld communication devices have had a similar effect. Cell phones, pagers, and wireless e-mail have created a workday that never ends (Hafner, 2000). These gadgets blur the boundaries between work time and family time to a degree unknown just a few years ago.

Some argue that these changes are good for families. In the not-so-distant past, working almost always meant being physically away from home. Now people can do much of their work at home in the presence of their loved ones. Some futurists even point out that homes may once again become workplaces and schools, healing the split between men and women and the split between parents and children that began over 100 years ago (Skolnick, 1996).

Others, however, are not so optimistic. The urge to electronically "stay in touch" with the workplace is robbing some families of uninterrupted time together. Family vacations, once a near-sacred ritual of withdrawal from the demands of everyday life, are no longer respites from work responsibilities, especially for families of professional and managerial workers. Many remote resort towns now have Internet cafes where hikers and tourists can check their e-mail for messages. One study found that 1 in 5 people nowadays take their laptop on vacation ("Poll: 1 in 5," 2007), and more and more people are now able to access their e-mail through their cell phones. Simply being hundreds of miles away from the office is no longer enough to keep work at bay. As electronic devices get smaller, the number of intrusive communication gadgets that people have at home—laptops, Treos, BlackBerries, multi-function cell phones—has grown substantially (Hafner, 2006).

Technology has the potential to significantly alter family dynamics in some indirect ways too. For instance, computer technology has made custody arrangements in divorce cases more creative over the last few decades in cases where noncustodial parents are forced to move far away to keep their jobs. With instant messaging and Webcams, noncustodial parents can "visit" their children from any place in the world. The legal system has just begun to address the possible benefits (and problems) of technology's bridging the physical and emotional distance caused by divorce (Clemetson, 2006). In 2004 Utah became the first state to allow judges to grant virtual visits in custody cases. At the time of this writing, several other states were considering similar bills.

In sum, many of the most difficult family issues we face today derive from technologies that provide benefits few people are willing to part with: longer, healthier lives, the ability to choose when and how many children to have, quicker access to information, ease of maintaining contact with others, and so on. Technological advances have forced us to face conditions that were unknown to previous generations, and we are unlikely to reverse the changes that have occurred, rendering moot the nostalgic hope that family difficulties could be solved by returning to a simpler, less technologically sophisticated time.

Institutional Diffusion

■ **institutional diffusion**
Changes in one social institution that create changes in other institutions.

Changes that occur in one social institution usually create changes in others, a phenomenon known as **institutional diffusion.** A booming economy leads to higher rates of employment, which can encourage children to leave home and become independent earlier, and families to move to better neighborhoods or a new part of the country. The prosperous postwar economy of the late 1940s and 1950s is a case in point. Many young couples in that era could afford to buy homes and start families, which encouraged earlier marriage and childbearing than in the previous generation that had come of age during the Great Depression.

In contrast, a slow-growing or stagnant economy encourages people to maintain close networks with other relatives and may discourage young people from moving out of their parents' home. During periods of extreme economic distress when rates of unemployment tend to be high, patterns of decision making within families are likely to shift as the breadwinning role moves from one person to another (Hareven, 2000).

Outside the small percentage of families who are independently wealthy, families today generally need two permanent, well-paying jobs to ensure that they remain financially secure. If good jobs become scarcer and are replaced by low-paying and sporadic employment, even two earners may not be enough to safeguard a family from poverty. Furthermore, women and minorities are disproportionately affected by economic downturns, which produce low wages and underemployment. Most families remain at the mercy of economic change, along with a variety of other trends in the larger society.

Changes in the economy may even influence the act of giving birth. The increasing importance of work in women's lives has created a desire on the part of many pregnant women to choose when they will deliver. In 2003, 1 of every 5 U.S. births was artificially induced (allowing mothers to know the delivery date in advance), up from 1 in 10 in 1990 (Cassidy, 2006). Consequently, over the past decade, the average U.S. pregnancy has shortened from 40 weeks to 39 weeks, and the percentage of babies born "near term" (at 34 to 36 weeks' gestation) has increased from 7.3% to 8.8%. Child development experts worry that shorter gestation periods increase the likelihood of babies being born with low birth weights, which may create developmental problems for these children later in life (Stein, 2006).

At the same time, the effects of changes in the institution of family extend to other institutions, such as law, politics, and schools. No teacher today can fail to witness the psychological effects of divorce and remarriage that many students experience. Many school districts bend residency rules to accommodate children in joint-custody situations, hold separate teacher conferences for divorced parents, and make duplicate copies of students' papers, assignments, and report cards to send to both parents (Keller, 1997). In addition, as more families find themselves unable to cope with the social problems their children face, schools are being called on to provide services that were once the sole province of families. They teach moral values, consumer skills, and technological "literacy," provide adequate nutrition, and administer programs to help students avoid drug and alcohol abuse, teen pregnancy, and sexually transmitted diseases.

Other institutions have been slower to adapt to family changes. Despite some efforts to accommodate family obligations, the workplace, for the most part, is still built on the assumption that job commitment takes precedence over family time. Furthermore, women still face wage gaps, segregated labor markets, glass ceilings, and other workplace disadvantages (Gerson, 2000).

Social Movements

Social change is not just something that *happens* to a society or to families, however. Sometimes change is brought about purposefully by individuals or groups of individuals. These changes are not a by-product of population pressures, technological innovation, cultural and institutional diffusion, or economic change. Rather, they are the result of a concerted effort on the part of people who feel that things aren't the way they ought to be.

When groups of people with common goals and bonds of solidarity make a sustained attempt to bring about change through collective action, targeted at the government or other opponents, they are part of a **social movement** (Staggenborg, 1998). People who participate in social movements take part in a variety of actions, such as violent protest, peaceful demonstrations, lobbying, circulation of petitions, donations, or simple identification with a movement through wearing its symbols or espousing the cause. But underlying all social movements is change: the desire to enact it, stop it, or reverse it.

■ **social movement**
Groups of people with common goals and bonds of solidarity who make a sustained attempt to bring about change through collective action, targeted at the government or other opponents.

Family life may seem far removed from these concerted efforts to change society, but in fact some of the most persistent and far-reaching social movements in the 20th century have had a profound impact on families. The labor movement, the movement to create safe working environments, the women's movement, the environmental movement, the civil rights movement, the abortion rights and anti-abortion movements, the gay and lesbian rights movement, and the religious right movement have all directly or indirectly affected people's ability to create, sustain, and direct their family lives. Others specifically relate to family, such as MOMS Rising, an organized movement that seeks to create a "family friendly" society by lobbying legislators on such issues as family leave, after school programs, affordable health care, and living wages.

Ideology

To be effective, a social movement must have an **ideology,** a coherent system of beliefs, values, and ideas that justifies its existence (Turner & Killian, 1987; Zurcher & Snow, 1981). People are almost never neutral about family matters, which lie at the heart of religious, political, and philosophical belief systems. Controversial issues such as welfare, homosexual rights, abortion, sex education, corporal punishment, and divorce often divide people into clear ideological camps.

■ **ideology**
A coherent system of beliefs, values, and ideas that justifies a social movement.

The fervor and energy people bring with them to various protests and demonstrations illustrate the cultural and personal importance of family in this society.

■ traditionalist family ideology
Belief system in which the primary cause of family problems is thought to be the disappearance of "family values" and the prevalence of moral decay among people who are either selfish or behaviorally corrupt.

Social movements that touch upon the institution of family fall into two broad ideology categories. A **traditionalist family ideology** rests on the assumption that U.S. families are in serious decline. To traditionalists, the primary cause of family problems is the disappearance of "family values" and the prevalence of moral decay among people who are either selfish (such as women who would rather work than stay at home to raise their children) or behaviorally corrupt (such as people who have premarital or extramarital sex). In addition, traditionalists believe that the foundation of family is duty and obligation. People have a duty to be chaste before legal marriage and monogamous afterward, to have children only within a legal marriage, to live for children and not do anything that has a negative effect on them, and to maintain a permanent marriage "for the children's sake" (Scanzoni, 1991). These are the arrangements and expectations that traditionalists consider "normal" and highly desirable. Hence, they would support movements seeking to reverse the trend toward quick and easy divorce and mothers' participation in the paid labor force; to prevent homosexuals from legally marrying; and to restrict easy access to welfare, abortion, and sex education in schools.

A good example of a traditionalist movement is the anti-abortion, or "pro-life," movement. Its ideology rests on several assumptions about the nature of childhood and motherhood (Luker, 1984): Each conception is an act of God, and so abortion violates God's will; life begins at conception; the fetus is an individual who has a constitutional right to life; and every human life should be valued (Michener, DeLamater, & Schwartz, 1986).

Although abortion remains legal in this country and the majority of adults support its availability, at least under certain circumstances, the anti-abortion movement has achieved some success. Since 1996, nearly every state has enacted some sort of restriction on abortion. In 1980 there were 428 abortions for every 1,000 live births. Today, that figure is a little more than 300 (U.S. Bureau of the Census, 2008). In 2007 the U.S. Supreme Court upheld the Partial Birth Abortion Act, which prohibits a particular late-term abortion procedure.

About 87% of all U.S. counties (and over 90% of counties in the Midwest and South) have no abortion provider, and the number of abortion providers decreased by 25% between 1992 and 2005 (Jones, Zolna, Henshaw, & Finer, 2008). By 1995 only 12% of obstetrics and gynecology residents were routinely trained in abortion techniques. The percentage remains low today, although pressure from medical student advocacy groups has led some programs to reinstate abortion in the curriculum (cited in Edwards, 2001).

In contrast to the traditionalist view, the theme of a **progressive family ideology** is that families are not declining but instead are caught up in the continual process of evolution and transition that has been occurring for centuries. Progressives agree with traditionalists that the family is a vital social institution, but they also believe it is a social construction—a product of the attitudes and behaviors of the people touched by it—not a universal form that exists for all times and all societies. In other words, all societies may have something they call "family," but its structure, form, and nature vary widely. The stresses and strains that people experience in their families result not from forsaking a traditionalist vision but instead from the paradox of adhering to traditional norms while behaving in distinctly nontraditional ways. For progressives:

> The [traditionalists] have it backward when they argue that the collapse of traditional family values is at the heart of our social decay. The losses in real earnings and in breadwinner jobs, the persistence of low-wage work for women and the corporate greed that has accompanied global economic restructuring have wreaked far more havoc on [families] than have the combined effects of feminism, sexual revolution, gay liberation . . . and every other value flip of the past half-century. (Stacey, 1994, pp. 120–121)

Rather than issuing inflexible rules, progressives seek to discover what works and what doesn't work for families across a variety of circumstances (Scanzoni, 1991). Progressive family ideology pays a lot of attention to the place of women in society: It makes little sense to speak of the well-being of families until adults can be economically secure without regard to gender, until men become more involved in household tasks and child rearing, and until the nation commits to high-quality support for young children (Scanzoni, 1991). For instance, progressives argue that, because both women's employment and day care are here to stay, social movements must aim to reduce their costs and maximize their benefits for *both* adults and children. If women's economic well-being improves, kids will ultimately be better off. If children participate in high-quality day care programs, their parents (women and men alike) will be better off.

Ironically, partisan politics and the needs of special interests often blur the boundaries between traditionalist and progressive ideologies. The Family and Medical Leave Act of 1993 granted full-time workers unpaid leaves of absence for childbirth, adoption, and family emergencies (see Chapter 9). Although such a bill would seem to fit a traditionalist ideology, which emphasizes the interests of children, many traditionalist

■ **progressive family ideology**
Belief system that maintains that families are not declining but instead are caught up in the continual process of evolution and transition that has been occurring for centuries.

lawmakers were initially opposed to the bill because they felt the policy would impose undue hardships on businesses. These legislators were successful in diluting the original bill, reducing the amount of time workers could take off, and eliminating many workers from coverage. As a result, this law has had little effect on the lives of the working families it was intended to help (Marks, 1997).

Clearly, dividing ideologies into broad "traditionalist" and "progressive" categories is an oversimplification. We cannot assume that everyone fits neatly into one category or the other. Indeed, the same person may be rather "traditional" on some issues but "progressive" on others. Yet we must remember that fundamental ideological and practical conflicts do separate these two positions and can influence the sorts of changes that society experiences.

Movements and Countermovements

Social movements usually arise in response to social problems. For instance, the main focus of the women's movement at the turn of the 19th century was gender inequality and oppression in the legal and political arena. It aimed to secure women's right to divorce, to retain custody of children after a divorce, to retain property, to work and keep their wages, and to vote.

■ **countermovement**
A social movement aimed at preventing or reversing the changes sought or accomplished by an earlier movement.

The women's movement that gained strength in the mid-20th century had a somewhat different focus, prompted by a different social environment. Beginning in the 1960s, women—particularly white, middle-class, well-educated women—were becoming increasingly aware of the gap between their capabilities and the limiting domestic roles to which they were consigned. Women began to realize that the best way to improve their lives was to campaign for increased reproductive freedom, lobby for changes in rape and domestic violence laws, and increase their economic and social opportunities. Through organizations like the National Organization for Women and the National Abortion and Reproductive Rights Action League, women gained the political clout to have their voices heard.

Some women of color and working-class women have found today's women's movement irrelevant to their immediate needs and concerns. And the major goal of full equality for women has not yet been met. Nevertheless, the movement has been quite successful in securing important economic, political, legal, and familial changes. The vast majority of people believe that the movement has improved the lives of working women, though there's less agreement as to whether it's improved the lives of full-time homemakers, men, or children (Figure 15.2).

There will always be some people who feel threatened by any social movement seeking to change the existing social arrangements. Hence, movements for social reform often spawn organized **countermovements,** which aim to prevent or reverse the changes sought or accomplished by an earlier movement. Countermovements are most likely to emerge when the reform movements against which they are

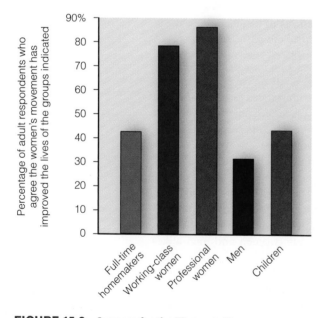

FIGURE 15.2 Support for the Women's Movement
Source: National Opinion Research Center, 1998.

reacting become large and effective in pursuing their goals and therefore come to be seen as threats to personal and social interests (Chafetz & Dworkin, 1987; Mottl, 1980).

The emergence of the "religious right" or "Christian right" in the 1980s and 1990s, for instance, was provoked by a growing perception that the women's movement of the 1960s and 1970s had created enormous social upheaval, breaking down traditional roles and values and challenging the institution of family (Klatch, 1991). The religious right's stated positions—pro-family, pro-motherhood, and anti–equal rights for women—were clearly designed to turn back the feminist agenda. The leaders of the religious right went so far as to articulate the notion that gender equality was responsible for women's unhappiness and the weakening of U.S. families (Faludi, 1991). The rising divorce rate and the increased number of working mothers were seen as eroding the moral bases of family life (Klatch, 1991). As one minister said, "We're not here to get into politics. We're here to turn the clock back to 1954 in this country" (quoted in Faludi, 1991, p. 230).

Over the last few decades, the religious right has successfully shifted the political and social mood of the country. It first gained legitimacy in 1980, when presidential candidate Ronald Reagan and several senate candidates it supported won election. It reasserted its influence in 1994 with the takeover of Congress by conservative Republicans. And it gained even more power and visibility with the election and reelection of George W. Bush, who promoted many religious-right themes. At one point, the seven highest-ranking Republicans in the U.S. Senate were all staunch supporters of the religious right (Theocracy Watch, 2005). Even Barack Obama courted the religious right during the 2008 presidential campaign.

In the 2000s, the religious right has turned its focus to opposing the increasing visibility of homosexuality in U.S. society. It was mobilized, in particular, by a U.S. Supreme Court decision that deemed laws banning homosexual contact unconstitutional and by legislative actions in Massachusetts and California that allowed same-sex couples to marry. Through the Eagle Forum, the Christian Coalition, American Values, the Family Research Council, the National Right to Life Committee, the Traditional Values Coalition, Concerned Women for America, Focus on the Family, the Alliance for Marriage, and many smaller organizations around the United States, the religious right has achieved some notable triumphs at the state and local level. It has succeeded in influencing public school curricula as well as promoting anti–gay rights legislation and defense-of-marriage acts.

RECENT AND FUTURE FAMILY TRENDS

Knowing something about the nature of social change and the dynamics and structure of social movements allows us to explain how the institution of family has changed and is changing. It also helps us to extrapolate from current trends to get a glimpse of what family life might look like in the future. But trying to discern the future can be a futile endeavor, according to sociologist Kathleen Gerson (2000):

> The looking glass remains opaque not simply because our analytic tools are imprecise. The human capacity for growth and creativity, for responding in unintended ways to new contingencies, renders prediction a risky business (p. 180).

In fact, when discussing future trends and outcomes, sociologists usually talk about *projections* rather than *predictions,* acknowledging that it's not possible to predict the future with any certainty. At best, sociologists can analyze current trends and factors and determine what family life will look like if these trends were to continue. Let's consider a few key family trends in recent decades and where each might be headed.

Definitions of Family

In recent years we've seen the meaning of family expand beyond the traditional definition. Although nuclear families will always be an important cornerstone in this society, they will reflect less and less the reality of family life for most U.S. residents in years to come. Hence the term *family* will most likely be used with increasing looseness in the future. In part, the liberal use of the word is a testament to its profound cultural and personal importance. To metaphorically refer to a sports team or a work group as a family is to symbolically reinforce the power that family holds over our lives. Aside from such usage of the term, the trend toward including various nontraditional relationships under the legal rubric of *family* will be at the forefront of emotional debates for years to come.

For instance, each year more and more major corporations decide to grant financial benefits to unmarried domestic partners. Huge corporations don't set such policies frivolously, and few of them have any desire to make a political statement about the acceptability of certain lifestyles. Instead, these companies have concluded that such policies make good financial sense because they increase workers' motivation and, hence, their productivity and loyalty. To the extent that an inclusive definition of family continues to make good business sense, the list of economically and socially "legitimate" types of families will continue to expand.

Marriage

In the distant past, spouses didn't require much of each other to make a marriage work. Marriages were primarily economic arrangements. If two partners found that they could tolerate each other's company and were mildly compatible, that was enough. Today, people expect a lot more from their marriages; they want deep intimacy, sexual compatibility, friendship, and self-fulfillment. These heightened expectations coupled with increasing longevity have made it all the more difficult for people to keep less-than-perfect marriages together. Furthermore, in the face of increased economic opportunities for women outside the home, their financial incentives to be married have decreased. Cohabitation and voluntary singlehood have become more commonplace and acceptable. When people do get married, they're waiting longer to do so. And although the divorce rate has stabilized and even dipped recently, all indications are that it will remain a fundamental element of family life into the foreseeable future.

■ TAKING A CLOSER LOOK

The Abolition of Marriage?

What will become of marriage in the future? There is no doubt that marriage still has some distinct advantages for individuals and for society, enumerated in Chapter 8. Nonetheless, some people have gone so far as to suggest that we should rethink our long-standing tradition of organizing society around married couples. Feminist scholar Martha Fineman (1995) has proposed that marriage, as a legal category, ought to be abolished. Our values surrounding marriage are so ingrained that it is virtually impossible for most people to seriously imagine society without it. But the institution of marriage has undergone so many significant changes and challenges in recent decades that Fineman and other critics suggest a radical rethinking of marriage may be in order.

Fineman proposes that people be allowed to engage in ceremonial marriage, but such an event would have no legal (that is, no court-enforceable) consequences. The decision to define the relationship as a "marriage" would be left to the individuals involved, who may or may not seek religious ratification.

Fineman imagines a future in which the interactions of married people will be governed by the same rules that regulate all other interactions in society—namely, those of property, contract, and criminal law. Equality between adults would be asserted and assumed. No special legal or economic privileges would be granted to husbands over wives or to married couples over unmarried couples. Voluntary, adult sexual interactions would be of no interest to the state because the state would no longer have a preferred model of family intimacy to protect.

Under this legal system, the treatment of children would no longer be based on the marital status of their parents. Children would be protected by the same laws that apply to all citizens, so parents would no longer have the right to hit their children. The category of "illegitimate" children would disappear and, with it, the stigma attached to being born "out of wedlock." In this proposed legal scheme, the core of family would be the relationship between dependents and the people who care for them, regardless of their blood or marital ties.

Similarly, sociologist Anthony Giddens (2007) suggests that, as a global society, we ought to be moving away from a traditional family structure toward what he calls "emotional democracies" in which the protection of children becomes the primary feature of legislation and policy. Parents should be legally obligated to provide emotionally and economically for their children until adulthood, no matter what their living arrangements happen to be.

The caregiving family would become a privileged and protected entity, entitled to special, preferred treatment. Tax breaks would be awarded, regardless of marital status, to stable lower- and middle-income households financially responsible for children, the elderly, or the handicapped. The motivation behind these changes would be not to eliminate marriage entirely but to encourage and sustain stable caregiving households (Johnson, 1996).

Such radical suggestions are unlikely to be implemented any time soon, however, given the hold that marriage still has on our national psyche. The vast majority of the adult population will probably continue to marry. Marriage, for all its problems and pitfalls, is here to stay.

Gender Equity

For the past few decades, U.S. men and women have been slowly moving toward a blending of gender and family roles and away from traditional notions of wives and husbands, mothers and fathers. There is a growing recognition in this society that the best way to ensure that families with or without children will remain stable is to increase economic opportunities for women as well as men. As couples in which both partners work continue to be the norm, employers will have more and more trouble ignoring the importance of their employees' need to balance their work and family lives. Perhaps we'll soon see the disappearance of the 9-to-5, Monday-through-Friday workweek, an acknowledgment of how employees' needs change through the life course, and a more flexible and less gender-specific definition of what it means to be a good worker.

As working families become more common, fewer people can publicly condemn working mothers as negligent parents. Most people today already say that they believe, at least in principle, in the ideal of equal opportunities for men and women. If current trends continue, more people will endorse such a belief in the future.

With regard to household work, sociologist Scott Coltrane (1996b) argues that changes in the gender-based division of labor will propel us toward equality between men and women at home. When men take on more of the mundane domestic tasks, the balance of power in the household begins to shift. When fathers take on more child care responsibilities, they begin to develop the sort of nurturing sensitivities traditionally associated with mothers. When parents share responsibilities, children thrive intellectually and emotionally and grow up holding less-rigid gender stereotypes.

Some fathers are already becoming more engaged in child care and are more likely to want an active role in raising their children. We can expect that men in the future will place even more value on spending time with their children. Of course, not everyone's attitudes will conform to this ideal. Nevertheless, Coltrane (1996a) expects that household tasks will become less tied to gender in the future.

These changes in the home and the workplace have the potential to transform the meaning of gender in future generations and to reduce gender-based inequality and discrimination in the present generation. But the road toward gender equity will not be completely free of potholes. As we saw in Chapter 9, most jobs are still based on the assumption that an employee can and should work long hours without worrying about child care and other household needs. Most employed women continue to work in traditionally "female" occupations and still earn substantially lower wages than men. In addition, the vast majority of women are still responsible for the majority of housework and child care.

Furthermore, work is still structured around a male model of 20 years of schooling, followed by 40 years of employment, and then retirement (Skolnick, 1996). This model doesn't work for many women, who must combine work and domestic responsibilities. They often have to step out of the paid labor force to raise a family and return to it later when the children are grown, thereby sacrificing huge chunks of earning potential (Crittenden, 2001).

Some sociologists feel that despite changing attitudes and the growth of well-intentioned "family-friendly" workplace policies, family status rather than gender may become the most potent discriminating characteristic among workers in the future. These sociologists argue that the social and economic gap between "career-oriented" workers (those single people and couples who forgo having children in pursuit of career advancement) and "child-oriented" workers (those single people and couples who forgo careers in the interests of their families) will inevitably widen. They fear that employers interested in productivity will favor career-oriented workers over workers who want to spend more time maintaining their families, regardless of the workers' gender (Hunt & Hunt, 1990). If future employers still assume that the most committed employees are those unfettered by family demands, both women and men who openly express a desire to spend more time with their families will risk being passed over for promotions and interesting assignments.

Life Expectancy

Medical advances in the treatment of ailments like heart disease and cancer will likely contribute to a continued decline in mortality rates and an increase in life expectancy. Low death rates coupled with low birthrates will result in an increasing proportion of the population being over 75, the "graying" of the United States described in Chapter 12. Once, only the most durable and healthiest people lived to this age. However, improved medical technology has increased the longevity of even frail people. Hence, society is doubly likely to face increasing demands to care for its elderly population.

The aging of the U.S. population will have serious implications for the way people live their lives within families. Financial responsibility for the care of elderly family members, as well as demands for emotional and social support, will likely still fall on families. Certain issues most families have not yet faced will become more common as well. What, for instance, will be the role of great-grandparents in family life? How will they be incorporated into the family structure? Will they be regarded as an obstacle to younger generations' independence, as a "social problem" for family members and for the community, or as valued members of a vastly extended family? What about five-generation families in which a grandparent can also be a grandchild? Such structures will surely require adjustments in patterns of family life and will be a focal point of public policy in the years to come.

Increasing longevity could combine with advances in reproductive technology to shatter what were once thought to be impenetrable age boundaries of biological parenthood. In 1997 a 63-year-old Los Angeles woman gave birth to a normal baby girl who was created from her husband's sperm and an anonymous donor's egg. She became the oldest woman on record to give birth. The possibility that someone could become a mother at a time when most women are thinking about becoming grandmothers raises difficult questions about parent–child relationships and, indeed, the assumptions underlying family. What, for instance, would prevent a couple from waiting until they retire to have children? If they are in good health, they can expect to live more than 20 years into retirement. Moreover, with no job to take their time and energy, they wouldn't have to worry about balancing the demands of work and family as so many younger parents must.

Critics, however, argue that older parents place excessive strains on themselves and their children. They may be unable to keep up with the demands of teenagers, and children may worry that their parents will die at any moment. It should be noted, however, that becoming a parent at age 60 or 70 has always been a biological option for men, especially well-to-do men. The late actor Tony Randall and his wife had their first baby when she was 26 and he was going on 77. So-called *start-over dads* have always been commonplace, and their parenthood has never raised the sorts of ethical questions raised by postmenopausal women bearing children.

FAMILY POLICY

With all the heated political rhetoric we hear these days about the changing state of the American family, you might expect the government would have an identified set of family-related objectives and specific measures to achieve them. Unlike most Western industrialized countries, however, the United States has no formal family policy to guide us into the future.

One reason for this lack is the country's powerful cultural belief in individualism and privacy (see Chapter 1). Law and policy have traditionally been directed toward individuals rather than families. To some people, the very notion of a government plan regarding families is disturbing because it implies state intrusion into family life.

Also inhibiting the development of a family policy in the United States is the diverse nature of families themselves. Regional, state, racial, religious, ethnic, and generational variation in values have precluded agreement on what families are, not to mention what the government should be doing for them.

Certainly, at one level, all our government policies—on taxes, education, welfare, health care, and so on—affect families, even if they're not designed specifically to do so. However, the federal government has no systematic and developed plan regarding families. Instead, we have a mishmash of state laws and regulations that lack coherence.

■ GOING GLOBAL

European Family Policies

In contrast to the United States, most European countries have an extensive policy structure for families, which includes national health insurance or services, cash benefits for families based on the number and age of children, guaranteed minimum child support payments, and sometimes housing subsidies for low- and middle-income families (Kamerman & Kahn, 1995). Although specific services and philosophies vary from country to country, the common goal is to support families, particularly families with children, at home and in the community:

> The French want not only to protect the economic well-being of children in vulnerable families but also to ensure that women continue to have children even while entering the labor force in ever-increasing numbers. The Germans and Austrians want to acknowledge and affirm the value of children and of "family work." The Finns . . . see their policies as supporting the values of parental choice and family work. . . . The Italians stress maternal protection and support for child well-being. The Swedes, and to a lesser degree the Danes, have sought to promote gender equity, child well-being, responsiveness to labor market demands, and support for a strong work ethic. (Kamerman & Kahn, 1995, p. 25)

The policy differences between Europe and the United States are noteworthy because European children tend to be better off physically, by most statistical measures, than U.S. children (Figure 15.3). Furthermore, in most but not all European countries, school achievement in reading, math, and science is higher than in the United States, and schools have fewer problems with disruptive students (UNICEF, 2007). Later on, fewer European adolescents have babies or abortions than do adolescents in the United States (Kamerman & Kahn, 1995).

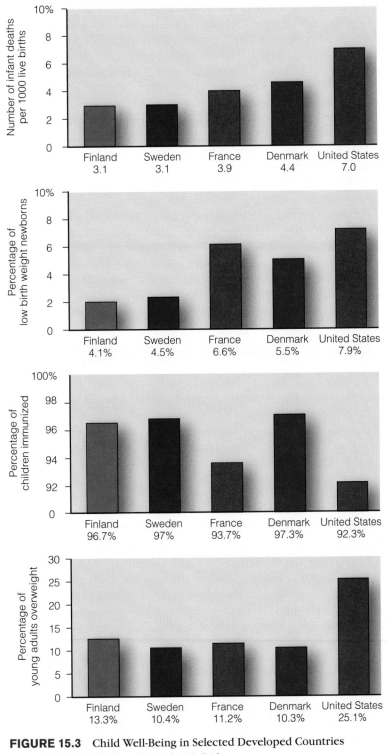

FIGURE 15.3   Child Well-Being in Selected Developed Countries
Source: UNICEF, 2007, figs. 2.1a, 2.1b, 2.2, 5.1d.

In the United States, much of the government support for families with children is limited to programs that serve children with behavioral problems, poor children, or children from deprived groups. Such programs provide important safety-net income or remedial services. However, U.S. policies don't offer basic preventive and development services that can enhance the socialization of children and avert problems as they become adult members of society.

Despite the lack of a formal family policy, the U.S. government and state governments are always considering family-related legislation on such issues as abortion, parental responsibility, family leave, domestic partnerships, welfare, support for the elderly, and tax benefits for families (Schneider, 1996). However, the lack of coherence among all these different initiatives leaves some critical areas unaddressed and creates confusion in other areas about our society's real values and goals.

Decisions made piecemeal over the next few years within legislatures, government agencies, and the courts will likely determine the nation's course in regard to families well into the 21st century. In large part, the long-term fate of U.S. families will depend on how we define certain social trends. If trends like the increase in dual-earner and single-parent families are labeled as harmful to family life, then policies will probably develop that oppose family diversity and discourage "nontraditional" households. If, on the other hand, such developments are viewed as inevitable—and perhaps even beneficial—then social policies will likely develop to support the needs of new and diverse family forms (Gerson, 1998).

At the forefront of the political debate over these issues will be fundamental questions about government's role in family life, such as the following:

■ *Should we emphasize "traditional" family values?* One direction the government might take is to promote and support traditional views on family issues regarding marriage, sexual activity outside marriage, maternal child care at home, and so on. Public policies, including taxes, would give preference to married couples with children and discourage or place restrictions on divorce, illegitimacy, and single and gay parenting. Schools would teach children that sex outside of marriage is wrong, and states would repeal no-fault divorce laws. However, at a time when the country is becoming more diverse, a complete return to "traditional families" at the expense of "nontraditional" families seems unlikely.

■ *Should we promote parental responsibility?* This policy approach would make family planning and sex education a national priority, discouraging people who aren't prepared financially or emotionally from becoming parents unexpectedly. It would strictly enforce existing laws that hold parents responsible for raising children and accountable for their children's legal transgressions. Failure to pay child support, for instance, would be considered a form of child neglect. Divorce and custody arrangements would make the financial well-being of children—not of parents—the highest priority. However, this perspective would further complicate the decision to bear and raise children at a time when many people are already struggling to meet the demands of children and work.

■ *Should we expand the government's responsibility for helping families raise children?* We have programs designed to help the elderly (Social Security, Medicare), so why not make similar provisions for children? Following models that exist in other industrialized countries, the government could take steps to lift all children out of poverty. The government would subsidize child care, preschool, health care, and paid parental leave when babies are born. It would also require employers to pay women the same wages that men earn in similar jobs. It would encourage employment practices, such as a shorter workweek, that would help to undercut the career advantage of people who don't place a priority on family life. However, such a policy would require a more pronounced government role in people's lives at a time when our political climate seems to emphasize limited government and reduced public spending.

Regardless of which direction government policy ultimately takes, we will need to debate many specific legal issues in the foreseeable future (Minow & Shanley, 1996):

- *The place of biology in reproduction, custody, and access.* What, if any, claims should those people with biological ties to a child have on decisions about the child's conception, gestation, birth, and custody? Should grandparents have legally protected access to their grandchildren in the event of a divorce?

- *Sexual orientation.* What relations between adult homosexual partners should the state permit or promote? Should homosexual parents be restricted in their ability to nurture children?

- *The preference or privilege accorded to legally recognized families compared to families formed informally.* Should those in legally executed marriages and adoptions receive social and economic benefits denied those in informal, legally unrecognized arrangements?

- *The role of the economic marketplace in forming family relationships.* Should people be able to contract for the conception or generation of a child? For a child available for adoption? For sexual services? For a spouse?

- *The role of government money in providing support for families.* Should the government subsidize child care, care of ill or disabled family members, or nursing homes for all enfeebled U.S. citizens? Should it subsidize job training for people forced off welfare or for displaced homemakers? Should it subsidize greater choice in children's education in the form of charter schools or school voucher systems?

- *The relationship between the workplace and family life.* Should workplaces be structured to favor or support one family type over others? Should workloads in the paid labor force be made more flexible to accommodate the demands of caring for children or elderly relatives or of performing other family duties?

- *The relative power of family members in family-related decision making.* What is the legal or philosophical basis for granting greater power to one member of an adult partnership over the other, as in decisions over abortion and child custody? Should children have as much say as parents in custody decisions? In medical treatment decisions, how should the views of all involved—patients, spouses, cohabiting partners, and other relatives—be collected and given force?

- *Dependency, disability, and illness.* Who should be responsible for the daily care and financial support of such dependents as children, elderly people, and people with severe disabilities or illnesses? What degree of closeness in a family relationship should determine such responsibilities?

Each of these issues has arisen because of new technologies, changing social practices, and conflict over norms and ethics. Their resolution will not be easy because family life is the result of a complex interplay among individuals, institutions, cultural values, and conscious political choices.

WHAT DOES IT ALL MEAN?

Families are a topic about which everyone has some expertise. It is tempting, therefore, to assume that we can know everything that needs to be known about families simply by looking at our own lives. Of course, such a subjective view can never be sufficient.

At the same time, though, you have seen in this book that many, if not most, families have certain patterns and features in common with each other and with your family. It's the patterns and commonalities that are intriguing to sociologists because they suggest a much larger reality than the private experience of individual people in individual families.

Furthermore, families, though private and unique, are always tightly intertwined with larger political, historical, economic, cultural, and environmental forces. We can never understand our own families without understanding the social structure within which our families are situated.

Will families exist in the future? Yes. But we must keep certain important points in mind:

■ It has never been and never will be possible to think of "the family" or "the American family." Family diversity has always characterized family life and will continue to do so in the next century.

■ The experiences that individuals have within their own families will always be filtered by their race or ethnicity, social class, gender, sexual orientation, religion, and other social characteristics.

■ None of the shifts in family life can be understood in isolation. Each change takes place within a particular cultural and historical context. Furthermore, each aspect of family life touches on others. We can't begin to understand parent–child relationships, for instance, without understanding something about marriage, gender, demography, culture, domestic and global economics, work, even biology.

As I wrap up this book, I have feelings of both failure and success. On one hand, I've provided few, if any, iron-clad answers to the crucial questions that drive discussions and debates over families in U.S. society. People can't even agree on what a family is or what the relative importance of biology and culture are in forming family experiences. No one knows for sure what the perfect balance of family privacy and public accountability should be, or whether individual rights or family responsibilities should be granted more importance in society. People still argue vehemently over whether U.S. families are declining in significance or merely adapting to changing social circumstances and whether or not divorce or having two working parents hurts children.

My failure in showing consensus on any of these issues is not based on my ignorance. None of these important questions have clear, simple answers. Sociological research can provide invaluable information on general tendencies and truths as they apply to the majority of the population, but it can never predict the family experiences of every single person. Sure, some kids suffer when their parents divorce, but others do fine. Some kids with homosexual parents thrive, while others don't. The same can be said for kids whose heterosexual parents still live together. Yes, the cultural value of family privacy creates serious and dangerous problems, but it also prevents other problems from occurring. Black families, Latino/a families, Native American families, Asian families, white families, religious families, atheist families, rich families, middle-class families, and poor families are indeed different, but they're also similar in many ways.

Well, maybe the lack of clear, unequivocal answers isn't a failure after all (Whew!). Maybe what I've done is succeed in showing you that *no* family issue or experience has an easy explanation. Sociological theory and research are valuable and useful tools in understanding the nature of these phenomena, but no two people will ever experience their families in exactly the same way. No two families will ever deal with economic, political, religious, cultural, and educational institutions in the same way. There's an important lesson here: Be wary and skeptical of commentators, critics, politicians, and fellow citizens bearing simple answers to complex family questions. Instead, understand families—your family, friends' families, and families in general—for what they truly are: familiar yet confusing, boring yet thrilling, simple yet complex, painful yet wonderful, exasperating yet comforting, frightening yet exciting.

So what can you expect in your own family life in the next decade or so? Family relationships occupy such a crucial position in our lives that we all have a powerful desire to know what's in store for us. But after spending most of this chapter offering speculative thoughts about what families may look like in the future, I can be 100% certain of only two things:

■ Families will be the same as they've always been.

■ Families will never be the same again.

In some not-yet-known ways, as families move further into the 21st century, they will be nearly unrecognizable to contemporary observers. No doubt we will encounter some new, frightening things that we haven't yet had to deal with. In other ways, though, families will be much the same as they are today. People will still worry about the same things they've always worried about and criticize families on the same grounds on which they've always criticized them.

Consider this account of a family event that, although it took place fairly recently, is likely to become a common, unremarkable occurrence in the future:

> At the recent wedding of my stepson, my husband sat companionably between his former wife (the mother of the groom) and me. The groom, in his toast, warmly acknowledged the bride's ex-husband (the father of her son), who was there with his long-time partner, who sat next to the lesbian couple with their new baby. The new husband of my husband's ex-wife introduced us to the daughters of his two previous marriages, one of whom described the difficulties of living with your ex-husband in the apartment right above you. All in all, a typical post-modern family—one typical of Republicans as well as Democrats, conservatives as well as liberals, rich as well as poor. (Tavris, 1996, p. 27)

Complicated step-relationships and "nontraditional" living arrangements abound. But notice also that age-old things like long-term, committed relationships and child rearing remain important aspects of family life. In short, even though the structure of people's family relationships may look quite different than they do today, people will always have a need for intimacy and commitment and a desire to nurture offspring and therefore will always have a need to construct some sort of family—whatever it may look like.

Barring some cataclysmic fascist revolution like that depicted in *The Handmaid's Tale*, people in the future will continue to face choices about the things people currently contemplate: whom to date, whether to marry, whether to have children, whether to remain married. The growing racial, ethnic, cultural, and sexual diversity of the population will create substantial variation in the ways people make these choices in the future, but the fundamental needs of human intimacy remain.

As you reflect on the material covered in this chapter, think about the following questions:

1. What do you consider to be the most important social changes that have affected U.S. families over the past decade? Have these changes been mostly positive or negative? What effects have these changes had on *your own* family?

2. In what ways do contemporary U.S. families resemble families of 40 or 50 years ago? In other words, what elements of family life have remained the same over time?

3. What do you think will be the most crucial issues facing families over the next two decades? What role, if any, should the federal government play in addressing these issues?

4. Now that you've finished this book, how have your perceptions of your own family changed? What about your expectations for your future family life?

SUMMARY

- When massive social changes occur in a society, their effects are often strongly felt in families. Sometimes these changes occur as the result of major demographic shifts, technological innovations, diffusion between cultures and institutions, or economic change; other times they are brought about purposefully by individuals or groups of individuals who feel that some aspect of society isn't functioning the way it should.

- Although future families will face some issues very different from those faced today, they will also, in many ways, struggle with the same questions and dilemmas families have always struggled with.

- Unlike other industrialized countries, the United States lacks a national family policy. Ironically, some of our most cherished "family values" (for instance, family privacy and autonomy) prevent the establishment of a coherent state policy.

- At the forefront of political debate over future family trends will be the government's role in family life.

Go to the Online Learning Center at **www.mhhe.com/newman1** to test your knowledge of the chapter concepts and key terms.

KEY TERMS

countermovement 430	institutional diffusion 426	social movement 427
ideology 427	progressive family ideology 429	traditionalist family ideology 428

SEE FOR YOURSELF

One of the themes of this chapter has been that change is a permanent characteristic of the institution of family. Such change is sometimes the by-product of changes that occur in other areas of society. Other times, the change comes from the purposeful actions of groups of individuals.

First, visit the Web sites of several groups or organizations that reflect traditionalist family ideologies (e.g., the Eagle Forum, the Family Research Council, the National Right to Life Committee, the Traditional Values Coalition) and progressive family ideologies (e.g., the National Organization for Women, the Council on Contemporary Families, the National Abortion and Reproductive Rights Action League). What are the mission statements of these groups? Are they interested in a single issue, or are their concerns more general? Are their positions and claims supported by trustworthy research? What strategies do they use to spread their message and recruit new members?

Social movements don't simply exist online; they require people's actions to sustain them. Most communities contain people who are active in a major movement for social change (or countermovement) that has at its core concern over family roles and responsibilities: the women's movement, the welfare reform movement, the anti-abortion or abortion rights movement, and so on. See if you can find a few people who participate in one such movement. Ask them to describe their experiences. What was their reason for joining the movement in the first place? How does the movement reflect their image of what a family ought to be? What sorts of movement-related activities do they participate in? Is their participation regular or sporadic? What are the goals they want to accomplish? Do they feel the movement has been effective in accomplishing its goals? If not, why not? What else needs to be done?

Next try to attend a gathering in which a movement addressing family needs is involved. It might be an organizational or group gathering, a town council meeting, a protest march, or a demonstration. What happened at this event? What seemed to be the overall atmosphere? Was it festive? Solemn? Angry? Businesslike? Was any opposition present?

After gathering your data, reflect on the relative effectiveness of family social movements. Do you think they make a difference? Can you think of better ways to create the change they seek? Overall, what do these movements tell us about the nature of families and their relationship to broader elements of social change?

Glossary

adolescence The awkward and tumultuous stage of life between childhood and adulthood.

ageism Prejudice and discrimination against the elderly.

agents of socialization Sources of socialization such as family, school, peers, friends, and television that provide children with cultural information concerning behaviors and beliefs.

androgynous socialization Bringing up children to have both male and female traits and behaviors.

annulment A declaration that a marriage is null and void because a key term of the marriage contract has not been put into effect.

antinatalism Policies designed to prevent or at least limit the childbearing of certain people.

assimilation The process by which members of minority groups change their own ways to conform to those of the dominant culture.

baby boom An era roughly from the late 1940s to the early 1960s marked by high marriage rates, low divorce rates, and high birthrates.

back stage Private region of social life where people can be authentic and can knowingly and sometimes cynically violate their front stage performances.

battered child syndrome A condition first identified in the early 1960s that included traumatic head injuries and fractures of the long bones, inflicted most commonly upon children under the age of 3.

battered woman syndrome A state of mind that occurs when a woman's exposure to long-term physical and mental abuse makes her feel psychologically trapped in a relationship.

bilateral descent Kinship system in which family connections are traced through both the mother's and the father's line.

bilateral no-fault divorce A divorce that occurs when both spouses want to end the marriage amicably.

bundling An 18th-century practice in which an unmarried woman and an unmarried man, fully clothed, slept together in the same bed.

calling A highly ritualized system of dating and courtship.

childhood A stage of development that precedes adolescence and adulthood; a social category subject to definitions and expectations that vary across cultures.

collectivist cultures Cultures in which members tend to subordinate their individual goals to the goals of the larger group, and to value obligation to others over personal freedom.

commitment Personal dedication to a relationship; a desire to maintain and improve it for the benefit of both partners.

common-law marriage Agreements by which couples who have not had their relationships validated religiously or civilly are considered legally married if they've lived together long enough.

commuter marriage Marriage in which spouses spend at least several nights a week in separate residences.

companionate love The quiet, predictable affection that people experience later in a relationship.

compulsory heterosexuality A characteristic of culture wherein heterosexuality is accepted as the normal, taken-for-granted mode of sexual expression.

conflict perspective A theoretical perspective that examines society in terms of conflict and struggle, focusing on how social structure promotes divisions and inequalities between groups.

content analysis The study of recorded communication—books, speeches, poems, songs, television commercials, and the like—to determine variations in social trends over time.

convenience sampling A nonrandom method of sampling in which participants are selected on the basis of convenience.

corporal punishment Nonabusive disciplinary violence inflicted on children either by school officials or parents.

countermovement A social movement aimed at preventing or reversing the changes sought or accomplished by an earlier movement.

cultural capital Reputations, connections, skills, knowledge, and so on that can be exchanged for economic benefit.

cycle of violence The tendency for people who are abused as children to grow up to be abusing parents and violent spouses themselves.

dating The recognized means by which most people move from being single to being coupled.

dependence The degree to which one person in a relationship relies on the other for important resources.

dependent variable A factor that is assumed to depend on, be caused by, or change as a result of another variable.

displaced homemakers Women who didn't work outside the home during their marriage or worked only part time and who are therefore at significant risk of economic disadvantage after a divorce.

downward mobility Process by which families fall out of the middle class and experience economic insecurity.

elder care The day-to-day care of people too old to take care of themselves.

empty nest syndrome The pervasive belief that middle-aged parents, particularly stay-at-home mothers, suffer severe emotional crises when all their children grow up and leave home.

endogamy Rules that limit marital choices to people within one's social group, principally race, ethnicity, religion, and social class.

equity The level of perceived fairness or justice that exists in a relationship.

ethnicity The nonbiological traits—such as shared ancestry, culture, history, language, patterns of behavior, and beliefs—that provide members of a group with a sense of common identity.

exogamy Rules that require an individual to marry someone *outside* certain social groups to which he or she belongs.

expanded families Large kinship networks in Latino/a communities in which even though relatives don't live in the same household, they live in the same neighborhood and interact on a regular basis.

experiment A research method designed to elicit some sort of behavior; typically under closely controlled laboratory conditions.

extended family Relatives outside the nuclear family, such as grandparents, aunts, uncles, and cousins.

family A group of two or more people related by blood, marriage, or adoption and residing together.

family autonomy The ability of families to make their own decisions about their future or about the treatment of their members.

family decline perspective An approach to understanding families that regards recent changes in family life as a sign that the overall importance of family as a social institution is eroding.

family privacy The ability of families to keep their everyday activities confidential and to be protected from outside interference.

family transformation perspective An approach to understanding families that maintains that family—both as a living arrangement and as a social institution—is not disappearing but instead is becoming more diverse and complex as it adapts to changing social and economic circumstances.

feminist theory A theoretical perspective that attempts to explain women's subordination in families by arguing that men's power within families is part of a wider system of male domination.

feminization of love The process by which love comes to be culturally defined in terms of feminine characteristics such as emotional expression, talking about feelings, vulnerability, warmth, and affection.

feminization of poverty The greater likelihood that women, as compared to men, will live in poverty.

fictive kin People other than legal or blood relatives who play family roles by providing for the emotional and other needs of others.

field research A type of research in which the researcher goes out and observes events as they actually occur.

front stage   Region of social life where people carry out interaction performances and maintain appropriate public appearances in front of others.

gender   The psychological, social, and cultural aspects of maleness and femaleness—that is, the characteristics we call masculinity and femininity.

guilt gap   Gender difference in the amount of concern men and women express over the effect their employment will have on their children.

historical analysis   A research method that relies on existing historical documents as a source of data.

household   All persons or groups of persons who occupy a dwelling intended to be living quarters.

hypodescent rule   A determinant of racial identity of people with mixed-race backgrounds, whereby an individual is always assigned the status of the subordinate group.

hypothesis   A researchable prediction that specifies the relationship between two or more variables.

ideology   A coherent system of beliefs, values, and ideas that justifies a social movement.

ideology of separate spheres   The widespread belief that women's place *should be* in the home (the private sphere) and men's *should be* in the work world outside the home (the public sphere).

implementation power   The ability to decide how a course of action will be accomplished.

incomplete institution   A characterization of remarriages that posits that they lack the guiding norms, values, and role expectations typical of first marriages.

independent variable   A factor that is presumed to cause changes in or to influence another variable.

indicators   Measurable events, characteristics, or behaviors commonly thought to reflect a particular variable.

individualist cultures   Cultures in which individual rights, self-realization, personal autonomy, and personal identity are likely to take precedence over family obligations.

infertility   Couples who want genetically related children but are unable to have them.

institutional diffusion   Changes in one social institution that create changes in other institutions.

interdependence   The degree to which partners rely on each other to provide needed resources such as affection, companionship, sex, and money.

intersexuals   Individuals in whom biological sexual differentiation is either incomplete or ambiguous.

intimacy   The state of being emotionally and affectionately close to another person.

intimate self-disclosure   A willingness to go beyond providing basic background information to reveal some very personal facts, thoughts, and feelings.

investment   Anything that a person can offer to a relationship, such as time, money, interest, or personal characteristics, that creates feelings of entitlement or deservedness.

joint custody   A postdivorce arrangement in which both parents have a say in major decisions affecting the child's life (legal custody) or share in the physical care of the child (physical custody).

juvenilization of poverty   The greater likelihood that children, as compared to adults, will live in poverty.

kinship   Who is related to whom across generations.

legal custody   Determination of which parent has the right to make major religious, medical, and educational decisions for his or her children after a divorce.

life course   The sequence of socially defined, age-related events and roles that occur over an individual's life.

masochism thesis   A psychological explanation, popular in the 1950s and 1960s, that claimed women stayed in abusive relationships because they derived pleasure from being humiliated and hurt.

maternity   The state of being pregnant and giving birth.

matrilineal descent   Kinship system in which family connections are traced through the mother's line.

Medicaid   The federal health insurance program that covers people with low incomes.

medicalization of childbirth   The process by which labor and delivery moved from the home to the hospital, carried out under the supervision of medical professionals.

Medicare   The federal health insurance program that covers people who are either over age 65 or who are under 65 but disabled.

melting pot   A metaphor popular in the late 19th and early 20th centuries that depicted U.S. society as a place where different ethnicities and nationalities would blend together to form a new cultural pattern.

middle-class families   Families that typically consist of college-educated managers, supervisors, executives, owners of small businesses, and professionals (e.g., lawyers, doctors, teachers, and engineers).

monogamy   The marriage of one man to one woman.

multicultural society   A society in which groups maintain not only their ethnic identities but also their own languages, arts, music, foods, literature, religions, and family forms.

mutual dependency and need fulfillment   A relationship stage that endures beyond the point of shared self-disclosures where partners begin to interpret their level of commitment as serious.

new rich   Families that have made, not inherited, their fortunes.

no-fault divorce   A provision in divorce laws that eliminates the requirement that one partner be found guilty; instead marriages can be declared unworkable and simply terminated.

nuclear family   Small family unit consisting of a married couple with or without children, or at least one parent and his or her children.

orchestration power   The ability to decide what course of action will be taken.

othermother   An adult woman who raises a child when relatives conclude that the child's biological mother is not old enough or emotionally ready to fulfill her parental duties.

parental investment   The relative contribution mothers and fathers make to the genetic fitness of their offspring.

passionate love   The intense, sexually thrilling feelings of attraction that mark the beginning of a relationship.

patrilineal descent   Kinship system in which family connections are traced through the father's line.

physical custody   Legal determination of where children will live on a day-to-day basis after a divorce.

polyandry   A marriage consisting of one wife and multiple husbands.

polygamy   A marriage in which an individual has more than one spouse at the same time.

polygyny   A marriage consisting of one husband and multiple wives.

poor families   Families that typically consist of people who either work for minimum wages or who are chronically unemployed. They are sometimes referred to as the *lower class* or *underclass*.

poverty line   The minimum amount of money a family needs to survive.

power   The ability to impose one's will on others.

principle of least interest   Power in a relationship rests with the partner who loves less and has the least interest in continuing it.

private culture   A couple's unique way of dealing with the demands of everyday life, such as how important decisions will be made, what are appropriate expressions of sexuality, how the individuals will communicate with one another, and how household labor will be allocated.

progressive family ideology   Belief system that maintains that families are not declining but instead are caught up in the continual process of evolution and transition that has been occurring for centuries.

pronatalism   A cultural belief that married couples should reproduce or should want to reproduce.

puberty   The maturing of the genital organs, the onset of reproductive capabilities, and the development of secondary sex characteristics such as breasts and hips in girls and facial hair and deepening of the voice in boys.

race   A category of individuals labeled and treated as similar because of some common inborn biological traits, such as skin color, texture of hair, and shape of eyes, nose, or head.

random selection   Sampling procedure in which each person in a population has an equal chance of being selected.

rapport   A general sense of compatibility in the early stages of a relationship.

recreational sex   Sexual pleasure for its own sake.

relational sex   Sex within the context of an ongoing relationship.

religion   A system of beliefs about the purpose of the universe and the intervention of God (or some other divine force) in human lives that serves as a major source of cultural knowledge, plays a key role in the development of people's ideas about right and wrong, and aids in the formation of people's identities.

replication   The practice of researchers performing similar studies to see whether they obtain the same results as a previous study.

representative sample   A small subgroup that is typical of the population as a whole.

sample   A subgroup of individuals selected from the larger population for study.

sex   A person's biological maleness or femaleness: chromosomes, sex glands, hormones, internal sex organs, external genitalia, reproductive capacities, and germ cells produced.

sexual dichotomy   The division of sex into two and only two categories: male and female.

sexual double standard   A cultural belief that celebrates men who have lots of sex while punishing women for the same behavior.

social class   A group of people who share a similar position in society based on their wealth and income.

social construction of family   The meaning we attach to family is a matter of collective definition and human agreement.

social desirability bias   The tendency for study participants to report what they believe are the most socially acceptable or appropriate answers.

social exchange theory   A theoretical perspective that assumes humans' intimate choices are motivated by the same forces that drive economic marketplaces: a desire to maximize rewards and minimize costs.

social institutions   Patterned ways of solving problems and meeting the needs of a particular society.

social mobility   The movement of people from one class level to another.

social movement   Groups of people with common goals and bonds of solidarity who make a sustained attempt to bring about change through collective action, targeted at the government or other opponents.

Social Security   A federal social insurance program that provides benefits for retirement, disability, survivorship, and death.

socialization   The process by which individuals learn the values, attitudes, and behaviors appropriate for them in a given society.

sociobiology   A theoretical perspective suggesting that all human behaviors are influenced to some degree by strong biological forces and that biology always interacts with culture to create certain family forms; the fundamental assertion of this perspective is that we are endowed by nature with a desire to ensure that our genetic material is passed on to future generations (also known as *evolutionary psychology*).

sole custody   Legal or physical custody of children is granted solely to one parent.

split household   A family arrangement common among 19th-century Chinese immigrants in which financial support was provided by one member (the father) who lived far from the rest of the family.

stratification   The ranking of entire groups of people that perpetuates unequal rewards and life chances in a society.

structural functionalism   A theoretical perspective that assumes that society is structured to maintain its stability; families serve as an individual's primary source of emotional and practical training in society, a necessary institution for the survival of the larger society.

survey   A form of social research in which researchers ask respondents a series of questions, either orally or through a questionnaire.

symbolic interactionism   A theoretical perspective that attempts to understand society by looking at day-to-day interactions of people as individuals, pairs, or groups; the larger group or society to which we belong influences the symbols we use to communicate—language, gestures, posture, and so on.

theory   A set of statements or propositions that seek to explain or predict a particular aspect of social life.

traditionalist family ideology   Belief system in which the primary cause of family problems is thought to be the disappearance of "family values" and the prevalence of moral decay among people who are either selfish or behaviorally corrupt.

transsexuals   People who identify with a different sex, sometimes (though not always) strongly enough to undergo hormone treatment or surgery to change their sex.

unilateral no-fault divorce   A divorce provision whereby one spouse can simply go to court and obtain an uncontested divorce for no particular reason.

units of analysis   Who or what a researcher is studying, such as individuals, couples, nuclear families, households, or extended families.

unobtrusive research   A form of social research in which the researcher examines the evidence of social behavior that people create or leave behind.

upper-class families   Prestigious families that own vast amounts of property and other forms of wealth, and that consist of major shareholders and owners of large corporations, top financiers, and rich celebrities and politicians.

variable   Any characteristic, attitude, behavior, or event to which we can assign two or more values or attributes.

voluntary childlessness   Couples biologically capable of having children that choose not to do so.

wage gap   A persistent difference in the amount of money women earn compared to men, regardless of the occupation.

working-class families   Families that typically consist of industrial and factory workers, office workers, clerks, and farm and manual laborers; most working-class people don't own their own homes and don't attend college.

References

Abell, E., Clawson, M., Washington, W. N., Bost, K. K., & Vaughn, B. E. 1996. "Parenting values, attitudes, behaviors and goals of African American mothers from a low-income population in relation to social and societal contexts." *Journal of Family Issues, 17,* 593–613.

Acker, J. 1978. "Issues in the sociological study of women's work." In A. H. Stromberg & S. Harkees (Eds.), *Women working.* Palo Alto, CA: Mayfield.

Acock, A. C., & Demo, D. H. 1994. *Family diversity and well-being.* Thousand Oaks, CA: Sage.

Adelson, J. 1996. "Splitting up." *Commentary,* September, 63–66.

Administration for Children and Families. 2006a. "ACF healthy marriage mission." U.S. Department of Health and Human Services. www.acf.hhs.gov/healthymarriage/about/mission.html#ms. Accessed June 1, 2006.

———. 2006b. "Child maltreatment: 2004." U.S. Department of Health and Human Services. www.acf.hhs.gov/programs/cb/pubs/cm04/index.htm. Accessed August 7, 2006.

Administration on Aging. 2001. "The National Elder Abuse Incidence Study: Executive Summary." www.aoa.gov. Accessed May 5, 2001.

Adopting.org. 2006. "The open records debate, page 1." www.adopting.org/adoptions/the-open-records-debate-2.html. Accessed July 27, 2006.

Ahrons, C. 1998. *The good divorce.* New York: Harper Paperback.

———. 2007. "No easy answers: Why the popular view of divorce is wrong." In S. J. Ferguson (Ed.), *Shifting the center.* New York: McGraw-Hill.

Ahrons, C. R., & Rodgers, R. H. 1987. *Divorced families: A multidisciplinary developmental view.* New York: Norton.

Akers, P. 1996. "Deadbeat dads meet your counterpart, walkaway wives." *American Enterprise,* May–June.

Aldous, J. 1995. "New views of grandparents in intergenerational context." *Journal of Family Issues, 16,* 104–122.

Aldous, J., & Dumon, W. 1990. "Family policy in the 1980's: Controversy and consensus." *Journal of Marriage and the Family, 52,* 1136–1151.

Alksnis, C., Desmarais, S., & Wood, E. 1996. "Gender differences in scripts for different types of dates." *Sex Roles, 34,* 321–336.

Allen, A. L. 1988. *Uneasy access: Privacy for women in a free society.* Totowa, NJ: Rowman & Littlefield.

Allen, R. E., & Hanson, R. W. 2005. "Episiotomy in low-risk vaginal deliveries." *Journal of the American Board of Family Practice, 18,* 8–12.

Aloi, D. 2005. "Mothers face disadvantages in getting hired, Cornell study says." Cornell University News Service. www.news.cornell.edu/stories/Aug05/soc.mothers.dea.html. Accessed July 18, 2006.

Altman, I., & Taylor, D. A. 1973. *Social penetration: The development of interpersonal relationships.* New York: Holt, Rinehart & Winston.

Amato, P. R. 1993. "Children's adjustment to divorce: Theories, hypotheses and empirical support." *Journal of Marriage and the Family, 55,* 23–38.

———. 2000. "The consequences of divorce for adults and children." *Journal of Marriage and the Family, 62,* 1269–1288.

———. 2001. "What children learn from divorce." *Population Today.* January. www.prb.org/pt/2001/

Jan2001/children_divorce.html. Accessed July 16, 2001.

American Association of Retired Persons. 2001. "In the middle: A report on multicultural boomers coping with family and aging issues." http://assets.aarp .org/rgcenter/il/in_the_middle.pdf. Accessed April 4, 2008.

———. 2002. "The grandparenting study, 2002 report." http://assets.aarp.org/rgcenter/general/gp_2002.pdf. Accessed August 1, 2006.

American Civil Liberties Union. 1994. "NorPlant: A new contraceptive with the potential for abuse." www.aclu.org/reproductiverights/contraception/ 16528res19940131.html. Accessed July 25, 2006.

———. 2003. "Judge imposes birth control to prevent Michigan woman from having more children." www.aclu.org/reproductiverights/contraception/ 16429prs20030708.html. Accessed August 8, 2007.

American Religion Data Archive. 2002. "2002 Religion and Public Life Survey." Survey finding. www .thearda.com/index.asp?finding=8. Accessed June 14, 2006.

———. 2004. "General Social Survey, 2004." www .thearda.com/Archive/Files/Analysis/GSS2004/ GSS2004_VAR132_1.asp. Accessed June 14, 2006.

America's Model Miss. 2007. "Girls just wanna have fun Pageant." www.americasmodelmiss.com/index .html. Accessed August 22, 2007.

Ammar, N. H., Orloff, L. E., Dutton, M. A., & Aguilar-Hass, G. 2005. "Calls to police and police responses: A case study of Latina immigrant women in the USA." *International Journal of Police Science and Management, 7,* 230–244.

Ammerman, N. T. 1987. *Bible believers: Fundamentalists in the modern world.* New Brunswick, NJ: Rutgers University Press.

Amnesty International. 2004. "Female genital mutilation." www.amnesty.org/ailib/intcam/femgen/ fgm1htm. Accessed June 25, 2006.

Anderson, A., & Middleton, L. 2006. "What is this thing called love?" *New Scientist,* April 29.

Anderson, R. S. 1988. "Why adoptees search: Motives and more." *Child Welfare, 67,* 15–19.

Angier, N. 1997a. "New debate over surgery on genitals." *New York Times,* May 13.

———. 1997b. "Sexual identity not pliable after all, report says." *New York Times,* March 14.

Angier, N., & Chang, K. 2005. "Gray matter and the sexes: Still a scientific gray area." *New York Times,* January 24.

Appell, L. W. R. 1988. "Menstruation among the Rungus of Borneo: An unmarked category." In T. Buckley & A. Gottlieb (Eds.), *Blood magic: The anthropology of menstruation.* Berkeley: University of California Press.

Applbaum, K. D. 1995. "Marriage with the proper stranger: Arranged marriage in metropolitan Japan." *Ethnology, 34,* 37–51.

Archer, D. 1985. "Social deviance." In G. Lindzey & E. Aronson (Eds.), *Handbook of social psychology* (3rd ed., Vol. 2). New York: Random House.

Arditti, J. A. 1999. "Rethinking relationships between divorced mothers and their children: Capitalizing on family strengths." *Family Relations, 48,* 109–119.

Arditti, J. A., & Madden-Derdich, D. 1997. "Joint and sole custody mothers: Implications for research and practice." *Families in Society, 78,* 36–45.

Arendell, T. 1987. "Women and the economics of divorce in the contemporary United States." *Signs, 13,* 121–135.

———. 1992. "After divorce: Investigations into father absence." *Gender and Society, 6,* 562–586.

———. 1995. *Fathers and divorce.* Thousand Oaks, CA: Sage.

Ariès, P. 1962. *Centuries of childhood.* New York: Vintage.

Aron, A., & Aron, E. N. 1986. *The heart of social psychology.* Lexington, MA: Lexington Books.

Arrighi, B. A. 1997. *America's shame: Women and children in shelter and the degradation of family roles.* Westport, CT: Praeger.

Arrighi, B. A., & Maume, D. J. 2000. "Workplace subordination and men's avoidance of housework." *Journal of Family Issues, 21,* 464–488.

Ashford, L. 2005. "Taking stock of women's progress." Population Reference Bureau. www.prb.org/pdf05/ TakingStockWomens.pdf. Accessed July 2, 2007.

Associated Press State & Local Wire. 2006. "Granholm denies clemency request for 20 women prisoners." http://web.lexis-nexis.com. May 20. Accessed August 7, 2006.

Atwood, M. 1985. *The handmaid's tale.* New York: Fawcett.

Babbie, E. 1992. *The practice of social research.* Belmont, CA: Wadsworth.

———. 2007. *The practice of social research*. Belmont, CA: Thomson Learning.

"Babyklappe." 2007. www.everything2.com/index .pl?node_id=1208451. Accessed June 11, 2007.

Bachu, A., & O'Connell, M. 2000. "Fertility of American women—June, 1998." *Current Population Reports,* P20-526. Washington, DC: Government Printing Office.

Bailey, B. L. 1988. *From front porch to back seat*. Baltimore: Johns Hopkins University Press.

Baker, P. L. 1997. "And I went back: Battered women's negotiation of choice." *Journal of Contemporary Ethnography, 26,* 55–74.

Ballard, C. 1987. "A humanist sociology approach to teaching social research." *Teaching Sociology, 15,* 7–14.

Balswick, J. O., & Balswick, J. K. 1995. "Gender relations and marital power." In B. B. Ingoldsby & S. Smith (Eds.), *Families in multicultural perspective*. New York: Guilford Press.

Baltzell, E. D. 1958. *Philadelphia gentleman: The making of a national upper class*. Glencoe, IL: Free Press.

Bank, B. J. 1995. "Friendships in Australia and the United States: From feminization to a more heroic image." *Gender & Society, 9,* 79–98.

Barker, O. 2002. "8 minutes to a love connection in this rush-rush culture, 'speed dating' is fast route to everlasting romance." *USA Today Online*. www .usatoday.com/usatonline/20021212/4694919s.htm. Accessed December 13, 2002.

Barkin, S., Scheindlin, B., Ip, E. H., Richardson, I., & Finch, S. 2007. "Determinants of parental discipline practices: A national sample from primary care practices." *Clinical Pediatrics, 46,* 64–69.

The Barna Group. 2005. Church attendance. www .barna.org/FlexPage.aspx?PageCMD=Print. Accessed May 25, 2005.

———. 2007. "Barna's annual tracking study shows Americans stay spiritually active, but Biblical views wane." www.barna.org/FlexPage.aspx?Page= BarnaUpdate&BarnaUpdateID=271. Accessed June 4, 2007.

Barnett, R., & Baruch, G. 1987. "Determinants of fathers' participation in family work." *Journal of Marriage and the Family, 49,* 29–40.

Barry, J. B. 1993. "Daddytrack." *Utne Reader,* May–June, 70–73.

Bartholet, E. 1993. *Family bonds*. Boston: Houghton Mifflin.

Bassuk, E. L., Rubin, L., & Lauriat, A. S. 1986. "Characteristics of sheltered homeless families." *American Journal of Public Health, 76,* 1079–1101.

Bauserman, R. 2002. "Child adjustment in joint-custody versus sole-custody arrangements: A meta-analytic review." *Journal of Family Psychology, 16,* 91–102.

Beah, I. 2007. "George Clooney: Using star power to illuminate the crisis in Darfur." *Time,* May 14.

Bearak, B. 2006. "The bride price." *New York Times,* July 6.

Becerra, R. N. 1992. "Mexican American families." In J. M. Henslin (Ed.), *Marriage and family in a changing society*. New York: Free Press.

Becker, G. S. 1981. *A treatise on the family*. Cambridge, MA: Harvard University Press.

Becker, P. E., & Moen, P. 1999. "Scaling back: Dual-earner couples' work–family strategies." *Journal of Marriage and the Family, 61,* 995–1007.

Beekman, D. 1977. *The mechanical baby: A popular history of the theory and practice of child raising*. Westport, CT: Lawrence Hill.

Beer, W. R. 1988. *Relative strangers: Studies of stepfamily processes*. Totowa, NJ: Rowman & Littlefield.

Begley, S. 2007. "The anatomy of violence." *Newsweek,* April 30.

Beil, L. 2007. "Abstinence education faces uncertain future." *New York Times,* July 18.

Bell, S. T., Kuriloff, P. J., & Lottes, I. 1994. "Understanding attributions of blame in stranger rape and date rape situations: An examination of gender, race, identification, and students' social perceptions of rape victims." *Journal of Applied Social Psychology, 24,* 1719–1734.

Bellah, R. N. 1995. "The quest for self." In A. Etzioni (Ed.), *Rights and the common good*. New York: St. Martin's Press.

Bellah, R. N., Madsen, R., Sullivan, W. M., Swidler, A., & Tipton, S. M. 1985. *Habits of the heart*. New York: Harper & Row.

Bell-Rowbotham, B., & Lero, D. 2001. "Responses to extension of parental leaves." Centre for Families, Work and Well-Being. www.uoguelph.ca/cfww/ response.htm. Accessed July 10, 2001.

Belluck, P. 2000a. "Parents try to reclaim their children's time." *New York Times,* June 13.

———. 2000b. "States declare war on divorce rates, before any 'I do's'." *New York Times,* April 25.

———.2002. "Doctors' new practices offer deluxe service for deluxe fee." *New York Times,* January 15.

———. 2008. "Gay couples find marriage a mixed bag." *New York Times,* June 15.

Bem, S. L. 1974. "The measurement of psychological androgyny." *Journal of Consulting and Clinical Psychology, 42,* 155–162.

Bender, D. R. 1979. "A refinement of the concept of household: Families, co-residence, and domestic functions." *American Anthropologist, 69,* 493–504.

Bengtson, V. L. 2001. "Beyond the nuclear family: The increasing importance of multigenerational bonds." *Journal of Marriage and the Family, 63,* 1–17.

Bennett, N. G., Bloom, D. E., & Craig, P. H. 1986. *Black and white marriage patterns: Why so different?* Discussion paper No. 500. New Haven, CT: Economic Growth Center, Yale University.

Berardo, F. M. 1998. "Family privacy: Issues and concepts." *Journal of Family Issues, 19,* 4–19.

Bergen, R. K. 1999. "Marital rape." Violence Against Women Online Resources. www.vaw.umn.edu/documents/vawnet/mrape/mrape.html#id75958. Accessed June 13, 2005.

Berger, L. 2000. "What children do when home and alone." *New York Times,* April 11.

Berger, P. L., & Kellner, H. 1964. "Marriage and the construction of reality: An exercise in the microsociology of knowledge." *Diogenes, 46,* 1–23.

Berkin, C. 1996. *First generations: Women in colonial America.* New York: Hill & Wang.

Bernard, J. 1981. "The good provider role: Its rise and fall." *American Psychologist, 36,* 1–12.

———. 1982. *The future of marriage.* New York: Bantam.

Berns, N. 2004. *Framing the victim: Domestic violence, media, and social problems.* Hawthorne, NY: Aldine de Gruyter.

Berscheid, E., & Peplau, L. A. 1983. "The emerging science of relationships." In H. H. Kelley, E. Berscheid, A. Christensen, J. H. Harvey, T. L. Huston, G. Levinger, E. McClintock, & D. R. Peterson (Eds.), *Close relationships: Perspectives on the meaning of intimacy.* New York: Freeman.

Berthelsen, C. 1999. "Suit says advanced-placement classes show bias." *New York Times,* July 28.

Besharov, D. J., & Laumann-Billings, L. A. 2006. "Child abuse reporting." In P. A. Adler & P. Adler (Eds.), *Constructions of deviance.* Belmont, CA: Wadsworth.

Best, J. 1993. *Threatened children.* Chicago: University of Chicago Press.

Bhattacharya, J., DeLeire, T., Haider, S., & Currie, J. 2003. "Heat or eat? Cold-weather shocks and nutrition in poor American families." *American Journal of Public Health, 93,* 1149–1154.

Bianchi, S. M. 1999. "Feminization and juvenilization of poverty: Trends, relative risks, causes, and consequences." *Annual Review of Sociology, 25,* 307–333.

———. 2000. "Maternal employment and time with children: Dramatic change or surprising continuity?" *Demography, 37,* 401–414.

Bianchi, S. M., & Casper, L. M. 2000. "American families." *Population Bulletin, 55,* 1–44.

Bianchi, S. M., Milkie, M. A., Sayer, L. C., & Robinson, J. P. 2000. "Is anyone doing the housework? Trends in the gender division of household labor." *Social Forces, 79,* 191–228.

Bianchi, S. M., Robinson, J. P., & Milkie, M. A. 2006. *Changing rhythms of American family life.* New York: Russell Sage Foundation.

Birchler, G. R., Weiss, R. L., & Vincent, J. P. 1975. "Multimethod analysis of social reinforcement exchange between maritally distressed and non-distressed spouse and stranger dyads." *Journal of Personality and Social Psychology, 31,* 349–360.

Bird, P. 2005. "Jury convicts parents in baby's death." *Indianapolis Star,* May 13.

Blackwell, J. E. 1985. *The black community: Diversity and unity.* New York: Harper & Row.

Blaisure, K. R., & Allen, K. R. 2000. "Feminism and marital equality." In N. V. Benokraitis (Ed.), *Feuds about families.* Upper Saddle River, NJ: Prentice Hall.

Blau, P. M. 1964. *Exchange and power in social life.* New York: Wiley.

Blau, P. M., & Duncan, O. D. 1967. *The American occupational structure.* New York: Wiley.

Blood, R. O., & Wolfe, D. M. 1960. *Husbands and wives.* New York: Free Press.

Bloomer, S. R., Sipe, T. A., & Ruedt, D. E. 2002. "Child support payment and child visitation: Perspectives from nonresident fathers and resident mothers." *Journal of Sociology and Social Welfare, 29,* 77–91.

Blumstein, P., & Kollock, P. 1988. "Personal relationships." *Annual Review of Sociology, 14,* 467–490.

Blumstein, P., & Schwartz, P. 1983. *American couples.* New York: Morrow.

"The body counters." 1993. *People Weekly,* April 12, 34–37.

Bollenbacher, V., & Burtt, S. 1997. "Discipline, assault, and justice: Violent parents and the law." *Law & Policy, 19,* 344–361.

Bolton, M. K. 2000. *The third shift: Managing hard choices in our careers, homes, and lives as women.* San Francisco: Jossey-Bass.

Bonney, J. F., Kelley, M. L., & Levant, R. F. 1999. "A model of fathers' behavioral involvement in child care in dual-earner families." *Journal of Family Psychology, 13,* 401–415.

Booth, A., & Amato, P. R. 2001. "Parental predivorce relations and offspring postdivorce well-being." *Journal of Marriage and the Family, 63,* 197–212.

Booth, A., & Johnson, D. 1988. "Premarital cohabitation and marital success." *Journal of Family Issues, 9,* 255–272.

Boudreau, F. A. 1993. "Elder abuse." In R. L. Hampton & T. P. Gullotta (Eds.), *Family violence: Prevention and treatment.* Newbury Park, CA: Sage.

Boulding, E. 1976. "Familial constraint on women's work roles." *Signs, 1,* 95–118.

Bound, J., Duncan, G., Laren, D., & Oleinick, L. 1991. "Poverty dynamics in widowhood." *Journal of Gerontology, 46,* 115–124.

Boushey, H. 2005. "Are women opting out? Debunking the myth." Center for Economic and Policy Research. www.cepr.net/publications/opt_out _2005_11.pdf. Accessed July 20, 2006.

Bowe, J. 2006. "Gay donor or gay dad?" *New York Times Magazine,* November 19.

Bowker, L. H. 1993. "A battered woman's problems are social, not psychological." In R. J. Gelles & D. R. Loeske (Eds.), *Current controversies on family violence.* Newbury Park, CA: Sage.

Boydston, J. 2001. "Cult of true womanhood." www .pbs.org/stantonanthony/resources/culthood.html. Accessed July 10, 2001.

Boyes, R. 2007. "'Dump your children here' box to stop mothers killing their babies." *TimesOnline.* www.timesonline.co.uk/tol/news/world/europe/ article1572569.ece. Accessed June 12, 2007.

Brabant, S., & Mooney, L. A. 1999. "The social construction of family life in the Sunday comics: Race as a consideration." *Journal of Comparative Family Studies, 30,* 113–133.

Bradbury, T. N., Fincham, F. D., & Beach, S. R. H. 2000. "Research on the nature and determinants of marital satisfaction: A decade in review." *Journal of Marriage and the Family, 62,* 964–981.

Bradley, M. 2006. "In 'family friendly' workplaces, singles feel overlooked." *Christian Science Monitor,* June 12.

Bradsher, K. 1999. "Fear of crime trumps fear of lost youth." *New York Times,* November 21.

Bramlett, M. D., & Mosher, W. D. 2002. "Cohabitation, marriage, divorce, and remarriage in the United States." National Center for Health Statistics. www .cdc.gov/nchs/data/series/sr_23/sr23_022.pdf. Accessed August 11, 2006.

"Breaking the rules of engagement." 2002. *American Demographics,* July–August.

Brehm, S. 1992. *Intimate relationships.* New York: McGraw-Hill.

Brien, M. J., Lillard, L. A., & Waite, L. J. 1999. "Interrelated family-building behaviors: Cohabitation, marriage, and nonmarital conception." *Demography, 36,* 535–551.

Brines, J. 1994. "Economic dependency, gender and the division of labor at home." *American Journal of Sociology, 100,* 652–688.

Brines, J., & Joyner, K. 1999. "The ties that bind: Principles of cohesion in cohabitation and marriage." *American Sociological Review, 64,* 333–355.

Brinig, M. F. 2000. *From contract to covenant: Beyond the law and economics of the family.* Cambridge, MA: Harvard University Press.

Broad, D. D. 1996. "The social register: Directory of America's upper class." *Sociological Spectrum, 16,* 173–181.

Brookings Institution. 2006. "From poverty, opportunity: Putting the market to work for lower income families." www.brookings.edu/metro/pubs/20060718 _PovOp.pdf. Accessed July 18, 2006.

Brooks, C. 2002. "Religious influence and the politics of family decline concern: Trends, sources, and U.S. political behavior." *American Sociological Review, 67,* 191–211.

Brooks, D. 2004. "Columbine: Parents of a killer." *New York Times,* May 15.

Broom, L., & Kitsuse, J. I. 1956. *The managed casualty.* Berkeley: University of California Press.

Brown, P. 1998. "Biology and the social construction of the 'race' concept." In J. Ferrante & P. Brown (Eds.), *The social construction of race and ethnicity in the United States.* New York: Longman.

Brown, P. L. 2000. "'Sudden wealth syndrome' brings new stress." *New York Times,* March 10.

Brown, R. 1986. *Social psychology.* New York: Free Press.

Brown, S. L., & Booth, A. 1996. "Cohabitation versus marriage: A comparison of relationship quality." *Journal of Marriage and the Family, 58,* 668–678.

Browne, A. 1993. "Family violence and homelessness: The relevance of trauma histories in the lives of homeless women." *American Journal of Orthopsychiatry, 63,* 370–384.

Browning, C. R., & Laumann, E. O. 1997. "Sexual contact between children and adults: A life course perspective." *American Sociological Review, 62,* 540–560.

Brush, L. D. 2000. "Battering, traumatic stress, and welfare-to-work transition." *Violence Against Women, 6,* 1039–1065.

Bryjak, G. J., & Soroka, M. P. 1992. *Sociology: Cultural diversity in a changing world.* Boston: Allyn & Bacon.

Buckley, T., & Gottlieb, A. 1988. "A critical appraisal of theories of menstrual symbolism." In T. Buckley & A. Gottlieb (Eds.), *Blood magic: The anthropology of menstruation.* Berkeley: University of California Press.

Budig, M. J., & England, P. 2001. "The wage penalty for motherhood." *American Sociological Review, 66,* 204–225.

Bulanda, J. R., & Brown, S. L. 2006. "Race-ethnic differences in marital quality and divorce." Working Paper Series 06–08. Center for Family and Demographic Research. www.bgsu.edu/organizations/cfdr/research/pdf/2006/2006-8.pdf. Accessed August 11, 2006.

Bumiller, E. 1992. "First comes marriage—then maybe love." In J. M. Henslin (Ed.), *Marriage and family in a changing society.* New York: Free Press.

Bumpass, L., Sweet, J. A., & Cherlin, A. 1991. "The role of cohabitation in declining rates of marriage." *Journal of Marriage and the Family, 53,* 913–927.

Burke, T. W., & Owen, S. S. 2006. "Same-sex domestic violence: Is anyone listening?" *The Gay & Lesbian Review,* January–February.

Burnham, M. 1993. "An impossible marriage: Slave law and family law." In M. Minow (Ed.), *Family matters: Readings on family lives and the law.* New York: New Press.

Buss, D. M. 1994. *The evolution of desire: Strategies of human mating.* New York: Basic Books.

Buss, D. M., Shackelford, T. K., Kirkpatrick, L. A., & Larsen, R. J. 2001. "A half century of mate preferences: The cultural evolution of values." *Journal of Marriage and the Family, 63,* 491–514.

Bussell, D. A. 1994. "Ethical issues in observational family research." *Family Process, 33,* 361–376.

Butler, A. 1996. "The effect of welfare benefit levels on poverty among single-parent families." *Social Problems, 43,* 94–115.

Cadge, W., & Ecklund, E. H. 2007. "Immigration and religion." *Annual Review of Sociology, 33,* 17.1–17.21.

Cahill, H. A. 2001. "Male appropriation and medicalization of childbirth: An historical analysis." *Journal of Advanced Nursing, 33,* 334–342.

Caldwell, C. 2006. "A family or a crowd?" *New York Times Magazine,* February 26.

Call, V. R. A., & Heaton, T. B. 1997. "Religious influence on marital stability." *Journal for the Scientific Study of Religion, 36,* 382–392.

Call, V., Sprecher, S., & Schwartz, P. 1995. "The incidence and frequency of marital sex in a national sample." *Journal of Marriage and the Family, 57,* 639–652.

Campbell, R., & Wasco, S. M. 2005. "Understanding rape and sexual assault: 20 years of progress and future directions." *Interpersonal Violence, 20,* 127–131.

Cancian, F. 1987. *Love in America.* Cambridge, MA: Cambridge University Press.

———. 1993. "Gender politics: Love and power in the private and public spheres." In B. J. Fox (Ed.), *Family patterns: Gender relations.* Toronto: Oxford University Press.

Cancian, F., & Gordon, S. C. 1988. "Changing emotion norms in marriage: Love and anger in U.S. women's magazines since 1900." *Gender and Society, 2,* 308–342.

Cancian, F., & Oliker, S. J. 2000. *Caring and gender.* Thousand Oaks, CA: Pine Forge Press.

Cancian, M., & Meyer, D. R. 2000. "Work after welfare: Women's work effort, occupation, and economic well-being." *Social Work Research, 24,* 69–86.

"Can't sue negligent officials in abuse cases, court rules." 1989. *Los Angeles Times,* February 22.

Cantor, M. G. 1991. "The American family on television: From Molly Goldberg to Bill Cosby." *Journal of Comparative Family Studies, 22,* 205–216.

Capps, D. 1992. "Religion and child abuse: Perfect together." *Journal for the Scientific Study of Religion, 31,* 1–14.

Carbone, J. 2000. *From partners to parents: The second revolution in family law.* New York: Columbia University Press.

Carey, B. 2007a. "Can Johnny come out and (be taught to) play?" *New York Times,* January 14.

———. 2007b. "Poor behavior is linked to time in day care." *New York Times,* March 26.

Carli, L. L. 1997. "Biology does not create gender differences in personality." In M. R. Walsh (Ed.), *Women, men and gender: Ongoing debates.* New Haven: Yale University Press.

Carr, B. J. 1988. *Crisis in intimacy.* Pacific Grove, CA: Brooks/Cole.

Carrington, C. 1999. *No place like home: Relationships and family life among lesbians and gay men.* Chicago: University of Chicago Press.

"The case for staying home." 2004. *Time,* March 22.

Casper, L. M., & Bianchi, S. M. 2007. "Grandparenting." In S. J. Ferguson (Ed.), *Shifting the center.* New York: McGraw-Hill.

Caspi, A., Wright, B. R. E., Moffitt, T. E., & Silva, P. A. 1998. "Early failure in the labor market: Childhood and adolescent predictors of unemployment in the transition to adulthood." *American Sociology Review, 63,* 424–451

Cassidy, T. 2006. "Birth, controlled." *New York Times Magazine,* March 26.

Cast, A. D., Schweinbruber, D., & Berns, N. 2006. "Childhood physical punishment and problem solving in marriage." *Journal of Interpersonal Violence, 21,* 244–261.

Catalano, S. 2006. "Intimate partner violence in the United States." Bureau of Justice Statistics. www.ujp/usdoj.gov/bjs/pub/pdf/ipvus.pdf. Accessed April 28, 2007.

Cate, R. M., & Lloyd, S. A. 1992. *Courtship.* Newbury Park, CA: Sage.

Cazenave, N. A. 1984. "Race, socioeconomic status, and age: The social context of American masculinity." *Sex Roles, 11,* 639–656.

Cazenave, N. A., & Straus, M. A. 1990. "Race, class, network embeddedness, and family violence: A search for potent support systems." In M. A. Straus & R. J. Gelles (Eds.), *Physical violence in American families.* New Brunswick, NJ: Transaction.

Center for Law and Social Policy. 2006. "Couples and marriage policy." www.clasp.org/publications.pfp?id=6&type=1#0. Accessed May 30, 2006.

Center on Budget and Policy Priorities. 1999. "Average incomes of very poor families fell during early years of welfare reform, study finds." www.cbpp.org/8-22-99wel.htm. Accessed June 23, 2000.

Centers for Disease Control and Prevention. 2005a. "Assisted reproductive technology success rate: National summary and fertility clinic reports." www.cdc.gov/ART/ART2003/PDF/ART2003.pdf. Accessed July 24, 2006.

———. 2005b. "Births, marriages, divorces, and deaths: Provisional data for 2004." National Vital Statistics Report. www.cdc.gov/nchs/data/nvsr/nvsr53/nvsr53-21.pdf. Accessed August 11, 2006.

———. 2006a. "Dating abuse fact sheet. National Center for Injury Prevention and Control. www.cdc.gov/ncipc/dvp/DatingViolence.htm. Accessed June 1, 2006.

———. 2006b. "Intimate partner violence: Fact sheet." www.cdc.gov/ncipc/factsheets/ipvfacts.htm. Accessed August 4, 2006.

———. 2006c. "Tracking Fetal Alcohol Syndrome." www.cdc.gov/ncbddd/fas/fassurv.htm. Accessed July 26, 2006.

———. 2006d. "Trends in the prevalence of sexual behaviors." National Youth Risk Behavior Survey: 1991–2005. www.cdc.gov/healthyyouth/yrbs/pdf/trends/2005_YRBS_Sexual_Behaviors.pdf. Accessed July 7, 2006.

Chafetz, J. S. 1978. *A primer on the construction and testing of theories in sociology.* Itasca, IL: Peacock.

Chafetz, J. S., & Dworkin, A. G. 1987. "In the face of threat: Organized anti-feminism in comparative perspective." *Gender and Society, 1,* 33–60.

Chandra, A., Martinez, G. M., Mosher, W. D., Abma, J. C., & Jones, J. 2005. "Fertility, family planning, and reproductive health of U.S. women: Data from the 2002 National Survey of Family Growth." National Center for Health Statistics. www.cdc.gov/nchs/data/series/sr_23/sr23_025.pdf. Accessed July 23, 2006.

Chang, T. 2006. "S. Korea to spend 32 trillion won to boost birthrate, tackle aging problem." *Yonhap News Agency,* June 7.

Chatters, L. M., Taylor, R. J., & Jayakody, R. 1994. "Fictive kinship relations in black extended families." *Journal of Comparative Family Studies, 25,* 297–313.

Chauncey, G. 2007. "Why do gays want to marry?" In A. S. Skolnick & J. H. Skolnick (Eds.), *Family in transition.* Boston: Allyn & Bacon.

Cheever, S. 2006. "Baby battle." In L. M. Steiner (Ed.), *Mommy wars.* New York: Random House.

Cherlin, A. J. 1978. "Remarriage as an incomplete institution." *American Journal of Sociology, 84,* 634–650.

———. 1990. "The strange career of the 'Harvard–Yale study.'" *Public Opinion Quarterly, 54,* 117–124.

———. 1992. *Marriage, divorce, remarriage.* Cambridge, MA: Harvard University Press.

———. 1999. *Public and private families.* Boston: McGraw-Hill.

———. 2007. "The deinstitutionalization of American marriage." In S. J. Ferguson (Ed.), *Shifting the center: Understanding contemporary families.* New York: McGraw-Hill.

Cherlin, A. J., Chase-Landale, P. L., & McRae, C. 1998. "Effects of parental divorce on mental health throughout the life course." *American Sociological Review, 63,* 239–249.

Cherlin, A. J., & Furstenberg, F. F. 1987. *The new American grandparent: A place in the family, a life apart.* New York: Basic Books.

———. 1994. "Stepfamilies in the United States: A reconsideration." *Annual Review of Sociology, 20,* 359–381.

———. 1997. "The future of grandparenthood." In M. Hutter (Ed.), *The family experience.* Boston: Allyn & Bacon.

Cherlin, A. J., Furstenberg, F. F., Chase-Landale, P. L., Kiernan, K. E., Robins, P. K., Morrison, D. R., & Teitler, J. O. 1991. "Longitudinal studies of effects of divorce on children in Great Britain and the United States." *Science, 252,* 1386–1389.

CHILD, Inc. 2006. "Religious exemptions from health care for children." www.childrenshealthcare.org. Accessed June 15, 2006.

"Child abuse cases surge in Japan." 2001. *Associated Press Online,* June 21.

Child Welfare League of America. 2006. "Child abuse and neglect." National Data Analysis System Issue Brief. http://hdas.cwla.org/include/PDF/ChildAbuseNeglect_Final_IB.PDF. Accessed August 7, 2006.

Childbirth Connection. 2006. "Technology-intensive childbirth is the norm for great majority of primarily healthy women." *Listening to Mothers II National Survey.* http://childbirthconnection.org/pdf.asp?PDFDownload=LTMII_pressrelease. Accessed February 22, 2007.

Children's Rights Council. 2004. "Child custody statistics 2004." www.gocrc.com/research/custody-stats.html. Accessed August 17, 2006.

———. 2005. "Joint custody and shared parenting statutes." www.gocrc.com/research/legislation.html. Accessed August 17, 2006.

Childress, S. 2006. "My mother the narc." *Newsweek,* April 10.

Ching C. L., & Burke, S. 1999. "An assessment of college students' attitudes and empathy toward rape." *College Student Journal, 33,* 573–584.

Chira, S. 1995. "Struggling to find stability when divorce is a pattern." *New York Times,* March 19.

Chong, E., & Haberland, N. 2005. "Child marriage: A cause for global action." *Transitions to Adulthood Brief #14.* Population Council. www.popcouncil.org/pdfs/TABriefs/GFD_Brief-14_GLOBALACTION.pdf. Accessed December 20, 2006.

Christensen, B. J. 1990. *Utopia against the family.* San Francisco: Ignatius Press.

Ciancanelli, P., & Berch, B. 1987. "Gender and the GNP." In B. B. Hess & M. M. Ferree (Eds.), *Analyzing gender: A handbook of social science research.* Newbury Park, CA: Sage.

Clarity, J. F. 1995. "Irish voting in close race on divorce." *New York Times,* November 25.

Clark, C. S. 1996. "Marriage and divorce." *CQ Researcher,* May 10.

Clark, G. 1994. *Onions are my husband: Survival and accumulation by West African market women.* Chicago: University of Chicago Press.

Clark, M. S., & Mills, J. 1979. "Interpersonal attraction in exchange and communal relationships." *Journal of Personal and Social Psychology, 37,* 12–24.

Clarkberg, M., & Moen, P. 2001. "Understanding the time-squeeze: Married couples' preferred and actual work-hour strategies." *American Behavioral Scientist, 44,* 1115–1136.

Clawson, D., & Gertsel, N. 2007. "Caring for our young: Child care in Europe and the United States." In A. S. Skolnick & J. H. Skolnick (Eds.), *Family in transition.* Boston: Allyn & Bacon.

DeMaris, A., & Longmore, M. A. 1996. "Ideology, power and equity: Testing competing explanations for the perception of fairness in household labor." *Social Forces, 74,* 1043–1071.

deMause, L. 1975. "Our forebears made childhood a nightmare." *Psychology Today, 8,* 85–88.

D'Emilio, J., & Freedman, E. B. 1988. *Intimate matters: A history of sexuality in America.* New York: Harper & Row.

Demos, J. 1986. *Past, present and personal: The family and life course in American history.* New York: Oxford University Press.

DeNavas-Walt, C., Proctor, B. D., & Smith, J. 2007. "Income, poverty, and health insurance coverage in the United States: 2006." U.S. Census Bureau, *Current Population Reports,* P60–233. www.census .gov/prod/2007pubs/p60-233.pdf. Accessed August 27, 2007.

Denno, D. W. 2003. "Why the Model Penal Code's sexual offense provisions should be pulled and replaced." *Ohio State Journal of Criminal Law, 1,* 207–218.

Denzin, N. 1989. *The research act: A theoretical introduction to sociological methods.* Englewood Cliffs, NJ: Prentice Hall.

DeParle, J. 1996. "Slamming the door." *New York Times Magazine,* October 20.

———. 1997. "Learning poverty first hand." *New York Times Magazine,* April 27.

———. 1999. "Bold effort leaves much unchanged for the poor." *New York Times,* December 30.

DePaulo, B. 2006. *Singled out: How singles are stereotyped, stigmatized, and ignored, and still live happily ever after.* New York: St. Martin's.

Derlega, V. J., Harris, M. S., & Chaikin, A. L. 1973. "Self-disclosure reciprocity, liking and the deviant." *Journal of Experimental Social Psychology, 9,* 277–284.

Deutsch, F. M. 1999. *Halving it all: How equally shared parenting works.* Cambridge, MA: Harvard University Press.

DeVoe, J. F., Peter, K., Kaufman, P., Miller, A., Noonan, M., Snyder, T. D., & Baum, K. 2004. "Indicators of school crime and safety: 2004." www.ojp.usdoj.gov/ bjs/pub/pdf/iscs04ex.pdf. Accessed June 21, 2005.

Dey, J. G., & Hill, C. 2007. "Behind the pay gap." American Association of University Women Educational Fund. www.aauw.org. Accessed April 22, 2007.

Diekmann, A., & Engelhardt, H. 1999. "The social inheritence [sic] of divorce: Effects of parent's family type in postwar Germany." *American Sociological Review, 64,* 783–793.

Dill, B. T. 1995. "Our mothers' grief: Racial ethnic women and the maintenance of families." In M. L. Anderson & P. H. Collins (Eds.), *Race, class, and gender: An anthology.* Belmont, CA: Wadsworth.

Dill, B. T., Baca Zinn, M., & Patton, S. 1994. "Feminism, race and the politics of family values." *Report from the Institute for Philosophy and Public Policy, 13,* 13–18.

Dion, K. K., & Dion, K. L. 1996. "Cultural perspectives on romantic love." *Personal Relationships, 3,* 5–17.

Domhoff, G. W. 1998. *Who rules America? Power and politics in the year 2000.* Mountain View, CA: Mayfield.

Douglas, W. 2003. *Television families: Is something wrong in suburbia?* Mahwah, NJ: Lawrence Erlbaum.

Douglas, W., & Olsen, B. M. 1996. "Subversion of the American family? An examination of children and parents in television families." *Communication Research, 23,* 73–99.

Downs, D. A. 1996. *More than victims: Battered women, the syndrome society, and the law.* Chicago: University of Chicago Press.

Draut, T., & Silva, J. 2004. "Generation broke: The growth of debt among young Americans." *Demos.* www.demos-usa.org/pubs/Generation_Broke.pdf. Accessed July 31, 2006.

Dugger, C. W. 1996. "Immigrant cultures raising issues of child punishment." *New York Times,* February 29.

———. 2004. "Devastated by AIDS, Africa sees life expectancy plunge." *New York Times,* July 16.

Dujon, D., Gradford, J., & Stevens, D. 1995. "Reports from the front: Welfare mothers up in arms." In M. L. Anderson & P. H. Collins (Eds.), *Race, class, and gender: An anthology.* Belmont, CA: Wadsworth.

Dunbar, N. E., & Burgoon, J. K. 2005. "Perceptions of power and interactional dominance in interpersonal relationships." *Journal of Social and Personal Relationships, 22,* 207–233.

Duncan, G. J., & Chase-Landale, P. L. 2001. "For better and for worse: Welfare reform and the well-being of children and families." In G. J. Duncan & P. L. Chase-Landale (Eds.), *For better and for worse.* New York: Russell Sage Foundation.

Duncan, G. J., Yeung, W. J., Brooks-Gunn, J., & Smith, J. R. 1998. "How much does childhood poverty affect the life chances of children?" *American Sociological Review, 63,* 406–423.

Durkheim, E. 1951. *Suicide.* New York: Free Press. (Original work published 1897)

————. 1965. *The elementary forms of the religious life.* Trans. by J. W. Swain. New York: Free Press. (Original work published 1915)

Durrant, J. E. 2003. "Legal reform and attitudes toward physical punishment in Sweden." *The International Journal of Children's Rights, 11,* 147–173.

Dye, J. L. 2005. "Fertility of American women: June 2004." *Current Population Reports.* P20–555. Washington, DC: U.S. Bureau of the Census.

Economic Policy Institute. 2006. *The state of working America, 2006–2007.* www.stateofworkingamerica .org. Accessed December 24, 2006.

Economic Roundtable. 2000. "The cage of poverty." www.economicrt.org/publications.html#recent. Accessed July 28, 2001.

————. 2003. "Prisoners of hope: Welfare to work." www.economicrt.org/download/prisoners_of_hope .html. Accessed June 29, 2006.

————. 2005. "Hopeful workers, marginal jobs: LA's off-the-books labor force." www.economicrt.org/ summaries/hopeful_workers_marginal_jobs _synopsis.html. Accessed June 29, 2006.

Edin, K., & Jencks, C. 1992. "Reforming welfare." In C. Jencks (Ed.), *Rethinking social policy: Race, poverty and the underclass.* Cambridge, MA: Harvard University Press.

Edin, K., & Kefalas, M. 2005. *Promises I can keep: Why poor women put motherhood before marriage.* Berkeley: University of California Press.

Edin, K., & Lein, L. 1997. "Work, welfare, and single mothers' economic strategies." *American Sociological Review, 62,* 253–266.

Edwards, T. M. 2001. "How med students put abortion back in the classroom." *Time,* May 7.

Eggebeen, D. J., & Hogan, D. P. 1990. "Giving between generations in American families." *Human Nature, 1,* 211–232.

Eggen, D. 2007. "Violent crime up for second year." *Washington Post,* June 2.

Ehrenreich, B. 1983. *The hearts of men: American dreams and the flight from commitment.* New York: Anchor.

————. 1994. "Oh, those family values." *Time,* July 8.

Ehrenreich, B., & English, D. 1979. *For her own good: 150 years of experts' advice to women.* Garden City, NY: Anchor.

Elder, G. H., Jr. 1998. "The life course and human development." In W. Damon & R. M. Lerner (Eds.), *Handbook of child psychology: Theoretical models of human development* (Vol. 1). New York: Wiley.

Elder, G. H., Jr., & Eccles, J. S. 1995. "Inner-city parents under economic pressure: Perspectives on the strategies of parenting." *Journal of Marriage and the Family, 57,* 771–784.

Eldridge, R. I., & Sutton, P. D. 2007. "Births, marriages, divorces, and deaths: Provisional data for October 2006." *National Vital Statistics Reports, 55,* 1–6. May, 2007. Hyattsville, MD: National Center for Health Statistics.

Elkind, D. 1994. *Ties that stress: The new family imbalance.* Cambridge, MA: Harvard University Press.

Elliot, P. 1996. "Shattering illusions: Same-sex domestic violence." *Journal of Gay and Lesbian Social Services, 4,* 1–8.

Emerson, R. 1962. "Power-dependence relations." *American Sociological Review, 27,* 31–41.

Engels, F. 1972. *The origin of the family, private property and the state.* New York: International Publishers. (Originally published 1884)

England, P., & Thomas, R. J. 2007. "The decline of the date and the rise of the college hook-up." In A. S. Skolnick & J. H. Skolnick (Eds.), *Family in transition.* Boston: Allyn & Bacon.

Espiritu, Y. L. 2004. "Asian American panethnicity: Bridging institutions and identities." In C. A. Gallagher (Ed.), *Rethinking the color line: Readings in race and ethnicity.* New York: McGraw-Hill.

Estioko-Griffin, A., & Griffin, P. B. 1997. "Woman the hunter: The Agta." In C. B. Brettell & C. F. Sargent (Eds.), *Gender in cross-cultural perspective.* Upper Saddle River, NJ: Prentice Hall.

Ettelbrick, P. L. 1992. "Since when is marriage a path to liberation?" In S. Sherman (Ed.), *Lesbian and gay marriage.* Philadelphia: Temple University Press.

Etzioni, A. 1993. "How to make marriage matter." *Time,* September 6.

Evan B. Donaldson Adoption Institute. 2002. "National Adoption Attitudes Survey." www.adoptioninstitute .org/Survey/Adoption_Exec_Summary.pdf. Accessed July 24, 2006.

S. E. Tolnay (Eds.), *The changing American family: Sociological and demographic perspectives.* Boulder, CO: Westview Press.

Furstenberg, F., & Nord, C. 1985. "Parenting apart: Patterns of childrearing after marital disruption." *Journal of Marriage and the Family, 47,* 893–904.

Fuscaldo, G. 2005. "Spare embryos: 3000 reasons to rethink the significance of genetic relatedness." *Reproductive Biomedicine Online, 10,* 164–168. www.rbmonline.com/Article/1550. Accessed December 21, 2005.

Fyfe, J. J., Klinger, D. A., & Flavin, J. M. 1997. "Differential police treatment of male-on-female spousal violence." *Criminology, 35,* 455–473.

Gabriel, T. 1996. "High-tech pregnancies test hope's limit." *New York Times,* January 7.

Galambos, N. L., & Maggs, J. L. 1991. "Children in self-care: Figures, facts and fictions." In J. V. Lerner & N. L. Galambos (Eds.), *Employed mothers and their children.* New York: Garland.

Galliher, J. F., Brekhus, W. H., & Keys, D. P. 2004. *Laud Humphreys: Prophet of homosexuality and sociology.* Madison: University of Wisconsin Press.

Galston, W. A. 1995a. "A liberal-democratic case for the two-parent family." In A. Etzioni (Ed.), *Rights and the common good.* New York: St. Martin's Press.

———. 1995b. "Needed: A not-so-fast divorce law." *New York Times,* December 27.

Gangestad, S. W. 1993. "Sexual selection and physical attractiveness: Implications of mating dynamics." *Human Nature, 4,* 205–236.

Ganong, L. H., & Coleman, M. 1994. *Remarried family relationships.* Thousand Oaks, CA: Sage.

Gans, H. J. 1995. *The war against the poor.* New York: Basic Books.

Garcia-Moreno, C., Jansen, H., Ellsberg, M., Heise, L., & Watts, C. H. 2006. "Prevalence of intimate partner violence: Findings from the WHO multi-country study on women's health and domestic violence." *The Lancet, 368,* 1260–1269.

Garfinkel, J. 2003. "Boutique medical practices face legal, legislative foes." *Cincinnati Business Courier.* www.bizjournals.com/cincinnati/stories/2003/ 02/24/focus2.html. February 24. Accessed July 12, 2004.

Gelles, R. J. 1995. *Contemporary families: A sociological view.* Thousand Oaks, CA: Sage.

Gelles, R. J., & Straus, M. A. 1988. *Intimate violence.* New York: Touchstone.

"Gender neutral name game." 2007. *Utne Reader,* September–October.

Gerencher, K. 2001. "The economic value of housework: New survey to track women-dominated labor." Center for Partnership Studies. www.partnershipway .org/html/subpages/articles/valueofhousework.htm. Accessed July 20, 2006.

Gerson, K. 1985. *Hard choices: How women decide about work, career and motherhood.* Berkeley: University of California Press.

———. 1993. *No man's land: Men's changing commitments to family and work.* New York: Basic Books.

———. 1998. "Dismantling the 'gendered family': Breadwinning, gender, and the family values debate." *Contemporary Sociology, 27,* 228–230.

———. 2000. "Resolving family dilemmas and conflicts: Beyond utopia." *Contemporary Society, 29,* 180–187.

———. 2002. "Moral dilemmas, moral strategies, and the transformation of gender." *Gender & Society, 16,* 8–28.

Gerson, K., & Jacobs, J. A. 2007. "The work-home crunch." In S. J. Ferguson (Ed.), *Shifting the center.* New York: McGraw-Hill.

Gertsel, N. 1987. "Divorce and stigma." *Social Problems, 34,* 172–186.

Gettelman, E. 2005. "A new order in the court." *Mother Jones,* July–August.

Gibbs, N. R. 1993. "Bringing up father." *Time,* June 28.

Gibbs, N. R., & Roche, T. 1999. "The Columbine tapes." *Time,* December 20.

Giddens, A. 2007. "The global revolution in family and personal life." In A. S. Skolnick & J. H. Skolnick (Eds.), *Family in transition.* Boston: Allyn & Bacon.

Gies, F., & Gies, J. 1989. *Marriage and the family in the middle ages.* New York: Harper & Row.

Gillespie, C. K. 1989. *Justifiable homicide.* Columbus: Ohio State University Press.

Gillham, B., Tanner, G., Cheyne, B., Freeman, I., Rooney, M., & Lambie, A. 1997. "Unemployment rates, single parent density, and indices of child poverty: Their relationship to different categories of child abuse and neglect." *Child Abuse and Neglect, 22,* 79–90.

Gilliam, W. S. 2005. "Prekindergarteners left behind: Expulsion rates in state prekindergarten systems." Foundation for Child Development. www.fcd-us.org/PDFs/NationalPreKExpulsionPaper03.02 _new.pdf. Accessed May 17, 2005.

Gillis, J. R. 1996. *A world of their own making: Myth, ritual and the quest for family values.* New York: Basic Books.

Gilliom, J. 2001. *Overseers of the poor: Surveillance, resistance, and the limits of privacy.* Chicago: University of Chicago Press.

Ginther, D. K., & Zavodny, M. 2001. "Is the male marriage premium due to selection? The effect of shotgun weddings on the return to marriage." *Journal of Population Economics, 14,* 313–328.

Giroux, H. A. 1998. "Nymphet fantasies: Child beauty pageants and the politics of innocence." *Social Text, 16,* 31–53.

Gittins, D. 2001. "The family question." In S. Ferguson (Ed.), *Shifting the center.* Mountain View, CA: Mayfield.

Glass, J. 2000. "Envisioning the integration of family and work: Toward a kinder, gentler workplace." *Contemporary Society, 29,* 129–143.

Glass, J., & Fujimoto, T. 1994. "Housework, paid work, and depression among husbands and wives." *Journal of Health and Social Behavior, 35,* 179–191.

Glazer, S. 2003. "Mothers' movement." *CQ Researcher, 13,* 297–320.

———. 2006. "Future of feminism." *CQ Researcher, 16,* 313–336.

Glenn, N. 2000. "Who's who in the family wars: A characterization of the major ideological factions." In N. V. Benokraitis (Ed.), *Feuds about families.* Upper Saddle River, NJ: Prentice Hall.

Glenn, N. D., & Supancic, M. 1984. "The social and demographic correlates of divorce and separation in the United States: An update and reconsideration." *Journal of Marriage and the Family, 46,* 563–575.

Glenn, N. D., & Sylvester, T. 2006. "The denial: Downplaying the consequences of family structure for children." Institute for American Values. www .familyscholarslibrary.org/assets/pdf/thedenial.pdf. Accessed May 31, 2006.

Glenn, N. D., & Yap, S. G. H. 1994. "Chinese American families." In R. L. Taylor (Ed.), *Minority families in the United States.* Englewood Cliffs, NJ: Prentice Hall.

Goffman, E. 1959. *Presentation of self in everyday life.* Garden City, NY: Doubleday.

Gold, S. N., & Heffner, C. L. 1998. "Sexual addiction: Many conceptions, minimal data." *Clinical Psychology Review, 18,* 367–381.

Goldberg, C. 1999. "Spouse abuse crackdown, surprisingly, nets many women." *New York Times,* November 23.

———. 2000. "Massachusetts is set apart in ratio of older mothers." *New York Times,* June 21.

Golden, L. 1998. "Working time and the impact of policy institutions: Reforming the overtime hours law and regulation." *Review of Social Economy, 56,* 522–541.

———. 2001. "Flexible work schedules: Which workers get them?" *American Behavioral Scientist, 44,* 1157–1178.

Goldscheider, F. K., & Waite, L. J. 1991. *New families, no families?* Berkeley: University of California Press.

Goldstein, J. 1999. "Kinship networks that cross racial lines: The exception or the rule?" *Demography, 36,* 399–407.

Goode, W. J. 1971. "Force and violence in the family." *Journal of Marriage and the Family, 33,* 624–636.

———. 1981. "Why men resist." In B. Thorne & M. Yalom (Eds.), *Rethinking the family: Some feminist questions.* New York: Longman.

———. 1993. *World changes in divorce patterns.* New Haven, CT: Yale University Press.

Goodstein, L. 2003. "Survey finds slight rise in Jews' intermarrying." *New York Times,* September 11.

Goodstein, L., & Connelly, M. 1998. "Teen-age poll finds support for tradition." *New York Times,* April 30.

Gootman, E. 2006. "Those preschoolers are looking older." *New York Times,* October 19.

Gordon, L. 1997. "Killing in self-defense." *The Nation,* March 24, 25–28.

Gordon, M. 1964. *Assimilation in American life.* New York: Oxford University Press.

Gordon, M. 1981. "Was Waller ever right? The rating and dating complex reconsidered." *Journal of Marriage and the Family, 43,* 67–76.

Gove, W. R. 1980. "Mental illness and psychiatric treatment among women." *Psychology of Women Quarterly, 4,* 345–362.

Gove, W. R., Style, C. B., & Hughes, M. 1990. "The effect of marriage on the well-being of adults: A theoretical analysis." *Journal of Family Issues, 11,* 4–35.

Graefe, D. R., & Lichter, D. T. 1999. "Life course transitions of American children: Parental cohabitation, marriage, and single motherhood." *Demography, 36,* 205–217.

Hawkins, D. N., & Booth, A. 2005. "Unhappily ever after: Effects of long-term, low-quality marriages on well-being." *Social Forces, 84,* 445–465.

Hays, C. L. 1995. "Increasing shift work challenges child care." *New York Times,* June 8.

Hays, S. 1996. *The cultural contradictions of motherhood.* New Haven, CT: Yale University Press.

———. 2003. *Flat broke with children.* New York: Oxford University Press.

"Healthier hearts through marriage." 2006. *The Advocate,* March 28.

Healy, P. O. 2005. "Drinking tests becoming part of school day." *New York Times,* March 3.

Heaton, T. B., Jacobson, C. K., & Fu, X. N. 1992. "Religiosity of married couples and childlessness." *Review of Religious Research, 33,* 244–255.

Heaton, T., Jacobson, C. K., & Holland, K. 1999. "Persistence and change in decisions to remain childless." *Journal of Marriage and the Family, 61,* 531–539.

Hegtvedt, K. A., Clay-Warner, J., & Ferrigno, E. D. 2002. "Reactions to injustice: Factors affecting workers' resentment toward family-friendly policies." *Social Psychology Quarterly, 65,* 386–400.

Heintz, A. J., & Melendez, R. M. 2006. "Intimate partner violence and HIV/STD risk among lesbian, gay, bisexual, and transgender individuals." *Journal of Interpersonal Violence, 21,* 193–208.

Hendrick, S. S. 1981. "Self-disclosure and marital satisfaction." *Journal of Personality and Social Psychology, 40,* 1150–1159.

Hendrick, S. S., & Hendrick, C. 1992a. *Liking, loving, and relating.* Monterey, CA: Brooks/Cole.

———. 1992b. *Romantic love.* Newbury Park, CA: Sage.

Herbert, B. 2005. "A new civil rights movement." *New York Times,* December 26.

Hertz, R. 1986. *More equal than others: Women and men in dual-career marriages.* Berkeley: University of California Press.

———. 1999. "Working to place family at the center of life: Dual-earner and single-parent strategies." *Annals of the American Academy of Political and Social Science, 562,* 16–31.

Hetherington, E. M. 2002. "Marriage and divorce American style." *American Prospect.* April 8.

Hetherington, E. M., & Kelly, J. 2003. *For better or worse: Divorce reconsidered.* New York: Norton.

Hewlett, S. A., & Luce, C. B. 2005. "Off-ramps and on-ramps: Keeping talented women on the road to success." *Harvard Business Review,* March, 1–10.

Heymann, J., Earle, A., Simmons, S., Breslow, S. M., & Kuehnhoff, A. 2004. "The work, family, and equity index: Where does the United States stand globally?" The Project on Global Working Families. www.hsph.harvard.edu/globalworkingfamilies/images/report.pdf. Accessed April 4, 2007.

Hibbler, D. K., & Shinew, K. J. 2005. "The social life of interracial couples." In R. H. Lauer & J. C. Lauer (Eds.), *Sociology: Windows on society.* Los Angeles: Roxbury.

Hill, N. E. 1997. "Does parenting differ based on social class? African American women's perceived socialization for achievement." *American Journal of Community Psychology, 25,* 67–97.

Hill, S. A. 2005. *Black intimacies: A gender perspective on families and relationships.* Walnut Creek, CA: Altamira.

Hill, S. A., & Sprague, J. 1999. "Parenting in black and white families: The interaction of gender with race and class." *Gender & Society, 13,* 480–502.

Hines, P. M., Garcia-Preto, N., McGoldrick, M., Almeida, R., & Weltman, S. 1997. "Intergenerational relationships across cultures." In A. S. Skolnick & J. H. Skolnick (Eds.), *Family in transition* (9th ed.). New York: Longman.

Hirshman, L. R. 2006. *Get to work.* New York: Viking.

Hitchcock, J. T., & Minturn, L. 1963. "The Rajputs of Khalapur." In B. Witing (Ed.), *Six cultures: Studying child rearing.* New York: Wiley.

Hobart, C. 1991. "Conflict in remarriages." *Journal of Divorce and Remarriage, 15,* 69–86.

Hochman, N. K. S. 1997. "Fathers play larger roles in custody." *New York Times,* April 20.

Hochschild, A. R. 1997. *The time bind: When work becomes home and home becomes work.* New York: Metropolitan Books.

Hochschild, A. R., & Machung, A. 1989. *The second shift: Working parents and the revolution at home.* New York: Viking.

Hofstede, G. 1984. *Culture's consequences: International differences in work-related values.* Beverly Hills, CA: Sage.

Holl, J. L., Slack, K. S., & Stevens, A. B. 2005. "Welfare reform and health insurance: Consequences for parents." *American Journal of Public Health, 95,* 279–285.

Hollway, W. 1993. "Heterosexual sex: Power and desire for the other." In B. J. Fox (Ed.), *Family patterns, gender relations.* Toronto: Oxford University Press.

Holmes, S. A. 1996. "Quality of life is up for many blacks." *New York Times,* November 18.

———. 2000. "New policy on census says those listed as white and minority will be counted as minority." *New York Times,* March 11.

Holter, H. 1970. *Sex roles and social structure.* Oslo: Universitetsforlaget.

Holtzworth-Munroe, A., & Jacobson, N. S. 1985. "Causal attributions of married couples: When do they search for causes? What do they conclude when they do?" *Journal of Personality and Social Psychology, 48,* 1398–1412.

Holzer, H. J., Schanzenbach, D. W., Duncan, G. J., & Ludwig, J. 2007. "The economic costs of poverty in the United States: Subsequent effects of children growing up poor." Center for American Progress. www.americanprogress.org/issues/2007/01/poverty_report.html. Accessed February 5, 2007.

Homans, G. 1961. *Social behavior: Its elementary forms.* New York: Harcourt Brace Jovanovich.

"Home sweet home." 1995. *The Economist,* September, 25–33.

Homola, V. 2006. "Germany: Turkish man sentenced in 'honor killing' of sister." *New York Times,* April 14.

Hopper, J. 1993. "The rhetoric of motives in divorce." *Journal of Marriage and the Family, 55,* 801–813.

Horowitz, R. 1997. "The expanded family and family honor." In M. Hutter (Ed.), *The family experience: A reader in cultural diversity.* Boston: Allyn & Bacon.

Horton, R. 1995. "Is homosexuality inherited?" *New York Review of Books,* July 13, 36–41.

Horwitz, A. V. 1994. "Predictors of adult sibling social support for the seriously mentally ill: An exploratory study." *Journal of Family Issues, 15,* 272–289.

Horwitz, A. V., McLaughlin, J., & White, H. R. 1997. "How the negative and positive aspects of partner relationships affect the mental health of young married people." *Journal of Health and Social Behavior, 39,* 124–136.

Houseknecht, S., & Sastry, J. 1996. "Family decline and child well-being: A comparative assessment." *Journal of Marriage and the Family, 58,* 726–739.

Howard, J. A., & Hollander, J. 1997. *Gendered situations, gendered selves.* Newbury Park, CA: Sage.

Howell-White, S. 1999. *Birth alternatives: How women select childbirth care.* Westport, CT: Greenwood Press.

Huber, E., & Stephens, J. D. 2000. "Partisan governance, women's employment, and the social democratic service state." *American Sociological Review, 65,* 323–342.

Hughes, D., & Chen, L. 1997. "When and what parents tell children about race: An examination of race-related socialization among African American families." *Applied Developmental Science, 1,* 200–214.

Human Development Report. 1995. "The revolution of gender equality." United Nations Development Programme. www.undp.org/dhro/e95over.htm. Accessed January 5, 2001.

Humphreys, L. 1970. *The tearoom trade.* Chicago: Aldine.

Hunt, J. G., & Hunt, L. L. 1990. "The dualities of careers and families: New integrations or new polarizations?" In C. Carlson (Ed.), *Perspectives on the family: History, class and feminism.* Belmont, CA: Wadsworth.

Hunter, A. G. 1997. "Counting on grandmothers: Black mothers' and fathers' reliance on grandmothers for parenting support." *Journal of Family Issues, 18,* 251–269.

Hunter, J. 1991. *Culture wars: The struggle to define America.* New York: Basic Books.

Hurst, M. D. 2005. "Dating abuse." *Education Week,* June 22.

Hurtado, A. 1995. "Variations, combinations, and evolutions: Latino families in the United States." In R. E. Zambrana (Ed.), *Understanding Latino families.* Thousand Oaks, CA: Sage.

Huss, M. T., Tomkins, A. J., Garbin, C. P., Schopp, R. F., & Kilian, A. 2006. "Battered women who kill their abusers: An examination of commonsense notions, cognitions, and judgments." *Journal of Interpersonal Violence, 21,* 1063–1080.

Hyde, J. S. 1984. "How large are gender differences in aggression? A developmental meta-analysis." *Developmental Psychology, 20,* 722–736.

Hyman, A., Schillinger, D., & Lo, B. 1995. "Laws mandating reporting of domestic violence." *Journal of the American Medical Association, 273,* 1781–1787.

Hynie, M., & Lydon, J. E. 1995. "Women's perceptions of female contraceptive behavior: Experimental evidence of the sexual double standard." *Psychology of Women Quarterly, 19,* 563–581.

Iggulden, C., & Iggulden, H. 2007. *The dangerous book for boys.* New York: Collins.

Ignatius, A. 1988. "China's birthrate is out of control again as one-child policy fails in rural areas." *Wall Street Journal,* July 14.

"Indiana woman says 'Big Brother' made her unwelcome at home." 2000. *Lafayette Journal and Courier,* August 23.

Inglehart, R., Basañez, M., & Moreno, A. 1998. *Human values and beliefs: A cross-cultural sourcebook.* Ann Arbor: University of Michigan Press.

Ingraham, C. 1999. *White weddings: Romancing heterosexuality in popular culture.* New York: Routledge.

Ingrassia, M., & McCormick, J. 1994. "Why leave children with bad parents?" *Newsweek,* April 25.

Injury Prevention Web. 2000. "Injury prevention policy: Child death review and injury prevention." www.safetypolicy.org/pm/death.htm. Accessed July 15, 2001.

"The institution of marriage is weakening." 1999. *Society, 36,* 2–3.

Ishii-Kuntz, M. 1989. "Collectivism or individualism? Changing patterns of Japanese attitudes." *Sociology and Social Research, 73,* 174–179.

———. 1999. "Japan and its planning toward family caregiving." In V. M. Lechner & M. B. Neal (Eds.), *Work and caring for the elderly: International perspectives.* Philadelphia, PA: Brunner/Mazel.

Jackson, S. M., & Cram, F. 2003. "Disrupting the sexual double standard: Young women's talk about heterosexuality." *British Journal of Social Psychology, 42,* 113–127.

Jacobs, J. A., & Labov, T. G. 2002. "Gender differentials in intermarriage among sixteen race and ethnic groups." *Sociological Forum, 17,* 621–646.

Jacobs, S. 2005. "Senate bill would require four- to six-month delay; parents would get counseling." *Atlanta Journal-Constitution,* March 4.

Jacobson, C. K., & Heaton, T. B. 2003. "Inter-group marriage and United States military service." *Journal of Political and Military Sociology, 31,* 1–22.

Jankowiak, W. R., & Fischer, E. F. 1992. "A cross-cultural perspective on romantic love." *Ethnology, 31,* 149–155.

Jarrell, A. 2000. "The face of teenage sex grows younger." *New York Times,* April 3.

Jayson, S. 2006. "Not so afraid to commit after all; Study of attitudes about family looks inside male psyche." *USA Today,* June 1.

Jehl, D. 1999. "Arab honor's price: A woman's blood." *New York Times,* June 20.

Jeremiah Project. 2007. "Children with guns don't kill people." www.jeremiahproject.com/prophecy/nomorals.html. Accessed June 28, 2007.

Jha, P., Kumar, R., Vasa, P., Dhingra, N., Thiruchelvam, D., & Moineddin, R. 2006. "Low male-to-female sex ratio of children born in India: National survey of 1.1 million households." *The Lancet, 367,* 211–218.

John, D., Shelton, B. A., & Luschen, K. 1995. "Race, ethnicity, gender and perceptions of fairness." *Journal of Family Issues, 16,* 357–379.

Johnson, C. 1994. "Gender, legitimate authority, and leader–subordinate conversations." *American Sociological Review, 59,* 122–135.

Johnson, D. 1999. "Seeking Little League skills at $70 an hour." *New York Times,* June 24.

Johnson, F. 1996. "Wedded to an illusion." *Harper's Magazine,* November.

Johnson, J. M. 1995. "Horror stories and the construction of child abuse." In J. Best (Ed.), *Images of issues.* New York: Aldine de Gruyter.

Johnson, J. O. 2005. "Who's minding the kids? Child care arrangements: Winter 2002." *Current Population Reports,* P70–101. Washington, DC: U.S. Bureau of the Census.

Johnson, M. P., & Ferraro, K. J. 2005. "Research on domestic violence: Making distinctions." In A. S. Skolnick & J. H. Skolnick (Eds.), *Family in transition.* Boston: Allyn & Bacon.

Johnson, S. M., & O'Conner, E. 2002. *The gay baby boom.* New York: NYU Press.

Jones, A. 1980. *Women who kill.* New York: Fawcett Columbine.

Jones, A. 2002. "The National Nursing Home Survey: 1999 summary." National Center for Health Statistics. *Vital and Health Statistics* Series 13, #152. www.cdc.gov/nchs/data/series/sr_13/sr13_152.pdf. Accessed August 2, 2006..

Jones, R. K., & Brayfield, A. 1997. "Life's greatest joy? European attitudes toward the centrality of children." *Social Forces, 75,* 1239–1270.

Jones, R. K., Zolna, M. R. S., Henshaw, S. K., & Finer, L. B. 2008. "Abortion in the United States: Incidence and access to services, 2005." *Perspectives on Sexual and Reproductive Health, 40,* 6–16.

Jones, N. A., & Smith, A. S. 2001. "The two or more races population: 2000." *Census 2000 Brief,*

C2KBR/01-6. www.census.gov/prod/2001pubs/c2kbr01-6.pdf. Accessed September 22, 2004.

Jost, K. 2006. "Transgender issues." *CQ Researcher, 16,* 385–405.

Joyce, A. 2005. "Workplace improves for gay, transgender employees, rights group says." *Washington Post,* June 6.

Julian, T. W., McKenry, P. C., & McKelvey, M. W. 1994. "Cultural variations in parenting: Perceptions of Caucasian, African-American, Hispanic, and Asian-American parents." *Family Relations, 43,* 30–37.

Kagan, J. 1976. *Raising children in modern America: Problems and prospective solutions.* Boston: Little, Brown.

Kahn, J. 2004. "The most populous nation faces a population crisis." *New York Times,* May 30.

———. 2007. "Harsh birth control steps fuel violence in China." *New York Times,* May 22.

Kain, E. 1990. *The myth of family decline.* Lexington, MA: Lexington Books.

Kalmijn, M. 1991. "Status homogamy in the United States." *American Journal of Sociology, 97,* 496–523.

———. 1998. "Intermarriage and homogamy: Causes, patterns, trends." *Annual Review of Sociology, 24,* 395–421.

Kalmijn, M., & Flap, H. 2001. "Assortive meeting and mating: Unintended consequences of organized settings for partner choices." *Social Forces, 79,* 1289–1312.

Kamerman, S. B., & Kahn, A. J. 1995. *Starting right: How America neglects its youngest children and what we can do about it.* New York: Oxford University Press.

Kana'iaupuni, S. M., Donato, K. M., Thompson-Colón, T., & Stainback, M. 2005. "Counting on kin: Social networks, social support, and child health status." *Social Forces, 83,* 1137–1164.

Kanter, G. K., & Straus, M. A. 1990. "The 'drunken bum' theory of wife beating." In M. A. Straus & R. J. Gelles (Eds.), *Physical violence in American families.* New Brunswick, NJ: Transaction.

Kantor, J. 2006. "On the job, nursing mothers are finding a 2-class system." *New York Times,* September 1.

Karraker, K. H., Vogel, D. A., & Lake, M. A. 1995. "Parents' gender-stereotyped perceptions of newborns: The eye of the beholder revisited." *Sex Roles, 33,* 687–701.

Kart, C. S. 1990. *The realities of aging.* Boston: Allyn & Bacon.

Karush, S. 2001. "Russia's population drain could open a floodgate of consequences." *Los Angeles Times,* May 6.

Kaser-Boyd, N. 2004. "Battered women syndrome: Clinical factors, evaluation, and expert testimony." In B. J. Cling (Ed.), *Sexualized violence against women and children: A psychology and law perspective.* New York: Guilford Press.

Kataoka-Yahiro, M. R., Ceria, C., & Yoder, M. 2004. "Grandparent caregiving role in Filipino-American families." *Journal of Cultural Diversity, 11,* 110–117.

Kaufman, G. 1999. "The portrayal of men's family roles in television commercials." *Sex Roles, 41,* 439–458.

Kaufman, J., & Zigler, E. 1987. "Do abused children become abusive parents?" *American Journal of Orthopsychiatry, 57,* 186–192.

Keller, B. 1997. "Divorce increasingly puts schools in the middle of family conflicts." *Education Week,* April 9.

Kelley, J., & DeGraaf, N. D. 1997. "National context, parental socialization, and religious belief: Results from 15 nations." *American Sociological Review, 62,* 639–659.

Kelly, J. B., & Emery, R. E. 2007. "Children's adjustment following divorce: Risk and resilience perspectives." In A. S. Skolnick & J. H. Skolnick (Eds.), *Family in transition.* Boston: Allyn & Bacon.

Kempe, C. H., Silverman, F. N., Steele, B. F., Droegemueller, W., & Silver, H. K. 1962. "The battered-child syndrome." *Journal of the American Medical Association, 18,* 17–24.

Kendall, D. 2002. *The power of good deeds: Privileged women and the social reproduction of the upper class.* Lanham, MD: Rowman & Littlefield.

Kennedy, K. 2006. "College grads moving back home to boomer parents—and staying." *Newsday.com.* www.newsday.com. Accessed July 31, 2006.

Kennedy, R. 2002. "Interracial intimacy." *Atlantic Monthly,* December.

Kerr, D. 2004. "Family transformations and the well-being of children: Recent evidence from Canadian longitudinal data." *Journal of Comparative Family Studies, 35,* 73–90.

Kershner, R. 1996. "Adolescent attitudes about rape." *Adolescence, 31,* 29–33.

Kessler, S. J., & McKenna, W. 1978. *Gender: An ethnomethodological approach.* Chicago: University of Chicago Press.

Kessler-Harris, A. 1982. *Out to work: A history of wage-earning women in the United States.* New York: Oxford University Press.

Kibria, N. 1994. "Vietnamese families in the United States." In R. L. Taylor (Ed.), *Minority families in the United States.* Englewood Cliffs, NJ: Prentice Hall.

Kiernan, K. 2002. "Cohabitation in western Europe: Trends, issues, and implications." In A. Booth & A. C. Crouter (Eds.), *Just living together: Implications of cohabitation on families, children, and social policy.* Mahwah, NJ: Erlbaum.

Kilborn, P. T. 2005. "The five-bedroom, six-figure rootless life." *New York Times,* June 1.

Kimmel, M. 2004. *The gendered society.* New York: Oxford University Press.

Kincaid, S. B., & Caldwell, R. A. 1995. "Marital separation: Causes, coping, and consequences." *Journal of Divorce and Remarriage, 22,* 109–128.

Kinsey, A. C., Pomeroy, W. B., & Martin, C. E. 1948. *Sexual behavior in the human male.* Philadelphia: Saunders.

Kinsey Institute. 2007. "Kinsey's heterosexual-homosexual rating scale." www.indiana.edu/~kinsey/research/ak-hhscale.html. Accessed March 12, 2007.

Kipnis, L. 2004. *Against love: A polemic.* New York: Vintage.

Kirkman, M. 2003. "Infertile women and the narrative work of mourning: Barriers to the revision of autobiographical narratives of motherhood." *Narrative Inquiry, 13,* 243–262.

Kirn, W., & King, W. 1997. "The ties that bind." *Time,* August 18.

Kirp, D. L. 2004. "And the rich get smarter." *New York Times,* April 30.

Kishor, S., & Johnson, K. 2004. "Profiling domestic violence: A multi-country study." www.measuredhs.com/pubs/pdf/OD31/DV.pdf. Accessed June 1, 2005.

Kitamura, T., & Kijima, N. 1999. "Frequencies of child abuse in Japan: Hidden by prevalent crime." *International Journal of Offender Therapy and Comparative Criminology, 43,* 21–33.

Kitano, H. L. 1976. *Japanese Americans: The evolution of a subculture.* Englewood Cliffs, NJ: Prentice Hall.

Kitano, H. L., & Daniels, R. 1988. *Asian Americans: Emerging minorities.* Englewood Cliffs, NJ: Prentice Hall.

Kitano, H. L., Yeung, W., Chai, L., & Hatanaka, H. 1984. "Asian American interracial marriage." *Journal of Marriage and the Family, 46,* 179–190.

Klatch, R. 1991. "Complexities of conservatism: How conservatives understand the world." In A. Wolfe (Ed.), *America at century's end.* Berkeley: University of California Press.

Klawitter, M. M. 1994. "Who gains, who loses from changing U.S. child support policies?" *Policy Sciences, 27,* 197–219.

Klein, D. M., & White, J. M. 1996. *Family theories.* Thousand Oaks, CA: Sage.

Kluger, J. 2008. "Why we love." *Time,* January 28.

Knowlton, B. 2007. "General stands by stance against gay troops." *New York Times,* March 13.

Kobrin, J. E. 1991. "Cross-cultural perspectives and research directions for the twenty-first century." *Child Abuse and Neglect, 15,* 67–77.

Kohlberg, L. A. 1966. "A cognitive-developmental analysis of children's sex-role concepts and attitudes." In E. Maccoby (Ed.), *The development of sex differences.* Stanford, CA: Stanford University Press.

Kohn, M. 1979. "The effects of social class on parental values and practices." In D. Reiss & H. A. Hoffman (Eds.), *The American family: Dying or developing.* New York: Plenum.

Kohut, A. 1999. "Globalization and the wage gap." *New York Times,* December 3.

Kolata, G. 2006. "So big and healthy nowadays, Grandpa wouldn't know you." *New York Times,* July 30.

Kollock, P., & Blumstein, P. 1988. "Personal relationships." *Annual Review of Sociology, 14,* 467–490.

Kollock, P., Blumstein, P., & Schwartz, P. 1985. "Sex and power in interaction: Conversational privileges and duties." *American Sociological Review, 50,* 34–46.

———. 1994. "The judgment of equity in intimate relationships." *Social Psychology Quarterly, 57,* 340–351.

Komarovsky, M. 1962. *Blue-collar marriage.* New Haven, CT: Vintage.

Komter, A. 1989. "Hidden power in marriage." *Gender & Society, 3,* 187–216.

Kranichfeld, M. L. 1987. "Rethinking family power." *Journal of Family Issues, 8,* 42–56.

Krauss, C. 2004. "In aging Quebec, town pays to keep the babies coming." *New York Times,* March 2.

Kreider, R. M. 2005. "Number, timing, and duration of marriages and divorces: 2001." *Current Population*

Reports, P70–97. www.census.gov/prod/2055pubs/p70-97.pdf. Accessed August 11, 2006.

Kreider, R. M., & Fields, J. 2005. "Living arrangements of children: 2001." *Current Population Reports,* P70–104. www.census.gov/prod/2005pubs/;70-104.pdf. Accessed August 18, 2006.

Kristof, N. D. 1996a. "Do Korean men still beat their wives? Definitely." *New York Times,* December 5.

———. 1996b. "Japan is a woman's world, once the front door is shut." *New York Times,* June 19.

———. 1996c. "Who needs love! In Japan, many couples don't." *New York Times,* February 11.

———. 1997. "Once prized, Japan's elderly feel dishonored and fearful." *New York Times,* August 4.

———. 2003. "Believe it or not." *New York Times,* August 15.

Krugman, P. 2006. "Left behind economics." *New York Times,* July 14.

Kudson-Martin, C., & Mahoney, A. R. 1998. "Language processes in the construction of equality in marriages." *Family Relations, 47,* 81–91.

Kurz, D. 1989. "Social science perspectives on wife abuse: Current debates and future directions." *Gender & Society, 3,* 489–505.

———. 1995. *For richer, for poorer: Mothers confront divorce.* New York: Routledge.

Lacey, M. 2003. "Rights group calls for end to inheriting African wives." *New York Times,* March 5.

Lalasz, R. 2005. "Full-time work no guarantee of livelihood for many U.S. families." Population Reference Bureau Report, January. www.prb.org. Accessed January 19, 2005.

Lamp, F. 1988. "Heavenly bodies: Menses, moon, and rituals of license among the Temne of Sierra Leone." In T. Buckley & A. Gottlieb (Eds.), *Blood magic: The anthropology of menstruation.* Berkeley: University of California Press.

Landers, A. 1993. "What's in a name? A lot of discord." *Lafayette Journal and Courier,* December 31.

Landis-Kleine, C., Foley, L. A., Nall, L., Padgett, P., & Walters-Palmer, L. 1995. "Attitudes toward marriage and divorce held by young adults." *Journal of Divorce and Remarriage, 23,* 63–73.

Laner, M. R. 1989. *Dating: Delights, discontents and dilemmas.* Salem, WI: Sheffield.

Lang, S. 1998. *Men as women, women as men: Changing gender in Native American cultures.* Austin: University of Texas Press.

Langan, P. A., & Dawson, J. M. 1995. "Spouse murder defendants in large urban counties." Bureau of Justice Statistics. NCJ-153256. www.ojp.usdoj.gov/bjs/pub/ascii/spousmur.txt. Accessed August 18, 2007.

Langman, L. 1988. "Social stratification." In M. B. Sussman & S. K. Steinmetz (Eds.), *Handbook of marriage and the family.* New York: Plenum.

Lansford, J. E., Ceballo, R., Abbey, A., & Stewart, A. J. 2001. "Does family structure matter? A comparison of adoptive, two-parent biological, single-mother, stepfather, and stepmother households." *Journal of Marriage and the Family, 63,* 840–851.

Lanvers, U. 2004. "Gender in discourse behaviour in parent-child dyads: A literature review." *Child: Care, Health, and Development, 30,* 481–493.

Lareau, A. 2003. *Unequal childhoods: Class, race, and family life.* Berkeley: University of California Press.

LaRossa, R. 1992. "Fatherhood and social change." In M. S. Kimmel & M. A. Messner (Eds.), *Men's lives.* New York: Macmillan.

Larson, L. E., & Goltz, J. W. 1989. "Religious participation and marital commitment." *Review of Religious Research, 30,* 387–400.

Larzelere, R. E., & Klein, D. M. 1987. "Methodology." In M. B. Sussman & S. K. Steinmetz (Eds.), *Handbook of marriage and the family.* New York: Plenum.

Lasch, C. 1977. *Haven in a heartless world: The family besieged.* New York: Norton.

Laumann, E. O., Gagnon, J. H., Michael, R. T., & Michaels, S. 1994. *The social organization of sexuality.* Chicago: University of Chicago Press.

Lawton, L. E., & Bures, R. 2001. "Parental divorce and the 'switching' of religious identity." *Journal for the Scientific Study of Religion, 40,* 99–111.

Lee, F. R. 2005. "Driven by costs, fertility clients head overseas." *New York Times,* January 25.

Lee, G. R., & Stone, L. H. 1980. "Mate-selection systems and criteria: Variation according to family structure." *Journal of Marriage and the Family, 42,* 319–326.

Lee, J. 2006. "For insurance, adult children ride piggyback." *New York Times,* September 17.

Lee, J., & Bean, F. D. 2004. "America's changing color lines: Immigration, race/ethnicity, and multiracial identification." *Annual Review of Sociology, 30,* 221–242.

Lee, S. M. 1993. "Racial classifications in the U.S. Census: 1890–1990." *Ethnic and Racial Studies, 16,* 75–94.

Mitford, J. 1993. *The American way of birth.* New York: Plume.

Moen, P., & Yu, Y. 2000. "Effective work/life strategies: Working couples, work conditions, gender and life quality." *Social Problems, 47,* 291–326.

Mogelonsky, M. 1996. "The rocky road to adulthood." *American Demographics,* May, 26–34.

Money, Meaning & Choice Institute. 2006. "Sudden wealth syndrome." www.mmcinstitute.com/sws_print.html. Accessed June 28, 2006.

Montgomery, R. 2006. "Regulating the rights of the unborn." *Kansas City Star,* July 9.

Moore, K., Manlove, J., Glei, D., & Morrison, D. R. 1998. "Nonmarital school-age motherhood: Family, individual, and school characteristics." *Journal of Adolescent Research, 13,* 433–457.

Moore, M. L. 1992. "The family as portrayed on prime-time television, 1947–1990: Structure and characteristics." *Sex Roles, 26,* 41–61.

Moore, S. A. D. 2003. "Understanding the connection between domestic violence, crime, and poverty: How welfare reform may keep battered women from leaving abusive relationships." *Texas Journal of Women and the Law, 12,* 451–484.

Moorman, J. E. 1987. "The history and future of the relationship between education and first marriage." Unpublished paper. Washington, DC: U.S. Bureau of the Census.

Moreau, R., & Yousafzai, S. 2006. "A war on schoolgirls." *Newsweek,* June 26.

Morgan, R. 1996. *Sisterhood is global.* New York: The Feminist Press at the City University of New York.

Morgan, L., & Kunkel, S. 1998. *Aging and society.* Thousand Oaks, CA: Pine Forge Press.

Mottl, T. L. 1980. "The analysis of countermovements." *Social Problems, 27,* 620–635.

Moynihan, D. P. 1965. *The Negro family: The case for national action.* Washington, DC: Office of Planning and Research, Department of Labor.

Mulkern, A. C. 2004. "Canada offers preview of gay-marriage impacts." *Denver Post,* July 4.

Murdock, G. P. 1949. *Social structure.* New York: Free Press.

———. 1957. "World ethnography sample." *American Anthropologist, 59,* 664–687.

Murstein, B. I. 1974. *Love, sex, and marriages through the ages.* New York: Springer.

———. 1987. "A clarification and extension of the SVR theory of dyadic pairing." *Journal of Marriage and the Family, 49,* 929–933.

Nack, W., & Munson, L. 1995. "Sports' dirty secret." *Sports Illustrated,* July 31.

Nanda, S. 1994. *Cultural anthropology.* Belmont, CA: Wadsworth.

Nason-Clark, N. 2004. "When terror strikes at home: The interface between religion and domestic violence." *Journal for the Scientific Study of Religion, 43,* 303–310.

National Alliance for Caregiving. 2005. "Caregiving in the U.S." www.caregiving.org/data/04execsumm.pdf. Accessed August 2, 2006.

National Alliance to End Homelessness. 2007. "Homelessness counts." www.endhomelessness.org/content/general/detail/1440. Accessed June 24, 2007.

National Center for Education Statistics. 2005. "Annual earnings of young adults." Table 22-1. http://nces.ed.gov/programs/coe/2006/section2/table.asp?tableID=473. Accessed July 31, 2006.

National Center for Fair and Open Testing. 2007. "2006 college bound seniors' average SAT scores." www.fairtest.org/univ/Score_Release_2006/SAT_Scores_2006_Chart.pdf. Accessed January 16, 2007.

National Center for Health Statistics. 2003. "Health, United States, 2003." www.cdc.gov/nchs/products/pubs/pubd/hus/trendtables.htm. Accessed September 23, 2004.

National Center on Elder Abuse. 2001. "What are the major types of elder abuse?" www.elderabusecenter.org. Accessed May 5, 2001.

———. 2005. "Elder abuse prevalence and incidence—Fact sheet." www.elderabusecenter.org/pdf/publication/FinalStatistics050331.pdf. Accessed August 8, 2006.

National Committee on Pay Equity. 1999. "The wage gap: 1998." www.feminist.com/fairpay. Accessed July 1, 2000.

———. 2006. "The wage gap over time: In real dollars, women see a continuing gap." www.pay-equity.org/info-time.html. Accessed July 17, 2006.

National Conference of State Legislatures. 2005. "Same sex marriage." www.ncsl.org/programs/cyf/samesex.htm#DOMA. Accessed June 3, 2005.

———. 2007. "State laws regarding marriages between first cousins." www.ncsl.org/programs/cyf/cousins.htm. Accessed March 20, 2007.

National Court-Appointed Special Advocate Association. 2000. "Statistics on child abuse and neglect, foster care, adoption, and CASA programs." CASAnet Resources. www.casanet.org/library/abuse/abuse-stats.98.htm#Foster%20Care. Accessed August 8, 2006.

———. 2006. "Children need protection and care more than ever." www.casanet.org/download/ncasa_publications/0603_statistics_sheet_0021.pdf. Accessed August 8, 2006.

National Low Income Housing Coalition. 2006. "Out of reach 2006." www.nlihc.org/oor/oor2006/?CFID=12522815&CFTOKEN=54970147. Accessed May 26, 2007.

National Marriage Project. 2001. "Mission, goals and organization." http://marriage.rutgers.edu/about.htm. Accessed July 7, 2001.

———. 2005. "The state of our unions 2005: The social health of marriages in America." http://marriage.rutgers.edu/publications/soou/soou2005.pdf. Accessed May 29, 2006.

National Opinion Research Center. 1998. "General Social Survey, 1972–1998." www.icpsr.umich.edu/GSS/. Tables generated August 27, 2007.

———. 2006. "General Social Survey, 1972–2004." http://webapp.icpsr.umich.edu/GSS/. Tables generated July 20, 2006.

National Partnership for Women and Families. 2005. "Expecting better: A state-by-state analysis of parental leave programs." www.nationalpartnership.org/portals/p3/library/PaidLeave/ParentalLeaveReportMay05.pdf. Accessed June 1, 2005.

———. 2006. "Facts about the FMLA: What does it do? Who uses it, and how?" www.nationalpartnership.org/portals/p3/library/FamilyMedicalLeave/FMLAWhatWhoHow.pdf. Accessed July 18, 2006.

National Public Radio. 2005. "Jobless with a college degree: The numbers rise." Weekend Edition. March 19. www.npr.org/templates/story/story.php?storyId=4542578. Accessed May 20, 2005.

Navarro, M. 2006. "Families add 3rd generation to households." *New York Times,* May 25.

Neal, A. G., Groat, H. T., & Wicks, J. W. 1989. "Attitudes about having children: A study of 600 couples in the early years of marriage." *Journal of Marriage and the Family, 59,* 313–328.

Nelson, T. J. 2004. "Low-income fathers." *Annual Review of Sociology, 30,* 427–451.

Neugarten, B. L. 1980. "Grow old along with me! The best is yet to be." In B. Hess (Ed.), *Growing old in America.* New Brunswick, NJ: Transaction Books.

New York Times. 2006. "State laws on same-sex marriage." http://graphics8.nytimes.com/images/2006/10/13/us/politics/14marriage_graphic.gif.

Newman, D. 2006. *Sociology: Exploring the architecture of everyday life.* Thousand Oaks, CA: Pine Forge Press.

———. 2007. *Identities and inequalities.* New York: McGraw-Hill.

Newman, K. 1999a. *Falling from grace: Downward mobility in the age of affluence.* Berkeley: University of California Press.

———. 1999b. *No shame in my game: The working poor in the inner city.* New York: Knopf.

———. 2005. "Family values against the odds." In A. S. Skolnick & J. H. Skolnick (Eds.), *Family in transition.* Boston: Allyn & Bacon.

Nichols, M. 2005. "Is 'lesbian bed death' for real?" *The Gay & Lesbian Review,* July–August, 18–20.

Nickman, S. L. 2005. "Children in adoptive families: Overview and update." *Journal of the American Academy of Child and Adolescent Psychiatry, 44,* 987–995.

Nock, S. L. 1995. "A comparison of marriages and cohabiting relationships." *Journal of Family Issues, 16,* 53–76.

———. 1998a. "The consequences of premarital fatherhood." *American Sociological Review, 63,* 250–263.

———. 1998b "Too much privacy?" *Journal of Family Issues, 19,* 101–118.

———. 1999. "The problem with marriage." *Society, 36,* 20–27.

Noller, P. 1993. "Gender and emotional communication in marriage: Different cultures or differential social power?" *Journal of Language and Social Psychology, 12,* 132–152.

Nugman, G. 2002. "World divorce rates." www.divorcereform.org/gul.html. Accessed July 6, 2003.

"Obesity letters having effect in Arkansas." 2006. *New York Times,* June 4.

O'Brien, M., & Huston, A. C. 1985. "Development of sex-typed play behavior in toddlers." *Developmental Psychology, 21,* 866–871.

"Ohio court removes child from parents because of her gender." 2000. www.gpac.org. Accessed August 26, 2000.

Oliker, S. J. 1995. "Work commitment and constraint among mothers on welfare." *Journal of Contemporary Ethnography, 24,* 165–194.

Olson, E. 1981. "Socioeconomic and psychocultural contexts of child abuse and neglect in Turkey." In J. Kobrin (Ed.), *Child abuse and neglect: Cross-cultural perspectives.* Berkeley: University of California Press.

Onishi, N. 2007. "Betrothed at first sight: A Korean-Vietnamese courtship." *New York Times,* February 22.

Ordover, N. 1996. "Eugenics, the gay gene, and the science of backlash." *Socialist Review, 26,* 125–144.

Orenstein, P. 2007. "Baby lust." *New York Times Magazine,* April 1.

O'Rourke, M. 2006. "Desperate feminist wives: Why wanting equality makes women unhappy." *Slate,* March 6.

Ortner, S. B. 1998. "Identities: The hidden life of class." *Journal of Anthropological Research, 54,* 1–17.

Ostrander, S. 1984. *Women of the upper class.* Philadelphia: Temple University Press.

O'Sullivan, L. F., & Gaines, M. E. 1998. "Decision-making in college students' heterosexual dating relationships: Ambivalence about engaging in sexual activity." *Journal of Social and Personal Relationships, 15,* 347–363.

Owen, M. 1996. *A world of widows.* London: Zed Books.

Palmore, E. 1975. *The honorable elders: A cross-cultural analysis of aging in Japan.* Durham, NC: Duke University Press.

Pandya, S. 2001. "Nursing homes fact sheet." American Association of Retired Persons. www.aarp.org/research/longtermcare/nursinghomes/aresearch-import--669-FS1OR.html. Accessed August 2, 2006.

Pappas, M. 2006. "Divorce New York style." *New York Times,* February 19.

Parcel, T. L., & Menaghan, E. G., 1990. "Maternal working conditions and children's verbal facility: Studying the intergenerational transmission of inequality from mothers to young children." *Social Psychology Quarterly, 53,* 132–147.

———. 1994. "Early parental work, family social capital, and early childhood outcomes." *American Journal of Sociology, 99,* 972–1009.

"Parental leave." 2007. Wikipedia. http://en.wikipedia.org/wiki/Parental_leave. Accessed April 4, 2007.

Park, K. 2002. "Stigma management among the voluntarily childless." *Sociological Perspectives, 45,* 21–45.

Parke, R. D. 2004. "Fathers, families, and the future: A plethora of plausible predictions." *Merrill-Palmer Quarterly, 50,* 456–470.

Parke, R. D., & Buriel, R. 2002. "Socialization concerns in African American, American Indian, Asian American, and Latino Families." In N. V. Benokraitis (Ed.), *Contemporary ethnic families in the United States: Characteristics, variations, and dynamics.* Upper Saddle River, NJ: Prentice Hall.

Parlee, M. B. 1989. "Conversational politics." In L. Richardson & V. Taylor (Eds.), *Feminist frontiers.* New York: Random House.

Parrott, S., & Sherman, A. 2006. "TANF at 10: Program results are more mixed than often understood." Center on Budget and Policy Priorities. www.cbpp.org/8-17-06tanf.pdf. Accessed August 22, 2006.

Parsons, T., & Bales, R. F. 1955. *Family socialization and interaction process.* Glencoe, IL: Free Press.

Pasupathi, M. 2002. "Arranged marriages: What's love got to do with it?" In M. Yalom & L. L. Carstensen (Eds.), *Inside the American couple: New thinking, new challenges.* Berkeley: University of California Press.

Pattillo-McCoy, M. 1999. *Black picket fences: Privilege and peril among the black middle class.* Chicago: University of Chicago Press.

Patton, W., & Mannison, M. 1995. "Sexual coercion in high school dating." *Sex Roles, 33,* 447–457.

Paul, P. 2001. "Childless by choice." *American Demographics,* November.

Pear, R. 2000. "A million parents lost Medicaid, study says." *New York Times,* June 20.

———. 2006. "New rules force states to limit welfare rolls." *New York Times,* June 28.

Pearce, D. 1978. "Feminization of poverty—women, work and welfare." *Urban & Social Change Review, 11,* 28–36.

Pearce, L. D., & Axinn, W. G. 1998. "The impact of family religious life on the quality of mother–child relations." *American Sociological Review, 63,* 810–828.

Penner, D. 1995. "Aid recipients defy stereotypes, seek a better way." *Indianapolis Star,* April 16.

Penton-Voak, I. S., Perrett, D. I., Castles, D. L., Kobayashi, T., Burt, D. M., Murray, L. K., & Minamisawa,

R. 1999. "Menstrual cycles alter face preference." *Nature, 399,* 741–742.

Peplau, L. A. 2003. "Human sexuality: How do men and women differ?" *Current Directions in Psychological Science, 12,* 37–40.

Peterson, R. R. 1996. "A re-evaluation of the economic consequences of divorce." *American Sociological Review, 61,* 528–536.

Pew Forum on Religion and Public Life. 2002. "Americans struggle with religion's role at home and abroad." Survey report. http://people-press.org/reports. Accessed January 18, 2003.

Pew Research Center. 2007. "As marriage and parenthood drift apart, public is concerned about social impact." http://pewresearch.org/pubs/526/marriage-parenthood. Accessed July 1, 2007.

Pfizer, Inc. 2002. "Global study of sexual attitudes and behaviors." www.pfizerglobalstudy.com/study/study-results.asp. Accessed May 22, 2007.

Pfohl, S. J. 1977. "The discovery of child abuse." *Social Problems, 24,* 310–323.

Philipson, I. 2000. "Work as family: The workplace as repository of women's unmet emotional needs." Working paper, Center for Working Families. Berkeley, CA: University of California, Berkeley.

Pienta, A. M., Hayward, M. D., & Jenkins, K. R. 2000. "Health consequences of marriage for the retirement years." *Journal of Family Issues, 21,* 559–586.

Pillemer, K. A. 1993. "Abuse is caused by the deviance and dependence of abusive caregivers." In R. J. Gelbs & D. R. Loeske (Eds.), *Current controversies in family violence.* Newbury Park, CA: Sage.

Piper, A. 1992. "Passing for white, passing for black." *Transition, 58,* 4–32.

Pittman, J. F., & Blanchard, D. 1996. "The effects of work history and timing of marriage on the division of household labor: A life-course perspective." *Journal of Marriage and the Family, 58,* 78–90.

Pleck, E. 1987. *Domestic tyranny.* New York: Oxford University Press.

"Poll: 1 in 5 take laptops on vacation, check voicemail." 2007. *Greencastle Banner Graphic,* June 2.

Pollitt, K. 1991. "Fetal rights: A new assault on feminism." In J. H. Skolnick & E. Currie (Eds.), *Crisis in American institutions.* New York: HarperCollins.

Ponticelli, C. M. 1999. "Crafting stories of sexual identity reconstruction." *Social Psychology Quarterly, 62,* 157–172.

Popenoe, D. 1993. "American family decline, 1960–1990: A review and appraisal." *Journal of Marriage and the Family, 55,* 527–555.

———. 1996. "Where's Papa?" *Utne Reader,* September–October, 63–66.

———. 1999. "Can the nuclear family be revived?" *Society, 36,* 28–30.

Popenoe, D., & Whitehead, B. D. 2004. "Ten important research findings on marriage and choosing a marriage partner." National Marriage Project Information Brief. http://marriage.rutgers.edu/Publications/pubTenThingsYoungAdults.pdf. Accessed May 30, 2006.

Population Council. 2004. "Forced sexual relations among married young women in developing countries." www.popcouncil.org/pdfs/popsyn/PopulationSynthesis1.pdf. Accessed June 24, 2006.

Population Reference Bureau. 2007. "2007 World Population Data Sheet." www.prb.org/pdf07/07WPDS_Eng.pdf. Accessed April 5, 2008.

Porter, E. 2004. "Hourly pay in U.S. not keeping pace with price rises." *New York Times,* July 18.

Porter, E. 2006. "Stretched to limit, women still march to work." *New York Times,* March 2.

Potuchek, J. L. 1997. *Who supports the family? Gender and breadwinning in dual-earner marriages.* Stanford, CA: Stanford University Press.

Prah, P. M. 2006. "Domestic violence." *CQ Researcher, 16,* 1–24.

Press, E. 2007. "Family-leave values." *New York Times Magazine,* July 29.

Preston, S. H. 1984. "Children and the elderly in the U.S." *Scientific American,* December, 44–49.

Previti, D., & Amato, P. R. 2004. "Is infidelity a cause or a consequence of poor marital quality?" *Journal of Social and Personal Relationships, 21,* 217–230.

Public Policy Institute. 2002. "Family caregiving and long-term care." www.aarp.org/research/housing-mobility/caregiving/aresearch-import-779-FS91.html. Accessed January 4, 2007.

Pyke, K. 1994. "Women's employment as a gift or burden? Marital power across marriage, divorce, and remarriage." *Gender and Society, 8,* 73–91.

———. 1996. "Class-based masculinities: The interdependence of gender, class, and interpersonal power." *Gender and Society, 10,* 527–549.

Pyke, K., & Bengston, V. L. 1996. "Caring more or less: Individualistic and collectivist systems of family eldercare." *Journal of Marriage and the Family, 58,* 379–392.

Qian, Z., & Lichter, D. T. 2007. "Social boundaries and marital assimilation: Interpreting trends in racial and ethnic marriage." *American Sociological Review, 72,* 68–94.

Quadagno, J. 1999. *Aging and the life course.* New York: McGraw-Hill.

Rabin, R. 2006. "Breast-feed or else." *New York Times,* June 13.

Rackl, L., & Herrmann, A. 2005. "Couples are out, groups are in." *Chicago Sun-Times,* March 20.

Rafferty, Y., & Rollins, N. 1989. *Learning in limbo: The educational deprivation of homeless children.* New York: Advocates for Children.

Raley, R. K. 1995. "Black–white differences in kin contact and exchange among never married adults." *Journal of Family Issues, 16,* 77–103.

Raley, S., & Bianchi, S. 2006. "Sons, daughters, and family processes: Does gender of children matter?" *Annual Review of Sociology, 32,* 401–421.

Ramachandran, N. 2005. "The parent trap: Boomerang kids." *U.S. News & World Report,* December 12.

Rangarajan, A., & Razafindrakoto, C. 2004. "Unemployment insurance as a potential safety net for TANF leavers: Evidence from five states." U.S. Department of Health and Human Services report. http://aspe.hhs.gov/hsp/wtw-grants-eval98/ui04/. Accessed June 30, 2006.

Rank, M. 1994. *Life on the edge: The realities of welfare in America.* New York: Columbia University Press.

Rapp, R. 1999. "Family and class in contemporary America: Notes toward an understanding of ideology." In S. Coontz (Ed.), *American families: A multicultural reader.* New York: Routledge.

Rasekh, Z., Bauer, H. M., Manos, M. M., & Iacopino, V. 1998. "Women's health and human rights in Afghanistan." *Journal of the American Medical Association, 280,* 449–455.

Recer, P. 2000. "Gene mutation may extend human life." *Lafayette Journal and Courier,* December 15.

Reddy, G. 2005. *With respect to sex: Negotiating Hijra identity in South Asia.* Chicago: University of Chicago Press.

Reich, R. B. 2004. "Marriage aid that misses the point." *Washington Post,* January 22.

Reinharz, S. 1992. *Feminist methods in social research.* New York: Oxford University Press.

Reinholtz, R. K., Muehlenhard, C. L., Phelps, J. L., & Satterfield, A. T. 1995. "Sexual discourse and sexual intercourse: How the way we communicate affects the way we think about sexual coercion." In P. J. Kalfleisch & M. J. Cody (Eds.), *Gender, power and communication in human relationships.* Hillsdale, NJ: Erlbaum.

Reinisch, J. M., Rosenblum, L. A., Rubin, D. B., & Schulsinger, M. F. 1997. "Sex differences emerge during the first year of life." In M. R. Walsh (Ed.), *Women, men and gender: Ongoing debates.* New Haven: Yale University Press.

Reiss, I. L. 1960. "Toward a sociology of the heterosexual love relationship." *Marriage and Family Living, 22,* 139–145.

Reiss, I. L., & Lee, G. R. 1988. *Family systems in America.* New York: Holt, Rinehart & Winston.

Renzetti, C. M., & Curran, D. J. 2003. *Women, men, and society.* Boston: Allyn & Bacon.

"Report on black America finds college gender gap." 2000. *New York Times,* July 26.

Reskin, B., & Hartmann, H. 1986. *Women's work, men's work: Sex segregation on the job.* Washington, DC: National Academy Press.

Rhodes, K. V., Drum, M., Anliker, E., Frankel, R. M., Howes, D. S., & Levinson, W. 2006. "Lowering the threshold for discussions of domestic violence." *Archives of Internal Medicine, 166,* 1107–1114.

Ribbens, J. 1994. *Mothers and their children.* London: Sage.

Ridgeway, C. L. 1997. "Interaction and the conservation of gender inequality: Considering employment." *American Sociological Review, 62,* 218–235.

Ridgeway, C. L., & Smith-Lovin, L. 1999. "The gender system and interaction." *Annual Review of Sociology, 25,* 191–216.

Riley, G. 1991. *Divorce: An American tradition.* New York: Oxford University Press.

Riley, M. W. 1983. "The family in an aging society: A matrix of latent relationships." *Journal of Family Issues, 4,* 439–454.

Rimer, S. 1998. "Tradition of care thrives in black families." *New York Times,* March 15.

Risman, B. J. 1989. "Can men mother? Life as a single father." In B. J. Risman & P. Schwartz (Eds.), *Gender in intimate relationships.* Belmont, CA: Wadsworth.

Risman, B., & Myers, K. 1997. "As the twig is bent: Children reared in feminist households." *Qualitative Sociology, 20,* 229–252.

Rivera, L. 2000. "Welfare to what? Barriers to adult literacy for homeless women in Massachusetts." Paper presented at the Society for the Study of Social Problems, August, Washington, DC.

Robbins, R., Scherman, A., Holeman, H., & Wilson, J. 2005. "Roles of American Indian grandparents in times of cultural crisis." *Journal of Cultural Diversity, 12,* 62–68.

Roberts, A. R. 1996. "Battered women who kill: A comparative study of incarcerated participants with a community sample of battered women." *Journal of Family Violence, 11,* 291–304.

Roberts, S. 2006. "It's official: To be married means to be outnumbered." *New York Times,* October 15.

———. 2007. "51% of women are now living without spouse." *New York Times,* January 16.

Robinson, L. 1994. "Religious orientation in enduring marriage: An exploratory study." *Review of Religious Research, 35,* 207–218.

Rogers, S. 1975. "Female forms of power and the myth of male dominance." *American Ethnologist, 2,* 727–756.

Roland, A. 1988. *In search of self in India and Japan.* Princeton, NJ: Princeton University Press.

Roof, W. C. 1999. *Spiritual marketplace: Baby boomers and the remaking of American religion.* Princeton, NJ: Princeton University Press.

Rosato, D. 2004. "Flights of fancy, part 2: Airlines class warfare." *Money Magazine,* August.

Rose, A. 1996. "How I became a single woman." *The New Yorker,* April 8.

Rose, S., & Frieze, I. H. 1989. "Young singles' scripts for a first date." *Gender & Society, 3,* 258–268.

Roselli, C. E., Resko, J. A., & Stormshak, F. 2006. "Expression of steroid hormone receptors in the fetal sheep brain during the critical period for sexual differentiation." *Brain Research, 1110,* 76–80.

Rosellini, L. 1992. "Sexual desire." *U.S. News and World Report,* July 6, 60–66.

Rosen, C. 2006. "Romance on the Internet." In K. R. Gilbert (Ed.), *Annual Editions: The Family 06/07.* Dubuque, IA: McGraw-Hill.

Rosen, J. 1997. "Abraham's drifting children." *New York Times Book Review,* March 30.

Rosenblatt, P. C., Karis, T. A., & Powell, R. D. 1995. *Multiracial couples.* Thousand Oaks, CA: Sage.

Rossi, A. 1968. "Transition to parenthood." *Journal of Marriage and the Family, 30,* 26–39.

———. 1977. "A bio-social perspective on parenting." *Daedalus, 106,* 1–31.

Rothman, E. K. 1984. *Hands and hearts: A history of courtship in America.* New York: Basic Books.

Rubin, J. Z., Provenzano, F. J., & Luria, Z. 1974. "The eye of the beholder: Parents' views on sex of newborns." *American Journal of Orthopsychiatry, 44,* 512–519.

Rubin, L. 1976. *Worlds of pain.* New York: Basic Books.

———. 1990. *Erotic wars: What happened to the sexual revolution?* New York: Harper Perennial.

———. 1992. "The empty nest." In J. M. Heaslin (Ed.), *Marriage and family in a changing society.* New York: Free Press.

———. 1995. *Families on the fault line.* New York: Harper Perennial.

Rubin, Z. 1973. *Liking and loving.* New York: Holt, Rinehart & Winston.

Runté, M., & Mills, A. J. 2004. "Paying the toll: A feminist post-structural critique of the discourse bridging work and family." *Culture and Organization, 10,* 237–249.

Rusbult, C. E. 1983. "A longitudinal test of the investment model: The development (and deterioration) of satisfaction and commitment in heterosexual involvement." *Journal of Personality and Social Psychology, 45,* 101–117.

Russell, D. E. H. 1998. "Wife rape and the law." In M. E. Odem & J. Clay-Warner (Eds.), *Confronting rape and sexual assault.* Wilmington, DE: SR Books.

Russell, G. 1999. "Primary caregiving fathers." In M. E. Lamb (Ed.), *Parenting and child development in "nontraditional" families.* Mahwah, NJ: Erlbaum.

Rutter, V. 1995. "Adolescence: Whose hell is it?" *Psychology Today,* January–February.

———. 1997. "Lessons from stepfamilies." In K. R. Gilbert (Ed.), *Annual editions: Marriage and family 97/98.* Guilford, CT: Dushkin.

Saenz, R. 2004. "Latinos and the changing face of America." Population Reference Bureau Report. August. www.prb.org. Accessed September 3, 2004.

Saenz, R., Hwang, S. S., Aguirre, B. E., & Anderson, R. N. 1995. "Persistence and change in Asian identity among children of intermarried couples." *Sociological Perspectives, 38,* 175–194.

Safilios-Rothschild, C. 1976. "A macro- and micro-examination of family power and love: An exchange model." *Journal of Marriage and the Family, 38,* 355–362.

Safire, W. 1995. "News about Jews." *New York Times,* July 17.

Sahadi, J. 2006. "The taxing truth about marriage." *CNN Money,* February 14.

Salholz, E. 1986. "Too late for Prince Charming?" *Newsweek,* June 2.

Sanchez-Ayendez, M. 1998. "The Puerto Rican family." In C. H. Mindel, R. W. Habenstein, & R. Wright (Eds.), *Ethnic families in America.* Upper Saddle River, NJ: Prentice Hall.

Sandberg, J. F., & Hofferth, S. L. 2001. "Changes in children's time with parents: United States 1981–1997." *Demography, 38,* 423–436.

Sandefur, G. 1996. "Welfare doesn't cause illegitimacy and single parenthood." *Chronicle of Higher Education,* October 4.

Sanghavi, D. M. 2006. "Wanting babies like themselves, some parents choose genetic defects." *New York Times,* December 5.

Santovec, M. L. 2004. "Dual orientations help 'helicopter' parents let go." *Recruitment and Retention in Higher Education, 18,* 1–8.

Saul, L. 1972. "Personal and social psychopathology and the primary prevention of violence." *American Journal of Psychiatry, 128,* 1578–1581.

Saulny, S., & Sander, L. 2007. "Soul-searching by suspect's neighbors." *New York Times,* January 21.

Savin-Williams, R. C., & Esterberg, K. G. 2000. "Lesbian, gay, and bisexual families." In D. H. Demo, K. R. Allen, & M. A. Fine (Eds.), *Handbook of family diversity.* New York: Oxford University Press.

Scanzoni, J. 1991. "Balancing the policy interests of children and adults." In E. A. Anderson & R. C. Hula (Eds.), *The reconstruction of family policy.* Westport, CT: Greenwood Press.

———. 2000. *Designing families: The search for self and community in the information age.* Thousand Oaks, CA: Pine Forge Press.

Scanzoni, J., Polonko, K., Teachman, J., & Thompson, L. 1989. *The sexual bond: Rethinking families and close relationships.* Newbury Park, CA: Sage.

Scheper-Hughes, N. 1989. "Lifeboat ethics: Mother love and child death in northeast Brazil." *National History, 98,* 8–16.

Scheuble, L., & Johnson, D. 2005. "Married women's situational use of last names: An empirical study." *Sex Roles, 53,* 143–151.

Schnaiberg, A., & Goldenberg, S. 1989. "From empty nest to crowded nest: The dynamics of incompletely launched young adults." *Social Problems, 36,* 251–269.

Schneider, M. B. 1996. "A campaign truth: Values matter." *Indianapolis Star,* September 29.

Schoenborn, C. A. 2004. "Marital status and health: United States, 1999–2002." Centers for Disease Control and Prevention. *Vital and Health Statistics, 351.* http://www.cdc.gov/nchs/data/ad/ad351.pdf. Accessed March 25, 2007.

Schofield, H. 2005. "France announces new measures to encourage large families." *Agence France Presse—English,* September 22.

Scholinski, D. 1997. "The last time I wore a dress." *Utne Reader,* November–December.

Schooler, C. 1996. "Cultural and social structural explanations of cross-national psychological differences." *Annual Review of Sociology, 22,* 323–349.

Schuller, R. A., & Vidmar, N. 1992. "Battered woman syndrome evidence in the courtroom." *Law and Human Behavior, 16,* 273–291.

Schutt, R. K. 2006. *Investigating the social world.* Thousand Oaks, CA: Pine Forge.

Schwartz, C. R., & Mare, R. D. 2005. "Trends in educational assertive marriage from 1940 to 2003." *Demography, 42,* 621–646.

Schwartz, C. R., Revkin, A. C., & Wald, M. L. 2005. "In reviving New Orleans, a challenge of many tiers." *New York Times,* September 12.

Schwartz, P. 1987. "The family as a changed institution." *Journal of Family Issues, 8,* 455–459.

———. 1994. *Love between equals.* New York: Free Press.

———. 2000. "Creating sexual pleasure and sexual justice in the twenty-first century." *Contemporary Sociology, 29,* 213–219.

———. 2007. "Peer marriage." In S. J. Ferguson (Ed.), *Shifting the center.* New York: McGraw-Hill.

Schwartz, P., & Rutter, V. 1998. *The gender of sexuality.* Thousand Oaks, CA: Sage.

Schweingruber, D., Anahita, S., & Berns, N. 2004. "'Popping the question' when the answer is known: The engagement proposal as performance." *Sociological Focus, 37,* 143–161.

Scott, A. O. 2001. "'The wedding planner': Some things just can't be planned." *New York Times,* January 26.

Scott, E. K., Edin, K., London, A. S., & Mazelis, J. M. 2001. "My children come first: Welfare-reliant women's post-TANF views of work-family trade-offs and marriage." In G. J. Duncan & P. L. Chase-Landale (Eds.), *For better and for worse.* New York: Russell Sage Foundation.

Scott, L. D. 2003. "The relation of racial identity and racial socialization to coping with discrimination among African American adolescents." *Journal of Black Studies, 33,* 520–538.

Sedlak, A. J., & Broadhurst, D. D. 1996. *Third national incidence study of child abuse and neglect.* Washington, DC: U.S. Department of Health and Human Services.

Sedney, M. A. 1987. "Development of androgyny: Parental influences." *Psychology of Women Quarterly, 11,* 311–326.

Seelye, K. Q., & Elder, J. 2003. "Strong support is found for ban on gay marriage." *New York Times,* December 21.

Seff, M. A. 1995. "Cohabitation and the law." *Marriage and Family Review, 21,* 141–168.

Seigel, J. S. 1993. *A generation of change: A profile of America's older population.* New York: Russell Sage Foundation.

Seiler, N. 2002. "Is teen marriage a solution?" Center for Law and Social Policy. www.clasp.org/publications/teenmarriage02-20.pdf. Accessed July 31, 2006.

Seltzer, J. A. 1994. "Consequences of marital dissolution for children." *Annual Review of Sociology, 20,* 235–266.

———. 2007. "Families formed outside of marriage." In S. J. Ferguson (Ed.), *Shifting the center.* New York: McGraw-Hill.

Sen, S. 2007. "The newest parent trap." *Newsweek,* July 16.

Sennett, R. 1984. *Families against the city: Middle-class homes in industrial Chicago.* Cambridge, MA: Harvard University Press.

Sennett, R., & Cobb, J. 1972. *Hidden injuries of class.* New York: Vintage.

Seto, A., & Dahlen, P. 2005. "Understanding women in the role of caregivers for older adults in Japan." *Adultspan, 4,* 69–78.

Shanahan, M. J. 2000. "Pathways to adulthood in changing societies: Variability and mechanisms in life course perspective." *Annual Review of Sociology, 26,* 667–692.

Shapo, H. S. 2006. "Assisted reproduction and the law: Disharmony on a divisive social issue." *Northwestern University Law Review, 100,* 465–479.

Shellenbarger, S. 2006. "Parents crash HR office: 'Hire my kid'." *Seattle Times,* April 9.

Shelton, B. A. 1992. *Women, men, time.* New York: Greenwood.

Shelton, B. A., & John, D. 1993. "Ethnicity, race, and difference: A comparison of white, black, and Hispanic men's household labor time." In J. C. Hood (Ed.), *Men, work, and family.* Newbury Park, CA: Sage.

Sheridan, M. B. 2000. "In Mexico, women take a siesta from housework." *Los Angeles Times,* July 23.

Sherkat, D. E., & Ellison, C. G. 1999. "Recent developments and current controversies in the sociology of religion." *Annual Review of Sociology, 25,* 363–394.

Sherman, S. 1992. *Lesbian and gay marriage: Private commitments, public ceremonies.* Philadelphia: Temple University Press.

Shipler, D. K. 2004. *The working poor: Invisible in America.* New York: Knopf.

Shotland, R. L., & Straw, M. K. 1976. "Bystander response to an assault: When a man attacks a woman." *Journal of Personality and Social Psychology, 34,* 990–999.

Shorto, R. 2008. "No babies?" *The New York Times Magazine,* June 29.

Siegel, R. B. 1996. "The rule of love: Wife beating as prerogative and privacy." *Yale Law Journal, 105,* 2116–2207.

———. 2004. "A short history of sexual harassment." In C. A. MacKinnon & R. B. Siegel (Eds.), *Directions in sexual harassment law.* New Haven: Yale University Press.

Silverman, J. G., Raj, A., Mucci, L. A., & Hathaway, J. E. 2001. "Dating violence against adolescent girls and associated substance use, unhealthy weight control, sexual risk behavior, pregnancy, and suicidality." *Journal of the American Medical Association, 286,* 572–579.

Simmons, T., & Dye, J. L. 2003. "Grandparents living with grandchildren: 2000." Census 2000 Brief. C2KBR-31. www.census.gov/prod/2003pubs/C2KBR-31.pdf. Accessed August 1, 2006.

Simmons, T., & O'Connell, M. 2003. "Married-couple and unmarried-partner households: 2000." U.S.

Bureau of the Census. www.census.gov/prod/2003pubs/censr-5.pdf. Accessed July 25, 2006.

Simon, R. W., Eder, D., & Evans, C. 1992. "The development of feeling norms underlying romantic love among adolescent females." *Social Psychology Quarterly, 55,* 29–46.

Simon, R. W., & Marcussen, K. 1999. "Marital transitions, marital beliefs, and mental health." *Journal of Health and Social Behavior, 40,* 111–125.

Simons, L. G., Simons, R. L., & Conger, R. D. 2004. "Identifying the mechanisms whereby family religiosity influences the probability of adolescent antisocial behavior." *Journal of Comparative Family Studies, 35,* 547–563.

Sims, C. 1998. "Using gifts as bait, Peru sterilizes poor women." *New York Times,* February 15.

———. 2000. "Japan's employers are giving bonuses for having babies." *New York Times,* May 30.

Singh, S., & Darroch, J. E. 2000. "Adolescent pregnancy and childbearing: Levels and trends in developed countries." *Family Planning Perspectives, 32,* 14–23.

Sinha, J. B. P., Sinha, T. N., Verma, J., & Sinha, R. B. N. 2001. "Collectivism co-existing with individualism: An Indian scenario." *Asian Journal of Social Psychology, 4,* 133–145.

Sink, M. 1999. "Family of one Columbine victim files lawsuit against parents of gunmen." *New York Times,* May 28.

Skolnick, A. S. 1991. *Embattled paradise.* New York: Basic Books.

———. 1996. *The intimate environment: Exploring marriage and the family* (6th ed.). New York: HarperCollins.

Skolnick, A. S., & Skolnick, J. H. 2007. "Introduction." In A. S. Skolnick & J. H. Skolnick (Eds.), *Family in transition.* Boston: Allyn & Bacon.

Smiley, J. 2000. "Why do we marry?" *Utne Reader,* September–October.

Smith, C. S. 2005. "Abduction, often violent, a Kyrgyz wedding rite." *New York Times,* April 30.

Smock, P. J. 2000. "Cohabitation in the United States: An appraisal of research themes, findings, and implications." *Annual Review of Sociology 26,* 1–20.

Smock, P. J., & Gupta, S. 2002. "Cohabitation in contemporary North America." In A. Booth & A. C. Crouter (Eds.), *Just living together: Implications of cohabitation on families, children, and social policy.* Mahwah, NJ: Erlbaum.

Smock, P. J., Manning, W. D., & Gupta, S. 1999. "The effect of marriage and divorce on women's economic well-being." *American Sociological Review, 64,* 794–812.

Snow, E. A. 1997. *Inside Bruegel: The play of images in children's games.* San Francisco: North Point Press.

Snyder, H. N. 2000. "Sexual assault of young children as reported to law enforcement: Victim, incident, and offender characteristics." NCJ182990. www.ojp.usdoj.gov/bjs/pub/pdf/saycrle.pdf. Accessed June 1, 2001.

Somers, M. D. 1993. "A comparison of voluntarily child-free adults and parents." *Journal of Marriage and the Family, 55,* 643–650.

South, S. J. 1991. "Sociodemographic differentials in mate selection processes." *Journal of Marriage and the Family, 53,* 928–940.

———. 1992. "For love or money? Sociodemographic determinants of the expected benefits from marriage." In S. J. South & S. E. Tolnay (Eds.), *The changing American family: Sociological and demographic perspectives.* Boulder, CO: Westview Press.

South, S. J., & Lloyd, K. M. 1992. "Marriage opportunities and family formation: Further implications of imbalanced sex ratios." *Journal of Marriage and the Family, 54,* 440–451.

———. 1995. "Spousal alternatives and marital dissolution." *American Sociological Review, 60,* 21–35.

South, S. J., & Spitze, G. D. 1994. "Housework in marital and nonmarital households." *American Sociological Review, 59,* 327–347.

Spar, D. L. 2006. *The baby business: How money, science, and politics drive the commerce of conception.* Boston: Harvard Business School Press.

Spilerman, S. 2004. "The impact of parental wealth on early living standards in Israel." *American Journal of Sociology, 110,* 92–122.

Spock, B. 2004. *Dr. Spock's baby and child care.* New York: Pocket Books.

Sprague, S. J. E., 2002. "Protecting family autonomy: An essay." *American Journal of Family Law, 16,* 87–92.

Sprecher, S., McKinney, K., & Orbuch, T. L. 1987. "Has the double standard disappeared? An experimental test." *Social Psychology Quarterly, 50,* 24–31.

Springen, K. 2007. "Indecent exposure?" *Newsweek,* June 11.

Squadron, D. 2005. "United we stand (in line)." *New York Times,* June 5.

Stacey, J. 1994. "Dan Quayle's revenge: The new family values crusaders." *The Nation,* July 25–August 1, 119–122.

———. 1996. *In the name of the family.* Boston: Beacon Press.

———. 2001. "Gay and lesbian families are here." In S. J. Ferguson (Ed.), *Shifting the center: Understanding contemporary families.* Mountain View, CA: Mayfield.

Stacey, J., & Biblarz, T. J. 2001. "(How) does the sexual orientation of parents matter?" *American Sociological Review, 66,* 159–183.

Stack, C. 1974. *All our kin: Strategies for survival in a black community.* New York: Harper & Row.

Staggenborg, S. 1998. *Gender, family and social movements.* Thousand Oaks, CA: Pine Forge Press.

Stanford, E. P., Peddecord, M., & Lockery, S. 1990. "Variations among the elderly in black, Hispanic and white families." In T. Brubaker (Ed.), *Family relations in later life.* Newbury Park, CA: Sage.

Stanley, S. M., & Markman, H. J. 1992. "Assessing commitment in personal relationships." *Journal of Marriage and the Family, 54,* 595–609.

Staples, B. 1999. "The final showdown on interracial marriage." *New York Times,* July 6.

Staples, R. 1992. "African American families." In J. M. Henslin (Ed.), *Marriage and family in a changing society.* New York: Free Press.

Steen, S., & Schwartz, P. 1995. "Communication, gender, and power: Homosexual couples as a case study." In M. A. Fitzpatrick & A. L. Vangelisti (Eds.), *Explaining family interactions.* Thousand Oaks, CA: Sage.

Stehle, B. F. 1985. *Incurably romantic.* Philadelphia: Temple University Press.

Stein, R. 2006. "More babies arriving a few weeks early." *Indianapolis Star,* May 21.

Steinberg, S. R., & Kincheloe, J. L. 1997. "Introduction: No more secrets—Kinderculture information saturation and the postmodern childhood." In S. R. Steinberg & J. L. Kincheloe (Eds.), *Kinderculture: The corporate construction of childhood.* Boulder, CO: Westview Press.

Steinhauer, J. 2007. "A proposal to ban spanking sparks debate." *New York Times,* January 21.

Steinmetz, S. K., Clavan, S., & Stein, K. F. 1990. *Marriage and family realities: Historical and contemporary perspectives.* New York: Harper & Row.

Stephens, L. S. 1996. "Will Johnny see Daddy this week? An empirical test of three theoretical perspectives on post-divorce contact." *Journal of Family Issues, 17,* 466–494.

Stephens, W. N. 1963. *The family in cross-cultural perspective.* New York: University Press of America.

Stepp, L. S. 2005. "Study: Half of all teens have had oral sex." *Washington Post,* September 16.

Stets, J., & Straus, M. A. 1990. "The marriage license as a hitting license: A comparison of assaults in dating, cohabiting, and married couples." In M. A. Straus & R. J. Gelles (Eds.), *Physical violence in American families.* New Brunswick, NJ: Transaction.

Stevenson, B., & Wolfers, J. 2007. "Marriage and divorce: Changes and their driving forces." Working Paper 12944. National Bureau of Economic Research. http://bpp.wharton.upenn.edu/jwolfers/Papers/MarriageandDivorce(JEP).pdf. Accessed May 12, 2007.

Stewart, A. J., Copeland, A. P., Chester, A. L., Malley, J. E., & Barenbaum, N. B. 1997. *Separating together: How divorce transforms families.* New York: Guilford Press.

Stoddard, T. B. 1992. "Why gay people should seek the right to marry." In S. Sherman (Ed.), *Lesbian and gay marriage.* Philadelphia: Temple University Press.

Stolberg, S. G. 2001. "Science, studies and motherhood." *New York Times,* April 22.

Stoller, E. P., & Gibson, R. C. 1994. *Worlds of difference: Inequality in the aging experience.* Thousand Oaks, CA: Pine Forge Press.

Stolzenberg, R. M., Blair-Loy, M., & Waite, L. J. 1995. "Religious participation in early adulthood: Age and family life cycle effects on church membership." *American Sociological Review, 60,* 84–103.

Stone, L. 1979. *The family, sex and marriage in England 1500–1800.* New York: Harper Torch Books.

Story, L. 2005. "Many women at elite colleges set career path to motherhood." *New York Times,* September 20.

"The strange world of JonBenet." 1997. *Newsweek,* January 20.

Straus, M. A. 1990. "Ordinary violence, child abuse, and wife beating: What do they have in common?" In M. A. Straus & R. J. Gelles (Eds.), *Physical violence in American families.* New Brunswick, NJ: Transaction.

———. 1994. *Beating the devil out of them.* New York: Lexington Books.

Straus, M. A., & Gelles, R. J. 1990. "How violent are American families? Estimates from the National Family Violence Resurvey and other studies." In M. A. Straus & R. J. Gelles (Eds.), *Physical violence in American families.* New Brunswick, NJ: Transaction.

Straus, M. A., Gelles, R. J., & Steinmetz, S. K. 1980. *Behind closed doors: Violence in the American family.* New York: Doubleday/Anchor.

Strom, R., Collinsworth, P., Strom, P., & Griswold, D. 1992-1993. "Strengths and needs of black grandparents." *International Journal of Aging and Human Development, 36,* 255–268.

Strom, S. 2001. "On the wane in Japan: Slavish daughters-in-law." *New York Times,* April 22.

———. 2003. "In middle class, health benefits become luxury." *New York Times,* November 16.

Stromberg, L. 1999. "Boy in blue tutu." *Utne Reader,* July–August.

"Study of poor children shows powerful choice: Heat over food." 1992. *New York Times,* September 9.

Suarez, Z. 1998. "The Cuban-American family." In C. H. Mindel, R. W. Habenstein, & R. Wright (Eds.), *Ethnic families in America: Patterns and variations.* Upper Saddle River, NJ: Prentice Hall.

Sullivan, O. 1997. "The division of housework among 'remarried' couples." *Journal of Family Issues, 18,* 205–223.

Super, C. M. 1976. "Environmental effects on motor development." *Developmental Medicine and Child Neurology, 18,* 561–567.

Swarns, R. L. 1997. "In a policy shift, more parents are arrested for child neglect." *New York Times,* October 25.

———. 2004. "Hispanics resist racial grouping by census." *New York Times,* October 24.

Swartz, M. 2007. "Shop stewards on Fantasy Island?" *New York Times Magazine,* June 10.

Szinovacz, M. E., & Egley, L. C. 1995. "Comparing one-partner and couple data on sensitive marital behaviors: The case of marital violence." *Journal of Marriage and the Family, 57,* 995–1010.

Takagi, D. Y. 1994. "Japanese American families." In R. L. Taylor (Ed.), *Minority families in the United States.* Englewood Cliffs, NJ: Prentice Hall.

Talbot, M. 2000. "A mighty fortress." *New York Times Magazine,* February 27.

Tavris, C. 1992. *Mismeasure of women.* New York: Touchstone.

———. 1996. "Goodbye, Ozzie and Harriet." *New York Times Book Review,* September 22.

Taylor, B. A., & Behnke, A. 2005. "Fathering across the border: Latino fathers in Mexico and the U.S." *Fathering, 3,* 99–120.

Taylor, R. L. 2007. "Diversity within African American families." In A. S. Skolnick & J. H. Skolnick (Eds.), *Family in transition.* Boston: Allyn & Bacon.

Teachman, J. D. 1991. "Contributions to children by divorced fathers." *Social Problems, 38,* 358–371.

Teachman, J. D., Tedrow, L. M., & Crowder, K. D. 2000. "The changing demography of America's families." *Journal of Marriage and the Family, 62,* 1234–1247.

"Temiar marriage and family." 2007. *World Culture Encyclopedia.* www.everyculture.com/East-Southeast-Asia/Temiar-Marriage-and-Family.html. Accessed March 20, 2007.

Terman, L. 1938. *Psychological factors in marital happiness.* New York: McGraw-Hill.

Terry, D. 1996. "In Wisconsin, a rarity of a fetal-harm case." *New York Times,* August 17.

Testa, M., & Krogh, M. 1995. "The effect of employment on marriage among black males in inner-city Chicago." In M. B. Tucker & C. Mitchell-Kernan (Eds.), *The decline in marriage among African Americans.* New York: Russell Sage.

Theocracy Watch. 2005. "The rise of the religious right in the Republican party." www.theocracywatch.org. Accessed June 22, 2005.

Thibaut, J., & Kelley, H. 1959. *The social psychology of groups.* New York: Wiley.

Thompson, L., & Walker, A. J. 1989. "Gender in families: Women and men in marriage, work, and parenthood." *Journal of Marriage and the Family, 51,* 845–871.

Thompson, M., Zimbardo, P., & Hutchinson, G. 2005. "Consumers are having second thoughts about on line dating." www.weattract.com/images/weAttract_whitepaper_v1_4.pdf. Accessed July 4, 2006.

Thorne, B., & Yalom, M. 1982. *Rethinking the family: Some feminist questions.* New York: Longman.

Thornton, M. 1997. "Strategies of racial socialization among black parents: Mainstreaming, minority, and cultural messages." In R. Taylor, J. Jackson, & L. Chatters (Eds.), *Family life in black America.* Thousand Oaks, CA: Sage.

Thornton, A., Axinn, W. G., & Hill, D. H. 1992. "Reciprocal effects of religiosity, cohabitation, and marriage." *American Journal of Sociology, 98,* 628–651.

Thornton, A., & Camburn, D. 1989. "Religious participation and adolescent sexual behavior and attitudes." *Journal of Marriage and the Family, 51,* 641–653.

Tjaden, P., & Thoennes, N. 2000. "Extent, nature, and consequences of intimate partner violence." National Institute of Justice Report #NCJ 181867. www.ncjrs.org/pdffiles1/nij/181867.pdf. Accessed October 12, 2004.

Tolman, D. L. 2006. "Dilemmas of desire: Teenage girls talk about sexuality." In D. M. Newman & J. O'Brien (Eds.), *Sociology: Exploring the architecture of everyday life (Readings).* Thousand Oaks, CA: Pine Forge Press.

Tolnay, S. E., & Crowder, K. D. 1999. "Regional origin and family stability in Northern cities: The role of context." *American Sociological Review, 64,* 97–112.

Toner, R., & Connelly, M. 2005. "Poll finds broad pessimism on Social Security benefits." *New York Times,* June 19.

Toscano, V. 2005. "Misguided retribution: Criminalization of women who take drugs." *Social and Legal Studies, 14,* 359–386.

Treas, J., & Bengston, V. L. 1982. "The demography of mid- and late-life transitions." *Annals of the American Academy of Political and Social Science, 464,* 11–21.

Triandis, H. C. 1995. *Individualism and collectivism.* Boulder, CO: Westview Press.

"Trip home to stand up for their community." 2000. *New York Times,* June 18.

Trost, J. 1988. "Conceptualising the family." *International Sociology, 3,* 301–308.

Tucker, M. B., & Mitchell-Kernan, C. 1995. "Trends in African American family formation: A theoretical and statistical overview." In M. B. Tucker & C. Mitchell-Kernan (Eds.), *The decline in marriage among African Americans.* New York: Russell Sage.

Turner, J. H. 1972. *Patterns of social organization.* New York: McGraw-Hill.

Turner, R. W., & Killian, L. M. 1987. *Collective behavior.* Englewood Cliffs, NJ: Prentice Hall.

Tuttle, W. 1993. *Daddy's gone to war: The Second World War in the lives of America's children.* New York: Oxford University Press.

Twigg, J., & Grand, A. 1998. "Contrasting legal conceptions of family obligation and financial reciprocity in the support of older people: France and England." *Ageing and Society, 18,* 131–146.

Tyagi, A. W. 2004. "Why women have to work." *Time,* March 22.

"Tying the knot: The changing face of marriage in Japan." 1998. Trends in Japan. http://web-japan.org/trends98/honbun/ntj980729.html. Accessed December 18, 2006.

Tyre, P. 2005. "House calls." *Newsweek,* February 7.

Uchitelle, L. 2005. "College degree still pays, but it's leveling off." *New York Times,* January 13.

———. 2006a. *The disposable American: Layoffs and their consequences.* New York: Knopf.

———. 2006b. "Raising the floor on pay." *New York Times,* December 20.

———. 2006c. "Very rich are leaving the merely rich behind." *New York Times,* November 27.

———. 2008. "The wage that meant middle class." *New York Times,* April 20.

Udry, J. R. 2000. "Biological limits of gender construction." *American Sociological Review, 65,* 443–457.

Uhlenberg, P. 1996. "Mutual attraction: Demography and life-course analysis." *The Gerontologist, 36,* 226–229.

Ulrich, L. T. 1990. *A midwife's tale: The life of Martha Ballard, based on her diary, 1785–1812.* New York: Knopf.

Umberson, D., Chen, M. D., House, J. S., Hopkins, K., & Slaten, E. 1996. "The effect of social relationships on psychological well-being: Are men and women really so different?" *American Sociological Review, 61,* 837–857.

Umberson, D., Wortman, C. B., & Kessler, R. C. 1992. "Widowhood and depression: Explaining long-term gender differences in vulnerability." *Journal of Health and Social Behavior, 33,* 10–24.

UNICEF. 2000. *Domestic violence against women and girls.* Innocenti Digest #6. www.unicef-icdc.org. Accessed July 16, 2001.

———. 2005. "Early marriage: A harmful traditional practice." www.unicef.org/publications/files/Early_Marriage_12.lo.pdf. Accessed July 11, 2006.

———. 2007. "Child poverty in perspective: An overview of child well-being in rich countries." *Innocenti Report Card* 7. www.unicef.org/media/files/ChildPovertyReport.pdf. Accessed May 21, 2007.

United Nations. 2007. "Situations of concern." Office of the Special Representative of the Secretary-General for Children and Armed Conflict. www.un.org/children/conflict/english/conflicts2.html. Accessed July 16, 2007.

United Nations Population Fund. 2005. "Child marriage fact sheet." www.unfpa.org/swp/2005/presskit/factsheets/facts_child_marriage.htm. Accessed July 11, 2006.

Upton, R. L. Forthcoming. *The next one changes everything*. Ann Arbor: University of Michigan Press.

U.S. Bureau of Justice Statistics. 2001. "The sexual victimization of college women." BJS Press release. www.ojp.usdoj.gov/bjs/pub/press/svcw.pr. Accessed January 28, 2001.

———. 2006. "Criminal victimization in the United States, 2004." Statistical tables. NCJ213257. www.ojp.usdoj.gov/bjs/pub/pdf/cvus0402.pdf. Accessed June 1, 2006.

U.S. Bureau of Labor Statistics. 2004. "Time-use survey—First results announced by BLS." USDL04-1797. www.bls.gov/tus/. Accessed September 15, 2004.

———. 2005a. "Employed persons by full- and part-time status and sex, 1970–2004 annual averages." Table 20. www.bls.gov/cps/wlf-table20-2005.pdf. Accessed July 17, 2006.

———. 2005b. "Workers on flexible and shift schedules in 2004 summary." www.bls.gov/news.release/flex.nr0.htm. Accessed July 19, 2006.

———. 2006. "Employment characteristics of families summary." Table 1. www.bls.gov/news.release/famee.nr0.htm. Accessed June 20, 2006.

U.S. Bureau of the Census. 1994. *Statistical abstract of the United States*. www2.census.gov/prod2/statecomp/documents/1994-04.pdf. Accessed July 24, 2007.

———. 1999. *Statistical abstract of the United States*. Washington, DC: U.S. Government Printing Office.

———. 2000. *Statistical abstract of the United States*. Washington, DC: U.S. Government Printing Office.

———. 2001a. "The 'nuclear family' rebounds, Census Bureau reports." Report #CB01-69. www.census.gov/Press-Release/www/2001/cb01-69.html. Accessed April 14, 2001.

———. 2001b. "Profile of general demographic characteristics for the United States: 2000." Table DP-1. www.census.gov/Press-Release/www2001/tables/dp_us_2000.pdf. Accessed May 15, 2001.

———. 2006a. "America's families and living arrangements, 2006." www.census.gov/population/www/socdemo/hh-fam/cps2006.html. Accessed June 28, 2007.

———. 2006b. *Statistical abstract of the United States*. http://www.census.gov/compendia/statab/2006/2006edition.html. Accessed May 24, 2006.

———. 2007. *Statistical abstract of the United States*. http://www.census.gov/compendia/statab/2007edition.html. Accessed December 24, 2006.

———. 2008. *Statistical abstract of the United States*. http://www.census.gov/compendia/statab/2008edition.html. Accessed January 5, 2008.

U.S. Conference of Mayors. 2006. "Hunger and homelessness survey." www.usmayors.org/uscm/hungersurvey/2006/report06.pdf. Accessed June 24, 2007.

U.S. Department of Labor. 2006. "Household data, annual averages." Table 39. www.bls.gov/cps/cpsaat39.pdf. Accessed March 31, 2007.

———. 2007. "Family and Medical Leave Act regulations: A report on the Department of Labor's request for information." www.dol.gov/ESA/WHD/FMLA2007Report/Chapter11.pdf. Accessed July 9, 2007.

U.S. Department of State. 2003. "Report illustrates quality of life has improved for Afghan women, children, and refugees." www.state.gov/r/pa/prs/ps/2003/22721.htm. Accessed June 15, 2006.

"U.S. divorce statistics." 2006. *Divorce Magazine*. www.divorcemag.com/statistics/statsUS.shtml. Accessed August 16, 2006.

U.S. General Accounting Office. 2003. "Women's earnings: Work patterns partially explain difference between men's and women's earnings." GAO-04-35. Washington, DC: Government Printing Office.

Utne, M. K., Hatfield, E., Traupmann, J., & Greenberger, D. 1984. "Equity, marital satisfaction, and stability." *Journal of Social and Personal Relationships, 1,* 323–332.

Vandell, D. L., & Wolfe, B. 2000. "Childcare quality: Does it matter and does it need to be improved?" NICHD Study of Early Child Care Research Network. http://aspe.hhs.gov/hsp/ccquality00/index.htm. Accessed July 28, 2006.

van den Berghe, P. 1979. *Human family systems*. New York: Elsevier.

Vanek, J. 1980. "Work, leisure and family roles: Farm households in the United States: 1920–1955." *Journal of Family History, 5,* 422–431.

VanYperen, N. W., & Buunk, B. P. 1990. "A longitudinal study of equity and satisfaction in intimate relationships." *European Journal of Social Psychology, 20,* 287–309.

Vartanian, T. P., & McNamara, J. M. 2000. "Work and economic outcomes after welfare." *Journal of Sociology and Social Welfare, 27,* 41–77.

Vaughan, D. 1986. *Uncoupling.* New York: Vintage.

Veevers, J. 1980. *Childless by choice.* Toronto: Butterworth.

Vela, D. G. 1996. *The role of religion/spirituality in building strong families: Respondents' perceptions: A qualitative grounded theory.* Dissertation, University of Nebraska. UMI Dissertation Services.

Ventura, S. J., Mathews, T. J., & Hamilton, B. E. 2001. "Births to teenagers in the United States, 1940–2000." *National Vital Statistics Report, 49.* September 25.

Vincent, J. P., Weiss, R. L., & Birchler, G. R. 1975. "Dyadic problem solving behavior as a function of marital distress and spousal vs. stranger interactions." *Behavior Therapy, 6,* 475–487.

Vincent, N. 2006. *Self-made man: One woman's journey into manhood and back again.* New York: Viking.

"Vladimir Putin on raising Russia's birth rate." 2006. *Population and Development Review, 32,* 385–389.

Vobejda, B. 1996. "Study rebuts 'danger' of day care." *Indianapolis Star,* April 21.

Vora, S. 2007. "Money doesn't talk." *New York Times,* January 14.

Vorauer, J. D., & Ratner, R. K. 1996. "Who's going to make the first move? Pluralistic ignorance as an impediment to relationship formation." *Journal of Social and Personal Relationships, 13,* 483–506.

Voyandoff, P. 1990. "Economic distress and family relations: A review of the eighties." *Journal of Marriage and the Family, 52,* 1099–1115.

Waite, L. J. 2000a. "Cohabitation: A communitarian perspective." In M. K. Whyte (Ed.), *Marriage in America: A communitarian perspective.* Lanham, MD: Rowman & Littlefield.

———. 2000b. "Social science finds: 'Marriage matters'." In N. V. Benokraitis (Ed.), *Feuds about families.* Upper Saddle River, NJ: Prentice Hall.

Waite, L. J., & Gallagher, M. 2000. *The case for marriage: Why married people are happier, healthier, and better off financially.* New York: Doubleday.

Waldman, A. 2003. "Broken taboos doom lovers in an Indian village." *New York Times,* March 28.

Walker, L. 1979. *The battered woman.* New York: Harper & Row.

Wallerstein, J., Lewis, J., & Blakeslee, S. 2000. *The unexpected legacy of divorce: A 25-year landmark study.* New York: Hyperion.

Walsh, A., & Gordon, R. A. 1995. *Biosociology: An emerging paradigm.* Westport, CT: Praeger.

Walsh, F. 1998. *Strengthening family resilience.* New York: Guilford Press.

Walton, J. 1990. *Sociology and critical inquiry.* Belmont, CA: Wadsworth.

Warren, C. A. B. 1987. *Madwives: Schizophrenic women in the 1950's.* New Brunswick, NJ: Rutgers University Press.

Warren, E., & Tyagi, A. W. 2007. "Why middle-class mothers and fathers are going broke." In A. S. Skolnick & J. H. Skolnick (Eds.), *Family in transition.* Boston: Allyn & Bacon.

Waters, M. C., & Jiménez, T. R. 2005. "Assessing immigrant assimilation: New empirical and theoretical challenges." *Annual Review of Sociology, 31,* 105–125.

Watson, I. 2005. "As elections near, Iranian women stage protest." NPR Morning Edition. June 13. www .npr.org/templates/story/story.php?storyID= 4700486. Accessed June 13, 2005.

Wattenberg, E. 1986. "The fate of baby boomers and their children." *Social Work, 31,* 20–28.

Webb, E. J., Campbell, D. T., Schwartz, R. D., & Sechrest, L. 1966. *Unobtrusive measures: Nonreactive research in the social sciences.* Chicago: Rand McNally.

Wegar, K. 2000. "Adoption, family ideology, and social stigma: Bias in community attitudes, adoption research, and practice." *Family Relations, 49,* 363–370.

Weger, H. 2005. "Disconfirming communication and self-verification in marriage: Associations among the demand/withdraw interaction pattern, feeling understood, and marital satisfaction." *Journal of Personal and Social Relationships, 22,* 19–31.

Weibel-Orlando, J. 1997. "Grandparenting styles: Native American perspectives." In M. Hutter (Ed.), *The family experience.* Boston: Allyn & Bacon.

Weil, E. 2006. "What if it's (sort of) a boy and (sort of) a girl?" *New York Times,* September 24.

Weinberg, M. S., Williams, C. J., & Pryor, D. W. 2003. "Becoming bisexual." In P. A. Adler & P. Adler (Eds.), *Constructions of deviance: Social power, context, and interaction.* Belmont, CA: Wadsworth.

Weiss, J. 2000. *To have and to hold: Marriage, the baby boom and social change.* Chicago: University of Chicago Press.

Weitzman, L. J. 1985. *The divorce revolution: The unexpected consequences for women and children in America.* New York: Free Press.

West, C., & Zimmerman, D. H. 1987. "Doing gender." *Gender & Society, 1,* 125–151.

Weston, K. 1991. *Families we choose: Lesbians, gays and kinship.* New York: Columbia University Press.

White, L., & Edwards, J. N. 1990. "Emptying the nest and parental well-being: An analysis of national panel data." *American Sociological Review, 55,* 235–242.

White, L., & Gilbreth, J. G. 2001. "When children have two fathers: Effects of relationships with stepfathers and noncustodial fathers on adolescent outcomes." *Journal of Marriage and the Family, 63,* 155–167.

White, L., & Keith, B. 1990. "The effect of shift work on the quality and stability of marital relations." *Journal of Marriage and the Family, 52,* 453–462.

White, L., & Riedmann, A. 1992. "When the Brady Bunch grows up: Step/half- and full sibling relationships in adulthood." *Journal of Marriage and the Family, 54,* 197–208.

Whiteford, L. M., & Gonzalez, L. 1995. "Stigma: The hidden burden of infertility." *Social Science and Medicine, 40,* 27–36.

Whitehead, B. D. 1997. *The divorce culture.* New York: Knopf.

Whitehead, B. D, & Pearson, M. 2006. "Making a love connection: Teen relationships, pregnancy, and marriage." Washington, DC: National Campaign to Prevent Teen Pregnancy.

Whyte, M. K. 1990. *Dating, mating and marriage.* New York: Aldine de Gruyter.

———. 1992. "Choosing mates—the American way." *Society,* March–April, 71–77.

Widom, C. S., & Maxfield, M. G. 2001. An update on the "cycle of violence." National Institute of Justice Research in Brief. www.ojp.usdoj.gov/nij/pubs-sum/184894.htm. Accessed July 15, 2001.

Wilcox, W. B. 1998. "Conservative Protestant child-rearing: Authoritarian or authoritative?" *American Sociological Review, 63,* 796–809.

———. 2000. "Conservative Protestant child discipline: The case of parental yelling." *Social Forces, 79,* 865–891

Wilcox, W. B., Chaves, M., & Franz, D. 2004. "Focused on the family? Religious traditions, family discourse, and pastoral practice." *Journal for the Scientific Study of Religion, 43,* 491–504.

Wildman, S. M., & Davis, A. D. 2002. "Making systems of privilege visible." In P. S. Rothenberg (Ed.), *White privilege: Essential readings on the other side of racism.* New York: Worth.

Wilgoren, J. 1999. "Quality daycare, early, is tied to achievements as an adult." *New York Times,* October 22.

———. 2000. "The bell rings and students stay." *New York Times,* January 24.

———. 2005. "At center of clash, rowdy children in coffee shops." *New York Times,* November 9.

Williams, C. 2004. "Still a man's world: Men who do 'women's work'." In D. M. Newman & J. O'Brien (Eds.), *Sociology: Exploring the architecture of everyday life (Readings).* Thousand Oaks, CA: Pine Forge Press.

———. 2006. *Inside toyland: Working, shopping, and social inequality.* Berkeley: University of California Press.

Williams, J. 2000. *Unbending gender: Why family and work conflict and what to do about it.* New York: Oxford.

Williams, J. C. 2006. "One sick child away from being fired: When 'opting out' is not an option." University of California Hastings College of the Law. www.uchastings.edu/site_files/WLL/onesickchild.pdf. Accessed July 20, 2006.

Williamson, R. C. 1984. "A partial replication of the Kohn-Gecas-Nye thesis in a German sample." *Journal of Marriage and the Family, 46,* 971–979.

Willie, C. V. 1981. *A new look at the black family.* Bayside, NY: General Hall.

Wills, E. 2005. "Parent trap." *Chronicle of Higher Education,* July 22.

Wilmoth, J., & Koso, G. 1997. "Does marital history matter? The effect of marital status on wealth outcomes among pre-retirement age adults." Paper presented at the annual meetings of the North Central Sociological Association, Cincinnati, Ohio, April.

Wilson, J., & Musick, M. 1996. "Religion and marital dependency." *Journal for the Scientific Study of Religion, 35,* 30–40.

Winkler, A. E. 1998. "Earnings of husbands and wives in dual-earner families." *Monthly Labor Review Online.* http://stats.bls.gov/opub/mlr/1998/04/art4abs.htm. Accessed July 1, 2001.

Winton, C. A. 1995. *Frameworks for studying families.* Guilford, CT: Dushkin.

Winton, M. A., & Mara, B. A. 2001. *Child abuse & neglect: Multidisciplinary approaches.* Needham Heights, MA: Allyn & Bacon.

Wolak, J., Mitchell, K., & Finkelhor, D. 2006. "Online victimization of youth: Five years later." National Center for Missing and Exploited Children. www.missingkids.com/en_US/publications/NC167.pdf. Accessed August 10, 2006.

Wolf, M. E., Ly, U., Hobart, M. A., & Kernic, M. A. 2003. "Barriers to seeking police help for intimate partner violence." *Journal of Family Violence, 18,* 121–129.

Wolf, R. 2005. "Some may face choice: Whether to heat or 'eat'." *USA Today,* December 13.

Wolfe, A. 1998. *One nation, after all: What middle-class Americans really think about.* New York: Penguin.

Wolfson, E. 2006. "The freedom to marry: Keep dancing." *The Advocate.* www.advocate.com/print_article_ektid33556.asp. Accessed July 25, 2006.

Wong, D. 2004. "Singapore unveils incentives to halt falling birth rate." *Financial Times Asia Edition,* August 26.

Wong, M. G. 1998. "The Chinese-American family." In C. H. Mindel, R. W. Habenstein, & R. Wright (Eds.), *Ethnic families in America: Patterns and variations.* Upper Saddle River, NJ: Prentice Hall.

Woodward, K. L., Quade, V., & Kantrowitz, B. 1995. "Q: When is a marriage not a marriage?" *Newsweek,* March 13.

World Values Survey. 2007. "Online data analysis." www.worldvaluessurvey.org. Accessed July 25, 2007.

Wright, E. O., Baxter, J., & Birkelund, G. E. 1995. "The gender gap in workplace authority: A cross-national study." *American Sociological Review, 60,* 407–435.

Wright, E. O., Costello, C., Hachen, D., & Sprague, J. 1982. "The American class structure." *American Sociological Review, 47,* 709–726.

Wright, E. O., Shire, K., Hwang, S. L., Dolan, M., & Baxter, J. 1992. "The non-effects of class on the gendered division of labor in the home: A comparative study of Sweden and the United States." *Gender and Society, 6,* 252–282.

Wu, L. L. 1996. "Effects of family instability, income, and income instability on the risk of a premarital birth." *American Sociological Review, 61,* 386–406.

Wu, L. L., & Martinson, B. C. 1993. "Family structure and the risk of premarital birth." *American Sociological Review, 58,* 210–232.

Wu, Z., & Penning, M. 1997. "Marital instability after midlife." *Journal of Family Issues, 13,* 459–478.

WuDunn, S. 1996. "A taboo creates a land of Romeos and Juliets." *New York Times,* September 11.

Wuthnow, R. 1998. *After heaven: Spirituality in America since the 1950s.* Berkeley: University of California Press.

Xiao, H. 2000. "Class, gender, and parental values in the 1990s." *Gender & Society, 14,* 785–803.

Yabroff, J. 2008. "Birth, the American way." *Newsweek,* January 28.

Yamato, R. 2006. "Changing attitudes toward elderly dependence in postwar Japan." *Current Sociology, 54,* 273–291.

Yardley, J. 2006. "Dead bachelors in remote China still find wives." *New York Times,* October 5.

Yee, B. W. K. 1992. "Elders in Southeast Asian refugee families." *Generations,* Summer, 24–27.

Yellin, J. 2006. "Single, female, and desperate no more." *New York Times,* June 4.

Yi, Z., & Deqing, W. 2000. "Regional analysis of divorce in China since 1980." *Demography, 37,* 215–219.

Yllo, K. 1993. "Through a feminist lens: Gender, power and violence." In R. J. Gelles & D. R. Loeske (Eds.), *Current controversies on family violence.* Newbury Park, CA: Sage.

Yllo, K., & Straus, M. A. 1990. "Patriarchy and violence against wives: The impact of structural and normative factors." In M. A. Straus & R. J. Gelles (Eds.), *Physical violence in American families.* New Brunswick, NJ: Transaction.

Yusufali, A. 2001. "What the Koran says about women." www.csmonitor.com/2001/1219/p10s1-wogi.htm Accessed June 16, 2006.

Zelizer, V. 1985. *Pricing the priceless child.* New York: Basic Books.

———. 2005. *The purchase of intimacy.* Princeton: Princeton University Press.

Zernike, K. 2007. "Why are there so many single Americans?" *New York Times,* January 21.

Zhan, H. J. 2004. "Willingness and expectations: Inter-generational differences in attitudes toward filial responsibility in China." *Marriage & Family Review, 36,* 175–200.

Zhang, S. D., & Odenwald, W. F. 1995. "Misexpression of the white gene triggers male–male courtship in Drosphilia." *Proceedings of the National Academy of Sciences, 92,* 5525–5529.

Zimmer, N. 2006. "Elgin to consider meaning of family." *The Courier News.* May 9.

Zogby International. 2006. "Opinions of military personnel on gays in the military." www.zogby.com/CSSMM_Report-Final.pdf. Accessed March 21, 2007.

Zoll, R. 2005. "Poll reveals U.S. leads in religious devotion." *Indianapolis Star,* June 7.

Zuger, A. 2005. "For a retainer, lavish care by 'boutique doctors'." *New York Times,* October 30.

Zurcher, L. A., & Snow, D. A. 1981. "Collective behavior: Social movements." In M. Rosenberg & R. H. Turner (Eds.), *Social psychology: Sociological perspectives.* New York: Basic Books.

Zvonkovic, A. M., Greaves, K. M., Schmiege, C. J., & Hall, L. D. 1996. "The marital construction of gender through work and family decisions: A qualitative analysis." *Journal of Marriage and the Family, 58,* 91–100.

Zweig, M. 2000. *The working class majority: America's best kept secret.* Ithaca, NY: Cornell University Press.

Photo Credits

Chapter 1

Page 2: (top) © Jay Freis/Digital Vision/Alamy, (center, bottom) © Jay Freis/Photodisc/Getty Images; **3:** (top) © Jay Freis/Digital Vision/Alamy, (center): © Stan Fellerman/Alamy, (bottom right) © Image Source/Getty Images; **11:** (left) © Schindler Family Photo/AP Images, (right) © Getty Images; **21:** © Ariana Lindquist/The New York Times/Redux Pictures

Chapter 2

28: © Fox Searchlight/The Kobal Collection/Gregory, Doane; **39:** © Lambert/Getty Images; **41:** © Lewis Wickes Hine/Corbis; **46:** (both) © Fox/Photofest

Chapter 3

54: © Rob Crandall/Image Works; **61:** © Sally Ryan/The New York Times/Redux Pictures; **63:** © Stephanie Sinclair/VII Photo Agency-New York

Chapter 4

80: © Jim Wilson/The New York Times/Redux Pictures; **86:** (left) © Bettmann/Corbis, (right) © AP Images; **87:** (left) © Narong Sangnak/epa/Corbis, (right) © Mariette Pathy Allen; **89:** © Jorgen Schytte/Peter Arnold; **95:** © Frank Pedrick/Image Works

Chapter 5

106: © Erica Berger/Corbis; **113:** © Mansell/Mansell/Time & Life Pictures/Getty Images; **116:** © John A. Lacko/The New York Times/Redux; **119:** © Seattle Post-Intelligencer Collection; Museum of History and Industry/Corbis

Chapter 6

132: © John Sturrock/Alamy; **136:** (left) © Buccina Studios/Photodisc, (right) © Jeff Greenberg/PhotoEdit; **140:** (left) © Jason Reid/Reuters/Corbis, (right) © Alison Wright/Corbis; **141:** (all) © Melanie Burford/Dallas Morning News/Corbis; **149:** (left) © Sally and Richard Greenhill/Alamy, (right) © Emiliano Rodriguez/Alamy

Chapter 7

164: © Sven Hagolani/zefa/Corbis; **168:** (top) © Daily Record, Danielle Austen/AP Images, (bottom) © Mika/zefa/Corbis; **169:** (top left) © Colin Young-Wolff/PhotoEdit, (top right) © Claire Greenway/Getty Images, (bottom) © John Rowley/Digital Vision/Getty Images; **172:** © Erica Simone Leeds 2007; **178:** © Rahav Segev/The New York Times/Redux Pictures

Chapter 8

202: © Pamela Chen/Syracuse Newspapers/Image Works; **208:** © Bettmann/Corbis

Chapter 9

236: © Big Cheese Photo LLC/Alamy; **241:** © Genevieve Naylor/Corbis; **246:** © Marissa Roth/The New York Times/Redux Pictures; **260:** © John Lund/Getty Images

Chapter 10

266: © Nevada Wier/Corbis; **270:** © Sylwia Kapuscinski/The New York Times/Redux Pictures; **279:** © Dung Vo Trung/Corbis; **280:** (center) © Rune Hellestad/Corbis, (bottom) © Peter Turnley/Corbis; **281:** (top) © Karen Kasmauski/Corbis, (center) © Floris Leeuwenberg/Corbis, (bottom) © Heiner Heine/Imagebroker/Alamy; **286:** © Bob Fritz/The New York Times/Redux Pictures

Chapter 11

294: © Karen Kasmauski/Corbis; **304:** (top) © Alain Nogue/Corbis, (bottom) © Benjamin Lowy/Corbis; **305:** (top left) © Patrick Chauvel/Corbis, (top right) © Manish Swarup/AP Images, (bottom left) © Andrew Lichtenstein/Corbis, (bottom right) © Christine Spengler/Sygma/Corbis; **308:** © Jupiterimages/

BananaStock/Alamy; **314:** © Carol Beckwith/Robert Estall Photo Agency/Alamy; **315:** © Robert Mulder/Godong/Corbis

Chapter 12

322: © Mark Hamilton/zefa/Corbis; **331:** © Stewart Cairns/The New York Times/Redux Pictures; **335:** © Ryan McVay/Getty Images; **339:** © Hideo Haga/HAGA/Image Works

Chapter 13

348: © Sami Sarkis/Getty Images; **362:** © Bill Aron/PhotoEdit; **375:** © Washington County Sheriff's Department/AP Images; **376:** (top right) © John Springer Collection/Corbis, (bottom left) © Bettmann/Corbis, (bottom right) © H. Armstrong Roberts/Corbis; **377:** (left) © Bettmann/Corbis, (right) © Mark Peterson/Corbis, (bottom) © Roy McMahon/Corbis

Chapter 14

384: © The McGraw-Hill Companies/Jill Braaten, photographer; **389:** © Bettmann/Corbis; **393:** © Joe Sohm/Visions of America, LLC/Alamy; **412:** © Timothy A. Clary/Getty Images

Chapter 15

418: © Mark Richards/PhotoEdit; **424:** © Alessandro BianchiI/Reuters/Corbis; **428:** © Nati Harnik/AP Images

Name Index

Subject Index